MznLnx

Missing Links Exam Preps

Exam Prep for

Economics

Samuelson, Nordhaus, 18th Edition

The MznLnx Exam Prep is your link from the texbook and lecture to your exams.
The MznLnx Exam Preps are unauthorized and comprehensive reviews of your textbooks.

MznLnx

Rico
Publications

Exam Prep for Economics
18th Edition
Samuelson, Nordhaus

Publisher: Raymond Houge
Assistant Editor: Michael Rouger
Text and Cover Designer: Lisa Buckner
Marketing Manager: Sara Swagger
Project Manager, Editorial Production: Jerry Emerson
Art Director: Vernon Lowerui

Product Manager: Dave Mason
Editorial Assitant: Rachel Guzmanji
Pedagogy: Debra Long
Cover Image: Jim Reed/Getty Images
Text and Cover Printer: City Printing, Inc.
Compositor: Media Mix, Inc.

Printed in the United States
ISBN:

For more information about our products, contact us at:
Dave.Mason@RicoPublications.com

For permission to use material from this text or product, submit a request online to:
Dave.Mason@RicoPublications.com

Contents

Contents (Cont.)

TO THE STUDENT

COMPREHENSIVE

The *MznLnx* Exam Prep series is designed to help you pass your exams. Editors at MznLnx review your textbooks and then prepare these practice exams to help you master the textbook material. Unlike study guides, workbooks, and practice tests provided by the texbook publisher and textbook authors, *MznLnx* gives you ***all*** of the material in each chapter in exam form, not just samples, so you can be sure to nail your exam.

MECHANICAL

The MznLnx Exam Prep series creates exams that will help you learn the subject matter as well as test you on your understanding. Each question is designed to help you master the concept. Just working through the exams, you gain an understanding of the subject--its a simple mechanical process that produces success.

INTEGRATED STUDY GUIDE AND REVIEW

MznLnx is not just a set of exams designed to test you, its also a comprehensive review of the subject content. Each exam question is also a review of the concept, making sure that you will get the answer correct without having to go to other sources of material. You learn as you go! Its the easiest way to pass an exam.

HUMOR

Studying can be tedious and dry. MznLnx's instructional design includes moderate humor within the exam questions on occassion, to break the tedium and revitalize the brain

1. The _________ is a heterodox school of economics that emphasizes the spontaneous organizing power of the price mechanism. It holds that the complexity of subjective human choices makes mathematical modelling of the evolving market extremely difficult and advocates a laissez faire approach to the economy. _________ economists advocate the enforcement of voluntary contractual agreements between economic agents, but otherwise the smallest imposition of coercive force on commercial transactions.

a. ACCRA Cost of Living Index
b. ACEA agreement
c. Economic calculation problem
d. Austrian School

2. _________s is the social science that studies the production, distribution, and consumption of goods and services. The term _________s comes from the Ancient Greek oá¼°κονομΐ¯α from oá¼¶κος (oikos, 'house') + νΐŒμος (nomos, 'custom' or 'law'), hence 'rules of the house(hold)'. Current _________ models developed out of the broader field of political economy in the late 19th century, owing to a desire to use an empirical approach more akin to the physical sciences.

a. Inflation
b. Energy economics
c. Opportunity cost
d. Economic

3. A _________ is an object whose consumption increases the utility of the consumer, for which the quantity demanded exceeds the quantity supplied at zero price. _________s are usually modeled as having diminishing marginal utility. The first individual purchase has high utility; the second has less.

a. Good
b. Merit good
c. Composite good
d. Pie method

4. _________ was a survey conducted by the U.S. Department of Justice to gauge the prevalence of alcohol and illegal drug use among prior arrestees. It was a reformulation of the prior Drug Use Forecasting (DUF) program, focused on five drugs in particular: cocaine, marijuana, methamphetamine, opiates, and PCP.

Participants were randomly selected from arrest records in major metropolitan areas; because no personally identifying information is taken from each record chosen, the resulting data can be correlated to arrest rates, but not to the total population of persons charged.

a. ACEA agreement
b. AD-IA Model
c. ACCRA Cost of Living Index
d. Arrestee Drug Abuse Monitoring

5. _________ was a Scottish moral philosopher and a pioneer of political economy. One of the key figures of the Scottish Enlightenment, Smith is the author of The Theory of Moral Sentiments and An Inquiry into the Nature and Causes of the Wealth of Nations. The latter, usually abbreviated as The Wealth of Nations, is considered his magnum opus and the first modern work of economics.

a. Adolf Hitler
b. Alan Greenspan
c. Adam Smith
d. Adolph Fischer

6. _________s is concerned with the tasks of developing and applying quantitative or statistical methods to the study and elucidation of economic principles. _________s combines economic theory with statistics to analyze and test economic relationships. Theoretical _________s considers questions about the statistical properties of estimators and tests, while applied _________s is concerned with the application of _________ methods to assess economic theories.

a. Economic
b. Econometric
c. Experimental economics
d. Evolutionary economics

7. The _________ was written by the English economist John Maynard Keynes. The book, generally considered to be his magnum opus, is largely credited with creating the terminology and shape of modern macroeconomics. Published in February 1936 it sought to bring about a revolution, commonly referred to as the 'Keynesian Revolution', in the way economists thought - especially in relation to the proposition that a market economy tends naturally to restore itself to full employment after temporary shocks.

a. The General Theory of Employment, Interest and Money
b. Black Book of Communism
c. Human Action
d. General Theory of Employment, Interest and Money

8. The _________ was a worldwide economic downturn starting in most places in 1929 and ending at different times in the 1930s or early 1940s for different countries. It was the largest and most important economic depression in the 20th century, and is used in the 21st century as an example of how far the world's economy can fall. The _________ originated in the United States; historians most often use as a starting date the stock market crash on October 29, 1929, known as Black Tuesday.

a. British Empire Economic Conference
b. Jarrow March
c. Great Depression
d. Wall Street Crash of 1929

9. _________ is a fee paid on borrowed assets. It is the price paid for the use of borrowed money , or, money earned by deposited funds . Assets that are sometimes lent with _________ include money, shares, consumer goods through hire purchase, major assets such as aircraft, and even entire factories in finance lease arrangements.

a. Asset protection
b. Internal debt
c. Insolvency
d. Interest

10. _________, 1st Baron Keynes was a renowned economist from Britain whose many ideas on economic and political theories as well as on many governments' monetary policies influenced America. He advocated a government that played an active role in the lives of people regarding business, economy, etc. In this role, the government would use fiscal measures to reduce the consequences of recessions, economic depressions and booms.

a. Adam Smith
b. Adolf Hitler
c. John Maynard Keynes
d. Adolph Fischer

11. _________ is a branch of economics that deals with the performance, structure, and behavior of a national or regional economy as a whole. Along with microeconomics, _________ is one of the two most general fields in economics. It is the study of the behavior and decision-making of entire economies.

a. Macroeconomics
b. New Trade Theory
c. Tobit model
d. Nominal value

12. A _________ is an economy based on the division of labor in which the prices of goods and services are determined in a free price system set by supply and demand. This is often contrasted with a planned economy, in which a central government determines the price of goods and services using a fixed price system. Market economies are contrasted with mixed economy where the price system is not entirely free but under some government control that is not extensive enough to constitute a planned economy.

a. Market economy
b. Network Economy
c. Nutritional Economics
d. Commons-based peer production

13. _________ is a branch of economics that studies how individuals, households and firms and some states make decisions to allocate limited resources, typically in markets where goods or services are being bought and sold. _________ examines how these decisions and behaviours affect the supply and demand for goods and services, which determines prices; and how prices, in turn , determine the supply and demand of goods and services.

Whereas macroeconomics involves the 'sum total of economic activity, dealing with the issues of growth, inflation and unemployment, and with national economic policies relating to these issues' and the effects of government actions on them.

a. Countercyclical
b. Microeconomics
c. Recession
d. New Keynesian economics

14. An Inquiry into the Nature and Causes of the _________ is the magnum opus of the Scottish economist Adam Smith. It is a clearly written account of economics at the dawn of the Industrial Revolution, as well as a rhetorical piece written for the generally educated individual of the 18th century - advocating a free market economy as more productive and more beneficial to society.

The work is credited as a watershed in history and economics due to its comprehensive, largely accurate characterization of economic mechanisms that survive in modern economics; and also for its effective use of rhetorical technique, including structuring the work to contrast real world examples of free and fettered markets.

a. The Rise and Fall of the Great Powers
b. Black Book of Communism
c. Wealth of Nations
d. The Bell Curve

15. A _________ arises when one infers that something is true of the whole from the fact that it is true of some part of the whole (or even of every proper part.) For example: 'This fragment of metal cannot be broken with a hammer, therefore the machine of which it is a part cannot be broken with a hammer.' This is clearly fallacious, because many machines can be broken into their constituent parts without any of those parts being breakable.

This fallacy is often confused with the fallacy of hasty generalization, in which an unwarranted inference is made from a statement about a sample to a statement about the population from which it is drawn.

a. 130-30 fund
b. 1921 recession
c. 100-year flood
d. Fallacy of composition

16. To _________ is to impose a financial charge or other levy upon a taxpayer by a state or the functional equivalent of a state.

_________es are also imposed by many subnational entities. _________es consist of direct _________ or indirect _________, and may be paid in money or as its labour equivalent (often but not always unpaid.)

a. Tax
b. 130-30 fund
c. 100-year flood
d. 1921 recession

17. A _________ is a reduction in taxes. Economic stimulus via _________s, along with interest rate intervention and deficit spending, are one of the central tenets of Keynesian economics.

The immediate effects of a _________ are, generally, a decrease in the real income of the government and an increase in the real income of those whose tax rate has been lowered.

a. Direct taxes
b. Withholding tax
c. Popiwek
d. Tax cut

18. _________ is a socioeconomic structure and political ideology that promotes the establishment of an egalitarian, classless, stateless society based on common ownership and control of the means of production and property in general. In political science, the term '_________' is sometimes used to refer to communist states, a form of government in which the state operates under a one-party system and declares allegiance to Marxism-Leninism or a derivative thereof, even if the party does not actually claim that it has already reached _________.

Forerunners of communist ideas existed in antiquity and particularly in the 18th and early 19th century France, with thinkers such as Jean-Jacques Rousseau and the more radical Gracchus Babeuf.

a. Democratic centralism
b. New Communist Movement
c. Social fascism
d. Communism

19. The _________, sometimes called the fundamental _________, is one of the fundamental economic theories in the operation of any economy. It asserts that there is scarcity, that the finite resources available are insufficient to satisfy all human wants. The problem then becomes how to determine what is to be produced and how the factors of production (such as capital and labour) are to be allocated.

a. Eclectic paradigm
b. Economic problem
c. Endogenous growth theory
d. Economic nationalism

20. In economics, _________ is how a natione;s total economy is distributed among its population. ._________ has always been a central concern of economic theory and economic policy. Classical economists such as Adam Smith, Thomas Malthus and David Ricardo were mainly concerned with factor _________, that is, the distribution of income between the main factors of production, land, labour and capital.

a. Equipment trust certificate
b. Eco commerce
c. Authorised capital
d. Income distribution

21. _________ is the branch of economics that incorporates value judgments (that is, normative judgements) about what the economy ought to be like or what particular policy actions ought to be recommended to achieve a desirable goal. _________ looks at the desirability of certain aspects of the economy. It underlies expressions of support for particular economic policies.

a. Double bottom line
b. Nanoeconomics
c. Broad money
d. Normative economics

22. _________ is the branch of economics that concerns the description and explanation of economic phenomena (Wong, 1987, p. 920.) It focuses on facts and cause-and-effect relationships and includes the development and testing of economics theories.

a. 100-year flood
b. 130-30 fund
c. Regulatory economics
d. Positive economics

23. _________ in economic theory is the use of modern economic tools to study problems that are traditionally in the province of political science.

In particular, it studies the behavior of politicians and government officials as mostly self-interested agents and their interactions in the social system either as such or under alternative constitutional rules. These can be represented a number of ways, including standard constrained utility maximization, game theory, or decision theory.

a. Rational ignorance
b. Public choice
c. Paradox of voting
d. Public interest theory

24. In economics, the term _________ of income or _________ refers to a simple economic model which describes the reciprocal circulation of income between producers and consumers. In the _________ model, the inter-dependent entities of producer and consumer are referred to as 'firms' and 'households' respectively and provide each other with factors in order to facilitate the flow of income. Firms provide consumers with goods and services in exchange for consumer expenditure and 'factors of production' from households.

a. 100-year flood
b. 1921 recession
c. Circular flow
d. 130-30 fund

25. A _________ or directed economy is an economic system in which the government or workers' councils manages the economy. It is an economic system in which the central government makes all decisions on the production and consumption of goods and services. Its most extensive form is referred to as a _________, centrally planned economy, or command and control economy.

a. Nutritional Economics
b. Command economy
c. Subsistence economy
d. Transition economy

26. An _________ or Å"conomic system is a system that involves the production, distribution and consumption of goods and services between the entities in a particular society. It is the method used by society to produce and distribute goods and services. The _________ is composed of people and institutions, including their relationships to productive resources, such as through the convention of property.

a. Information economy
b. Intention economy
c. Economic system
d. Indicative planning

27. _________ is a term used to describe a policy of allowing events to take their own course. The term is a French phrase literally meaning 'let do'. It is a doctrine that states that government generally should not intervene in the marketplace.

a. Heroic capitalism
b. Theory of Productive Forces
c. Laissez-faire
d. Communization

28. _________ is used to assign the available resources in an economic way. It is part of resource management.

In strategic planning,is a plan for using available resources, for example human resources, especially in the near term, to achieve goals for the future.

a. 100-year flood
b. 1921 recession
c. 130-30 fund
d. Resource allocation

29. _________ is an economic system in which wealth, and the means of producing wealth, are privately owned. Through _________, the land, labor, and capital are owned, operated, and traded for the purpose of generating profits, without force or fraud, by private individuals either singly or jointly, and investments, distribution, income, production, pricing and supply of goods, commodities and services are determined by voluntary private decision in a market economy. A distinguishing feature of _________ is that each person owns his or her own labor and therefore is allowed to sell the use of it to employers.

a. Creative capitalism
b. Late capitalism
c. Socialism for the rich and capitalism for the poor
d. Capitalism

30. A _________ is any systematic process enabling many market players to bid and ask: helping bidders and sellers interact and make deals. It is not just the price mechanism but the entire system of regulation, qualification, credentials, reputations and clearing that surrounds that mechanism and makes it operate in a social context.

Because a _________ relies on the assumption that players are constantly involved and unequally enabled, a _________ is distinguished specifically from a voting system where candidates seek the support of voters on a less regular basis.

a. Market system
b. Contestable market
c. Price mechanism
d. Competitive equilibrium

31. In law and economics, the _________, describes the economic efficiency of an economic allocation or outcome in the presence of externalities. The theorem states that when trade in an externality is possible and there are no transaction costs, bargaining will lead to an efficient outcome regardless of the initial allocation of property rights. In practice, obstacles to bargaining or poorly defined property rights can prevent Coasian bargaining.

a. Prior appropriation water rights
b. Means test
c. Coase theorem
d. General Mining Act of 1872

32. In economics, _________ are the resources employed to produce goods and services. They facilitate production but do not become part of the product (as with raw materials) or significantly transformed by the production process (as with fuel used to power machinery.) To 19th century economists, the _________ were land (natural resources, gifts from nature), labor (the ability to work), and capital goods (human-made tools and equipment.)

a. Factors of production
b. Hicks-neutral technical change
c. Long-run
d. Product Pipeline

33. _________ is the term denoting either an entrance or changes which are inserted into a system and which activate/modify a process. It is an abstract concept, used in the modeling, system(s) design and system(s) exploitation. It is usually connected with other terms, e.g., _________ field, _________ variable, _________ parameter, _________ value, _________ signal, _________ device and _________ file.

a. Input
b. AD-IA Model
c. ACCRA Cost of Living Index
d. ACEA agreement

34. _________s (economically referred to as land or raw materials) occur naturally within environments that exist relatively undisturbed by mankind, in a natural form. A _________'s is often characterized by amounts of biodiversity existent in various ecosystems.

Mining, petroleum extraction, fishing, hunting, and forestry are generally considered natural-resource industries.

a. Natural resource
b. 130-30 fund
c. 100-year flood
d. 1921 recession

35. In microeconomics, _________ is quite simply the conversion of inputs into outputs. It is an economic process that uses resources to create a good or service that is suitable for exchange. This can include manufacturing, storing, shipping, and packaging.

a. MET
b. Solved
c. Red Guards
d. Production

36. In economics, a _________ is a function that specifies the output of a firm, an industry, or an entire economy for all combinations of inputs. A meta-_________ compares the practice of the existing entities converting inputs X into output y to determine the most efficient practice _________ of the existing entities, whether the most efficient feasible practice production or the most efficient actual practice production. In either case, the maximum output of a technologically-determined production process is a mathematical function of input factors of production.

a. Post-Fordism
b. Production function
c. Short-run
d. Constant elasticity of substitution

37. A _________ is an expression that compares quantities relative to each other. The most common examples involve two quantities, but any number of quantities can be compared. _________s are represented mathematically by separating each quantity with a colon, for example the _________ 2:3, which is read as the _________ 'two to three'.

a. 100-year flood
b. 130-30 fund
c. Y-intercept
d. Ratio

38. _________ is the increase in the amount of the goods and services produced by an economy over time. It is conventionally measured as the percent rate of increase in real gross domestic product, or real GDP. Growth is usually calculated in real terms, i.e. inflation-adjusted terms, in order to net out the effect of inflation on the price of the goods and services produced.

a. ACCRA Cost of Living Index
b. ACEA agreement
c. AD-IA Model
d. Economic growth

39. In economics, a _________ is a good that is non-rivaled and non-excludable. This means, respectively, that consumption of the good by one individual does not reduce availability of the good for consumption by others; and that no one can be effectively excluded from using the good. In the real world, there may be no such thing as an absolutely non-rivaled and non-excludable good; but economists think that some goods approximate the concept closely enough for the analysis to be economically useful.

a. Happiness economics
b. Demand-pull theory
c. Neoclassical synthesis
d. Public good

40. _________ is a common concept in economics, and gives rise to derived concepts such as consumer debt. Generally _________ is defined by opposition to production. But the precise definition can vary because different schools of economists define production quite differently.

a. Cash or share options
b. Federal Reserve Bank Notes
c. Foreclosure data providers
d. Consumption

41. In economics, economic output is divided into physical goods and intangible services. Consumption of _________ is assumed to produce utility. It is often used when referring to a _________ Tax.

a. Composite good
b. Private good
c. Manufactured goods
d. Goods and services

42. A _________ is defined in economics as a good that exhibits these properties:

- Excludable - it is reasonably possible to prevent a class of consumers (e.g. those who have not paid for it) from consuming the good.
- Rivalrous - consumptions by one consumer prevents simultaneous consumption by other consumers. _________s satisfies an individual want while public good satisfies a collective want of the society.

A _________ is the opposite of a public good, as they are almost exclusively made for profit.

An example of the _________ is bread: bread eaten by a given person cannot be consumed by another (rivalry), and it is easy for a baker to refuse to trade a loaf (excludable

a. Positional goods
b. Pie method
c. Demerit good
d. Private good

43. _________ is that which is owed; usually referencing assets owed, but the term can also cover moral obligations and other interactions not requiring money. In the case of assets, _________ is a means of using future purchasing power in the present before a summation has been earned. Some companies and corporations use _________ as a part of their overall corporate finance strategy.

a. Debenture
b. Debt
c. Hard money loan
d. Collateral Management

44. _________ in economics refers to metrics and measures of output from production processes, per unit of input. Labor _________, for example, is typically measured as a ratio of output per labor-hour, an input. _________ may be conceived of as a metrics of the technical or engineering efficiency of production.

a. Piece work
b. Production-possibility frontier
c. Fordism
d. Productivity

45. _________ is a situation in which the limited resources of a firm are allocated in accordance with the wishes of consumers. An allocatively efficient economy produces an 'optimal mix' of commodities. A firm is allocatively efficient when its price is equal to its marginal costs (that is, P = MC) in a perfect market.

a. ACEA agreement
b. ACCRA Cost of Living Index
c. Allocative efficiency
d. Economic efficiency

46. _________ or economic opportunity loss is the value of the next best alternative foregone as the result of making a decision. _________ analysis is an important part of a company's decision-making processes but is not treated as an actual cost in any financial statement. The next best thing that a person can engage in is referred to as the _________ of doing the best thing and ignoring the next best thing to be done.

a. Economic
b. Economic ideology
c. Industrial organization
d. Opportunity cost

47. _________ occurs when the economy is operating at its production possibility frontier (PPF.) This takes place when production of one good is achieved at the lowest cost possible, given the production of the other good(s.) Equivalently, it is when the highest possible output of one good is produced, given the production level of the other good(s.)

a. Discretionary spending
b. Free contract
c. Preclusive purchasing
d. Productive efficiency

48. A _________ is a situation that involves losing one quality or aspect of something in return for gaining another quality or aspect. It implies a decision to be made with full comprehension of both the upside and downside of a particular choice.

In economics the term is expressed as opportunity cost, referring the most preferred alternative given up.

a. Friedman-Savage utility function
b. Nonmarket
c. Whitemail
d. Trade-off

49. _________ and Keynesian Theory) is a macroeconomic theory based on the ideas of 20th-century British economist John Maynard Keynes. _________ argues that private sector decisions sometimes lead to inefficient macroeconomic outcomes and therefore advocates active policy responses by the public sector, including monetary policy actions by the central bank and fiscal policy actions by the government to stabilize output over the business cycle.

The theories forming the basis of _________ were first presented in The General Theory of Employment, Interest and Money, published in 1936.

a. Deflation
b. Rational choice theory
c. Market failure
d. Keynesian economics

50. _________ Theory (or _________ Theory) is a class of macroeconomic models in which business cycle fluctuations to a large extent can be accounted for by real (in contrast to nominal) shocks. (The four primary economic fluctuations are secular (trend), business cycle, seasonal, and random.) Unlike other leading theories of the business cycle, it sees recessions and periods of economic growth as the efficient response to exogenous changes in the real economic environment.

a. Real business cycle
b. Monetary policy reaction function
c. Balanced-growth equilibrium
d. SIMIC

51. In economics, a _________ is a general slowdown in economic activity over a sustained period of time, or a business cycle contraction. During _________s, many macroeconomic indicators vary in a similar way. Production as measured by Gross Domestic Product (GDP), employment, investment spending, capacity utilization, household incomes and business profits all fall during _________s.

a. Leading indicators
b. Monetary economics
c. Treasury View
d. Recession

52. In economics, the _________ measures the payments that flow between any individual country and all other countries. It is used to summarize all international economic transactions for that country during a specific time period, usually a year. The _________ is determined by the country's exports and imports of goods, services, and financial capital, as well as financial transfers.

a. Skyscraper Index
b. Gross domestic product per barrel
c. Balance of payments
d. Gross world product

53. The term _________ refers to economy-wide fluctuations in production or economic activity over several months or years. These fluctuations occur around a long-term growth trend, and typically involve shifts over time between periods of relatively rapid economic growth (expansion or boom), and periods of relative stagnation or decline (contraction or recession.)

These fluctuations are often measured using the growth rate of real gross domestic product.

a. Nominal value
b. Consumer theory
c. Tobit model
d. Business cycle

54. A _________ is the transfer of wealth from one party (such as a person or company) to another. A _________ is usually made in exchange for the provision of goods, services or both, or to fulfill a legal obligation.

The simplest and oldest form of _________ is barter, the exchange of one good or service for another.

a. Going concern
b. Soft count
c. Social gravity
d. Payment

55. _________ in political thought refers to economic theories of social organization advocating collective ownership and administration of the means of production and distribution of goods, and a society characterized by equality for all individuals, with an egalitarian method of compensation. Modern _________ originated in the late 19th-century intellectual and working class political movement that criticized the effects of industrialization and private ownership on society. Karl Marx posited that _________ would be achieved via class struggle and a proletarian revolution after a transitional stage from capitalism called the dictatorship of the proletariat.

a. Adolph Fischer
b. Socialism
c. Adam Smith
d. Adolf Hitler

56. An inverse or negative relationship is a mathematical relationship in which one variable, say y, decreases as another, say x, increases. For a linear (straight-line) relation, this can be expressed as y = a-bx, where -b is a constant value less than zero and a is a constant. For example, there is an _________ between education and unemployment -- that is, as education increases, the rate of unemployment decreases.

a. AD-IA Model
b. ACEA agreement
c. ACCRA Cost of Living Index
d. Inverse relationship

57. In mathematics, a _________ system is a system which is not linear, that is, a system which does not satisfy the superposition principle, or whose output is not proportional to its input. Less technically, a _________ system is any problem where the variable(s) to be solved for cannot be written as a linear combination of independent components. A nonhomogeneous system, which is linear apart from the presence of a function of the independent variables, is _________ according to a strict definition, but such systems are usually studied alongside linear systems, because they can be transformed to a linear system of multiple variables.

a. Nonlinear system
b. 100-year flood
c. 130-30 fund
d. Nonlinear

58. In economics, the _________ is a single mathematical function used to express consumer spending. It was developed by John Maynard Keynes and detailed most famously in his book The General Theory of Employment, Interest, and Money. The function is used to calculate the amount of total consumption in an economy.

a. Liquidity preference
b. Consumption function
c. DAD-SAS model
d. Procyclical

59. The _________ or gross domestic income (GDI), a basic measure of an economy's economic performance, is the market value of all final goods and services produced within the borders of a nation in a year. _________ can be defined in three ways, all of which are conceptually identical. First, it is equal to the total expenditures for all final goods and services produced within the country in a stipulated period of time (usually a 365-day year.)

a. Monopolistic competition
b. Countercyclical
c. Market structure
d. Gross Domestic Product

60. In economics, _________ is the ratio of the percent change in one variable to the percent change in another variable. It is a tool for measuring the responsiveness of a function to changes in parameters in a relative way. Commonly analyzed are _________ of substitution, price and wealth.

a. ACEA agreement
b. ACCRA Cost of Living Index
c. Elasticity of demand
d. Elasticity

61. _________ is an economic model based on price, utility and quantity in a market. It predicts that in a competitive market, price will function to equalize the quantity demanded by consumers, and the quantity supplied by producers, resulting in an economic equilibrium of price and quantity. The model incorporates other factors changing equilibrium as a shift of demand and/or supply.

a. Rational addiction
b. Deferred gratification
c. Supply and demand
d. Joint demand

62. Economics:

- _________,the desire to own something and the ability to pay for it
- _________ curve,a graphic representation of a _________ schedule
- _________ deposit, the money in checking accounts
- _________ pull theory,the theory that inflation occurs when _________ for goods and services exceeds existing supplies
- _________ schedule,a table that lists the quantity of a good a person will buy it each different price
- _________ side economics,the school of economics at believes government spending and tax cuts open economy by raising _________

.

a. Variability
b. McKesson ' Robbins scandal
c. Demand
d. Production

1. _________ was a survey conducted by the U.S. Department of Justice to gauge the prevalence of alcohol and illegal drug use among prior arrestees. It was a reformulation of the prior Drug Use Forecasting (DUF) program, focused on five drugs in particular: cocaine, marijuana, methamphetamine, opiates, and PCP.

Participants were randomly selected from arrest records in major metropolitan areas; because no personally identifying information is taken from each record chosen, the resulting data can be correlated to arrest rates, but not to the total population of persons charged.

a. ACCRA Cost of Living Index
b. AD-IA Model
c. ACEA agreement
d. Arrestee Drug Abuse Monitoring

2. _________ is an economic system in which wealth, and the means of producing wealth, are privately owned. Through _________, the land, labor, and capital are owned, operated, and traded for the purpose of generating profits, without force or fraud, by private individuals either singly or jointly, and investments, distribution, income, production, pricing and supply of goods, commodities and services are determined by voluntary private decision in a market economy. A distinguishing feature of _________ is that each person owns his or her own labor and therefore is allowed to sell the use of it to employers.

a. Socialism for the rich and capitalism for the poor
b. Creative capitalism
c. Late capitalism
d. Capitalism

3. A _________ or directed economy is an economic system in which the government or workers' councils manages the economy. It is an economic system in which the central government makes all decisions on the production and consumption of goods and services. Its most extensive form is referred to as a _________, centrally planned economy, or command and control economy.

a. Nutritional Economics
b. Subsistence economy
c. Transition economy
d. Command economy

4. _________s is the social science that studies the production, distribution, and consumption of goods and services. The term _________s comes from the Ancient Greek οá¼°κονομÎ¯α from οá¼¶κος (oikos, 'house') + νÏŒμος (nomos, 'custom' or 'law'), hence 'rules of the house(hold)'. Current _________ models developed out of the broader field of political economy in the late 19th century, owing to a desire to use an empirical approach more akin to the physical sciences.

a. Energy economics
b. Opportunity cost
c. Inflation
d. Economic

5. An _________ or Å“conomic system is a system that involves the production, distribution and consumption of goods and services between the entities in a particular society. It is the method used by society to produce and distribute goods and services. The _________ is composed of people and institutions, including their relationships to productive resources, such as through the convention of property.

a. Economic system
b. Indicative planning
c. Information economy
d. Intention economy

6. _________ is a term used to describe a policy of allowing events to take their own course. The term is a French phrase literally meaning 'let do'. It is a doctrine that states that government generally should not intervene in the marketplace.

a. Laissez-faire
b. Theory of Productive Forces
c. Heroic capitalism
d. Communization

7. A _________ is an economy based on the division of labor in which the prices of goods and services are determined in a free price system set by supply and demand. This is often contrasted with a planned economy, in which a central government determines the price of goods and services using a fixed price system. Market economies are contrasted with mixed economy where the price system is not entirely free but under some government control that is not extensive enough to constitute a planned economy.

a. Network Economy
b. Commons-based peer production
c. Nutritional Economics
d. Market economy

8. _________ is a term from economics referring to the use of money exchanged by buyers and sellers with an open and understood system of value and time trade offs to produce the best distribution of goods and services. The use of the _________ does not imply a free market: there can be captive or controlled markets which seek to use supply and demand, or some other form of charging for scarcity, both in social situations and in engineering.

The _________ assumes perfect competition and is regulated by demand and supply.

a. Product-Market Growth Matrix
b. Partial equilibrium
c. Two-sided markets
d. Market mechanism

9. _________ is the incidence or process of transferring ownership of a business, enterprise, agency or public service from the public sector (government) to the private sector (business.) In a broader sense, _________ refers to transfer of any government function to the private sector including governmental functions like revenue collection and law enforcement.

The term '_________' also has been used to describe two unrelated transactions.

a. Compound empowerment
b. Performance reports
c. Privatization
d. Ricardian equivalence

10. _________ in economic theory is the use of modern economic tools to study problems that are traditionally in the province of political science.

In particular, it studies the behavior of politicians and government officials as mostly self-interested agents and their interactions in the social system either as such or under alternative constitutional rules. These can be represented a number of ways, including standard constrained utility maximization, game theory, or decision theory.

a. Paradox of voting
b. Rational ignorance
c. Public choice
d. Public interest theory

11. _________ was a Scottish moral philosopher and a pioneer of political economy. One of the key figures of the Scottish Enlightenment, Smith is the author of The Theory of Moral Sentiments and An Inquiry into the Nature and Causes of the Wealth of Nations. The latter, usually abbreviated as The Wealth of Nations, is considered his magnum opus and the first modern work of economics.

a. Adam Smith
b. Adolph Fischer
c. Adolf Hitler
d. Alan Greenspan

12. An Inquiry into the Nature and Causes of the _________ is the magnum opus of the Scottish economist Adam Smith. It is a clearly written account of economics at the dawn of the Industrial Revolution, as well as a rhetorical piece written for the generally educated individual of the 18th century - advocating a free market economy as more productive and more beneficial to society.

The work is credited as a watershed in history and economics due to its comprehensive, largely accurate characterization of economic mechanisms that survive in modern economics; and also for its effective use of rhetorical technique, including structuring the work to contrast real world examples of free and fettered markets.

a. The Rise and Fall of the Great Powers
b. Black Book of Communism
c. The Bell Curve
d. Wealth of Nations

13. There are two main interpretations of the idea of a _________:

- A model in which the state assumes primary responsibility for the welfare of its citizens. This responsibility in theory ought to be comprehensive, because all aspects of welfare are considered and universally applied to citizens as a 'right'. _________ can also mean the creation of a 'social safety net' of minimum standards of varying forms of welfare. Here is found some confusion between a '_________' and a 'welfare society' in common debate about the definition of the term.
- The provision of welfare in society. In many '_________s', especially in continental Europe, welfare is not actually provided by the state, but by a combination of independent, voluntary, mutualist and government services. The functional provider of benefits and services may be a central or state government, a state-sponsored company or agency, a private corporation, a charity or another form of non-profit organization. However, this phenomenon has been more appropriately termed a 'welfare society,' and the term 'welfare system' has been used to describe the range of _________ and welfare society mixes that are found.

The English term '_________' is believed by Asa Briggs to have been coined by Archbishop William Temple during the Second World War, contrasting wartime Britain with the 'warfare state' of Nazi Germany. Friedrich Hayek contends that the term derived from the older German word Wohlfahrtsstaat, which itself was used by nineteenth century historians to describe a variant of the ideal of Polizeistaat . It was fully developed by the German academic Sozialpolitiker--'socialists of the chair'--from 1870 and first implemented through Bismarck's 'state socialism'. Bismarck's policies have also been seen as the creation of a _________.

a. 130-30 fund
b. Welfare state
c. 100-year flood
d. 1921 recession

14. _________ has several particular meanings:

- in mathematics
  - _________ function
  - Euler _________
  - _________
  - _________ subgroup
  - method of _________s (partial differential equations)
- in physics and engineering
  - any _________ curve that shows the relationship between certain input- and output parameters, e.g.
  - an I-V or current-voltage _________ is the current in a circuit as a function of the applied voltage
  - Receiver-Operator _________
- in fiction
  - in Dungeons ' Dragons, _________ is another name for ability score

a. Technocracy | b. Russian financial crisis
c. Demand | d. Characteristic

15. A _________ is an economic system that incorporates a mixture of private and government ownership or control, or a mixture of capitalism and socialism.

There is not one single definition for a _________, but relevant aspects include: a degree of private economic freedom (including privately owned industry) intermingled with centralized economic planning and government regulation (which may include regulation of the market for environmental concerns and social welfare, or state ownership and management of some of the means of production for national or social objectives.)

For some states, there is not a consensus on whether they are capitalist, socialist, or mixed economies.

a. Planned liberalism | b. Hunter-gatherer
c. Dual economy | d. Mixed economy

16. The _________ , established in 1848, is the world's oldest futures and options exchange. More than 50 different options and futures contracts are traded by over 3,600 _________ members through open outcry and eTrading. Volumes at the exchange in 2003 were a record breaking 454 million contracts.

a. New York Mercantile Exchange | b. 130-30 fund
c. Chicago Board of Trade | d. 100-year flood

17. _________s are a type of administrative division, in some countries managed by a local government. They vary greatly in size, spanning entire regions or counties, several municipalities, or subdivisions of municipalities.

In Austria, a _________ or Bezirk is an administrative division normally encompassing several municipalities, roughly equivalent to the Landkreis in Germany.

a. 1921 recession
b. 130-30 fund
c. 100-year flood
d. District

18. A _________ is the space, actual or metaphorical, in which a market operates. The term is also used in a trademark law context to denote the actual consumer environment, ie. the 'real world' in which products and services are provided and consumed.

a. 130-30 fund
b. 100-year flood
c. 1921 recession
d. Marketplace

19. The _________ is the world's largest physical commodity futures exchange, located in New York City. Its two principal divisions are the _________ and Commodity Exchange, Inc (COMEX) which were once separate but are now merged. The parent company of the _________, Inc., New York Mercantile ExchangeX Holdings, Inc.

a. Commodity Exchange
b. 130-30 fund
c. New York Mercantile Exchange
d. 100-year flood

20. A _________ is any systematic process enabling many market players to bid and ask: helping bidders and sellers interact and make deals. It is not just the price mechanism but the entire system of regulation, qualification, credentials, reputations and clearing that surrounds that mechanism and makes it operate in a social context.

Because a _________ relies on the assumption that players are constantly involved and unequally enabled, a _________ is distinguished specifically from a voting system where candidates seek the support of voters on a less regular basis.

a. Competitive equilibrium
b. Contestable market
c. Price mechanism
d. Market system

21. _________ is a broad label that refers to any individuals or households that use goods and services generated within the economy. The concept of a _________ is used in different contexts, so that the usage and significance of the term may vary.

Typically when business people and economists talk of _________s they are talking about person as _________, an aggregated commodity item with little individuality other than that expressed in the buy/not-buy decision.

a. Consumer
b. 130-30 fund
c. 100-year flood
d. 1921 recession

22. _________ are final goods specifically intended for the mass market. For instance, _________ do not include investment assets, like precious antiques, even though these antiques are final goods.

Manufactured goods are goods that have been processed by way of machinery.

a. G-20 Leaders Summit on Financial Markets and the World Economy
b. Consumer goods
c. Fiscal stimulus plans
d. Bulgarian-American trade

23. The _________, sometimes called the fundamental _________, is one of the fundamental economic theories in the operation of any economy. It asserts that there is scarcity, that the finite resources available are insufficient to satisfy all human wants. The problem then becomes how to determine what is to be produced and how the factors of production (such as capital and labour) are to be allocated.

a. Endogenous growth theory
b. Economic problem
c. Economic nationalism
d. Eclectic paradigm

24. In economics, _________ are the resources employed to produce goods and services. They facilitate production but do not become part of the product (as with raw materials) or significantly transformed by the production process (as with fuel used to power machinery.) To 19th century economists, the _________ were land (natural resources, gifts from nature), labor (the ability to work), and capital goods (human-made tools and equipment.)

a. Hicks-neutral technical change
b. Long-run
c. Product Pipeline
d. Factors of production

25. _________ theory is a branch of theoretical economics. It seeks to explain the behavior of supply, demand and prices in a whole economy with several or many markets. It is often assumed that agents are price takers and in that setting two common notions of equilibrium exist: Walrasian (or competitive) equilibrium, and its generalization; a price equilibrium with transfers.

a. New Keynesian economics
b. Human capital
c. Rational choice theory
d. General equilibrium

26. In economics, economic equilibrium is simply a state of the world where economic forces are balanced and in the absence of external influences the (equilibrium) values of economic variables will not change. It is the point at which quantity demanded and quantity supplied are equal. _________, for example, refers to a condition where a market price is established through competition such that the amount of goods or services sought by buyers is equal to the amount of goods or services produced by sellers.

a. Product-Market Growth Matrix
b. Regulated market
c. Marketization
d. Market equilibrium

27. _________ describes a deliberate attempt to interfere with the free and fair operation of the market and create artificial, false or misleading appearances with respect to the price of a security, commodity or currency. _________ is prohibited under Section 9(a)(2) of the Securities Exchange Act of 1934, and in Australia under Section s 1041A of the Corporations Act 2001. The Act defines _________ as transactions which create an artificial price or maintain an artificial price for a tradable security.

a. Net domestic product
b. Legal monopoly
c. Market manipulation
d. Managerial economics

28. _________ is an economic concept with commonplace familiarity. It is the price that a good or service is offered at, or will fetch, in the marketplace. It is of interest mainly in the study of microeconomics.

a. Noisy market hypothesis
b. Market anomaly
c. Paper trading
d. Market price

29. _________ in economics and business is the result of an exchange and from that trade we assign a numerical monetary value to a good, service or asset. If Alice trades Bob 4 apples for an orange, the _________ of an orange is 4 apples. Inversely, the _________ of an apple is 1/4 oranges.

a. Price
b. Price book
c. Premium pricing
d. Price war

30. A _________ is message sent to consumers and producers in the form of a price charged for a commodity; this is seen as indicating a signal for producers to increase supplies and/or consumers to reduce demand.

For example, in a free price system, rising prices may indicate a shortage of supply, increase in demand, or a rise in input costs. Regardless of the underlying reason--and without the consumer needing to know the cause--the price increase communicates the notion that consumer demand (at this new, higher price) should recede or that supplies should increase.

a. Mohring effect
b. Market demand schedule
c. Threshold population
d. Price signal

31. In economics, _________ is the process by which a firm determines the price and output level that returns the greatest profit. There are several approaches to this problem. The total revenue--total cost method relies on the fact that profit equals revenue minus cost, and the marginal revenue--marginal cost method is based on the fact that total profit in a perfectly competitive market reaches its maximum point where marginal revenue equals marginal cost.
a. Profit maximization
b. Profit margin
c. 100-year flood
d. Normal profit

32. _________ is an economic model based on price, utility and quantity in a market. It predicts that in a competitive market, price will function to equalize the quantity demanded by consumers, and the quantity supplied by producers, resulting in an economic equilibrium of price and quantity. The model incorporates other factors changing equilibrium as a shift of demand and/or supply.
a. Deferred gratification
b. Rational addiction
c. Joint demand
d. Supply and demand

33. Competition law, known in the United States as _________ law, has three main elements:

- prohibiting agreements or practices that restrict free trading and competition between business entities. This includes in particular the repression of cartels.
- banning abusive behaviour by a firm dominating a market, or anti-competitive practices that tend to lead to such a dominant position. Practices controlled in this way may include predatory pricing, tying, price gouging, refusal to deal, and many others.
- supervising the mergers and acquisitions of large corporations, including some joint ventures. Transactions that are considered to threaten the competitive process can be prohibited altogether, or approved subject to 'remedies' such as an obligation to divest part of the merged business or to offer licences or access to facilities to enable other businesses to continue competing.

The substance and practice of competition law varies from jurisdiction to jurisdiction. Protecting the interests of consumers (consumer welfare) and ensuring that entrepreneurs have an opportunity to compete in the market economy are often treated as important objectives. Competition law is closely connected with law on deregulation of access to markets, state aids and subsidies, the privatisation of state owned assets and the establishment of independent sector regulators. In recent decades, competition law has been viewed as a way to provide better public services.

a. Intellectual property law
b. United Kingdom competition law
c. Anti-Inflation Act
d. Antitrust

34. In economics, the term _________ of income or _________ refers to a simple economic model which describes the reciprocal circulation of income between producers and consumers. In the _________ model, the inter-dependent entities of producer and consumer are referred to as 'firms' and 'households' respectively and provide each other with factors in order to facilitate the flow of income. Firms provide consumers with goods and services in exchange for consumer expenditure and 'factors of production' from households.

a. 130-30 fund
b. 100-year flood
c. 1921 recession
d. Circular flow

35. Economics:

- _________,the desire to own something and the ability to pay for it
- _________ curve,a graphic representation of a _________ schedule
- _________ deposit, the money in checking accounts
- _________ pull theory,the theory that inflation occurs when _________ for goods and services exceeds existing supplies
- _________ schedule,a table that lists the quantity of a good a person will buy it each different price
- _________ side economics,the school of economics at believes government spending and tax cuts open economy by raising _________

.

a. Variability
b. Production
c. McKesson ' Robbins scandal
d. Demand

36. A _________ is an object whose consumption increases the utility of the consumer, for which the quantity demanded exceeds the quantity supplied at zero price. _________s are usually modeled as having diminishing marginal utility. The first individual purchase has high utility; the second has less.

a. Composite good
b. Pie method
c. Merit good
d. Good

37. In microeconomics, _________ is quite simply the conversion of inputs into outputs. It is an economic process that uses resources to create a good or service that is suitable for exchange. This can include manufacturing, storing, shipping, and packaging.

a. Red Guards
b. Production
c. Solved
d. MET

38. The _________ consists of a number of economic theories which describe the nature of the firm, company including its existence, its behaviour, and its relationship with the market.

In simplified terms, the _________ aims to answer these questions:

1. Existence - why do firms emerge, why are not all transactions in the economy mediated over the market?
2. Boundaries - why the boundary between firms and the market is located exactly there? Which transactions are performed internally and which are negotiated on the market?
3. Organization - why are firms structured in such specific way? What is the interplay of formal and informal relationships?

Despite looking simple, these questions are not answered by the established economic theory, which usually views firms as given, and treats them as black boxes without any internal structure.

The First World War period saw a change of emphasis in economic theory away from industry-level analysis which mainly included analysing markets to analysis at the level of the firm, as it became increasingly clear that perfect competition was no longer an adequate model of how firms behaved. Economic theory till then had focussed on trying to understand markets alone and there had been little study on understanding why firms or organisations exist.

a. Technology gap
b. Theory of the firm
c. Khazzoom-Brookes postulate
d. Policy Ineffectiveness Proposition

39. A _________ product is a product designed for cheapness and short-term convenience rather than medium to long-term durability, with most products only intended for single use. The term is also sometimes used for products that may last several months (ex. _________ air filters) to distinguish from similar products that last indefinitely (ex.

a. 1921 recession
b. Disposable
c. 130-30 fund
d. 100-year flood

40. _________ is gross income minus income tax on that income.

Discretionary income is income after subtracting taxes and normal expenses (such as rent or mortgage, utilities, insurance, medical, transportation, property maintenance, child support, inflation, food and sundries, 'c.) to maintain a certain standard of living.

a. Stamp Act
b. Taxation as theft
c. Disposable personal income
d. Disposable income

41. _________ are the prices that the factors of production of a finished item attract.

There has been some economic debate as to what determines these prices. Classical and Marxist economists argued that the _________ decided the value of a product and so value was intrinsic within the product.

a. Marginal product
b. Productivity model
c. Factor prices
d. Marginal product of labor

42. In economics, _________ is how a natione;s total economy is distributed among its population. ._________ has always been a central concern of economic theory and economic policy. Classical economists such as Adam Smith, Thomas Malthus and David Ricardo were mainly concerned with factor _________, that is, the distribution of income between the main factors of production, land, labour and capital.

a. Eco commerce
b. Equipment trust certificate
c. Authorised capital
d. Income distribution

43. A variety of measures of _________ and output are used in economics to estimate total economic activity in a country or region, including gross domestic product (GDP), gross national product (GNP), and net _________

There are three main ways of calculating these numbers; the output approach, the income approach and the expenditure approach. In theory, the three must yield the same, because total expenditures on goods and services must equal the total income paid to the producers (Gnational income), and that must also equal the total value of the output of goods and services (GNP.)

a. Gross world product
b. Volume index
c. GNI per capita
d. National income

44. A _________ represents the combinations of goods and services that a consumer can purchase given current prices and his income. Consumer theory uses the concepts of a _________ and a preference map to analyze consumer choices. Both concepts have a ready graphical representation in the two-good case.

a. Joint demand
b. Revealed preference
c. Budget constraint
d. Quality bias

45. In economics, a _________ is a function that specifies the output of a firm, an industry, or an entire economy for all combinations of inputs. A meta-_________ compares the practice of the existing entities converting inputs X into output y to determine the most efficient practice _________ of the existing entities, whether the most efficient feasible practice production or the most efficient actual practice production. In either case, the maximum output of a technologically-determined production process is a mathematical function of input factors of production.

a. Short-run
b. Constant elasticity of substitution
c. Production function
d. Post-Fordism

46. In economics, the _________ is the term economists use to describe the self-regulating nature of the marketplace. The _________ is a metaphor coined by the economist Adam Smith in The Wealth of Nations.

Adam Smith mentions the metaphor in Book IV of The Wealth of Nations, arguing that people in any society will certainly employ their capital in foreign trading only if the profits available by that method far exceed those available locally, and that in such a case it is better for society as a whole if they so did.

a. AD-IA Model
b. ACEA agreement
c. ACCRA Cost of Living Index
d. Invisible hand

47. _________ is a mechanism that allows people easily to buy and sell products. Services are often included in the scope of the term. _________ regulation is an economic term that describes restrictions in the market.

a. Fixed exchange rate system
b. Market dominance
c. Product market
d. Financialization

48. In economics, an _________ or spillover of an economic transaction is an impact on a party that is not directly involved in the transaction. In such a case, prices do not reflect the full costs or benefits in production or consumption of a product or service. A positive impact is called an external benefit, while a negative impact is called an external cost.

a. Environmental tariff
b. Existence value
c. Environmental impact assessment
d. Externality

49. _________ is a situation in which the limited resources of a firm are allocated in accordance with the wishes of consumers. An allocatively efficient economy produces an 'optimal mix' of commodities. A firm is allocatively efficient when its price is equal to its marginal costs (that is, P = MC) in a perfect market.

a. ACEA agreement
b. Allocative efficiency
c. Economic efficiency
d. ACCRA Cost of Living Index

50. In law and economics, the _________, describes the economic efficiency of an economic allocation or outcome in the presence of externalities. The theorem states that when trade in an externality is possible and there are no transaction costs, bargaining will lead to an efficient outcome regardless of the initial allocation of property rights. In practice, obstacles to bargaining or poorly defined property rights can prevent Coasian bargaining.

a. General Mining Act of 1872
b. Prior appropriation water rights
c. Means test
d. Coase theorem

51. _________ is the increase in the amount of the goods and services produced by an economy over time. It is conventionally measured as the percent rate of increase in real gross domestic product, or real GDP. Growth is usually calculated in real terms, i.e. inflation-adjusted terms, in order to net out the effect of inflation on the price of the goods and services produced.

a. ACEA agreement
b. ACCRA Cost of Living Index
c. AD-IA Model
d. Economic growth

52. The _________ was a period in the late 18th and early 19th centuries when major changes in agriculture, manufacturing, mining, and transportation had a profound effect on the socioeconomic and cultural conditions in Britain. The changes subsequently spread throughout Europe, North America, and eventually the world. The onset of the _________ marked a major turning point in human society; almost every aspect of daily life was eventually influenced in some way.

a. Adolf Hitler
b. Adolph Fischer
c. Adam Smith
d. Industrial Revolution

53. In economics, a _________ exists when the production or use of goods and services by the market is not efficient. That is, there exists another outcome where all involved can be made better off. _________s can be viewed as scenarios where individuals' pursuit of pure self-interest leads to results that are not efficient - that can be improved upon from the societal point-of-view.

a. Fixed exchange rate
b. Financial economics
c. Market failure
d. General equilibrium

54. In economics, a _________ exists when a specific individual or enterprise has sufficient control over a particular product or service to determine significantly the terms on which other individuals shall have access to it. Monopolies are thus characterized by a lack of economic competition for the good or service that they provide and a lack of viable substitute goods. The verb 'monopolize' refers to the process by which a firm gains persistently greater market share than what is expected under perfect competition.

a. 100-year flood
b. 130-30 fund
c. 1921 recession
d. Monopoly

55. In neoclassical economics and microeconomics, _________ describes the perfect being a market in which there are many small firms, all producing homogeneous goods. In the short term, such markets are productively inefficient as output will not occur where mc is equal to ac, but allocatively efficient, as output under _________ will always occur where mc is equal to mr, and therefore where mc equals ar. However, in the long term, such markets are both allocatively and productively efficient.

a. Law of supply
b. Co-operative economics
c. General equilibrium
d. Perfect competition

56. _________ is exchange of capital, goods, and services across international borders or territories. In most countries, it represents a significant share of gross domestic product (GDP.) While _________ has been present throughout much of history , its economic, social, and political importance has been on the rise in recent centuries.

a. Incoterms
b. Intra-industry trade
c. Import license
d. International trade

57. _________ is a term used to describe how different aspects between economies are integrated. The basics of this theory were written by the Hungarian Economist Béla Balassa in the 1960s. As _________ increases, the barriers of trade between markets diminishes.

a. Economic integration
b. Import license
c. Import
d. Inward investment

58. In economics, a _________ is a mechanism that allows people to easily buy and sell (trade) financial securities (such as stocks and bonds), commodities (such as precious metals or agricultural goods), and other fungible items of value at low transaction costs and at prices that reflect the efficient-market hypothesis.

_________s have evolved significantly over several hundred years and are undergoing constant innovation to improve liquidity.

Both general markets (where many commodities are traded) and specialized markets (where only one commodity is traded) exist.

a. Noise trader
b. Market anomaly
c. Convertible arbitrage
d. Financial market

59. _________ in its literal sense is the process of transformation of local or regional phenomena into global ones. It can be described as a process by which the people of the world are unified into a single society and function together.

This process is a combination of economic, technological, sociocultural and political forces.

a. Globally Integrated Enterprise
b. Helsinki Process on Globalisation and Democracy
c. Global Cosmopolitanism
d. Globalization

60. In economics, economic output is divided into physical goods and intangible services. Consumption of _________ is assumed to produce utility. It is often used when referring to a _________ Tax.

a. Composite good
b. Manufactured goods
c. Private good
d. Goods and services

61. _________ is subcontracting a process, such as product design or manufacturing, to a third-party company. The decision to outsource is often made in the interest of lowering cost or making better use of time and energy costs, redirecting or conserving energy directed at the competencies of a particular business, or to make more efficient use of land, labor, capital, (information) technology and resources. _________ became part of the business lexicon during the 1980s.

a. Electronic business
b. Additional Funds Needed
c. Averch-Johnson effect
d. Outsourcing

62. _________ is the economic policy of restraining trade between states, through methods such as tariffs on imported goods, restrictive quotas, and a variety of other restrictive government regulations designed to discourage imports, and prevent foreign take-over of local markets and companies. This policy is closely aligned with anti-globalization, and contrasts with free trade, where government barriers to trade are kept to a minimum. The term is mostly used in the context of economics, where _________ refers to policies or doctrines which 'protect' businesses and workers within a country by restricting or regulating trade with foreign nations.

a. Google economy
b. Digital economy
c. Knowledge economy
d. Protectionism

63. In economics, _________ refers to the ability of a party to produce a good or service using fewer real resources than another entity producing the same good or service..A party has an _________ when using the same input as another party, it can produce a greater output. Since _________ is determined by a simple comparison of labor productivities, it is possible for a party to have no _________ in anything. It can be contrasted with the concept of comparative advantage which refers to the ability to produce a particular good at a lower opportunity cost.

a. International economics
b. Index number
c. ACCRA Cost of Living Index
d. Absolute advantage

64. In economics a _________ is an entity that owes a debt to someone else. The entity may be an individual, a firm, a government, a company or other legal person. The counterparty is called a creditor.

a. Decision process tool
b. Duration gap
c. Senior stretch loan
d. Debtor

65. A _________ is the transfer of wealth from one party (such as a person or company) to another. A _________ is usually made in exchange for the provision of goods, services or both, or to fulfill a legal obligation.

The simplest and oldest form of _________ is barter, the exchange of one good or service for another.

a. Soft count
b. Going concern
c. Social gravity
d. Payment

66. _________ in economics refers to metrics and measures of output from production processes, per unit of input. Labor _________, for example, is typically measured as a ratio of output per labor-hour, an input. _________ may be conceived of as a metrics of the technical or engineering efficiency of production.

a. Fordism
b. Piece work
c. Productivity
d. Production-possibility frontier

67. The _________ is the central banking system of the United States. Created in 1913 by the enactment of the Federal Reserve Act (signed by Woodrow Wilson), it is a quasi-public and quasi-private (government entity with private components) banking system that comprises (1) the presidentially appointed Board of Governors of the _________ in Washington, D.C.; (2) the Federal Open Market Committee; (3) twelve regional Federal Reserve Banks located in major cities throughout the nation acting as fiscal agents for the U.S. Treasury, each with its own nine-member board of directors; (4) numerous other private U.S. member banks, which subscribe to required amounts of non-transferable stock in their regional Federal Reserve Banks; and (5) various advisory councils. Since February 2006, Ben Bernanke has served as the Chairman of the Board of Governors of the

_________.

a. Federal Reserve System Open Market Account
b. Federal Reserve System
c. Term auction facility
d. Monetary Policy Report to the Congress

68. The term financial crisis is applied broadly to a variety of situations in which some financial institutions or assets suddenly lose a large part of their value. In the 19th and early 20th centuries, many _________ were associated with banking panics, and many recessions coincided with these panics. Other situations that are often called _________ include stock market crashes and the bursting of other financial bubbles, currency crises, and sovereign defaults.

a. Microeconomics
b. General equilibrium
c. Georgism
d. Financial crises

69. In economics, _________ is inflation that is very high or 'out of control', a condition in which prices increase rapidly as a currency loses its value. Definitions used by the media vary from a cumulative inflation rate over three years approaching 100% to 'inflation exceeding 50% a month.' In informal usage the term is often applied to much lower rates. As a rule of thumb, normal inflation is reported per year, but _________ is often reported for much shorter intervals, often per month.

a. 1921 recession
b. 130-30 fund
c. 100-year flood
d. Hyperinflation

70. In economics, _________ is the total amount of money available in an economy at a particular point in time. There are several ways to define 'money', but standard measures usually include currency in circulation and demand deposits.

_________ data are recorded and published, usually by the government or the central bank of the country.

a. Neutrality of money
b. Veil of money
c. Velocity of money
d. Money supply

71. The _________ is the market for securities, where companies and governments can raise longterm funds. It is a market in which money is lent for periods longer than a year. The _________ includes the stock market and the bond market.

a. Financial instrument
b. Multi-family office
c. Capital Market
d. Performance attribution

72. _________ is money accepted for exchange of goods in an economy. The prevalence of one money over another arises, usually, when a government designates through decrees that the government shall accept only particular notes and coins in payment for taxes. Typically, money of _________ consists of stamped coins and minted paper bills.

a. Security thread
b. Currency
c. Local currency
d. Totnes pound

73. A _________ is a monetary authority which is required to maintain a fixed exchange rate with a foreign currency. This policy objective requires the conventional objectives of a central bank to be subordinated to the exchange rate target.

The main qualities of an orthodox _________ are:

- A _________'s foreign currency reserves must be sufficient to ensure that all holders of its notes and coins (and all banks creditor of a Reserve Account at the _________) can convert them into the reserve currency (usually 110-115% of the monetary base M0.)
- A _________ maintains absolute, unlimited convertibility between its notes and coins and the currency against which they are pegged (the anchor currency), at a fixed rate of exchange, with no restrictions on current-account or capital-account transactions.
- A _________ only earns profit from interests on foreign reserves (less the expense of note-issuing), and does not engage in forward-exchange transactions. These foreign reserves exist (1) because local notes have been issued in exchange, or (2) because commercial banks must by regulation deposit a minimum reserve at the _________. (1) generates a seignorage revenue. (2) is the revenue on minimum reserves (revenue of investment activities less cost of minimum reserves remuneration)
- A _________ has no discretionary powers to effect monetary policy and does not lend to the government. Governments cannot print money, and can only tax or borrow to meet their spending commitments.
- A _________ does not act as a lender of last resort to commercial banks, and does not regulate reserve requirements.
- A _________ does not attempt to manipulate interest rates by establishing a discount rate like a central bank. The peg with the foreign currency tends to keep interest rates and inflation very closely aligned to those in the country against whose currency the peg is fixed.

The _________ in question will no longer issue fiat money but instead will only issue one unit of local currency for each unit (or decided amount) of foreign currency it has in its vault (often a hard currency such as the U.S. dollar or the euro.) The surplus on the balance of payments of that country is reflected by higher deposits local banks hold at the central bank as well as (initially) higher deposits of the (net) exporting firms at their local banks.

a. Petrodollar
b. Reserve currency
c. Currency competition
d. Currency board

74. A _________, which is also called a balance-of-payments crisis, occurs when the value of a currency changes quickly, undermining its ability to serve as a medium of exchange or a store of value. It is a type of financial crisis and is often associated with a real economic crisis. Currency crises can be especially destructive to small open economies or bigger, but not sufficiently stable ones.

a. Speculative attack
b. Currency crisis
c. 130-30 fund
d. 100-year flood

75. The term _________ is applied broadly to a variety of situations in which some financial institutions or assets suddenly lose a large part of their value. In the 19th and early 20th centuries, many financial crises were associated with banking panics, and many recessions coincided with these panics. Other situations that are often called financial crises include stock market crashes and the bursting of other financial bubbles, currency crises, and sovereign defaults.

a. Market failure
b. Financial crisis
c. Macroeconomics
d. Co-operative economics

76. In economics, _________ is a rise in the general level of prices of goods and services in an economy over a period of time. When the general price level rises, each unit of currency buys fewer goods and services; consequently, _________ is also a decline in the real value of money--a loss of purchasing power in the medium of exchange which is also the monetary unit of account in the economy. A chief measure of general price-level _________ is the general _________ rate, which is the percentage change in a general price index (normally the Consumer Price Index) over time.

a. Energy economics
b. Inflation
c. Economic
d. Opportunity cost

77. A _________ is an expression that compares quantities relative to each other. The most common examples involve two quantities, but any number of quantities can be compared. _________s are represented mathematically by separating each quantity with a colon, for example the _________ 2:3, which is read as the _________ 'two to three'.

a. 100-year flood
b. 130-30 fund
c. Y-intercept
d. Ratio

78. A _________ is the exclusive authority to determine how a resource is used, whether that resource is owned by government or by individuals. All economic goods have a _________s attribute. This attribute has three broad components

1. The right to use the good
2. The right to earn income from the good
3. The right to transfer the good to others

The concept of _________s as used by economists and legal scholars are related but distinct. The distinction is largely seen in the economists' focus on the ability of an individual or collective to control the use of the good.

a. Property right
b. Post-sale restraint
c. High-reeve
d. Holder in due course

79. _________ is a common concept in economics, and gives rise to derived concepts such as consumer debt. Generally _________ is defined by opposition to production. But the precise definition can vary because different schools of economists define production quite differently.

a. Consumption
b. Federal Reserve Bank Notes
c. Foreclosure data providers
d. Cash or share options

80. In economic theory, _________ is the competitive situation in any market where the conditions necessary for perfect competition are not satisfied. It is a market structure that does not meet the conditions of perfect competition.

Forms of _________ include:

- Monopoly, in which there is only one seller of a good.
- Oligopoly, in which there is a small number of sellers.
- Monopolistic competition, in which there are many sellers producing highly differentiated goods.
- Monopsony, in which there is only one buyer of a good.
- Oligopsony, in which there is a small number of buyers.

There may also be _________ in markets due to buyers or sellers lacking information about prices and the goods being traded.

There may also be _________ due to a time lag in a market.

a. Imperfect competition
b. ACCRA Cost of Living Index
c. ACEA agreement
d. AD-IA Model

81. _________ is used to assign the available resources in an economic way. It is part of resource management.

In strategic planning,is a plan for using available resources, for example human resources, especially in the near term, to achieve goals for the future.

a. 100-year flood
b. Resource allocation
c. 1921 recession
d. 130-30 fund

82. _________ is the concept or idea of fairness in economics, particularly as to taxation or welfare economics.

In welfare economics, _________ may be distinguished from economic efficiency in overall evaluation of social welfare. Although '_________' has broader uses, it may be posed as a counterpart to economic inequality in yielding a 'good' distribution of welfare.

a. ACEA agreement
b. ACCRA Cost of Living Index
c. Equity
d. AD-IA Model

83. In calculus, a function f defined on a subset of the real numbers with real values is called _________, if for all x and y such that x >≤ y one has f(x) >≤ f(y), so f preserves the order. In layman's terms, the sign of the slope is always positive (the curve tending upwards) or zero (i.e., non-decreasing, or asymptotic, or depicted as a horizontal, flat line) Likewise, a function is called monotonically decreasing (non-increasing) if, whenever x >≤ y, then f(x) >≥ f(y), so it reverses the order.

a. Monotonic
b. 130-30 fund
c. 100-year flood
d. 1921 recession

84. In economics, a _________ occurs when, due to the economies of scale of a particular industry, the maximum efficiency of production and distribution is realized through a single supplier.

Natural monopolies arise where the largest supplier in an industry, often the first supplier in a market, has an overwhelming cost advantage over other actual or potential competitors. This tends to be the case in industries where capital costs predominate, creating economies of scale which are large in relation to the size of the market, and hence high barriers to entry; examples include water services and electricity.

a. Collective goods
b. Common-pool resource
c. Privatizing profits and socializing losses
d. Natural monopoly

85. Many _________ are related to the environmental consequences of production and use

- Systemic risk describes the risks to the overall economy arising from the risks which the banking system takes. That the private costs of banking failure may be smaller than the social costs justifies banking regulations, although regulations could create a moral hazard.

- Anthropogenic climate change is attributed to greenhouse gas emissions from burning oil, gas, and coal. Global warming has been ranked as the #1 externality of all economic activity, in the magnitude of potential harms and yet remains unmitigated.

a. Negative externalities
b. Green certificate
c. Total Economic Value
d. White certificates

86. Examples of _________ include:

- A beekeeper keeps the bees for their honey. A side effect or externality associated with his activity is the pollination of surrounding crops by the bees. The value generated by the pollination may be more important than the value of the harvested honey.

- An individual planting an attractive garden in front of his house may provide benefits to others living in the area, and even financial benefits in the form of increased property values for all property owners.

- An individual buying a product that is interconnected in a network (e.g., a video cellphone) will increase the usefulness of such phones to other people who have a video cellphone. When each new user of a product increases the value of the same product owned by others, the phenomenon is called a network externality or a network effect. Network externalities often have 'tipping points' where, suddenly, the product reaches general acceptance and near-universal usage, a phenomenon which can be seen in the near universal take-up of cellphones in some Scandinavian countries.

- Knowledge spillover of inventions and information - once an invention (or most other forms of practical information) is discovered or made more easily accessible, others benefit by exploiting the invention or information. Copyright and intellectual property law are mechanisms to allow the inventor or creator to benefit from a temporary, state-protected monopoly in return for 'sharing' the information through publication or other means.

a. Total Economic Value
b. Weighted average cost of carbon
c. Positive externalities
d. Negative externalities

87. _________s are externalities of economic activity or processes upon those who are not directly involved in it. Odours from a rendering plant are negative _________s upon its neighbours; the beauty of a homeowner's flower garden is a positive _________ upon neighbours.

In the same way, the economic benefits of increased trade are the _________s anticipated in the formation of multilateral alliances of many of the regional nation states: e.g. SARC (South Asian Regional Cooperation), ASpillover effectAN (Association of South East Asian Nations)

In reference to psychology, the _________ is when other people's emotions affect the emotions of those around them.

a. Cobb-Douglas
b. Public good
c. Spillover effect
d. Business sector

88. In economics, a _________ is a good that is non-rivaled and non-excludable. This means, respectively, that consumption of the good by one individual does not reduce availability of the good for consumption by others; and that no one can be effectively excluded from using the good. In the real world, there may be no such thing as an absolutely non-rivaled and non-excludable good; but economists think that some goods approximate the concept closely enough for the analysis to be economically useful.

a. Happiness economics
b. Neoclassical synthesis
c. Demand-pull theory
d. Public good

89. _________ is that which is owed; usually referencing assets owed, but the term can also cover moral obligations and other interactions not requiring money. In the case of assets, _________ is a means of using future purchasing power in the present before a summation has been earned. Some companies and corporations use _________ as a part of their overall corporate finance strategy.

a. Debt
b. Collateral Management
c. Debenture
d. Hard money loan

90. A _________ or a flexible exchange rate is a type of exchange rate regime wherein a currency's value is allowed to fluctuate according to the foreign exchange market. A currency that uses a _________ is known as a floating currency. The opposite of a _________ is a fixed exchange rate.

a. Floating currency
b. Floating exchange rate
c. Trade Weighted US dollar Index
d. Foreign exchange market

91. The _________ is a measure of statistical dispersion, commonly used as a measure of inequality of income distribution or inequality of wealth distribution. It is defined as a ratio with values between 0 and 1: A low _________ indicates more equal income or wealth distribution, while a high _________ indicates more unequal distribution. 0 corresponds to perfect equality (everyone having exactly the same income) and 1 corresponds to perfect inequality (where one person has all the income, while everyone else has zero income.)

a. Leapfrogging
b. Suits index
c. Gini coefficient
d. Compensating variation

92. In economics, the _________ is used to illustrate the idea that increases in the rate of taxation do not necessarily increase tax revenue. (For instance, whereas a 0% income tax rate will generate no revenue, neither will a 100% rate, as citizens will have no incentive to make money.) Increasing taxes beyond the peak of the curve point will decrease tax revenue.

a. 130-30 fund
b. 100-year flood
c. Laffer curve
d. 1921 recession

93. _________ is the prospect that a party insulated from risk may behave differently from the way it would behave if it were fully exposed to the risk. In insurance, _________ that occurs without conscious or malicious action is called morale hazard.

_________ is related to information asymmetry, a situation in which one party in a transaction has more information than another.

a. Moral hazard
b. 100-year flood
c. 130-30 fund
d. 1921 recession

94. In mathematics, a _________ is a constant multiplicative factor of a certain object. For example, in the expression $9x^2$, the _________ of x^2 is 9.

The object can be such things as a variable, a vector, a function, etc.

a. Coefficient
b. 100-year flood
c. 1921 recession
d. 130-30 fund

95. In finance, the _________s between two currencies specifies how much one currency is worth in terms of the other. It is the value of a foreign natione;s currency in terms of the home natione;s currency. For example an _________ of 102 Japanese yen to the United States dollar means that JPY 102 is worth the same as USD 1.

a. ACCRA Cost of Living Index
b. Interbank market
c. Exchange rate
d. ACEA agreement

96. In mathematics, an _________ is a statement about the relative size or order of two objects, or about whether they are the same or not

- The notation a < b means that a is less than b.
- The notation a > b means that a is greater than b.
- The notation a ≠ b means that a is not equal to b, but does not say that one is greater than the other or even that they can be compared in size.

In each statement above, a is not equal to b. These relations are known as strict inequalities. The notation a < b may also be read as 'a is strictly less than b'.

a. Inequality
b. ACCRA Cost of Living Index
c. AD-IA Model
d. ACEA agreement

97. Economic _________ is defined as an excess distribution to any factor in a production process above that which is required to induce the factor into the process or any excess above that which is necessary to keep the factor in its current use..

Classical Factor _________ is primarily concerned with the fee paid for the use of fixed (e.g. natural) resources. The classical definition is expressed as any excess payment above that required to induce or provide for production.

a. 130-30 fund
b. Rent
c. 100-year flood
d. 1921 recession

98. To _________ is to impose a financial charge or other levy upon a taxpayer by a state or the functional equivalent of a state.

_________es are also imposed by many subnational entities. _________es consist of direct _________ or indirect _________, and may be paid in money or as its labour equivalent (often but not always unpaid.)

a. 100-year flood
b. 130-30 fund
c. 1921 recession
d. Tax

99. To tax is to impose a financial charge or other levy upon a taxpayer by a state or the functional equivalent of a state.

_________ are also imposed by many subnational entities. _________ consist of direct tax or indirect tax, and may be paid in money or as its labour equivalent (often but not always unpaid.)

a. 130-30 fund
b. 1921 recession
c. 100-year flood
d. Taxes

100. The term _________ refers to economy-wide fluctuations in production or economic activity over several months or years. These fluctuations occur around a long-term growth trend, and typically involve shifts over time between periods of relatively rapid economic growth (expansion or boom), and periods of relative stagnation or decline (contraction or recession.)

These fluctuations are often measured using the growth rate of real gross domestic product.

a. Tobit model
b. Business cycle
c. Consumer theory
d. Nominal value

101. A _________, reserve bank, or monetary authority is the entity responsible for the monetary policy of a country or of a group of member states. It is a bank that can lend money to other banks in times of need. Its primary responsibility is to maintain the stability of the national currency and money supply, but more active duties include controlling subsidized-loan interest rates, and acting as a lender of last resort to the banking sector during times of financial crisis (private banks often being integral to the national financial system.)

a. 100-year flood
b. Central bank
c. 1921 recession
d. 130-30 fund

102. _________ is a term that refers both to:

- a formal discipline used to help appraise, or assess, the case for a project or proposal, which itself is a process known as project appraisal; and
- an informal approach to making decisions of any kind.

Under both definitions the process involves, whether explicitly or implicitly, weighing the total expected costs against the total expected benefits of one or more actions in order to choose the best or most profitable option. The formal process is often referred to as either CBA (_________) or BCost-benefit analysis

A hallmark of CBA is that all benefits and all costs are expressed in money terms, and are adjusted for the time value of money, so that all flows of benefits and flows of project costs over time (which tend to occur at different points in time) are expressed on a common basis in terms of their e;present value.e; Closely related, but slightly different, formal techniques include Cost-effectiveness analysis, Economic impact analysis, Fiscal impact analysis and Social Return on Investment(SROI) analysis. The latter builds upon the logic of _________, but differs in that it is explicitly designed to inform the practical decision-making of enterprise managers and investors focused on optimising their social and environmental impacts.

a. Cost-benefit analysis
b. 100-year flood
c. Decision theory
d. 130-30 fund

103. _________ refers to an absence of excessive fluctuations in the macroeconomy. An economy with fairly constant output growth and low and stable inflation would be considered economically stable. An economy with frequent large recessions, a pronounced business cycle, very high or variable inflation, or frequent financial crises would be considered economically unstable.

a. Export-led growth
b. Export subsidy
c. Economic stability
d. Income effect

104. The term _________ refers to government debt, expenditures and revenues, or to finance (particularly financial revenue) in general.

- _________ deficit is the budget deficit of federal or local government
- _________ policy is the discretionary spending of governments. Contrasts with monetary policy.
- _________ year and _________ quarter are reporting periods for firms and other agencies.

.

a. Fiscal
b. Bucket shop
c. Drawdown
d. Procter ' Gamble

105. In economics, _________ is the use of government spending and revenue collection to influence the economy.

_________ can be contrasted with the other main type of economic policy, monetary policy, which attempts to stabilize the economy by controlling interest rates and the supply of money. The two main instruments of _________ are government spending and taxation.

a. 100-year flood
b. Fiscalism
c. Sustainable investment rule
d. Fiscal policy

106. In economics, _________ is the transfer of income, wealth or property from some individuals to others.

One premise of _________ is that money should be distributed to benefit the poorer members of society, and that the rich have an obligation to assist the poor, thus creating a more financially egalitarian society. Another argument is that the rich exploit the poor or otherwise gain unfair benefits.

a. Redistribution
b. 1921 recession
c. 130-30 fund
d. 100-year flood

107. _________ in economics are wage and price controls, most commonly instituted as a response to inflation, and usually below market level.

This type of policy dates to the Old Testament, in which Israelites were instructed not to charge interest to other Israelites. It was tried during the Roman Empire.

a. Inflationary Spikes
b. Employment Cost Index
c. Inflation swap
d. Incomes policies

108. _________, 1st Baron Keynes was a renowned economist from Britain whose many ideas on economic and political theories as well as on many governments' monetary policies influenced America. He advocated a government that played an active role in the lives of people regarding business, economy, etc. In this role, the government would use fiscal measures to reduce the consequences of recessions, economic depressions and booms.

a. Adolf Hitler
b. Adam Smith
c. Adolph Fischer
d. John Maynard Keynes

109. _________ and Keynesian Theory) is a macroeconomic theory based on the ideas of 20th-century British economist John Maynard Keynes. _________ argues that private sector decisions sometimes lead to inefficient macroeconomic outcomes and therefore advocates active policy responses by the public sector, including monetary policy actions by the central bank and fiscal policy actions by the government to stabilize output over the business cycle.

The theories forming the basis of _________ were first presented in The General Theory of Employment, Interest and Money, published in 1936.

a. Market failure
b. Deflation
c. Keynesian economics
d. Rational choice theory

110. The _________ was a fundamental reworking of economic theory concerning the factors determining employment levels in the overall economy. The revolution was set against the orthodox classical economic framework, which based on Say's Law argued that unless special conditions prevailed the free market would naturally establish full employment equilibrium with no need for government intervention. Employers will be able to make a profit by employing all available workers as long as workers drop their wages below the value of the total output they are able to produce - and classical economics assumed that in a free market workers would be willing to lower their wage demands accordingly , because they are rational agents who would rather work for less than face unemployment.

a. Keynesian revolution
b. Speculative demand
c. Neo-Keynesian economics
d. Military Keynesianism

111. A _________ is a tax by which the tax rate increases as the taxable amount increases. 'Progressive' describes a distribution effect on income or expenditure, referring to the way the rate progresses from low to high, where the average tax rate is less than the marginal tax rate. It can be applied to individual taxes or to a tax system as a whole; a year, multi-year, or lifetime.

a. Progressive tax
b. 130-30 fund
c. Proportional tax
d. 100-year flood

112. In economics, a _________ is a general slowdown in economic activity over a sustained period of time, or a business cycle contraction. During _________s, many macroeconomic indicators vary in a similar way. Production as measured by Gross Domestic Product (GDP), employment, investment spending, capacity utilization, household incomes and business profits all fall during _________s.

a. Monetary economics
b. Leading indicators
c. Treasury View
d. Recession

113. In economics, a _________ is a redistribution of income in the market system. These payments are considered to be nonexhaustive because they do not directly absorb resources or create output. Examples of certain _________s include welfare (financial aid), social security, and government subsidies for certain businesses (firms.)

a. 130-30 fund
b. 100-year flood
c. 1921 recession
d. Transfer payment

114. In economics, _________ is the total demand for final goods and services in the economy (Y) at a given time and price level. It is the amount of goods and services in the economy that will be purchased at all possible price levels. This is the demand for the gross domestic product of a country when inventory levels are static.

a. Aggregate expenditure
b. Aggregate supply
c. Aggregation problem
d. Aggregate demand

115. The term surplus is used in economics for several related quantities. The _________ is the amount that consumers benefit by being able to purchase a product for a price that is less than they would be willing to pay. The producer surplus is the amount that producers benefit by selling at a market price mechanism that is higher than they would be willing to sell for.

a. Necessity good
b. Microeconomic reform
c. Marginal rate of technical substitution
d. Consumer surplus

116. _________ was an American economist, statistician and public intellectual, and a recipient of the Nobel Memorial Prize in Economic Sciences. He is best known among scholars for his theoretical and empirical research, especially consumption analysis, monetary history and theory, and for his demonstration of the complexity of stabilization policy. A global public followed his restatement of a political philosophy that insisted on minimizing the role of government in favor of the private sector.

a. Adolph Fischer
b. Adolf Hitler
c. Milton Friedman
d. Adam Smith

117. _________ is the public sector analogy to market failure and occurs when a government intervention causes a more inefficient allocation of goods and resources than would occur without that intervention. Likewise, the government's failure to intervene in a market failure that would result in a socially preferable mix of output is referred to as passive _________ (Weimer and Vining, 2004.) Just as with market failures, there are many different kinds of _________s that describe corresponding distortions.

a. Government-granted monopoly
b. Privatizing profits and socializing losses
c. Natural monopoly
d. Government failure

118. _________ is the socio-economic status of unfree peasants under feudalism, and specifically relates to Manorialism. It was a condition of bondage or modified slavery which developed primarily during the High Middle Ages in Europe. _________ was the enforced labour of serfs on the fields of landowners, in return for protection and the right to work on their leased fields.

a. Rural tenancy
b. Landwirtschaftliche Produktionsgenossenschaft
c. Metayage
d. Serfdom

119. _________ in political thought refers to economic theories of social organization advocating collective ownership and administration of the means of production and distribution of goods, and a society characterized by equality for all individuals, with an egalitarian method of compensation. Modern _________ originated in the late 19th-century intellectual and working class political movement that criticized the effects of industrialization and private ownership on society. Karl Marx posited that _________ would be achieved via class struggle and a proletarian revolution after a transitional stage from capitalism called the dictatorship of the proletariat.

a. Adam Smith
b. Socialism
c. Adolph Fischer
d. Adolf Hitler

1. In economics, _________ is the total demand for final goods and services in the economy (Y) at a given time and price level. It is the amount of goods and services in the economy that will be purchased at all possible price levels. This is the demand for the gross domestic product of a country when inventory levels are static.
a. Aggregate demand
b. Aggregate expenditure
c. Aggregate supply
d. Aggregation problem

2. In economics, _________ is the total supply of goods and services produced by a national economy during a specific time period. It is the total amount of goods and services in the economy available at all possible price levels.
a. Aggregate expenditure
b. Aggregate demand
c. Aggregation problem
d. Aggregate supply

3. _________ is a broad label that refers to any individuals or households that use goods and services generated within the economy. The concept of a _________ is used in different contexts, so that the usage and significance of the term may vary.

Typically when business people and economists talk of _________s they are talking about person as _________, an aggregated commodity item with little individuality other than that expressed in the buy/not-buy decision.

a. 130-30 fund
b. Consumer
c. 1921 recession
d. 100-year flood

4. A _________ is an object whose consumption increases the utility of the consumer, for which the quantity demanded exceeds the quantity supplied at zero price. _________s are usually modeled as having diminishing marginal utility. The first individual purchase has high utility; the second has less.
a. Composite good
b. Pie method
c. Merit good
d. Good

5. In economics, economic output is divided into physical goods and intangible services. Consumption of _________ is assumed to produce utility. It is often used when referring to a _________ Tax.
a. Composite good
b. Manufactured goods
c. Goods and services
d. Private good

6. _________ is an economic concept with commonplace familiarity. It is the price that a good or service is offered at, or will fetch, in the marketplace. It is of interest mainly in the study of microeconomics.
a. Market anomaly
b. Noisy market hypothesis
c. Market price
d. Paper trading

7. _________ in economics and business is the result of an exchange and from that trade we assign a numerical monetary value to a good, service or asset. If Alice trades Bob 4 apples for an orange, the _________ of an orange is 4 apples. Inversely, the _________ of an apple is 1/4 oranges.
a. Price
b. Price war
c. Premium pricing
d. Price book

8. _________ is defined as the measure of responsiveness in the quantity demanded for a commodity as a result of change in price of the same commodity. It is a measure of how consumers react to a change in price. In other words, it is percentage change in quantity demanded as per the percentage change in price of the same commodity.

a. 100-year flood
b. 130-30 fund
c. Price elasticity of demand
d. 1921 recession

9. In economics, the _________ is defined as a numerical measure of the responsiveness of the quantity supplied of product (A) to a change in price of product (A) alone. It is the measure of the way quantity supplied reacts to a change in price.

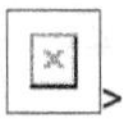

For example, if, in response to a 10% rise in the price of a good, the quantity supplied increases by 20%, the _________ would be 20%/10% = 2.

a. Price elasticity of supply
b. Demand shaping
c. Passive income
d. Hedonimetry

10. A _________ or market-based mechanism is any of a wide variety of ways to match up buyers and sellers.

An example of a _________ uses announced bid and ask prices. Generally speaking, when two parties wish to engage in a trade, the purchaser will announce a price he is willing to pay (the bid price) and seller will announce a price he is willing to accept (the ask price.)

a. Horizontal market
b. Market equilibrium
c. Marketization
d. Price mechanism

11. _________ is an economic model based on price, utility and quantity in a market. It predicts that in a competitive market, price will function to equalize the quantity demanded by consumers, and the quantity supplied by producers, resulting in an economic equilibrium of price and quantity. The model incorporates other factors changing equilibrium as a shift of demand and/or supply.

a. Supply and demand
b. Rational addiction
c. Joint demand
d. Deferred gratification

12. Competition law, known in the United States as _________ law, has three main elements:

- prohibiting agreements or practices that restrict free trading and competition between business entities. This includes in particular the repression of cartels.
- banning abusive behaviour by a firm dominating a market, or anti-competitive practices that tend to lead to such a dominant position. Practices controlled in this way may include predatory pricing, tying, price gouging, refusal to deal, and many others.
- supervising the mergers and acquisitions of large corporations, including some joint ventures. Transactions that are considered to threaten the competitive process can be prohibited altogether, or approved subject to 'remedies' such as an obligation to divest part of the merged business or to offer licences or access to facilities to enable other businesses to continue competing.

The substance and practice of competition law varies from jurisdiction to jurisdiction. Protecting the interests of consumers (consumer welfare) and ensuring that entrepreneurs have an opportunity to compete in the market economy are often treated as important objectives. Competition law is closely connected with law on deregulation of access to markets, state aids and subsidies, the privatisation of state owned assets and the establishment of independent sector regulators. In recent decades, competition law has been viewed as a way to provide better public services.

a. United Kingdom competition law
b. Antitrust
c. Anti-Inflation Act
d. Intellectual property law

13. Economics:

- _________,the desire to own something and the ability to pay for it
- _________ curve,a graphic representation of a _________ schedule
- _________ deposit, the money in checking accounts
- _________ pull theory,the theory that inflation occurs when _________ for goods and services exceeds existing supplies
- _________ schedule,a table that lists the quantity of a good a person will buy it each different price
- _________ side economics,the school of economics at believes government spending and tax cuts open economy by raising _________

.

a. McKesson ' Robbins scandal
b. Demand
c. Production
d. Variability

14. In economics, _________ is the ratio of the percent change in one variable to the percent change in another variable. It is a tool for measuring the responsiveness of a function to changes in parameters in a relative way. Commonly analyzed are _________ of substitution, price and wealth.

a. Elasticity
b. ACCRA Cost of Living Index
c. ACEA agreement
d. Elasticity of demand

15. Price _________ is defined as the measure of responsiveness in the quantity demanded for a commodity as a result of change in price of the same commodity. It is a measure of how consumers react to a change in price. In other words, it is percentage change in quantity demanded by the percentage change in price of the same commodity.

a. ACEA agreement
b. ACCRA Cost of Living Index
c. Elasticity
d. Elasticity of demand

16. In microeconomics, _________ is quite simply the conversion of inputs into outputs. It is an economic process that uses resources to create a good or service that is suitable for exchange. This can include manufacturing, storing, shipping, and packaging.

a. Solved
b. MET
c. Red Guards
d. Production

17. _________ is a concept with somewhat disparate meanings in several fields. It also has a common meaning which has a loose connection with some of those more definite meanings.

Casually, it is typically used to denote a lack of order, or purpose, or cause.

a. 100-year flood
b. 130-30 fund
c. 1921 recession
d. Randomness

18. In economics, the _________ can be defined as the graph depicting the relationship between the price of a certain commodity, and the amount of it that consumers are willing and able to purchase at that given price. It is a graphic representation of a demand schedule. The _________ for all consumers together follows from the _________ of every individual consumer: the individual demands at each price are added together.

a. Kuznets curve
b. Demand curve
c. Wage curve
d. Cost curve

19. In economics, a _________ is a table that lists the quantity of a good a person will buy it each different price See Demand curve.

a. Rational irrationality
b. Demand schedule
c. Free contract
d. Federal Reserve districts

20. The _________ or gross domestic income (GDI), a basic measure of an economy's economic performance, is the market value of all final goods and services produced within the borders of a nation in a year. _________ can be defined in three ways, all of which are conceptually identical. First, it is equal to the total expenditures for all final goods and services produced within the country in a stipulated period of time (usually a 365-day year.)

a. Monopolistic competition
b. Gross domestic product
c. Market structure
d. Countercyclical

21. Necessary _________s:

If x is a necessary _________ of y, then the presence of y necessarily implies the presence of x. The presence of x, however, does not imply that y will occur.

Sufficient _________s:

If x is a sufficient _________ of y, then the presence of x necessarily implies the presence of y.

a. Philosophy of economics
b. Political philosophy
c. Materialism
d. Cause

22. In economics, the _________ is the change in consumption resulting from a change in real income.

Another important item that can change is the money income of the consumer. The _________ is the phenomenon observed through changes in purchasing power.

a. Export subsidy
b. Equilibrium wage
c. Inflation hedge
d. Income effect

23. _________ in economics refers to metrics and measures of output from production processes, per unit of input. Labor _________, for example, is typically measured as a ratio of output per labor-hour, an input. _________ may be conceived of as a metrics of the technical or engineering efficiency of production.

a. Productivity
b. Fordism
c. Piece work
d. Production-possibility frontier

24. In economics, the _________ measures the payments that flow between any individual country and all other countries. It is used to summarize all international economic transactions for that country during a specific time period, usually a year. The _________ is determined by the country's exports and imports of goods, services, and financial capital, as well as financial transfers.

a. Gross world product
b. Skyscraper Index
c. Gross domestic product per barrel
d. Balance of payments

25. A _________ is the transfer of wealth from one party (such as a person or company) to another. A _________ is usually made in exchange for the provision of goods, services or both, or to fulfill a legal obligation.

The simplest and oldest form of _________ is barter, the exchange of one good or service for another.

a. Soft count
b. Social gravity
c. Going concern
d. Payment

26. In economics, _________ refers to how the marginal contribution of a factor of production usually decreases as more of the factor is used. According to this relationship, in a production system with fixed and variable inputs, beyond some point, each additional unit of the variable input yields smaller and smaller increases in output. Conversely, producing one more unit of output costs more and more in variable inputs.

a. Derivatives law
b. Patent troll
c. Diminishing returns
d. Community property

27. _________ is the term denoting either an entrance or changes which are inserted into a system and which activate/modify a process. It is an abstract concept, used in the modeling, system(s) design and system(s) exploitation. It is usually connected with other terms, e.g., _________ field, _________ variable, _________ parameter, _________ value, _________ signal, _________ device and _________ file.

a. AD-IA Model
b. ACCRA Cost of Living Index
c. ACEA agreement
d. Input

28. _________ is a term that is used to describe the overall process of invention, innovation and diffusion of technology or processes. The term is redundant with technological development, technological achievement, and technological progress. In essence _________ is the invention of a technology (or a process), the continuous process of improving a technology (in which it often becomes cheaper) and its diffusion throughout industry or society.

a. 1921 recession
b. 130-30 fund
c. 100-year flood
d. Technological change

29. In algebra, a _________ is a function depending on n that associates a scalar, det(A), to an n×n square matrix A. The fundamental geometric meaning of a _________ is a scale factor for measure when A is regarded as a linear transformation. _________s are important both in calculus, where they enter the substitution rule for several variables, and in multilinear algebra.

For a fixed nonnegative integer n, there is a unique _________ function for the n×n matrices over any commutative ring R. In particular, this function exists when R is the field of real or complex numbers.

a. 130-30 fund
b. Determinant
c. 100-year flood
d. 1921 recession

30. _________ theory is a branch of theoretical economics. It seeks to explain the behavior of supply, demand and prices in a whole economy with several or many markets. It is often assumed that agents are price takers and in that setting two common notions of equilibrium exist: Walrasian (or competitive) equilibrium, and its generalization; a price equilibrium with transfers.

a. Human capital
b. New Keynesian economics
c. General equilibrium
d. Rational choice theory

31. In economics, economic equilibrium is simply a state of the world where economic forces are balanced and in the absence of external influences the (equilibrium) values of economic variables will not change. It is the point at which quantity demanded and quantity supplied are equal. _________, for example, refers to a condition where a market price is established through competition such that the amount of goods or services sought by buyers is equal to the amount of goods or services produced by sellers.

a. Market equilibrium
b. Product-Market Growth Matrix
c. Marketization
d. Regulated market

32. The _________ is a heterodox school of economics that emphasizes the spontaneous organizing power of the price mechanism. It holds that the complexity of subjective human choices makes mathematical modelling of the evolving market extremely difficult and advocates a laissez faire approach to the economy. _________ economists advocate the enforcement of voluntary contractual agreements between economic agents, but otherwise the smallest imposition of coercive force on commercial transactions.

a. Austrian School
b. ACCRA Cost of Living Index
c. ACEA agreement
d. Economic calculation problem

33. In economics, the term _________ of income or _________ refers to a simple economic model which describes the reciprocal circulation of income between producers and consumers. In the _________ model, the inter-dependent entities of producer and consumer are referred to as 'firms' and 'households' respectively and provide each other with factors in order to facilitate the flow of income. Firms provide consumers with goods and services in exchange for consumer expenditure and 'factors of production' from households.

a. 1921 recession
b. 100-year flood
c. 130-30 fund
d. Circular flow

34. _________ to the arrival of new individuals into a habitat or population. It is a biological concept and is important in population ecology, differentiated from emigration and migration.

_________ is a modern phenomenon.

a. Immigration
b. ACCRA Cost of Living Index
c. AD-IA Model
d. ACEA agreement

35. _________ is a term in economics, where demand for one good or service occurs as a result of demand for another. This may occur as the former is a part of production of the second. For example, demand for coal leads to _________ for mining, as coal must be mined for coal to be consumed.

a. Rate risk
b. Leontief production function
c. Derived demand
d. Days Sales Outstanding

36. _________s is the social science that studies the production, distribution, and consumption of goods and services. The term _________s comes from the Ancient Greek oá¼°κονομÎ¯α from oá¼¶κος (oikos, 'house') + vÏŒμος (nomos, 'custom' or 'law'), hence 'rules of the house(hold)'. Current _________ models developed out of the broader field of political economy in the late 19th century, owing to a desire to use an empirical approach more akin to the physical sciences.

a. Energy economics
b. Inflation
c. Opportunity cost
d. Economic

37. _________ is the increase in the amount of the goods and services produced by an economy over time. It is conventionally measured as the percent rate of increase in real gross domestic product, or real GDP. Growth is usually calculated in real terms, i.e. inflation-adjusted terms, in order to net out the effect of inflation on the price of the goods and services produced.

a. ACCRA Cost of Living Index
b. ACEA agreement
c. AD-IA Model
d. Economic growth

38. _________ is a term from economics referring to the use of money exchanged by buyers and sellers with an open and understood system of value and time trade offs to produce the best distribution of goods and services. The use of the _________ does not imply a free market: there can be captive or controlled markets which seek to use supply and demand, or some other form of charging for scarcity, both in social situations and in engineering.

The _________ assumes perfect competition and is regulated by demand and supply.

a. Product-Market Growth Matrix
b. Partial equilibrium
c. Market mechanism
d. Two-sided markets

39. _________ is the controlled distribution of resources and scarce goods or services. _________ controls the size of the ration, one's allotted portion of the resources being distributed on a particular day or at a particular time.

In economics, it is often common to use the word '_________' to refer to one of the roles that prices play in markets, while _________ is called 'non-price _________.' Using prices to ration means that those with the most money (or other assets) and who want a product the most are first to receive it.

a. 100-year flood
b. Rationing
c. 1921 recession
d. 130-30 fund

40. A _________ or directed economy is an economic system in which the government or workers' councils manages the economy. It is an economic system in which the central government makes all decisions on the production and consumption of goods and services. Its most extensive form is referred to as a _________, centrally planned economy, or command and control economy.

a. Transition economy
b. Subsistence economy
c. Nutritional Economics
d. Command economy

41. The _________, sometimes called the fundamental _________, is one of the fundamental economic theories in the operation of any economy. It asserts that there is scarcity, that the finite resources available are insufficient to satisfy all human wants. The problem then becomes how to determine what is to be produced and how the factors of production (such as capital and labour) are to be allocated.

a. Endogenous growth theory
b. Economic nationalism
c. Economic problem
d. Eclectic paradigm

42. In economics, the _________ is a historical inverse relation between the rate of unemployment and the rate of inflation in an economy. Stated simply, the lower the unemployment in an economy, the higher the rate of increase in nominal wages in the economy. Rate of Change of Wages against Unemployment, United Kingdom 1913-1948 from Phillips (1958)

William Phillips, a New Zealand born economist, wrote a paper in 1958 titled The Relationship between Unemployment and the Rate of Change of Money Wages in the United Kingdom 1861-1957, which was published in the quarterly journal Economica.

a. Cost curve
b. Demand curve
c. Lorenz curve
d. Phillips curve

1. _________ is a branch of economics that studies how individuals, households and firms and some states make decisions to allocate limited resources, typically in markets where goods or services are being bought and sold. _________ examines how these decisions and behaviours affect the supply and demand for goods and services, which determines prices; and how prices, in turn , determine the supply and demand of goods and services.

Whereas macroeconomics involves the 'sum total of economic activity, dealing with the issues of growth, inflation and unemployment, and with national economic policies relating to these issues' and the effects of government actions on them.

a. Recession
b. Countercyclical
c. New Keynesian economics
d. Microeconomics

2. _________ in economics and business is the result of an exchange and from that trade we assign a numerical monetary value to a good, service or asset. If Alice trades Bob 4 apples for an orange, the _________ of an orange is 4 apples. Inversely, the _________ of an apple is 1/4 oranges.

a. Price book
b. Premium pricing
c. Price war
d. Price

3. _________ is a mechanism that allows people easily to buy and sell products. Services are often included in the scope of the term. _________ regulation is an economic term that describes restrictions in the market.

a. Financialization
b. Fixed exchange rate system
c. Market dominance
d. Product market

4. _________ in economic theory is the use of modern economic tools to study problems that are traditionally in the province of political science.

In particular, it studies the behavior of politicians and government officials as mostly self-interested agents and their interactions in the social system either as such or under alternative constitutional rules. These can be represented a number of ways, including standard constrained utility maximization, game theory, or decision theory.

a. Public choice
b. Rational ignorance
c. Paradox of voting
d. Public interest theory

5. _________ is an economic model based on price, utility and quantity in a market. It predicts that in a competitive market, price will function to equalize the quantity demanded by consumers, and the quantity supplied by producers, resulting in an economic equilibrium of price and quantity. The model incorporates other factors changing equilibrium as a shift of demand and/or supply.

a. Rational addiction
b. Supply and demand
c. Joint demand
d. Deferred gratification

6. Economics:

- _________,the desire to own something and the ability to pay for it
- _________ curve,a graphic representation of a _________ schedule
- _________ deposit, the money in checking accounts
- _________ pull theory,the theory that inflation occurs when _________ for goods and services exceeds existing supplies
- _________ schedule,a table that lists the quantity of a good a person will buy it each different price
- _________ side economics,the school of economics at believes government spending and tax cuts open economy by raising _________

.

a. McKesson ' Robbins scandal
b. Demand
c. Variability
d. Production

7. In economics, _________ is the ratio of the percent change in one variable to the percent change in another variable. It is a tool for measuring the responsiveness of a function to changes in parameters in a relative way. Commonly analyzed are _________ of substitution, price and wealth.

a. ACCRA Cost of Living Index
b. ACEA agreement
c. Elasticity of demand
d. Elasticity

8. In economics, _________ is the total demand for final goods and services in the economy (Y) at a given time and price level. It is the amount of goods and services in the economy that will be purchased at all possible price levels. This is the demand for the gross domestic product of a country when inventory levels are static.

a. Aggregation problem
b. Aggregate supply
c. Aggregate demand
d. Aggregate expenditure

9. In mathematics, a _________ is a constant multiplicative factor of a certain object. For example, in the expression $9x^2$, the _________ of x^2 is 9.

The object can be such things as a variable, a vector, a function, etc.

a. 100-year flood
b. 1921 recession
c. 130-30 fund
d. Coefficient

10. _________ is a broad label that refers to any individuals or households that use goods and services generated within the economy. The concept of a _________ is used in different contexts, so that the usage and significance of the term may vary.

Typically when business people and economists talk of _________s they are talking about person as _________, an aggregated commodity item with little individuality other than that expressed in the buy/not-buy decision.

a. 100-year flood
b. 130-30 fund
c. Consumer
d. 1921 recession

11. A _________ is an object whose consumption increases the utility of the consumer, for which the quantity demanded exceeds the quantity supplied at zero price. _________s are usually modeled as having diminishing marginal utility. The first individual purchase has high utility; the second has less.

a. Good
b. Merit good
c. Composite good
d. Pie method

12. In economics, economic output is divided into physical goods and intangible services. Consumption of _________ is assumed to produce utility. It is often used when referring to a _________ Tax.

a. Manufactured goods
b. Private good
c. Composite good
d. Goods and services

13. In economics, _________ describes demand that is not very sensitive to a change in price.

a. Inflation hedge
b. Export-led growth
c. Effective unemployment rate
d. Inelastic

14. _________ is defined as the measure of responsiveness in the quantity demanded for a commodity as a result of change in price of the same commodity. It is a measure of how consumers react to a change in price. In other words, it is percentage change in quantity demanded as per the percentage change in price of the same commodity.

a. 130-30 fund
b. 100-year flood
c. 1921 recession
d. Price elasticity of demand

15. Necessary _________s:

If x is a necessary _________ of y, then the presence of y necessarily implies the presence of x. The presence of x, however, does not imply that y will occur.

Sufficient _________s:

If x is a sufficient _________ of y, then the presence of x necessarily implies the presence of y.

a. Cause
b. Materialism
c. Political philosophy
d. Philosophy of economics

16. Price _________ is defined as the measure of responsiveness in the quantity demanded for a commodity as a result of change in price of the same commodity. It is a measure of how consumers react to a change in price. In other words, it is percentage change in quantity demanded by the percentage change in price of the same commodity.

a. ACEA agreement
b. ACCRA Cost of Living Index
c. Elasticity
d. Elasticity of demand

17. _________ in economics refers to metrics and measures of output from production processes, per unit of input. Labor _________, for example, is typically measured as a ratio of output per labor-hour, an input. _________ may be conceived of as a metrics of the technical or engineering efficiency of production.

a. Production-possibility frontier
b. Piece work
c. Productivity
d. Fordism

18. _________ is an economic concept with commonplace familiarity. It is the price that a good or service is offered at, or will fetch, in the marketplace. It is of interest mainly in the study of microeconomics.

a. Market anomaly
b. Noisy market hypothesis
c. Paper trading
d. Market price

19. Competition law, known in the United States as _________ law, has three main elements:

- prohibiting agreements or practices that restrict free trading and competition between business entities. This includes in particular the repression of cartels.
- banning abusive behaviour by a firm dominating a market, or anti-competitive practices that tend to lead to such a dominant position. Practices controlled in this way may include predatory pricing, tying, price gouging, refusal to deal, and many others.
- supervising the mergers and acquisitions of large corporations, including some joint ventures. Transactions that are considered to threaten the competitive process can be prohibited altogether, or approved subject to 'remedies' such as an obligation to divest part of the merged business or to offer licences or access to facilities to enable other businesses to continue competing.

The substance and practice of competition law varies from jurisdiction to jurisdiction. Protecting the interests of consumers (consumer welfare) and ensuring that entrepreneurs have an opportunity to compete in the market economy are often treated as important objectives. Competition law is closely connected with law on deregulation of access to markets, state aids and subsidies, the privatisation of state owned assets and the establishment of independent sector regulators. In recent decades, competition law has been viewed as a way to provide better public services.

a. United Kingdom competition law
b. Intellectual property law
c. Anti-Inflation Act
d. Antitrust

20. In economics, the _________ can be defined as the graph depicting the relationship between the price of a certain commodity, and the amount of it that consumers are willing and able to purchase at that given price. It is a graphic representation of a demand schedule. The _________ for all consumers together follows from the _________ of every individual consumer: the individual demands at each price are added together.

a. Cost curve
b. Wage curve
c. Kuznets curve
d. Demand curve

21. In economics, the _________ is the change in consumption resulting from a change in real income.

Another important item that can change is the money income of the consumer. The _________ is the phenomenon observed through changes in purchasing power.

a. Equilibrium wage
b. Income effect
c. Export subsidy
d. Inflation hedge

22. _________ is a fee paid on borrowed assets. It is the price paid for the use of borrowed money , or, money earned by deposited funds . Assets that are sometimes lent with _________ include money, shares, consumer goods through hire purchase, major assets such as aircraft, and even entire factories in finance lease arrangements.

a. Asset protection
b. Internal debt
c. Interest
d. Insolvency

23. A _________ is:

- Rewrite _________, in generative grammar and computer science
- Standardization, a formal and widely-accepted statement, fact, definition, or qualification
- Operation, a determinate _________ for performing a mathematical operation and obtaining a certain result (Mathematics, Logic)
    - Unary operation
    - Binary operation
- _________ of inference, a function from sets of formulae to formulae (Mathematics, Logic)
- _________ of thumb, principle with broad application that is not intended to be strictly accurate or reliable for every situation. Also often simply referred to as a _________
- Moral, an atomic element of a moral code for guiding choices in human behavior
- Heuristic, a quantized '_________' which shows a tendency or probability for successful function
- A regulation, as in sports
- A Production _________, as in computer science
- Procedural law, a _________set governing the application of laws to cases
    - A law, which may informally be called a '_________'
    - A court ruling, a decision by a court
- In the U.S. Government, a regulation mandated by Congress, but written or expanded upon by the Executive Branch.
- Norm (sociology), an informal but widely accepted _________, concept, truth, definition, or qualification (social norms, legal norms, coding norms)
- Norm (philosophy), a kind of sentence or a reason to act, feel or believe
- 'Rulership' is the concept of governance by a government:
    - Military _________, governance by a military body
    - Monastic _________, a collection of precepts that guides the life of monks or nuns in a religious order where the superior holds the place of Christ
- Slide _________

- '_________,' a song by Ayumi Hamasaki
- '_________,' a song by rapper Nas
- '_________s,' an album by the band The Whitest Boy Alive
- _________s: Pyaar Ka Superhit Formula, a 2003 Bollywood film
- ruler, an instrument for measuring lengths
- _________, a component of an astrolabe, circumferator or similar instrument
- The _________s, a bestselling self-help book
- _________ Project (Run Up-to-date Linux Everywhere), a project that aims to use up-to-date Linux software on old PCs
- _________ engine, a software system that helps managing business _________s
- Ja _________, a hip hop artist
    - R.U.L.E., a 2005 greatest hits album by rapper Ja _________
- '_________s,' a KMFDM song

a. Rule
b. Procter ' Gamble
c. Demand
d. Technocracy

24. _________ is the total money received from the sale of any given quantity of output.

The _________ is calculated by taking the price of the sale times the quantity sold, i.e.

_________ = price X quantity.

.

a. Ceteris paribus
b. Small numbers game
c. Market development funds
d. Total revenue

25. _________ exists when sales of identical goods or services are transacted at different prices from the same provider. In a theoretical market with perfect information, no transaction costs or prohibition on secondary exchange (or re-selling) to prevent arbitrage, _________ can only be a feature of monopoly and oligopoly markets, where market power can be exercised. Otherwise, the moment the seller tries to sell the same good at different prices, the buyer at the lower price can arbitrage by selling to the consumer buying at the higher price but with a tiny discount.

a. Price discrimination
b. Loss leader
c. Lerner Index
d. Transfer pricing

26. The _________ is the apparent contradiction that although water is on the whole more useful, in terms of survival, than diamonds, diamonds command a higher price in the market. The economist Adam Smith is often considered to be the classic presenter of this paradox. Nicolaus Copernicus, John Locke, John Law and others had previously tried to explain the disparity.

a. 100-year flood
b. St. Petersburg paradox
c. 130-30 fund
d. Paradox of value

27. In law and economics, the _________, describes the economic efficiency of an economic allocation or outcome in the presence of externalities. The theorem states that when trade in an externality is possible and there are no transaction costs, bargaining will lead to an efficient outcome regardless of the initial allocation of property rights. In practice, obstacles to bargaining or poorly defined property rights can prevent Coasian bargaining.

a. Prior appropriation water rights
b. Means test
c. Coase theorem
d. General Mining Act of 1872

28. In economics, the _________ is defined as a numerical measure of the responsiveness of the quantity supplied of product (A) to a change in price of product (A) alone. It is the measure of the way quantity supplied reacts to a change in price.

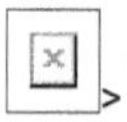

For example, if, in response to a 10% rise in the price of a good, the quantity supplied increases by 20%, the _________ would be 20%/10% = 2.

a. Passive income
b. Hedonimetry
c. Price elasticity of supply
d. Demand shaping

29. To _________ is to impose a financial charge or other levy upon a taxpayer by a state or the functional equivalent of a state.

_________es are also imposed by many subnational entities. _________es consist of direct _________ or indirect _________, and may be paid in money or as its labour equivalent (often but not always unpaid.)

a. Tax
b. 1921 recession
c. 100-year flood
d. 130-30 fund

30. To tax is to impose a financial charge or other levy upon a taxpayer by a state or the functional equivalent of a state.

_________ are also imposed by many subnational entities. _________ consist of direct tax or indirect tax, and may be paid in money or as its labour equivalent (often but not always unpaid.)

a. 100-year flood
b. Taxes
c. 1921 recession
d. 130-30 fund

31. In economics, _________ are the resources employed to produce goods and services. They facilitate production but do not become part of the product (as with raw materials) or significantly transformed by the production process (as with fuel used to power machinery.) To 19th century economists, the _________ were land (natural resources, gifts from nature), labor (the ability to work), and capital goods (human-made tools and equipment.)

a. Long-run
b. Hicks-neutral technical change
c. Product Pipeline
d. Factors of production

32. In microeconomics, _________ is quite simply the conversion of inputs into outputs. It is an economic process that uses resources to create a good or service that is suitable for exchange. This can include manufacturing, storing, shipping, and packaging.

a. Solved
b. MET
c. Production
d. Red Guards

33. A _________ is a measure of the average price of consumer goods and services purchased by households. A _________ measures a price change for a constant market basket of goods and services from one period to the next within the same area (city, region, or nation.) It is a price index determined by measuring the price of a standard group of goods meant to represent the typical market basket of a typical urban consumer.

a. Lipstick index
b. Consumer price index
c. CPI
d. Cost-of-living index

34. In economics, the _________ measures the payments that flow between any individual country and all other countries. It is used to summarize all international economic transactions for that country during a specific time period, usually a year. The _________ is determined by the country's exports and imports of goods, services, and financial capital, as well as financial transfers.

a. Gross domestic product per barrel
b. Skyscraper Index
c. Gross world product
d. Balance of payments

35. _________s is the social science that studies the production, distribution, and consumption of goods and services. The term _________s comes from the Ancient Greek οá¼°κονομΐ α from οá¼¶κος (oikos, 'house') + νΪŒμος (nomos, 'custom' or 'law'), hence 'rules of the house(hold)'. Current _________ models developed out of the broader field of political economy in the late 19th century, owing to a desire to use an empirical approach more akin to the physical sciences.

a. Energy economics
b. Economic
c. Inflation
d. Opportunity cost

36. In economic models, the _________ time frame assumes no fixed factors of production. Firms can enter or leave the marketplace, and the cost (and availability) of land, labor, raw materials, and capital goods can be assumed to vary. In contrast, in the short-run time frame, certain factors are assumed to be fixed, because there is not sufficient time for them to change.

a. Price/performance ratio
b. Long-run
c. Diseconomies of scale
d. Productivity world

37. A _________ is the transfer of wealth from one party (such as a person or company) to another. A _________ is usually made in exchange for the provision of goods, services or both, or to fulfill a legal obligation.

The simplest and oldest form of _________ is barter, the exchange of one good or service for another.

a. Soft count
b. Going concern
c. Social gravity
d. Payment

38. A _________ is a normalized average (typically a weighted average) of prices for a given class of goods or services in a given region, during a given interval of time. It is a statistic designed to help to compare how these prices, taken as a whole, differ between time periods or geographical locations.

Price indices have several potential uses.

a. Product sabotage
b. Two-part tariff
c. Transactional Net Margin Method
d. Price index

39. The _________ is the labour pool in employment. It is generally used to describe those working for a single company or industry, but can also apply to a geographic region like a city, country, state, etc. The term generally excludes the employers or management, and implies those involved in manual labour.

a. Collective bargaining
b. Departmentalization
c. Grenelle agreements
d. Workforce

40. _________ is a term that is used to describe the overall process of invention, innovation and diffusion of technology or processes. The term is redundant with technological development, technological achievement, and technological progress. In essence _________ is the invention of a technology (or a process), the continuous process of improving a technology (in which it often becomes cheaper) and its diffusion throughout industry or society.

a. 100-year flood
b. 1921 recession
c. Technological change
d. 130-30 fund

41. In economics, tax incidence is the analysis of the effect of a particular tax on the distribution of economic welfare. Tax incidence is said to 'fall' upon the group that, at the end of the day, bears the burden of the tax. The key concept is that the tax incidence or _________ does not depend on where the revenue is collected, but on the price elasticity of demand and price elasticity of supply.

a. 1921 recession
b. Tax burden
c. 100-year flood
d. 130-30 fund

42. In economics, an _________ or spillover of an economic transaction is an impact on a party that is not directly involved in the transaction. In such a case, prices do not reflect the full costs or benefits in production or consumption of a product or service. A positive impact is called an external benefit, while a negative impact is called an external cost.

a. Environmental impact assessment
b. Environmental tariff
c. Externality
d. Existence value

43. _________ was a survey conducted by the U.S. Department of Justice to gauge the prevalence of alcohol and illegal drug use among prior arrestees. It was a reformulation of the prior Drug Use Forecasting (DUF) program, focused on five drugs in particular: cocaine, marijuana, methamphetamine, opiates, and PCP.

Participants were randomly selected from arrest records in major metropolitan areas; because no personally identifying information is taken from each record chosen, the resulting data can be correlated to arrest rates, but not to the total population of persons charged.

a. ACEA agreement
b. ACCRA Cost of Living Index
c. Arrestee Drug Abuse Monitoring
d. AD-IA Model

44. A _________ is the lowest hourly, daily or monthly wage that employers may legally pay to employees or workers. Equivalently, it is the lowest wage at which workers may sell their labor. Although _________ laws are in effect in a great many jurisdictions, there are differences of opinion about the benefits and drawbacks of a _________.

a. Marginal propensity to consume
b. Microfoundations
c. Permanent war economy
d. Minimum wage

45. A _________ is a government- or group-imposed limit on how low a price can be charged for a product. In order for a _________ to be effective, it must be greater than the equilibrium price. An ineffective _________, below equilibrium price.

A _________ can be set below the free-market equilibrium price.

a. Price floor
b. Price markdown
c. Two-part tariff
d. Flat rate

46. Economic _________ is defined as an excess distribution to any factor in a production process above that which is required to induce the factor into the process or any excess above that which is necessary to keep the factor in its current use..

Classical Factor _________ is primarily concerned with the fee paid for the use of fixed (e.g. natural) resources. The classical definition is expressed as any excess payment above that required to induce or provide for production.

a. 1921 recession
b. Rent
c. 100-year flood
d. 130-30 fund

47. _________ refers to laws or ordinances that set price controls on the renting of residential housing. It functions as a price ceiling.

_________ exists in approximately 40 countries around the world.

a. National Housing Conference
b. Rent control
c. 100-year flood
d. Tenant rights

48. _________ was a Scottish moral philosopher and a pioneer of political economy. One of the key figures of the Scottish Enlightenment, Smith is the author of The Theory of Moral Sentiments and An Inquiry into the Nature and Causes of the Wealth of Nations. The latter, usually abbreviated as The Wealth of Nations, is considered his magnum opus and the first modern work of economics.

a. Alan Greenspan
b. Adolf Hitler
c. Adam Smith
d. Adolph Fischer

49. A _________ product is a product designed for cheapness and short-term convenience rather than medium to long-term durability, with most products only intended for single use. The term is also sometimes used for products that may last several months (ex. _________ air filters) to distinguish from similar products that last indefinitely (ex.

a. 100-year flood
b. 130-30 fund
c. 1921 recession
d. Disposable

50. _________ is gross income minus income tax on that income.

Discretionary income is income after subtracting taxes and normal expenses (such as rent or mortgage, utilities, insurance, medical, transportation, property maintenance, child support, inflation, food and sundries, 'c.) to maintain a certain standard of living.

a. Taxation as theft
b. Stamp Act
c. Disposable income
d. Disposable personal income

51. In economics, the people in the _________ are the suppliers of labor. The _________ is all the nonmilitary people who are employed or unemployed. In 2005, the worldwide _________ was over 3 billion people.

a. Labor force
b. Departmentalization
c. Grenelle agreements
d. Distributed workforce

52. A variety of measures of _________ and output are used in economics to estimate total economic activity in a country or region, including gross domestic product (GDP), gross national product (GNP), and net _________

There are three main ways of calculating these numbers; the output approach, the income approach and the expenditure approach. In theory, the three must yield the same, because total expenditures on goods and services must equal the total income paid to the producers (Gnational income), and that must also equal the total value of the output of goods and services (GNP.)

a. Gross world product
b. Volume index
c. National income
d. GNI per capita

53. A _________ is a government imposed limit on how high a price can be charged on a product. For a _________ to be effective, it must differ from the free market price. In the graph at right, the supply and demand curves intersect to determine the free-market quantity and price.

a. Price ceiling
b. Fire sale
c. Product sabotage
d. Pricing

54. A _________ represents the combinations of goods and services that a consumer can purchase given current prices and his income. Consumer theory uses the concepts of a _________ and a preference map to analyze consumer choices. Both concepts have a ready graphical representation in the two-good case.

a. Joint demand
b. Revealed preference
c. Quality bias
d. Budget constraint

55. _________ is the controlled distribution of resources and scarce goods or services. _________ controls the size of the ration, one's allotted portion of the resources being distributed on a particular day or at a particular time.

In economics, it is often common to use the word '_________' to refer to one of the roles that prices play in markets, while _________ is called 'non-price _________.' Using prices to ration means that those with the most money (or other assets) and who want a product the most are first to receive it.

a. 130-30 fund
b. 1921 recession
c. 100-year flood
d. Rationing

56. The underground economy or _________ is a market where all commerce is conducted without regard to taxation, law or regulations of trade. The term is also often known as the underdog, shadow economy, black economy, parallel economy or phantom trades.

In modern societies the underground economy covers a vast array of activities.

a. Protectionism
b. Social market economy
c. Market economy
d. Black market

1. In economics, _________ is the total demand for final goods and services in the economy (Y) at a given time and price level. It is the amount of goods and services in the economy that will be purchased at all possible price levels. This is the demand for the gross domestic product of a country when inventory levels are static.

a. Aggregate demand
b. Aggregation problem
c. Aggregate supply
d. Aggregate expenditure

2. In production, returns to scale refers to changes in output subsequent to a proportional change in all inputs (where all inputs increase by a constant factor.) If output increases by that same proportional change then there are _________ If output increases by less than that proportional change, there are decreasing returns to scale (DRS.)

a. Lexicographic preferences
b. Constant returns to scale
c. Consumer sovereignty
d. Long term

3. _________ is a broad label that refers to any individuals or households that use goods and services generated within the economy. The concept of a _________ is used in different contexts, so that the usage and significance of the term may vary.

Typically when business people and economists talk of _________s they are talking about person as _________, an aggregated commodity item with little individuality other than that expressed in the buy/not-buy decision.

a. Consumer
b. 1921 recession
c. 130-30 fund
d. 100-year flood

4. _________ is the study of when, why, how, where and what people do or do not buy products. It blends elements from psychology, sociology,social psychology, anthropology and economics. It attempts to understand the buyer decision making process, both individually and in groups.

a. Shopping Neutral
b. Consumption smoothing
c. Consumer behavior
d. Situational theory of publics

5. Economics:

- _________,the desire to own something and the ability to pay for it
- _________ curve,a graphic representation of a _________ schedule
- _________ deposit, the money in checking accounts
- _________ pull theory,the theory that inflation occurs when _________ for goods and services exceeds existing supplies
- _________ schedule,a table that lists the quantity of a good a person will buy it each different price
- _________ side economics,the school of economics at believes government spending and tax cuts open economy by raising _________

.

a. Production
b. Variability
c. McKesson ' Robbins scandal
d. Demand

6. In economics, the _________ of a good or of a service is the utility of the specific use to which an agent would put a given increase in that good or service, or of the specific use that would be abandoned in response to a given decrease. In other words, _________ is the utility of the marginal use -- which, on the assumption of economic rationality, would be the least urgent use of the good or service, from the best feasible combination of actions in which its use is included. Under the mainstream assumptions, the _________ of a good or service is the posited quantified change in utility obtained by increasing or by decreasing use of that good or service.

a. 100-year flood
b. 1921 recession
c. 130-30 fund
d. Marginal utility

7. _________ in economics and business is the result of an exchange and from that trade we assign a numerical monetary value to a good, service or asset. If Alice trades Bob 4 apples for an orange, the _________ of an orange is 4 apples. Inversely, the _________ of an apple is 1/4 oranges.

a. Premium pricing
b. Price
c. Price war
d. Price book

8. _________ is defined as the measure of responsiveness in the quantity demanded for a commodity as a result of change in price of the same commodity. It is a measure of how consumers react to a change in price. In other words, it is percentage change in quantity demanded as per the percentage change in price of the same commodity.

a. 130-30 fund
b. Price elasticity of demand
c. 100-year flood
d. 1921 recession

9. _________ is an economic model based on price, utility and quantity in a market. It predicts that in a competitive market, price will function to equalize the quantity demanded by consumers, and the quantity supplied by producers, resulting in an economic equilibrium of price and quantity. The model incorporates other factors changing equilibrium as a shift of demand and/or supply.

a. Deferred gratification
b. Rational addiction
c. Joint demand
d. Supply and demand

10. In economics, _________ is a measure of the relative satisfaction from consumption of various goods and services. Given this measure, one may speak meaningfully of increasing or decreasing _________, and thereby explain economic behavior in terms of attempts to increase one's _________. For illustrative purposes, changes in _________ are sometimes expressed in units called utils.

a. Utility function
b. Ordinal utility
c. Expected utility hypothesis
d. Utility

11. In economics, the _________ can be defined as the graph depicting the relationship between the price of a certain commodity, and the amount of it that consumers are willing and able to purchase at that given price. It is a graphic representation of a demand schedule. The _________ for all consumers together follows from the _________ of every individual consumer: the individual demands at each price are added together.

a. Cost curve
b. Demand curve
c. Wage curve
d. Kuznets curve

12. In economics, _________ is the ratio of the percent change in one variable to the percent change in another variable. It is a tool for measuring the responsiveness of a function to changes in parameters in a relative way. Commonly analyzed are _________ of substitution, price and wealth.

a. ACEA agreement
b. ACCRA Cost of Living Index
c. Elasticity of demand
d. Elasticity

13. Price _________ is defined as the measure of responsiveness in the quantity demanded for a commodity as a result of change in price of the same commodity. It is a measure of how consumers react to a change in price. In other words, it is percentage change in quantity demanded by the percentage change in price of the same commodity.

a. Elasticity
b. ACCRA Cost of Living Index
c. ACEA agreement
d. Elasticity of demand

14. In economics, the _________ is the change in consumption resulting from a change in real income.

Another important item that can change is the money income of the consumer. The _________ is the phenomenon observed through changes in purchasing power.

a. Equilibrium wage
b. Export subsidy
c. Inflation hedge
d. Income effect

15. In economics, _________ and economies of scale are related terms that describe what happens as the scale of production increases. They are different terms and should not be used interchangeably.

_________ refers to a technical property of production that examines changes in output subsequent to a proportional change in all inputs (where all inputs increase by a constant factor.)

a. Constant returns to scale
b. Returns to scale
c. Customer equity
d. Necessity good

16. _________ is a way of expressing knowledge or belief that an event will occur or has occurred. In mathematics the concept has been given an exact meaning in _________ theory, that is used extensively in such areas of study as mathematics, statistics, finance, gambling, science, and philosophy to draw conclusions about the likelihood of potential events and the underlying mechanics of complex systems.

The word _________ does not have a consistent direct definition.

a. 100-year flood
b. 1921 recession
c. 130-30 fund
d. Probability

17. _________ was a survey conducted by the U.S. Department of Justice to gauge the prevalence of alcohol and illegal drug use among prior arrestees. It was a reformulation of the prior Drug Use Forecasting (DUF) program, focused on five drugs in particular: cocaine, marijuana, methamphetamine, opiates, and PCP.

Participants were randomly selected from arrest records in major metropolitan areas; because no personally identifying information is taken from each record chosen, the resulting data can be correlated to arrest rates, but not to the total population of persons charged.

a. ACCRA Cost of Living Index
b. ACEA agreement
c. AD-IA Model
d. Arrestee Drug Abuse Monitoring

18. In economics, _________ is a theory of utility under which the utility (roughly, satisfaction) gained from a particular good or service can be measured and that the magnitude of the measurement is meaningful. Under _________ theory, the util is a unit of measurement much like the metre or second. A util has a fixed size, making comparisons based on ratios of utils possible.

a. Cardinal utility
b. 130-30 fund
c. Weakly additive
d. 100-year flood

19. _________ is a common concept in economics, and gives rise to derived concepts such as consumer debt. Generally _________ is defined by opposition to production. But the precise definition can vary because different schools of economists define production quite differently.

a. Federal Reserve Bank Notes
b. Cash or share options
c. Foreclosure data providers
d. Consumption

20. _________ is a branch of economics that deals with the performance, structure, and behavior of a national or regional economy as a whole. Along with microeconomics, _________ is one of the two most general fields in economics. It is the study of the behavior and decision-making of entire economies.

a. New Trade Theory
b. Macroeconomics
c. Nominal value
d. Tobit model

21. _________ theory states that while the utility of a particular good and service cannot be measured using an objective scale, a consumer is capable of ranking different alternatives available. Goods are often considered in 'bundles' or 'baskets'. For example, does individual A prefer 3 apples and 2 oranges or 3 oranges and 2 apples? When a large number of baskets of goods are compared, the preferences of the individual can be seen.

a. Ordinal utility
b. Utility
c. Expected utility hypothesis
d. Utility function

22. _________ can be generally defined as the course of action or inaction taken by governmental entities with regard to a particular issue or set of issues. Other scholars define it as a system of 'courses of action, regulatory measures, laws, and funding priorities concerning a given topic promulgated by a governmental entity or its representatives.' _________ is commonly embodied 'in constitutions, legislative acts, and judicial decisions.'

In the United States, this concept refers not only to the end result of policies, but more broadly to the decision-making and analysis of governmental decisions. _________ is also considered an academic discipline, as it is studied by professors and students at _________ schools of major universities throughout the country.

a. 100-year flood
b. Public policy
c. 130-30 fund
d. 1921 recession

23. _________ was a Scottish moral philosopher and a pioneer of political economy. One of the key figures of the Scottish Enlightenment, Smith is the author of The Theory of Moral Sentiments and An Inquiry into the Nature and Causes of the Wealth of Nations. The latter, usually abbreviated as The Wealth of Nations, is considered his magnum opus and the first modern work of economics.

a. Adam Smith
b. Adolph Fischer
c. Alan Greenspan
d. Adolf Hitler

24. A _________ product is a product designed for cheapness and short-term convenience rather than medium to long-term durability, with most products only intended for single use. The term is also sometimes used for products that may last several months (ex. _________ air filters) to distinguish from similar products that last indefinitely (ex.

a. 130-30 fund
b. 100-year flood
c. Disposable
d. 1921 recession

25. _________ is gross income minus income tax on that income.

Discretionary income is income after subtracting taxes and normal expenses (such as rent or mortgage, utilities, insurance, medical, transportation, property maintenance, child support, inflation, food and sundries, 'c.) to maintain a certain standard of living.

a. Disposable income
b. Disposable personal income
c. Taxation as theft
d. Stamp Act

26. A variety of measures of _________ and output are used in economics to estimate total economic activity in a country or region, including gross domestic product (GDP), gross national product (GNP), and net _________

There are three main ways of calculating these numbers; the output approach, the income approach and the expenditure approach. In theory, the three must yield the same, because total expenditures on goods and services must equal the total income paid to the producers (Gnational income), and that must also equal the total value of the output of goods and services (GNP.)

a. GNI per capita
b. National income
c. Volume index
d. Gross world product

27. A _________ represents the combinations of goods and services that a consumer can purchase given current prices and his income. Consumer theory uses the concepts of a _________ and a preference map to analyze consumer choices. Both concepts have a ready graphical representation in the two-good case.

a. Budget constraint
b. Revealed preference
c. Joint demand
d. Quality bias

28. The _________ is a heterodox school of economics that emphasizes the spontaneous organizing power of the price mechanism. It holds that the complexity of subjective human choices makes mathematical modelling of the evolving market extremely difficult and advocates a laissez faire approach to the economy. _________ economists advocate the enforcement of voluntary contractual agreements between economic agents, but otherwise the smallest imposition of coercive force on commercial transactions.

a. Austrian School
b. Economic calculation problem
c. ACEA agreement
d. ACCRA Cost of Living Index

29. _________ and behavioral finance are closely related fields that have evolved to be a separate branch of economic and financial analysis which applies scientific research on human and social, cognitive and emotional factors to better understand economic decisions by consumers, borrowers, investors, and how they affect market prices, returns and the allocation of resources.

The field is primarily concerned with the bounds of rationality (selfishness, self-control) of economic agents. Behavioral models typically integrate insights from psychology with neo-classical economic theory.

a. Georgism
b. Mainstream economics
c. Neoclassical economics
d. Behavioral economics

30. A _________ is an object whose consumption increases the utility of the consumer, for which the quantity demanded exceeds the quantity supplied at zero price. _________s are usually modeled as having diminishing marginal utility. The first individual purchase has high utility; the second has less.

a. Pie method
b. Composite good
c. Merit good
d. Good

31. In economics, economic output is divided into physical goods and intangible services. Consumption of _________ is assumed to produce utility. It is often used when referring to a _________ Tax.

a. Composite good
b. Private good
c. Manufactured goods
d. Goods and services

32. In microeconomic theory, an _________ is a graph showing different bundles of goods, each measured as to quantity, between which a consumer is indifferent. That is, at each point on the curve, the consumer has no preference for one bundle over another. In other words, they are all equally preferred.

a. Expenditure minimization problem
b. Indifference map
c. Engel curve
d. Indifference curve

33. _________ is an economic concept with commonplace familiarity. It is the price that a good or service is offered at, or will fetch, in the marketplace. It is of interest mainly in the study of microeconomics.

a. Noisy market hypothesis
b. Market anomaly
c. Paper trading
d. Market price

34. Competition law, known in the United States as _________ law, has three main elements:

- prohibiting agreements or practices that restrict free trading and competition between business entities. This includes in particular the repression of cartels.
- banning abusive behaviour by a firm dominating a market, or anti-competitive practices that tend to lead to such a dominant position. Practices controlled in this way may include predatory pricing, tying, price gouging, refusal to deal, and many others.
- supervising the mergers and acquisitions of large corporations, including some joint ventures. Transactions that are considered to threaten the competitive process can be prohibited altogether, or approved subject to 'remedies' such as an obligation to divest part of the merged business or to offer licences or access to facilities to enable other businesses to continue competing.

The substance and practice of competition law varies from jurisdiction to jurisdiction. Protecting the interests of consumers (consumer welfare) and ensuring that entrepreneurs have an opportunity to compete in the market economy are often treated as important objectives. Competition law is closely connected with law on deregulation of access to markets, state aids and subsidies, the privatisation of state owned assets and the establishment of independent sector regulators. In recent decades, competition law has been viewed as a way to provide better public services.

a. Anti-Inflation Act
b. United Kingdom competition law
c. Antitrust
d. Intellectual property law

35. _________s is the social science that studies the production, distribution, and consumption of goods and services. The term _________s comes from the Ancient Greek oá¼°κονομÎ¯α from oá¼¶κος (oikos, 'house') + νÏŒμος (nomos, 'custom' or 'law'), hence 'rules of the house(hold)'. Current _________ models developed out of the broader field of political economy in the late 19th century, owing to a desire to use an empirical approach more akin to the physical sciences.

a. Inflation
b. Opportunity cost
c. Energy economics
d. Economic

36. _________ in economics refers to metrics and measures of output from production processes, per unit of input. Labor _________, for example, is typically measured as a ratio of output per labor-hour, an input. _________ may be conceived of as a metrics of the technical or engineering efficiency of production.

a. Piece work
b. Productivity
c. Fordism
d. Production-possibility frontier

37. In economics, the _________ of demand measures the responsiveness of the demand of a good to the change in the income of the people demanding the good. It is calculated as the ratio of the percent change in demand to the percent change in income. For example, if, in response to a 10% increase in income, the demand of a good increased by 20%, the _________ of demand would be 20%/10% = 2.

a. ACEA agreement
b. ACCRA Cost of Living Index
c. AD-IA Model
d. Income elasticity

38. _________ is the income of individuals or nations after adjusting for inflation. It is calculated by subtracting inflation from the nominal income. Real variables, such as _________, real GDP, and real interest rate are variables that are measured in physical units, while nominal variables such as nominal income, nominal GDP, and nominal interest rate are measured in monetary units.

a. Real income
b. Family income
c. Net national income
d. Windfall gain

39. Necessary _________s:

If x is a necessary _________ of y, then the presence of y necessarily implies the presence of x. The presence of x, however, does not imply that y will occur.

Sufficient _________s:

If x is a sufficient _________ of y, then the presence of x necessarily implies the presence of y.

a. Cause
b. Materialism
c. Philosophy of economics
d. Political philosophy

40. In economics, an _________ or spillover of an economic transaction is an impact on a party that is not directly involved in the transaction. In such a case, prices do not reflect the full costs or benefits in production or consumption of a product or service. A positive impact is called an external benefit, while a negative impact is called an external cost.

a. Existence value
b. Externality
c. Environmental tariff
d. Environmental impact assessment

41. In consumer theory, an _________ is a good that decreases in demand when consumer income rises, unlike normal goods, for which the opposite is observed. It is a good that consumers demand increases when their income increases. Inferiority, in this sense, is an observable fact relating to affordability rather than a statement about the quality of the good.

a. Independent goods
b. Export-oriented
c. Inferior good
d. Information good

42. _________ are those things that are neither used with, nor instead of, the item of interest. Their use is independent of the use of the good being considered. A person's demand of nails is independent of his or her demand for bread.

a. Export-oriented
b. Inferior good
c. Information good
d. Independent goods

43. In economics, a _________ is a good or service whose consumption is considered unhealthy, degrading, or otherwise socially undesirable due to the perceived negative effects on the consumers themselves. It is over-consumed if left to market forces. Examples of _________s include tobacco, alcoholic beverages, recreational drugs, gambling, junk food and prostitution.

a. Search good
b. Demerit good
c. Durable good
d. Credence good

44. The concept of a _________ introduced in economics introduced by Richard Musgrave (1957, 1959) is a commodity which is judged that an individual or society should have on the basis of some concept of need, rather than ability and willingness to pay. The term is, perhaps, less often used today than it was in the 1960s to 1980s but the concept still lies behind many economic actions by governments which are not performed specifically for financial reasons or by supporting incomes (eg via tax rebates.) Examples include the provision of food stamps to support nutrition, the delivery of health services to improve quality of life and reduce morbidity, subsidized housing and arguably education.

a. Positional goods
b. Merit good
c. Final good
d. Private good

45. _________ is a voluntary transfer of resources from one country to another, given at least partly with the objective of benefiting the recipient country. It may have other functions as well: it may be given as a signal of diplomatic approval, or to strengthen a military ally, to reward a government for behaviour desired by the donor, to extend the donor's cultural influence, to provide infrastructure needed by the donor for resource extraction from the recipient country, or to gain other kinds of commercial access. Humanitarianism and altruism are, nevertheless, significant motivations for the giving of _________.

a. ACCRA Cost of Living Index
b. ACEA agreement
c. AD-IA Model
d. AID

46. The _________ is the apparent contradiction that although water is on the whole more useful, in terms of survival, than diamonds, diamonds command a higher price in the market. The economist Adam Smith is often considered to be the classic presenter of this paradox. Nicolaus Copernicus, John Locke, John Law and others had previously tried to explain the disparity.

a. Paradox of value
b. 100-year flood
c. St. Petersburg paradox
d. 130-30 fund

47. _________ is the a method of technical and economic research of the systems for purpose to optimize a parity between system's consumer functions or properties and expenses to achieve those functions or properties.

This methodology for continuous perfection of production, industrial technologies, organizational structures was developed by Juryj Sobolev in 1948 at the 'Perm telephone factory'

- 1948 Juryj Sobolev - the first success in application of a method analysis at the 'Perm telephone factory' .
- 1949 - the first application for the invention as result of use of the new method.

Today in economically developed countries practically each enterprise or the company use methodology of the kind of functional-cost analysis as a practice of the quality management, most full satisfying to principles of standards of series ISO 9000.

- Interest of consumer not in products itself, but the advantage which it will receive from its usage.
- The consumer aspires to reduce his expenses
- Functions needed by consumer can be executed in the various ways, and, hence, with various efficiency and expenses. Among possible alternatives of realization of functions exist such in which the parity of quality and the price is the optimal for the consumer.

The goal of _________ is achievement of the highest consumer satisfaction of production at simultaneous decrease in all kinds of industrial expenses Classical _________ has three English synonyms - Value Engineering, Value Management, Value Analysis.

a. Willingness to pay
b. Monopoly wage
c. Function cost analysis
d. Staple financing

48. An Inquiry into the Nature and Causes of the _________ is the magnum opus of the Scottish economist Adam Smith. It is a clearly written account of economics at the dawn of the Industrial Revolution, as well as a rhetorical piece written for the generally educated individual of the 18th century - advocating a free market economy as more productive and more beneficial to society.

The work is credited as a watershed in history and economics due to its comprehensive, largely accurate characterization of economic mechanisms that survive in modern economics; and also for its effective use of rhetorical technique, including structuring the work to contrast real world examples of free and fettered markets.

a. The Bell Curve
b. Black Book of Communism
c. The Rise and Fall of the Great Powers
d. Wealth of Nations

49. The term surplus is used in economics for several related quantities. The _________ is the amount that consumers benefit by being able to purchase a product for a price that is less than they would be willing to pay. The producer surplus is the amount that producers benefit by selling at a market price mechanism that is higher than they would be willing to sell for.

a. Necessity good
b. Marginal rate of technical substitution
c. Microeconomic reform
d. Consumer surplus

50. _________ is a term that refers both to:

- a formal discipline used to help appraise, or assess, the case for a project or proposal, which itself is a process known as project appraisal; and
- an informal approach to making decisions of any kind.

Under both definitions the process involves, whether explicitly or implicitly, weighing the total expected costs against the total expected benefits of one or more actions in order to choose the best or most profitable option. The formal process is often referred to as either CBA (_________) or BCost-benefit analysis

A hallmark of CBA is that all benefits and all costs are expressed in money terms, and are adjusted for the time value of money, so that all flows of benefits and flows of project costs over time (which tend to occur at different points in time) are expressed on a common basis in terms of their e;present value.e; Closely related, but slightly different, formal techniques include Cost-effectiveness analysis, Economic impact analysis, Fiscal impact analysis and Social Return on Investment(SROI) analysis. The latter builds upon the logic of _________, but differs in that it is explicitly designed to inform the practical decision-making of enterprise managers and investors focused on optimising their social and environmental impacts.

a. 100-year flood
b. 130-30 fund
c. Decision theory
d. Cost-benefit analysis

51. The _________, a unit of the United States Department of Labor, is the principal fact-finding agency for the U.S. government in the broad field of labor economics and statistics. The BLS is an independent national statistical agency that collects, processes, analyzes, and disseminates essential statistical data to the American public, the U.S. Congress, other Federal agencies, State and local governments, business, and labor representatives. The BLS also serves as a statistical resource to the Department of Labor.

a. Gross world product
b. Gross national product
c. Gross Regional Product
d. Bureau of Labor Statistics

52. In microeconomic theory a preference map or _________ is the collection of indifference curves possessed by an individual. Similar in nature to a topographical map, the contour lines of such a map demonstrating progressively more desirable options as they move upward or to the right. Because of the nature of indifference curves they cannot intersect and are effectively infinite in number, their sum defining all possible combinations of values.

a. Expenditure minimization problem
b. Engel curve
c. Elasticity of substitution
d. Indifference map

53. In economics, the _________ is the rate at which a consumer is ready to give up one good in exchange for another good while maintaining the same level of satisfaction.

Under the standard assumption of neoclassical economics that goods and services are continuously divisible, the marginal rates of substitution will be the same regardless of the direction of exchange, and will correspond to the slope of an indifference curve (more precisely, to the slope multiplied by -1) passing through the consumption bundle in question, at that point: mathematically, it is the implicit derivative. MRS of Y for X is the amount of Y for which a consumer is willing to exchange for X locally.

a. Demand vacuum
b. Quality bias
c. Marginal rate of substitution
d. Supply and demand

54. A _________ is an expression that compares quantities relative to each other. The most common examples involve two quantities, but any number of quantities can be compared. _________s are represented mathematically by separating each quantity with a colon, for example the _________ 2:3, which is read as the _________ 'two to three'.

a. 100-year flood
b. 130-30 fund
c. Y-intercept
d. Ratio

55. _________ theory is a branch of theoretical economics. It seeks to explain the behavior of supply, demand and prices in a whole economy with several or many markets. It is often assumed that agents are price takers and in that setting two common notions of equilibrium exist: Walrasian (or competitive) equilibrium, and its generalization; a price equilibrium with transfers.

a. General equilibrium
b. Rational choice theory
c. New Keynesian economics
d. Human capital

56. In economics, economic equilibrium is simply a state of the world where economic forces are balanced and in the absence of external influences the (equilibrium) values of economic variables will not change. It is the point at which quantity demanded and quantity supplied are equal. _________, for example, refers to a condition where a market price is established through competition such that the amount of goods or services sought by buyers is equal to the amount of goods or services produced by sellers.

a. Marketization
b. Product-Market Growth Matrix
c. Market equilibrium
d. Regulated market

1. In microeconomics, _________ is quite simply the conversion of inputs into outputs. It is an economic process that uses resources to create a good or service that is suitable for exchange. This can include manufacturing, storing, shipping, and packaging.

a. Solved
b. Production
c. MET
d. Red Guards

2. _________ is a term used to define maximum possible output of an economy. According to UNCTAD, no agreed-upon definition exists. UNCTAD itself proposes: 'the productive resources, entrepreneurial capabilities and production linkages which together determine the capacity of a country to produce goods and services.' The term '_________' is also used in binary economics to mean income-generating capacity be it of a factory, land, patent or the labour skills of an individual.

a. Productive capacity
b. Multifactor productivity
c. Constant elasticity of substitution
d. Price/performance ratio

3. In law and economics, the _________, describes the economic efficiency of an economic allocation or outcome in the presence of externalities. The theorem states that when trade in an externality is possible and there are no transaction costs, bargaining will lead to an efficient outcome regardless of the initial allocation of property rights. In practice, obstacles to bargaining or poorly defined property rights can prevent Coasian bargaining.

a. Prior appropriation water rights
b. Means test
c. General Mining Act of 1872
d. Coase theorem

4. _________ is the term denoting either an entrance or changes which are inserted into a system and which activate/modify a process. It is an abstract concept, used in the modeling, system(s) design and system(s) exploitation. It is usually connected with other terms, e.g., _________ field, _________ variable, _________ parameter, _________ value, _________ signal, _________ device and _________ file.

a. AD-IA Model
b. ACEA agreement
c. Input
d. ACCRA Cost of Living Index

5. In economics, the _________ or marginal physical product is the extra output produced by one more unit of an input (for instance, the difference in output when a firm's labour is increased from five to six units.) Assuming that no other inputs to production change, the _________ of a given input (X) can be expressed as:

_________ = ΔY/ΔX = (the change of Y)/(the change of X.)

-
    -
        - Pending approval by Thomas Sowell***

In neoclassical economics, this is the mathematical derivative of the production function.... Note that the 'product' (Y) is typically defined ignoring external costs and benefits.

a. Factor prices
b. Labor problem
c. Marginal product
d. Productive capacity

6. The _________ of a variable factor of Production identifies what outputs are possible using various levels of the variable input. This can be displayed in either a chart that lists the output level corresponding to various levels of input, or a graph that summarizes the data into a '_________ curve'. The diagram shows a typical _________ curve. In this example, output increases as more inputs are employed up until point A. The maximum output possible with this Production process is Qm. (If there are other inputs used in the process, they are assumed to be fixed).

a. Total product
b. Convexity
c. Tightness
d. Consequence

7. In economics and finance, _________ is the change in total cost that arises when the quantity produced changes by one unit. It is the cost of producing one more unit of a good. Mathematically, the _________ function is expressed as the first derivative of the total cost (TC) function with respect to quantity (Q.)

a. Variable cost
b. Khozraschyot
c. Marginal cost
d. Quality costs

8. In economics, a _________ is a function that specifies the output of a firm, an industry, or an entire economy for all combinations of inputs. A meta-_________ compares the practice of the existing entities converting inputs X into output y to determine the most efficient practice _________ of the existing entities, whether the most efficient feasible practice production or the most efficient actual practice production. In either case, the maximum output of a technologically-determined production process is a mathematical function of input factors of production.

a. Short-run
b. Post-Fordism
c. Constant elasticity of substitution
d. Production function

9. In economics, _________ refers to how the marginal contribution of a factor of production usually decreases as more of the factor is used. According to this relationship, in a production system with fixed and variable inputs, beyond some point, each additional unit of the variable input yields smaller and smaller increases in output. Conversely, producing one more unit of output costs more and more in variable inputs.

a. Derivatives law
b. Community property
c. Patent troll
d. Diminishing returns

10. In economics, a _________ is a graph of the costs of production as a function of total quantity produced. In a free market economy, productively efficient firms use these curves to find the optimal point of production, where they make the most profits. There are a few different types of _________s, each relevant to a different area of economics.

a. Demand curve
b. Kuznets curve
c. Cost curve
d. Phillips curve

11. A _________ is a standard monetary unit of measurement of the market value/cost of goods, services, or assets. It is one of three well-known functions of money. It lends meaning to profits, losses, liability, or assets.

a. ACEA agreement
b. Unit of account
c. ACCRA Cost of Living Index
d. AD-IA Model

12. A _________ is an expression that compares quantities relative to each other. The most common examples involve two quantities, but any number of quantities can be compared. _________s are represented mathematically by separating each quantity with a colon, for example the _________ 2:3, which is read as the _________ 'two to three'.

a. 130-30 fund
b. Ratio
c. Y-intercept
d. 100-year flood

13. _________, in microeconomics, are the cost advantages that a business obtains due to expansion. They are factors that cause a producere;s average cost per unit to fall as scale is increased. _________ is a long run concept and refers to reductions in unit cost as the size of a facility, or scale, increases.

a. Economies of scale
b. Isoquant
c. Economic production quantity
d. Underinvestment employment relationship

14. In economics, _________ are the resources employed to produce goods and services. They facilitate production but do not become part of the product (as with raw materials) or significantly transformed by the production process (as with fuel used to power machinery.) To 19th century economists, the _________ were land (natural resources, gifts from nature), labor (the ability to work), and capital goods (human-made tools and equipment.)

a. Factors of production
b. Long-run
c. Product Pipeline
d. Hicks-neutral technical change

15. In calculus, a function f defined on a subset of the real numbers with real values is called _________, if for all x and y such that x >≤ y one has f(x) >≤ f(y), so f preserves the order. In layman's terms, the sign of the slope is always positive (the curve tending upwards) or zero (i.e., non-decreasing, or asymptotic, or depicted as a horizontal, flat line) Likewise, a function is called monotonically decreasing (non-increasing) if, whenever x >≤ y, then f(x) >≥ f(y), so it reverses the order.

a. 1921 recession
b. 130-30 fund
c. Monotonic
d. 100-year flood

16. In economics, _________ and economies of scale are related terms that describe what happens as the scale of production increases. They are different terms and should not be used interchangeably.

_________ refers to a technical property of production that examines changes in output subsequent to a proportional change in all inputs (where all inputs increase by a constant factor.)

a. Returns to scale
b. Necessity good
c. Customer equity
d. Constant returns to scale

17. _________ is a term used in economics to describe an economy where capital per worker is increasing. A process of increasing the amount of capital per worker. It is an increase in the capital intensity.

a. Capital expenditure
b. Capital deepening
c. Capital formation
d. Firm-specific infrastructure

18. In production, returns to scale refers to changes in output subsequent to a proportional change in all inputs (where all inputs increase by a constant factor.) If output increases by that same proportional change then there are _________ If output increases by less than that proportional change, there are decreasing returns to scale (DRS.)

a. Lexicographic preferences
b. Consumer sovereignty
c. Long term
d. Constant returns to scale

19. In neoclassical economics and microeconomics, _________ describes the perfect being a market in which there are many small firms, all producing homogeneous goods. In the short term, such markets are productively inefficient as output will not occur where mc is equal to ac, but allocatively efficient, as output under _________ will always occur where mc is equal to mr, and therefore where mc equals ar. However, in the long term, such markets are both allocatively and productively efficient.

a. Law of supply
b. Perfect competition
c. Co-operative economics
d. General equilibrium

20. The _________ consists of a number of economic theories which describe the nature of the firm, company including its existence, its behaviour, and its relationship with the market.

In simplified terms, the _________ aims to answer these questions:

1. Existence - why do firms emerge, why are not all transactions in the economy mediated over the market?
2. Boundaries - why the boundary between firms and the market is located exactly there? Which transactions are performed internally and which are negotiated on the market?
3. Organization - why are firms structured in such specific way? What is the interplay of formal and informal relationships?

Despite looking simple, these questions are not answered by the established economic theory, which usually views firms as given, and treats them as black boxes without any internal structure.

The First World War period saw a change of emphasis in economic theory away from industry-level analysis which mainly included analysing markets to analysis at the level of the firm, as it became increasingly clear that perfect competition was no longer an adequate model of how firms behaved. Economic theory till then had focussed on trying to understand markets alone and there had been little study on understanding why firms or organisations exist.

a. Policy Ineffectiveness Proposition
b. Khazzoom-Brookes postulate
c. Theory of the firm
d. Technology gap

21. _________ , as defined by the _________ Association of America (Information technologyAA), is 'the study, design, development, implementation, support or management of computer-based information systems, particularly software applications and computer hardware.' _________ deals with the use of electronic computers and computer software to convert, store, protect, process, transmit, and securely retrieve information.

Today, the term _________ has ballooned to encompass many aspects of computing and technology, and the term has become very recognizable. The _________ umbrella can be quite large, covering many fields.

a. AD-IA Model
b. ACEA agreement
c. ACCRA Cost of Living Index
d. Information technology

22. _________ is the production of large amounts of standardized products, including and especially on assembly lines. The concepts of _________ are applied to various kinds of products, from fluids and particulates handled in bulk to discrete solid parts to assemblies of such parts

_________ of assemblies typically uses electric-motor-powered moving tracks or conveyor belts to move partially complete products to workers, who perform simple repetitive tasks.

a. 130-30 fund
b. 100-year flood
c. 1921 recession
d. Mass production

23. In economic theory, _________ is the competitive situation in any market where the conditions necessary for perfect competition are not satisfied. It is a market structure that does not meet the conditions of perfect competition.

Forms of _________ include:

- Monopoly, in which there is only one seller of a good.
- Oligopoly, in which there is a small number of sellers.
- Monopolistic competition, in which there are many sellers producing highly differentiated goods.
- Monopsony, in which there is only one buyer of a good.
- Oligopsony, in which there is a small number of buyers.

There may also be _________ in markets due to buyers or sellers lacking information about prices and the goods being traded.

There may also be _________ due to a time lag in a market.

a. AD-IA Model
b. ACEA agreement
c. ACCRA Cost of Living Index
d. Imperfect competition

24. In economic models, the _________ time frame assumes no fixed factors of production. Firms can enter or leave the marketplace, and the cost (and availability) of land, labor, raw materials, and capital goods can be assumed to vary. In contrast, in the short-run time frame, certain factors are assumed to be fixed, because there is not sufficient time for them to change.

a. Productivity world
b. Price/performance ratio
c. Diseconomies of scale
d. Long-run

25. In economics, the concept of the _________ refers to the decision-making time frame of a firm in which at least one factor of production is fixed. Costs which are fixed in the _________ have no impact on a firms decisions. For example a firm can raise output by increasing the amount of labour through overtime.

a. Productivity model
b. Product Pipeline
c. Short-run
d. Hicks-neutral technical change

26. A _________ is an object whose consumption increases the utility of the consumer, for which the quantity demanded exceeds the quantity supplied at zero price. _________s are usually modeled as having diminishing marginal utility. The first individual purchase has high utility; the second has less.

a. Composite good
b. Pie method
c. Merit good
d. Good

27. In economics, economic output is divided into physical goods and intangible services. Consumption of _________ is assumed to produce utility. It is often used when referring to a _________ Tax.

a. Manufactured goods
b. Private good
c. Composite good
d. Goods and services

28. A _________ is an economy based on the division of labor in which the prices of goods and services are determined in a free price system set by supply and demand. This is often contrasted with a planned economy, in which a central government determines the price of goods and services using a fixed price system. Market economies are contrasted with mixed economy where the price system is not entirely free but under some government control that is not extensive enough to constitute a planned economy.

a. Network Economy
b. Nutritional Economics
c. Commons-based peer production
d. Market economy

29. The process of _________ involves the introduction of a good or service that is new or substantially improved. This includes, but is not limited to, improvements in functional characteristics, technical abilities, or ease of use.

a. Dogs of the Dow
b. Microcap stock
c. Refusal to deal
d. Product innovation

30. _________ is a term that is used to describe the overall process of invention, innovation and diffusion of technology or processes. The term is redundant with technological development, technological achievement, and technological progress. In essence _________ is the invention of a technology (or a process), the continuous process of improving a technology (in which it often becomes cheaper) and its diffusion throughout industry or society.

a. 1921 recession
b. 100-year flood
c. 130-30 fund
d. Technological change

31. The _________ is the largest national economy in the world. Its gross domestic product (GDP) was estimated as $14.2 trillion in 2008. The U.S. economy maintains a high level of output per person (GDP per capita, $46,800 in 2008, ranked at around number ten in the world.)

a. ACEA agreement
b. ACCRA Cost of Living Index
c. AD-IA Model
d. Economy of the United States

32. In economics, the _________ measures the payments that flow between any individual country and all other countries. It is used to summarize all international economic transactions for that country during a specific time period, usually a year. The _________ is determined by the country's exports and imports of goods, services, and financial capital, as well as financial transfers.

a. Skyscraper Index
b. Gross domestic product per barrel
c. Gross world product
d. Balance of payments

33. A _________ is the transfer of wealth from one party (such as a person or company) to another. A _________ is usually made in exchange for the provision of goods, services or both, or to fulfill a legal obligation.

The simplest and oldest form of _________ is barter, the exchange of one good or service for another.

a. Soft count
b. Social gravity
c. Going concern
d. Payment

34. _________ in economics refers to metrics and measures of output from production processes, per unit of input. Labor _________, for example, is typically measured as a ratio of output per labor-hour, an input. _________ may be conceived of as a metrics of the technical or engineering efficiency of production.

a. Fordism
b. Productivity
c. Production-possibility frontier
d. Piece work

35. In economics, a _________ exists when the production or use of goods and services by the market is not efficient. That is, there exists another outcome where all involved can be made better off. _________s can be viewed as scenarios where individuals' pursuit of pure self-interest leads to results that are not efficient - that can be improved upon from the societal point-of-view.

a. General equilibrium
b. Fixed exchange rate
c. Market failure
d. Financial economics

36. _________ is a broad label that refers to any individuals or households that use goods and services generated within the economy. The concept of a _________ is used in different contexts, so that the usage and significance of the term may vary.

Typically when business people and economists talk of _________s they are talking about person as _________, an aggregated commodity item with little individuality other than that expressed in the buy/not-buy decision.

a. 100-year flood
b. Consumer
c. 1921 recession
d. 130-30 fund

37. The _________ is the central banking system of the United States. Created in 1913 by the enactment of the Federal Reserve Act (signed by Woodrow Wilson), it is a quasi-public and quasi-private (government entity with private components) banking system that comprises (1) the presidentially appointed Board of Governors of the _________ in Washington, D.C.; (2) the Federal Open Market Committee; (3) twelve regional Federal Reserve Banks located in major cities throughout the nation acting as fiscal agents for the U.S. Treasury, each with its own nine-member board of directors; (4) numerous other private U.S. member banks, which subscribe to required amounts of non-transferable stock in their regional Federal Reserve Banks; and (5) various advisory councils. Since February 2006, Ben Bernanke has served as the Chairman of the Board of Governors of the _________.

a. Monetary Policy Report to the Congress
b. Term auction facility
c. Federal Reserve System Open Market Account
d. Federal Reserve System

38. _________ is the pricing technique of setting a relatively low initial entry price, often lower than the eventual market price, to attract new customers. The strategy works on the expectation that customers will switch to the new brand because of the lower price. _________ is most commonly associated with a marketing objective of increasing market share or sales volume, rather than to make profit in the short term.

a. Transfer pricing
b. Contribution margin-based pricing
c. Fire sale
d. Penetration pricing

39. _________ is one of the four Ps of the marketing mix. The other three aspects are product, promotion, and place. It is also a key variable in microeconomic price allocation theory.

a. Pricing
b. Guaranteed Maximum Price
c. Point of total assumption
d. Premium pricing

40. In the theory of artificial neural networks _________ networks are a case of competitive learning in recurrent neural networks. Output nodes in the network inhibit each other and activate themselves through reflexive connections. After some time, only one node in the output layer will be active.

a. 130-30 fund
b. 100-year flood
c. Winner-take-all
d. 1921 recession

41. In economics, _________ is equal to total cost divided by the number of goods produced (the output quantity, Q.) It is also equal to the sum of average variable costs (total variable costs divided by Q) plus average fixed costs (total fixed costs divided by Q.) _________s may be dependent on the time period considered (increasing production may be expensive or impossible in the short term, for example.)

a. Average fixed cost
b. Average variable cost
c. Explicit cost
d. Average cost

42. In economics, an _________ or spillover of an economic transaction is an impact on a party that is not directly involved in the transaction. In such a case, prices do not reflect the full costs or benefits in production or consumption of a product or service. A positive impact is called an external benefit, while a negative impact is called an external cost.

a. Existence value
b. Environmental impact assessment
c. Environmental tariff
d. Externality

43. In economics, _________ (TFP) is a variable which accounts for effects in total output not caused by inputs. For example, a year with unusually good weather will tend to have higher output, because bad weather hinders agricultural output. A variable like weather does not directly relate to unit inputs, so weather is considered a _________ variable.

a. Flow to Equity-Approach
b. Total-factor productivity
c. Human rights
d. 35-hour working week

44. _________s is the social science that studies the production, distribution, and consumption of goods and services. The term _________s comes from the Ancient Greek oá¼°κονομΐα from oá¼¶κος (oikos, 'house') + νÏŒμος (nomos, 'custom' or 'law'), hence 'rules of the house(hold)'. Current _________ models developed out of the broader field of political economy in the late 19th century, owing to a desire to use an empirical approach more akin to the physical sciences.

a. Opportunity cost
b. Energy economics
c. Inflation
d. Economic

45. _________ is the increase in the amount of the goods and services produced by an economy over time. It is conventionally measured as the percent rate of increase in real gross domestic product, or real GDP. Growth is usually calculated in real terms, i.e. inflation-adjusted terms, in order to net out the effect of inflation on the price of the goods and services produced.

a. ACCRA Cost of Living Index
b. Economic growth
c. ACEA agreement
d. AD-IA Model

46. In economics, _________ is a rise in the general level of prices of goods and services in an economy over a period of time. When the general price level rises, each unit of currency buys fewer goods and services; consequently, _________ is also a decline in the real value of money--a loss of purchasing power in the medium of exchange which is also the monetary unit of account in the economy. A chief measure of general price-level _________ is the general _________ rate, which is the percentage change in a general price index (normally the Consumer Price Index) over time.

a. Energy economics
b. Opportunity cost
c. Economic
d. Inflation

47. In finance, _________ rate of profit or sometimes just return, is the ratio of money gained or lost on an investment relative to the amount of money invested. The amount of money gained or lost may be referred to as interest, profit/loss, gain/loss, or net income/loss. The money invested may be referred to as the asset, capital, principal, or the cost basis of the investment.

a. Current ratio
b. Sortino ratio
c. Cost accrual ratio
d. Rate of return

48. _________ is a term used in national accounts statistics and macroeconomics. It basically refers to the net additions to the (physical) capital stock in an accounting period, or, to the value of the increase of the capital stock; though it may occasionally also refer to the (growth of the) total stock of capital formed.

Thus, in UNSNA, _________ equals fixed capital investment, the increase in the value of inventories held, plus (net) lending to foreign countries, during an accounting period.

a. Capital intensity
b. Consumption of fixed capital
c. Capital flight
d. Capital formation

49. _________s (economically referred to as land or raw materials) occur naturally within environments that exist relatively undisturbed by mankind, in a natural form. A _________'s is often characterized by amounts of biodiversity existent in various ecosystems.

Mining, petroleum extraction, fishing, hunting, and forestry are generally considered natural-resource industries.

a. 100-year flood
b. 1921 recession
c. 130-30 fund
d. Natural resource

50. The _________ 4(16) Economica 386-405 by Ronald Coase is a brief but highly influential essay that offers an economic explanation of why individuals choose to form partnerships, companies and other business entities rather than trading bilaterally through contracts on a market.

Given that 'production could be carried on without any organization that is, firms at all', Coase asks, why and under what conditions should we expect firms to emerge? Since modern firms can only emerge when an entrepreneur of some sort begins to hire people, Coase's analysis proceeds by considering the conditions under which it makes sense for an entrepreneur to seek hired help instead of contracting out for some particular task.

The traditional economic theory of the time suggested that, because the market is 'efficient' (that is, those who are best at providing each good or service most cheaply are already doing so), it should always be cheaper to contract out than to hire.

a. Legal tender
b. Nature of the firm
c. Holder in due course
d. Greenfield agreement

51. The _________ was an early English joint-stock company that was formed initially for pursuing trade with the East Indies, but that ended up trading with the Indian subcontinent and China. The oldest among several similarly formed European East India Companies, the Company was granted an English Royal Charter, under the name Governor and Company of Merchants of London Trading into the East Indies, by Elizabeth I on 31 December 1600. After a rival English company challenged its monopoly in the late 17th century, the two companies were merged in 1708 to form the United Company of Merchants of England Trading to the East Indies, commonly styled the Honourable _________, and abbreviated, HEast India Company; the Company was colloquially referred to as John Company, and in India as Company Bahadur .

a. East India Company
b. AD-IA Model
c. ACEA agreement
d. ACCRA Cost of Living Index

52. _________ is a concept whereby a person's financial liability is limited to a fixed sum, most commonly the value of a person's investment in a company or partnership with _________. A shareholder in a limited company is not personally liable for any of the debts of the company, other than for the value of his investment in that company. The same is true for the members of a _________ partnership and the limited partners in a limited partnership.

a. Deficiency judgment
b. Personal Responsibility and Work Opportunity Reconciliation Act of 1996
c. Limited liability
d. Nexus of contracts

53. _________ is an equity (stock) exchange located at 11 Wall Street in lower Manhattan, New York, USA. It is the largest stock exchange in the world by dollar value of its listed companies' securities. As of October 2008, the combined capitalization of all domestic _________ listed companies was US$10.1 trillion.

a. New York Stock Exchange
b. 130-30 fund
c. 100-year flood
d. 1921 recession

54. A _________ is a type of business entity in which partners (owners) share with each other the profits or losses of the business _________s are often favored over corporations for taxation purposes, as the _________ structure does not generally incur a tax on profits before it is distributed to the partners (i.e. there is no dividend tax levied.) However, depending on the _________ structure and the jurisdiction in which it operates, owners of a _________ may be exposed to greater personal liability than they would as shareholders of a corporation.

For a country-by-country listing of types of _________s, companies, etc., see Types of business entity.

a. Feoffee
b. Due diligence
c. Minimum wage law
d. Partnership

55. A mutual _________ or stockholder is an individual or company (including a corporation) that legally owns one or more shares of stock in a joint stock company. A company's _________s collectively own that company. Thus, the typical goal of such companies is to enhance _________ value.

a. Prime Standard
b. Relative valuation
c. Shareholder
d. Profit warning

56. A _________ is a corporation or mutual organization which provides trading facilities for stock brokers and traders, to trade stocks and other securities. It may be a physical trading room where the traders gather, or a formalised communications network. Creation of a _________ is a strategy of economic development.

a. Primary shares
b. SEAQ
c. 100-year flood
d. Stock Exchange

57. A _________, or simply proprietorship is a type of business entity which legally has no separate existence from its owner. Hence, the limitations of liability enjoyed by a corporation and limited liability partnerships do not apply to sole proprietors. All debts of the business are debts of the owner.

a. Sole proprietorship
b. Golden parachute
c. Corporate tax
d. Golden hello

58. _________ is a situation in which the limited resources of a firm are allocated in accordance with the wishes of consumers. An allocatively efficient economy produces an 'optimal mix' of commodities. A firm is allocatively efficient when its price is equal to its marginal costs (that is, P = MC) in a perfect market.

a. ACCRA Cost of Living Index
b. Allocative efficiency
c. Economic efficiency
d. ACEA agreement

59. _________s are payments made by a corporation to its shareholders. It is the portion of corporate profits paid out to stockholders. When a corporation earns a profit or surplus, that money can be put to two uses: it can either be re-invested in the business (called retained earnings), or it can be paid to the shareholders as a _________.

a. Dividend puzzle
b. Dividend yield
c. Dividend cover
d. Dividend

60. _________ is subcontracting a process, such as product design or manufacturing, to a third-party company. The decision to outsource is often made in the interest of lowering cost or making better use of time and energy costs, redirecting or conserving energy directed at the competencies of a particular business, or to make more efficient use of land, labor, capital, (information) technology and resources. _________ became part of the business lexicon during the 1980s.

a. Electronic business
b. Averch-Johnson effect
c. Outsourcing
d. Additional Funds Needed

1. In economics, and cost accounting, _________ describes the total economic cost of production and is made up of variable costs, which vary according to the quantity of a good produced and include inputs such as labor and raw materials, plus fixed costs, which are independent of the quantity of a good produced and include inputs (capital) that cannot be varied in the short term, such as buildings and machinery. _________ in economics includes the total opportunity cost of each factor of production in addition to fixed and variable costs.

The rate at which _________ changes as the amount produced changes is called marginal cost.

a. 130-30 fund
b. 1921 recession
c. 100-year flood
d. Total cost

2. _________s is the social science that studies the production, distribution, and consumption of goods and services. The term _________s comes from the Ancient Greek oá¼°κονομÎ¯α from oá¼¶κος (oikos, 'house') + νÏŒμος (nomos, 'custom' or 'law'), hence 'rules of the house(hold)'. Current _________ models developed out of the broader field of political economy in the late 19th century, owing to a desire to use an empirical approach more akin to the physical sciences.

a. Opportunity cost
b. Inflation
c. Economic
d. Energy economics

3. In economics and finance, _________ is the change in total cost that arises when the quantity produced changes by one unit. It is the cost of producing one more unit of a good. Mathematically, the _________ function is expressed as the first derivative of the total cost (TC) function with respect to quantity (Q.)

a. Quality costs
b. Khozraschyot
c. Marginal cost
d. Variable cost

4. In microeconomics, _________ is quite simply the conversion of inputs into outputs. It is an economic process that uses resources to create a good or service that is suitable for exchange. This can include manufacturing, storing, shipping, and packaging.

a. Production
b. Red Guards
c. MET
d. Solved

5. The _________ consists of a number of economic theories which describe the nature of the firm, company including its existence, its behaviour, and its relationship with the market.

In simplified terms, the _________ aims to answer these questions:

1. Existence - why do firms emerge, why are not all transactions in the economy mediated over the market?
2. Boundaries - why the boundary between firms and the market is located exactly there? Which transactions are performed internally and which are negotiated on the market?
3. Organization - why are firms structured in such specific way? What is the interplay of formal and informal relationships?

Despite looking simple, these questions are not answered by the established economic theory, which usually views firms as given, and treats them as black boxes without any internal structure.

The First World War period saw a change of emphasis in economic theory away from industry-level analysis which mainly included analysing markets to analysis at the level of the firm, as it became increasingly clear that perfect competition was no longer an adequate model of how firms behaved. Economic theory till then had focussed on trying to understand markets alone and there had been little study on understanding why firms or organisations exist.

a. Policy Ineffectiveness Proposition
b. Khazzoom-Brookes postulate
c. Technology gap
d. Theory of the firm

6. In economics, _________ are business expenses that are not dependent on the activities of the business They tend to be time-related, such as salaries or rents being paid per month. This is in contrast to variable costs, which are volume-related (and are paid per quantity.)

In management accounting, _________ are defined as expenses that do not change in proportion to the activity of a business, within the relevant period or scale of production.

a. Quality costs
b. Cost-Volume-Profit Analysis
c. Cost of poor quality
d. Fixed costs

7. In business, _________, Overhead cost or _________ expense refers to an ongoing expense of operating a business. The term _________ is usually used to group expenses that are necessary to the continued functioning of the business, but do not directly generate profits.

_________ expenses are all costs on the income statement except for direct labor and direct materials.

a. ACEA agreement
b. AD-IA Model
c. ACCRA Cost of Living Index
d. Overhead

8. In economics and business decision-making, _________ are costs that cannot be recovered once they have been incurred. _________ are sometimes contrasted with variable costs, which are the costs that will change due to the proposed course of action, and prospective costs which are costs that will be incurred if an action is taken.

In traditional microeconomic theory, only variable costs are relevant to a decision.

a. Hyperbolic discounting
b. Post-purchase rationalization
c. Halo effect
d. Sunk costs

9. _________s are expenses that change in proportion to the activity of a business. In other words, _________ is the sum of marginal costs. It can also be considered normal costs.

a. Quality costs
b. Cost allocation
c. Cost-Volume-Profit Analysis
d. Variable cost

10. In economics, a _________ is a graph of the costs of production as a function of total quantity produced. In a free market economy, productively efficient firms use these curves to find the optimal point of production, where they make the most profits. There are a few different types of _________s, each relevant to a different area of economics.

a. Cost curve
b. Demand curve
c. Kuznets curve
d. Phillips curve

11. A _________ is:

- Rewrite _________, in generative grammar and computer science
- Standardization, a formal and widely-accepted statement, fact, definition, or qualification
- Operation, a determinate _________ for performing a mathematical operation and obtaining a certain result (Mathematics, Logic)
  - Unary operation
  - Binary operation
- _________ of inference, a function from sets of formulae to formulae (Mathematics, Logic)
- _________ of thumb, principle with broad application that is not intended to be strictly accurate or reliable for every situation. Also often simply referred to as a _________
- Moral, an atomic element of a moral code for guiding choices in human behavior
- Heuristic, a quantized '_________' which shows a tendency or probability for successful function
- A regulation, as in sports
- A Production _________, as in computer science
- Procedural law, a _________set governing the application of laws to cases
  - A law, which may informally be called a '_________'
  - A court ruling, a decision by a court
- In the U.S. Government, a regulation mandated by Congress, but written or expanded upon by the Executive Branch.
- Norm (sociology), an informal but widely accepted _________, concept, truth, definition, or qualification (social norms, legal norms, coding norms)
- Norm (philosophy), a kind of sentence or a reason to act, feel or believe
- 'Rulership' is the concept of governance by a government:
  - Military _________, governance by a military body
  - Monastic _________, a collection of precepts that guides the life of monks or nuns in a religious order where the superior holds the place of Christ
- Slide _________

- '_________,' a song by Ayumi Hamasaki
- '_________,' a song by rapper Nas
- '_________s,' an album by the band The Whitest Boy Alive
- _________s: Pyaar Ka Superhit Formula, a 2003 Bollywood film
- ruler, an instrument for measuring lengths
- _________, a component of an astrolabe, circumferator or similar instrument
- The _________s, a bestselling self-help book
- _________ Project (Run Up-to-date Linux Everywhere), a project that aims to use up-to-date Linux software on old PCs
- _________ engine, a software system that helps managing business _________s
- Ja _________, a hip hop artist
  - R.U.L.E., a 2005 greatest hits album by rapper Ja _________
- '_________s,' a KMFDM song

a. Demand
b. Technocracy
c. Rule
d. Procter ' Gamble

12. In economics, _________ is equal to total cost divided by the number of goods produced (the output quantity, Q.) It is also equal to the sum of average variable costs (total variable costs divided by Q) plus average fixed costs (total fixed costs divided by Q.) _________s may be dependent on the time period considered (increasing production may be expensive or impossible in the short term, for example.)

a. Average variable cost
b. Average cost
c. Average fixed cost
d. Explicit cost

13. _________ is an economics term used to describe the total fixed costs (TFC) divided by the quantity (Q) of units produced.

$$AFC = \frac{TFC}{Q}$$

_________ is a per-unit measure of fixed costs. As the total number of goods produced increases, the _________ decreases because the same amount of fixed costs are being spread over a larger number of units.

a. Inventory valuation
b. Average variable cost
c. Explicit cost
d. Average fixed cost

14. _________ is an economics term to describe a firms variable costs (labor, electricity, etc.) divided by the quantity (Q) of total units of output.

$$\mathrm{AVC} = \frac{\mathrm{TVC}}{\mathrm{Q}}$$

Where:

- TVC = Total Variable Cost
- _________ = Average variable cost
- Q = Quantity of Units Produced

_________ plus average fixed cost equals average total cost:

_________ + AFC = ATC.

.

a. Average fixed cost
b. Inventory valuation
c. Explicit cost
d. Average variable cost

15. In law and economics, the _________, describes the economic efficiency of an economic allocation or outcome in the presence of externalities. The theorem states that when trade in an externality is possible and there are no transaction costs, bargaining will lead to an efficient outcome regardless of the initial allocation of property rights. In practice, obstacles to bargaining or poorly defined property rights can prevent Coasian bargaining.

a. Prior appropriation water rights
b. General Mining Act of 1872
c. Means test
d. Coase theorem

16. _________ are the prices that the factors of production of a finished item attract.

There has been some economic debate as to what determines these prices. Classical and Marxist economists argued that the _________ decided the value of a product and so value was intrinsic within the product.

a. Marginal product of labor
b. Marginal product
c. Productivity model
d. Factor prices

17. In algebra, a _________ is a function depending on n that associates a scalar, det(A), to an n×n square matrix A. The fundamental geometric meaning of a _________ is a scale factor for measure when A is regarded as a linear transformation. _________s are important both in calculus, where they enter the substitution rule for several variables, and in multilinear algebra.

For a fixed nonnegative integer n, there is a unique _________ function for the n×n matrices over any commutative ring R. In particular, this function exists when R is the field of real or complex numbers.

a. 1921 recession
b. 130-30 fund
c. Determinant
d. 100-year flood

18. _________ in economics and business is the result of an exchange and from that trade we assign a numerical monetary value to a good, service or asset. If Alice trades Bob 4 apples for an orange, the _________ of an orange is 4 apples. Inversely, the _________ of an apple is 1/4 oranges.

a. Premium pricing
b. Price
c. Price war
d. Price book

19. In economics, a _________ is a function that specifies the output of a firm, an industry, or an entire economy for all combinations of inputs. A meta-_________ compares the practice of the existing entities converting inputs X into output y to determine the most efficient practice _________ of the existing entities, whether the most efficient feasible practice production or the most efficient actual practice production. In either case, the maximum output of a technologically-determined production process is a mathematical function of input factors of production.

a. Constant elasticity of substitution
b. Post-Fordism
c. Short-run
d. Production function

20. In economics, _________ refers to how the marginal contribution of a factor of production usually decreases as more of the factor is used. According to this relationship, in a production system with fixed and variable inputs, beyond some point, each additional unit of the variable input yields smaller and smaller increases in output. Conversely, producing one more unit of output costs more and more in variable inputs.

a. Community property
b. Diminishing returns
c. Derivatives law
d. Patent troll

21. _________ is the simplest of the pharmacoeconomics tools and is applied when comparing two drugs of equal efficacy and equal tolerability

Therapeutic equivalence must be referenced by the author conducting the study and should have been done prior to the _________ work. Since equal efficacy and equal tolerability is already demonstrated, there is no requirement to find a common efficacy denominator as would be the case when conducting a cost-effectiveness study. The author is not precluded from doing so through the use of 'cost/cure' or 'cost/year of life gained'.

a. Liquidating dividend
b. Bord halfpenny
c. Linkage principle
d. Cost-minimization

22. _________ is the term denoting either an entrance or changes which are inserted into a system and which activate/modify a process. It is an abstract concept, used in the modeling, system(s) design and system(s) exploitation. It is usually connected with other terms, e.g., _________ field, _________ variable, _________ parameter, _________ value, _________ signal, _________ device and _________ file.

a. ACCRA Cost of Living Index
b. Input
c. ACEA agreement
d. AD-IA Model

23. In economics, the _________ or marginal physical product is the extra output produced by one more unit of an input (for instance, the difference in output when a firm's labour is increased from five to six units.) Assuming that no other inputs to production change, the _________ of a given input (X) can be expressed as:

_________ = ΔY/ΔX = (the change of Y)/(the change of X.)

-
  -
    - Pending approval by Thomas Sowell***

In neoclassical economics, this is the mathematical derivative of the production function.... Note that the 'product' (Y) is typically defined ignoring external costs and benefits.

a. Factor prices
b. Labor problem
c. Marginal product
d. Productive capacity

24. The _________ of a decision depends on both the cost of the alternative chosen and the benefit that the best alternative would have provided if chosen. _________ differs from accounting cost because it includes opportunity cost.

a. Epstein-Zin preferences
b. Inventory analysis
c. Economic cost
d. Isocost

25. _________ is a company's financial statement that indicates how the revenue is transformed into the net income The purpose of the _________ is to show managers and investors whether the company made or lost money during the period being reported.

The important thing to remember about an _________ is that it represents a period of time.

a. ACEA agreement
b. Income statement
c. AD-IA Model
d. ACCRA Cost of Living Index

26. _________ is equal to the income that a firm has after subtracting costs and expenses from the total revenue. _________ can be distributed among holders of common stock as a dividend or held by the firm as retained earnings. _________ is an accounting term.

a. Salvage value
b. Net income
c. Net profit
d. Historical cost

27. In financial accounting, a _________ or statement of financial position is a summary of a person's or organization's balances. Assets, liabilities and ownership equity are listed as of a specific date, such as the end of its financial year. A _________ is often described as a snapshot of a company's financial condition.

a. 1921 recession
b. 100-year flood
c. Balance sheet
d. 130-30 fund

28. In Marxian economics, _________ originally referred to the means of production. Individuals, organizations and governments use _________ in the production of other goods or commodities. _________ include factories, machinery, tools, equipment, and various buildings which are used to produce other products for consumption.

a. Capital deepening
b. Capital goods
c. Wealth inequality in the United States
d. Capital intensive

29. In financial accounting, _________ or cost of sales includes the direct costs attributable to the production of the goods sold by a company. This amount includes the materials cost used in creating the goods along with the direct labour costs used to produce the good. It excludes indirect expenses such as distribution costs and sales force costs.

a. 100-year flood
b. 130-30 fund
c. 1921 recession
d. Cost of goods sold

30. _________ is a term used in accounting, economics and finance to spread the cost of an asset over the span of several years.

In simple words we can say that _________ is the reduction in the value of an asset due to usage, passage of time, wear and tear, technological outdating or obsolescence, depletion, inadequacy, rot, rust, decay or other such factors.

In accounting, _________ is a term used to describe any method of attributing the historical or purchase cost of an asset across its useful life, roughly corresponding to normal wear and tear.

a. Salvage value
b. Historical cost
c. Net income per employee
d. Depreciation

31. A _________ is an object whose consumption increases the utility of the consumer, for which the quantity demanded exceeds the quantity supplied at zero price. _________s are usually modeled as having diminishing marginal utility. The first individual purchase has high utility; the second has less.

a. Merit good
b. Composite good
c. Pie method
d. Good

32. In business and accounting, _________ are everything of value that is owned by a person or company. It is a claim on the property your income of a borrower. The balance sheet of a firm records the monetary value of the _________ owned by the firm.

a. Assets
b. ACEA agreement
c. Amortization schedule
d. ACCRA Cost of Living Index

33. The accounting equation relates assets, _________, and owner's equity:

Assets = _________ + Owner's Equity

The accounting equation is the mathematical structure of the balance sheet.

The Australian Accounting Research Foundation defines _________ as: 'future sacrifice of economic benefits that the entity is presently obliged to make to other entities as a result of past transactions and other past events.'

Probably the most accepted accounting definition of liability is the one used by the International Accounting Standards Board (IASB.) The following is a quotation from IFRS Framework:

A liability is a present obligation of the enterprise arising from past events, the settlement of which is expected to result in an outflow from the enterprise of resources embodying economic benefits

-

Regulations as to the recognition of _________ are different all over the world, but are roughly similar to those of the IASB.

a. Community property
b. Competition law theory
c. Coase theorem
d. Liabilities

34. In business, _________ is the total liabilitiess minus total outside assets of an individual or a company. For a company, this is called shareholders' prefernce and may be referred to as book value. _________ is stated as at a particular year in time.

a. Sinking fund
b. Bond credit rating
c. Net worth
d. Post earnings announcement drift

35. _________, or corporate _________ are political and business scandals which arise with the disclosure of misdeeds by trusted executives of large public corporations. Such misdeeds typically involve complex methods for misusing or misdirecting funds, overstating revenues, understating expenses, overstating the value of corporate assets or underreporting the existence of liabilities, sometimes with the cooperation of officials in other corporations or affiliates.

In public companies, this type of 'creative accounting' can amount to fraud and investigations are typically launched by government oversight agencies, such as the Securities and Exchange Commission (SEC) in the United States.

a. Accounting scandals
b. ACCRA Cost of Living Index
c. AD-IA Model
d. ACEA agreement

36. In finance, a _________ is a debt security, in which the authorized issuer owes the holders a debt and, depending on the terms of the _________, is obliged to pay interest (the coupon) and/or to repay the principal at a later date, termed maturity. A _________ is a formal contract to repay borrowed money with interest at fixed intervals.

Thus a _________ is like a loan: the issuer is the borrower (debtor), the holder is the lender (creditor), and the coupon is the interest.

a. Zero-coupon
b. Bond
c. Prize Bond
d. Callable

37. In accounting, _________ is the original monetary value of an economic item. In some circumstances, assets and liabilities may be shown at their _________, as if there had been no change in value since the date of acquisition. The balance sheet value of the item may therefore differ from the 'true' value.
a. Salvage value
b. Deferred financing costs
c. Net income per employee
d. Historical cost

38. _________ or economic opportunity loss is the value of the next best alternative foregone as the result of making a decision. _________ analysis is an important part of a company's decision-making processes but is not treated as an actual cost in any financial statement. The next best thing that a person can engage in is referred to as the _________ of doing the best thing and ignoring the next best thing to be done.
a. Economic
b. Economic ideology
c. Industrial organization
d. Opportunity cost

39. _________ is an economic concept with commonplace familiarity. It is the price that a good or service is offered at, or will fetch, in the marketplace. It is of interest mainly in the study of microeconomics.
a. Market price
b. Noisy market hypothesis
c. Paper trading
d. Market anomaly

40. _________s (economically referred to as land or raw materials) occur naturally within environments that exist relatively undisturbed by mankind, in a natural form. A _________'s is often characterized by amounts of biodiversity existent in various ecosystems.

Mining, petroleum extraction, fishing, hunting, and forestry are generally considered natural-resource industries.

a. 1921 recession
b. Natural resource
c. 100-year flood
d. 130-30 fund

41. _________ is the a method of technical and economic research of the systems for purpose to optimize a parity between system's consumer functions or properties and expenses to achieve those functions or properties.

This methodology for continuous perfection of production, industrial technologies, organizational structures was developed by Juryj Sobolev in 1948 at the 'Perm telephone factory'

- 1948 Juryj Sobolev - the first success in application of a method analysis at the 'Perm telephone factory' .
- 1949 - the first application for the invention as result of use of the new method.

Today in economically developed countries practically each enterprise or the company use methodology of the kind of functional-cost analysis as a practice of the quality management, most full satisfying to principles of standards of series ISO 9000.

- Interest of consumer not in products itself, but the advantage which it will receive from its usage.
- The consumer aspires to reduce his expenses
- Functions needed by consumer can be executed in the various ways, and, hence, with various efficiency and expenses. Among possible alternatives of realization of functions exist such in which the parity of quality and the price is the optimal for the consumer.

The goal of _________ is achievement of the highest consumer satisfaction of production at simultaneous decrease in all kinds of industrial expenses Classical _________ has three English synonyms - Value Engineering, Value Management, Value Analysis.

a. Function cost analysis
b. Staple financing
c. Willingness to pay
d. Monopoly wage

42. Competition law, known in the United States as _________ law, has three main elements:

- prohibiting agreements or practices that restrict free trading and competition between business entities. This includes in particular the repression of cartels.
- banning abusive behaviour by a firm dominating a market, or anti-competitive practices that tend to lead to such a dominant position. Practices controlled in this way may include predatory pricing, tying, price gouging, refusal to deal, and many others.
- supervising the mergers and acquisitions of large corporations, including some joint ventures. Transactions that are considered to threaten the competitive process can be prohibited altogether, or approved subject to 'remedies' such as an obligation to divest part of the merged business or to offer licences or access to facilities to enable other businesses to continue competing.

The substance and practice of competition law varies from jurisdiction to jurisdiction. Protecting the interests of consumers (consumer welfare) and ensuring that entrepreneurs have an opportunity to compete in the market economy are often treated as important objectives. Competition law is closely connected with law on deregulation of access to markets, state aids and subsidies, the privatisation of state owned assets and the establishment of independent sector regulators. In recent decades, competition law has been viewed as a way to provide better public services.

a. Antitrust
b. Intellectual property law
c. Anti-Inflation Act
d. United Kingdom competition law

43. _________ is a broad label that refers to any individuals or households that use goods and services generated within the economy. The concept of a _________ is used in different contexts, so that the usage and significance of the term may vary.

Typically when business people and economists talk of _________s they are talking about person as _________, an aggregated commodity item with little individuality other than that expressed in the buy/not-buy decision.

a. 1921 recession
b. Consumer
c. 100-year flood
d. 130-30 fund

44. The term surplus is used in economics for several related quantities. The _________ is the amount that consumers benefit by being able to purchase a product for a price that is less than they would be willing to pay. The producer surplus is the amount that producers benefit by selling at a market price mechanism that is higher than they would be willing to sell for.

a. Marginal rate of technical substitution
b. Consumer surplus
c. Necessity good
d. Microeconomic reform

45. In retail systems, the _________ represents the specific value that represents unit price purchased. This value is used as a key factor in determining profitability and in some stock market theories it is used in establishing the value of stock holding.

_________s appear in several forms, such as Actual Cost, Last Cost, Average Cost and Net realizable value.

a. Customer Demand Planning
b. Ten bagger
c. Facilitation payment
d. Cost Price

46. In economics, _________ are the resources employed to produce goods and services. They facilitate production but do not become part of the product (as with raw materials) or significantly transformed by the production process (as with fuel used to power machinery.) To 19th century economists, the _________ were land (natural resources, gifts from nature), labor (the ability to work), and capital goods (human-made tools and equipment.)

a. Factors of production
b. Product Pipeline
c. Hicks-neutral technical change
d. Long-run

47. A security is a fungible, negotiable instrument representing financial value. _________ are broadly categorized into debt _________; equity _________, e.g., common stocks; and derivative (finance) contracts such as forwards, futures, options and swaps. The company or other entity issuing the security is called the issuer.

a. Settlement risk
b. Pass-Through Certificates
c. Red herring prospectus
d. Securities

48. In economics, the _________ also known as MPL or MPN is the change in output from hiring one additional unit of labor. It is the increase in output added by the last unit of labor. Assuming that no other inputs to production change, the marginal product of a given input (X) can be expressed as:

MP = ΔY/ΔX = (the change of Y)/(the change of X.)

a. Product Pipeline
b. Marginal product of labor
c. Production function
d. Marginal product

49. In economics, an _________ is a contour line drawn through the set of points at which the same quantity of output is produced while changing the quantities of two or more inputs. While an indifference curve helps to answer the utility-maximizing problem of consumers, the _________ deals with the cost-minimization problem of producers. _________s are typically drawn on capital-labor graphs, showing the tradeoff between capital and labor in the production function, and the decreasing marginal returns of both inputs.

a. Underinvestment employment relationship
b. Economies of scale
c. Economic production quantity
d. Isoquant

50. A _________ is an expression that compares quantities relative to each other. The most common examples involve two quantities, but any number of quantities can be compared. _________s are represented mathematically by separating each quantity with a colon, for example the _________ 2:3, which is read as the _________ 'two to three'.

a. Y-intercept
b. 130-30 fund
c. Ratio
d. 100-year flood

1. The _________ consists of a number of economic theories which describe the nature of the firm, company including its existence, its behaviour, and its relationship with the market.

In simplified terms, the _________ aims to answer these questions:

1. Existence - why do firms emerge, why are not all transactions in the economy mediated over the market?
2. Boundaries - why the boundary between firms and the market is located exactly there? Which transactions are performed internally and which are negotiated on the market?
3. Organization - why are firms structured in such specific way? What is the interplay of formal and informal relationships?

Despite looking simple, these questions are not answered by the established economic theory, which usually views firms as given, and treats them as black boxes without any internal structure.

The First World War period saw a change of emphasis in economic theory away from industry-level analysis which mainly included analysing markets to analysis at the level of the firm, as it became increasingly clear that perfect competition was no longer an adequate model of how firms behaved. Economic theory till then had focussed on trying to understand markets alone and there had been little study on understanding why firms or organisations exist.

a. Policy Ineffectiveness Proposition
b. Technology gap
c. Theory of the firm
d. Khazzoom-Brookes postulate

2. _________ is an economic model based on price, utility and quantity in a market. It predicts that in a competitive market, price will function to equalize the quantity demanded by consumers, and the quantity supplied by producers, resulting in an economic equilibrium of price and quantity. The model incorporates other factors changing equilibrium as a shift of demand and/or supply.

a. Deferred gratification
b. Joint demand
c. Rational addiction
d. Supply and demand

3. Economics:

- _________,the desire to own something and the ability to pay for it
- _________ curve,a graphic representation of a _________ schedule
- _________ deposit, the money in checking accounts
- _________ pull theory,the theory that inflation occurs when _________ for goods and services exceeds existing supplies
- _________ schedule,a table that lists the quantity of a good a person will buy it each different price
- _________ side economics,the school of economics at believes government spending and tax cuts open economy by raising _________

a. Demand
b. Production
c. McKesson ' Robbins scandal
d. Variability

4. In economics, the _________ can be defined as the graph depicting the relationship between the price of a certain commodity, and the amount of it that consumers are willing and able to purchase at that given price. It is a graphic representation of a demand schedule. The _________ for all consumers together follows from the _________ of every individual consumer: the individual demands at each price are added together.

a. Kuznets curve
b. Cost curve
c. Demand curve
d. Wage curve

5. In neoclassical economics and microeconomics, _________ describes the perfect being a market in which there are many small firms, all producing homogeneous goods. In the short term, such markets are productively inefficient as output will not occur where mc is equal to ac, but allocatively efficient, as output under _________ will always occur where mc is equal to mr, and therefore where mc equals ar. However, in the long term, such markets are both allocatively and productively efficient.

a. Perfect competition
b. Law of supply
c. General equilibrium
d. Co-operative economics

6. In economics, _________ is the process by which a firm determines the price and output level that returns the greatest profit. There are several approaches to this problem. The total revenue--total cost method relies on the fact that profit equals revenue minus cost, and the marginal revenue--marginal cost method is based on the fact that total profit in a perfectly competitive market reaches its maximum point where marginal revenue equals marginal cost.

a. Profit margin
b. Normal profit
c. Profit maximization
d. 100-year flood

7. A _________ is:

- Rewrite _________, in generative grammar and computer science
- Standardization, a formal and widely-accepted statement, fact, definition, or qualification
- Operation, a determinate _________ for performing a mathematical operation and obtaining a certain result (Mathematics, Logic)
    - Unary operation
    - Binary operation
- _________ of inference, a function from sets of formulae to formulae (Mathematics, Logic)
- _________ of thumb, principle with broad application that is not intended to be strictly accurate or reliable for every situation. Also often simply referred to as a _________
- Moral, an atomic element of a moral code for guiding choices in human behavior
- Heuristic, a quantized '_________' which shows a tendency or probability for successful function
- A regulation, as in sports
- A Production _________, as in computer science
- Procedural law, a _________set governing the application of laws to cases
    - A law, which may informally be called a '_________'
    - A court ruling, a decision by a court
- In the U.S. Government, a regulation mandated by Congress, but written or expanded upon by the Executive Branch.
- Norm (sociology), an informal but widely accepted _________, concept, truth, definition, or qualification (social norms, legal norms, coding norms)
- Norm (philosophy), a kind of sentence or a reason to act, feel or believe
- 'Rulership' is the concept of governance by a government:
    - Military _________, governance by a military body
    - Monastic _________, a collection of precepts that guides the life of monks or nuns in a religious order where the superior holds the place of Christ
- Slide _________

- '_________,' a song by Ayumi Hamasaki
- '_________,' a song by rapper Nas
- '_________s,' an album by the band The Whitest Boy Alive
- _________s: Pyaar Ka Superhit Formula, a 2003 Bollywood film
- ruler, an instrument for measuring lengths
- _________, a component of an astrolabe, circumferator or similar instrument
- The _________s, a bestselling self-help book
- _________ Project (Run Up-to-date Linux Everywhere), a project that aims to use up-to-date Linux software on old PCs
- _________ engine, a software system that helps managing business _________s
- Ja _________, a hip hop artist
    - R.U.L.E., a 2005 greatest hits album by rapper Ja _________
- '_________s,' a KMFDM song

a. Demand
b. Technocracy
c. Procter ' Gamble
d. Rule

8. In economic theory, _________ is the competitive situation in any market where the conditions necessary for perfect competition are not satisfied. It is a market structure that does not meet the conditions of perfect competition.

Forms of _________ include:

- Monopoly, in which there is only one seller of a good.
- Oligopoly, in which there is a small number of sellers.
- Monopolistic competition, in which there are many sellers producing highly differentiated goods.
- Monopsony, in which there is only one buyer of a good.
- Oligopsony, in which there is a small number of buyers.

There may also be _________ in markets due to buyers or sellers lacking information about prices and the goods being traded.

There may also be _________ due to a time lag in a market.

a. AD-IA Model
b. ACCRA Cost of Living Index
c. ACEA agreement
d. Imperfect competition

9. In economics and finance, _________ is the change in total cost that arises when the quantity produced changes by one unit. It is the cost of producing one more unit of a good. Mathematically, the _________ function is expressed as the first derivative of the total cost (TC) function with respect to quantity (Q.)

a. Khozraschyot
b. Quality costs
c. Variable cost
d. Marginal cost

10. _________ in economics and business is the result of an exchange and from that trade we assign a numerical monetary value to a good, service or asset. If Alice trades Bob 4 apples for an orange, the _________ of an orange is 4 apples. Inversely, the _________ of an apple is 1/4 oranges.

a. Premium pricing
b. Price
c. Price war
d. Price book

11. Monopoly power is an example of market failure which occurs when one or more of the participants has the ability to influence the price or other outcomes in some general or specialized market. The most commonly discussed form of market power is that of a monopoly, but other forms such as monopsony, and more moderate versions of these two extremes, exist. Market participants that have market power are sometimes referred to as 'price makers', while those without are sometimes called '_________'.

a. Market power
b. Market concentration
c. Price takers
d. Monopolization

12. In economics, an _________ or spillover of an economic transaction is an impact on a party that is not directly involved in the transaction. In such a case, prices do not reflect the full costs or benefits in production or consumption of a product or service. A positive impact is called an external benefit, while a negative impact is called an external cost.

a. Environmental impact assessment
b. Existence value
c. Environmental tariff
d. Externality

13. In economics, the _________ is the change in consumption resulting from a change in real income.

Another important item that can change is the money income of the consumer. The _________ is the phenomenon observed through changes in purchasing power.

a. Equilibrium wage
b. Export subsidy
c. Inflation hedge
d. Income effect

14. In law and economics, the _________, describes the economic efficiency of an economic allocation or outcome in the presence of externalities. The theorem states that when trade in an externality is possible and there are no transaction costs, bargaining will lead to an efficient outcome regardless of the initial allocation of property rights. In practice, obstacles to bargaining or poorly defined property rights can prevent Coasian bargaining.

a. Means test
b. Coase theorem
c. Prior appropriation water rights
d. General Mining Act of 1872

15. _________s is the social science that studies the production, distribution, and consumption of goods and services. The term _________s comes from the Ancient Greek οἁ¼°κονομΓ¯α from οἁ¼¶κος (oikos, 'house') + vÏŒμος (nomos, 'custom' or 'law'), hence 'rules of the house(hold)'. Current _________ models developed out of the broader field of political economy in the late 19th century, owing to a desire to use an empirical approach more akin to the physical sciences.

a. Opportunity cost
b. Energy economics
c. Inflation
d. Economic

16. In economics, _________ is the difference between a company's total revenue and its opportunity costs. It is the increase in wealth that an investor has from making an investment, taking into consideration all costs associated with that investment including the opportunity cost of capital.

Profit is the factor income of the entrepreneur.

a. Economic profit
b. Accounting profit
c. ACCRA Cost of Living Index
d. Operating profit

17. In economics, and cost accounting, _________ describes the total economic cost of production and is made up of variable costs, which vary according to the quantity of a good produced and include inputs such as labor and raw materials, plus fixed costs, which are independent of the quantity of a good produced and include inputs (capital) that cannot be varied in the short term, such as buildings and machinery. _________ in economics includes the total opportunity cost of each factor of production in addition to fixed and variable costs.

The rate at which _________ changes as the amount produced changes is called marginal cost.

a. Total cost
b. 130-30 fund
c. 100-year flood
d. 1921 recession

18. In economics, a _________ is a graph of the costs of production as a function of total quantity produced. In a free market economy, productively efficient firms use these curves to find the optimal point of production, where they make the most profits. There are a few different types of _________s, each relevant to a different area of economics.

a. Kuznets curve
b. Demand curve
c. Phillips curve
d. Cost curve

19. In microeconomics, _________ is quite simply the conversion of inputs into outputs. It is an economic process that uses resources to create a good or service that is suitable for exchange. This can include manufacturing, storing, shipping, and packaging.

a. MET
b. Solved
c. Red Guards
d. Production

20. _________ is an economic concept with commonplace familiarity. It is the price that a good or service is offered at, or will fetch, in the marketplace. It is of interest mainly in the study of microeconomics.

a. Paper trading
b. Noisy market hypothesis
c. Market price
d. Market anomaly

21. Competition law, known in the United States as _________ law, has three main elements:

- prohibiting agreements or practices that restrict free trading and competition between business entities. This includes in particular the repression of cartels.
- banning abusive behaviour by a firm dominating a market, or anti-competitive practices that tend to lead to such a dominant position. Practices controlled in this way may include predatory pricing, tying, price gouging, refusal to deal, and many others.
- supervising the mergers and acquisitions of large corporations, including some joint ventures. Transactions that are considered to threaten the competitive process can be prohibited altogether, or approved subject to 'remedies' such as an obligation to divest part of the merged business or to offer licences or access to facilities to enable other businesses to continue competing.

The substance and practice of competition law varies from jurisdiction to jurisdiction. Protecting the interests of consumers (consumer welfare) and ensuring that entrepreneurs have an opportunity to compete in the market economy are often treated as important objectives. Competition law is closely connected with law on deregulation of access to markets, state aids and subsidies, the privatisation of state owned assets and the establishment of independent sector regulators. In recent decades, competition law has been viewed as a way to provide better public services.

a. Anti-Inflation Act
b. Antitrust
c. Intellectual property law
d. United Kingdom competition law

22. _________ theory is a branch of theoretical economics. It seeks to explain the behavior of supply, demand and prices in a whole economy with several or many markets. It is often assumed that agents are price takers and in that setting two common notions of equilibrium exist: Walrasian (or competitive) equilibrium, and its generalization; a price equilibrium with transfers.

a. New Keynesian economics
b. General equilibrium
c. Human capital
d. Rational choice theory

23. In economic models, the _________ time frame assumes no fixed factors of production. Firms can enter or leave the marketplace, and the cost (and availability) of land, labor, raw materials, and capital goods can be assumed to vary. In contrast, in the short-run time frame, certain factors are assumed to be fixed, because there is not sufficient time for them to change.

a. Diseconomies of scale
b. Price/performance ratio
c. Productivity world
d. Long-run

24. In economics, economic equilibrium is simply a state of the world where economic forces are balanced and in the absence of external influences the (equilibrium) values of economic variables will not change. It is the point at which quantity demanded and quantity supplied are equal. _________, for example, refers to a condition where a market price is established through competition such that the amount of goods or services sought by buyers is equal to the amount of goods or services produced by sellers.

a. Marketization
b. Product-Market Growth Matrix
c. Regulated market
d. Market equilibrium

25. In economics, the concept of the _________ refers to the decision-making time frame of a firm in which at least one factor of production is fixed. Costs which are fixed in the _________ have no impact on a firms decisions. For example a firm can raise output by increasing the amount of labour through overtime.

a. Productivity model
b. Product Pipeline
c. Hicks-neutral technical change
d. Short-run

26. In economics, _________ is the total demand for final goods and services in the economy (Y) at a given time and price level. It is the amount of goods and services in the economy that will be purchased at all possible price levels. This is the demand for the gross domestic product of a country when inventory levels are static.

a. Aggregation problem
b. Aggregate expenditure
c. Aggregate supply
d. Aggregate demand

27. _________ is defined as the measure of responsiveness in the quantity demanded for a commodity as a result of change in price of the same commodity. It is a measure of how consumers react to a change in price. In other words, it is percentage change in quantity demanded as per the percentage change in price of the same commodity.

a. 1921 recession
b. 130-30 fund
c. 100-year flood
d. Price elasticity of demand

28. In economics, the _________ measures the payments that flow between any individual country and all other countries. It is used to summarize all international economic transactions for that country during a specific time period, usually a year. The _________ is determined by the country's exports and imports of goods, services, and financial capital, as well as financial transfers.

a. Balance of payments
b. Skyscraper Index
c. Gross domestic product per barrel
d. Gross world product

29. In economics, _________ is the ratio of the percent change in one variable to the percent change in another variable. It is a tool for measuring the responsiveness of a function to changes in parameters in a relative way. Commonly analyzed are _________ of substitution, price and wealth.

a. Elasticity of demand
b. ACCRA Cost of Living Index
c. ACEA agreement
d. Elasticity

30. Price _________ is defined as the measure of responsiveness in the quantity demanded for a commodity as a result of change in price of the same commodity. It is a measure of how consumers react to a change in price. In other words, it is percentage change in quantity demanded by the percentage change in price of the same commodity.

a. ACCRA Cost of Living Index
b. Elasticity
c. ACEA agreement
d. Elasticity of demand

31. _________ is a term used by economists to describe a condition in which firms can freely enter the market for an economic good by establishing production and beginning to sell the product.

_________ is implied by the perfect competition condition that there is an unlimited number of buyers and sellers in a market. In comparison to perfect competition, however, _________ is a condition often more applicable to real world conditions.

a. 100-year flood
b. 130-30 fund
c. 1921 recession
d. Free entry

32. A _________ is the transfer of wealth from one party (such as a person or company) to another. A _________ is usually made in exchange for the provision of goods, services or both, or to fulfill a legal obligation.

The simplest and oldest form of _________ is barter, the exchange of one good or service for another.

a. Payment
b. Going concern
c. Soft count
d. Social gravity

33. _________ is a situation in which the limited resources of a firm are allocated in accordance with the wishes of consumers. An allocatively efficient economy produces an 'optimal mix' of commodities. A firm is allocatively efficient when its price is equal to its marginal costs (that is, P = MC) in a perfect market.

a. Economic efficiency
b. ACCRA Cost of Living Index
c. ACEA agreement
d. Allocative efficiency

34. In economics, _________ is the total supply of goods and services produced by a national economy during a specific time period. It is the total amount of goods and services in the economy available at all possible price levels.

a. Aggregate expenditure
b. Aggregate demand
c. Aggregation problem
d. Aggregate supply

35. In economics, _________ refers to how the marginal contribution of a factor of production usually decreases as more of the factor is used. According to this relationship, in a production system with fixed and variable inputs, beyond some point, each additional unit of the variable input yields smaller and smaller increases in output. Conversely, producing one more unit of output costs more and more in variable inputs.

a. Derivatives law
b. Patent troll
c. Community property
d. Diminishing returns

36. In economics supernormal profit _________ or pure profit or excess profits, is a profit exceeding the normal profit. Normal profit equals the opportunity cost of labour and capital, while supernormal profit is the amount exceeds the normal return from these input factors in production.

_________ is usually generated by an oligopoly or a monopoly; however, these firms often try to hide this from the market to reduce risk of competition or antitrust investigation.

a. ACCRA Cost of Living Index
b. Abnormal profit
c. Economic profit
d. Accounting profit

37. In economics, _________ are the resources employed to produce goods and services. They facilitate production but do not become part of the product (as with raw materials) or significantly transformed by the production process (as with fuel used to power machinery.) To 19th century economists, the _________ were land (natural resources, gifts from nature), labor (the ability to work), and capital goods (human-made tools and equipment.)

a. Hicks-neutral technical change
b. Product Pipeline
c. Long-run
d. Factors of production

38. In economics, the _________ is defined as a numerical measure of the responsiveness of the quantity supplied of product (A) to a change in price of product (A) alone. It is the measure of the way quantity supplied reacts to a change in price.

>

For example, if, in response to a 10% rise in the price of a good, the quantity supplied increases by 20%, the _________ would be 20%/10% = 2.

a. Passive income
b. Price elasticity of supply
c. Demand shaping
d. Hedonimetry

39. Economic _________ is defined as an excess distribution to any factor in a production process above that which is required to induce the factor into the process or any excess above that which is necessary to keep the factor in its current use..

Classical Factor _________ is primarily concerned with the fee paid for the use of fixed (e.g. natural) resources. The classical definition is expressed as any excess payment above that required to induce or provide for production.

a. 100-year flood
b. Rent
c. 1921 recession
d. 130-30 fund

40. The supply of labor is the number of total hours that workers wish to work at a given real wage rate.

_________ curves are derived from the 'labor-leisure' trade-off. More hours worked earn higher incomes but necessitate a cut in the amount of leisure that workers enjoy.

a. Creative capitalism
b. Human trafficking
c. Late capitalism
d. Labor supply

41. Competitive market equilibrium is the traditional concept of economic equilibrium, appropriate for the analysis of commodity markets with flexible prices and many traders, and serving as the benchmark of efficiency in economic analysis. It relies crucially on the assumption of a competitive environment where each trader decides upon a quantity that is so small compared to the total quantity traded in the market that their individual transactions have no influence on the prices.Competitive markets are an ideal, a standard that other market structures are evaluated by.

A _________ consists of a vector of prices and an allocation such that given the prices, each trader by maximizing his objective function (profit, preferences) subject to his technological possibilities and resource constraints plans to trade into his part of the proposed allocation, and such that the prices make all net trades compatible with one another ('clear the market') by equating aggregate supply and demand for the commodities which are traded.

a. Market system
b. Product-Market Growth Matrix
c. Partial equilibrium
d. Competitive equilibrium

42. In economics, the _________ of a good or of a service is the utility of the specific use to which an agent would put a given increase in that good or service, or of the specific use that would be abandoned in response to a given decrease. In other words, _________ is the utility of the marginal use -- which, on the assumption of economic rationality, would be the least urgent use of the good or service, from the best feasible combination of actions in which its use is included. Under the mainstream assumptions, the _________ of a good or service is the posited quantified change in utility obtained by increasing or by decreasing use of that good or service.

a. 1921 recession
b. 100-year flood
c. 130-30 fund
d. Marginal utility

43. _________ is an important concept in economics with broad applications in game theory, engineering and the social sciences. The term is named after Vilfredo Pareto, an Italian economist who used the concept in his studies of economic efficiency and income distribution. Informally, pareto efficient situations are those in which any change to make any person better off would make someone else worse off.

a. Matching pennies
b. Lump of labour
c. Pareto efficiency
d. Perfect rationality

44. In economics, _________ is a measure of the relative satisfaction from consumption of various goods and services. Given this measure, one may speak meaningfully of increasing or decreasing _________, and thereby explain economic behavior in terms of attempts to increase one's _________. For illustrative purposes, changes in _________ are sometimes expressed in units called utils.

a. Ordinal utility
b. Expected utility hypothesis
c. Utility function
d. Utility

45. The term surplus is used in economics for several related quantities. The consumer surplus is the amount that consumers benefit by being able to purchase a product for a price that is less than they would be willing to pay. The _________ is the amount that producers benefit by selling at a market price mechanism that is higher than they would be willing to sell for.

a. Schedule delay
b. Long term
c. Returns to scale
d. Producer surplus

46. _________ is a broad label that refers to any individuals or households that use goods and services generated within the economy. The concept of a _________ is used in different contexts, so that the usage and significance of the term may vary.

Typically when business people and economists talk of _________s they are talking about person as _________, an aggregated commodity item with little individuality other than that expressed in the buy/not-buy decision.

a. 100-year flood
b. 130-30 fund
c. 1921 recession
d. Consumer

47. A _________ is an object whose consumption increases the utility of the consumer, for which the quantity demanded exceeds the quantity supplied at zero price. _________s are usually modeled as having diminishing marginal utility. The first individual purchase has high utility; the second has less.

a. Merit good
b. Pie method
c. Composite good
d. Good

48. In economics, economic output is divided into physical goods and intangible services. Consumption of _________ is assumed to produce utility. It is often used when referring to a _________ Tax.

a. Manufactured goods
b. Private good
c. Goods and services
d. Composite good

49. _________ in economics refers to metrics and measures of output from production processes, per unit of input. Labor _________, for example, is typically measured as a ratio of output per labor-hour, an input. _________ may be conceived of as a metrics of the technical or engineering efficiency of production.

a. Piece work
b. Productivity
c. Fordism
d. Production-possibility frontier

50. A _________ is an economy based on the division of labor in which the prices of goods and services are determined in a free price system set by supply and demand. This is often contrasted with a planned economy, in which a central government determines the price of goods and services using a fixed price system. Market economies are contrasted with mixed economy where the price system is not entirely free but under some government control that is not extensive enough to constitute a planned economy.

a. Nutritional Economics
b. Commons-based peer production
c. Network Economy
d. Market economy

51. In economics, a _________ exists when the production or use of goods and services by the market is not efficient. That is, there exists another outcome where all involved can be made better off. _________s can be viewed as scenarios where individuals' pursuit of pure self-interest leads to results that are not efficient - that can be improved upon from the societal point-of-view.

a. Financial economics
b. Fixed exchange rate
c. Market failure
d. General equilibrium

52. _________ refers to various economic systems where the means of production are publicly owned, but the market is utilized. In a traditional market socialist economy, prices would be determined by a government planning ministry, and enterprises would either be state-owned or cooperatively-owned and managed by their employees. The People's Republic of China currently has a form of _________ referred to as the socialist market economy.

a. Democratic socialism
b. Red fist
c. Working class
d. Market socialism

53. _________ is one of the four Ps of the marketing mix. The other three aspects are product, promotion, and place. It is also a key variable in microeconomic price allocation theory.

a. Premium pricing
b. Point of total assumption
c. Guaranteed Maximum Price
d. Pricing

54. In economics, _________ is equal to total cost divided by the number of goods produced (the output quantity, Q.) It is also equal to the sum of average variable costs (total variable costs divided by Q) plus average fixed costs (total fixed costs divided by Q.) _________s may be dependent on the time period considered (increasing production may be expensive or impossible in the short term, for example.)

a. Average variable cost
b. Average fixed cost
c. Explicit cost
d. Average cost

55. _________ in political thought refers to economic theories of social organization advocating collective ownership and administration of the means of production and distribution of goods, and a society characterized by equality for all individuals, with an egalitarian method of compensation. Modern _________ originated in the late 19th-century intellectual and working class political movement that criticized the effects of industrialization and private ownership on society. Karl Marx posited that _________ would be achieved via class struggle and a proletarian revolution after a transitional stage from capitalism called the dictatorship of the proletariat.

a. Adam Smith
b. Socialism
c. Adolph Fischer
d. Adolf Hitler

56. In economics, the _________ is the term economists use to describe the self-regulating nature of the marketplace. The _________ is a metaphor coined by the economist Adam Smith in The Wealth of Nations.

Adam Smith mentions the metaphor in Book IV of The Wealth of Nations, arguing that people in any society will certainly employ their capital in foreign trading only if the profits available by that method far exceed those available locally, and that in such a case it is better for society as a whole if they so did.

a. ACCRA Cost of Living Index
b. Invisible hand
c. AD-IA Model
d. ACEA agreement

57. Examples of _________ include:

- A beekeeper keeps the bees for their honey. A side effect or externality associated with his activity is the pollination of surrounding crops by the bees. The value generated by the pollination may be more important than the value of the harvested honey.

- An individual planting an attractive garden in front of his house may provide benefits to others living in the area, and even financial benefits in the form of increased property values for all property owners.

- An individual buying a product that is interconnected in a network (e.g., a video cellphone) will increase the usefulness of such phones to other people who have a video cellphone. When each new user of a product increases the value of the same product owned by others, the phenomenon is called a network externality or a network effect. Network externalities often have 'tipping points' where, suddenly, the product reaches general acceptance and near-universal usage, a phenomenon which can be seen in the near universal take-up of cellphones in some Scandinavian countries.

- Knowledge spillover of inventions and information - once an invention (or most other forms of practical information) is discovered or made more easily accessible, others benefit by exploiting the invention or information. Copyright and intellectual property law are mechanisms to allow the inventor or creator to benefit from a temporary, state-protected monopoly in return for 'sharing' the information through publication or other means.

a. Negative externalities
b. Weighted average cost of carbon
c. Total Economic Value
d. Positive externalities

58. Although information has been bought and sold since ancient times, the idea of an information marketplace is relatively recent. The nature of such markets is still evolving, which complicates development of sustainable business models. However, certain attributes of _________ are beginning to be understood, such as diminished participation costs, opportunities for customization, shifting customer relations, and a need for order.

a. Underground economy
b. Intention economy
c. Open economy
d. Information markets

59. In microeconomics, _________ is the extra revenue that an additional unit of product will bring. It is the additional income from selling one more unit of a good; sometimes equal to price. It can also be described as the change in total revenue/change in number of units sold.

a. Long term
b. Reservation price
c. Market demand schedule
d. Marginal revenue

1. The _________ or gross domestic income (GDI), a basic measure of an economy's economic performance, is the market value of all final goods and services produced within the borders of a nation in a year. _________ can be defined in three ways, all of which are conceptually identical. First, it is equal to the total expenditures for all final goods and services produced within the country in a stipulated period of time (usually a 365-day year.)

a. Monopolistic competition
b. Gross domestic product
c. Market structure
d. Countercyclical

2. In economic theory, _________ is the competitive situation in any market where the conditions necessary for perfect competition are not satisfied. It is a market structure that does not meet the conditions of perfect competition.

Forms of _________ include:

- Monopoly, in which there is only one seller of a good.
- Oligopoly, in which there is a small number of sellers.
- Monopolistic competition, in which there are many sellers producing highly differentiated goods.
- Monopsony, in which there is only one buyer of a good.
- Oligopsony, in which there is a small number of buyers.

There may also be _________ in markets due to buyers or sellers lacking information about prices and the goods being traded.

There may also be _________ due to a time lag in a market.

a. ACCRA Cost of Living Index
b. AD-IA Model
c. Imperfect competition
d. ACEA agreement

3. _________ is a common market structure where many competing producers sell products that are differentiated from one another (ie. the products are substitutes, but are not exactly alike.) Many markets are monopolistically competitive, common examples include the markets for restaurants, cereal, clothing, shoes and service industries in large cities.

a. Monopolistic competition
b. Perfect competition
c. Financial crisis
d. Mathematical economics

4. In economics, a _________ exists when a specific individual or enterprise has sufficient control over a particular product or service to determine significantly the terms on which other individuals shall have access to it. Monopolies are thus characterized by a lack of economic competition for the good or service that they provide and a lack of viable substitute goods. The verb 'monopolize' refers to the process by which a firm gains persistently greater market share than what is expected under perfect competition.

a. Monopoly
b. 1921 recession
c. 100-year flood
d. 130-30 fund

5. An _________ is a market form in which a market or industry is dominated by a small number of sellers (oligopolists.) Because there are few participants in this type of market, each oligopolist is aware of the actions of the others. The decisions of one firm influence, and are influenced by, the decisions of other firms.

a. ACCRA Cost of Living Index
b. ACEA agreement
c. Oligopsony
d. Oligopoly

6. In economics, _________ and economies of scale are related terms that describe what happens as the scale of production increases. They are different terms and should not be used interchangeably.

_________ refers to a technical property of production that examines changes in output subsequent to a proportional change in all inputs (where all inputs increase by a constant factor.)

a. Necessity good
b. Returns to scale
c. Constant returns to scale
d. Customer equity

7. _________ is a situation in which the limited resources of a firm are allocated in accordance with the wishes of consumers. An allocatively efficient economy produces an 'optimal mix' of commodities. A firm is allocatively efficient when its price is equal to its marginal costs (that is, P = MC) in a perfect market.

a. Allocative efficiency
b. Economic efficiency
c. ACEA agreement
d. ACCRA Cost of Living Index

8. In economics, the _________ measures the payments that flow between any individual country and all other countries. It is used to summarize all international economic transactions for that country during a specific time period, usually a year. The _________ is determined by the country's exports and imports of goods, services, and financial capital, as well as financial transfers.

a. Skyscraper Index
b. Balance of payments
c. Gross world product
d. Gross domestic product per barrel

9. _________ has several particular meanings:

- in mathematics
  - _________ function
  - Euler _________
  - _________
  - _________ subgroup
  - method of _________s (partial differential equations)
- in physics and engineering
  - any _________ curve that shows the relationship between certain input- and output parameters, e.g.
  - an I-V or current-voltage _________ is the current in a circuit as a function of the applied voltage
  - Receiver-Operator _________
- in fiction
  - in Dungeons ' Dragons, _________ is another name for ability score

.

a. Demand
b. Russian financial crisis
c. Technocracy
d. Characteristic

10. A _________ is the transfer of wealth from one party (such as a person or company) to another. A _________ is usually made in exchange for the provision of goods, services or both, or to fulfill a legal obligation.

The simplest and oldest form of _________ is barter, the exchange of one good or service for another.

a. Soft count
b. Going concern
c. Social gravity
d. Payment

11. _________ is an economic concept with commonplace familiarity. It is the price that a good or service is offered at, or will fetch, in the marketplace. It is of interest mainly in the study of microeconomics.

a. Market anomaly
b. Paper trading
c. Noisy market hypothesis
d. Market price

12. Competition law, known in the United States as _________ law, has three main elements:

- prohibiting agreements or practices that restrict free trading and competition between business entities. This includes in particular the repression of cartels.
- banning abusive behaviour by a firm dominating a market, or anti-competitive practices that tend to lead to such a dominant position. Practices controlled in this way may include predatory pricing, tying, price gouging, refusal to deal, and many others.
- supervising the mergers and acquisitions of large corporations, including some joint ventures. Transactions that are considered to threaten the competitive process can be prohibited altogether, or approved subject to 'remedies' such as an obligation to divest part of the merged business or to offer licences or access to facilities to enable other businesses to continue competing.

The substance and practice of competition law varies from jurisdiction to jurisdiction. Protecting the interests of consumers (consumer welfare) and ensuring that entrepreneurs have an opportunity to compete in the market economy are often treated as important objectives. Competition law is closely connected with law on deregulation of access to markets, state aids and subsidies, the privatisation of state owned assets and the establishment of independent sector regulators. In recent decades, competition law has been viewed as a way to provide better public services.

a. Intellectual property law
b. Anti-Inflation Act
c. Antitrust
d. United Kingdom competition law

13. Economics:

- _________,the desire to own something and the ability to pay for it
- _________ curve,a graphic representation of a _________ schedule
- _________ deposit, the money in checking accounts
- _________ pull theory,the theory that inflation occurs when _________ for goods and services exceeds existing supplies
- _________ schedule,a table that lists the quantity of a good a person will buy it each different price
- _________ side economics,the school of economics at believes government spending and tax cuts open economy by raising _________

.

a. Demand
b. McKesson ' Robbins scandal
c. Production
d. Variability

14. In economics, the _________ can be defined as the graph depicting the relationship between the price of a certain commodity, and the amount of it that consumers are willing and able to purchase at that given price. It is a graphic representation of a demand schedule. The _________ for all consumers together follows from the _________ of every individual consumer: the individual demands at each price are added together.

a. Cost curve
b. Wage curve
c. Kuznets curve
d. Demand curve

15. _________ in economics and business is the result of an exchange and from that trade we assign a numerical monetary value to a good, service or asset. If Alice trades Bob 4 apples for an orange, the _________ of an orange is 4 apples. Inversely, the _________ of an apple is 1/4 oranges.

a. Price war
b. Premium pricing
c. Price book
d. Price

16. A _________ is a set of exclusive rights granted by a state to an inventor or his assignee for a limited period of time in exchange for a disclosure of an invention.

The procedure for granting _________s, the requirements placed on the _________ee and the extent of the exclusive rights vary widely between countries according to national laws and international agreements. Typically, however, a _________ application must include one or more claims defining the invention which must be new, inventive, and useful or industrially applicable.

a. Bona fide occupational qualification
b. Bank regulation
c. Long service leave
d. Patent

17. _________ is defined as the measure of responsiveness in the quantity demanded for a commodity as a result of change in price of the same commodity. It is a measure of how consumers react to a change in price. In other words, it is percentage change in quantity demanded as per the percentage change in price of the same commodity.

a. 100-year flood
b. 130-30 fund
c. 1921 recession
d. Price elasticity of demand

18. In marketing, _________ is the process of distinguishing the differences of a product or offering from others, to make it more attractive to a particular target market. This involves differentiating it from competitors' products as well as one's own product offerings.

Differentiation is a source of competitive advantage.

a. Technology acceptance model
b. Market segment
c. Pricing science
d. Product differentiation

19. In economics, _________ is the ratio of the percent change in one variable to the percent change in another variable. It is a tool for measuring the responsiveness of a function to changes in parameters in a relative way. Commonly analyzed are _________ of substitution, price and wealth.

a. Elasticity of demand
b. Elasticity
c. ACEA agreement
d. ACCRA Cost of Living Index

20. Price _________ is defined as the measure of responsiveness in the quantity demanded for a commodity as a result of change in price of the same commodity. It is a measure of how consumers react to a change in price. In other words, it is percentage change in quantity demanded by the percentage change in price of the same commodity.

a. ACEA agreement
b. Elasticity
c. ACCRA Cost of Living Index
d. Elasticity of demand

21. A _________ is:

- Rewrite _________, in generative grammar and computer science
- Standardization, a formal and widely-accepted statement, fact, definition, or qualification
- Operation, a determinate _________ for performing a mathematical operation and obtaining a certain result (Mathematics, Logic)
  - Unary operation
  - Binary operation
- _________ of inference, a function from sets of formulae to formulae (Mathematics, Logic)
- _________ of thumb, principle with broad application that is not intended to be strictly accurate or reliable for every situation. Also often simply referred to as a _________
- Moral, an atomic element of a moral code for guiding choices in human behavior
- Heuristic, a quantized '_________' which shows a tendency or probability for successful function
- A regulation, as in sports
- A Production _________, as in computer science
- Procedural law, a _________set governing the application of laws to cases
  - A law, which may informally be called a '_________'
  - A court ruling, a decision by a court
- In the U.S. Government, a regulation mandated by Congress, but written or expanded upon by the Executive Branch.
- Norm (sociology), an informal but widely accepted _________, concept, truth, definition, or qualification (social norms, legal norms, coding norms)
- Norm (philosophy), a kind of sentence or a reason to act, feel or believe
- 'Rulership' is the concept of governance by a government:
  - Military _________, governance by a military body
  - Monastic _________, a collection of precepts that guides the life of monks or nuns in a religious order where the superior holds the place of Christ
- Slide _________

- '_________,' a song by Ayumi Hamasaki
- '_________,' a song by rapper Nas
- '_________s,' an album by the band The Whitest Boy Alive
- _________s: Pyaar Ka Superhit Formula, a 2003 Bollywood film
- ruler, an instrument for measuring lengths
- _________, a component of an astrolabe, circumferator or similar instrument
- The _________s, a bestselling self-help book
- _________ Project (Run Up-to-date Linux Everywhere), a project that aims to use up-to-date Linux software on old PCs
- _________ engine, a software system that helps managing business _________s
- Ja _________, a hip hop artist
  - R.U.L.E., a 2005 greatest hits album by rapper Ja _________
- '_________s,' a KMFDM song

a. Procter ' Gamble
b. Demand
c. Technocracy
d. Rule

22. In economics, _________ is a measure of the relative satisfaction from consumption of various goods and services. Given this measure, one may speak meaningfully of increasing or decreasing _________, and thereby explain economic behavior in terms of attempts to increase one's _________. For illustrative purposes, changes in _________ are sometimes expressed in units called utils.

a. Expected utility hypothesis
b. Utility function
c. Ordinal utility
d. Utility

23. A _________ is an object whose consumption increases the utility of the consumer, for which the quantity demanded exceeds the quantity supplied at zero price. _________s are usually modeled as having diminishing marginal utility. The first individual purchase has high utility; the second has less.

a. Good
b. Pie method
c. Merit good
d. Composite good

24. In economics, economic output is divided into physical goods and intangible services. Consumption of _________ is assumed to produce utility. It is often used when referring to a _________ Tax.

a. Goods and services
b. Composite good
c. Manufactured goods
d. Private good

25. In economics, _________ describes the state of a market with respect to competition.

- Perfect competition, in which the market consists of a very large number of firms producing a homogeneous product.
- Monopolistic competition where there are a large number of independent firms which have a very small proportion of the market share.
- Oligopoly, in which a market is dominated by a small number of firms which own more than 40% of the market share.
- Oligopsony, a market dominated by many sellers and a few buyers.
- Monopoly, where there is only one provider of a product or service.
- Natural monopoly, a monopoly in which economies of scale cause efficiency to increase continuously with the size of the firm. A firm is a natural monopoly if it is able to serve the entire market demand at a lower cost than any combination of two or more smaller, more specialized firms.
- Monopsony, when there is only one buyer in a market.

The imperfectly competitive structure is quite identical to the realistic market conditions where some monopolistic competitors, monopolists, oligopolists, and duopolists exist and dominate the market conditions. The elements of _________ include the number and size distribution of firms, entry conditions, and the extent of differentiation.

These somewhat abstract concerns tend to determine some but not all details of a specific concrete market system where buyers and sellers actually meet and commit to trade.

a. Human capital
b. Monopolistic competition
c. Market structure
d. Labour economics

26. In neoclassical economics and microeconomics, _________ describes the perfect being a market in which there are many small firms, all producing homogeneous goods. In the short term, such markets are productively inefficient as output will not occur where mc is equal to ac, but allocatively efficient, as output under _________ will always occur where mc is equal to mr, and therefore where mc equals ar. However, in the long term, such markets are both allocatively and productively efficient.

a. Law of supply
b. Co-operative economics
c. General equilibrium
d. Perfect competition

27. _________ in economics refers to metrics and measures of output from production processes, per unit of input. Labor _________, for example, is typically measured as a ratio of output per labor-hour, an input. _________ may be conceived of as a metrics of the technical or engineering efficiency of production.

a. Fordism
b. Production-possibility frontier
c. Piece work
d. Productivity

28. In economics, a _________ is a graph of the costs of production as a function of total quantity produced. In a free market economy, productively efficient firms use these curves to find the optimal point of production, where they make the most profits. There are a few different types of _________s, each relevant to a different area of economics.

a. Kuznets curve
b. Phillips curve
c. Cost curve
d. Demand curve

29. In calculus, a function f defined on a subset of the real numbers with real values is called _________, if for all x and y such that x >≤ y one has f(x) >≤ f(y), so f preserves the order. In layman's terms, the sign of the slope is always positive (the curve tending upwards) or zero (i.e., non-decreasing, or asymptotic, or depicted as a horizontal, flat line) Likewise, a function is called monotonically decreasing (non-increasing) if, whenever x >≤ y, then f(x) >≥ f(y), so it reverses the order.

a. 130-30 fund
b. Monotonic
c. 1921 recession
d. 100-year flood

30. In economics, a _________ occurs when, due to the economies of scale of a particular industry, the maximum efficiency of production and distribution is realized through a single supplier.

Natural monopolies arise where the largest supplier in an industry, often the first supplier in a market, has an overwhelming cost advantage over other actual or potential competitors. This tends to be the case in industries where capital costs predominate, creating economies of scale which are large in relation to the size of the market, and hence high barriers to entry; examples include water services and electricity.

a. Privatizing profits and socializing losses
b. Collective goods
c. Common-pool resource
d. Natural monopoly

31. In algebra, a _________ is a function depending on n that associates a scalar, det(A), to an n×n square matrix A. The fundamental geometric meaning of a _________ is a scale factor for measure when A is regarded as a linear transformation. _________s are important both in calculus, where they enter the substitution rule for several variables, and in multilinear algebra.

For a fixed nonnegative integer n, there is a unique _________ function for the n×n matrices over any commutative ring R. In particular, this function exists when R is the field of real or complex numbers.

a. Determinant
b. 1921 recession
c. 100-year flood
d. 130-30 fund

32. In microeconomics, _________ is quite simply the conversion of inputs into outputs. It is an economic process that uses resources to create a good or service that is suitable for exchange. This can include manufacturing, storing, shipping, and packaging.

a. Production
b. Solved
c. MET
d. Red Guards

33. _________, in strategic management and marketing is, according to Carlton O'Neal, the percentage or proportion of the total available market or market segment that is being serviced by a company. It can be expressed as a company's sales revenue (from that market) divided by the total sales revenue available in that market. It can also be expressed as a company's unit sales volume (in a market) divided by the total volume of units sold in that market.

a. Product differentiation
b. Pricing science
c. Market share
d. Customer to customer

34. _________, in microeconomics, are the cost advantages that a business obtains due to expansion. They are factors that cause a producere;s average cost per unit to fall as scale is increased. _________ is a long run concept and refers to reductions in unit cost as the size of a facility, or scale, increases.

a. Isoquant
b. Underinvestment employment relationship
c. Economic production quantity
d. Economies of scale

35. In economics and especially in the theory of competition, _________ are obstacles in the path of a firm that make it difficult to enter a given market.

_________ are the source of a firm's pricing power - the ability of a firm to raise prices without losing all its customers.

The term refers to hindrances that an individual may face while trying to gain entrance into a profession or trade.

a. Limit price
b. Group boycott
c. Barriers to entry
d. Social dumping

36. The _________ is an economic and political union of 27 member states, located primarily in Europe. It was established by the Treaty of Maastricht on 1 November 1993, upon the foundations of the pre-existing European Economic Community. With a population of almost 500 million, the _________ generates an estimated 30% share (US$18.4 trillion in 2008) of the nominal gross world product.

a. ACCRA Cost of Living Index
b. ACEA agreement
c. European Court of Justice
d. European Union

37. _________ is a type of trade policy that allows traders to act and transact without interference from government. Thus, the policy permits trading partners mutual gains from trade, with goods and services produced according to the theory of comparative advantage.

Under a _________ policy, prices are a reflection of true supply and demand, and are the sole determinant of resource allocation.

a. 100-year flood
b. Free trade
c. 1921 recession
d. 130-30 fund

38. _________ is a designated group of countries that have agreed to eliminate tariffs, quotas and preferences on most (if not all) goods and services traded between them. It can be considered the second stage of economic integration. Countries choose this kind of economic integration form if their economical structures are complementary.

a. 130-30 fund
b. 100-year flood
c. Free trade area
d. MERCOSUR

39. In economics, an _________ is any good (e.g. a commodity) or service brought into one country from another country in a legitimate fashion, typically for use in trade.It is a good that is brought in from another country for sale. _________ goods or services are provided to domestic consumers by foreign producers. An _________ in the receiving country is an export to the sending country.

a. Incoterms
b. Import quota
c. Economic integration
d. Import

40. An _________ is a financial institution that raises capital, trades in securities and manages corporate mergers and acquisitions. _________s profit from companies and governments by raising money through issuing and selling securities in the capital markets (both equity, bond) and insuring bonds (selling credit default swaps), as well as providing advice on transactions such as mergers and acquisitions. To perform these services in the United States, an adviser must be a licensed broker-dealer, and is subject to SEC (FINRA) regulation see SEC.

a. Annual percentage rate
b. Interbanca
c. Investment bank
d. Anonymous internet banking

41. _________ is the economic policy of restraining trade between states, through methods such as tariffs on imported goods, restrictive quotas, and a variety of other restrictive government regulations designed to discourage imports, and prevent foreign take-over of local markets and companies. This policy is closely aligned with anti-globalization, and contrasts with free trade, where government barriers to trade are kept to a minimum. The term is mostly used in the context of economics, where _________ refers to policies or doctrines which 'protect' businesses and workers within a country by restricting or regulating trade with foreign nations.

a. Google economy
b. Knowledge economy
c. Protectionism
d. Digital economy

42. _________ is a term that is used to describe the overall process of invention, innovation and diffusion of technology or processes. The term is redundant with technological development, technological achievement, and technological progress. In essence _________ is the invention of a technology (or a process), the continuous process of improving a technology (in which it often becomes cheaper) and its diffusion throughout industry or society.

a. 1921 recession
b. 100-year flood
c. 130-30 fund
d. Technological change

43. A _________ strategy is the planned method of delivering goods or services to a target market and distributing them there. When importing or exporting services, it refers to establishing and managing contracts in a foreign country.

Many companies successfully operate in a niche market without ever expanding into new markets.

a. Customer centricity
b. Deep discount broker
c. Forfaiting
d. Market entry

44. The _________ consists of a number of economic theories which describe the nature of the firm, company including its existence, its behaviour, and its relationship with the market.

In simplified terms, the _________ aims to answer these questions:

1. Existence - why do firms emerge, why are not all transactions in the economy mediated over the market?
2. Boundaries - why the boundary between firms and the market is located exactly there? Which transactions are performed internally and which are negotiated on the market?
3. Organization - why are firms structured in such specific way? What is the interplay of formal and informal relationships?

Despite looking simple, these questions are not answered by the established economic theory, which usually views firms as given, and treats them as black boxes without any internal structure.

The First World War period saw a change of emphasis in economic theory away from industry-level analysis which mainly included analysing markets to analysis at the level of the firm, as it became increasingly clear that perfect competition was no longer an adequate model of how firms behaved. Economic theory till then had focussed on trying to understand markets alone and there had been little study on understanding why firms or organisations exist.

a. Theory of the firm
b. Khazzoom-Brookes postulate
c. Technology gap
d. Policy Ineffectiveness Proposition

45. _________ is the price at which an asset would trade in a competitive Walrasian auction setting. _________ is often used interchangeably with open _________, fair value or fair _________, although these terms have distinct definitions in different standards, and may differ in some circumstances.

International Valuation Standards defines _________ as 'the estimated amount for which a property should exchange on the date of valuation between a willing buyer and a willing seller in an arm's-length transaction after proper marketing wherein the parties had each acted knowledgeably, prudently, and without compulsion.'

_________ is a concept distinct from market price, which is 'the price at which one can transact', while _________ is 'the true underlying value' according to theoretical standards.

a. Secured loan
b. Netting
c. Personal financial management
d. Market value

46. In microeconomics, _________ is the extra revenue that an additional unit of product will bring. It is the additional income from selling one more unit of a good; sometimes equal to price. It can also be described as the change in total revenue/change in number of units sold.

a. Market demand schedule
b. Long term
c. Reservation price
d. Marginal revenue

47. _________ is the a method of technical and economic research of the systems for purpose to optimize a parity between system's consumer functions or properties and expenses to achieve those functions or properties.

This methodology for continuous perfection of production, industrial technologies, organizational structures was developed by Juryj Sobolev in 1948 at the 'Perm telephone factory'

- 1948 Juryj Sobolev - the first success in application of a method analysis at the 'Perm telephone factory' .
- 1949 - the first application for the invention as result of use of the new method.

Today in economically developed countries practically each enterprise or the company use methodology of the kind of functional-cost analysis as a practice of the quality management, most full satisfying to principles of standards of series ISO 9000.

- Interest of consumer not in products itself, but the advantage which it will receive from its usage.
- The consumer aspires to reduce his expenses
- Functions needed by consumer can be executed in the various ways, and, hence, with various efficiency and expenses. Among possible alternatives of realization of functions exist such in which the parity of quality and the price is the optimal for the consumer.

The goal of _________ is achievement of the highest consumer satisfaction of production at simultaneous decrease in all kinds of industrial expenses Classical _________ has three English synonyms - Value Engineering, Value Management, Value Analysis.

a. Monopoly wage
b. Willingness to pay
c. Staple financing
d. Function cost analysis

48. _________ is the total money received from the sale of any given quantity of output.

The _________ is calculated by taking the price of the sale times the quantity sold, i.e.

_________ = price X quantity.

.

a. Total revenue
b. Market development funds
c. Ceteris paribus
d. Small numbers game

49. In economics, the _________ is the change in consumption resulting from a change in real income.

Another important item that can change is the money income of the consumer. The _________ is the phenomenon observed through changes in purchasing power.

a. Equilibrium wage
b. Income effect
c. Inflation hedge
d. Export subsidy

50. _________ is an economic model based on price, utility and quantity in a market. It predicts that in a competitive market, price will function to equalize the quantity demanded by consumers, and the quantity supplied by producers, resulting in an economic equilibrium of price and quantity. The model incorporates other factors changing equilibrium as a shift of demand and/or supply.

a. Joint demand
b. Rational addiction
c. Deferred gratification
d. Supply and demand

51. In economics, _________ is the total demand for final goods and services in the economy (Y) at a given time and price level. It is the amount of goods and services in the economy that will be purchased at all possible price levels. This is the demand for the gross domestic product of a country when inventory levels are static.

a. Aggregation problem
b. Aggregate expenditure
c. Aggregate supply
d. Aggregate demand

52. In economics and finance, _________ is the change in total cost that arises when the quantity produced changes by one unit. It is the cost of producing one more unit of a good. Mathematically, the _________ function is expressed as the first derivative of the total cost (TC) function with respect to quantity (Q.)

a. Variable cost
b. Quality costs
c. Khozraschyot
d. Marginal cost

53. In economics, a firm is said to reap _________s when a lack of viable market competition allows it to set its prices above the equilibrium price for a good or service without losing profits to competitors. _________ is a type of economic profit, that is, it is a profit greater than the normal profit that is typical in a perfectly competitive industry. The resulting price is known as the monopoly price.

a. Borrowing base
b. Monopoly Profit
c. First-price sealed-bid auction
d. Cleanup clause

54. _________ theory is a branch of theoretical economics. It seeks to explain the behavior of supply, demand and prices in a whole economy with several or many markets. It is often assumed that agents are price takers and in that setting two common notions of equilibrium exist: Walrasian (or competitive) equilibrium, and its generalization; a price equilibrium with transfers.

a. Rational choice theory
b. General equilibrium
c. Human capital
d. New Keynesian economics

55. In economics, economic equilibrium is simply a state of the world where economic forces are balanced and in the absence of external influences the (equilibrium) values of economic variables will not change. It is the point at which quantity demanded and quantity supplied are equal. _________, for example, refers to a condition where a market price is established through competition such that the amount of goods or services sought by buyers is equal to the amount of goods or services produced by sellers.

a. Regulated market
b. Product-Market Growth Matrix
c. Market equilibrium
d. Marketization

56. In economics, _________ is the process by which a firm determines the price and output level that returns the greatest profit. There are several approaches to this problem. The total revenue--total cost method relies on the fact that profit equals revenue minus cost, and the marginal revenue--marginal cost method is based on the fact that total profit in a perfectly competitive market reaches its maximum point where marginal revenue equals marginal cost.

a. Normal profit
b. Profit margin
c. 100-year flood
d. Profit maximization

57. In economics and business decision-making, _________ are costs that cannot be recovered once they have been incurred. _________ are sometimes contrasted with variable costs, which are the costs that will change due to the proposed course of action, and prospective costs which are costs that will be incurred if an action is taken.

In traditional microeconomic theory, only variable costs are relevant to a decision.

a. Post-purchase rationalization
b. Hyperbolic discounting
c. Halo effect
d. Sunk costs

58. _________ was a Scottish-born American industrialist, businessman, and a major philanthropist. He was an immigrant as a child with his parents. He built Pittsburgh's Carnegie Steel Company, which was later merged with Elbert H. Gary's Federal Steel Company and several smaller companies to create U.S. Steel.

a. Andrew Carnegie
b. Oskar Morgenstern
c. Alfred Marshall
d. Eli Whitney

59. _________ is a term used to describe the lavish spending on goods and services acquired mainly for the purpose of displaying income or wealth. In the mind of a conspicuous consumer, such display serves as a means of attaining or maintaining social status. A very similar but more colloquial term is 'keeping up with the Joneses'.

a. Diderot effect
b. Consumption smoothing
c. Consumer behavior
d. Conspicuous consumption

60. In American history, the _________ refers to substantial growth in population in the United States and extravagant displays of wealth and excess of America's upper-class during the post-Civil War and post-Reconstruction era, in the late 19th century (1865-1901.) The wealth polarization derived primarily from industrial and population expansion. The businessmen of the Second Industrial Revolution created industrial towns and cities in the Northeast with new factories, and contributed to the creation of an ethnically diverse industrial working class which produced the wealth owned by rising super-rich industrialists and financiers such as Cornelius Vanderbilt, John D. Rockefeller, Andrew Carnegie, Henry Flagler, and J.P. Morgan.

a. Adolph Fischer
b. Gilded Age
c. Adolf Hitler
d. Adam Smith

61. _________ was an American industrialist and philanthropist. Rockefeller revolutionized the petroleum industry and defined the structure of modern philanthropy. In 1870, he founded the Standard Oil Company and ran it until he officially retired in 1897.

a. Adolf Hitler
b. Adolph Fischer
c. Adam Smith
d. John Davison Rockefeller

62. _________ was a predominant American integrated oil producing, transporting, refining, and marketing company. Established in 1870 as an Ohio Corporation, it was the largest oil refiner in the world and operated as a major company trust and was one of the world's first and largest multinational corporations until it was broken up by the United States Supreme Court in 1911. John D. Rockefeller was a founder, chairman and major shareholder, and the company made him a billionaire and eventually the richest man in history.

a. 1921 recession
b. 130-30 fund
c. 100-year flood
d. Standard Oil

63. _________ is a common concept in economics, and gives rise to derived concepts such as consumer debt. Generally _________ is defined by opposition to production. But the precise definition can vary because different schools of economists define production quite differently.

a. Foreclosure data providers
b. Consumption
c. Federal Reserve Bank Notes
d. Cash or share options

1. Competition law, known in the United States as _________ law, has three main elements:

- prohibiting agreements or practices that restrict free trading and competition between business entities. This includes in particular the repression of cartels.
- banning abusive behaviour by a firm dominating a market, or anti-competitive practices that tend to lead to such a dominant position. Practices controlled in this way may include predatory pricing, tying, price gouging, refusal to deal, and many others.
- supervising the mergers and acquisitions of large corporations, including some joint ventures. Transactions that are considered to threaten the competitive process can be prohibited altogether, or approved subject to 'remedies' such as an obligation to divest part of the merged business or to offer licences or access to facilities to enable other businesses to continue competing.

The substance and practice of competition law varies from jurisdiction to jurisdiction. Protecting the interests of consumers (consumer welfare) and ensuring that entrepreneurs have an opportunity to compete in the market economy are often treated as important objectives. Competition law is closely connected with law on deregulation of access to markets, state aids and subsidies, the privatisation of state owned assets and the establishment of independent sector regulators. In recent decades, competition law has been viewed as a way to provide better public services.

a. United Kingdom competition law
b. Anti-Inflation Act
c. Intellectual property law
d. Antitrust

2. In economics, the _________ of an industry is used as an indicator of the relative size of firms in relation to the industry as a whole. It is calculated as the sum of the percent market share of the top n industries. This may also assist in determining the market structure of the industry.

a. Pacman conjecture
b. Quasi-rent
c. Monopolization
d. Concentration ratio

3. In economic theory, _________ is the competitive situation in any market where the conditions necessary for perfect competition are not satisfied. It is a market structure that does not meet the conditions of perfect competition.

Forms of _________ include:

- Monopoly, in which there is only one seller of a good.
- Oligopoly, in which there is a small number of sellers.
- Monopolistic competition, in which there are many sellers producing highly differentiated goods.
- Monopsony, in which there is only one buyer of a good.
- Oligopsony, in which there is a small number of buyers.

There may also be _________ in markets due to buyers or sellers lacking information about prices and the goods being traded.

There may also be _________ due to a time lag in a market.

a. AD-IA Model
b. ACCRA Cost of Living Index
c. ACEA agreement
d. Imperfect competition

4. In economics, _________ is the ability of a firm to alter the market price of a good or service. A firm with _________ can raise prices without losing all customers to competitors.

When a firm has _________ it faces a downward-sloping demand curve.

a. Price makers
b. Revenue-cap regulation
c. Pacman conjecture
d. Market power

5. In economics, _________ describes the state of a market with respect to competition.

- Perfect competition, in which the market consists of a very large number of firms producing a homogeneous product.
- Monopolistic competition where there are a large number of independent firms which have a very small proportion of the market share.
- Oligopoly, in which a market is dominated by a small number of firms which own more than 40% of the market share.
- Oligopsony, a market dominated by many sellers and a few buyers.
- Monopoly, where there is only one provider of a product or service.
- Natural monopoly, a monopoly in which economies of scale cause efficiency to increase continuously with the size of the firm. A firm is a natural monopoly if it is able to serve the entire market demand at a lower cost than any combination of two or more smaller, more specialized firms.
- Monopsony, when there is only one buyer in a market.

The imperfectly competitive structure is quite identical to the realistic market conditions where some monopolistic competitors, monopolists, oligopolists, and duopolists exist and dominate the market conditions. The elements of _________ include the number and size distribution of firms, entry conditions, and the extent of differentiation.

These somewhat abstract concerns tend to determine some but not all details of a specific concrete market system where buyers and sellers actually meet and commit to trade.

a. Human capital
b. Monopolistic competition
c. Labour economics
d. Market structure

6. _________ is a common market structure where many competing producers sell products that are differentiated from one another (ie. the products are substitutes, but are not exactly alike.) Many markets are monopolistically competitive, common examples include the markets for restaurants, cereal, clothing, shoes and service industries in large cities.

a. Mathematical economics
b. Monopolistic competition
c. Financial crisis
d. Perfect competition

7. In economics, a _________ occurs when, due to the economies of scale of a particular industry, the maximum efficiency of production and distribution is realized through a single supplier.

Natural monopolies arise where the largest supplier in an industry, often the first supplier in a market, has an overwhelming cost advantage over other actual or potential competitors. This tends to be the case in industries where capital costs predominate, creating economies of scale which are large in relation to the size of the market, and hence high barriers to entry; examples include water services and electricity.

a. Collective goods
b. Natural monopoly
c. Privatizing profits and socializing losses
d. Common-pool resource

8. An _________ is a market form in which a market or industry is dominated by a small number of sellers (oligopolists.) Because there are few participants in this type of market, each oligopolist is aware of the actions of the others. The decisions of one firm influence, and are influenced by, the decisions of other firms.

a. Oligopsony
b. Oligopoly
c. ACCRA Cost of Living Index
d. ACEA agreement

9. In economics, a _________ exists when a specific individual or enterprise has sufficient control over a particular product or service to determine significantly the terms on which other individuals shall have access to it. Monopolies are thus characterized by a lack of economic competition for the good or service that they provide and a lack of viable substitute goods. The verb 'monopolize' refers to the process by which a firm gains persistently greater market share than what is expected under perfect competition.

a. 100-year flood
b. 130-30 fund
c. 1921 recession
d. Monopoly

10. A _________ is an expression that compares quantities relative to each other. The most common examples involve two quantities, but any number of quantities can be compared. _________s are represented mathematically by separating each quantity with a colon, for example the _________ 2:3, which is read as the _________ 'two to three'.

a. 130-30 fund
b. Y-intercept
c. 100-year flood
d. Ratio

11. In neoclassical economics and microeconomics, _________ describes the perfect being a market in which there are many small firms, all producing homogeneous goods. In the short term, such markets are productively inefficient as output will not occur where mc is equal to ac, but allocatively efficient, as output under _________ will always occur where mc is equal to mr, and therefore where mc equals ar. However, in the long term, such markets are both allocatively and productively efficient.

a. Law of supply
b. Co-operative economics
c. Perfect competition
d. General equilibrium

12. In economics and especially in the theory of competition, _________ are obstacles in the path of a firm that make it difficult to enter a given market.

_________ are the source of a firm's pricing power - the ability of a firm to raise prices without losing all its customers.

The term refers to hindrances that an individual may face while trying to gain entrance into a profession or trade.

a. Group boycott
b. Barriers to entry
c. Limit price
d. Social dumping

13.

The _________ is an independent agency of the United States government, created, directed, and empowered by Congressional statute , and with the majority of its commissioners appointed by the current President. The _________ works towards six strategic goals in the areas of broadband, competition, the spectrum, the media, public safety and homeland security, and modernizing the _________.

a. 1921 recession
b. 130-30 fund
c. Federal Communications Commission
d. 100-year flood

14. _________ is a field of economics that studies the strategic behavior of firms, the structure of markets and their interactions. The study of _________ adds to the perfectly competitive model real-world frictions such as limited information, transaction cost, cost of adjusting prices, government actions, and barriers to entry by new firms into a market. It then considers how firms are organized and how they compete.

a. Economic ideology
b. Economic
c. Inflation
d. Industrial organization

15. The _________ refers to the 'common well-being' or 'general welfare.' The _________ is central to policy debates, politics, democracy and the nature of government itself. While nearly everyone claims that aiding the common well-being or general welfare is positive, there is little, if any, consensus on what exactly constitutes the _________.

There are different views on how many members of the public must benefit from an action before it can be declared to be in the _________: at one extreme, an action has to benefit every single member of society in order to be truly in the _________; at the other extreme, any action can be in the _________ as long as it benefits some of the population and harms none.

a. Second-class citizen
b. Stealth tax
c. Power Elite
d. Public interest

16. The phrase _________, according to the Organization for Economic Co-operation and Development, refers to 'creative work undertaken on a systematic basis in order to increase the stock of knowledge, including knowledge of man, culture and society, and the use of this stock of knowledge to devise new applications [sic]'

New product design and development is more than often a crucial factor in the survival of a company. In an industry that is fast changing, firms must continually revise their design and range of products. This is necessary due to continuous technology change and development as well as other competitors and the changing preference of customers.

a. 130-30 fund
b. 100-year flood
c. Research and development
d. 1921 recession

17. _________ refers to the state of not requiring any outside aid, support for survival; it is therefore a type of personal or collective autonomy. On a large scale, a totally self-sufficient economy that does not trade with the outside world is called an autarky.

The term _________ is usually applied to varieties of sustainable living in which nothing is consumed outside of what is produced by the self-sufficient individuals.

a. Global Reporting Initiative
b. Sustainable forest management
c. Sustainability science
d. Self-sufficiency

18. _________ is a fee paid on borrowed assets. It is the price paid for the use of borrowed money , or, money earned by deposited funds . Assets that are sometimes lent with _________ include money, shares, consumer goods through hire purchase, major assets such as aircraft, and even entire factories in finance lease arrangements.

a. Interest
b. Internal debt
c. Insolvency
d. Asset protection

19. The phrase _________ and acquisitions refers to the aspect of corporate strategy, corporate finance and management dealing with the buying, selling and combining of different companies that can aid, finance, or help a growing company in a given industry grow rapidly without having to create another business entity.

An acquisition, also known as a takeover or a buyout, is the buying of one company (the 'target') by another. An acquisition may be friendly or hostile.

a. Political economy
b. Peace dividend
c. Differential accumulation
d. Mergers

20. In microeconomics, _________ is quite simply the conversion of inputs into outputs. It is an economic process that uses resources to create a good or service that is suitable for exchange. This can include manufacturing, storing, shipping, and packaging.

a. MET
b. Solved
c. Red Guards
d. Production

21. A _________ is a counterfeit agreement among industries. It is an informal organization of producers that agree to coordinate prices and production. _________s usually occur in an oligopolistic industry, where there is a small number of sellers and usually involve homogeneous products.

a. Cartel
b. 100-year flood
c. Shill
d. Shanzhai

22. _________ is the transition of a national economy from monopoly control by groups of large businesses to a free market economy. This change rarely arises naturally, and is generally the result of regulation by a governing body.

A modern example of _________ is the economic restructuring of Germany after the fall of the Third Reich in 1945.

a. Monopolization
b. Decartelization
c. Market power
d. Complementary monopoly

23. _________ is an agreement, usually secretive, which occurs between two or more persons to deceive, mislead or to obtain an objective forbidden by law typically involving fraud or gaining an unfair advantage. It is an agreement among firms to divide the market, set prices kickbacks, or misrepresenting the independence of the relationship between the colluding parties.' All acts effected by _________ are considered void.

a. Bid rigging
b. Collusion
c. Net Book Agreement
d. Dividing territories

24. The _________ consists of a number of economic theories which describe the nature of the firm, company including its existence, its behaviour, and its relationship with the market.

In simplified terms, the _________ aims to answer these questions:

1. Existence - why do firms emerge, why are not all transactions in the economy mediated over the market?
2. Boundaries - why the boundary between firms and the market is located exactly there? Which transactions are performed internally and which are negotiated on the market?
3. Organization - why are firms structured in such specific way? What is the interplay of formal and informal relationships?

Despite looking simple, these questions are not answered by the established economic theory, which usually views firms as given, and treats them as black boxes without any internal structure.

The First World War period saw a change of emphasis in economic theory away from industry-level analysis which mainly included analysing markets to analysis at the level of the firm, as it became increasingly clear that perfect competition was no longer an adequate model of how firms behaved. Economic theory till then had focussed on trying to understand markets alone and there had been little study on understanding why firms or organisations exist.

a. Khazzoom-Brookes postulate
b. Policy Ineffectiveness Proposition
c. Technology gap
d. Theory of the firm

25. In economics, a firm is said to reap _________s when a lack of viable market competition allows it to set its prices above the equilibrium price for a good or service without losing profits to competitors. _________ is a type of economic profit, that is, it is a profit greater than the normal profit that is typical in a perfectly competitive industry. The resulting price is known as the monopoly price.

a. Borrowing base
b. Cleanup clause
c. First-price sealed-bid auction
d. Monopoly profit

26. _________ in economics and business is the result of an exchange and from that trade we assign a numerical monetary value to a good, service or asset. If Alice trades Bob 4 apples for an orange, the _________ of an orange is 4 apples. Inversely, the _________ of an apple is 1/4 oranges.

a. Price
b. Premium pricing
c. Price war
d. Price book

27. _________ is an agreement between business competitors to sell the same product or service at the same price. In general, it is an agreement intended to ultimately push the price of a product as high as possible, leading to profits for all the sellers. Price-fixing can also involve any agreement to fix, peg, discount or stabilize prices.

a. Price fixing
b. Moral victory
c. Non-price competition
d. Cut-throat competition

28. _________ is a term used in business to indicate a state of intense competitive rivalry accompanied by a multi-lateral series of price reduction. One competitor will lower its price, then others will lower their prices to match. If one of them reduces their price again, a new round of reductions starts.

a. Big ticket item
b. Price war
c. Transactional Net Margin Method
d. Discounts and allowances

29. In economics, _________ is the process by which a firm determines the price and output level that returns the greatest profit. There are several approaches to this problem. The total revenue--total cost method relies on the fact that profit equals revenue minus cost, and the marginal revenue--marginal cost method is based on the fact that total profit in a perfectly competitive market reaches its maximum point where marginal revenue equals marginal cost.

a. Normal profit
b. Profit maximization
c. Profit margin
d. 100-year flood

30. _________ occurs when cartels are illegal or overt collusion is absent. Put another way, two firms agree to play a certain strategy without explicitly saying so. This is also known as price leadership, as firms may stay within the law but still tacitly collude by monitoring each other's prices and keeping them the same.

a. Product innovation
b. Poverty penalty
c. Staple port
d. Tacit collusion

31. Economics:

- _________,the desire to own something and the ability to pay for it
- _________ curve,a graphic representation of a _________ schedule
- _________ deposit, the money in checking accounts
- _________ pull theory,the theory that inflation occurs when _________ for goods and services exceeds existing supplies
- _________ schedule,a table that lists the quantity of a good a person will buy it each different price
- _________ side economics,the school of economics at believes government spending and tax cuts open economy by raising _________

.

a. McKesson ' Robbins scandal
b. Variability
c. Production
d. Demand

32. In economics, the _________ can be defined as the graph depicting the relationship between the price of a certain commodity, and the amount of it that consumers are willing and able to purchase at that given price. It is a graphic representation of a demand schedule. The _________ for all consumers together follows from the _________ of every individual consumer: the individual demands at each price are added together.

a. Kuznets curve
b. Cost curve
c. Wage curve
d. Demand curve

33. The Organization of the Petroleum Exporting Countries is a cartel of twelve countries made up of Algeria, Angola, Ecuador, Iran, Iraq, Kuwait, Libya, Nigeria, Qatar, Saudi Arabia, the United Arab Emirates, and Venezuela. The cartel has maintained its headquarters in Vienna since 1965, and hosts regular meetings among the oil ministers of its Member Countries. Indonesia withdrew its membership in _________ in 2008 after it became a net importer of oil, but stated it would likely return if it became a net exporter in the world.

a. ACEA agreement
b. OPEC
c. AD-IA Model
d. ACCRA Cost of Living Index

34. In marketing, _________ is the process of distinguishing the differences of a product or offering from others, to make it more attractive to a particular target market. This involves differentiating it from competitors' products as well as one's own product offerings.

Differentiation is a source of competitive advantage.

a. Pricing science
b. Technology acceptance model
c. Product differentiation
d. Market segment

35. _________ has several particular meanings:

- in mathematics
    - _________ function
    - Euler _________
    - _________
    - _________ subgroup
    - method of _________s (partial differential equations)
- in physics and engineering
    - any _________ curve that shows the relationship between certain input- and output parameters, e.g.
    - an I-V or current-voltage _________ is the current in a circuit as a function of the applied voltage
    - Receiver-Operator _________
- in fiction
    - in Dungeons ' Dragons, _________ is another name for ability score

.

a. Russian financial crisis
b. Characteristic
c. Technocracy
d. Demand

36. _________ - The Concept of Countervailing Power is a book by John Kenneth Galbraith, written in 1952.

Not as well-known as some of his other works, it contains a critique of the view that markets, left to their own devices, will provide socially optimal solutions. Galbraith agrees with F. A. Hayek as far as the assertion goes that 'the price system will fulfil [its] function only if competition prevails, that is, if the individual producer has to adapt to price changes and cannot control them.'

Galbraith builds on work by Prof. E. H.

a. American capitalism
b. Assets and Liabilities of Commercial Banks in the United States
c. Economics in One Lesson
d. Omnipotent Government

37. _________ is an economic system in which wealth, and the means of producing wealth, are privately owned. Through _________, the land, labor, and capital are owned, operated, and traded for the purpose of generating profits, without force or fraud, by private individuals either singly or jointly, and investments, distribution, income, production, pricing and supply of goods, commodities and services are determined by voluntary private decision in a market economy. A distinguishing feature of _________ is that each person owns his or her own labor and therefore is allowed to sell the use of it to employers.

a. Creative capitalism
b. Late capitalism
c. Socialism for the rich and capitalism for the poor
d. Capitalism

38. A _________ or directed economy is an economic system in which the government or workers' councils manages the economy. It is an economic system in which the central government makes all decisions on the production and consumption of goods and services. Its most extensive form is referred to as a _________, centrally planned economy, or command and control economy.

a. Transition economy
b. Command economy
c. Nutritional Economics
d. Subsistence economy

39. A true _________ is a specific type of oligopoly where only two producers exist in one market. In reality, this definition is generally used where only two firms have dominant control over a market. In the field of industrial organization, it is the most commonly studied form of oligopoly due to its simplicity.

a. Megacorpstate
b. Duopoly
c. 130-30 fund
d. 100-year flood

40. _________ is a branch of applied mathematics that is used in the social sciences (most notably economics), biology, engineering, political science, international relations, computer science, and philosophy. _________ attempts to mathematically capture behavior in strategic situations, in which an individual's success in making choices depends on the choices of others. While initially developed to analyze competitions in which one individual does better at another's expense (zero sum games), it has been expanded to treat a wide class of interactions, which are classified according to several criteria.

a. Discriminatory price auction
b. Dollar auction
c. Proper equilibrium
d. Game theory

41. In economic models, the _________ time frame assumes no fixed factors of production. Firms can enter or leave the marketplace, and the cost (and availability) of land, labor, raw materials, and capital goods can be assumed to vary. In contrast, in the short-run time frame, certain factors are assumed to be fixed, because there is not sufficient time for them to change.

a. Diseconomies of scale
b. Productivity world
c. Price/performance ratio
d. Long-run

42. _________s is the social science that studies the production, distribution, and consumption of goods and services. The term _________s comes from the Ancient Greek οá¼°κονομÎ¯α from οá¼¶κος (oikos, 'house') + νÏŒμος (nomos, 'custom' or 'law'), hence 'rules of the house(hold)'. Current _________ models developed out of the broader field of political economy in the late 19th century, owing to a desire to use an empirical approach more akin to the physical sciences.

a. Inflation
b. Opportunity cost
c. Energy economics
d. Economic

43. _________ exists when sales of identical goods or services are transacted at different prices from the same provider. In a theoretical market with perfect information, no transaction costs or prohibition on secondary exchange (or re-selling) to prevent arbitrage, _________ can only be a feature of monopoly and oligopoly markets, where market power can be exercised. Otherwise, the moment the seller tries to sell the same good at different prices, the buyer at the lower price can arbitrage by selling to the consumer buying at the higher price but with a tiny discount.

a. Loss leader
b. Lerner Index
c. Transfer pricing
d. Price discrimination

44. _________ is an economic concept with commonplace familiarity. It is the price that a good or service is offered at, or will fetch, in the marketplace. It is of interest mainly in the study of microeconomics.

a. Market anomaly
b. Market price
c. Paper trading
d. Noisy market hypothesis

45. In mathematics, a _________ system is a system which is not linear, that is, a system which does not satisfy the superposition principle, or whose output is not proportional to its input. Less technically, a _________ system is any problem where the variable(s) to be solved for cannot be written as a linear combination of independent components. A nonhomogeneous system, which is linear apart from the presence of a function of the independent variables, is _________ according to a strict definition, but such systems are usually studied alongside linear systems, because they can be transformed to a linear system of multiple variables.

a. Nonlinear
b. Nonlinear system
c. 130-30 fund
d. 100-year flood

46. A public utility (usually just utility) is an organization that maintains the infrastructure for a public service (often also providing a service using that infrastructure.) _________ are subject to forms of public control and regulation ranging from local community-based groups to state-wide government monopolies. Common arguments in favor of regulation include the desire to control market power, facilitate competition, promote investment or system expansion, or stabilize markets.

a. 130-30 fund
b. 100-year flood
c. 1921 recession
d. Public utilities

47. In economics, _________ refers to the ability of a party to produce a good or service using fewer real resources than another entity producing the same good or service..A party has an _________ when using the same input as another party, it can produce a greater output. Since _________ is determined by a simple comparison of labor productivities, it is possible for a a party to have no _________ in anything. It can be contrasted with the concept of comparative advantage which refers to the ability to produce a particular good at a lower opportunity cost.

a. International economics
b. Index number
c. ACCRA Cost of Living Index
d. Absolute advantage

48. _________ is the removal or simplification of government rules and regulations that constrain the operation of market forces. _________ does not mean elimination of laws against fraud, but eliminating or reducing government control of how business is done, thereby moving toward a more free market.

The stated rationale for '_________' is often that fewer and simpler regulations will lead to a raised level of competitiveness, therefore higher productivity, more efficiency and lower prices overall.

a. Macroeconomic policy instruments
b. Fundamental psychological law
c. Secular basis
d. Deregulation

49. In economics, an _________ or spillover of an economic transaction is an impact on a party that is not directly involved in the transaction. In such a case, prices do not reflect the full costs or benefits in production or consumption of a product or service. A positive impact is called an external benefit, while a negative impact is called an external cost.

a. Existence value
b. Environmental impact assessment
c. Environmental tariff
d. Externality

50. A _________ is the transfer of wealth from one party (such as a person or company) to another. A _________ is usually made in exchange for the provision of goods, services or both, or to fulfill a legal obligation.

The simplest and oldest form of _________ is barter, the exchange of one good or service for another.

a. Social gravity
b. Soft count
c. Going concern
d. Payment

51. _________ is a concept based on the fact that rationality of individuals is limited by the information they have, the cognitive limitations of their minds, and the finite amount of time they have to make decisions. This contrasts with the concept of rationality as optimization. Another way to look at _________ is that, because decision-makers lack the ability and resources to arrive at the optimal solution, they instead apply their rationality only after having greatly simplified the choices available.

a. Dynamic inconsistency
b. Dollar auction
c. Generalized game theory
d. Bounded rationality

52. _________ is a broad label that refers to any individuals or households that use goods and services generated within the economy. The concept of a _________ is used in different contexts, so that the usage and significance of the term may vary.

Typically when business people and economists talk of _________s they are talking about person as _________, an aggregated commodity item with little individuality other than that expressed in the buy/not-buy decision.

a. 100-year flood
b. 1921 recession
c. 130-30 fund
d. Consumer

53. A _________ is:

- Rewrite _________, in generative grammar and computer science
- Standardization, a formal and widely-accepted statement, fact, definition, or qualification
- Operation, a determinate _________ for performing a mathematical operation and obtaining a certain result (Mathematics, Logic)
    - Unary operation
    - Binary operation
- _________ of inference, a function from sets of formulae to formulae (Mathematics, Logic)
- _________ of thumb, principle with broad application that is not intended to be strictly accurate or reliable for every situation. Also often simply referred to as a _________
- Moral, an atomic element of a moral code for guiding choices in human behavior
- Heuristic, a quantized '_________' which shows a tendency or probability for successful function
- A regulation, as in sports
- A Production _________, as in computer science
- Procedural law, a _________set governing the application of laws to cases
    - A law, which may informally be called a '_________'
    - A court ruling, a decision by a court
- In the U.S. Government, a regulation mandated by Congress, but written or expanded upon by the Executive Branch.
- Norm (sociology), an informal but widely accepted _________, concept, truth, definition, or qualification (social norms, legal norms, coding norms)
- Norm (philosophy), a kind of sentence or a reason to act, feel or believe
- 'Rulership' is the concept of governance by a government:
    - Military _________, governance by a military body
    - Monastic _________, a collection of precepts that guides the life of monks or nuns in a religious order where the superior holds the place of Christ
- Slide _________

- '_________,' a song by Ayumi Hamasaki
- '_________,' a song by rapper Nas
- '_________s,' an album by the band The Whitest Boy Alive
- _________s: Pyaar Ka Superhit Formula, a 2003 Bollywood film
- ruler, an instrument for measuring lengths
- _________, a component of an astrolabe, circumferator or similar instrument
- The _________s, a bestselling self-help book
- _________ Project (Run Up-to-date Linux Everywhere), a project that aims to use up-to-date Linux software on old PCs
- _________ engine, a software system that helps managing business _________s
- Ja _________, a hip hop artist
    - R.U.L.E., a 2005 greatest hits album by rapper Ja _________
- '_________s,' a KMFDM song

a. Technocracy
b. Procter ' Gamble
c. Demand
d. Rule

54. A mutual _________ or stockholder is an individual or company (including a corporation) that legally owns one or more shares of stock in a joint stock company. A company's _________s collectively own that company. Thus, the typical goal of such companies is to enhance _________ value.

a. Shareholder
b. Profit warning
c. Prime Standard
d. Relative valuation

55. _________ is a specific term used in companies' financial reporting from the company-whole point of view. Because that use excludes the effects of changing ownership interest, an economic measure of _________ is necessary for financial analysis from the shareholders' point of view

_________ is defined by the Financial Accounting Standards Board, or FASB, as e;the change in equity [net assets] of a business enterprise during a period from transactions and other events and circumstances from nonowner sources. It includes all changes in equity during a period except those resulting from investments by owners and distributions to owners.e;

_________ is the sum of net income and other items that must bypass the income statement because they have not been realized, including items like an unrealized holding gain or loss from available for sale securities and foreign currency translation gains or losses.

a. Windfall gain
b. Real income
c. Net national income
d. Comprehensive income

56. _________ is one of the four Ps of the marketing mix. The other three aspects are product, promotion, and place. It is also a key variable in microeconomic price allocation theory.

a. Premium pricing
b. Pricing
c. Point of total assumption
d. Guaranteed Maximum Price

57. The _________ is a heterodox school of economics that emphasizes the spontaneous organizing power of the price mechanism. It holds that the complexity of subjective human choices makes mathematical modelling of the evolving market extremely difficult and advocates a laissez faire approach to the economy. _________ economists advocate the enforcement of voluntary contractual agreements between economic agents, but otherwise the smallest imposition of coercive force on commercial transactions.

a. Economic calculation problem
b. ACCRA Cost of Living Index
c. Austrian School
d. ACEA agreement

58. _________s is concerned with the tasks of developing and applying quantitative or statistical methods to the study and elucidation of economic principles. _________s combines economic theory with statistics to analyze and test economic relationships. Theoretical _________s considers questions about the statistical properties of estimators and tests, while applied _________s is concerned with the application of _________ methods to assess economic theories.

a. Experimental economics
b. Evolutionary economics
c. Econometric
d. Economic

59. _________ is the development of economic wealth of countries or regions for the well-being of their inhabitants. It is the process by which a nation improves the economic, political, and social well being of its people. From a policy perspective, _________ can be defined as efforts that seek to improve the economic well-being and quality of life for a community by creating and/or retaining jobs and supporting or growing incomes and the tax base.

a. Economic methodology
b. Inflation
c. Experimental economics
d. Economic Development

60. _________, 1st Baron Keynes was a renowned economist from Britain whose many ideas on economic and political theories as well as on many governments' monetary policies influenced America. He advocated a government that played an active role in the lives of people regarding business, economy, etc. In this role, the government would use fiscal measures to reduce the consequences of recessions, economic depressions and booms.

a. Adolf Hitler
b. Adam Smith
c. Adolph Fischer
d. John Maynard Keynes

61. _________ in political thought refers to economic theories of social organization advocating collective ownership and administration of the means of production and distribution of goods, and a society characterized by equality for all individuals, with an egalitarian method of compensation. Modern _________ originated in the late 19th-century intellectual and working class political movement that criticized the effects of industrialization and private ownership on society. Karl Marx posited that _________ would be achieved via class struggle and a proletarian revolution after a transitional stage from capitalism called the dictatorship of the proletariat.

a. Adolf Hitler
b. Socialism
c. Adolph Fischer
d. Adam Smith

62. _________ is a defined term that an economy with an increased emphasis on informational activities and information industry.

The vagueness of the term has three major sources. First, not surprisingly, there is no agreed-upon definition regarding the threshold of when an economy is _________ and when it is not.

a. Information economy
b. Autarky
c. Intention economy
d. Indicative planning

63. _________ , as defined by the _________ Association of America (Information technologyAA), is 'the study, design, development, implementation, support or management of computer-based information systems, particularly software applications and computer hardware.' _________ deals with the use of electronic computers and computer software to convert, store, protect, process, transmit, and securely retrieve information.

Today, the term _________ has ballooned to encompass many aspects of computing and technology, and the term has become very recognizable. The _________ umbrella can be quite large, covering many fields.

a. ACEA agreement
b. ACCRA Cost of Living Index
c. Information technology
d. AD-IA Model

64. _________ are legal property rights over creations of the mind, both artistic and commercial, and the corresponding fields of law. Under _________ law, owners are granted certain exclusive rights to a variety of intangible assets, such as musical, literary, and artistic works; ideas, discoveries and inventions; and words, phrases, symbols, and designs. Common types of _________ include copyrights, trademarks, patents, industrial design rights and trade secrets.

a. Expedited Funds Availability Act
b. Independent contractor
c. Ease of Doing Business Index
d. Intellectual property

65. A _________ is a set of exclusive rights granted by a state to an inventor or his assignee for a limited period of time in exchange for a disclosure of an invention.

The procedure for granting _________s, the requirements placed on the _________ee and the extent of the exclusive rights vary widely between countries according to national laws and international agreements. Typically, however, a _________ application must include one or more claims defining the invention which must be new, inventive, and useful or industrially applicable.

a. Bona fide occupational qualification
b. Long service leave
c. Bank regulation
d. Patent

66. A _________ is the exclusive authority to determine how a resource is used, whether that resource is owned by government or by individuals. All economic goods have a _________s attribute. This attribute has three broad components

1. The right to use the good
2. The right to earn income from the good
3. The right to transfer the good to others

The concept of _________s as used by economists and legal scholars are related but distinct. The distinction is largely seen in the economists' focus on the ability of an individual or collective to control the use of the good.

a. Holder in due course
b. High-reeve
c. Post-sale restraint
d. Property right

67. _________ in economic theory is the use of modern economic tools to study problems that are traditionally in the province of political science.

In particular, it studies the behavior of politicians and government officials as mostly self-interested agents and their interactions in the social system either as such or under alternative constitutional rules. These can be represented a number of ways, including standard constrained utility maximization, game theory, or decision theory.

a. Rational ignorance
b. Paradox of voting
c. Public interest theory
d. Public choice

68. The _________ was an evolution of developed countries from an industrial/manufacturing-based wealth producing economy into a service sector asset based economy, brought about by globalization and currency manipulation by governments and their central banks. Some analysts claimed that this change in the economic structure of the United States had created a state of permanent steady growth, low unemployment, and immunity to boom and bust macroeconomic cycles. They believed that the change rendered obsolete many business practices.

a. New economy
b. 1921 recession
c. 100-year flood
d. 130-30 fund

69. The _________ of a decision depends on both the cost of the alternative chosen and the benefit that the best alternative would have provided if chosen. _________ differs from accounting cost because it includes opportunity cost.

a. Epstein-Zin preferences
b. Economic cost
c. Inventory analysis
d. Isocost

70. The term surplus is used in economics for several related quantities. The _________ is the amount that consumers benefit by being able to purchase a product for a price that is less than they would be willing to pay. The producer surplus is the amount that producers benefit by selling at a market price mechanism that is higher than they would be willing to sell for.

a. Necessity good
b. Marginal rate of technical substitution
c. Microeconomic reform
d. Consumer surplus

71. In economics, a _________ is a loss of economic efficiency that can occur when equilibrium for a good or service is not Pareto optimal. In other words, either people who would have more marginal benefit than marginal cost are not buying the good or service, or people who would have more marginal cost than marginal benefit are buying the product.

Causes of _________ can include monopoly pricing, externalities, taxes or subsidies, and binding price ceilings or floors.

a. Contract curve
b. Leapfrogging
c. Distributive efficiency
d. Deadweight loss

72. _________ was an American economist, statistician and public intellectual, and a recipient of the Nobel Memorial Prize in Economic Sciences. He is best known among scholars for his theoretical and empirical research, especially consumption analysis, monetary history and theory, and for his demonstration of the complexity of stabilization policy. A global public followed his restatement of a political philosophy that insisted on minimizing the role of government in favor of the private sector.

a. Adolf Hitler
b. Adam Smith
c. Adolph Fischer
d. Milton Friedman

73. In economics, _________ is how a natione;s total economy is distributed among its population. ._________ has always been a central concern of economic theory and economic policy. Classical economists such as Adam Smith, Thomas Malthus and David Ricardo were mainly concerned with factor _________, that is, the distribution of income between the main factors of production, land, labour and capital.

a. Equipment trust certificate
b. Authorised capital
c. Eco commerce
d. Income distribution

74. _________ is the incidence or process of transferring ownership of a business, enterprise, agency or public service from the public sector (government) to the private sector (business.) In a broader sense, _________ refers to transfer of any government function to the private sector including governmental functions like revenue collection and law enforcement.

The term '_________' also has been used to describe two unrelated transactions.

a. Compound empowerment
b. Ricardian equivalence
c. Performance reports
d. Privatization

75. In economics, _________ is the transfer of income, wealth or property from some individuals to others.

One premise of _________ is that money should be distributed to benefit the poorer members of society, and that the rich have an obligation to assist the poor, thus creating a more financially egalitarian society. Another argument is that the rich exploit the poor or otherwise gain unfair benefits.

a. 1921 recession
b. 100-year flood
c. 130-30 fund
d. Redistribution

1. _________s is the social science that studies the production, distribution, and consumption of goods and services. The term _________s comes from the Ancient Greek οá¼°κονομÎ¯α from οá¼¶κος (oikos, 'house') + νÏŒμος (nomos, 'custom' or 'law'), hence 'rules of the house(hold)'. Current _________ models developed out of the broader field of political economy in the late 19th century, owing to a desire to use an empirical approach more akin to the physical sciences.

a. Inflation
b. Energy economics
c. Opportunity cost
d. Economic

2. In game theory, _________ is a solution concept of a game involving two or more players, in which each player is assumed to know the equilibrium strategies of the other players, and no player has anything to gain by changing only his or her own strategy unilaterally. If each player has chosen a strategy and no player can benefit by changing his or her strategy while the other players keep theirs unchanged, then the current set of strategy choices and the corresponding payoffs constitute a _________.

Stated simply, Amy and Bill are in _________ if Amy is making the best decision she can, taking into account Bill's decision, and Bill is making the best decision he can, taking into account Amy's decision.

a. Linear production game
b. Nash equilibrium
c. Lump of labour
d. Proper equilibrium

3. The Organization of the Petroleum Exporting Countries is a cartel of twelve countries made up of Algeria, Angola, Ecuador, Iran, Iraq, Kuwait, Libya, Nigeria, Qatar, Saudi Arabia, the United Arab Emirates, and Venezuela. The cartel has maintained its headquarters in Vienna since 1965, and hosts regular meetings among the oil ministers of its Member Countries. Indonesia withdrew its membership in _________ in 2008 after it became a net importer of oil, but stated it would likely return if it became a net exporter in the world.

a. ACCRA Cost of Living Index
b. OPEC
c. AD-IA Model
d. ACEA agreement

4. _________ is a type of risk faced by investors, corporations, and governments. It is a risk that can be understood and managed with proper aforethought and investment.

Broadly, _________ refers to the complications businesses and governments may face as a result of what are commonly referred to as political decisions--or e;any political change that alters the expected outcome and value of a given economic action by changing the probability of achieving business objectives.e; .

a. Black-Derman-Toy model
b. Capital adequacy ratio
c. Pull to par
d. Political risk

5. _________ is a branch of applied mathematics that is used in the social sciences (most notably economics), biology, engineering, political science, international relations, computer science, and philosophy. _________ attempts to mathematically capture behavior in strategic situations, in which an individual's success in making choices depends on the choices of others. While initially developed to analyze competitions in which one individual does better at another's expense (zero sum games), it has been expanded to treat a wide class of interactions, which are classified according to several criteria.

a. Game theory
b. Discriminatory price auction
c. Dollar auction
d. Proper equilibrium

6. In microeconomics, _________ is quite simply the conversion of inputs into outputs. It is an economic process that uses resources to create a good or service that is suitable for exchange. This can include manufacturing, storing, shipping, and packaging.

a. Red Guards
b. MET
c. Solved
d. Production

7. In economics and finance, _________ is the practice of taking advantage of a price differential between two or more markets: striking a combination of matching deals that capitalize upon the imbalance, the profit being the difference between the market prices. When used by academics, an _________ is a transaction that involves no negative cash flow at any probabilistic or temporal state and a positive cash flow in at least one state; in simple terms, a risk-free profit. A person who engages in _________ is called an arbitrageur--such as a bank or brokerage firm.

a. Options Price Reporting Authority
b. Alternext
c. Arbitrage
d. Electronic trading

8. A _________ is an object whose consumption increases the utility of the consumer, for which the quantity demanded exceeds the quantity supplied at zero price. _________s are usually modeled as having diminishing marginal utility. The first individual purchase has high utility; the second has less.

a. Good
b. Composite good
c. Merit good
d. Pie method

9. In economics, economic output is divided into physical goods and intangible services. Consumption of _________ is assumed to produce utility. It is often used when referring to a _________ Tax.

a. Composite good
b. Private good
c. Manufactured goods
d. Goods and services

10. _________ is the term denoting either an entrance or changes which are inserted into a system and which activate/modify a process. It is an abstract concept, used in the modeling, system(s) design and system(s) exploitation. It is usually connected with other terms, e.g., _________ field, _________ variable, _________ parameter, _________ value, _________ signal, _________ device and _________ file.

a. Input
b. ACEA agreement
c. AD-IA Model
d. ACCRA Cost of Living Index

11. _________ in economics and business is the result of an exchange and from that trade we assign a numerical monetary value to a good, service or asset. If Alice trades Bob 4 apples for an orange, the _________ of an orange is 4 apples. Inversely, the _________ of an apple is 1/4 oranges.

a. Price
b. Price book
c. Premium pricing
d. Price war

12. In finance, _________ is a financial action that does not promise safety of the initial investment along with the return on the principal sum. _________ typically involves the lending of money or the purchase of assets, equity or debt but in a manner that has not been given thorough analysis or is deemed to have low margin of safety or a significant risk of the loss of the principal investment. The term, '_________,' which is formally defined as above in Graham and Dodd's 1934 text, Security Analysis, contrasts with the term 'investment,' which is a financial operation that, upon thorough analysis, promises safety of principal and a satisfactory return.

a. Global Financial Centres Index
b. Municipal Bond Arbitrage
c. Speculation
d. Hybrid market

13. In economics, the _________ is the term economists use to describe the self-regulating nature of the marketplace. The _________ is a metaphor coined by the economist Adam Smith in The Wealth of Nations.

Adam Smith mentions the metaphor in Book IV of The Wealth of Nations, arguing that people in any society will certainly employ their capital in foreign trading only if the profits available by that method far exceed those available locally, and that in such a case it is better for society as a whole if they so did.

a. ACEA agreement
b. ACCRA Cost of Living Index
c. AD-IA Model
d. Invisible hand

14. _________ is an economic concept with commonplace familiarity. It is the price that a good or service is offered at, or will fetch, in the marketplace. It is of interest mainly in the study of microeconomics.

a. Market price
b. Noisy market hypothesis
c. Paper trading
d. Market anomaly

15. Competition law, known in the United States as _________ law, has three main elements:

- prohibiting agreements or practices that restrict free trading and competition between business entities. This includes in particular the repression of cartels.
- banning abusive behaviour by a firm dominating a market, or anti-competitive practices that tend to lead to such a dominant position. Practices controlled in this way may include predatory pricing, tying, price gouging, refusal to deal, and many others.
- supervising the mergers and acquisitions of large corporations, including some joint ventures. Transactions that are considered to threaten the competitive process can be prohibited altogether, or approved subject to 'remedies' such as an obligation to divest part of the merged business or to offer licences or access to facilities to enable other businesses to continue competing.

The substance and practice of competition law varies from jurisdiction to jurisdiction. Protecting the interests of consumers (consumer welfare) and ensuring that entrepreneurs have an opportunity to compete in the market economy are often treated as important objectives. Competition law is closely connected with law on deregulation of access to markets, state aids and subsidies, the privatisation of state owned assets and the establishment of independent sector regulators. In recent decades, competition law has been viewed as a way to provide better public services.

a. Anti-Inflation Act
b. Antitrust
c. Intellectual property law
d. United Kingdom competition law

16. _________ is a situation in which the limited resources of a firm are allocated in accordance with the wishes of consumers. An allocatively efficient economy produces an 'optimal mix' of commodities. A firm is allocatively efficient when its price is equal to its marginal costs (that is, P = MC) in a perfect market.

a. ACCRA Cost of Living Index
b. Allocative efficiency
c. Economic efficiency
d. ACEA agreement

17. _________ is a common concept in economics, and gives rise to derived concepts such as consumer debt. Generally _________ is defined by opposition to production. But the precise definition can vary because different schools of economists define production quite differently.

a. Cash or share options
b. Consumption
c. Foreclosure data providers
d. Federal Reserve Bank Notes

18. In economics, the _________ of a good or of a service is the utility of the specific use to which an agent would put a given increase in that good or service, or of the specific use that would be abandoned in response to a given decrease. In other words, _________ is the utility of the marginal use -- which, on the assumption of economic rationality, would be the least urgent use of the good or service, from the best feasible combination of actions in which its use is included. Under the mainstream assumptions, the _________ of a good or service is the posited quantified change in utility obtained by increasing or by decreasing use of that good or service.

a. Marginal utility
b. 100-year flood
c. 1921 recession
d. 130-30 fund

19. In economics, _________ is a measure of the relative satisfaction from consumption of various goods and services. Given this measure, one may speak meaningfully of increasing or decreasing _________, and thereby explain economic behavior in terms of attempts to increase one's _________. For illustrative purposes, changes in _________ are sometimes expressed in units called utils.

a. Expected utility hypothesis
b. Ordinal utility
c. Utility function
d. Utility

20. A _________ product is a product designed for cheapness and short-term convenience rather than medium to long-term durability, with most products only intended for single use. The term is also sometimes used for products that may last several months (ex. _________ air filters) to distinguish from similar products that last indefinitely (ex.

a. Disposable
b. 130-30 fund
c. 1921 recession
d. 100-year flood

21. _________ is gross income minus income tax on that income.

Discretionary income is income after subtracting taxes and normal expenses (such as rent or mortgage, utilities, insurance, medical, transportation, property maintenance, child support, inflation, food and sundries, 'c.) to maintain a certain standard of living.

a. Disposable personal income
b. Stamp Act
c. Taxation as theft
d. Disposable income

22. A variety of measures of _________ and output are used in economics to estimate total economic activity in a country or region, including gross domestic product (GDP), gross national product (GNP), and net _________

There are three main ways of calculating these numbers; the output approach, the income approach and the expenditure approach. In theory, the three must yield the same, because total expenditures on goods and services must equal the total income paid to the producers (Gnational income), and that must also equal the total value of the output of goods and services (GNP.)

a. Gross world product
b. GNI per capita
c. Volume index
d. National income

23. A _________ represents the combinations of goods and services that a consumer can purchase given current prices and his income. Consumer theory uses the concepts of a _________ and a preference map to analyze consumer choices. Both concepts have a ready graphical representation in the two-good case.

a. Quality bias
b. Joint demand
c. Budget constraint
d. Revealed preference

24. _________ is a broad label that refers to any individuals or households that use goods and services generated within the economy. The concept of a _________ is used in different contexts, so that the usage and significance of the term may vary.

Typically when business people and economists talk of _________s they are talking about person as _________, an aggregated commodity item with little individuality other than that expressed in the buy/not-buy decision.

a. Consumer
b. 130-30 fund
c. 100-year flood
d. 1921 recession

25. The term surplus is used in economics for several related quantities. The _________ is the amount that consumers benefit by being able to purchase a product for a price that is less than they would be willing to pay. The producer surplus is the amount that producers benefit by selling at a market price mechanism that is higher than they would be willing to sell for.

a. Microeconomic reform
b. Marginal rate of technical substitution
c. Necessity good
d. Consumer surplus

26. _________ is a company's financial statement that indicates how the revenue is transformed into the net income The purpose of the _________ is to show managers and investors whether the company made or lost money during the period being reported.

The important thing to remember about an _________ is that it represents a period of time.

a. ACCRA Cost of Living Index
b. ACEA agreement
c. AD-IA Model
d. Income statement

27. The _________ is a heterodox school of economics that emphasizes the spontaneous organizing power of the price mechanism. It holds that the complexity of subjective human choices makes mathematical modelling of the evolving market extremely difficult and advocates a laissez faire approach to the economy. _________ economists advocate the enforcement of voluntary contractual agreements between economic agents, but otherwise the smallest imposition of coercive force on commercial transactions.

a. ACCRA Cost of Living Index
b. Economic calculation problem
c. ACEA agreement
d. Austrian School

28. _________ is the branch of economics concerned with 'the allocation and deployment of economic resources, both spatially and across time, in an uncertain environment' . It is additionally characterised by its 'concentration on monetary activities', in which 'money of one type or another is likely to appear on both sides of a trade' . The questions within _________ are typically framed in terms of 'time, uncertainty, options and information' .

a. Financial economics
b. Price revolution
c. Public economics
d. Fixed exchange rate

29. In economics, a _________ is a mechanism that allows people to easily buy and sell (trade) financial securities (such as stocks and bonds), commodities (such as precious metals or agricultural goods), and other fungible items of value at low transaction costs and at prices that reflect the efficient-market hypothesis.

_________s have evolved significantly over several hundred years and are undergoing constant innovation to improve liquidity.

Both general markets (where many commodities are traded) and specialized markets (where only one commodity is traded) exist.

a. Convertible arbitrage
b. Noise trader
c. Market anomaly
d. Financial market

30. _________, in law and economics, is a form of risk management primarily used to hedge against the risk of a contingent loss. _________ is defined as the equitable transfer of the risk of a loss, from one entity to another, in exchange for a premium, and can be thought of as a guaranteed small loss to prevent a large, possibly devastating loss. An insurer is a company selling the _________; an insured or policyholder is the person or entity buying the _________.

a. ACEA agreement
b. ACCRA Cost of Living Index
c. AD-IA Model
d. Insurance

31. In economics, a _________ exists when the production or use of goods and services by the market is not efficient. That is, there exists another outcome where all involved can be made better off. _________s can be viewed as scenarios where individuals' pursuit of pure self-interest leads to results that are not efficient - that can be improved upon from the societal point-of-view.

a. Fixed exchange rate
b. General equilibrium
c. Financial economics
d. Market failure

32. In general _________ refers to any non-human asset made by humans and then used in production. Often, it refers to economic capital in some ambiguous combination of infrastructural capital and natural capital. As these are combined in process-specific and firm-specific ways that neoclassical macroeconomics does not differentiate at its level of analysis, it is common to refer only to physical vs. human capital and seek so-called 'balanced growth' that develops both in tandem

Such analyses, however, fails to make distinctions considered critical by many modern economists.

a. Factor cost
b. Net domestic product
c. Physical capital
d. Linkage principle

33. A mutual _________ or stockholder is an individual or company (including a corporation) that legally owns one or more shares of stock in a joint stock company. A company's _________s collectively own that company. Thus, the typical goal of such companies is to enhance _________ value.

a. Profit warning
b. Prime Standard
c. Shareholder
d. Relative valuation

34. _________ or the economics of information is a branch of microeconomic theory that studies how information affects an economy and economic decisions. Information has special characteristics. It is easy to create but hard to trust.

a. ACEA agreement
b. ACCRA Cost of Living Index
c. Information Economics
d. AD-IA Model

35. Although information has been bought and sold since ancient times, the idea of an information marketplace is relatively recent. The nature of such markets is still evolving, which complicates development of sustainable business models. However, certain attributes of _________ are beginning to be understood, such as diminished participation costs, opportunities for customization, shifting customer relations, and a need for order.

a. Open economy
b. Information markets
c. Underground economy
d. Intention economy

36. _________, anti-selection insurance, statistics, and risk management. It refers to a market process in which 'bad' results occur when buyers and sellers have asymmetric information (i.e. access to different information): the 'bad' products or customers are more likely to be selected. A bank that sets one price for all its checking account customers runs the risk of being adversely selected against by its low-balance, high-activity (and hence least profitable) customers.

a. Adverse selection
b. AD-IA Model
c. ACEA agreement
d. ACCRA Cost of Living Index

37. A _________ is a situation in microeconomics where a competitive market allowing the exchange of a commodity would be Pareto-efficient, but no such market exists.

A variety of factors can lead to _________s:

A classic example of a _________ is the case of an externality like pollution, where decision makers are not responsible for some of the consequences of their actions. When a factory discharges polluted water into a river, that pollution can hurt people who fish in or get their drinking water from the river downstream, but the factory owner may have no incentive to consider those consequences.

a. Deadweight loss
b. Distributive efficiency
c. Wage share
d. Missing market

38. _________ is the prospect that a party insulated from risk may behave differently from the way it would behave if it were fully exposed to the risk. In insurance, _________ that occurs without conscious or malicious action is called morale hazard.

_________ is related to information asymmetry, a situation in which one party in a transaction has more information than another.

a. 130-30 fund
b. 100-year flood
c. 1921 recession
d. Moral hazard

39. _________ is a policy or ideology of violence intended to intimidate or cause terror for the purpose of 'exerting pressure on decision making by state bodies.' The term 'terror' is largely used to indicate clandestine, low-intensity violence that targets civilians and generates public fear. Thus 'terror' is distinct from asymmetric warfare, and violates the concept of a common law of war in which civilian life is regarded. The term '-ism' is used to indicate an ideology --typically one that claims its attacks are in the domain of a 'just war' concept, though most condemn such as crimes against humanity.
a. 1921 recession
b. 130-30 fund
c. 100-year flood
d. Terrorism

40. An _________ is a market form in which a market or industry is dominated by a small number of sellers (oligopolists.) Because there are few participants in this type of market, each oligopolist is aware of the actions of the others. The decisions of one firm influence, and are influenced by, the decisions of other firms.
a. ACCRA Cost of Living Index
b. Oligopsony
c. Oligopoly
d. ACEA agreement

41. Wisconsin originated the idea of _________ in the U.S. in 1932. In the United States, there are 50 state _________ programs plus one each in the District of Columbia and Puerto Rico. Through the Social Security Act of 1935, the Federal Government of the United States effectively coerced the individual states into adopting _________ plans.
a. AD-IA Model
b. ACCRA Cost of Living Index
c. ACEA agreement
d. Unemployment insurance

42. _________ is the term for economic policies followed as a part of military operations during wartime. The purpose of _________ is to capture critical economic resources so that the military can operate at full efficiency and/or deprive the enemy forces of those resources so that they cannot fight the war properly. The Russians demonstrated the use of economical warfare in the Battle of Stalingrad by cutting off the Germans' supply lines and starving them to death.
a. ACEA agreement
b. AD-IA Model
c. ACCRA Cost of Living Index
d. Economic warfare

43. A true _________ is a specific type of oligopoly where only two producers exist in one market. In reality, this definition is generally used where only two firms have dominant control over a market. In the field of industrial organization, it is the most commonly studied form of oligopoly due to its simplicity.
a. Megacorpstate
b. Duopoly
c. 130-30 fund
d. 100-year flood

44. _________ is a term used in business to indicate a state of intense competitive rivalry accompanied by a multi-lateral series of price reduction. One competitor will lower its price, then others will lower their prices to match. If one of them reduces their price again, a new round of reductions starts.
a. Price war
b. Transactional Net Margin Method
c. Discounts and allowances
d. Big ticket item

45. _________ was a survey conducted by the U.S. Department of Justice to gauge the prevalence of alcohol and illegal drug use among prior arrestees. It was a reformulation of the prior Drug Use Forecasting (DUF) program, focused on five drugs in particular: cocaine, marijuana, methamphetamine, opiates, and PCP.

Participants were randomly selected from arrest records in major metropolitan areas; because no personally identifying information is taken from each record chosen, the resulting data can be correlated to arrest rates, but not to the total population of persons charged.

a. ACCRA Cost of Living Index
b. ACEA agreement
c. AD-IA Model
d. Arrestee Drug Abuse Monitoring

46. A _________ is a counterfeit agreement among industries. It is an informal organization of producers that agree to coordinate prices and production. _________s usually occur in an oligopolistic industry, where there is a small number of sellers and usually involve homogeneous products.

a. 100-year flood
b. Shanzhai
c. Shill
d. Cartel

47. _________ is the transition of a national economy from monopoly control by groups of large businesses to a free market economy. This change rarely arises naturally, and is generally the result of regulation by a governing body.

A modern example of _________ is the economic restructuring of Germany after the fall of the Third Reich in 1945.

a. Complementary monopoly
b. Market power
c. Monopolization
d. Decartelization

48. _________ is an agreement, usually secretive, which occurs between two or more persons to deceive, mislead or to obtain an objective forbidden by law typically involving fraud or gaining an unfair advantage. It is an agreement among firms to divide the market, set prices kickbacks, or misrepresenting the independence of the relationship between the colluding parties.' All acts effected by _________ are considered void.

a. Dividing territories
b. Net Book Agreement
c. Collusion
d. Bid rigging

49. _________ was a Scottish moral philosopher and a pioneer of political economy. One of the key figures of the Scottish Enlightenment, Smith is the author of The Theory of Moral Sentiments and An Inquiry into the Nature and Causes of the Wealth of Nations. The latter, usually abbreviated as The Wealth of Nations, is considered his magnum opus and the first modern work of economics.

a. Alan Greenspan
b. Adam Smith
c. Adolf Hitler
d. Adolph Fischer

50. A _________ is a group of people who share or are motivated by at least one common issue or interest, or work together on a specific project(s) to achieve a common objective. _________s are also characterised by attempts to share and exercise political and social power and to make decisions on a consensus-driven and egalitarian basis. _________s differ from cooperatives in that they are not necessarily focused upon an economic benefit or saving (but can be that as well.)

a. 130-30 fund
b. 100-year flood
c. 1921 recession
d. Collective

51. In organized labor, _________ is the method whereby workers organize together (usually in unions) to meet, converse, and negotiate upon the work conditions with their employers normally resulting in a written contract setting forth the wages, hours, and other conditions to be observed for a stipulated period.It is the practice in which union and company representatives meet to negotiate a new labor contract. In various national labor and employment law contexts, _________ takes on a more specific legal meaning and so, in a broad sense, however, it is the coming together of workers to negotiate their employment.

A collective agreement is a labor contract between an employer and one or more unions.

a. Designated Suppliers Program
b. Demarcation dispute
c. Strikebreaker
d. Collective bargaining

52. Competitive market equilibrium is the traditional concept of economic equilibrium, appropriate for the analysis of commodity markets with flexible prices and many traders, and serving as the benchmark of efficiency in economic analysis. It relies crucially on the assumption of a competitive environment where each trader decides upon a quantity that is so small compared to the total quantity traded in the market that their individual transactions have no influence on the prices.Competitive markets are an ideal, a standard that other market structures are evaluated by.

A _________ consists of a vector of prices and an allocation such that given the prices, each trader by maximizing his objective function (profit, preferences) subject to his technological possibilities and resource constraints plans to trade into his part of the proposed allocation, and such that the prices make all net trades compatible with one another ('clear the market') by equating aggregate supply and demand for the commodities which are traded.

a. Market system
b. Partial equilibrium
c. Product-Market Growth Matrix
d. Competitive equilibrium

53. In the theory of artificial neural networks _________ networks are a case of competitive learning in recurrent neural networks. Output nodes in the network inhibit each other and activate themselves through reflexive connections. After some time, only one node in the output layer will be active.

a. 100-year flood
b. 130-30 fund
c. 1921 recession
d. Winner-take-all

54. _________ refers to the objective and subjective components of the believability of a source or message.

Traditionally, _________ has two key components: trustworthiness and expertise, which both have objective and subjective components. Trustworthiness is a based more on subjective factors, but can include objective measurements such as established reliability.

a. 1921 recession
b. 130-30 fund
c. 100-year flood
d. Credibility

55. _________ is a type of trade policy that allows traders to act and transact without interference from government. Thus, the policy permits trading partners mutual gains from trade, with goods and services produced according to the theory of comparative advantage.

Under a _________ policy, prices are a reflection of true supply and demand, and are the sole determinant of resource allocation.

a. Free trade
b. 1921 recession
c. 130-30 fund
d. 100-year flood

56. _________ is the economic policy of restraining trade between states, through methods such as tariffs on imported goods, restrictive quotas, and a variety of other restrictive government regulations designed to discourage imports, and prevent foreign take-over of local markets and companies. This policy is closely aligned with anti-globalization, and contrasts with free trade, where government barriers to trade are kept to a minimum. The term is mostly used in the context of economics, where _________ refers to policies or doctrines which 'protect' businesses and workers within a country by restricting or regulating trade with foreign nations.

a. Protectionism
b. Google economy
c. Knowledge economy
d. Digital economy

1. The _________ consists of a number of economic theories which describe the nature of the firm, company including its existence, its behaviour, and its relationship with the market.

In simplified terms, the _________ aims to answer these questions:

1. Existence - why do firms emerge, why are not all transactions in the economy mediated over the market?
2. Boundaries - why the boundary between firms and the market is located exactly there? Which transactions are performed internally and which are negotiated on the market?
3. Organization - why are firms structured in such specific way? What is the interplay of formal and informal relationships?

Despite looking simple, these questions are not answered by the established economic theory, which usually views firms as given, and treats them as black boxes without any internal structure.

The First World War period saw a change of emphasis in economic theory away from industry-level analysis which mainly included analysing markets to analysis at the level of the firm, as it became increasingly clear that perfect competition was no longer an adequate model of how firms behaved. Economic theory till then had focussed on trying to understand markets alone and there had been little study on understanding why firms or organisations exist.

a. Technology gap
b. Policy Ineffectiveness Proposition
c. Theory of the firm
d. Khazzoom-Brookes postulate

2. A _________ product is a product designed for cheapness and short-term convenience rather than medium to long-term durability, with most products only intended for single use. The term is also sometimes used for products that may last several months (ex. _________ air filters) to distinguish from similar products that last indefinitely (ex.

a. Disposable
b. 1921 recession
c. 100-year flood
d. 130-30 fund

3. _________ is gross income minus income tax on that income.

Discretionary income is income after subtracting taxes and normal expenses (such as rent or mortgage, utilities, insurance, medical, transportation, property maintenance, child support, inflation, food and sundries, 'c.) to maintain a certain standard of living.

a. Disposable personal income
b. Stamp Act
c. Taxation as theft
d. Disposable income

4. _________ is the returns received on factors of production: rent is return on land, wages on labor, interest on capital, and profit on entrepreneurship. It is also known as Net Factor Payments (NFP.)

Part of current account with balance of trade (exports minus imports of goods and services) and net transfer payments (such as foreign aid.)

a. 130-30 fund
b. 100-year flood
c. Redistributive justice
d. Factor income

5. A variety of measures of _________ and output are used in economics to estimate total economic activity in a country or region, including gross domestic product (GDP), gross national product (GNP), and net _________

There are three main ways of calculating these numbers; the output approach, the income approach and the expenditure approach. In theory, the three must yield the same, because total expenditures on goods and services must equal the total income paid to the producers (Gnational income), and that must also equal the total value of the output of goods and services (GNP.)

a. Volume index
b. GNI per capita
c. Gross world product
d. National income

6. The _________ captures an expanded spectrum of values and criteria for measuring organizational (and societal) success: economic, ecological and social. With the ratification of the United Nations and ICLEI _________ standard for urban and community accounting in early 2007, this became the dominant approach to public sector full cost accounting. Similar UN standards apply to natural capital and human capital measurement to assist in measurements required by _________, e.g. the ecoBudget standard for reporting ecological footprint.

a. Social welfare function
b. Triple bottom line
c. Missing market
d. Leapfrogging

7. A _________ represents the combinations of goods and services that a consumer can purchase given current prices and his income. Consumer theory uses the concepts of a _________ and a preference map to analyze consumer choices. Both concepts have a ready graphical representation in the two-good case.

a. Joint demand
b. Revealed preference
c. Quality bias
d. Budget constraint

8. _________ is a specific term used in companies' financial reporting from the company-whole point of view. Because that use excludes the effects of changing ownership interest, an economic measure of _________ is necessary for financial analysis from the shareholders' point of view

_________ is defined by the Financial Accounting Standards Board, or FASB, as e;the change in equity [net assets] of a business enterprise during a period from transactions and other events and circumstances from nonowner sources. It includes all changes in equity during a period except those resulting from investments by owners and distributions to owners.e;

_________ is the sum of net income and other items that must bypass the income statement because they have not been realized, including items like an unrealized holding gain or loss from available for sale securities and foreign currency translation gains or losses.

a. Net national income
b. Real income
c. Windfall gain
d. Comprehensive income

9. In economics, _________ is how a natione;s total economy is distributed among its population. ._________ has always been a central concern of economic theory and economic policy. Classical economists such as Adam Smith, Thomas Malthus and David Ricardo were mainly concerned with factor _________, that is, the distribution of income between the main factors of production, land, labour and capital.

a. Income distribution
b. Authorised capital
c. Eco commerce
d. Equipment trust certificate

10. A _________ is an economy based on the division of labor in which the prices of goods and services are determined in a free price system set by supply and demand. This is often contrasted with a planned economy, in which a central government determines the price of goods and services using a fixed price system. Market economies are contrasted with mixed economy where the price system is not entirely free but under some government control that is not extensive enough to constitute a planned economy.

a. Commons-based peer production
b. Network Economy
c. Nutritional Economics
d. Market economy

11. Total _________ is defined by the United States' Bureau of Economic Analysis as

income received by persons from all sources. It includes income received from participation in production as well as from government and business transfer payments. It is the sum of compensation of employees (received), supplements to wages and salaries, proprietors' income with inventory valuation adjustment (IVA) and capital consumption adjustment (CCAdj), rental income of persons with CCAdj, _________ receipts on assets, and personal current transfer receipts, less contributions for government social insurance.

a. Greater fool theory
b. Bidding
c. Dividend Discount Model
d. Personal income

12. The _________ or gross domestic income (GDI), a basic measure of an economy's economic performance, is the market value of all final goods and services produced within the borders of a nation in a year. _________ can be defined in three ways, all of which are conceptually identical. First, it is equal to the total expenditures for all final goods and services produced within the country in a stipulated period of time (usually a 365-day year.)

a. Gross domestic product
b. Monopolistic competition
c. Market structure
d. Countercyclical

13. _________ is a fee paid on borrowed assets. It is the price paid for the use of borrowed money , or, money earned by deposited funds . Assets that are sometimes lent with _________ include money, shares, consumer goods through hire purchase, major assets such as aircraft, and even entire factories in finance lease arrangements.

a. Interest
b. Asset protection
c. Insolvency
d. Internal debt

14. _________ is a misspelled phrase from Latin 'pro capite' phrase meaning per head with pro meaning 'per' or 'for each' and capite meaning 'head.' Both words together equate to the phrase 'for each head.'

It is usually used in the field of statistics to indicate the average per person for any given concern, such as income, crime rate, etc.

It is also used in wills to indicate that each of the named beneficiaries should receive, by devise or bequest, equal shares of the estate. This is in contrast to a per stirpes division, in which each branch of the inheriting family inherits an equal share of the estate.

a. Sargan test
b. False positive rate
c. Population statistics
d. Per capita

15. _________ in economic theory is the use of modern economic tools to study problems that are traditionally in the province of political science.

In particular, it studies the behavior of politicians and government officials as mostly self-interested agents and their interactions in the social system either as such or under alternative constitutional rules. These can be represented a number of ways, including standard constrained utility maximization, game theory, or decision theory.

a. Public choice
b. Paradox of voting
c. Public interest theory
d. Rational ignorance

16. An _________, in economics, is the amount by which the real Gross domestic product exceeds potential GDP. The real GDP is also known as GDP 'adjusted for inflation', 'constant prices' GDP or 'constant dollar' GDP, because it measures the aggregate output in a country's income accounts in a given year, expressed in base-year prices. On the other hand, the potential GDP is the quantity of real GDP when a country's economy is at full-employment.

a. ACEA agreement
b. ACCRA Cost of Living Index
c. AD-IA Model
d. Inflationary gap

17. Economic _________ is defined as an excess distribution to any factor in a production process above that which is required to induce the factor into the process or any excess above that which is necessary to keep the factor in its current use..

Classical Factor _________ is primarily concerned with the fee paid for the use of fixed (e.g. natural) resources. The classical definition is expressed as any excess payment above that required to induce or provide for production.

a. 130-30 fund
b. Rent
c. 1921 recession
d. 100-year flood

18. In economics, a _________ is a redistribution of income in the market system. These payments are considered to be nonexhaustive because they do not directly absorb resources or create output. Examples of certain _________s include welfare (financial aid), social security, and government subsidies for certain businesses (firms.)

a. Transfer payment
b. 130-30 fund
c. 1921 recession
d. 100-year flood

19. A _________ is the transfer of wealth from one party (such as a person or company) to another. A _________ is usually made in exchange for the provision of goods, services or both, or to fulfill a legal obligation.

The simplest and oldest form of _________ is barter, the exchange of one good or service for another.

a. Payment
b. Going concern
c. Social gravity
d. Soft count

20. In business and accounting, _________ are everything of value that is owned by a person or company. It is a claim on the property your income of a borrower. The balance sheet of a firm records the monetary value of the _________ owned by the firm.

a. Amortization schedule
b. Assets
c. ACEA agreement
d. ACCRA Cost of Living Index

21. In statistics, the _________ problem occurs when one considers a set of statistical inferences simultaneously. Errors in inference, including confidence intervals that fail to include their corresponding population parameters are more likely to occur when one considers the family as a whole. Several statistical techniques have been developed to prevent this from happening, allowing significance levels for single and _________ to be directly compared.

a. Familywise error rate
b. Hypotheses suggested by the data
c. False discovery rate
d. Multiple comparisons

22. The _________ is 'the basic residential unit in which economic production, consumption, inheritance, child rearing, and shelter are organized and carried out'; [the _________] 'may or may not be synonomous with family'.

The _________ is the basic unit of analysis in many social, microeconomic and government models. The term refers to all individuals who live in the same dwelling.

a. 130-30 fund
b. Family economics
c. Household
d. 100-year flood

23. The accounting equation relates assets, _________, and owner's equity:

Assets = _________ + Owner's Equity

The accounting equation is the mathematical structure of the balance sheet.

The Australian Accounting Research Foundation defines _________ as: 'future sacrifice of economic benefits that the entity is presently obliged to make to other entities as a result of past transactions and other past events.'

Probably the most accepted accounting definition of liability is the one used by the International Accounting Standards Board (IASB.) The following is a quotation from IFRS Framework:

A liability is a present obligation of the enterprise arising from past events, the settlement of which is expected to result in an outflow from the enterprise of resources embodying economic benefits

-

Regulations as to the recognition of _________ are different all over the world, but are roughly similar to those of the IASB.

a. Competition law theory
b. Coase theorem
c. Community property
d. Liabilities

24. In business, _________ is the total liabilitiess minus total outside assets of an individual or a company. For a company, this is called shareholders' prefernce and may be referred to as book value. _________ is stated as at a particular year in time.

a. Bond credit rating
b. Post earnings announcement drift
c. Sinking fund
d. Net worth

25. In economics, the _________ measures the payments that flow between any individual country and all other countries. It is used to summarize all international economic transactions for that country during a specific time period, usually a year. The _________ is determined by the country's exports and imports of goods, services, and financial capital, as well as financial transfers.

a. Gross world product
b. Skyscraper Index
c. Balance of payments
d. Gross domestic product per barrel

26. _________ is a broad label that refers to any individuals or households that use goods and services generated within the economy. The concept of a _________ is used in different contexts, so that the usage and significance of the term may vary.

Typically when business people and economists talk of _________s they are talking about person as _________, an aggregated commodity item with little individuality other than that expressed in the buy/not-buy decision.

a. Consumer
b. 130-30 fund
c. 1921 recession
d. 100-year flood

27. _________ is a term in economics, where demand for one good or service occurs as a result of demand for another. This may occur as the former is a part of production of the second. For example, demand for coal leads to _________ for mining, as coal must be mined for coal to be consumed.

a. Rate risk
b. Leontief production function
c. Days Sales Outstanding
d. Derived demand

28. In economics, _________ are the resources employed to produce goods and services. They facilitate production but do not become part of the product (as with raw materials) or significantly transformed by the production process (as with fuel used to power machinery.) To 19th century economists, the _________ were land (natural resources, gifts from nature), labor (the ability to work), and capital goods (human-made tools and equipment.)

a. Long-run
b. Hicks-neutral technical change
c. Product Pipeline
d. Factors of production

29. _________ is the term denoting either an entrance or changes which are inserted into a system and which activate/modify a process. It is an abstract concept, used in the modeling, system(s) design and system(s) exploitation. It is usually connected with other terms, e.g., _________ field, _________ variable, _________ parameter, _________ value, _________ signal, _________ device and _________ file.

a. ACEA agreement
b. ACCRA Cost of Living Index
c. AD-IA Model
d. Input

30. In economics, the _________ is a graphical representation of the cumulative distribution function of a probability distribution; it is a graph showing the proportion of the distribution assumed by the bottom y% of the values. It is a curve that illustrates income distribution. It is often used to represent income distribution, where it shows for the bottom x% of households, what percentage y% of the total income they have.

a. Kuznets curve
b. Phillips curve
c. Demand curve
d. Lorenz curve

31. In economics, the _________ or marginal physical product is the extra output produced by one more unit of an input (for instance, the difference in output when a firm's labour is increased from five to six units.) Assuming that no other inputs to production change, the _________ of a given input (X) can be expressed as:

_________ = ΔY/ΔX = (the change of Y)/(the change of X.)

-
  -
    - Pending approval by Thomas Sowell***

In neoclassical economics, this is the mathematical derivative of the production function.... Note that the 'product' (Y) is typically defined ignoring external costs and benefits.

a. Marginal product
b. Labor problem
c. Factor prices
d. Productive capacity

32. _________ in economics and business is the result of an exchange and from that trade we assign a numerical monetary value to a good, service or asset. If Alice trades Bob 4 apples for an orange, the _________ of an orange is 4 apples. Inversely, the _________ of an apple is 1/4 oranges.

a. Premium pricing
b. Price war
c. Price book
d. Price

33. Applied microeconomics includes a range of specialized areas of study, many of which draw on methods from other fields. Applied work often uses little more than the basics of _________, supply and demand. Industrial organization and regulation examines topics such as the entry and exit of firms, innovation, role of trademarks.

a. Monopolistic competition
b. Financial crises
c. Microeconomics
d. Price theory

34. _________ is an economic model based on price, utility and quantity in a market. It predicts that in a competitive market, price will function to equalize the quantity demanded by consumers, and the quantity supplied by producers, resulting in an economic equilibrium of price and quantity. The model incorporates other factors changing equilibrium as a shift of demand and/or supply.

a. Rational addiction
b. Supply and demand
c. Joint demand
d. Deferred gratification

35. In economics, the term _________ of income or _________ refers to a simple economic model which describes the reciprocal circulation of income between producers and consumers. In the _________ model, the inter-dependent entities of producer and consumer are referred to as 'firms' and 'households' respectively and provide each other with factors in order to facilitate the flow of income. Firms provide consumers with goods and services in exchange for consumer expenditure and 'factors of production' from households.

a. 1921 recession
b. Circular flow
c. 130-30 fund
d. 100-year flood

36. Economics:

- _________,the desire to own something and the ability to pay for it
- _________ curve,a graphic representation of a _________ schedule
- _________ deposit, the money in checking accounts
- _________ pull theory,the theory that inflation occurs when _________ for goods and services exceeds existing supplies
- _________ schedule,a table that lists the quantity of a good a person will buy it each different price
- _________ side economics,the school of economics at believes government spending and tax cuts open economy by raising _________

.

a. Production
b. Demand
c. McKesson ' Robbins scandal
d. Variability

37. _________ is one of the four Ps of the marketing mix. The other three aspects are product, promotion, and place. It is also a key variable in microeconomic price allocation theory.

a. Guaranteed Maximum Price
b. Point of total assumption
c. Premium pricing
d. Pricing

38. In microeconomics, _________ is quite simply the conversion of inputs into outputs. It is an economic process that uses resources to create a good or service that is suitable for exchange. This can include manufacturing, storing, shipping, and packaging.

a. Production
b. MET
c. Red Guards
d. Solved

39. In microeconomics, _________ is the extra revenue that an additional unit of product will bring. It is the additional income from selling one more unit of a good; sometimes equal to price. It can also be described as the change in total revenue/change in number of units sold.

a. Reservation price
b. Market demand schedule
c. Marginal revenue
d. Long term

40. The marginal revenue productivity theory of wages, also referred to as the _________ of labor, is the change in total revenue earned by a firm that results from employing one more unit of labor. It is a neoclassical model that determines, under some conditions, the optimal number of workers to employ at an exogenously determined market wage rate.

The _________ of a worker is equal to the product of the marginal product of labor (MP) and the marginal revenue (MR), given by MR×MP = _________.

a. Marginal revenue productivity theory of wages
b. Coal depletion
c. Real prices and ideal prices
d. Marginal revenue product

41. In economics, the _________ can be defined as the graph depicting the relationship between the price of a certain commodity, and the amount of it that consumers are willing and able to purchase at that given price. It is a graphic representation of a demand schedule. The _________ for all consumers together follows from the _________ of every individual consumer: the individual demands at each price are added together.

a. Kuznets curve
b. Wage curve
c. Cost curve
d. Demand curve

42. In economics, _________ refers to how the marginal contribution of a factor of production usually decreases as more of the factor is used. According to this relationship, in a production system with fixed and variable inputs, beyond some point, each additional unit of the variable input yields smaller and smaller increases in output. Conversely, producing one more unit of output costs more and more in variable inputs.

a. Patent troll
b. Derivatives law
c. Community property
d. Diminishing returns

43. In economic theory, _________ is the competitive situation in any market where the conditions necessary for perfect competition are not satisfied. It is a market structure that does not meet the conditions of perfect competition.

Forms of _________ include:

- Monopoly, in which there is only one seller of a good.
- Oligopoly, in which there is a small number of sellers.
- Monopolistic competition, in which there are many sellers producing highly differentiated goods.
- Monopsony, in which there is only one buyer of a good.
- Oligopsony, in which there is a small number of buyers.

There may also be _________ in markets due to buyers or sellers lacking information about prices and the goods being traded.

There may also be _________ due to a time lag in a market.

a. ACCRA Cost of Living Index
b. ACEA agreement
c. Imperfect competition
d. AD-IA Model

44. _________ is a situation in which the limited resources of a firm are allocated in accordance with the wishes of consumers. An allocatively efficient economy produces an 'optimal mix' of commodities. A firm is allocatively efficient when its price is equal to its marginal costs (that is, P = MC) in a perfect market.

a. ACCRA Cost of Living Index
b. ACEA agreement
c. Allocative efficiency
d. Economic efficiency

45. In neoclassical economics and microeconomics, _________ describes the perfect being a market in which there are many small firms, all producing homogeneous goods. In the short term, such markets are productively inefficient as output will not occur where mc is equal to ac, but allocatively efficient, as output under _________ will always occur where mc is equal to mr, and therefore where mc equals ar. However, in the long term, such markets are both allocatively and productively efficient.

a. Co-operative economics
b. Law of supply
c. General equilibrium
d. Perfect competition

46. In economics, _________ is the process by which a firm determines the price and output level that returns the greatest profit. There are several approaches to this problem. The total revenue--total cost method relies on the fact that profit equals revenue minus cost, and the marginal revenue--marginal cost method is based on the fact that total profit in a perfectly competitive market reaches its maximum point where marginal revenue equals marginal cost.

a. Normal profit
b. 100-year flood
c. Profit margin
d. Profit maximization

47. A _________ is:

- Rewrite _________, in generative grammar and computer science
- Standardization, a formal and widely-accepted statement, fact, definition, or qualification
- Operation, a determinate _________ for performing a mathematical operation and obtaining a certain result (Mathematics, Logic)
    - Unary operation
    - Binary operation
- _________ of inference, a function from sets of formulae to formulae (Mathematics, Logic)
- _________ of thumb, principle with broad application that is not intended to be strictly accurate or reliable for every situation. Also often simply referred to as a _________
- Moral, an atomic element of a moral code for guiding choices in human behavior
- Heuristic, a quantized '_________' which shows a tendency or probability for successful function
- A regulation, as in sports
- A Production _________, as in computer science
- Procedural law, a _________set governing the application of laws to cases
    - A law, which may informally be called a '_________'
    - A court ruling, a decision by a court
- In the U.S. Government, a regulation mandated by Congress, but written or expanded upon by the Executive Branch.
- Norm (sociology), an informal but widely accepted _________, concept, truth, definition, or qualification (social norms, legal norms, coding norms)
- Norm (philosophy), a kind of sentence or a reason to act, feel or believe
- 'Rulership' is the concept of governance by a government:
    - Military _________, governance by a military body
    - Monastic _________, a collection of precepts that guides the life of monks or nuns in a religious order where the superior holds the place of Christ
- Slide _________

- '_________,' a song by Ayumi Hamasaki
- '_________,' a song by rapper Nas
- '_________s,' an album by the band The Whitest Boy Alive
- _________s: Pyaar Ka Superhit Formula, a 2003 Bollywood film
- ruler, an instrument for measuring lengths
- _________, a component of an astrolabe, circumferator or similar instrument
- The _________s, a bestselling self-help book
- _________ Project (Run Up-to-date Linux Everywhere), a project that aims to use up-to-date Linux software on old PCs
- _________ engine, a software system that helps managing business _________s
- Ja _________, a hip hop artist
    - R.U.L.E., a 2005 greatest hits album by rapper Ja _________
- '_________s,' a KMFDM song

a. Procter ' Gamble
b. Demand
c. Rule
d. Technocracy

48. _________ are the prices that the factors of production of a finished item attract.

There has been some economic debate as to what determines these prices. Classical and Marxist economists argued that the _________ decided the value of a product and so value was intrinsic within the product.

a. Marginal product of labor
b. Marginal product
c. Productivity model
d. Factor prices

49. In economics, _________ is the total supply of goods and services produced by a national economy during a specific time period. It is the total amount of goods and services in the economy available at all possible price levels.

a. Aggregate expenditure
b. Aggregation problem
c. Aggregate demand
d. Aggregate supply

50. In economics, _________ is the ratio of the percent change in one variable to the percent change in another variable. It is a tool for measuring the responsiveness of a function to changes in parameters in a relative way. Commonly analyzed are _________ of substitution, price and wealth.

a. Elasticity
b. ACEA agreement
c. ACCRA Cost of Living Index
d. Elasticity of demand

51. In economics, the _________ is defined as a numerical measure of the responsiveness of the quantity supplied of product (A) to a change in price of product (A) alone. It is the measure of the way quantity supplied reacts to a change in price.

>

For example, if, in response to a 10% rise in the price of a good, the quantity supplied increases by 20%, the _________ would be 20%/10% = 2.

a. Demand shaping
b. Hedonimetry
c. Passive income
d. Price elasticity of supply

52. _________ refers to the stock of skills and knowledge embodied in the ability to perform labor so as to produce economic value. It is the skills and knowledge gained by a worker through education and experience.Many early economic theories refer to it simply as labor, one of three factors of production, and consider it to be a fungible resource -- homogeneous and easily interchangeable. Other conceptions of labor dispense with these assumptions.

a. Human capital
b. Law of increasing costs
c. Price theory
d. General equilibrium

53. The supply of labor is the number of total hours that workers wish to work at a given real wage rate.

_________ curves are derived from the 'labor-leisure' trade-off. More hours worked earn higher incomes but necessitate a cut in the amount of leisure that workers enjoy.

a. Human trafficking
b. Late capitalism
c. Creative capitalism
d. Labor supply

54. In algebra, a _________ is a function depending on n that associates a scalar, det(A), to an n×n square matrix A. The fundamental geometric meaning of a _________ is a scale factor for measure when A is regarded as a linear transformation. _________s are important both in calculus, where they enter the substitution rule for several variables, and in multilinear algebra.

For a fixed nonnegative integer n, there is a unique _________ function for the n×n matrices over any commutative ring R. In particular, this function exists when R is the field of real or complex numbers.

a. 100-year flood
b. 130-30 fund
c. 1921 recession
d. Determinant

55. _________ in economics refers to metrics and measures of output from production processes, per unit of input. Labor _________, for example, is typically measured as a ratio of output per labor-hour, an input. _________ may be conceived of as a metrics of the technical or engineering efficiency of production.

a. Production-possibility frontier
b. Fordism
c. Piece work
d. Productivity

56. In economics, economic equilibrium is simply a state of the world where economic forces are balanced and in the absence of external influences the (equilibrium) values of economic variables will not change. It is the point at which quantity demanded and quantity supplied are equal. _________, for example, refers to a condition where a market price is established through competition such that the amount of goods or services sought by buyers is equal to the amount of goods or services produced by sellers.

a. Regulated market
b. Marketization
c. Product-Market Growth Matrix
d. Market equilibrium

57. The _________ on a portfolio of investments takes into account not only the capital appreciation on the portfolio, but also the income received on the portfolio. The income typically consists of interest, dividends, and securities lending fees. This contrasts with the price return, which takes into account only the capital gain on an investment.

a. Profitability index
b. Micro venture capital
c. Chinese wall
d. Total return

58. In economics, the _________ is the wage rate that produces neither an access supply of workers nor an excess demand for workers and labor market. See economic equilibrium.

a. Equilibrium wage
b. International free trade agreement
c. Effective unemployment rate
d. Economic stability

59. Competition law, known in the United States as _________ law, has three main elements:

- prohibiting agreements or practices that restrict free trading and competition between business entities. This includes in particular the repression of cartels.
- banning abusive behaviour by a firm dominating a market, or anti-competitive practices that tend to lead to such a dominant position. Practices controlled in this way may include predatory pricing, tying, price gouging, refusal to deal, and many others.
- supervising the mergers and acquisitions of large corporations, including some joint ventures. Transactions that are considered to threaten the competitive process can be prohibited altogether, or approved subject to 'remedies' such as an obligation to divest part of the merged business or to offer licences or access to facilities to enable other businesses to continue competing.

The substance and practice of competition law varies from jurisdiction to jurisdiction. Protecting the interests of consumers (consumer welfare) and ensuring that entrepreneurs have an opportunity to compete in the market economy are often treated as important objectives. Competition law is closely connected with law on deregulation of access to markets, state aids and subsidies, the privatisation of state owned assets and the establishment of independent sector regulators. In recent decades, competition law has been viewed as a way to provide better public services.

a. United Kingdom competition law
b. Anti-Inflation Act
c. Intellectual property law
d. Antitrust

60. In mathematics, an _________ is a statement about the relative size or order of two objects, or about whether they are the same or not

- The notation a < b means that a is less than b.
- The notation a > b means that a is greater than b.
- The notation a ≠ b means that a is not equal to b, but does not say that one is greater than the other or even that they can be compared in size.

In each statement above, a is not equal to b. These relations are known as strict inequalities. The notation a < b may also be read as 'a is strictly less than b'.

a. Inequality
b. ACEA agreement
c. AD-IA Model
d. ACCRA Cost of Living Index

61. In economics, the _________ is the term economists use to describe the self-regulating nature of the marketplace. The _________ is a metaphor coined by the economist Adam Smith in The Wealth of Nations.

Adam Smith mentions the metaphor in Book IV of The Wealth of Nations, arguing that people in any society will certainly employ their capital in foreign trading only if the profits available by that method far exceed those available locally, and that in such a case it is better for society as a whole if they so did.

a. ACEA agreement
b. ACCRA Cost of Living Index
c. AD-IA Model
d. Invisible hand

62. _________ is a term used to describe a policy of allowing events to take their own course. The term is a French phrase literally meaning 'let do'. It is a doctrine that states that government generally should not intervene in the marketplace.

a. Theory of Productive Forces
b. Laissez-faire
c. Communization
d. Heroic capitalism

63. _________ is the shortage of common things such as food, clothing, shelter and safe drinking water, all of which determine the quality of life. It may also include the lack of access to opportunities such as education and employment which aid the escape from _________ and/or allow one to enjoy the respect of fellow citizens. According to Mollie Orshansky who developed the _________ measurements used by the U.S. government, 'to be poor is to be deprived of those goods and services and pleasures which others around us take for granted.' Ongoing debates over causes, effects and best ways to measure _________, directly influence the design and implementation of _________-reduction programs and are therefore relevant to the fields of public administration and international development.

a. Growth Elasticity of Poverty
b. Liberal welfare reforms
c. Poverty map
d. Poverty

1. The _________ was a period in the late 18th and early 19th centuries when major changes in agriculture, manufacturing, mining, and transportation had a profound effect on the socioeconomic and cultural conditions in Britain. The changes subsequently spread throughout Europe, North America, and eventually the world. The onset of the _________ marked a major turning point in human society; almost every aspect of daily life was eventually influenced in some way.

a. Adam Smith
b. Adolf Hitler
c. Adolph Fischer
d. Industrial Revolution

2. The term _________s refers to wages that have been adjusted for inflation. This term is used in contrast to nominal wages or unadjusted wages.

The use of adjusted figures is in undertaking some form of economic analysis.

a. Real wage
b. Living wage
c. Federal Wage System
d. Profit sharing

3. In algebra, a _________ is a function depending on n that associates a scalar, det(A), to an n×n square matrix A. The fundamental geometric meaning of a _________ is a scale factor for measure when A is regarded as a linear transformation. _________s are important both in calculus, where they enter the substitution rule for several variables, and in multilinear algebra.

For a fixed nonnegative integer n, there is a unique _________ function for the n×n matrices over any commutative ring R. In particular, this function exists when R is the field of real or complex numbers.

a. 130-30 fund
b. 100-year flood
c. 1921 recession
d. Determinant

4. A _________ is an expression that compares quantities relative to each other. The most common examples involve two quantities, but any number of quantities can be compared. _________s are represented mathematically by separating each quantity with a colon, for example the _________ 2:3, which is read as the _________ 'two to three'.

a. Y-intercept
b. Ratio
c. 100-year flood
d. 130-30 fund

5. _________ is an economic model based on price, utility and quantity in a market. It predicts that in a competitive market, price will function to equalize the quantity demanded by consumers, and the quantity supplied by producers, resulting in an economic equilibrium of price and quantity. The model incorporates other factors changing equilibrium as a shift of demand and/or supply.

a. Deferred gratification
b. Rational addiction
c. Joint demand
d. Supply and demand

6. Economics:

- _________,the desire to own something and the ability to pay for it
- _________ curve,a graphic representation of a _________ schedule
- _________ deposit, the money in checking accounts
- _________ pull theory,the theory that inflation occurs when _________ for goods and services exceeds existing supplies
- _________ schedule,a table that lists the quantity of a good a person will buy it each different price
- _________ side economics,the school of economics at believes government spending and tax cuts open economy by raising _________

.

a. Production
b. Variability
c. Demand
d. McKesson ' Robbins scandal

7. In economics, _________ refers to how the marginal contribution of a factor of production usually decreases as more of the factor is used. According to this relationship, in a production system with fixed and variable inputs, beyond some point, each additional unit of the variable input yields smaller and smaller increases in output. Conversely, producing one more unit of output costs more and more in variable inputs.

a. Patent troll
b. Community property
c. Diminishing returns
d. Derivatives law

8. _________ in economics refers to metrics and measures of output from production processes, per unit of input. Labor _________, for example, is typically measured as a ratio of output per labor-hour, an input. _________ may be conceived of as a metrics of the technical or engineering efficiency of production.

a. Fordism
b. Productivity
c. Piece work
d. Production-possibility frontier

9. A _________, reserve bank, or monetary authority is the entity responsible for the monetary policy of a country or of a group of member states. It is a bank that can lend money to other banks in times of need. Its primary responsibility is to maintain the stability of the national currency and money supply, but more active duties include controlling subsidized-loan interest rates, and acting as a lender of last resort to the banking sector during times of financial crisis (private banks often being integral to the national financial system.)

a. 130-30 fund
b. 1921 recession
c. Central bank
d. 100-year flood

10. A _________ is a group of people who share or are motivated by at least one common issue or interest, or work together on a specific project(s) to achieve a common objective. _________s are also characterised by attempts to share and exercise political and social power and to make decisions on a consensus-driven and egalitarian basis. _________s differ from cooperatives in that they are not necessarily focused upon an economic benefit or saving (but can be that as well.)

a. 100-year flood
b. 1921 recession
c. 130-30 fund
d. Collective

11. In organized labor, _________ is the method whereby workers organize together (usually in unions) to meet, converse, and negotiate upon the work conditions with their employers normally resulting in a written contract setting forth the wages, hours, and other conditions to be observed for a stipulated period.It is the practice in which union and company representatives meet to negotiate a new labor contract. In various national labor and employment law contexts, _________ takes on a more specific legal meaning and so, in a broad sense, however, it is the coming together of workers to negotiate their employment.

A collective agreement is a labor contract between an employer and one or more unions.

a. Designated Suppliers Program
b. Strikebreaker
c. Demarcation dispute
d. Collective bargaining

12. _________ is money accepted for exchange of goods in an economy. The prevalence of one money over another arises, usually, when a government designates through decrees that the government shall accept only particular notes and coins in payment for taxes. Typically, money of _________ consists of stamped coins and minted paper bills.

a. Security thread
b. Local currency
c. Totnes pound
d. Currency

13. _________s is the social science that studies the production, distribution, and consumption of goods and services. The term _________s comes from the Ancient Greek οá¼°κονομÎ¯α from οá¼¶κος (oikos, 'house') + νÏŒμος (nomos, 'custom' or 'law'), hence 'rules of the house(hold)'. Current _________ models developed out of the broader field of political economy in the late 19th century, owing to a desire to use an empirical approach more akin to the physical sciences.

a. Inflation
b. Economic
c. Energy economics
d. Opportunity cost

14. _________ is the increase in the amount of the goods and services produced by an economy over time. It is conventionally measured as the percent rate of increase in real gross domestic product, or real GDP. Growth is usually calculated in real terms, i.e. inflation-adjusted terms, in order to net out the effect of inflation on the price of the goods and services produced.

a. ACEA agreement
b. ACCRA Cost of Living Index
c. AD-IA Model
d. Economic growth

15. _________ or government expenditure is classified by economists into three main types. Government purchases of goods and services for current use are classed as government consumption. Government purchases of goods and services intended to create future benefits, such as infrastructure investment or research spending, are classed as government investment.

a. 130-30 fund
b. 100-year flood
c. 1921 recession
d. Government spending

16. _________ is the term denoting either an entrance or changes which are inserted into a system and which activate/modify a process. It is an abstract concept, used in the modeling, system(s) design and system(s) exploitation. It is usually connected with other terms, e.g., _________ field, _________ variable, _________ parameter, _________ value, _________ signal, _________ device and _________ file.

a. AD-IA Model
b. ACEA agreement
c. ACCRA Cost of Living Index
d. Input

17. _________ is a common concept in economics, and gives rise to derived concepts such as consumer debt. Generally _________ is defined by opposition to production. But the precise definition can vary because different schools of economists define production quite differently.

a. Foreclosure data providers
b. Consumption
c. Cash or share options
d. Federal Reserve Bank Notes

18. In economics, the people in the _________ are the suppliers of labor. The _________ is all the nonmilitary people who are employed or unemployed. In 2005, the worldwide _________ was over 3 billion people.

a. Grenelle agreements
b. Labor force
c. Departmentalization
d. Distributed workforce

19. _________ is an economic system in which wealth, and the means of producing wealth, are privately owned. Through _________, the land, labor, and capital are owned, operated, and traded for the purpose of generating profits, without force or fraud, by private individuals either singly or jointly, and investments, distribution, income, production, pricing and supply of goods, commodities and services are determined by voluntary private decision in a market economy. A distinguishing feature of _________ is that each person owns his or her own labor and therefore is allowed to sell the use of it to employers.

a. Capitalism
b. Late capitalism
c. Creative capitalism
d. Socialism for the rich and capitalism for the poor

20. _________ is a negative term describing an claimed capitalist economy in which success in business depends on close relationships between businesspeople and government officials. It may be exhibited in the distribution of legal permits, government grants, special tax breaks, and so forth.

_________ is believed to arise when political cronyism spills over into the business world; self-serving friendships and family ties between businessmen and the government influence the economy and society to the extent that it corrupts public-serving economic and political ideals.

a. Crony capitalism
b. 130-30 fund
c. Good governance
d. 100-year flood

21. A _________ is a duty imposed on goods when they are moved across a political boundary. They are usually associated with protectionism, the economic policy of restraining trade between nations. For political reasons, _________s are usually imposed on imported goods, although they may also be imposed on exported goods.

a. 1921 recession
b. 130-30 fund
c. 100-year flood
d. Tariff

22. _________ refers to discriminatory employment practices such as bias in hiring, promotion, job assignment, termination, and compensation, and various types of harassment.

In many countries, laws prohibit employers from discriminating on the basis of race, color, sex, religion, national origin, physical or mental disability, or age. There is also a growing body of law preventing or occasionally justifying _________ based on sexual orientation or gender identity.

a. Energy Independence and Security Act of 2007
b. Employment discrimination
c. Irish competition law
d. Impotent poor

23. _________ is the period of time that an individual spends at paid occupational labor. Unpaid labors such as housework are not considered part of the working week. Many countries regulate the work week by law, such as stipulating minimum daily rest periods, annual holidays and a maximum number of working hours per week.

a. 100-year flood
b. 1921 recession
c. 130-30 fund
d. Working time

24. In economics, the _________ is the change in consumption resulting from a change in real income.

Another important item that can change is the money income of the consumer. The _________ is the phenomenon observed through changes in purchasing power.

a. Equilibrium wage
b. Income effect
c. Inflation hedge
d. Export subsidy

25. The supply of labor is the number of total hours that workers wish to work at a given real wage rate.

_________ curves are derived from the 'labor-leisure' trade-off. More hours worked earn higher incomes but necessitate a cut in the amount of leisure that workers enjoy.

a. Creative capitalism
b. Late capitalism
c. Human trafficking
d. Labor supply

26. _________ to the arrival of new individuals into a habitat or population. It is a biological concept and is important in population ecology, differentiated from emigration and migration.

_________ is a modern phenomenon.

a. ACEA agreement
b. ACCRA Cost of Living Index
c. AD-IA Model
d. Immigration

27. In economics, the _________ measures the payments that flow between any individual country and all other countries. It is used to summarize all international economic transactions for that country during a specific time period, usually a year. The _________ is determined by the country's exports and imports of goods, services, and financial capital, as well as financial transfers.

a. Skyscraper Index
b. Gross world product
c. Gross domestic product per barrel
d. Balance of payments

28. In economic theory, _________ is the competitive situation in any market where the conditions necessary for perfect competition are not satisfied. It is a market structure that does not meet the conditions of perfect competition.

Forms of _________ include:

- Monopoly, in which there is only one seller of a good.
- Oligopoly, in which there is a small number of sellers.
- Monopolistic competition, in which there are many sellers producing highly differentiated goods.
- Monopsony, in which there is only one buyer of a good.
- Oligopsony, in which there is a small number of buyers.

There may also be _________ in markets due to buyers or sellers lacking information about prices and the goods being traded.

There may also be _________ due to a time lag in a market.

a. ACCRA Cost of Living Index
b. Imperfect competition
c. AD-IA Model
d. ACEA agreement

29. A _________ is the transfer of wealth from one party (such as a person or company) to another. A _________ is usually made in exchange for the provision of goods, services or both, or to fulfill a legal obligation.

The simplest and oldest form of _________ is barter, the exchange of one good or service for another.

a. Payment
b. Soft count
c. Going concern
d. Social gravity

30. _________ is a term used in labor economics to analyze the relation between the wage rate and the unpleasantness, risk, or other undesirable attributes of a particular job. A _________, which is also called a compensating wage differential or an equalizing difference, is defined as the additional amount of income that a given worker must be offered in order to motivate them to accept a given undesirable job, relative to other jobs that worker could perform. One can also speak of the _________ for an especially desirable job, or one that provides special benefits, but in this case the differential would be negative: that is, a given worker would be willing to accept a lower wage for an especially desirable job, relative to other jobs.

a. Compensating differential
b. Search theory
c. 100-year flood
d. Wage dispersion

31. A _________ is:

- Rewrite _________, in generative grammar and computer science
- Standardization, a formal and widely-accepted statement, fact, definition, or qualification
- Operation, a determinate _________ for performing a mathematical operation and obtaining a certain result (Mathematics, Logic)
  - Unary operation
  - Binary operation
- _________ of inference, a function from sets of formulae to formulae (Mathematics, Logic)
- _________ of thumb, principle with broad application that is not intended to be strictly accurate or reliable for every situation. Also often simply referred to as a _________
- Moral, an atomic element of a moral code for guiding choices in human behavior
- Heuristic, a quantized '_________' which shows a tendency or probability for successful function
- A regulation, as in sports
- A Production _________, as in computer science
- Procedural law, a _________set governing the application of laws to cases
  - A law, which may informally be called a '_________'
  - A court ruling, a decision by a court
- In the U.S. Government, a regulation mandated by Congress, but written or expanded upon by the Executive Branch.
- Norm (sociology), an informal but widely accepted _________, concept, truth, definition, or qualification (social norms, legal norms, coding norms)
- Norm (philosophy), a kind of sentence or a reason to act, feel or believe
- 'Rulership' is the concept of governance by a government:
  - Military _________, governance by a military body
  - Monastic _________, a collection of precepts that guides the life of monks or nuns in a religious order where the superior holds the place of Christ
- Slide _________

- '_________,' a song by Ayumi Hamasaki
- '_________,' a song by rapper Nas
- '_________s,' an album by the band The Whitest Boy Alive
- _________s: Pyaar Ka Superhit Formula, a 2003 Bollywood film
- ruler, an instrument for measuring lengths
- _________, a component of an astrolabe, circumferator or similar instrument
- The _________s, a bestselling self-help book
- _________ Project (Run Up-to-date Linux Everywhere), a project that aims to use up-to-date Linux software on old PCs
- _________ engine, a software system that helps managing business _________s
- Ja _________, a hip hop artist
  - R.U.L.E., a 2005 greatest hits album by rapper Ja _________
- '_________s,' a KMFDM song

a. Demand
b. Procter ' Gamble
c. Technocracy
d. Rule

32. _________ refers to the stock of skills and knowledge embodied in the ability to perform labor so as to produce economic value. It is the skills and knowledge gained by a worker through education and experience.Many early economic theories refer to it simply as labor, one of three factors of production, and consider it to be a fungible resource -- homogeneous and easily interchangeable. Other conceptions of labor dispense with these assumptions.

a. General equilibrium
b. Law of increasing costs
c. Price theory
d. Human capital

33. In economics, _________ is the active redirecting resources from being consumed today so that they may create benefits in the future; the use of assets to earn income or profit._________ is the process of making an investment in order to earn a profit, for example equity investment either through a fund, a 401k plan, or individually. People often invest in order to build up their estate or to accumulate funds for retirement.

To try to predict good stocks to invest in, two main schools of thought exist: technical analysis and fundamentals analysis.

a. ACEA agreement
b. AD-IA Model
c. ACCRA Cost of Living Index
d. Investing

34. In economics supernormal profit _________ or pure profit or excess profits, is a profit exceeding the normal profit. Normal profit equals the opportunity cost of labour and capital, while supernormal profit is the amount exceeds the normal return from these input factors in production.

_________ is usually generated by an oligopoly or a monopoly; however, these firms often try to hide this from the market to reduce risk of competition or antitrust investigation.

a. ACCRA Cost of Living Index
b. Economic profit
c. Accounting profit
d. Abnormal profit

35. The _________ captures an expanded spectrum of values and criteria for measuring organizational (and societal) success: economic, ecological and social. With the ratification of the United Nations and ICLEI _________ standard for urban and community accounting in early 2007, this became the dominant approach to public sector full cost accounting. Similar UN standards apply to natural capital and human capital measurement to assist in measurements required by _________, e.g. the ecoBudget standard for reporting ecological footprint.

a. Triple bottom line
b. Leapfrogging
c. Social welfare function
d. Missing market

36. Economic _________ is defined as an excess distribution to any factor in a production process above that which is required to induce the factor into the process or any excess above that which is necessary to keep the factor in its current use..

Classical Factor _________ is primarily concerned with the fee paid for the use of fixed (e.g. natural) resources. The classical definition is expressed as any excess payment above that required to induce or provide for production.

a. 100-year flood
b. 130-30 fund
c. 1921 recession
d. Rent

37. The _________ was one of the first federations of labor unions in the United States. It was founded in Columbus, Ohio in 1886 by Samuel Gompers as a reorganization of its predecessor, the Federation of Organized Trades and Labor Unions. Gompers became president of the AFL in 1886 and was reelected every year except one until his death on December 13, 1924.

a. AD-IA Model
b. American Federation of Labor
c. ACEA agreement
d. ACCRA Cost of Living Index

38. In economics, _________ describes the state of a market with respect to competition.

- Perfect competition, in which the market consists of a very large number of firms producing a homogeneous product.
- Monopolistic competition where there are a large number of independent firms which have a very small proportion of the market share.
- Oligopoly, in which a market is dominated by a small number of firms which own more than 40% of the market share.
- Oligopsony, a market dominated by many sellers and a few buyers.
- Monopoly, where there is only one provider of a product or service.
- Natural monopoly, a monopoly in which economies of scale cause efficiency to increase continuously with the size of the firm. A firm is a natural monopoly if it is able to serve the entire market demand at a lower cost than any combination of two or more smaller, more specialized firms.
- Monopsony, when there is only one buyer in a market.

The imperfectly competitive structure is quite identical to the realistic market conditions where some monopolistic competitors, monopolists, oligopolists, and duopolists exist and dominate the market conditions. The elements of _________ include the number and size distribution of firms, entry conditions, and the extent of differentiation.

These somewhat abstract concerns tend to determine some but not all details of a specific concrete market system where buyers and sellers actually meet and commit to trade.

a. Human capital
b. Labour economics
c. Monopolistic competition
d. Market structure

39. The American Federation of Labor and Congress of Industrial Organizations, commonly _________, is a national trade union center, the largest federation of unions in the United States, made up of 65 national and international unions (including Canadian), together representing more than 10 million workers. It was formed in 1955 when the AFL and the CIO merged after a long estrangement. From 1955 until 2005, the _________'s member unions represented nearly all unionized workers in the United States.

a. AD-IA Model
b. ACCRA Cost of Living Index
c. AFL-CIO
d. ACEA agreement

40. Competition law, known in the United States as _________ law, has three main elements:

- prohibiting agreements or practices that restrict free trading and competition between business entities. This includes in particular the repression of cartels.
- banning abusive behaviour by a firm dominating a market, or anti-competitive practices that tend to lead to such a dominant position. Practices controlled in this way may include predatory pricing, tying, price gouging, refusal to deal, and many others.
- supervising the mergers and acquisitions of large corporations, including some joint ventures. Transactions that are considered to threaten the competitive process can be prohibited altogether, or approved subject to 'remedies' such as an obligation to divest part of the merged business or to offer licences or access to facilities to enable other businesses to continue competing.

The substance and practice of competition law varies from jurisdiction to jurisdiction. Protecting the interests of consumers (consumer welfare) and ensuring that entrepreneurs have an opportunity to compete in the market economy are often treated as important objectives. Competition law is closely connected with law on deregulation of access to markets, state aids and subsidies, the privatisation of state owned assets and the establishment of independent sector regulators. In recent decades, competition law has been viewed as a way to provide better public services.

a. Antitrust
b. United Kingdom competition law
c. Intellectual property law
d. Anti-Inflation Act

41. The _________ proposed by John L. Lewis in 1932, was a federation of unions that organized workers in industrial unions in the United States and Canada from 1935 to 1955. The Taft-Hartley Act of 1947 required union leaders to swear that they were not Communists. Many CIO leaders refused to obey that requirement, later found unconstitutional.

a. Foreign direct investment
b. Congress of Industrial Organizations
c. Multinational corporation
d. Chinese correction

42. _________ refers to organizing a union in a manner that seeks to unify workers in a particular industry along the lines of the particular craft or trade that they work in by class or skill level. It contrasts with industrial unionism, in which all workers in the same industry are organized into the same union, regardless of differences in skill.

_________ is perhaps best exemplified by many of the construction unions that formed the backbone of the old American Federation of Labor (which later merged with the industrial unions of the Congress of Industrial Organizations to form the AFL-CIO.)

a. 130-30 fund
b. 1921 recession
c. 100-year flood
d. Craft unionism

43. The _________ of 1938 (_________, ch. 676, 52 Stat. 1060, June 25, 1938, 29 U.S.C.ch.8), also called the Wages and Hours Bill, is United States federal law that applies to employees engaged in interstate commerce or employed by an enterprise engaged in commerce or in the production of goods for commerce, unless the employer can claim an exemption from coverage.

a. Hostile work environment
b. Generalized System of Preferences
c. Fair Labor Standards Act
d. Habitability

44. _________ is a field of economics that studies the strategic behavior of firms, the structure of markets and their interactions. The study of _________ adds to the perfectly competitive model real-world frictions such as limited information, transaction cost, cost of adjusting prices, government actions, and barriers to entry by new firms into a market. It then considers how firms are organized and how they compete.

a. Inflation
b. Economic ideology
c. Economic
d. Industrial Organization

45. A trade union or _________ is an organization of workers who have banded together to achieve common goals in key areas and working conditions. The trade union, through its leadership, bargains with the employer on behalf of union members (rank and file members) and negotiates labor contracts (Collective bargaining) with employers. This may include the negotiation of wages, work rules, complaint procedures, rules governing hiring, firing and promotion of workers, benefits, workplace safety and policies.

a. Business valuation standards
b. Demand-side technologies
c. Labor union
d. Basis of futures

46. In economics, _________ is the ability of a firm to alter the market price of a good or service. A firm with _________ can raise prices without losing all customers to competitors.

When a firm has _________ it faces a downward-sloping demand curve.

a. Pacman conjecture
b. Market power
c. Revenue-cap regulation
d. Price makers

47. _________ in economic theory is the use of modern economic tools to study problems that are traditionally in the province of political science.

In particular, it studies the behavior of politicians and government officials as mostly self-interested agents and their interactions in the social system either as such or under alternative constitutional rules. These can be represented a number of ways, including standard constrained utility maximization, game theory, or decision theory.

a. Public interest theory
b. Paradox of voting
c. Rational ignorance
d. Public choice

48. In a _________ there is both a monopoly (a single seller) and monopsony (a single buyer) in the same market.

In such market price and output will be determined by the non economic forces like bargaining power of both buyer and seller. A _________ model is often used in situations where the switching costs of both sides are prohibitively high.

a. Market concentration
b. Revenue-cap regulation
c. Price takers
d. Bilateral monopoly

49. In finance, the _________ of a financial asset measures the sensitivity of the asset's price to interest rate movements. There are various definitions of _________ and derived quantities, discussed below. If not otherwise specified, '_________' generally means the Macaulay _________, as defined below.

a. Time value of money
b. 100-year flood
c. Newtonian time
d. Duration

50. In economics, a _________ exists when a specific individual or enterprise has sufficient control over a particular product or service to determine significantly the terms on which other individuals shall have access to it. Monopolies are thus characterized by a lack of economic competition for the good or service that they provide and a lack of viable substitute goods. The verb 'monopolize' refers to the process by which a firm gains persistently greater market share than what is expected under perfect competition.

a. Monopoly
b. 130-30 fund
c. 1921 recession
d. 100-year flood

51. A _________ or labor union is an organization of workers who have banded together to achieve common goals in key areas and working conditions. The _________, through its leadership, bargains with the employer on behalf of union members (rank and file members) and negotiates labor contracts (Collective bargaining) with employers. This may include the negotiation of wages, work rules, complaint procedures, rules governing hiring, firing and promotion of workers, benefits, workplace safety and policies.

a. Case-Shiller Home Price Indices
b. Consumer goods
c. Guaranteed investment contracts
d. Trade union

52. _________ and Keynesian Theory) is a macroeconomic theory based on the ideas of 20th-century British economist John Maynard Keynes. _________ argues that private sector decisions sometimes lead to inefficient macroeconomic outcomes and therefore advocates active policy responses by the public sector, including monetary policy actions by the central bank and fiscal policy actions by the government to stabilize output over the business cycle.

The theories forming the basis of _________ were first presented in The General Theory of Employment, Interest and Money, published in 1936.

a. Market failure
b. Keynesian economics
c. Rational choice theory
d. Deflation

53. A variety of measures of _________ and output are used in economics to estimate total economic activity in a country or region, including gross domestic product (GDP), gross national product (GNP), and net _________

There are three main ways of calculating these numbers; the output approach, the income approach and the expenditure approach. In theory, the three must yield the same, because total expenditures on goods and services must equal the total income paid to the producers (Gnational income), and that must also equal the total value of the output of goods and services (GNP.)

a. National income
b. Volume index
c. Gross world product
d. GNI per capita

54. _________ in political thought refers to economic theories of social organization advocating collective ownership and administration of the means of production and distribution of goods, and a society characterized by equality for all individuals, with an egalitarian method of compensation. Modern _________ originated in the late 19th-century intellectual and working class political movement that criticized the effects of industrialization and private ownership on society. Karl Marx posited that _________ would be achieved via class struggle and a proletarian revolution after a transitional stage from capitalism called the dictatorship of the proletariat.

a. Adam Smith
b. Socialism
c. Adolph Fischer
d. Adolf Hitler

55. _________ is a specific term used in companies' financial reporting from the company-whole point of view. Because that use excludes the effects of changing ownership interest, an economic measure of _________ is necessary for financial analysis from the shareholders' point of view

_________ is defined by the Financial Accounting Standards Board, or FASB, as e;the change in equity [net assets] of a business enterprise during a period from transactions and other events and circumstances from nonowner sources. It includes all changes in equity during a period except those resulting from investments by owners and distributions to owners.e;

_________ is the sum of net income and other items that must bypass the income statement because they have not been realized, including items like an unrealized holding gain or loss from available for sale securities and foreign currency translation gains or losses.

a. Net national income
b. Real income
c. Windfall gain
d. Comprehensive income

56. _________, in law and economics, is a form of risk management primarily used to hedge against the risk of a contingent loss. _________ is defined as the equitable transfer of the risk of a loss, from one entity to another, in exchange for a premium, and can be thought of as a guaranteed small loss to prevent a large, possibly devastating loss. An insurer is a company selling the _________; an insured or policyholder is the person or entity buying the _________.

a. ACCRA Cost of Living Index
b. ACEA agreement
c. Insurance
d. AD-IA Model

57. The _________ was a landmark piece of legislation in the United States that outlawed racial segregation in schools, public places, and employment.

a. Civil Rights Act of 1964
b. Patent portfolio
c. Le Chapelier Law
d. Postcautionary principle

58. In statistics, the _________ problem occurs when one considers a set of statistical inferences simultaneously. Errors in inference, including confidence intervals that fail to include their corresponding population parameters are more likely to occur when one considers the family as a whole. Several statistical techniques have been developed to prevent this from happening, allowing significance levels for single and _________ to be directly compared.

a. Hypotheses suggested by the data
b. Familywise error rate
c. Multiple comparisons
d. False discovery rate

59. The _________, a unit of the United States Department of Labor, is the principal fact-finding agency for the U.S. government in the broad field of labor economics and statistics. The BLS is an independent national statistical agency that collects, processes, analyzes, and disseminates essential statistical data to the American public, the U.S. Congress, other Federal agencies, State and local governments, business, and labor representatives. The BLS also serves as a statistical resource to the Department of Labor.

a. Gross national product
b. Gross world product
c. Gross Regional Product
d. Bureau of Labor Statistics

1. _________s is the social science that studies the production, distribution, and consumption of goods and services. The term _________s comes from the Ancient Greek oá¼°κονομÎ¯α from oá¼¶κος (oikos, 'house') + vÏŒμος (nomos, 'custom' or 'law'), hence 'rules of the house(hold)'. Current _________ models developed out of the broader field of political economy in the late 19th century, owing to a desire to use an empirical approach more akin to the physical sciences.

a. Opportunity cost
b. Energy economics
c. Inflation
d. Economic

2. An _________ or Å"conomic system is a system that involves the production, distribution and consumption of goods and services between the entities in a particular society. It is the method used by society to produce and distribute goods and services. The _________ is composed of people and institutions, including their relationships to productive resources, such as through the convention of property.

a. Information economy
b. Intention economy
c. Indicative planning
d. Economic system

3. _________ is an economic concept with commonplace familiarity. It is the price that a good or service is offered at, or will fetch, in the marketplace. It is of interest mainly in the study of microeconomics.

a. Paper trading
b. Noisy market hypothesis
c. Market anomaly
d. Market price

4. Economic _________ is defined as an excess distribution to any factor in a production process above that which is required to induce the factor into the process or any excess above that which is necessary to keep the factor in its current use..

Classical Factor _________ is primarily concerned with the fee paid for the use of fixed (e.g. natural) resources. The classical definition is expressed as any excess payment above that required to induce or provide for production.

a. 130-30 fund
b. Rent
c. 1921 recession
d. 100-year flood

5. Competition law, known in the United States as _________ law, has three main elements:

- prohibiting agreements or practices that restrict free trading and competition between business entities. This includes in particular the repression of cartels.
- banning abusive behaviour by a firm dominating a market, or anti-competitive practices that tend to lead to such a dominant position. Practices controlled in this way may include predatory pricing, tying, price gouging, refusal to deal, and many others.
- supervising the mergers and acquisitions of large corporations, including some joint ventures. Transactions that are considered to threaten the competitive process can be prohibited altogether, or approved subject to 'remedies' such as an obligation to divest part of the merged business or to offer licences or access to facilities to enable other businesses to continue competing.

The substance and practice of competition law varies from jurisdiction to jurisdiction. Protecting the interests of consumers (consumer welfare) and ensuring that entrepreneurs have an opportunity to compete in the market economy are often treated as important objectives. Competition law is closely connected with law on deregulation of access to markets, state aids and subsidies, the privatisation of state owned assets and the establishment of independent sector regulators. In recent decades, competition law has been viewed as a way to provide better public services.

a. United Kingdom competition law
b. Antitrust
c. Intellectual property law
d. Anti-Inflation Act

6. In economics, the _________ measures the payments that flow between any individual country and all other countries. It is used to summarize all international economic transactions for that country during a specific time period, usually a year. The _________ is determined by the country's exports and imports of goods, services, and financial capital, as well as financial transfers.

a. Skyscraper Index
b. Gross domestic product per barrel
c. Balance of payments
d. Gross world product

7. _________ is an economic system in which wealth, and the means of producing wealth, are privately owned. Through _________, the land, labor, and capital are owned, operated, and traded for the purpose of generating profits, without force or fraud, by private individuals either singly or jointly, and investments, distribution, income, production, pricing and supply of goods, commodities and services are determined by voluntary private decision in a market economy. A distinguishing feature of _________ is that each person owns his or her own labor and therefore is allowed to sell the use of it to employers.

a. Socialism for the rich and capitalism for the poor
b. Capitalism
c. Late capitalism
d. Creative capitalism

8. In economics supernormal profit _________ or pure profit or excess profits, is a profit exceeding the normal profit. Normal profit equals the opportunity cost of labour and capital, while supernormal profit is the amount exceeds the normal return from these input factors in production.

_________ is usually generated by an oligopoly or a monopoly; however, these firms often try to hide this from the market to reduce risk of competition or antitrust investigation.

a. ACCRA Cost of Living Index
b. Accounting profit
c. Abnormal profit
d. Economic profit

9. _________ describes a deliberate attempt to interfere with the free and fair operation of the market and create artificial, false or misleading appearances with respect to the price of a security, commodity or currency. _________ is prohibited under Section 9(a)(2) of the Securities Exchange Act of 1934, and in Australia under Section s 1041A of the Corporations Act 2001. The Act defines _________ as transactions which create an artificial price or maintain an artificial price for a tradable security.

a. Legal monopoly
b. Market manipulation
c. Managerial economics
d. Net domestic product

10. A _________ is the transfer of wealth from one party (such as a person or company) to another. A _________ is usually made in exchange for the provision of goods, services or both, or to fulfill a legal obligation.

The simplest and oldest form of _________ is barter, the exchange of one good or service for another.

a. Social gravity
b. Going concern
c. Payment
d. Soft count

11. _________ in economics and business is the result of an exchange and from that trade we assign a numerical monetary value to a good, service or asset. If Alice trades Bob 4 apples for an orange, the _________ of an orange is 4 apples. Inversely, the _________ of an apple is 1/4 oranges.

a. Price war
b. Price
c. Price book
d. Premium pricing

12. In microeconomics, _________ is quite simply the conversion of inputs into outputs. It is an economic process that uses resources to create a good or service that is suitable for exchange. This can include manufacturing, storing, shipping, and packaging.

a. Solved
b. Red Guards
c. Production
d. MET

13. _________ is a term in economics, where demand for one good or service occurs as a result of demand for another. This may occur as the former is a part of production of the second. For example, demand for coal leads to _________ for mining, as coal must be mined for coal to be consumed.

a. Rate risk
b. Leontief production function
c. Days Sales Outstanding
d. Derived demand

14. In economics, _________ describes demand that is not very sensitive to a change in price.

a. Inelastic
b. Effective unemployment rate
c. Inflation hedge
d. Export-led growth

15. In economics, the _________ is used to illustrate the idea that increases in the rate of taxation do not necessarily increase tax revenue. (For instance, whereas a 0% income tax rate will generate no revenue, neither will a 100% rate, as citizens will have no incentive to make money.) Increasing taxes beyond the peak of the curve point will decrease tax revenue.

a. 1921 recession
b. 130-30 fund
c. 100-year flood
d. Laffer curve

16. In economics, economic equilibrium is simply a state of the world where economic forces are balanced and in the absence of external influences the (equilibrium) values of economic variables will not change. It is the point at which quantity demanded and quantity supplied are equal. _________, for example, refers to a condition where a market price is established through competition such that the amount of goods or services sought by buyers is equal to the amount of goods or services produced by sellers.

a. Regulated market
b. Marketization
c. Product-Market Growth Matrix
d. Market equilibrium

17. Economics:

- _________,the desire to own something and the ability to pay for it
- _________ curve,a graphic representation of a _________ schedule
- _________ deposit, the money in checking accounts
- _________ pull theory,the theory that inflation occurs when _________ for goods and services exceeds existing supplies
- _________ schedule,a table that lists the quantity of a good a person will buy it each different price
- _________ side economics,the school of economics at believes government spending and tax cuts open economy by raising _________

.

a. McKesson ' Robbins scandal
b. Production
c. Variability
d. Demand

18. To _________ is to impose a financial charge or other levy upon a taxpayer by a state or the functional equivalent of a state.

_________es are also imposed by many subnational entities. _________es consist of direct _________ or indirect _________, and may be paid in money or as its labour equivalent (often but not always unpaid.)

a. 1921 recession
b. Tax
c. 100-year flood
d. 130-30 fund

19. To tax is to impose a financial charge or other levy upon a taxpayer by a state or the functional equivalent of a state.

_________ are also imposed by many subnational entities. _________ consist of direct tax or indirect tax, and may be paid in money or as its labour equivalent (often but not always unpaid.)

a. Taxes
b. 130-30 fund
c. 1921 recession
d. 100-year flood

20. _________ is the shortage of common things such as food, clothing, shelter and safe drinking water, all of which determine the quality of life. It may also include the lack of access to opportunities such as education and employment which aid the escape from _________ and/or allow one to enjoy the respect of fellow citizens. According to Mollie Orshansky who developed the _________ measurements used by the U.S. government, 'to be poor is to be deprived of those goods and services and pleasures which others around us take for granted.' Ongoing debates over causes, effects and best ways to measure _________, directly influence the design and implementation of _________-reduction programs and are therefore relevant to the fields of public administration and international development.

a. Growth Elasticity of Poverty
b. Liberal welfare reforms
c. Poverty
d. Poverty map

21. A _________ is:

- Rewrite _________, in generative grammar and computer science
- Standardization, a formal and widely-accepted statement, fact, definition, or qualification
- Operation, a determinate _________ for performing a mathematical operation and obtaining a certain result (Mathematics, Logic)
    - Unary operation
    - Binary operation
- _________ of inference, a function from sets of formulae to formulae (Mathematics, Logic)
- _________ of thumb, principle with broad application that is not intended to be strictly accurate or reliable for every situation. Also often simply referred to as a _________
- Moral, an atomic element of a moral code for guiding choices in human behavior
- Heuristic, a quantized '_________' which shows a tendency or probability for successful function
- A regulation, as in sports
- A Production _________, as in computer science
- Procedural law, a _________set governing the application of laws to cases
    - A law, which may informally be called a '_________'
    - A court ruling, a decision by a court
- In the U.S. Government, a regulation mandated by Congress, but written or expanded upon by the Executive Branch.
- Norm (sociology), an informal but widely accepted _________, concept, truth, definition, or qualification (social norms, legal norms, coding norms)
- Norm (philosophy), a kind of sentence or a reason to act, feel or believe
- 'Rulership' is the concept of governance by a government:
    - Military _________, governance by a military body
    - Monastic _________, a collection of precepts that guides the life of monks or nuns in a religious order where the superior holds the place of Christ
- Slide _________

- '_________,' a song by Ayumi Hamasaki
- '_________,' a song by rapper Nas
- '_________s,' an album by the band The Whitest Boy Alive
- _________s: Pyaar Ka Superhit Formula, a 2003 Bollywood film
- ruler, an instrument for measuring lengths
- _________, a component of an astrolabe, circumferator or similar instrument
- The _________s, a bestselling self-help book
- _________ Project (Run Up-to-date Linux Everywhere), a project that aims to use up-to-date Linux software on old PCs
- _________ engine, a software system that helps managing business _________s
- Ja _________, a hip hop artist
    - R.U.L.E., a 2005 greatest hits album by rapper Ja _________
- '_________s,' a KMFDM song

a. Technocracy
b. Procter ' Gamble
c. Demand
d. Rule

22. In Marxian economics, _________ originally referred to the means of production. Individuals, organizations and governments use _________ in the production of other goods or commodities. _________ include factories, machinery, tools, equipment, and various buildings which are used to produce other products for consumption.

a. Capital deepening
b. Capital goods
c. Capital intensive
d. Wealth inequality in the United States

23. In economics, _________ are the resources employed to produce goods and services. They facilitate production but do not become part of the product (as with raw materials) or significantly transformed by the production process (as with fuel used to power machinery.) To 19th century economists, the _________ were land (natural resources, gifts from nature), labor (the ability to work), and capital goods (human-made tools and equipment.)

a. Product Pipeline
b. Factors of production
c. Long-run
d. Hicks-neutral technical change

24. A _________ is an object whose consumption increases the utility of the consumer, for which the quantity demanded exceeds the quantity supplied at zero price. _________s are usually modeled as having diminishing marginal utility. The first individual purchase has high utility; the second has less.

a. Composite good
b. Merit good
c. Pie method
d. Good

25. In economics, _________ is a rise in the general level of prices of goods and services in an economy over a period of time. When the general price level rises, each unit of currency buys fewer goods and services; consequently, _________ is also a decline in the real value of money--a loss of purchasing power in the medium of exchange which is also the monetary unit of account in the economy. A chief measure of general price-level _________ is the general _________ rate, which is the percentage change in a general price index (normally the Consumer Price Index) over time.

a. Inflation
b. Energy economics
c. Economic
d. Opportunity cost

26. In finance, _________ rate of profit or sometimes just return, is the ratio of money gained or lost on an investment relative to the amount of money invested. The amount of money gained or lost may be referred to as interest, profit/loss, gain/loss, or net income/loss. The money invested may be referred to as the asset, capital, principal, or the cost basis of the investment.

a. Current ratio
b. Sortino ratio
c. Cost accrual ratio
d. Rate of return

27. In business and accounting, _________ are everything of value that is owned by a person or company. It is a claim on the property your income of a borrower. The balance sheet of a firm records the monetary value of the _________ owned by the firm.

a. ACEA agreement
b. Amortization schedule
c. Assets
d. ACCRA Cost of Living Index

28. In financial accounting, a _________ or statement of financial position is a summary of a person's or organization's balances. Assets, liabilities and ownership equity are listed as of a specific date, such as the end of its financial year. A _________ is often described as a snapshot of a company's financial condition.

a. 1921 recession
b. Balance sheet
c. 100-year flood
d. 130-30 fund

29. _________ is a three-volume work on finance published by Austrian economist Eugen von Böhm-Bawerk.

The first two volumes were published in the 1880s when he was teaching at the University of Innsbruck.

The first volume of _________, titled History and Critique of Interest Theories (1884), is an exhaustive survey of the alternative treatments of the phenomenon of interest: use theories, productivity theories, abstinence theories, and many more.

a. The Bell Curve
b. Capital and interest
c. Development as Freedom
d. The General Theory of Employment, Interest and Money

30. In finance, the _________ is the system that allows the transfer of money between savers and borrowers.

Put another way: the _________ is a set of complex and closely interconnected financial institutions, markets, instruments, services, practices, and transactions.

a. Lean consumption
b. Financial system
c. Foreign investment
d. Hedonimetry

31. _________ is a fee paid on borrowed assets. It is the price paid for the use of borrowed money , or, money earned by deposited funds . Assets that are sometimes lent with _________ include money, shares, consumer goods through hire purchase, major assets such as aircraft, and even entire factories in finance lease arrangements.

a. Insolvency
b. Internal debt
c. Asset protection
d. Interest

32. An _________ is the price a borrower pays for the use of money they do not own, for instance a small company might borrow from a bank to kick start their business, and the return a lender receives for deferring the use of funds, by lending it to the borrower. _________s are normally expressed as a percentage rate over the period of one year.

_________s targets are also a vital tool of monetary policy and are used to control variables like investment, inflation, and unemployment.

a. Enterprise value
b. Arrow-Debreu model
c. Interest rate
d. ACCRA Cost of Living Index

33. In finance, a _________ is a debt security, in which the authorized issuer owes the holders a debt and, depending on the terms of the _________, is obliged to pay interest (the coupon) and/or to repay the principal at a later date, termed maturity. A _________ is a formal contract to repay borrowed money with interest at fixed intervals.

Thus a _________ is like a loan: the issuer is the borrower (debtor), the holder is the lender (creditor), and the coupon is the interest.

a. Zero-coupon
b. Callable
c. Prize Bond
d. Bond

34. In finance and economics _________ or nominal rate of interest refers to the rate of interest before adjustment for inflation (in contrast with the real interest rate); or, for interest rates 'as stated' without adjustment for the full effect of compounding (also referred to as the nominal annual rate.) An interest rate is called nominal if the frequency of compounding (e.g. a month) is not identical to the basic time unit (normally a year.)

The real interest rate includes compensation for the lender's lost value due to inflation, whereas the _________ excludes inflation.

a. Risk-free interest rate
b. Nominal interest rate
c. Fixed interest
d. London Interbank Offered Rate

35. _________ is the value on a given date of a future payment or series of future payments, discounted to reflect the time value of money and other factors such as investment risk. _________ calculations are widely used in business and economics to provide a means to compare cash flows at different times on a meaningful 'like to like' basis.

Money value fluctuates over time: $100 today are not worth $100 in five years.

a. Future value
b. Tax shield
c. Present value of costs
d. Present value

36. The '_________' is approximately the nominal interest rate minus the inflation rate Since the inflation rate over the course of a loan is not known initially, volatility in inflation represents a risk to both the lender and the borrower.

In economics and finance, an individual who lends money for repayment at a later point in time expects to be compensated for the time value of money, or not having the use of that money while it is lent.

a. Cost-push inflation
b. Core inflation
c. Reflation
d. Real interest rate

37. _________ is the a method of technical and economic research of the systems for purpose to optimize a parity between system's consumer functions or properties and expenses to achieve those functions or properties.

This methodology for continuous perfection of production, industrial technologies, organizational structures was developed by Juryj Sobolev in 1948 at the 'Perm telephone factory'

- 1948 Juryj Sobolev - the first success in application of a method analysis at the 'Perm telephone factory' .
- 1949 - the first application for the invention as result of use of the new method.

Today in economically developed countries practically each enterprise or the company use methodology of the kind of functional-cost analysis as a practice of the quality management, most full satisfying to principles of standards of series ISO 9000.

- Interest of consumer not in products itself, but the advantage which it will receive from its usage.
- The consumer aspires to reduce his expenses
- Functions needed by consumer can be executed in the various ways, and, hence, with various efficiency and expenses. Among possible alternatives of realization of functions exist such in which the parity of quality and the price is the optimal for the consumer.

The goal of _________ is achievement of the highest consumer satisfaction of production at simultaneous decrease in all kinds of industrial expenses Classical _________ has three English synonyms - Value Engineering, Value Management, Value Analysis.

a. Monopoly wage
b. Staple financing
c. Willingness to pay
d. Function cost analysis

38. _________ is a financial mechanism in which a debtor obtains the right to delay payments to a creditor, for a defined period of time, in exchange for a charge or fee. Essentially, the party that owes money in the present purchases the right to delay the payment until some future date. The discount, or charge, is simply the difference between the original amount owed in the present and the amount that has to be paid in the future to settle the debt.

a. Discounting
b. Maximum life span
c. Generalized linear model
d. Certified Risk Manager

39. A _________ is an annuity that has no definite end, or a stream of cash payments that continues forever. There are few actual perpetuities in existence (although the British government has issued them in the past, and they are known and still trade as consols.) A number of types of investments are effectively perpetuities, such as real estate and preferred stock, and techniques for valuing a _________ can be applied to establish price.

a. Discount rate
b. Current yield
c. Heath-Jarrow-Morton framework
d. Perpetuity

40. In algebra, a _________ is a function depending on n that associates a scalar, det(A), to an n×n square matrix A. The fundamental geometric meaning of a _________ is a scale factor for measure when A is regarded as a linear transformation. _________s are important both in calculus, where they enter the substitution rule for several variables, and in multilinear algebra.

For a fixed nonnegative integer n, there is a unique _________ function for the n×n matrices over any commutative ring R. In particular, this function exists when R is the field of real or complex numbers.

a. Determinant
b. 130-30 fund
c. 1921 recession
d. 100-year flood

41. An _________ is a person who has possession of an enterprise and assumes significant accountability for the inherent risks and the outcome. It is an ambitious leader who combines land, labor, and capital to create and market new goods or services. The term is a loanword from French and was first defined by the Irish economist Richard Cantillon.

a. ACCRA Cost of Living Index
b. ACEA agreement
c. Entrepreneur
d. Expansionary policies

42. _________ is the concept or idea of fairness in economics, particularly as to taxation or welfare economics.

In welfare economics, _________ may be distinguished from economic efficiency in overall evaluation of social welfare. Although '_________' has broader uses, it may be posed as a counterpart to economic inequality in yielding a 'good' distribution of welfare.

a. ACEA agreement
b. ACCRA Cost of Living Index
c. AD-IA Model
d. Equity

43. An _________ is a risk that meets the ideal criteria for efficient insurance. The concept of _________ underlies nearly all insurance decisions.

For a risk to be insurable, several things need to be true:

- The insurer must be able to charge a premium high enough to cover not only claims expenses, but also to cover the insurer's expenses. In other words, the risk cannot be catastrophic, or so large that no insurer could hope to pay for the loss.
- The nature of the loss must be definite and financially measurable. That is, there should not be room for argument as to whether or not payment is due, nor as to what amount the payment should be.

a. Actuary
b. Insurable risk
c. Ogden tables
d. Extreme value theory

44. In economics, a _________ occurs when, due to the economies of scale of a particular industry, the maximum efficiency of production and distribution is realized through a single supplier.

Natural monopolies arise where the largest supplier in an industry, often the first supplier in a market, has an overwhelming cost advantage over other actual or potential competitors. This tends to be the case in industries where capital costs predominate, creating economies of scale which are large in relation to the size of the market, and hence high barriers to entry; examples include water services and electricity.

a. Privatizing profits and socializing losses
b. Collective goods
c. Common-pool resource
d. Natural monopoly

45. _________ or economic opportunity loss is the value of the next best alternative foregone as the result of making a decision. _________ analysis is an important part of a company's decision-making processes but is not treated as an actual cost in any financial statement. The next best thing that a person can engage in is referred to as the _________ of doing the best thing and ignoring the next best thing to be done.

a. Opportunity cost
b. Economic
c. Economic ideology
d. Industrial organization

46. In finance, _________, also sometimes called market risk, aggregate risk is the risk associated with aggregate market returns. _________ is a risk of security that cannot be reduced through diversification. It should not be confused with systemic risk, which is the risk that the entire financial system will collapse as a result of some catastrophic event.

a. Systematic risk
b. Global Depository Receipt
c. Cleanup clause
d. Concentration risk

47. _________ is the development of economic wealth of countries or regions for the well-being of their inhabitants. It is the process by which a nation improves the economic, political, and social well being of its people. From a policy perspective, _________ can be defined as efforts that seek to improve the economic well-being and quality of life for a community by creating and/or retaining jobs and supporting or growing incomes and the tax base.

a. Experimental economics
b. Economic development
c. Economic methodology
d. Inflation

48. _________ represents the total cash investment that shareholders and debtholders have made in a company. There are two different but completely equivalent methods for calculating _________. The operating approach is calculated as:

_________ = Operating Net Working Capital + Net PP'E + Capitalized Operating Leases + Other Operating Assets + Operating Intangibles - Other Operating Liabilities - Cumulative Adjustment for Amortization of R'D

Equivalently, the financing approach is calculated as:

In symbols:

$$K = D + E - M$$

_________ is used in several important measurements of financial performance, including return on _________, economic value added, and free cash flow.

a. Operating margin
b. Invested capital
c. Asset turnover
d. Average propensity to consume

49. In economics, a _________ exists when a specific individual or enterprise has sufficient control over a particular product or service to determine significantly the terms on which other individuals shall have access to it. Monopolies are thus characterized by a lack of economic competition for the good or service that they provide and a lack of viable substitute goods. The verb 'monopolize' refers to the process by which a firm gains persistently greater market share than what is expected under perfect competition.

a. 100-year flood
b. 1921 recession
c. Monopoly
d. 130-30 fund

50. In law and economics, the _________, describes the economic efficiency of an economic allocation or outcome in the presence of externalities. The theorem states that when trade in an externality is possible and there are no transaction costs, bargaining will lead to an efficient outcome regardless of the initial allocation of property rights. In practice, obstacles to bargaining or poorly defined property rights can prevent Coasian bargaining.

a. Prior appropriation water rights
b. Means test
c. Coase theorem
d. General Mining Act of 1872

51. _________ is a common concept in economics, and gives rise to derived concepts such as consumer debt. Generally _________ is defined by opposition to production. But the precise definition can vary because different schools of economists define production quite differently.

a. Foreclosure data providers
b. Cash or share options
c. Federal Reserve Bank Notes
d. Consumption

52. In economics, _________ refers to how the marginal contribution of a factor of production usually decreases as more of the factor is used. According to this relationship, in a production system with fixed and variable inputs, beyond some point, each additional unit of the variable input yields smaller and smaller increases in output. Conversely, producing one more unit of output costs more and more in variable inputs.

a. Community property
b. Patent troll
c. Derivatives law
d. Diminishing returns

53. In economics, _________ is the total demand for final goods and services in the economy (Y) at a given time and price level. It is the amount of goods and services in the economy that will be purchased at all possible price levels. This is the demand for the gross domestic product of a country when inventory levels are static.

a. Aggregation problem
b. Aggregate expenditure
c. Aggregate supply
d. Aggregate demand

54. In economics, _________ is the total supply of goods and services produced by a national economy during a specific time period. It is the total amount of goods and services in the economy available at all possible price levels.

a. Aggregate demand
b. Aggregation problem
c. Aggregate supply
d. Aggregate expenditure

55. The _________ is 'the basic residential unit in which economic production, consumption, inheritance, child rearing, and shelter are organized and carried out'; [the _________] 'may or may not be synonomous with family'.

The _________ is the basic unit of analysis in many social, microeconomic and government models. The term refers to all individuals who live in the same dwelling.

a. Household
b. 130-30 fund
c. Family economics
d. 100-year flood

56. _________ is defined as the measure of responsiveness in the quantity demanded for a commodity as a result of change in price of the same commodity. It is a measure of how consumers react to a change in price. In other words, it is percentage change in quantity demanded as per the percentage change in price of the same commodity.

a. 130-30 fund
b. 1921 recession
c. Price elasticity of demand
d. 100-year flood

57. In economics, the _________ is defined as a numerical measure of the responsiveness of the quantity supplied of product (A) to a change in price of product (A) alone. It is the measure of the way quantity supplied reacts to a change in price.

>

For example, if, in response to a 10% rise in the price of a good, the quantity supplied increases by 20%, the _________ would be 20%/10% = 2.

a. Demand shaping
b. Passive income
c. Hedonimetry
d. Price elasticity of supply

58. _________ is an economic model based on price, utility and quantity in a market. It predicts that in a competitive market, price will function to equalize the quantity demanded by consumers, and the quantity supplied by producers, resulting in an economic equilibrium of price and quantity. The model incorporates other factors changing equilibrium as a shift of demand and/or supply.

a. Deferred gratification
b. Joint demand
c. Supply and demand
d. Rational addiction

59. _________ is a term used in economics to describe an economy where capital per worker is increasing. A process of increasing the amount of capital per worker. It is an increase in the capital intensity.

a. Capital expenditure
b. Firm-specific infrastructure
c. Capital formation
d. Capital deepening

60. In economics, _________ is the ratio of the percent change in one variable to the percent change in another variable. It is a tool for measuring the responsiveness of a function to changes in parameters in a relative way. Commonly analyzed are _________ of substitution, price and wealth.

a. ACEA agreement
b. Elasticity
c. ACCRA Cost of Living Index
d. Elasticity of demand

61. Price _________ is defined as the measure of responsiveness in the quantity demanded for a commodity as a result of change in price of the same commodity. It is a measure of how consumers react to a change in price. In other words, it is percentage change in quantity demanded by the percentage change in price of the same commodity.

a. Elasticity
b. ACCRA Cost of Living Index
c. ACEA agreement
d. Elasticity of demand

62. In economics, the _________ or marginal physical product is the extra output produced by one more unit of an input (for instance, the difference in output when a firm's labour is increased from five to six units.) Assuming that no other inputs to production change, the _________ of a given input (X) can be expressed as:

_________ = $\Delta Y/\Delta X$ = (the change of Y)/(the change of X.)

-
    -
        - Pending approval by Thomas Sowell***

In neoclassical economics, this is the mathematical derivative of the production function.... Note that the 'product' (Y) is typically defined ignoring external costs and benefits.

a. Marginal product
b. Labor problem
c. Productive capacity
d. Factor prices

63. _________ is the additional output resulting from the use of an additional unit of capital (ceteris paribus assuming all other factors are fixed.) It equals to 1 divided by the Incremental Capital-Output Ratio.

a. Loan officer
b. Buy-write
c. CAN SLIM
d. Marginal product of capital

64. In economics, the concept of the _________ refers to the decision-making time frame of a firm in which at least one factor of production is fixed. Costs which are fixed in the _________ have no impact on a firms decisions. For example a firm can raise output by increasing the amount of labour through overtime.

a. Short-run
b. Hicks-neutral technical change
c. Product Pipeline
d. Productivity model

65. In economic models, the _________ time frame assumes no fixed factors of production. Firms can enter or leave the marketplace, and the cost (and availability) of land, labor, raw materials, and capital goods can be assumed to vary. In contrast, in the short-run time frame, certain factors are assumed to be fixed, because there is not sufficient time for them to change.

a. Productivity world
b. Diseconomies of scale
c. Price/performance ratio
d. Long-run

66. The term _________s refers to wages that have been adjusted for inflation. This term is used in contrast to nominal wages or unadjusted wages.

The use of adjusted figures is in undertaking some form of economic analysis.

a. Profit sharing
b. Living wage
c. Federal Wage System
d. Real wage

67. A _________ is the minimum difference a person requires to be willing to take an uncertain bet, between the expected value of the bet and the certain value that he is indifferent to.

The certainty equivalent is the guaranteed payoff at which a person is 'indifferent' between accepting the guaranteed payoff and a higher but uncertain payoff. (It is the amount of the higher payout minus the _________.)

a. Risk premium
b. Ruin theory
c. Workers compensation
d. Linear model

68. A _________ is an expression that compares quantities relative to each other. The most common examples involve two quantities, but any number of quantities can be compared. _________s are represented mathematically by separating each quantity with a colon, for example the _________ 2:3, which is read as the _________ 'two to three'.

a. 100-year flood
b. 130-30 fund
c. Y-intercept
d. Ratio

69. The term '_________' refers to the concept of collecting information and attempting to spot a pattern in the information. In some fields of study, the term '_________' has more formally-defined meanings.

In project management _________ is a mathematical technique that uses historical results to predict future outcome.

a. Probit model
b. Coefficient of determination
c. Quantile regression
d. Trend analysis

70. _________ is a situation in which the limited resources of a firm are allocated in accordance with the wishes of consumers. An allocatively efficient economy produces an 'optimal mix' of commodities. A firm is allocatively efficient when its price is equal to its marginal costs (that is, P = MC) in a perfect market.

a. Allocative efficiency
b. Economic efficiency
c. ACEA agreement
d. ACCRA Cost of Living Index

71. In economics, a _________ is a mechanism that allows people to easily buy and sell (trade) financial securities (such as stocks and bonds), commodities (such as precious metals or agricultural goods), and other fungible items of value at low transaction costs and at prices that reflect the efficient-market hypothesis.

_________s have evolved significantly over several hundred years and are undergoing constant innovation to improve liquidity.

Both general markets (where many commodities are traded) and specialized markets (where only one commodity is traded) exist.

a. Financial market
b. Market anomaly
c. Convertible arbitrage
d. Noise trader

72. In economics, _________ is how a natione;s total economy is distributed among its population. ._________ has always been a central concern of economic theory and economic policy. Classical economists such as Adam Smith, Thomas Malthus and David Ricardo were mainly concerned with factor _________, that is, the distribution of income between the main factors of production, land, labour and capital.

a. Equipment trust certificate
b. Authorised capital
c. Eco commerce
d. Income distribution

73. The _________ is the market for securities, where companies and governments can raise longterm funds. It is a market in which money is lent for periods longer than a year. The _________ includes the stock market and the bond market.

a. Performance attribution
b. Multi-family office
c. Financial instrument
d. Capital market

74. In financial accounting, the _________ is one of the accounts in shareholders' equity. Sole proprietorships have a single _________ in the owner's equity. Partnerships maintain a _________ for each of the partners.

a. Compensation of employees
b. Capital account
c. Current account
d. Net national product

75. In economics, accounting and Marxian economics, _________ is often equated with investment of profit income, especially in real capital goods. The concentration and centralisation of capital are two of the results of such accumulation

But _________ can refer variously to

- working and consuming less than earned
- relying on the effects of compound interest to increase initial capital
- real investment in tangible means of production.
- financial investment in assets represented on paper.
- investment in non-productive physical assets such as residential real estate that appreciate in value.
- consuming less than produced by productive assets like farm land--saving or accumulating the residual
- 'human _________,' i.e., new education and training increasing the skills of the labour force.

Non-financial and financial _________ is usually needed for economic growth, since additional production usually requires additional funds to enlarge the scale of production. Smarter and more productive organization of production can also increase production without increased capital.

a. Productive force
b. Cultural Marxism
c. Marxian economics
d. Capital accumulation

76. _________ are the prices that the factors of production of a finished item attract.

There has been some economic debate as to what determines these prices. Classical and Marxist economists argued that the _________ decided the value of a product and so value was intrinsic within the product.

a. Productivity model
b. Marginal product
c. Marginal product of labor
d. Factor prices

77. In mathematics, an _________ is a statement about the relative size or order of two objects, or about whether they are the same or not

- The notation $a < b$ means that a is less than b.
- The notation $a > b$ means that a is greater than b.
- The notation $a \neq b$ means that a is not equal to b, but does not say that one is greater than the other or even that they can be compared in size.

In each statement above, a is not equal to b. These relations are known as strict inequalities. The notation $a < b$ may also be read as 'a is strictly less than b'.

a. AD-IA Model
b. ACCRA Cost of Living Index
c. ACEA agreement
d. Inequality

78. A _________ is an economy based on the division of labor in which the prices of goods and services are determined in a free price system set by supply and demand. This is often contrasted with a planned economy, in which a central government determines the price of goods and services using a fixed price system. Market economies are contrasted with mixed economy where the price system is not entirely free but under some government control that is not extensive enough to constitute a planned economy.

a. Commons-based peer production
b. Nutritional Economics
c. Network Economy
d. Market economy

79. _________ was a survey conducted by the U.S. Department of Justice to gauge the prevalence of alcohol and illegal drug use among prior arrestees. It was a reformulation of the prior Drug Use Forecasting (DUF) program, focused on five drugs in particular: cocaine, marijuana, methamphetamine, opiates, and PCP.

Participants were randomly selected from arrest records in major metropolitan areas; because no personally identifying information is taken from each record chosen, the resulting data can be correlated to arrest rates, but not to the total population of persons charged.

a. ACCRA Cost of Living Index
b. ACEA agreement
c. AD-IA Model
d. Arrestee Drug Abuse Monitoring

80. _________ theory is a branch of theoretical economics. It seeks to explain the behavior of supply, demand and prices in a whole economy with several or many markets. It is often assumed that agents are price takers and in that setting two common notions of equilibrium exist: Walrasian (or competitive) equilibrium, and its generalization; a price equilibrium with transfers.

a. Human capital
b. Rational choice theory
c. New Keynesian economics
d. General equilibrium

81. In economic theory, _________ is the competitive situation in any market where the conditions necessary for perfect competition are not satisfied. It is a market structure that does not meet the conditions of perfect competition.

Forms of _________ include:

- Monopoly, in which there is only one seller of a good.
- Oligopoly, in which there is a small number of sellers.
- Monopolistic competition, in which there are many sellers producing highly differentiated goods.
- Monopsony, in which there is only one buyer of a good.
- Oligopsony, in which there is a small number of buyers.

There may also be _________ in markets due to buyers or sellers lacking information about prices and the goods being traded.

There may also be _________ due to a time lag in a market.

a. AD-IA Model
b. Imperfect competition
c. ACCRA Cost of Living Index
d. ACEA agreement

82. In economics, the _________ is the term economists use to describe the self-regulating nature of the marketplace. The _________ is a metaphor coined by the economist Adam Smith in The Wealth of Nations.

Adam Smith mentions the metaphor in Book IV of The Wealth of Nations, arguing that people in any society will certainly employ their capital in foreign trading only if the profits available by that method far exceed those available locally, and that in such a case it is better for society as a whole if they so did.

a. ACCRA Cost of Living Index
b. ACEA agreement
c. AD-IA Model
d. Invisible hand

83. _________ is an important concept in economics with broad applications in game theory, engineering and the social sciences. The term is named after Vilfredo Pareto, an Italian economist who used the concept in his studies of economic efficiency and income distribution. Informally, pareto efficient situations are those in which any change to make any person better off would make someone else worse off.

a. Perfect rationality
b. Pareto efficiency
c. Lump of labour
d. Matching pennies

84. The _________ refers to the 'common well-being' or 'general welfare.' The _________ is central to policy debates, politics, democracy and the nature of government itself. While nearly everyone claims that aiding the common well-being or general welfare is positive, there is little, if any, consensus on what exactly constitutes the _________.

There are different views on how many members of the public must benefit from an action before it can be declared to be in the _________: at one extreme, an action has to benefit every single member of society in order to be truly in the _________; at the other extreme, any action can be in the _________ as long as it benefits some of the population and harms none.

a. Second-class citizen
b. Stealth tax
c. Public interest
d. Power Elite

85. _________ was a Scottish moral philosopher and a pioneer of political economy. One of the key figures of the Scottish Enlightenment, Smith is the author of The Theory of Moral Sentiments and An Inquiry into the Nature and Causes of the Wealth of Nations. The latter, usually abbreviated as The Wealth of Nations, is considered his magnum opus and the first modern work of economics.

a. Adam Smith
b. Adolf Hitler
c. Alan Greenspan
d. Adolph Fischer

86. In neoclassical economics and microeconomics, _________ describes the perfect being a market in which there are many small firms, all producing homogeneous goods. In the short term, such markets are productively inefficient as output will not occur where mc is equal to ac, but allocatively efficient, as output under _________ will always occur where mc is equal to mr, and therefore where mc equals ar. However, in the long term, such markets are both allocatively and productively efficient.

a. General equilibrium
b. Perfect competition
c. Law of supply
d. Co-operative economics

87. In economics, the term _________ of income or _________ refers to a simple economic model which describes the reciprocal circulation of income between producers and consumers. In the _________ model, the inter-dependent entities of producer and consumer are referred to as 'firms' and 'households' respectively and provide each other with factors in order to facilitate the flow of income. Firms provide consumers with goods and services in exchange for consumer expenditure and 'factors of production' from households.

a. 100-year flood
b. Circular flow
c. 1921 recession
d. 130-30 fund

88. _________ refers to the state of not requiring any outside aid, support for survival; it is therefore a type of personal or collective autonomy. On a large scale, a totally self-sufficient economy that does not trade with the outside world is called an autarky.

The term _________ is usually applied to varieties of sustainable living in which nothing is consumed outside of what is produced by the self-sufficient individuals.

a. Sustainability science
b. Global Reporting Initiative
c. Self-sufficiency
d. Sustainable forest management

89. A _________ is a type of economic equilibrium, where the clearance on the market of some specific goods is obtained independently from prices and quantities demanded and supplied in other markets. In other words, the prices of all substitutes and complements, as well as income levels of consumers are constant. Here the dynamic process is that prices adjust until supply equals demand.

a. Market system
b. Horizontal market
c. Market depth
d. Partial equilibrium

90. _________ is a broad label that refers to any individuals or households that use goods and services generated within the economy. The concept of a _________ is used in different contexts, so that the usage and significance of the term may vary.

Typically when business people and economists talk of _________s they are talking about person as _________, an aggregated commodity item with little individuality other than that expressed in the buy/not-buy decision.

a. 100-year flood
b. 130-30 fund
c. 1921 recession
d. Consumer

91. The _________ consists of a number of economic theories which describe the nature of the firm, company including its existence, its behaviour, and its relationship with the market.

In simplified terms, the _________ aims to answer these questions:

1. Existence - why do firms emerge, why are not all transactions in the economy mediated over the market?
2. Boundaries - why the boundary between firms and the market is located exactly there? Which transactions are performed internally and which are negotiated on the market?
3. Organization - why are firms structured in such specific way? What is the interplay of formal and informal relationships?

Despite looking simple, these questions are not answered by the established economic theory, which usually views firms as given, and treats them as black boxes without any internal structure.

The First World War period saw a change of emphasis in economic theory away from industry-level analysis which mainly included analysing markets to analysis at the level of the firm, as it became increasingly clear that perfect competition was no longer an adequate model of how firms behaved. Economic theory till then had focussed on trying to understand markets alone and there had been little study on understanding why firms or organisations exist.

a. Policy Ineffectiveness Proposition
b. Technology gap
c. Khazzoom-Brookes postulate
d. Theory of the firm

92. _________ is the term denoting either an entrance or changes which are inserted into a system and which activate/modify a process. It is an abstract concept, used in the modeling, system(s) design and system(s) exploitation. It is usually connected with other terms, e.g., _________ field, _________ variable, _________ parameter, _________ value, _________ signal, _________ device and _________ file.

a. ACCRA Cost of Living Index
b. AD-IA Model
c. ACEA agreement
d. Input

93. In economics, _________ is the process by which a firm determines the price and output level that returns the greatest profit. There are several approaches to this problem. The total revenue--total cost method relies on the fact that profit equals revenue minus cost, and the marginal revenue--marginal cost method is based on the fact that total profit in a perfectly competitive market reaches its maximum point where marginal revenue equals marginal cost.

a. 100-year flood
b. Normal profit
c. Profit margin
d. Profit maximization

94. A _________ is message sent to consumers and producers in the form of a price charged for a commodity; this is seen as indicating a signal for producers to increase supplies and/or consumers to reduce demand.

For example, in a free price system, rising prices may indicate a shortage of supply, increase in demand, or a rise in input costs. Regardless of the underlying reason--and without the consumer needing to know the cause--the price increase communicates the notion that consumer demand (at this new, higher price) should recede or that supplies should increase.

a. Threshold population
b. Market demand schedule
c. Mohring effect
d. Price signal

95. The _________ is a concept widely used in Welfare Economics, and analogous to the better-known Production-possibility frontier. It is a similar diagram which depicts not production of two goods, but rather the utility possibilities of two individuals.

In a competitive economy, any allocation over the _________ is a Pareto optimum, as the UPF is a representation of the Pareto contract curve in a different dimension (utilities versus goods.)

a. ACCRA Cost of Living Index
b. International Social Security Association
c. Utility-possibility frontier
d. Equivalent variation

1. _________ is exchange of capital, goods, and services across international borders or territories. In most countries, it represents a significant share of gross domestic product (GDP.) While _________ has been present throughout much of history , its economic, social, and political importance has been on the rise in recent centuries.

a. International trade
b. Import license
c. Intra-industry trade
d. Incoterms

2. In economics, _________ refers to the ability of a party to produce a good or service using fewer real resources than another entity producing the same good or service..A party has an _________ when using the same input as another party, it can produce a greater output. Since _________ is determined by a simple comparison of labor productivities, it is possible for a party to have no _________ in anything. It can be contrasted with the concept of comparative advantage which refers to the ability to produce a particular good at a lower opportunity cost.

a. ACCRA Cost of Living Index
b. Index number
c. Absolute advantage
d. International economics

3. Bartering is a medium in which goods or services are directly exchanged for other goods and/or services, without the use of money. It can be bilateral or multilateral, and usually exists parallel to monetary systems in most developed countries, though to a very limited extent. _________ usually replaces money as the method of exchange in times of monetary crisis, when the currency is unstable and devalued by hyperinflation.

a. Meitheal
b. Community-based economics
c. Barter
d. New Economics Foundation

4. _________s is the social science that studies the production, distribution, and consumption of goods and services. The term _________s comes from the Ancient Greek oá¼°κονομÎ¯α from oá¼¶κος (oikos, 'house') + vÏŒμος (nomos, 'custom' or 'law'), hence 'rules of the house(hold)'. Current _________ models developed out of the broader field of political economy in the late 19th century, owing to a desire to use an empirical approach more akin to the physical sciences.

a. Opportunity cost
b. Energy economics
c. Inflation
d. Economic

5. _________ is the increase in the amount of the goods and services produced by an economy over time. It is conventionally measured as the percent rate of increase in real gross domestic product, or real GDP. Growth is usually calculated in real terms, i.e. inflation-adjusted terms, in order to net out the effect of inflation on the price of the goods and services produced.

a. ACEA agreement
b. AD-IA Model
c. ACCRA Cost of Living Index
d. Economic growth

6. A _________ is the transfer of wealth from one party (such as a person or company) to another. A _________ is usually made in exchange for the provision of goods, services or both, or to fulfill a legal obligation.

The simplest and oldest form of _________ is barter, the exchange of one good or service for another.

a. Social gravity
b. Going concern
c. Soft count
d. Payment

7. A _________ is an object whose consumption increases the utility of the consumer, for which the quantity demanded exceeds the quantity supplied at zero price. _________s are usually modeled as having diminishing marginal utility. The first individual purchase has high utility; the second has less.

a. Pie method
b. Merit good
c. Composite good
d. Good

8. In economics, economic output is divided into physical goods and intangible services. Consumption of _________ is assumed to produce utility. It is often used when referring to a _________ Tax.

a. Manufactured goods
b. Composite good
c. Private good
d. Goods and services

9. _________s (economically referred to as land or raw materials) occur naturally within environments that exist relatively undisturbed by mankind, in a natural form. A _________'s is often characterized by amounts of biodiversity existent in various ecosystems.

Mining, petroleum extraction, fishing, hunting, and forestry are generally considered natural-resource industries.

a. Natural resource
b. 100-year flood
c. 1921 recession
d. 130-30 fund

10. Economics:

- _________,the desire to own something and the ability to pay for it
- _________ curve,a graphic representation of a _________ schedule
- _________ deposit, the money in checking accounts
- _________ pull theory,the theory that inflation occurs when _________ for goods and services exceeds existing supplies
- _________ schedule,a table that lists the quantity of a good a person will buy it each different price
- _________ side economics,the school of economics at believes government spending and tax cuts open economy by raising _________

.

a. McKesson ' Robbins scandal
b. Variability
c. Production
d. Demand

11. In finance, the _________s between two currencies specifies how much one currency is worth in terms of the other. It is the value of a foreign natione;s currency in terms of the home natione;s currency. For example an _________ of 102 Japanese yen to the United States dollar means that JPY 102 is worth the same as USD 1.

a. Exchange rate
b. ACCRA Cost of Living Index
c. ACEA agreement
d. Interbank market

12. _________ in economics refers to metrics and measures of output from production processes, per unit of input. Labor _________, for example, is typically measured as a ratio of output per labor-hour, an input. _________ may be conceived of as a metrics of the technical or engineering efficiency of production.

a. Piece work
b. Productivity
c. Fordism
d. Production-possibility frontier

13. The term '_________' refers to the concept of collecting information and attempting to spot a pattern in the information. In some fields of study, the term '_________' has more formally-defined meanings.

In project management _________ is a mathematical technique that uses historical results to predict future outcome.

a. Trend analysis
b. Coefficient of determination
c. Quantile regression
d. Probit model

14. _________ is the a method of technical and economic research of the systems for purpose to optimize a parity between system's consumer functions or properties and expenses to achieve those functions or properties.

This methodology for continuous perfection of production, industrial technologies, organizational structures was developed by Juryj Sobolev in 1948 at the 'Perm telephone factory'

- 1948 Juryj Sobolev - the first success in application of a method analysis at the 'Perm telephone factory' .
- 1949 - the first application for the invention as result of use of the new method.

Today in economically developed countries practically each enterprise or the company use methodology of the kind of functional-cost analysis as a practice of the quality management, most full satisfying to principles of standards of series ISO 9000.

- Interest of consumer not in products itself, but the advantage which it will receive from its usage.
- The consumer aspires to reduce his expenses
- Functions needed by consumer can be executed in the various ways, and, hence, with various efficiency and expenses. Among possible alternatives of realization of functions exist such in which the parity of quality and the price is the optimal for the consumer.

The goal of _________ is achievement of the highest consumer satisfaction of production at simultaneous decrease in all kinds of industrial expenses Classical _________ has three English synonyms - Value Engineering, Value Management, Value Analysis.

a. Function cost analysis
b. Willingness to pay
c. Staple financing
d. Monopoly wage

15. The _________ consists of a number of economic theories which describe the nature of the firm, company including its existence, its behaviour, and its relationship with the market.

In simplified terms, the _________ aims to answer these questions:

1. Existence - why do firms emerge, why are not all transactions in the economy mediated over the market?
2. Boundaries - why the boundary between firms and the market is located exactly there? Which transactions are performed internally and which are negotiated on the market?
3. Organization - why are firms structured in such specific way? What is the interplay of formal and informal relationships?

Despite looking simple, these questions are not answered by the established economic theory, which usually views firms as given, and treats them as black boxes without any internal structure.

The First World War period saw a change of emphasis in economic theory away from industry-level analysis which mainly included analysing markets to analysis at the level of the firm, as it became increasingly clear that perfect competition was no longer an adequate model of how firms behaved. Economic theory till then had focussed on trying to understand markets alone and there had been little study on understanding why firms or organisations exist.

a. Technology gap
b. Policy Ineffectiveness Proposition
c. Khazzoom-Brookes postulate
d. Theory of the firm

16. In economics, _________ and economies of scale are related terms that describe what happens as the scale of production increases. They are different terms and should not be used interchangeably.

_________ refers to a technical property of production that examines changes in output subsequent to a proportional change in all inputs (where all inputs increase by a constant factor.)

a. Constant returns to scale
b. Necessity good
c. Returns to scale
d. Customer equity

17. In economics, _________ refers to the ability of a person or a country to produce a particular good at a lower marginal cost and opportunity cost than another person or country. It is the ability to produce a product most efficiently given all the other products that could be produced. It can be contrasted with absolute advantage which refers to the ability of a person or a country to produce a particular good at a lower absolute cost than another.

a. Gravity model of trade
b. Hot money
c. Triffin dilemma
d. Comparative advantage

18. In economic theory, _________ is the competitive situation in any market where the conditions necessary for perfect competition are not satisfied. It is a market structure that does not meet the conditions of perfect competition.

Forms of _________ include:

- Monopoly, in which there is only one seller of a good.
- Oligopoly, in which there is a small number of sellers.
- Monopolistic competition, in which there are many sellers producing highly differentiated goods.
- Monopsony, in which there is only one buyer of a good.
- Oligopsony, in which there is a small number of buyers.

There may also be _________ in markets due to buyers or sellers lacking information about prices and the goods being traded.

There may also be _________ due to a time lag in a market.

a. AD-IA Model
b. ACCRA Cost of Living Index
c. Imperfect competition
d. ACEA agreement

19. In microeconomics, _________ is quite simply the conversion of inputs into outputs. It is an economic process that uses resources to create a good or service that is suitable for exchange. This can include manufacturing, storing, shipping, and packaging.

a. MET
b. Production
c. Solved
d. Red Guards

20. _________ was a survey conducted by the U.S. Department of Justice to gauge the prevalence of alcohol and illegal drug use among prior arrestees. It was a reformulation of the prior Drug Use Forecasting (DUF) program, focused on five drugs in particular: cocaine, marijuana, methamphetamine, opiates, and PCP.

Participants were randomly selected from arrest records in major metropolitan areas; because no personally identifying information is taken from each record chosen, the resulting data can be correlated to arrest rates, but not to the total population of persons charged.

a. ACCRA Cost of Living Index
b. AD-IA Model
c. ACEA agreement
d. Arrestee Drug Abuse Monitoring

21. _________ was a Scottish moral philosopher and a pioneer of political economy. One of the key figures of the Scottish Enlightenment, Smith is the author of The Theory of Moral Sentiments and An Inquiry into the Nature and Causes of the Wealth of Nations. The latter, usually abbreviated as The Wealth of Nations, is considered his magnum opus and the first modern work of economics.

a. Alan Greenspan
b. Adolph Fischer
c. Adam Smith
d. Adolf Hitler

22. _________ is a type of trade policy that allows traders to act and transact without interference from government. Thus, the policy permits trading partners mutual gains from trade, with goods and services produced according to the theory of comparative advantage.

Under a _________ policy, prices are a reflection of true supply and demand, and are the sole determinant of resource allocation.

a. Free trade
b. 1921 recession
c. 100-year flood
d. 130-30 fund

23. _________ in economics and business is the result of an exchange and from that trade we assign a numerical monetary value to a good, service or asset. If Alice trades Bob 4 apples for an orange, the _________ of an orange is 4 apples. Inversely, the _________ of an apple is 1/4 oranges.

a. Price book
b. Price war
c. Premium pricing
d. Price

24. A _________ is a hypothetical measure of overall prices for some set of goods and services, in a given region during a given interval, normalized relative to some base set. Typically, a _________ is approximated with a price index.

The classical dichotomy is the assumption that there is a relatively clean distinction between overall increases or decreases in prices and underlying, e;reale; economic variables.

a. Discouraged worker
b. Discretionary spending
c. Price level
d. Price elasticity of supply

25. A _________ is:

- Rewrite _________, in generative grammar and computer science
- Standardization, a formal and widely-accepted statement, fact, definition, or qualification
- Operation, a determinate _________ for performing a mathematical operation and obtaining a certain result (Mathematics, Logic)
    - Unary operation
    - Binary operation
- _________ of inference, a function from sets of formulae to formulae (Mathematics, Logic)
- _________ of thumb, principle with broad application that is not intended to be strictly accurate or reliable for every situation. Also often simply referred to as a _________
- Moral, an atomic element of a moral code for guiding choices in human behavior
- Heuristic, a quantized '_________' which shows a tendency or probability for successful function
- A regulation, as in sports
- A Production _________, as in computer science
- Procedural law, a _________set governing the application of laws to cases
    - A law, which may informally be called a '_________'
    - A court ruling, a decision by a court
- In the U.S. Government, a regulation mandated by Congress, but written or expanded upon by the Executive Branch.
- Norm (sociology), an informal but widely accepted _________, concept, truth, definition, or qualification (social norms, legal norms, coding norms)
- Norm (philosophy), a kind of sentence or a reason to act, feel or believe
- 'Rulership' is the concept of governance by a government:
    - Military _________, governance by a military body
    - Monastic _________, a collection of precepts that guides the life of monks or nuns in a religious order where the superior holds the place of Christ
- Slide _________

- '_________,' a song by Ayumi Hamasaki
- '_________,' a song by rapper Nas
- '_________s,' an album by the band The Whitest Boy Alive
- _________s: Pyaar Ka Superhit Formula, a 2003 Bollywood film
- ruler, an instrument for measuring lengths
- _________, a component of an astrolabe, circumferator or similar instrument
- The _________s, a bestselling self-help book
- _________ Project (Run Up-to-date Linux Everywhere), a project that aims to use up-to-date Linux software on old PCs
- _________ engine, a software system that helps managing business _________s
- Ja _________, a hip hop artist
    - R.U.L.E., a 2005 greatest hits album by rapper Ja _________
- '_________s,' a KMFDM song

a. Technocracy
b. Procter ' Gamble
c. Demand
d. Rule

26. _________ is an economic concept with commonplace familiarity. It is the price that a good or service is offered at, or will fetch, in the marketplace. It is of interest mainly in the study of microeconomics.

a. Market price
b. Noisy market hypothesis
c. Paper trading
d. Market anomaly

27. The term _________s refers to wages that have been adjusted for inflation. This term is used in contrast to nominal wages or unadjusted wages.

The use of adjusted figures is in undertaking some form of economic analysis.

a. Federal Wage System
b. Living wage
c. Profit sharing
d. Real wage

28. Competition law, known in the United States as _________ law, has three main elements:

- prohibiting agreements or practices that restrict free trading and competition between business entities. This includes in particular the repression of cartels.
- banning abusive behaviour by a firm dominating a market, or anti-competitive practices that tend to lead to such a dominant position. Practices controlled in this way may include predatory pricing, tying, price gouging, refusal to deal, and many others.
- supervising the mergers and acquisitions of large corporations, including some joint ventures. Transactions that are considered to threaten the competitive process can be prohibited altogether, or approved subject to 'remedies' such as an obligation to divest part of the merged business or to offer licences or access to facilities to enable other businesses to continue competing.

The substance and practice of competition law varies from jurisdiction to jurisdiction. Protecting the interests of consumers (consumer welfare) and ensuring that entrepreneurs have an opportunity to compete in the market economy are often treated as important objectives. Competition law is closely connected with law on deregulation of access to markets, state aids and subsidies, the privatisation of state owned assets and the establishment of independent sector regulators. In recent decades, competition law has been viewed as a way to provide better public services.

a. United Kingdom competition law
b. Anti-Inflation Act
c. Antitrust
d. Intellectual property law

29. _________ is a common concept in economics, and gives rise to derived concepts such as consumer debt. Generally _________ is defined by opposition to production. But the precise definition can vary because different schools of economists define production quite differently.

a. Cash or share options
b. Federal Reserve Bank Notes
c. Foreclosure data providers
d. Consumption

30. In international economics and international trade, _________ or _________ is the relative prices of a country's export to import. '_________' are sometimes used as a proxy for the relative social welfare of a country, but this heuristic is technically questionable and should be used with extreme caution. An improvement in a nation's _________ is good for that country in the sense that it has to pay less for the products it import.

a. Terms of trade
b. Commercial invoice
c. Kennedy Round
d. Common market

31. A _________ is an expression that compares quantities relative to each other. The most common examples involve two quantities, but any number of quantities can be compared. _________s are represented mathematically by separating each quantity with a colon, for example the _________ 2:3, which is read as the _________ 'two to three'.

a. Y-intercept
b. Ratio
c. 130-30 fund
d. 100-year flood

32. _________ or clearing trade is trade exclusively between two states, particularly, barter trade based on bilateral deals between governments, and without using hard currency for payment. _________ agreements often aim to keep trade deficits at minimum by keeping a clearing account where deficit would accumulate.

The Soviet Union conducted _________ with two nations, India and Finland.

a. 130-30 fund
b. 1921 recession
c. 100-year flood
d. Bilateral trade

33. _________ is a historical term indicating trade among three ports or regions. The trade evolved where a region had an export commodity that was required in the region from which its major imports came. _________ thus provided a mechanism for rectifying trade imbalances.

a. 1921 recession
b. 100-year flood
c. Triangular trade
d. 130-30 fund

34. _________ is widely regarded as the first modern school of economic thought. It is the idea that free markets can regulate themselves.Its major developers include Adam Smith, David Ricardo, Thomas Malthus and John Stuart Mill. Sometimes the definition of _________ is expanded to include William Petty, Johann Heinrich von Thünen.

a. Marginalism
b. Schools of economic thought
c. Tendency of the rate of profit to fall
d. Classical economics

35. In economics, _________ are the resources employed to produce goods and services. They facilitate production but do not become part of the product (as with raw materials) or significantly transformed by the production process (as with fuel used to power machinery.) To 19th century economists, the _________ were land (natural resources, gifts from nature), labor (the ability to work), and capital goods (human-made tools and equipment.)

a. Product Pipeline
b. Hicks-neutral technical change
c. Long-run
d. Factors of production

36. The _________ was a worldwide economic downturn starting in most places in 1929 and ending at different times in the 1930s or early 1940s for different countries. It was the largest and most important economic depression in the 20th century, and is used in the 21st century as an example of how far the world's economy can fall. The _________ originated in the United States; historians most often use as a starting date the stock market crash on October 29, 1929, known as Black Tuesday.

a. British Empire Economic Conference
b. Jarrow March
c. Wall Street Crash of 1929
d. Great Depression

37. In economics, _________ is how a natione;s total economy is distributed among its population. ._________ has always been a central concern of economic theory and economic policy. Classical economists such as Adam Smith, Thomas Malthus and David Ricardo were mainly concerned with factor _________, that is, the distribution of income between the main factors of production, land, labour and capital.

a. Equipment trust certificate
b. Authorised capital
c. Eco commerce
d. Income distribution

38. _________ is the economic policy of restraining trade between states, through methods such as tariffs on imported goods, restrictive quotas, and a variety of other restrictive government regulations designed to discourage imports, and prevent foreign take-over of local markets and companies. This policy is closely aligned with anti-globalization, and contrasts with free trade, where government barriers to trade are kept to a minimum. The term is mostly used in the context of economics, where _________ refers to policies or doctrines which 'protect' businesses and workers within a country by restricting or regulating trade with foreign nations.

a. Protectionism
b. Google economy
c. Knowledge economy
d. Digital economy

39. _________ theory is a branch of theoretical economics. It seeks to explain the behavior of supply, demand and prices in a whole economy with several or many markets. It is often assumed that agents are price takers and in that setting two common notions of equilibrium exist: Walrasian (or competitive) equilibrium, and its generalization; a price equilibrium with transfers.

a. New Keynesian economics
b. General equilibrium
c. Human capital
d. Rational choice theory

40. In economics, economic equilibrium is simply a state of the world where economic forces are balanced and in the absence of external influences the (equilibrium) values of economic variables will not change. It is the point at which quantity demanded and quantity supplied are equal. _________, for example, refers to a condition where a market price is established through competition such that the amount of goods or services sought by buyers is equal to the amount of goods or services produced by sellers.

a. Regulated market
b. Marketization
c. Product-Market Growth Matrix
d. Market equilibrium

41. The _________ was an act signed into law on June 17, 1930, that raised U.S. tariffs on over 20,000 imported goods to record levels. In the United States 1,028 economists signed a petition against this legislation, and after it was passed, many countries retaliated with their own increased tariffs on U.S. goods, and American exports and imports were reduced by more than half.

Although rated capacity had increased tremendously, actual output, income, and expenditure had not.

a. Patent Law Treaty
b. Loss of use
c. Judgment summons
d. Smoot-Hawley Tariff Act

42. _________ is an economic model based on price, utility and quantity in a market. It predicts that in a competitive market, price will function to equalize the quantity demanded by consumers, and the quantity supplied by producers, resulting in an economic equilibrium of price and quantity. The model incorporates other factors changing equilibrium as a shift of demand and/or supply.

a. Joint demand
b. Deferred gratification
c. Supply and demand
d. Rational addiction

43. A _________ is a general term that describes any government policy or regulation that restricts international trade. The barriers can take many forms, including the following terms that include many restrictions in international trade within multiple countries that import and export any items of trade.

- Import duty
- Import licenses
- Export licenses
- Import quotas
- Tariffs
- Subsidies
- Non-tariff barriers to trade
- Voluntary Export Restraints
- Local Content Requirements
- Embargo

Most _________s work on the same principle: the imposition of some sort of cost on trade that raises the price of the traded products. If two or more nations repeatedly use _________s against each other, then a trade war results.

a. National Foreign Trade Council
b. Trade barrier
c. Certificate of origin
d. Global financial system

44. _________ is the development of economic wealth of countries or regions for the well-being of their inhabitants. It is the process by which a nation improves the economic, political, and social well being of its people. From a policy perspective, _________ can be defined as efforts that seek to improve the economic well-being and quality of life for a community by creating and/or retaining jobs and supporting or growing incomes and the tax base.

a. Inflation
b. Experimental economics
c. Economic methodology
d. Economic development

45. A _________ is a duty imposed on goods when they are moved across a political boundary. They are usually associated with protectionism, the economic policy of restraining trade between nations. For political reasons, _________s are usually imposed on imported goods, although they may also be imposed on exported goods.

a. 1921 recession
b. Tariff
c. 100-year flood
d. 130-30 fund

46. The _________ of a decision depends on both the cost of the alternative chosen and the benefit that the best alternative would have provided if chosen. _________ differs from accounting cost because it includes opportunity cost.

a. Epstein-Zin preferences
b. Isocost
c. Inventory analysis
d. Economic cost

47. In economics, _________ is the transfer of income, wealth or property from some individuals to others.

One premise of _________ is that money should be distributed to benefit the poorer members of society, and that the rich have an obligation to assist the poor, thus creating a more financially egalitarian society. Another argument is that the rich exploit the poor or otherwise gain unfair benefits.

a. Redistribution
b. 100-year flood
c. 1921 recession
d. 130-30 fund

48. _________ in political thought refers to economic theories of social organization advocating collective ownership and administration of the means of production and distribution of goods, and a society characterized by equality for all individuals, with an egalitarian method of compensation. Modern _________ originated in the late 19th-century intellectual and working class political movement that criticized the effects of industrialization and private ownership on society. Karl Marx posited that _________ would be achieved via class struggle and a proletarian revolution after a transitional stage from capitalism called the dictatorship of the proletariat.

a. Adolph Fischer
b. Adolf Hitler
c. Adam Smith
d. Socialism

49. _________ is an economic theory that holds that the prosperity of a nation is dependent upon its supply of capital, and that the global volume of international trade is 'unchangeable.' Economic assets or capital, are represented by bullion (gold, silver, and trade value) held by the state, which is best increased through a positive balance of trade with other nations (exports minus imports.) _________ suggests that the ruling government should advance these goals by playing a protectionist role in the economy; by encouraging exports and discouraging imports, notably through the use of tariffs and subsidies.

_________ was the dominant school of thought throughout the early modern period (from the 16th to the 18th century.)

a. General equilibrium theory
b. Consumer theory
c. Mercantilism
d. Nominal value

50. The _________ is a term used for industries primarily concerned with the design or manufacture of clothing as well as the distribution and use of textiles.

Prior to the manufacturing processes were mechanized, textiles were produced in the home, and excess sold for extra money. Most cloth was made from either wool, cotton, or flax, depending on the era and location.

a. Textile industry
b. 130-30 fund
c. 100-year flood
d. Textile manufacture during the Industrial Revolution

51. _________ or government expenditure is classified by economists into three main types. Government purchases of goods and services for current use are classed as government consumption. Government purchases of goods and services intended to create future benefits, such as infrastructure investment or research spending, are classed as government investment.

a. Government spending
b. 100-year flood
c. 130-30 fund
d. 1921 recession

52. In economics, the people in the _________ are the suppliers of labor. The _________ is all the nonmilitary people who are employed or unemployed. In 2005, the worldwide _________ was over 3 billion people.

a. Grenelle agreements
b. Distributed workforce
c. Departmentalization
d. Labor force

53. The _________ is a trilateral trade bloc in North America created by the governments of the United States, Canada, and Mexico. The agreement creating the trade bloc came into force on January 1, 1994. It superseded the Canada-United States Free Trade Agreement between the U.S. and Canada.

a. Demand-side technologies
b. Federal Reserve Bank Notes
c. Case-Shiller Home Price Indices
d. North American Free Trade Agreement

54. In neoclassical economics and microeconomics, _________ describes the perfect being a market in which there are many small firms, all producing homogeneous goods. In the short term, such markets are productively inefficient as output will not occur where mc is equal to ac, but allocatively efficient, as output under _________ will always occur where mc is equal to mr, and therefore where mc equals ar. However, in the long term, such markets are both allocatively and productively efficient.

a. Law of supply
b. General equilibrium
c. Co-operative economics
d. Perfect competition

55. _________ is a fee paid on borrowed assets. It is the price paid for the use of borrowed money , or, money earned by deposited funds . Assets that are sometimes lent with _________ include money, shares, consumer goods through hire purchase, major assets such as aircraft, and even entire factories in finance lease arrangements.

a. Internal debt
b. Interest
c. Insolvency
d. Asset protection

56. _________ are duties imposed under WTO Rules to neutralize the negative effects of other duties. They are imposed when a foreign country subsidizes its exports, hurting domestic producers in the importing country

a. Certificate of origin
b. Kennedy Round
c. Market access
d. Countervailing duties

57. In economics, an _________ is any good (e.g. a commodity) or service brought into one country from another country in a legitimate fashion, typically for use in trade.It is a good that is brought in from another country for sale. _________ goods or services are provided to domestic consumers by foreign producers. An _________ in the receiving country is an export to the sending country.

a. Import
b. Economic integration
c. Incoterms
d. Import quota

58. _________ was the first United States Secretary of the Treasury, a Founding Father, economist, and political philosopher. He led calls for the Philadelphia Convention, was one of America's first Constitutional lawyers, and cowrote the Federalist Papers, a primary source for Constitutional interpretation.

Born on the British West Indian island of Nevis, Hamilton was educated in the Thirteen Colonies.

a. Adam Smith
b. Economic impact of immigration
c. American exceptionalism
d. Alexander Hamilton

59. The _________ is an economic reason for protectionism. The crux of the argument is that nascent industries often do not have the economies of scale that their older competitors from other countries may have, and thus need to be protected until they can attain similar economies of scale. It was first used by Alexander Hamilton in 1790 and later by Friedrich List, in 1841, to support protection for German manufacturing against British industry.

a. ACCRA Cost of Living Index
b. AD-IA Model
c. ACEA agreement
d. Infant industry argument

60. The supply of labor is the number of total hours that workers wish to work at a given real wage rate.

_________ curves are derived from the 'labor-leisure' trade-off. More hours worked earn higher incomes but necessitate a cut in the amount of leisure that workers enjoy.

a. Creative capitalism
b. Human trafficking
c. Late capitalism
d. Labor supply

61. _________ refers to discriminatory employment practices such as bias in hiring, promotion, job assignment, termination, and compensation, and various types of harassment.

In many countries, laws prohibit employers from discriminating on the basis of race, color, sex, religion, national origin, physical or mental disability, or age. There is also a growing body of law preventing or occasionally justifying _________ based on sexual orientation or gender identity.

a. Impotent poor
b. Energy Independence and Security Act of 2007
c. Irish competition law
d. Employment discrimination

62. _________ and Keynesian Theory) is a macroeconomic theory based on the ideas of 20th-century British economist John Maynard Keynes. _________ argues that private sector decisions sometimes lead to inefficient macroeconomic outcomes and therefore advocates active policy responses by the public sector, including monetary policy actions by the central bank and fiscal policy actions by the government to stabilize output over the business cycle.

The theories forming the basis of _________ were first presented in The General Theory of Employment, Interest and Money, published in 1936.

a. Deflation
b. Keynesian economics
c. Market failure
d. Rational choice theory

63. In finance, the _________ of a financial asset measures the sensitivity of the asset's price to interest rate movements. There are various definitions of _________ and derived quantities, discussed below. If not otherwise specified, '_________' generally means the Macaulay _________, as defined below.

a. Newtonian time
b. Time value of money
c. 100-year flood
d. Duration

64. In economics, an _________ is any good or commodity, transported from one country to another country in a legitimate fashion, typically for use in trade. _________ goods or services are provided to foreign consumers by domestic producers. _________ is an important part of international trade.

a. ACEA agreement
b. ACCRA Cost of Living Index
c. Export
d. AD-IA Model

65. The _________ is the official currency of 16 of the 27 member states of the European Union (EU.) The states, known collectively as the Eurozone, are Austria, Belgium, Cyprus, Finland, France, Germany, Greece, Ireland, Italy, Luxembourg, Malta, the Netherlands, Portugal, Slovakia, Slovenia, and Spain. The currency is also used in a further five European countries, with and without formal agreements and is consequently used daily by some 327 million Europeans.

a. Equity capital market
b. Import and Export Price Indices
c. IRS Code 3401
d. Euro

66. The _________ is an economic and political union of 27 member states, located primarily in Europe. It was established by the Treaty of Maastricht on 1 November 1993, upon the foundations of the pre-existing European Economic Community. With a population of almost 500 million, the _________ generates an estimated 30% share (US$18.4 trillion in 2008) of the nominal gross world product.

a. ACCRA Cost of Living Index
b. European Union
c. European Court of Justice
d. ACEA agreement

67. The _________ is the central banking system of the United States. Created in 1913 by the enactment of the Federal Reserve Act (signed by Woodrow Wilson), it is a quasi-public and quasi-private (government entity with private components) banking system that comprises (1) the presidentially appointed Board of Governors of the _________ in Washington, D.C.; (2) the Federal Open Market Committee; (3) twelve regional Federal Reserve Banks located in major cities throughout the nation acting as fiscal agents for the U.S. Treasury, each with its own nine-member board of directors; (4) numerous other private U.S. member banks, which subscribe to required amounts of non-transferable stock in their regional Federal Reserve Banks; and (5) various advisory councils. Since February 2006, Ben Bernanke has served as the Chairman of the Board of Governors of the _________.

a. Federal Reserve System
b. Federal Reserve System Open Market Account
c. Term auction facility
d. Monetary Policy Report to the Congress

68. The _________ was the outcome of the failure of negotiating governments to create the International Trade Organization (ITO.) GATT was formed in 1947 and lasted until 1994, when it was replaced by the World Trade Organization. The Bretton Woods Conference had introduced the idea for an organization to regulate trade as part of a larger plan for economic recovery after World War II.

a. GATT
b. Dutch-Scandinavian Economic Pact
c. General Agreement on Trade in Services
d. General Agreement on Tariffs and Trade

69. _________ in its literal sense is the process of transformation of local or regional phenomena into global ones. It can be described as a process by which the people of the world are unified into a single society and function together.

This process is a combination of economic, technological, sociocultural and political forces.

a. Helsinki Process on Globalisation and Democracy
b. Globally Integrated Enterprise
c. Global Cosmopolitanism
d. Globalization

70. The _________ commenced in September 1986 and continued until April 1994. The round, based on the General Agreement on Tariffs and Trade (GATT) ministerial meeting in Geneva (1982), was launched in Punta del Este in Uruguay (hence the name), followed by negotiations in Montreal, Geneva, Brussels, Washington, D.C., and Tokyo, with the 20 agreements finally being signed in Marrakech - the Marrakesh Agreement. The Round transformed the GATT into the World Trade Organization.

a. ACCRA Cost of Living Index
b. AD-IA Model
c. ACEA agreement
d. Uruguay Round

71. The _________ is an important selective, mainly private, international organization designed by its founders to supervise and liberalize international trade. The organization officially commenced on 1 January 1995, under the Marrakesh Agreement, succeeding the 1947 General Agreement on Tariffs and Trade (GATT.)

The _________ deals with regulation of trade between participating countries; it provides a framework for negotiating and formalising trade agreements, and a dispute resolution process aimed at enforcing participants' adherence to _________ agreements which are signed by representatives of member governments and ratified by their parliaments.

a. Bio-energy village
b. 2009 G-20 London summit protests
c. Backus-Kehoe-Kydland consumption correlation puzzle
d. World Trade Organization

72. _________ is money accepted for exchange of goods in an economy. The prevalence of one money over another arises, usually, when a government designates through decrees that the government shall accept only particular notes and coins in payment for taxes. Typically, money of _________ consists of stamped coins and minted paper bills.

a. Local currency
b. Totnes pound
c. Security thread
d. Currency

73. _________ is a branch of economics with three main subdisciplines international trade, monetary economics and international finance.

- International trade studies goods-and-services flows across international boundaries from supply-and-demand factors, economic integration, and policy variables such as tariff rates and trade quotas.
- International finance studies the flow of capital across international financial markets, and the effects of these movements on exchange rates.
- International monetary economics and macroeconomics studies money and macro flows across countries.

- Stanley W. Black (2008.) 'international monetary institutions,' The New Palgrave Dictionary of Economics. 2nd Edition.

a. Index number
b. ACCRA Cost of Living Index
c. International Economics
d. Economic depreciation

74. The _________ is an international organization that oversees the global financial system by following the macroeconomic policies of its member countries, in particular those with an impact on exchange rates and the balance of payments. It is an organization formed to stabilize international exchange rates and facilitate development. It also offers financial and technical assistance to its members, making it an international lender of last resort.

a. ACCRA Cost of Living Index
b. ACEA agreement
c. Office of Thrift Supervision
d. International Monetary Fund

75. The _________ is an international financial institution that provides financial and technical assistance to developing countries for development programs (e.g. bridges, roads, schools, etc.) with the stated goal of reducing poverty.

The _________ differs from the _________ Group, in that the _________ comprises only two institutions:

- International Bank for Reconstruction and Development (IBRD)
- International Development Association (IDA)

Whereas the latter incorporates these two in addition to three more:

- International Finance Corporation (IFC)
- Multilateral Investment Guarantee Agency (MIGA)
- International Centre for Settlement of Investment Disputes (ICSID)

John Maynard Keynes (right) represented the UK at the conference, and Harry Dexter White represented the US.

The _________ is one of two major financial institutions created as a result of the Bretton Woods Conference in 1944. The International Monetary Fund, a related but separate institution, is the second.

a. Bank-State-Branch
b. Financial costs of the 2003 Iraq War
c. Flow to Equity-Approach
d. World Bank

76. The term financial crisis is applied broadly to a variety of situations in which some financial institutions or assets suddenly lose a large part of their value. In the 19th and early 20th centuries, many _________ were associated with banking panics, and many recessions coincided with these panics. Other situations that are often called _________ include stock market crashes and the bursting of other financial bubbles, currency crises, and sovereign defaults.

a. Georgism
b. General equilibrium
c. Microeconomics
d. Financial crises

1. The _________ or gross domestic income (GDI), a basic measure of an economy's economic performance, is the market value of all final goods and services produced within the borders of a nation in a year. _________ can be defined in three ways, all of which are conceptually identical. First, it is equal to the total expenditures for all final goods and services produced within the country in a stipulated period of time (usually a 365-day year.)

a. Market structure
b. Monopolistic competition
c. Countercyclical
d. Gross domestic product

2. In economics, the _________ is used to illustrate the idea that increases in the rate of taxation do not necessarily increase tax revenue. (For instance, whereas a 0% income tax rate will generate no revenue, neither will a 100% rate, as citizens will have no incentive to make money.) Increasing taxes beyond the peak of the curve point will decrease tax revenue.

a. 130-30 fund
b. 1921 recession
c. 100-year flood
d. Laffer curve

3. _________ is a misspelled phrase from Latin 'pro capite' phrase meaning per head with pro meaning 'per' or 'for each' and capite meaning 'head.' Both words together equate to the phrase 'for each head.'

It is usually used in the field of statistics to indicate the average per person for any given concern, such as income, crime rate, etc.

It is also used in wills to indicate that each of the named beneficiaries should receive, by devise or bequest, equal shares of the estate. This is in contrast to a per stirpes division, in which each branch of the inheriting family inherits an equal share of the estate.

a. Population statistics
b. False positive rate
c. Sargan test
d. Per capita

4. An _________, in economics, is the amount by which the real Gross domestic product exceeds potential GDP. The real GDP is also known as GDP 'adjusted for inflation', 'constant prices' GDP or 'constant dollar' GDP, because it measures the aggregate output in a country's income accounts in a given year, expressed in base-year prices. On the other hand, the potential GDP is the quantity of real GDP when a country's economy is at full-employment.

a. ACEA agreement
b. Inflationary gap
c. ACCRA Cost of Living Index
d. AD-IA Model

5. In economics, a _________ is a redistribution of income in the market system. These payments are considered to be nonexhaustive because they do not directly absorb resources or create output. Examples of certain _________s include welfare (financial aid), social security, and government subsidies for certain businesses (firms.)

a. 1921 recession
b. Transfer payment
c. 100-year flood
d. 130-30 fund

6. _________ or government expenditure is classified by economists into three main types. Government purchases of goods and services for current use are classed as government consumption. Government purchases of goods and services intended to create future benefits, such as infrastructure investment or research spending, are classed as government investment.

a. Government spending
b. 1921 recession
c. 100-year flood
d. 130-30 fund

7. A _________ is the transfer of wealth from one party (such as a person or company) to another. A _________ is usually made in exchange for the provision of goods, services or both, or to fulfill a legal obligation.

The simplest and oldest form of _________ is barter, the exchange of one good or service for another.

a. Social gravity
b. Going concern
c. Soft count
d. Payment

8. Economic _________ is defined as an excess distribution to any factor in a production process above that which is required to induce the factor into the process or any excess above that which is necessary to keep the factor in its current use..

Classical Factor _________ is primarily concerned with the fee paid for the use of fixed (e.g. natural) resources. The classical definition is expressed as any excess payment above that required to induce or provide for production.

a. 1921 recession
b. 130-30 fund
c. 100-year flood
d. Rent

9. A _________ is:

- Rewrite _________, in generative grammar and computer science
- Standardization, a formal and widely-accepted statement, fact, definition, or qualification
- Operation, a determinate _________ for performing a mathematical operation and obtaining a certain result (Mathematics, Logic)
    - Unary operation
    - Binary operation
- _________ of inference, a function from sets of formulae to formulae (Mathematics, Logic)
- _________ of thumb, principle with broad application that is not intended to be strictly accurate or reliable for every situation. Also often simply referred to as a _________
- Moral, an atomic element of a moral code for guiding choices in human behavior
- Heuristic, a quantized '_________' which shows a tendency or probability for successful function
- A regulation, as in sports
- A Production _________, as in computer science
- Procedural law, a _________set governing the application of laws to cases
    - A law, which may informally be called a '_________'
    - A court ruling, a decision by a court
- In the U.S. Government, a regulation mandated by Congress, but written or expanded upon by the Executive Branch.
- Norm (sociology), an informal but widely accepted _________, concept, truth, definition, or qualification (social norms, legal norms, coding norms)
- Norm (philosophy), a kind of sentence or a reason to act, feel or believe
- 'Rulership' is the concept of governance by a government:
    - Military _________, governance by a military body
    - Monastic _________, a collection of precepts that guides the life of monks or nuns in a religious order where the superior holds the place of Christ
- Slide _________

- '_________,' a song by Ayumi Hamasaki
- '_________,' a song by rapper Nas
- '_________s,' an album by the band The Whitest Boy Alive
- _________s: Pyaar Ka Superhit Formula, a 2003 Bollywood film
- ruler, an instrument for measuring lengths
- _________, a component of an astrolabe, circumferator or similar instrument
- The _________s, a bestselling self-help book
- _________ Project (Run Up-to-date Linux Everywhere), a project that aims to use up-to-date Linux software on old PCs
- _________ engine, a software system that helps managing business _________s
- Ja _________, a hip hop artist
    - R.U.L.E., a 2005 greatest hits album by rapper Ja _________
- '_________s,' a KMFDM song

a. Rule
b. Demand
c. Procter ' Gamble
d. Technocracy

10. _________ describes a broad class of theories that try to explain the ways in which people form states and/or maintain social order. The notion of the _________ implies that the people give up some rights to a government or other authority in order to receive or maintain social order.

_________ theory formed a central pillar in the historically important notion that legitimate state authority must be derived from the consent of the governed.

a. 1921 recession
b. 130-30 fund
c. 100-year flood
d. Social contract

11. _________ is a common concept in economics, and gives rise to derived concepts such as consumer debt. Generally _________ is defined by opposition to production. But the precise definition can vary because different schools of economists define production quite differently.

a. Cash or share options
b. Federal Reserve Bank Notes
c. Foreclosure data providers
d. Consumption

12. The term '_________' refers to the concept of collecting information and attempting to spot a pattern in the information. In some fields of study, the term '_________' has more formally-defined meanings.

In project management _________ is a mathematical technique that uses historical results to predict future outcome.

a. Coefficient of determination
b. Quantile regression
c. Trend analysis
d. Probit model

13. Competition law, known in the United States as _________ law, has three main elements:

- prohibiting agreements or practices that restrict free trading and competition between business entities. This includes in particular the repression of cartels.
- banning abusive behaviour by a firm dominating a market, or anti-competitive practices that tend to lead to such a dominant position. Practices controlled in this way may include predatory pricing, tying, price gouging, refusal to deal, and many others.
- supervising the mergers and acquisitions of large corporations, including some joint ventures. Transactions that are considered to threaten the competitive process can be prohibited altogether, or approved subject to 'remedies' such as an obligation to divest part of the merged business or to offer licences or access to facilities to enable other businesses to continue competing.

The substance and practice of competition law varies from jurisdiction to jurisdiction. Protecting the interests of consumers (consumer welfare) and ensuring that entrepreneurs have an opportunity to compete in the market economy are often treated as important objectives. Competition law is closely connected with law on deregulation of access to markets, state aids and subsidies, the privatisation of state owned assets and the establishment of independent sector regulators. In recent decades, competition law has been viewed as a way to provide better public services.

a. Anti-Inflation Act
b. Intellectual property law
c. United Kingdom competition law
d. Antitrust

14. _________s is the social science that studies the production, distribution, and consumption of goods and services. The term _________s comes from the Ancient Greek oá¼°κονομÎ¯α from oá¼¶κος (oikos, 'house') + νÏŒμος (nomos, 'custom' or 'law'), hence 'rules of the house(hold)'. Current _________ models developed out of the broader field of political economy in the late 19th century, owing to a desire to use an empirical approach more akin to the physical sciences.

a. Economic
b. Inflation
c. Energy economics
d. Opportunity cost

15. The _________ was a regulatory body in the United States created by the Interstate Commerce Act of 1887, which was signed into law by President Grover Cleveland. The agency was abolished in 1995, and the agency's remaining functions were transferred to the Surface Transportation Board.

The Commission's five members were appointed by the President with the consent of the United States Senate.

a. ACCRA Cost of Living Index
b. Office of Thrift Supervision
c. ACEA agreement
d. Interstate Commerce Commission

16. _________ is a term used to describe a policy of allowing events to take their own course. The term is a French phrase literally meaning 'let do'. It is a doctrine that states that government generally should not intervene in the marketplace.

a. Heroic capitalism
b. Theory of Productive Forces
c. Laissez-faire
d. Communization

17. _________, often referred to by his initials _________, was the 32nd President of the United States. He was a central figure of the 20th century during a time of worldwide economic crisis and world war. Elected to four terms in office, he served from 1933 to 1945 and is the only U.S. president to have served more than two terms.

a. Franklin Delano Roosevelt
b. Adam Smith
c. Adolf Hitler
d. Adolph Fischer

18. _________ , also known as T.R., and to the public as Teddy, was the 26th President of the United States. A leader of the Republican Party and of the Progressive Party, he was a Governor of New York and a professional historian, naturalist, explorer, hunter, author, and soldier. He is most famous for his personality: his energy, his vast range of interests and achievements, his model of masculinity, and his 'cowboy' image.

a. Adolph Fischer
b. Theodore D. Roosevelt
c. Adam Smith
d. Adolf Hitler

19.

The _________ was the first United States Federal statute to limit cartels and monopolies. It falls under antitrust law.

The Act provides: 'Every contract, combination in the form of trust or otherwise, or conspiracy, in restraint of trade or commerce among the several States, or with foreign nations, is declared to be illegal'. The Act also provides: 'Every person who shall monopolize, or attempt to monopolize, or combine or conspire with any other person or persons, to monopolize any part of the trade or commerce among the several States, or with foreign nations, shall be deemed guilty of a felony [. . .]' The Act put responsibility upon government attorneys and district courts to pursue and investigate trusts, companies and organizations suspected of violating the Act. The Clayton Act extended the right to sue under the antitrust laws to 'any person who shall be injured in his business or property by reason of anything forbidden in the antitrust laws.' Under the Clayton Act, private parties may sue in U.S. district court and should they prevail, they may be awarded treble damages and the cost of suit, including reasonable attorney's fees.

a. Sherman Antitrust Act
b. 1921 recession
c. 100-year flood
d. 130-30 fund

20. _________ is a situation in which the limited resources of a firm are allocated in accordance with the wishes of consumers. An allocatively efficient economy produces an 'optimal mix' of commodities. A firm is allocatively efficient when its price is equal to its marginal costs (that is, P = MC) in a perfect market.

a. Allocative efficiency
b. ACEA agreement
c. ACCRA Cost of Living Index
d. Economic efficiency

21. _________ is an economic system in which wealth, and the means of producing wealth, are privately owned. Through _________, the land, labor, and capital are owned, operated, and traded for the purpose of generating profits, without force or fraud, by private individuals either singly or jointly, and investments, distribution, income, production, pricing and supply of goods, commodities and services are determined by voluntary private decision in a market economy. A distinguishing feature of _________ is that each person owns his or her own labor and therefore is allowed to sell the use of it to employers.

a. Late capitalism
b. Capitalism
c. Socialism for the rich and capitalism for the poor
d. Creative capitalism

22. In economic theory, _________ is the competitive situation in any market where the conditions necessary for perfect competition are not satisfied. It is a market structure that does not meet the conditions of perfect competition.

Forms of _________ include:

- Monopoly, in which there is only one seller of a good.
- Oligopoly, in which there is a small number of sellers.
- Monopolistic competition, in which there are many sellers producing highly differentiated goods.
- Monopsony, in which there is only one buyer of a good.
- Oligopsony, in which there is a small number of buyers.

There may also be _________ in markets due to buyers or sellers lacking information about prices and the goods being traded.

There may also be _________ due to a time lag in a market.

a. ACCRA Cost of Living Index
b. ACEA agreement
c. Imperfect competition
d. AD-IA Model

23. In economics, the _________ is the term economists use to describe the self-regulating nature of the marketplace. The _________ is a metaphor coined by the economist Adam Smith in The Wealth of Nations.

Adam Smith mentions the metaphor in Book IV of The Wealth of Nations, arguing that people in any society will certainly employ their capital in foreign trading only if the profits available by that method far exceed those available locally, and that in such a case it is better for society as a whole if they so did.

a. ACCRA Cost of Living Index
b. ACEA agreement
c. AD-IA Model
d. Invisible hand

24. _________ is a branch of economics that studies how individuals, households and firms and some states make decisions to allocate limited resources, typically in markets where goods or services are being bought and sold. _________ examines how these decisions and behaviours affect the supply and demand for goods and services, which determines prices; and how prices, in turn , determine the supply and demand of goods and services.

Whereas macroeconomics involves the 'sum total of economic activity, dealing with the issues of growth, inflation and unemployment, and with national economic policies relating to these issues' and the effects of government actions on them.

a. Microeconomics
b. Recession
c. Countercyclical
d. New Keynesian economics

25. _________ in economic theory is the use of modern economic tools to study problems that are traditionally in the province of political science.

In particular, it studies the behavior of politicians and government officials as mostly self-interested agents and their interactions in the social system either as such or under alternative constitutional rules. These can be represented a number of ways, including standard constrained utility maximization, game theory, or decision theory.

a. Paradox of voting
b. Public choice
c. Public interest theory
d. Rational ignorance

26. The _________ of June 30, 1906 is a United States federal law that provided federal inspection of meat products and forbade the manufacture, sale, or transportation of adulterated food products and poisonous patent medicines. The Act arose due to public education and exposés from authors such as Upton Sinclair and Samuel Hopkins Adams, social activist Florence Kelley, researcher Harvey W. Wiley, and President Theodore Roosevelt.

The _________ was initially concerned with ensuring products were labeled correctly.

a. Security and Freedom Through Encryption Act
b. 100-year flood
c. Sherman Silver Purchase Act
d. Pure food and drug act

27. A _________, reserve bank, or monetary authority is the entity responsible for the monetary policy of a country or of a group of member states. It is a bank that can lend money to other banks in times of need. Its primary responsibility is to maintain the stability of the national currency and money supply, but more active duties include controlling subsidized-loan interest rates, and acting as a lender of last resort to the banking sector during times of financial crisis (private banks often being integral to the national financial system.)

a. 130-30 fund
b. 1921 recession
c. 100-year flood
d. Central bank

28. The _________ is a measure of statistical dispersion, commonly used as a measure of inequality of income distribution or inequality of wealth distribution. It is defined as a ratio with values between 0 and 1: A low _________ indicates more equal income or wealth distribution, while a high _________ indicates more unequal distribution. 0 corresponds to perfect equality (everyone having exactly the same income) and 1 corresponds to perfect inequality (where one person has all the income, while everyone else has zero income.)

a. Suits index
b. Gini coefficient
c. Compensating variation
d. Leapfrogging

29. In economics, _________ is how a natione;s total economy is distributed among its population. ._________ has always been a central concern of economic theory and economic policy. Classical economists such as Adam Smith, Thomas Malthus and David Ricardo were mainly concerned with factor _________, that is, the distribution of income between the main factors of production, land, labour and capital.

a. Equipment trust certificate
b. Income distribution
c. Eco commerce
d. Authorised capital

30. In economics, _________ is the transfer of income, wealth or property from some individuals to others.

One premise of _________ is that money should be distributed to benefit the poorer members of society, and that the rich have an obligation to assist the poor, thus creating a more financially egalitarian society. Another argument is that the rich exploit the poor or otherwise gain unfair benefits.

a. 1921 recession
b. 130-30 fund
c. 100-year flood
d. Redistribution

31. In economics, a _________ exists when the production or use of goods and services by the market is not efficient. That is, there exists another outcome where all involved can be made better off. _________s can be viewed as scenarios where individuals' pursuit of pure self-interest leads to results that are not efficient - that can be improved upon from the societal point-of-view.

a. Financial economics
b. Fixed exchange rate
c. General equilibrium
d. Market failure

32. In economics, a _________ is a good that is non-rivaled and non-excludable. This means, respectively, that consumption of the good by one individual does not reduce availability of the good for consumption by others; and that no one can be effectively excluded from using the good. In the real world, there may be no such thing as an absolutely non-rivaled and non-excludable good; but economists think that some goods approximate the concept closely enough for the analysis to be economically useful.

a. Happiness economics
b. Demand-pull theory
c. Neoclassical synthesis
d. Public good

33. There are two main interpretations of the idea of a _________:

- A model in which the state assumes primary responsibility for the welfare of its citizens. This responsibility in theory ought to be comprehensive, because all aspects of welfare are considered and universally applied to citizens as a 'right'. _________ can also mean the creation of a 'social safety net' of minimum standards of varying forms of welfare. Here is found some confusion between a '_________' and a 'welfare society' in common debate about the definition of the term.
- The provision of welfare in society. In many '_________s', especially in continental Europe, welfare is not actually provided by the state, but by a combination of independent, voluntary, mutualist and government services. The functional provider of benefits and services may be a central or state government, a state-sponsored company or agency, a private corporation, a charity or another form of non-profit organization. However, this phenomenon has been more appropriately termed a 'welfare society,' and the term 'welfare system' has been used to describe the range of _________ and welfare society mixes that are found.

The English term '_________' is believed by Asa Briggs to have been coined by Archbishop William Temple during the Second World War, contrasting wartime Britain with the 'warfare state' of Nazi Germany. Friedrich Hayek contends that the term derived from the older German word Wohlfahrtsstaat, which itself was used by nineteenth century historians to describe a variant of the ideal of Polizeistaat . It was fully developed by the German academic Sozialpolitiker--'socialists of the chair'--from 1870 and first implemented through Bismarck's 'state socialism'. Bismarck's policies have also been seen as the creation of a _________.

a. 130-30 fund
b. 1921 recession
c. 100-year flood
d. Welfare state

34. In mathematics, a _________ is a constant multiplicative factor of a certain object. For example, in the expression $9x^2$, the _________ of x^2 is 9.

The object can be such things as a variable, a vector, a function, etc.

a. 130-30 fund
b. 1921 recession
c. 100-year flood
d. Coefficient

35. _________ is a term that refers both to:

- a formal discipline used to help appraise, or assess, the case for a project or proposal, which itself is a process known as project appraisal; and
- an informal approach to making decisions of any kind.

Under both definitions the process involves, whether explicitly or implicitly, weighing the total expected costs against the total expected benefits of one or more actions in order to choose the best or most profitable option. The formal process is often referred to as either CBA (_________) or BCost-benefit analysis

A hallmark of CBA is that all benefits and all costs are expressed in money terms, and are adjusted for the time value of money, so that all flows of benefits and flows of project costs over time (which tend to occur at different points in time) are expressed on a common basis in terms of their e;present value.e; Closely related, but slightly different, formal techniques include Cost-effectiveness analysis, Economic impact analysis, Fiscal impact analysis and Social Return on Investment(SROI) analysis. The latter builds upon the logic of _________, but differs in that it is explicitly designed to inform the practical decision-making of enterprise managers and investors focused on optimising their social and environmental impacts.

a. 100-year flood
b. Decision theory
c. 130-30 fund
d. Cost-benefit analysis

36. _________ is that which is owed; usually referencing assets owed, but the term can also cover moral obligations and other interactions not requiring money. In the case of assets, _________ is a means of using future purchasing power in the present before a summation has been earned. Some companies and corporations use _________ as a part of their overall corporate finance strategy.

a. Debt
b. Collateral Management
c. Hard money loan
d. Debenture

37. A _________ is an object whose consumption increases the utility of the consumer, for which the quantity demanded exceeds the quantity supplied at zero price. _________s are usually modeled as having diminishing marginal utility. The first individual purchase has high utility; the second has less.

a. Good
b. Pie method
c. Composite good
d. Merit good

38. In mathematics, an _________ is a statement about the relative size or order of two objects, or about whether they are the same or not

- The notation $a < b$ means that a is less than b.
- The notation $a > b$ means that a is greater than b.
- The notation $a \neq b$ means that a is not equal to b, but does not say that one is greater than the other or even that they can be compared in size.

In each statement above, a is not equal to b. These relations are known as strict inequalities. The notation $a < b$ may also be read as 'a is strictly less than b'.

a. ACEA agreement
b. ACCRA Cost of Living Index
c. AD-IA Model
d. Inequality

39. The _________ of monetary management established the rules for commercial and financial relations among the world's major industrial states in the mid 20th Century. The _________ was the first example of a fully negotiated monetary order intended to govern monetary relations among independent nation-states.

Preparing to rebuild the international economic system as World War II was still raging, 730 delegates from all 44 Allied nations gathered at the Mount Washington Hotel in Bretton Woods, New Hampshire, United States, for the United Nations Monetary and Financial Conference.

a. 1921 recession
b. Bretton Woods system
c. 100-year flood
d. 130-30 fund

40. The term _________ refers to economy-wide fluctuations in production or economic activity over several months or years. These fluctuations occur around a long-term growth trend, and typically involve shifts over time between periods of relatively rapid economic growth (expansion or boom), and periods of relative stagnation or decline (contraction or recession.)

These fluctuations are often measured using the growth rate of real gross domestic product.

a. Consumer theory
b. Nominal value
c. Tobit model
d. Business cycle

41. The term _________ refers to government debt, expenditures and revenues, or to finance (particularly financial revenue) in general.

- _________ deficit is the budget deficit of federal or local government
- _________ policy is the discretionary spending of governments. Contrasts with monetary policy.
- _________ year and _________ quarter are reporting periods for firms and other agencies.

.

a. Procter ' Gamble
b. Bucket shop
c. Drawdown
d. Fiscal

42. In economics, _________ is the use of government spending and revenue collection to influence the economy.

_________ can be contrasted with the other main type of economic policy, monetary policy, which attempts to stabilize the economy by controlling interest rates and the supply of money. The two main instruments of _________ are government spending and taxation.

a. Sustainable investment rule
b. Fiscalism
c. 100-year flood
d. Fiscal policy

43. The _________ was a worldwide economic downturn starting in most places in 1929 and ending at different times in the 1930s or early 1940s for different countries. It was the largest and most important economic depression in the 20th century, and is used in the 21st century as an example of how far the world's economy can fall. The _________ originated in the United States; historians most often use as a starting date the stock market crash on October 29, 1929, known as Black Tuesday.

a. British Empire Economic Conference
b. Wall Street Crash of 1929
c. Jarrow March
d. Great Depression

44. _________ and Keynesian Theory) is a macroeconomic theory based on the ideas of 20th-century British economist John Maynard Keynes. _________ argues that private sector decisions sometimes lead to inefficient macroeconomic outcomes and therefore advocates active policy responses by the public sector, including monetary policy actions by the central bank and fiscal policy actions by the government to stabilize output over the business cycle.

The theories forming the basis of _________ were first presented in The General Theory of Employment, Interest and Money, published in 1936.

a. Deflation
b. Rational choice theory
c. Market failure
d. Keynesian economics

45. A _________ is a general term that describes any government policy or regulation that restricts international trade. The barriers can take many forms, including the following terms that include many restrictions in international trade within multiple countries that import and export any items of trade.

- Import duty
- Import licenses
- Export licenses
- Import quotas
- Tariffs
- Subsidies
- Non-tariff barriers to trade
- Voluntary Export Restraints
- Local Content Requirements
- Embargo

Most _________s work on the same principle: the imposition of some sort of cost on trade that raises the price of the traded products. If two or more nations repeatedly use _________s against each other, then a trade war results.

a. Certificate of origin
b. Global financial system
c. National Foreign Trade Council
d. Trade barrier

46. In economics, _________ refers to the ability of a party to produce a good or service using fewer real resources than another entity producing the same good or service..A party has an _________ when using the same input as another party, it can produce a greater output. Since _________ is determined by a simple comparison of labor productivities, it is possible for a a party to have no _________ in anything. It can be contrasted with the concept of comparative advantage which refers to the ability to produce a particular good at a lower opportunity cost.

a. International economics
b. ACCRA Cost of Living Index
c. Absolute advantage
d. Index number

47. _________ is a voluntary transfer of resources from one country to another, given at least partly with the objective of benefiting the recipient country. It may have other functions as well: it may be given as a signal of diplomatic approval, or to strengthen a military ally, to reward a government for behaviour desired by the donor, to extend the donor's cultural influence, to provide infrastructure needed by the donor for resource extraction from the recipient country, or to gain other kinds of commercial access. Humanitarianism and altruism are, nevertheless, significant motivations for the giving of_________.

a. ACEA agreement
b. ACCRA Cost of Living Index
c. Aid
d. AD-IA Model

48. _________ is any long-term change in the patterns of average weather of a specific region or the Earth as a whole. _________ reflects abnormal variations to the Earth's climate and subsequent effects on other parts of the Earth, such as in the ice caps over durations ranging from decades to millions of years.

In recent usage, especially in the context of environmental policy, _________ usually refers to changes in modern climate

a. 130-30 fund
b. 1921 recession
c. 100-year flood
d. Climate change

49. _________ is a negative term describing an claimed capitalist economy in which success in business depends on close relationships between businesspeople and government officials. It may be exhibited in the distribution of legal permits, government grants, special tax breaks, and so forth.

_________ is believed to arise when political cronyism spills over into the business world; self-serving friendships and family ties between businessmen and the government influence the economy and society to the extent that it corrupts public-serving economic and political ideals.

a. Crony capitalism
b. 130-30 fund
c. Good governance
d. 100-year flood

50. _________ is the development of economic wealth of countries or regions for the well-being of their inhabitants. It is the process by which a nation improves the economic, political, and social well being of its people. From a policy perspective, _________ can be defined as efforts that seek to improve the economic well-being and quality of life for a community by creating and/or retaining jobs and supporting or growing incomes and the tax base.

a. Economic methodology
b. Experimental economics
c. Inflation
d. Economic development

51. _________ refers to the actions that governments take in the economic field. It covers the systems for setting interest rates and government deficit as well as the labour market, national ownership, and many other areas of government.

Such policies are often influenced by international institutions like the International Monetary Fund or World Bank as well as political beliefs and the consequent policies of parties.

a. AD-IA Model
b. Economic policy
c. ACCRA Cost of Living Index
d. ACEA agreement

52. The term _________ is applied broadly to a variety of situations in which some financial institutions or assets suddenly lose a large part of their value. In the 19th and early 20th centuries, many financial crises were associated with banking panics, and many recessions coincided with these panics. Other situations that are often called financial crises include stock market crashes and the bursting of other financial bubbles, currency crises, and sovereign defaults.

a. Co-operative economics
b. Macroeconomics
c. Market failure
d. Financial crisis

53. _________ was a survey conducted by the U.S. Department of Justice to gauge the prevalence of alcohol and illegal drug use among prior arrestees. It was a reformulation of the prior Drug Use Forecasting (DUF) program, focused on five drugs in particular: cocaine, marijuana, methamphetamine, opiates, and PCP.

Participants were randomly selected from arrest records in major metropolitan areas; because no personally identifying information is taken from each record chosen, the resulting data can be correlated to arrest rates, but not to the total population of persons charged.

a. ACCRA Cost of Living Index
b. ACEA agreement
c. Arrestee Drug Abuse Monitoring
d. AD-IA Model

54. As a subfield of public economics, _________ is concerned with 'understanding which functions and instruments are best centralized and which are best placed in the sphere of decentralized levels of government' (Oates, 1999.) In other words, it is the study of how competencies (expenditure side) and fiscal instruments (revenue side) are allocated across different (vertical) layers of the administration.

An important part of its subject matter is the system of transfer payments or grants by which a central government shares its revenues with lower levels of government.

a. 100-year flood
b. 1921 recession
c. Fiscal federalism
d. 130-30 fund

55. _________ was a Scottish moral philosopher and a pioneer of political economy. One of the key figures of the Scottish Enlightenment, Smith is the author of The Theory of Moral Sentiments and An Inquiry into the Nature and Causes of the Wealth of Nations. The latter, usually abbreviated as The Wealth of Nations, is considered his magnum opus and the first modern work of economics.

a. Adolph Fischer
b. Alan Greenspan
c. Adolf Hitler
d. Adam Smith

56. _________ in political thought refers to economic theories of social organization advocating collective ownership and administration of the means of production and distribution of goods, and a society characterized by equality for all individuals, with an egalitarian method of compensation. Modern _________ originated in the late 19th-century intellectual and working class political movement that criticized the effects of industrialization and private ownership on society. Karl Marx posited that _________ would be achieved via class struggle and a proletarian revolution after a transitional stage from capitalism called the dictatorship of the proletariat.

a. Adolf Hitler
b. Adolph Fischer
c. Adam Smith
d. Socialism

57. The _________ is a situation noted by the Marquis de Condorcet in the late 18th century, in which collective preferences can be cyclic, even if the preferences of individual voters are not. This is paradoxical, because it means that majority wishes can be in conflict with each other. When this occurs, it is because the conflicting majorities are each made up of different groups of individuals.

a. 100-year flood
b. 130-30 fund
c. Voting paradox
d. 1921 recession

58. The _________ is the apparent contradiction that although water is on the whole more useful, in terms of survival, than diamonds, diamonds command a higher price in the market. The economist Adam Smith is often considered to be the classic presenter of this paradox. Nicolaus Copernicus, John Locke, John Law and others had previously tried to explain the disparity.

a. St. Petersburg paradox
b. 100-year flood
c. Paradox of value
d. 130-30 fund

59. A _________ is a period used for calculating annual financial statements in businesses and other organizations. In many jurisdictions, regulatory laws regarding accounting and taxation require such reports once per twelve months, but do not require that the period reported on constitutes a calendar year (i.e., January through December.) _________s vary between businesses and countries.

a. 100-year flood
b. 1921 recession
c. Fiscal year
d. 130-30 fund

60. A _________ is a broad coalition government consisting of all parties (or all major parties) in the legislature, usually formed during a time of war or other national emergency.

During World War I the Conservative government of Sir Robert Borden invited the Liberal opposition to join the government as a means of dealing with the Conscription crisis of 1917. The Liberals, led by Sir Wilfrid Laurier refused; however, Borden was able to convince many individual Liberals to join what was called a Union Government, which defeated the Laurier Liberals in the fall 1917 election.

a. 130-30 fund
b. National Government
c. 100-year flood
d. 1921 recession

61. _________ is a company's financial statement that indicates how the revenue is transformed into the net income The purpose of the _________ is to show managers and investors whether the company made or lost money during the period being reported.

The important thing to remember about an _________ is that it represents a period of time.

a. Income statement
b. ACCRA Cost of Living Index
c. AD-IA Model
d. ACEA agreement

62. The phrase _________, according to the Organization for Economic Co-operation and Development, refers to 'creative work undertaken on a systematic basis in order to increase the stock of knowledge, including knowledge of man, culture and society, and the use of this stock of knowledge to devise new applications [sic]'

New product design and development is more than often a crucial factor in the survival of a company. In an industry that is fast changing, firms must continually revise their design and range of products. This is necessary due to continuous technology change and development as well as other competitors and the changing preference of customers.

a. 100-year flood
b. 1921 recession
c. Research and development
d. 130-30 fund

63. _________ is used to assign the available resources in an economic way. It is part of resource management.

In strategic planning,is a plan for using available resources, for example human resources, especially in the near term, to achieve goals for the future.

a. 100-year flood
b. 1921 recession
c. 130-30 fund
d. Resource allocation

64. In microeconomics, _________ is quite simply the conversion of inputs into outputs. It is an economic process that uses resources to create a good or service that is suitable for exchange. This can include manufacturing, storing, shipping, and packaging.

a. Red Guards
b. MET
c. Solved
d. Production

65. In economics, a _________ is a function that specifies the output of a firm, an industry, or an entire economy for all combinations of inputs. A meta-_________ compares the practice of the existing entities converting inputs X into output y to determine the most efficient practice _________ of the existing entities, whether the most efficient feasible practice production or the most efficient actual practice production. In either case, the maximum output of a technologically-determined production process is a mathematical function of input factors of production.

a. Short-run
b. Constant elasticity of substitution
c. Post-Fordism
d. Production function

66. The principle that taxes should vary according to an individual's level of wealth or income is the _________ principle.

a. ACCRA Cost of Living Index
b. ACEA agreement
c. Ability-to-pay
d. AD-IA Model

67. _________ is the concept or idea of fairness in economics, particularly as to taxation or welfare economics.

In welfare economics, _________ may be distinguished from economic efficiency in overall evaluation of social welfare. Although '_________' has broader uses, it may be posed as a counterpart to economic inequality in yielding a 'good' distribution of welfare.

a. AD-IA Model
b. ACEA agreement
c. ACCRA Cost of Living Index
d. Equity

68. The term direct tax has more than one meaning: a colloquial meaning and, in the United States, a constitutional law meaning. Certain taxes may be _________ in the colloquial sense but indirect taxes in the constitutional sense.

In the UK, direct tax refers to tax levied directly off of an organisation or an individual person, like income tax.

a. Honorarium
b. Taxation as theft
c. National War Tax Resistance Coordinating Committee
d. Direct taxes

69. An _________ is a tax levied on the financial income of people, corporations, or other legal entities. Various _________ systems exist, with varying degrees of tax incidence. Income taxation can be progressive, proportional, or regressive.

a. ACCRA Cost of Living Index
b. Income tax
c. ACEA agreement
d. AD-IA Model

70. The term _________ has more than one meaning.

In the colloquial sense, an _________, or goods and services tax (GST)) is a tax collected by an intermediary (such as a retail store) from the person who bears the ultimate economic burden of the tax (such as the customer.) The intermediary later files a tax return and forwards the tax proceeds to government with the return.

a. Optimal tax
b. User charge
c. Olivera-Tanzi effect
d. Indirect tax

71. A _________ is a tax by which the tax rate increases as the taxable amount increases. 'Progressive' describes a distribution effect on income or expenditure, referring to the way the rate progresses from low to high, where the average tax rate is less than the marginal tax rate. It can be applied to individual taxes or to a tax system as a whole; a year, multi-year, or lifetime.

a. Proportional tax
b. 130-30 fund
c. 100-year flood
d. Progressive tax

72. A _________ is a tax imposed so that the tax rate is fixed as the amount subject to taxation increases. In simple terms, it imposes an equal burden (relative to resources) on the rich and poor. 'Proportional' describes a distribution effect on income or expenditure, referring to the way the rate remains consistent (does not progress from 'low to high' or 'high to low' as income or consumption changes), where the marginal tax rate is equal to the average tax rate.

a. 130-30 fund
b. Regressive tax
c. 100-year flood
d. Proportional tax

73. A _________ is a tax imposed in such a manner that the tax rate decreases as the amount subject to taxation increases. In simple terms, a _________ imposes a greater burden (relative to resources) on the poor than on the rich -- there is an inverse relationship between the tax rate and the taxpayer's ability to pay as measured by assets, consumption, or income. 'Regressive' describes a distribution effect on income or expenditure, referring to the way the rate progresses from high to low, where the average tax rate exceeds the marginal tax rate.

a. 130-30 fund
b. Regressive tax
c. 100-year flood
d. Proportional tax

74. Under the system of feudalism, a _________, fief, feud, feoff often consisted of inheritable lands or revenue-producing property granted by a liege lord, generally to a vassal, in return for a form of allegiance, originally to give him the means to fulfill his military duties when called upon. However anything of value could be held in fief, such as an office, a right of exploitation (e.g., hunting, fishing) or any other type of revenue, rather than the land it comes from.

Originally, the feudal institution of vassalage did not imply the giving or receiving of landholdings (which were granted only as a reward for loyalty), but by the eighth century the giving of a landholding was becoming standard.

a. 1921 recession
b. 100-year flood
c. Fiefdom
d. 130-30 fund

75. To _________ is to impose a financial charge or other levy upon a taxpayer by a state or the functional equivalent of a state.

_________es are also imposed by many subnational entities. _________es consist of direct _________ or indirect _________, and may be paid in money or as its labour equivalent (often but not always unpaid.)

a. Tax
b. 130-30 fund
c. 100-year flood
d. 1921 recession

76. To tax is to impose a financial charge or other levy upon a taxpayer by a state or the functional equivalent of a state.

_________ are also imposed by many subnational entities. _________ consist of direct tax or indirect tax, and may be paid in money or as its labour equivalent (often but not always unpaid.)

a. 1921 recession
b. 130-30 fund
c. 100-year flood
d. Taxes

77. The _________ is 'the basic residential unit in which economic production, consumption, inheritance, child rearing, and shelter are organized and carried out'; [the _________] 'may or may not be synonomous with family'.

The _________ is the basic unit of analysis in many social, microeconomic and government models. The term refers to all individuals who live in the same dwelling.

a. 100-year flood
b. Household
c. Family economics
d. 130-30 fund

78. In business and accounting, _________ are everything of value that is owned by a person or company. It is a claim on the property your income of a borrower. The balance sheet of a firm records the monetary value of the _________ owned by the firm.

a. Amortization schedule
b. ACCRA Cost of Living Index
c. ACEA agreement
d. Assets

79. In statistics, the _________ problem occurs when one considers a set of statistical inferences simultaneously. Errors in inference, including confidence intervals that fail to include their corresponding population parameters are more likely to occur when one considers the family as a whole. Several statistical techniques have been developed to prevent this from happening, allowing significance levels for single and _________ to be directly compared.

a. Familywise error rate
b. Hypotheses suggested by the data
c. Multiple comparisons
d. False discovery rate

80. A _________ refers to any type debt instrument, such as a loan, bond, mortgage that does not have a fixed rate of interest over the life of the instrument. Such debt typically uses an index or other base rate for establishing the interest rate for each relevant period. One of the most common rates to use as the basis for applying interest rates is the London Inter-bank Offered Rate, or LIBOR

a. Floating interest rate
b. Money market
c. Disposal tax effect
d. Moneylender

81. The term _________ describes two different concepts:

- The first is a recognition of partial payment already made towards taxes due.
- The second is a state benefit paid to workers through the tax system, which has the effect of increasing (rather than reducing) net income.

Within the Australian, Canadian, United Kingdom, and United States tax systems, a _________ is a recognition of partial payment already made towards taxes due. A similar concept exists (fr:Avoir fiscal) in the French tax system. This situation arises, for example, when standard rate tax has been deducted at source , but the tax-payer is subject to further taxation at a higher rate. It also applies in dividend imputation systems.

a. 1921 recession
b. 100-year flood
c. Tax credit
d. 130-30 fund

82. A _________ product is a product designed for cheapness and short-term convenience rather than medium to long-term durability, with most products only intended for single use. The term is also sometimes used for products that may last several months (ex. _________ air filters) to distinguish from similar products that last indefinitely (ex.

a. 1921 recession
b. Disposable
c. 130-30 fund
d. 100-year flood

83. _________ is gross income minus income tax on that income.

Discretionary income is income after subtracting taxes and normal expenses (such as rent or mortgage, utilities, insurance, medical, transportation, property maintenance, child support, inflation, food and sundries, 'c.) to maintain a certain standard of living.

a. Taxation as theft
b. Stamp Act
c. Disposable personal income
d. Disposable income

84. A _________ is a tax system with a constant tax rate. Usually the term _________ would refer to household income (and sometimes corporate profits) being taxed at one marginal rate, in contrast with progressive taxes that may vary according to such parameters as income or usage levels. _________es generally offer simplicity in the tax code, which has been reported to increase compliance and decrease administration costs.

a. 130-30 fund
b. 100-year flood
c. Flat tax
d. 1921 recession

85. In a company, _________ is the sum of all financial records of salaries, wages, bonuses and deductions.

A paycheck, is traditionally a paper document issued by an employer to pay an employee for services rendered. While most commonly used in the United States, recently the physical paycheck has been increasingly replaced by electronic direct deposit to bank accounts.

a. Tax expense
b. 100-year flood
c. Payroll
d. Total Expense Ratio

86. A _________ is a tax on spending on goods and services. The term refers to a system with a tax base of consumption. It usually takes the form of an indirect tax, such as a sales tax or value added tax.

a. Consumption tax
b. 1921 recession
c. 100-year flood
d. 130-30 fund

87. _________, in law and economics, is a form of risk management primarily used to hedge against the risk of a contingent loss. _________ is defined as the equitable transfer of the risk of a loss, from one entity to another, in exchange for a premium, and can be thought of as a guaranteed small loss to prevent a large, possibly devastating loss. An insurer is a company selling the _________; an insured or policyholder is the person or entity buying the _________.

a. Insurance
b. ACEA agreement
c. ACCRA Cost of Living Index
d. AD-IA Model

88. _________s are payments made by a corporation to its shareholders. It is the portion of corporate profits paid out to stockholders. When a corporation earns a profit or surplus, that money can be put to two uses: it can either be re-invested in the business (called retained earnings), or it can be paid to the shareholders as a _________.

a. Dividend yield
b. Dividend cover
c. Dividend puzzle
d. Dividend

89. In finance, the _________s between two currencies specifies how much one currency is worth in terms of the other. It is the value of a foreign natione;s currency in terms of the home natione;s currency. For example an _________ of 102 Japanese yen to the United States dollar means that JPY 102 is worth the same as USD 1.

a. ACCRA Cost of Living Index
b. ACEA agreement
c. Interbank market
d. Exchange rate

90. _________ is an ad valorem tax that an owner is required to pay on the value of the property being taxed. _________ can be defined as 'generally, tax imposed by municipalities upon owners of property within their jurisdiction based on the value of such property.' There are three species or types of property: Land, Improvements to Land (immovable manmade objects; i.e., buildings), and Personal (movable manmade objects.) Real estate, real property or realty are all terms for the combination of land and improvements.

a. Bank regulation
b. Property tax
c. Community property
d. Chief Financial Officers Act of 1990

91. A _________ is a consumption tax charged at the point of purchase for certain goods and services. The tax is usually set as a percentage by the government charging the tax. There is usually a list of exemptions.

a. 1921 recession
b. Sales tax
c. 100-year flood
d. 130-30 fund

92. The supply of labor is the number of total hours that workers wish to work at a given real wage rate.

_________ curves are derived from the 'labor-leisure' trade-off. More hours worked earn higher incomes but necessitate a cut in the amount of leisure that workers enjoy.

a. Late capitalism
b. Labor supply
c. Human trafficking
d. Creative capitalism

93. _________ is a school of macroeconomic thought that argues that economic growth can be most effectively created using incentives for people to produce (supply) goods and services, such as adjusting income tax and capital gains tax rates, and by allowing greater flexibility by reducing regulation. Consumers will then benefit from a greater supply of goods and services at lower prices.

The term _________ was coined by journalist Jude Wanniski in 1975, and popularized the ideas of economists Robert Mundell and Arthur Laffer.

a. Clap note
b. Commodity trading advisors
c. Fiscal stimulus plans
d. Supply-side economics

94. _________ is the increase in the amount of the goods and services produced by an economy over time. It is conventionally measured as the percent rate of increase in real gross domestic product, or real GDP. Growth is usually calculated in real terms, i.e. inflation-adjusted terms, in order to net out the effect of inflation on the price of the goods and services produced.

a. AD-IA Model
b. ACEA agreement
c. ACCRA Cost of Living Index
d. Economic growth

95. In law and economics, the _________, describes the economic efficiency of an economic allocation or outcome in the presence of externalities. The theorem states that when trade in an externality is possible and there are no transaction costs, bargaining will lead to an efficient outcome regardless of the initial allocation of property rights. In practice, obstacles to bargaining or poorly defined property rights can prevent Coasian bargaining.

a. Coase theorem
b. Means test
c. Prior appropriation water rights
d. General Mining Act of 1872

96. A _________ is a tax that is a fixed amount no matter what the change in circumstance of the taxed entity. (A lump-sum subsidy or lump-sum redistribution is defined similarly.) It is a regressive tax, such that the lower income is, the higher percentage of income applicable to the tax.

a. Funding body
b. Budget deficit
c. Grant-in-aid
d. Lump-sum tax

97. _________, short for Ecological taxation, can refer to:

A policy that introduces taxes intended to promote ecologically sustainable activities via economic incentives. Such a policy can complement or avert the need for regulatory approaches. Often, such a policy intends to maintain overall tax revenue by proportionately reducing other taxes, e.g. on human labor and renewable resources, in which case it is known as the green tax shift towards ecological taxation.

a. Ecotax
b. AD-IA Model
c. ACCRA Cost of Living Index
d. ACEA agreement

98. _________ is a concept within public finance, a sub-discipline within economics, that refers to the combined overall economic impact of both government taxation and expenditures on the real economic income of individuals. While taxation reduces the economic well-being of individuals, government expenditures raise their economic well-being. _________ is the term for the overall impact of government taxing and spending considered together.

a. Funding body
b. Fiscal incidence
c. Lump-sum tax
d. Tax increment financing

99. In economics, _________ is the analysis of the effect of a particular tax on the distribution of economic welfare. _________ is said to 'fall' upon the group that, at the end of the day, bears the burden of the tax. The key concept is that the _________ or tax burden does not depend on where the revenue is collected, but on the price elasticity of demand and price elasticity of supply.

a. Tax incidence
b. 130-30 fund
c. 1921 recession
d. 100-year flood

1. _________ is a situation in which the limited resources of a firm are allocated in accordance with the wishes of consumers. An allocatively efficient economy produces an 'optimal mix' of commodities. A firm is allocatively efficient when its price is equal to its marginal costs (that is, P = MC) in a perfect market.

a. ACEA agreement
b. Economic efficiency
c. ACCRA Cost of Living Index
d. Allocative efficiency

2. Competition law, known in the United States as _________ law, has three main elements:

- prohibiting agreements or practices that restrict free trading and competition between business entities. This includes in particular the repression of cartels.
- banning abusive behaviour by a firm dominating a market, or anti-competitive practices that tend to lead to such a dominant position. Practices controlled in this way may include predatory pricing, tying, price gouging, refusal to deal, and many others.
- supervising the mergers and acquisitions of large corporations, including some joint ventures. Transactions that are considered to threaten the competitive process can be prohibited altogether, or approved subject to 'remedies' such as an obligation to divest part of the merged business or to offer licences or access to facilities to enable other businesses to continue competing.

The substance and practice of competition law varies from jurisdiction to jurisdiction. Protecting the interests of consumers (consumer welfare) and ensuring that entrepreneurs have an opportunity to compete in the market economy are often treated as important objectives. Competition law is closely connected with law on deregulation of access to markets, state aids and subsidies, the privatisation of state owned assets and the establishment of independent sector regulators. In recent decades, competition law has been viewed as a way to provide better public services.

a. United Kingdom competition law
b. Anti-Inflation Act
c. Intellectual property law
d. Antitrust

3. In economic theory, _________ is the competitive situation in any market where the conditions necessary for perfect competition are not satisfied. It is a market structure that does not meet the conditions of perfect competition.

Forms of _________ include:

- Monopoly, in which there is only one seller of a good.
- Oligopoly, in which there is a small number of sellers.
- Monopolistic competition, in which there are many sellers producing highly differentiated goods.
- Monopsony, in which there is only one buyer of a good.
- Oligopsony, in which there is a small number of buyers.

There may also be _________ in markets due to buyers or sellers lacking information about prices and the goods being traded.

There may also be _________ due to a time lag in a market.

a. AD-IA Model
b. Imperfect competition
c. ACCRA Cost of Living Index
d. ACEA agreement

4. The _________ was a regulatory body in the United States created by the Interstate Commerce Act of 1887, which was signed into law by President Grover Cleveland. The agency was abolished in 1995, and the agency's remaining functions were transferred to the Surface Transportation Board.

The Commission's five members were appointed by the President with the consent of the United States Senate.

a. ACEA agreement
b. Office of Thrift Supervision
c. ACCRA Cost of Living Index
d. Interstate Commerce Commission

5. In economics, the _________ is the term economists use to describe the self-regulating nature of the marketplace. The _________ is a metaphor coined by the economist Adam Smith in The Wealth of Nations.

Adam Smith mentions the metaphor in Book IV of The Wealth of Nations, arguing that people in any society will certainly employ their capital in foreign trading only if the profits available by that method far exceed those available locally, and that in such a case it is better for society as a whole if they so did.

a. AD-IA Model
b. ACEA agreement
c. ACCRA Cost of Living Index
d. Invisible hand

6. In economics, a _________ exists when the production or use of goods and services by the market is not efficient. That is, there exists another outcome where all involved can be made better off. _________s can be viewed as scenarios where individuals' pursuit of pure self-interest leads to results that are not efficient - that can be improved upon from the societal point-of-view.

a. Fixed exchange rate
b. Financial economics
c. General equilibrium
d. Market failure

7. In economics, _________ is the ability of a firm to alter the market price of a good or service. A firm with _________ can raise prices without losing all customers to competitors.

When a firm has _________ it faces a downward-sloping demand curve.

a. Market power
b. Revenue-cap regulation
c. Price makers
d. Pacman conjecture

8. In neoclassical economics and microeconomics, _________ describes the perfect being a market in which there are many small firms, all producing homogeneous goods. In the short term, such markets are productively inefficient as output will not occur where mc is equal to ac, but allocatively efficient, as output under _________ will always occur where mc is equal to mr, and therefore where mc equals ar. However, in the long term, such markets are both allocatively and productively efficient.

a. Co-operative economics
b. Perfect competition
c. Law of supply
d. General equilibrium

9. A _________ describes one of a number of pieces of legislation relating to the reduction of smog and air pollution in general. The use by governments to enforce clean air standards has contributed to an improvement in human health and longer life spans. Critics argue it has also sapped corporate profits and contributed to outsourcing, while defenders counter that improved environmental air quality has generated more jobs than it has eliminated.

a. 100-year flood
b. Smog
c. 130-30 fund
d. Clean Air Act

10. _________s is the social science that studies the production, distribution, and consumption of goods and services. The term _________s comes from the Ancient Greek οá¼°κονομÎ¯α from οá¼¶κος (oikos, 'house') + νÏŒμος (nomos, 'custom' or 'law'), hence 'rules of the house(hold)'. Current _________ models developed out of the broader field of political economy in the late 19th century, owing to a desire to use an empirical approach more akin to the physical sciences.

a. Energy economics
b. Economic
c. Inflation
d. Opportunity cost

11. _________ are conceptually similar to economies of scale. Whereas economies of scale primarily refer to efficiencies associated with supply-side changes, such as increasing or decreasing the scale of production, of a single product type, _________ refer to efficiencies primarily associated with demand-side changes, such as increasing or decreasing the scope of marketing and distribution, of different types of products. _________ are one of the main reasons for such marketing strategies as product bundling, product lining, and family branding.

a. Isoquant
b. Economies of scale
c. Economic production quantity
d. Economies of scope

12. In economics, a _________ is a mechanism that allows people to easily buy and sell (trade) financial securities (such as stocks and bonds), commodities (such as precious metals or agricultural goods), and other fungible items of value at low transaction costs and at prices that reflect the efficient-market hypothesis.

_________s have evolved significantly over several hundred years and are undergoing constant innovation to improve liquidity.

Both general markets (where many commodities are traded) and specialized markets (where only one commodity is traded) exist.

a. Convertible arbitrage
b. Noise trader
c. Market anomaly
d. Financial market

13. In economics, a _________ occurs when, due to the economies of scale of a particular industry, the maximum efficiency of production and distribution is realized through a single supplier.

Natural monopolies arise where the largest supplier in an industry, often the first supplier in a market, has an overwhelming cost advantage over other actual or potential competitors. This tends to be the case in industries where capital costs predominate, creating economies of scale which are large in relation to the size of the market, and hence high barriers to entry; examples include water services and electricity.

a. Collective goods
b. Privatizing profits and socializing losses
c. Common-pool resource
d. Natural monopoly

14. The _________ refers to the 'common well-being' or 'general welfare.' The _________ is central to policy debates, politics, democracy and the nature of government itself. While nearly everyone claims that aiding the common well-being or general welfare is positive, there is little, if any, consensus on what exactly constitutes the _________.

There are different views on how many members of the public must benefit from an action before it can be declared to be in the _________: at one extreme, an action has to benefit every single member of society in order to be truly in the _________; at the other extreme, any action can be in the _________ as long as it benefits some of the population and harms none.

a. Second-class citizen
b. Stealth tax
c. Power Elite
d. Public interest

15. A public utility (usually just utility) is an organization that maintains the infrastructure for a public service (often also providing a service using that infrastructure.) _________ are subject to forms of public control and regulation ranging from local community-based groups to state-wide government monopolies. Common arguments in favor of regulation include the desire to control market power, facilitate competition, promote investment or system expansion, or stabilize markets.

a. 1921 recession
b. 130-30 fund
c. 100-year flood
d. Public utilities

16. _________ is the removal or simplification of government rules and regulations that constrain the operation of market forces. _________ does not mean elimination of laws against fraud, but eliminating or reducing government control of how business is done, thereby moving toward a more free market.

The stated rationale for '_________' is often that fewer and simpler regulations will lead to a raised level of competitiveness, therefore higher productivity, more efficiency and lower prices overall.

a. Secular basis
b. Deregulation
c. Fundamental psychological law
d. Macroeconomic policy instruments

17. In economics and sociology, an _________ is any factor (financial or non-financial) that enables or motivates a particular course of action, or counts as a reason for preferring one choice to the alternatives. It is an expectation that encourages people to behave in a certain way. Since human beings are purposeful creatures, the study of _________ structures is central to the study of all economic activity (both in terms of individual decision-making and in terms of co-operation and competition within a larger institutional structure.)

a. Economic reform
b. Isocost
c. Epstein-Zin preferences
d. Incentive

18. _________ is a fee paid on borrowed assets. It is the price paid for the use of borrowed money , or, money earned by deposited funds . Assets that are sometimes lent with _________ include money, shares, consumer goods through hire purchase, major assets such as aircraft, and even entire factories in finance lease arrangements.

a. Interest
b. Internal debt
c. Asset protection
d. Insolvency

19. In economics, a _________ exists when a specific individual or enterprise has sufficient control over a particular product or service to determine significantly the terms on which other individuals shall have access to it. Monopolies are thus characterized by a lack of economic competition for the good or service that they provide and a lack of viable substitute goods. The verb 'monopolize' refers to the process by which a firm gains persistently greater market share than what is expected under perfect competition.

a. 100-year flood
b. 1921 recession
c. Monopoly
d. 130-30 fund

20. In finance, a _________ is a debt security, in which the authorized issuer owes the holders a debt and, depending on the terms of the _________, is obliged to pay interest (the coupon) and/or to repay the principal at a later date, termed maturity. A _________ is a formal contract to repay borrowed money with interest at fixed intervals.

Thus a _________ is like a loan: the issuer is the borrower (debtor), the holder is the lender (creditor), and the coupon is the interest.

a. Prize Bond
b. Callable
c. Zero-coupon
d. Bond

21. _________ is a broad label that refers to any individuals or households that use goods and services generated within the economy. The concept of a _________ is used in different contexts, so that the usage and significance of the term may vary.

Typically when business people and economists talk of _________s they are talking about person as _________, an aggregated commodity item with little individuality other than that expressed in the buy/not-buy decision.

a. Consumer
b. 100-year flood
c. 1921 recession
d. 130-30 fund

22. _________ is an equity (stock) exchange located at 11 Wall Street in lower Manhattan, New York, USA. It is the largest stock exchange in the world by dollar value of its listed companies' securities. As of October 2008, the combined capitalization of all domestic _________ listed companies was US$10.1 trillion.

a. 130-30 fund
b. 1921 recession
c. 100-year flood
d. New York Stock Exchange

23. _________ in economics and business is the result of an exchange and from that trade we assign a numerical monetary value to a good, service or asset. If Alice trades Bob 4 apples for an orange, the _________ of an orange is 4 apples. Inversely, the _________ of an apple is 1/4 oranges.

a. Price war
b. Price book
c. Premium pricing
d. Price

24. In economics, _________ and economies of scale are related terms that describe what happens as the scale of production increases. They are different terms and should not be used interchangeably.

_________ refers to a technical property of production that examines changes in output subsequent to a proportional change in all inputs (where all inputs increase by a constant factor.)

a. Necessity good
b. Constant returns to scale
c. Customer equity
d. Returns to scale

25. A security is a fungible, negotiable instrument representing financial value. _________ are broadly categorized into debt _________; equity _________, e.g., common stocks; and derivative (finance) contracts such as forwards, futures, options and swaps. The company or other entity issuing the security is called the issuer.

a. Red herring prospectus
b. Pass-Through Certificates
c. Securities
d. Settlement risk

26. A _________ is a corporation or mutual organization which provides trading facilities for stock brokers and traders, to trade stocks and other securities. It may be a physical trading room where the traders gather, or a formalised communications network. Creation of a _________ is a strategy of economic development.

a. Stock Exchange
b. Primary shares
c. 100-year flood
d. SEAQ

27. _________, in microeconomics, are the cost advantages that a business obtains due to expansion. They are factors that cause a producere;s average cost per unit to fall as scale is increased. _________ is a long run concept and refers to reductions in unit cost as the size of a facility, or scale, increases.

a. Underinvestment employment relationship
b. Economies of scale
c. Isoquant
d. Economic production quantity

28. In economics, an _________ or spillover of an economic transaction is an impact on a party that is not directly involved in the transaction. In such a case, prices do not reflect the full costs or benefits in production or consumption of a product or service. A positive impact is called an external benefit, while a negative impact is called an external cost.

a. Environmental impact assessment
b. Existence value
c. Environmental tariff
d. Externality

29. The phrase _________ and acquisitions refers to the aspect of corporate strategy, corporate finance and management dealing with the buying, selling and combining of different companies that can aid, finance, or help a growing company in a given industry grow rapidly without having to create another business entity.

An acquisition, also known as a takeover or a buyout, is the buying of one company (the 'target') by another. An acquisition may be friendly or hostile.

a. Political economy
b. Differential accumulation
c. Peace dividend
d. Mergers

30. _________ is an economic concept with commonplace familiarity. It is the price that a good or service is offered at, or will fetch, in the marketplace. It is of interest mainly in the study of microeconomics.

a. Paper trading
b. Market anomaly
c. Market price
d. Noisy market hypothesis

31. A _________ association is a financial institution that specializes in accepting savings deposits and making mortgage and other loans. The S'L or thrift term is mainly used in the United States; similar institutions in the United Kingdom, Ireland and some Commonwealth countries include building societies and trustee savings banks.

They are often mutually held, meaning that the depositors and borrowers are members with voting rights, and have the ability to direct the financial and managerial goals of the organization, similar to the policyholders of a mutual insurance company.

a. Fonds commun de placement
b. Participating policy
c. Collective investment scheme
d. Savings and loan

32. In economics, _________ is equal to total cost divided by the number of goods produced (the output quantity, Q.) It is also equal to the sum of average variable costs (total variable costs divided by Q) plus average fixed costs (total fixed costs divided by Q.) _________s may be dependent on the time period considered (increasing production may be expensive or impossible in the short term, for example.)

a. Average fixed cost
b. Explicit cost
c. Average cost
d. Average variable cost

33. _________ is one of the ways government regulate a monopoly market. Monopolists tend to produce less than the optimal quantity pushing the prices up. Government may use _________ as a tool to regulate prices monopolists may charge.

a. ACCRA Cost of Living Index
b. AD-IA Model
c. ACEA agreement
d. Average cost pricing

34. In economics, a _________ is a graph of the costs of production as a function of total quantity produced. In a free market economy, productively efficient firms use these curves to find the optimal point of production, where they make the most profits. There are a few different types of _________s, each relevant to a different area of economics.

a. Phillips curve
b. Cost curve
c. Demand curve
d. Kuznets curve

35. _________ is one of the four Ps of the marketing mix. The other three aspects are product, promotion, and place. It is also a key variable in microeconomic price allocation theory.

a. Premium pricing
b. Pricing
c. Guaranteed Maximum Price
d. Point of total assumption

36. A _________ is a price discrimination technique in which the price of a product or service is composed of two parts - a lump-sum fee as well as a per-unit charge. In general, price discrimination techniques only occur in partially or fully monopolistic markets. It is designed to enable the firm to capture more consumer surplus than it otherwise would in a non-discriminating pricing environment.

a. Price floor
b. Big ticket item
c. Penetration pricing
d. Two-part tariff

37. In algebra, a _________ is a function depending on n that associates a scalar, det(A), to an n×n square matrix A. The fundamental geometric meaning of a _________ is a scale factor for measure when A is regarded as a linear transformation. _________s are important both in calculus, where they enter the substitution rule for several variables, and in multilinear algebra.

For a fixed nonnegative integer n, there is a unique _________ function for the n×n matrices over any commutative ring R. In particular, this function exists when R is the field of real or complex numbers.

a. 100-year flood
b. 130-30 fund
c. 1921 recession
d. Determinant

38. A _________ is a duty imposed on goods when they are moved across a political boundary. They are usually associated with protectionism, the economic policy of restraining trade between nations. For political reasons, _________s are usually imposed on imported goods, although they may also be imposed on exported goods.

a. Tariff
b. 100-year flood
c. 1921 recession
d. 130-30 fund

39. The _________ consists of a number of economic theories which describe the nature of the firm, company including its existence, its behaviour, and its relationship with the market.

In simplified terms, the _________ aims to answer these questions:

1. Existence - why do firms emerge, why are not all transactions in the economy mediated over the market?
2. Boundaries - why the boundary between firms and the market is located exactly there? Which transactions are performed internally and which are negotiated on the market?
3. Organization - why are firms structured in such specific way? What is the interplay of formal and informal relationships?

Despite looking simple, these questions are not answered by the established economic theory, which usually views firms as given, and treats them as black boxes without any internal structure.

The First World War period saw a change of emphasis in economic theory away from industry-level analysis which mainly included analysing markets to analysis at the level of the firm, as it became increasingly clear that perfect competition was no longer an adequate model of how firms behaved. Economic theory till then had focussed on trying to understand markets alone and there had been little study on understanding why firms or organisations exist.

a. Theory of the firm
b. Policy Ineffectiveness Proposition
c. Khazzoom-Brookes postulate
d. Technology gap

40. Monopoly power is an example of market failure which occurs when one or more of the participants has the ability to influence the price or other outcomes in some general or specialized market. The most commonly discussed form of market power is that of a monopoly, but other forms such as monopsony, and more moderate versions of these two extremes, exist. Market participants that have market power are sometimes referred to as 'price makers', while those without are sometimes called '_________'.

a. Monopolization
b. Market concentration
c. Price takers
d. Market power

41. In economics, _________ is a measure of the relative satisfaction from consumption of various goods and services. Given this measure, one may speak meaningfully of increasing or decreasing _________, and thereby explain economic behavior in terms of attempts to increase one's _________. For illustrative purposes, changes in _________ are sometimes expressed in units called utils.

a. Expected utility hypothesis
b. Utility function
c. Utility
d. Ordinal utility

42. In economics, _________ is the transfer of income, wealth or property from some individuals to others.

One premise of _________ is that money should be distributed to benefit the poorer members of society, and that the rich have an obligation to assist the poor, thus creating a more financially egalitarian society. Another argument is that the rich exploit the poor or otherwise gain unfair benefits.

a. 130-30 fund
b. 100-year flood
c. 1921 recession
d. Redistribution

43. In economics, _________ refers to the ability of a party to produce a good or service using fewer real resources than another entity producing the same good or service..A party has an _________ when using the same input as another party, it can produce a greater output. Since _________ is determined by a simple comparison of labor productivities, it is possible for a a party to have no _________ in anything. It can be contrasted with the concept of comparative advantage which refers to the ability to produce a particular good at a lower opportunity cost.

a. Index number
b. International economics
c. ACCRA Cost of Living Index
d. Absolute advantage

44. In economics, the _________ measures the payments that flow between any individual country and all other countries. It is used to summarize all international economic transactions for that country during a specific time period, usually a year. The _________ is determined by the country's exports and imports of goods, services, and financial capital, as well as financial transfers.

a. Skyscraper Index
b. Gross world product
c. Gross domestic product per barrel
d. Balance of payments

45. _________ is a term that refers both to:

- a formal discipline used to help appraise, or assess, the case for a project or proposal, which itself is a process known as project appraisal; and
- an informal approach to making decisions of any kind.

Under both definitions the process involves, whether explicitly or implicitly, weighing the total expected costs against the total expected benefits of one or more actions in order to choose the best or most profitable option. The formal process is often referred to as either CBA (_________) or BCost-benefit analysis

A hallmark of CBA is that all benefits and all costs are expressed in money terms, and are adjusted for the time value of money, so that all flows of benefits and flows of project costs over time (which tend to occur at different points in time) are expressed on a common basis in terms of their e;present value.e; Closely related, but slightly different, formal techniques include Cost-effectiveness analysis, Economic impact analysis, Fiscal impact analysis and Social Return on Investment(SROI) analysis. The latter builds upon the logic of _________, but differs in that it is explicitly designed to inform the practical decision-making of enterprise managers and investors focused on optimising their social and environmental impacts.

a. Cost-benefit analysis
b. 130-30 fund
c. Decision theory
d. 100-year flood

46. A _________ is the transfer of wealth from one party (such as a person or company) to another. A _________ is usually made in exchange for the provision of goods, services or both, or to fulfill a legal obligation.

The simplest and oldest form of _________ is barter, the exchange of one good or service for another.

a. Payment
b. Soft count
c. Going concern
d. Social gravity

47. In 1940, President Franklin Roosevelt split the authority into two agencies, the Civil Aeronautics Administration (CAA) and the _________ The CAA was responsible for air traffic control, safety programs, and airway development. The _________ was entrusted with safety rulemaking, accident investigation, and economic regulation of the airlines.

a. Civil Aeronautics Board
b. 1921 recession
c. 100-year flood
d. 130-30 fund

48. _________ is the incidence or process of transferring ownership of a business, enterprise, agency or public service from the public sector (government) to the private sector (business.) In a broader sense, _________ refers to transfer of any government function to the private sector including governmental functions like revenue collection and law enforcement.

The term '_________' also has been used to describe two unrelated transactions.

a. Ricardian equivalence
b. Performance reports
c. Privatization
d. Compound empowerment

49. The _________ or cash market is a commodities or securities market in which goods are sold for cash and delivered immediately. Contracts bought and sold on these markets are immediately effective. _________s can operate wherever the infrastructure exists to conduct the transaction.

a. Spot market
b. Currency band
c. Foreign exchange trading
d. Triangular arbitrage

50. _________, or corporate _________ are political and business scandals which arise with the disclosure of misdeeds by trusted executives of large public corporations. Such misdeeds typically involve complex methods for misusing or misdirecting funds, overstating revenues, understating expenses, overstating the value of corporate assets or underreporting the existence of liabilities, sometimes with the cooperation of officials in other corporations or affiliates.

In public companies, this type of 'creative accounting' can amount to fraud and investigations are typically launched by government oversight agencies, such as the Securities and Exchange Commission (SEC) in the United States.

a. ACCRA Cost of Living Index
b. ACEA agreement
c. AD-IA Model
d. Accounting scandals

51.

The _________ was the first United States Federal statute to limit cartels and monopolies. It falls under antitrust law.

The Act provides: 'Every contract, combination in the form of trust or otherwise, or conspiracy, in restraint of trade or commerce among the several States, or with foreign nations, is declared to be illegal'. The Act also provides: 'Every person who shall monopolize, or attempt to monopolize, or combine or conspire with any other person or persons, to monopolize any part of the trade or commerce among the several States, or with foreign nations, shall be deemed guilty of a felony [. . .]' The Act put responsibility upon government attorneys and district courts to pursue and investigate trusts, companies and organizations suspected of violating the Act. The Clayton Act extended the right to sue under the antitrust laws to 'any person who shall be injured in his business or property by reason of anything forbidden in the antitrust laws.' Under the Clayton Act, private parties may sue in U.S. district court and should they prevail, they may be awarded treble damages and the cost of suit, including reasonable attorney's fees.

a. 130-30 fund
b. 1921 recession
c. 100-year flood
d. Sherman Antitrust Act

52. _________ is a term that is used to describe the overall process of invention, innovation and diffusion of technology or processes. The term is redundant with technological development, technological achievement, and technological progress. In essence _________ is the invention of a technology (or a process), the continuous process of improving a technology (in which it often becomes cheaper) and its diffusion throughout industry or society.

a. 1921 recession
b. 100-year flood
c. 130-30 fund
d. Technological change

53. _________ refers to when a retailer or wholesaler is e;tiede; to purchase from a supplier on the understanding that no other distributor will be appointed or receive supplies in a given area. When the sales outlets are owned by the supplier, _________ is because of vertical integration, where the outlets are independent _________ is illegal due to the Restrictive Trade Practices Act, however, if it is registered and approved it is allowed.

_________ can be a barrier to entry.

a. Exclusive dealing
b. AD-IA Model
c. ACCRA Cost of Living Index
d. ACEA agreement

54.

The _________ is an independent agency of the United States government, created, directed, and empowered by Congressional statute , and with the majority of its commissioners appointed by the current President. The _________ works towards six strategic goals in the areas of broadband, competition, the spectrum, the media, public safety and homeland security, and modernizing the _________.

a. 100-year flood
b. 130-30 fund
c. 1921 recession
d. Federal Communications Commission

55. _________ exists when sales of identical goods or services are transacted at different prices from the same provider. In a theoretical market with perfect information, no transaction costs or prohibition on secondary exchange (or re-selling) to prevent arbitrage, _________ can only be a feature of monopoly and oligopoly markets, where market power can be exercised. Otherwise, the moment the seller tries to sell the same good at different prices, the buyer at the lower price can arbitrage by selling to the consumer buying at the higher price but with a tiny discount.

a. Price discrimination
b. Lerner Index
c. Loss leader
d. Transfer pricing

56. _________ is the practice of selling a product or service at a very low price, intending to drive competitors out of the market, or create barriers to entry for potential new competitors. If competitors or potential competitors cannot sustain equal or lower prices without losing money, they go out of business or choose not to enter the business. The predatory merchant then has fewer competitors or is even a de facto monopoly, and can then raise prices above what the market would otherwise bear.

a. Third line forcing
b. Restraint of trade
c. Predatory pricing
d. Group boycott

57. _________ is an agreement between business competitors to sell the same product or service at the same price. In general, it is an agreement intended to ultimately push the price of a product as high as possible, leading to profits for all the sellers. Price-fixing can also involve any agreement to fix, peg, discount or stabilize prices.

a. Moral victory
b. Cut-throat competition
c. Non-price competition
d. Price fixing

58. _________ is an agreement between business competitors to sell the same product or service at the same price. In general, it is an agreement intended to ultimately push the price of a product as high as possible, leading to profits for all the sellers. _________ can also involve any agreement to fix, peg, discount or stabilize prices.

a. Moral victory
b. Non-price competition
c. Cut-throat competition
d. Price-fixing

59. _________ is a common law doctrine relating to the enforceability of contractual restrictions on freedom to conduct business. In an old leading case of Mitchell v. Reynolds (1711) Lord Smith L.C. said,

'it is the privilege of a trader in a free country, in all matters not contrary to law, to regulate his own mode of carrying it on according to his own discretion and choice.

a. Group boycott
b. Conscious parallelism
c. Restraint of trade
d. Third line forcing

60. _________ was a predominant American integrated oil producing, transporting, refining, and marketing company. Established in 1870 as an Ohio Corporation, it was the largest oil refiner in the world and operated as a major company trust and was one of the world's first and largest multinational corporations until it was broken up by the United States Supreme Court in 1911. John D. Rockefeller was a founder, chairman and major shareholder, and the company made him a billionaire and eventually the richest man in history.

a. 100-year flood
b. 1921 recession
c. 130-30 fund
d. Standard Oil

61. In economics, the _________ of an industry is used as an indicator of the relative size of firms in relation to the industry as a whole. It is calculated as the sum of the percent market share of the top n industries. This may also assist in determining the market structure of the industry.

a. Pacman conjecture
b. Quasi-rent
c. Concentration ratio
d. Monopolization

62. In economics, a _________ is the combination of two or more firms competing in the same market with the same good or service.See Horizontal integration.

a. Financial system
b. Market dominance
c. Federal Reserve districts
d. Horizontal merger

63. A _________ is an expression that compares quantities relative to each other. The most common examples involve two quantities, but any number of quantities can be compared. _________s are represented mathematically by separating each quantity with a colon, for example the _________ 2:3, which is read as the _________ 'two to three'.

a. 130-30 fund
b. Ratio
c. Y-intercept
d. 100-year flood

64. A _________ is officially defined as being 'any merger that is not horizontal or vertical; in general, it is the combination of firms in different industries or firms operating in different geographic areas'. _________s can serve various purposes, including extending corporate territories and extending a product range. One example of a _________ was the merger between the Walt Disney Company and the American Broadcasting Company.

a. Borrowing base
b. Factor cost
c. Cost-effectiveness analysis
d. Conglomerate merger

65. In economics, a firm is said to reap _________s when a lack of viable market competition allows it to set its prices above the equilibrium price for a good or service without losing profits to competitors. _________ is a type of economic profit, that is, it is a profit greater than the normal profit that is typical in a perfectly competitive industry. The resulting price is known as the monopoly price.

a. Cleanup clause
b. Borrowing base
c. Monopoly profit
d. First-price sealed-bid auction

66. _________, known in the United States as antitrust law, has three main elements:

- prohibiting agreements or practices that restrict free trading and competition between business entities. This includes in particular the repression of cartels.
- banning abusive behaviour by a firm dominating a market, or anti-competitive practices that tend to lead to such a dominant position. Practices controlled in this way may include predatory pricing, tying, price gouging, refusal to deal, and many others.
- supervising the mergers and acquisitions of large corporations, including some joint ventures. Transactions that are considered to threaten the competitive process can be prohibited altogether, or approved subject to 'remedies' such as an obligation to divest part of the merged business or to offer licences or access to facilities to enable other businesses to continue competing.

The substance and practice of _________ varies from jurisdiction to jurisdiction. Protecting the interests of consumers (consumer welfare) and ensuring that entrepreneurs have an opportunity to compete in the market economy are often treated as important objectives. _________ is closely connected with law on deregulation of access to markets, state aids and subsidies, the privatisation of state owned assets and the establishment of independent sector regulators. In recent decades, _________ has been viewed as a way to provide better public services.

a. Due diligence
b. Fee simple
c. Competition law
d. Hostile work environment

67. In economics, an _________ is any good (e.g. a commodity) or service brought into one country from another country in a legitimate fashion, typically for use in trade.It is a good that is brought in from another country for sale. _________ goods or services are provided to domestic consumers by foreign producers. An _________ in the receiving country is an export to the sending country.

a. Import quota
b. Import
c. Economic integration
d. Incoterms

68. _________, in strategic management and marketing is, according to Carlton O'Neal, the percentage or proportion of the total available market or market segment that is being serviced by a company. It can be expressed as a company's sales revenue (from that market) divided by the total sales revenue available in that market. It can also be expressed as a company's unit sales volume (in a market) divided by the total volume of units sold in that market.

a. Market share
b. Pricing science
c. Product differentiation
d. Customer to customer

1. The _________ is a protocol to the United Nations Framework Convention on Climate Change (UNFCCC or FCCC), an international environmental treaty produced at the United Nations Conference on treaty is intended to achieve 'stabilization of greenhouse gas concentrations in the atmosphere at a level that would prevent dangerous anthropogenic interference with the climate system.' The _________ establishes legally binding commitments for the reduction of four greenhouse gases (carbon dioxide, methane, nitrous oxide, sulphur hexafluoride), and two groups of gases (hydrofluorocarbons and perfluorocarbons) produced by 'Annex I' (industrialized) nations, as well as general commitments for all member countries. As of January 14 2009, 183 parties have ratified the protocol, which was initially adopted for use on 11 December 1997 in Kyoto, Japan and which entered into force on 16 February 2005. Under Kyoto, industrialized countries agreed to reduce their collective GHG emissions by 5.2% compared to the year 1990.

a. Kyoto Protocol
b. Green New Deal
c. Greenhouse gases
d. Carbon offset

2. _________s is the social science that studies the production, distribution, and consumption of goods and services. The term _________s comes from the Ancient Greek oá¼°κονομÎ¯α from oá¼¶κος (oikos, 'house') + νÏŒμος (nomos, 'custom' or 'law'), hence 'rules of the house(hold)'. Current _________ models developed out of the broader field of political economy in the late 19th century, owing to a desire to use an empirical approach more akin to the physical sciences.

a. Energy economics
b. Inflation
c. Opportunity cost
d. Economic

3. _________ is the increase in the amount of the goods and services produced by an economy over time. It is conventionally measured as the percent rate of increase in real gross domestic product, or real GDP. Growth is usually calculated in real terms, i.e. inflation-adjusted terms, in order to net out the effect of inflation on the price of the goods and services produced.

a. AD-IA Model
b. ACCRA Cost of Living Index
c. ACEA agreement
d. Economic growth

4. _________ is the concept of adding accumulated interest back to the principal, so that interest is earned on interest from that moment on. The act of declaring interest to be principal is called compounding (i.e., interest is compounded.) A loan, for example, may have its interest compounded every month: in this case, a loan with $100 principal and 1% interest per month would have a balance of $101 at the end of the first month.

a. Foreclosure data providers
b. Fama-French three factor model
c. General purpose technologies
d. Compound interest

5. In economics, _________ refers to how the marginal contribution of a factor of production usually decreases as more of the factor is used. According to this relationship, in a production system with fixed and variable inputs, beyond some point, each additional unit of the variable input yields smaller and smaller increases in output. Conversely, producing one more unit of output costs more and more in variable inputs.

a. Patent troll
b. Community property
c. Derivatives law
d. Diminishing returns

6. _________ is a fee paid on borrowed assets. It is the price paid for the use of borrowed money , or, money earned by deposited funds . Assets that are sometimes lent with _________ include money, shares, consumer goods through hire purchase, major assets such as aircraft, and even entire factories in finance lease arrangements.

a. Interest
b. Asset protection
c. Internal debt
d. Insolvency

7. A _________ is:

- Rewrite _________, in generative grammar and computer science
- Standardization, a formal and widely-accepted statement, fact, definition, or qualification
- Operation, a determinate _________ for performing a mathematical operation and obtaining a certain result (Mathematics, Logic)
  - Unary operation
  - Binary operation
- _________ of inference, a function from sets of formulae to formulae (Mathematics, Logic)
- _________ of thumb, principle with broad application that is not intended to be strictly accurate or reliable for every situation. Also often simply referred to as a _________
- Moral, an atomic element of a moral code for guiding choices in human behavior
- Heuristic, a quantized '_________' which shows a tendency or probability for successful function
- A regulation, as in sports
- A Production _________, as in computer science
- Procedural law, a _________set governing the application of laws to cases
  - A law, which may informally be called a '_________'
  - A court ruling, a decision by a court
- In the U.S. Government, a regulation mandated by Congress, but written or expanded upon by the Executive Branch.
- Norm (sociology), an informal but widely accepted _________, concept, truth, definition, or qualification (social norms, legal norms, coding norms)
- Norm (philosophy), a kind of sentence or a reason to act, feel or believe
- 'Rulership' is the concept of governance by a government:
  - Military _________, governance by a military body
  - Monastic _________, a collection of precepts that guides the life of monks or nuns in a religious order where the superior holds the place of Christ
- Slide _________

- '_________,' a song by Ayumi Hamasaki
- '_________,' a song by rapper Nas
- '_________s,' an album by the band The Whitest Boy Alive
- _________s: Pyaar Ka Superhit Formula, a 2003 Bollywood film
- ruler, an instrument for measuring lengths
- _________, a component of an astrolabe, circumferator or similar instrument
- The _________s, a bestselling self-help book
- _________ Project (Run Up-to-date Linux Everywhere), a project that aims to use up-to-date Linux software on old PCs
- _________ engine, a software system that helps managing business _________s
- Ja _________, a hip hop artist
  - R.U.L.E., a 2005 greatest hits album by rapper Ja _________
- '_________s,' a KMFDM song

a. Demand
b. Procter ' Gamble
c. Rule
d. Technocracy

8. The _________ was a period in the late 18th and early 19th centuries when major changes in agriculture, manufacturing, mining, and transportation had a profound effect on the socioeconomic and cultural conditions in Britain. The changes subsequently spread throughout Europe, North America, and eventually the world. The onset of the _________ marked a major turning point in human society; almost every aspect of daily life was eventually influenced in some way.

a. Adolf Hitler
b. Industrial Revolution
c. Adolph Fischer
d. Adam Smith

9. The _________ is a 1972 book modeling the consequences of a rapidly growing world population and finite resource supplies, commissioned by the Club of Rome. Its authors were Donella H. Meadows, Dennis L. Meadows, Jørgen Randers, and William W. Behrens III. The book used the World3 model to simulate the consequence of interactions between the Earth's and human systems.

a. The Wealth of Nations
b. Principles of Political Economy and Taxation
c. Limits to Growth
d. Fail-Safe Investing

10. _________ is a term that is used to describe the overall process of invention, innovation and diffusion of technology or processes. The term is redundant with technological development, technological achievement, and technological progress. In essence _________ is the invention of a technology (or a process), the continuous process of improving a technology (in which it often becomes cheaper) and its diffusion throughout industry or society.

a. 130-30 fund
b. 1921 recession
c. 100-year flood
d. Technological change

11. _________ is any long-term change in the patterns of average weather of a specific region or the Earth as a whole. _________ reflects abnormal variations to the Earth's climate and subsequent effects on other parts of the Earth, such as in the ice caps over durations ranging from decades to millions of years.

In recent usage, especially in the context of environmental policy, _________ usually refers to changes in modern climate

a. Climate change
b. 100-year flood
c. 1921 recession
d. 130-30 fund

12. _________ is a socioeconomic structure and political ideology that promotes the establishment of an egalitarian, classless, stateless society based on common ownership and control of the means of production and property in general. In political science, the term '_________' is sometimes used to refer to communist states, a form of government in which the state operates under a one-party system and declares allegiance to Marxism-Leninism or a derivative thereof, even if the party does not actually claim that it has already reached _________.

Forerunners of communist ideas existed in antiquity and particularly in the 18th and early 19th century France, with thinkers such as Jean-Jacques Rousseau and the more radical Gracchus Babeuf.

a. New Communist Movement
b. Social fascism
c. Democratic centralism
d. Communism

13. _________ is the development of economic wealth of countries or regions for the well-being of their inhabitants. It is the process by which a nation improves the economic, political, and social well being of its people. From a policy perspective, _________ can be defined as efforts that seek to improve the economic well-being and quality of life for a community by creating and/or retaining jobs and supporting or growing incomes and the tax base.

a. Inflation
b. Experimental economics
c. Economic methodology
d. Economic development

14. The term '_________' refers to the concept of collecting information and attempting to spot a pattern in the information. In some fields of study, the term '_________' has more formally-defined meanings.

In project management _________ is a mathematical technique that uses historical results to predict future outcome.

a. Probit model
b. Coefficient of determination
c. Quantile regression
d. Trend analysis

15. _________s (economically referred to as land or raw materials) occur naturally within environments that exist relatively undisturbed by mankind, in a natural form. A _________'s is often characterized by amounts of biodiversity existent in various ecosystems.

Mining, petroleum extraction, fishing, hunting, and forestry are generally considered natural-resource industries.

a. 100-year flood
b. Natural resource
c. 1921 recession
d. 130-30 fund

16. A natural resource is a _________ resource if it is replaced by natural processes at a rate comparable or faster than its rate of consumption by humans. Solar radiation, tides, winds and hydroelectricity are perpetual resources that are in no danger of long-term availability. _________ resources may also mean commodities such as wood, paper, and leather, if harvesting is performed in a sustainable manner.

a. 130-30 fund
b. 100-year flood
c. Renewable
d. 1921 recession

17. A natural resource is a _________ if it is replaced by natural processes at a rate comparable or faster than its rate of consumption by humans. Solar radiation, tides, winds and hydroelectricity are perpetual resources that are in no danger of long-term availability. _________s may also mean commodities such as wood, paper, and leather, if harvesting is performed in a sustainable manner.

a. 130-30 fund
b. 1921 recession
c. 100-year flood
d. Renewable resource

18. In microeconomics, _________ is quite simply the conversion of inputs into outputs. It is an economic process that uses resources to create a good or service that is suitable for exchange. This can include manufacturing, storing, shipping, and packaging.

a. Solved
b. Production
c. MET
d. Red Guards

19. In law and economics, the _________, describes the economic efficiency of an economic allocation or outcome in the presence of externalities. The theorem states that when trade in an externality is possible and there are no transaction costs, bargaining will lead to an efficient outcome regardless of the initial allocation of property rights. In practice, obstacles to bargaining or poorly defined property rights can prevent Coasian bargaining.

a. Prior appropriation water rights
b. Means test
c. Coase theorem
d. General Mining Act of 1872

20. _________ refers to the stock of skills and knowledge embodied in the ability to perform labor so as to produce economic value. It is the skills and knowledge gained by a worker through education and experience.Many early economic theories refer to it simply as labor, one of three factors of production, and consider it to be a fungible resource -- homogeneous and easily interchangeable. Other conceptions of labor dispense with these assumptions.

a. General equilibrium
b. Law of increasing costs
c. Human capital
d. Price theory

21. In microeconomic theory, an _________ is a graph showing different bundles of goods, each measured as to quantity, between which a consumer is indifferent. That is, at each point on the curve, the consumer has no preference for one bundle over another. In other words, they are all equally preferred.

a. Engel curve
b. Expenditure minimization problem
c. Indifference map
d. Indifference curve

22. In economics, an _________ is a contour line drawn through the set of points at which the same quantity of output is produced while changing the quantities of two or more inputs. While an indifference curve helps to answer the utility-maximizing problem of consumers, the _________ deals with the cost-minimization problem of producers. _________s are typically drawn on capital-labor graphs, showing the tradeoff between capital and labor in the production function, and the decreasing marginal returns of both inputs.

a. Economies of scale
b. Isoquant
c. Underinvestment employment relationship
d. Economic production quantity

23. _________ is the extension of the economic notion of capital (manufactured means of production) to environmental goods and services. _________ is thus the stock of natural ecosystems that yields a flow of valuable ecosystem goods or services into the future. For example, a stock of trees or fish provides a flow of new trees or fish, a flow which can be sustainable indefinitely.

a. Hubbert peak theory
b. Hydrogen economy
c. Natural capital
d. Non-conventional oil

24. In business and accounting, _________ are everything of value that is owned by a person or company. It is a claim on the property your income of a borrower. The balance sheet of a firm records the monetary value of the _________ owned by the firm.

a. Assets
b. Amortization schedule
c. ACCRA Cost of Living Index
d. ACEA agreement

25. In economics, the _________ measures the payments that flow between any individual country and all other countries. It is used to summarize all international economic transactions for that country during a specific time period, usually a year. The _________ is determined by the country's exports and imports of goods, services, and financial capital, as well as financial transfers.

a. Gross world product
b. Skyscraper Index
c. Gross domestic product per barrel
d. Balance of payments

26. _________ is a common concept in economics, and gives rise to derived concepts such as consumer debt. Generally _________ is defined by opposition to production. But the precise definition can vary because different schools of economists define production quite differently.

a. Cash or share options
b. Foreclosure data providers
c. Federal Reserve Bank Notes
d. Consumption

27. A _________ is the transfer of wealth from one party (such as a person or company) to another. A _________ is usually made in exchange for the provision of goods, services or both, or to fulfill a legal obligation.

The simplest and oldest form of _________ is barter, the exchange of one good or service for another.

a. Soft count
b. Social gravity
c. Payment
d. Going concern

28. _________ is an economic concept with commonplace familiarity. It is the price that a good or service is offered at, or will fetch, in the marketplace. It is of interest mainly in the study of microeconomics.

a. Market price
b. Market anomaly
c. Paper trading
d. Noisy market hypothesis

29. Competition law, known in the United States as _________ law, has three main elements:

- prohibiting agreements or practices that restrict free trading and competition between business entities. This includes in particular the repression of cartels.
- banning abusive behaviour by a firm dominating a market, or anti-competitive practices that tend to lead to such a dominant position. Practices controlled in this way may include predatory pricing, tying, price gouging, refusal to deal, and many others.
- supervising the mergers and acquisitions of large corporations, including some joint ventures. Transactions that are considered to threaten the competitive process can be prohibited altogether, or approved subject to 'remedies' such as an obligation to divest part of the merged business or to offer licences or access to facilities to enable other businesses to continue competing.

The substance and practice of competition law varies from jurisdiction to jurisdiction. Protecting the interests of consumers (consumer welfare) and ensuring that entrepreneurs have an opportunity to compete in the market economy are often treated as important objectives. Competition law is closely connected with law on deregulation of access to markets, state aids and subsidies, the privatisation of state owned assets and the establishment of independent sector regulators. In recent decades, competition law has been viewed as a way to provide better public services.

a. Intellectual property law
b. United Kingdom competition law
c. Anti-Inflation Act
d. Antitrust

30. _________ in economics and business is the result of an exchange and from that trade we assign a numerical monetary value to a good, service or asset. If Alice trades Bob 4 apples for an orange, the _________ of an orange is 4 apples. Inversely, the _________ of an apple is 1/4 oranges.

a. Price
b. Premium pricing
c. Price book
d. Price war

31. The _________ is a heterodox school of economics that emphasizes the spontaneous organizing power of the price mechanism. It holds that the complexity of subjective human choices makes mathematical modelling of the evolving market extremely difficult and advocates a laissez faire approach to the economy. _________ economists advocate the enforcement of voluntary contractual agreements between economic agents, but otherwise the smallest imposition of coercive force on commercial transactions.

a. Economic calculation problem
b. Austrian School
c. ACEA agreement
d. ACCRA Cost of Living Index

32. A _________ is a good that has the three following properties :

- It is non-rivalrous. Consumption of this good by anyone does not reduce the quantity available to other agents.
- It is non-excludable. It is impossible to prevent anyone from consuming that good.
- It is available worldwide.

This concept is an extension of Samuelson's notion of public goods to the economics of globalisation.

The theoretical concept of public goods does not distinguish with regard to the geographical region in which a good may be produced or consumed. However some theorists (such as Inge Kaul) use the term _________ to mean a public good which is non-rival and non-excludable throughout the whole world, as opposed to a public good which exists in just one national area. Knowledge is a canonical example of a _________.[Joseph E. Stiglitz, Knowledge as a _________ in _________s, ISBN 978-0-19-513052-2</ref>.]

a. Community indifference curve
b. Black-Litterman model
c. Monopoly price
d. Global public good

33. A _________ is an object whose consumption increases the utility of the consumer, for which the quantity demanded exceeds the quantity supplied at zero price. _________s are usually modeled as having diminishing marginal utility. The first individual purchase has high utility; the second has less.

a. Merit good
b. Composite good
c. Good
d. Pie method

34. In economics, economic output is divided into physical goods and intangible services. Consumption of _________ is assumed to produce utility. It is often used when referring to a _________ Tax.

a. Private good
b. Goods and services
c. Composite good
d. Manufactured goods

35. In economics, a _________ exists when the production or use of goods and services by the market is not efficient. That is, there exists another outcome where all involved can be made better off. _________s can be viewed as scenarios where individuals' pursuit of pure self-interest leads to results that are not efficient - that can be improved upon from the societal point-of-view.

a. General equilibrium
b. Fixed exchange rate
c. Financial economics
d. Market failure

36. In economics, a _________ is a good that is non-rivaled and non-excludable. This means, respectively, that consumption of the good by one individual does not reduce availability of the good for consumption by others; and that no one can be effectively excluded from using the good. In the real world, there may be no such thing as an absolutely non-rivaled and non-excludable good; but economists think that some goods approximate the concept closely enough for the analysis to be economically useful.

a. Neoclassical synthesis
b. Happiness economics
c. Demand-pull theory
d. Public good

37. _________ is that which is owed; usually referencing assets owed, but the term can also cover moral obligations and other interactions not requiring money. In the case of assets, _________ is a means of using future purchasing power in the present before a summation has been earned. Some companies and corporations use _________ as a part of their overall corporate finance strategy.

a. Debenture
b. Debt
c. Collateral Management
d. Hard money loan

38. A _________ is defined in economics as a good that exhibits these properties:

- Excludable - it is reasonably possible to prevent a class of consumers (e.g. those who have not paid for it) from consuming the good.
- Rivalrous - consumptions by one consumer prevents simultaneous consumption by other consumers. _________s satisfies an individual want while public good satisfies a collective want of the society.

A _________ is the opposite of a public good, as they are almost exclusively made for profit.

An example of the _________ is bread: bread eaten by a given person cannot be consumed by another (rivalry), and it is easy for a baker to refuse to trade a loaf (excludable

a. Positional goods
b. Pie method
c. Private Good
d. Demerit good

39. _________ in economics refers to metrics and measures of output from production processes, per unit of input. Labor _________, for example, is typically measured as a ratio of output per labor-hour, an input. _________ may be conceived of as a metrics of the technical or engineering efficiency of production.

a. Fordism
b. Piece work
c. Productivity
d. Production-possibility frontier

40. _________ is a situation in which the limited resources of a firm are allocated in accordance with the wishes of consumers. An allocatively efficient economy produces an 'optimal mix' of commodities. A firm is allocatively efficient when its price is equal to its marginal costs (that is, P = MC) in a perfect market.

a. ACEA agreement
b. Economic efficiency
c. ACCRA Cost of Living Index
d. Allocative efficiency

41. _________ is a term that refers both to:

- a formal discipline used to help appraise, or assess, the case for a project or proposal, which itself is a process known as project appraisal; and
- an informal approach to making decisions of any kind.

Under both definitions the process involves, whether explicitly or implicitly, weighing the total expected costs against the total expected benefits of one or more actions in order to choose the best or most profitable option. The formal process is often referred to as either CBA (_________) or BCost-benefit analysis

A hallmark of CBA is that all benefits and all costs are expressed in money terms, and are adjusted for the time value of money, so that all flows of benefits and flows of project costs over time (which tend to occur at different points in time) are expressed on a common basis in terms of their e;present value.e; Closely related, but slightly different, formal techniques include Cost-effectiveness analysis, Economic impact analysis, Fiscal impact analysis and Social Return on Investment(SROI) analysis. The latter builds upon the logic of _________, but differs in that it is explicitly designed to inform the practical decision-making of enterprise managers and investors focused on optimising their social and environmental impacts.

a. 100-year flood
b. 130-30 fund
c. Decision theory
d. Cost-benefit analysis

42. _________ is a broad label that refers to any individuals or households that use goods and services generated within the economy. The concept of a _________ is used in different contexts, so that the usage and significance of the term may vary.

Typically when business people and economists talk of _________s they are talking about person as _________, an aggregated commodity item with little individuality other than that expressed in the buy/not-buy decision.

a. 130-30 fund
b. 100-year flood
c. 1921 recession
d. Consumer

43. The term surplus is used in economics for several related quantities. The _________ is the amount that consumers benefit by being able to purchase a product for a price that is less than they would be willing to pay. The producer surplus is the amount that producers benefit by selling at a market price mechanism that is higher than they would be willing to sell for.

a. Microeconomic reform
b. Necessity good
c. Marginal rate of technical substitution
d. Consumer surplus

44. _________ is a survey-based economic technique for the valuation of non-market resources, such as environmental preservation or the impact of contamination. While these resources do give people utility, certain aspects of them do not have a market price as they are not directly sold--for example, people receive benefit from a beautiful view of a mountain, but it would be tough to value using price-based models. _________ surveys are one technique which is used to measure these aspects.

a. Habitat destruction
b. Positive externalities
c. Total Economic Value
d. Contingent valuation

45. A _________ describes one of a number of pieces of legislation relating to the reduction of smog and air pollution in general. The use by governments to enforce clean air standards has contributed to an improvement in human health and longer life spans. Critics argue it has also sapped corporate profits and contributed to outsourcing, while defenders counter that improved environmental air quality has generated more jobs than it has eliminated.

a. Clean Air Act
b. Smog
c. 130-30 fund
d. 100-year flood

46. Under the system of feudalism, a _________, fief, feud, feoff often consisted of inheritable lands or revenue-producing property granted by a liege lord, generally to a vassal, in return for a form of allegiance, originally to give him the means to fulfill his military duties when called upon. However anything of value could be held in fief, such as an office, a right of exploitation (e.g., hunting, fishing) or any other type of revenue, rather than the land it comes from.

Originally, the feudal institution of vassalage did not imply the giving or receiving of landholdings (which were granted only as a reward for loyalty), but by the eighth century the giving of a landholding was becoming standard.

a. 130-30 fund
b. Fiefdom
c. 100-year flood
d. 1921 recession

47. _________ describes a deliberate attempt to interfere with the free and fair operation of the market and create artificial, false or misleading appearances with respect to the price of a security, commodity or currency. _________ is prohibited under Section 9(a)(2) of the Securities Exchange Act of 1934, and in Australia under Section s 1041A of the Corporations Act 2001. The Act defines _________ as transactions which create an artificial price or maintain an artificial price for a tradable security.

a. Net domestic product
b. Legal monopoly
c. Managerial economics
d. Market manipulation

48. A public utility (usually just utility) is an organization that maintains the infrastructure for a public service (often also providing a service using that infrastructure.) _________ are subject to forms of public control and regulation ranging from local community-based groups to state-wide government monopolies. Common arguments in favor of regulation include the desire to control market power, facilitate competition, promote investment or system expansion, or stabilize markets.

a. 100-year flood
b. 1921 recession
c. 130-30 fund
d. Public utilities

49. _________ is the removal or simplification of government rules and regulations that constrain the operation of market forces. _________ does not mean elimination of laws against fraud, but eliminating or reducing government control of how business is done, thereby moving toward a more free market.

The stated rationale for '_________' is often that fewer and simpler regulations will lead to a raised level of competitiveness, therefore higher productivity, more efficiency and lower prices overall.

a. Macroeconomic policy instruments
b. Secular basis
c. Deregulation
d. Fundamental psychological law

50. _________ is the increase in the average temperature of the Earth's near-surface air and oceans since the mid-twentieth century and its projected continuation. Global surface temperature increased 0.74 ± 0.18 °C (1.33 ± 0.32 °F) during the last century. The Intergovernmental Panel on Climate Change (IPCC) concludes that anthropogenic greenhouse gases are responsible for most of the observed temperature increase since the middle of the twentieth century, and that natural phenomena such as solar variation and volcanoes probably had a small warming effect from pre-industrial times to 1950 and a small cooling effect afterward.

a. Consumer goods
b. Dividend unit
c. Controlled Foreign Corporations
d. Global warming

51. A _________ is the exclusive authority to determine how a resource is used, whether that resource is owned by government or by individuals. All economic goods have a _________s attribute. This attribute has three broad components

1. The right to use the good
2. The right to earn income from the good
3. The right to transfer the good to others

The concept of _________s as used by economists and legal scholars are related but distinct. The distinction is largely seen in the economists' focus on the ability of an individual or collective to control the use of the good.

a. High-reeve
b. Post-sale restraint
c. Holder in due course
d. Property right

52. To _________ is to impose a financial charge or other levy upon a taxpayer by a state or the functional equivalent of a state.

_________es are also imposed by many subnational entities. _________es consist of direct _________ or indirect _________, and may be paid in money or as its labour equivalent (often but not always unpaid.)

a. 100-year flood
b. 1921 recession
c. 130-30 fund
d. Tax

53. _________ is a practice of protecting the environment, on individual, organisational or governmental level, for the benefit of the natural environment and (or) humans.

Due to the pressures of population and technology the biophysical environment is being degraded, sometimes permanently. This has been recognised and governments began placing restraints on activities that caused environmental degradation.

a. ACEA agreement
b. AD-IA Model
c. Environmental Protection
d. ACCRA Cost of Living Index

1. _________ is a situation in which the limited resources of a firm are allocated in accordance with the wishes of consumers. An allocatively efficient economy produces an 'optimal mix' of commodities. A firm is allocatively efficient when its price is equal to its marginal costs (that is, P = MC) in a perfect market.

a. ACCRA Cost of Living Index
b. ACEA agreement
c. Economic efficiency
d. Allocative efficiency

2. A _________ product is a product designed for cheapness and short-term convenience rather than medium to long-term durability, with most products only intended for single use. The term is also sometimes used for products that may last several months (ex. _________ air filters) to distinguish from similar products that last indefinitely (ex.

a. 100-year flood
b. 130-30 fund
c. Disposable
d. 1921 recession

3. _________ is gross income minus income tax on that income.

Discretionary income is income after subtracting taxes and normal expenses (such as rent or mortgage, utilities, insurance, medical, transportation, property maintenance, child support, inflation, food and sundries, 'c.) to maintain a certain standard of living.

a. Disposable personal income
b. Taxation as theft
c. Disposable income
d. Stamp Act

4. In mathematics, an _________ is a statement about the relative size or order of two objects, or about whether they are the same or not

- The notation a < b means that a is less than b.
- The notation a > b means that a is greater than b.
- The notation a ≠ b means that a is not equal to b, but does not say that one is greater than the other or even that they can be compared in size.

In each statement above, a is not equal to b. These relations are known as strict inequalities. The notation a < b may also be read as 'a is strictly less than b'.

a. ACCRA Cost of Living Index
b. AD-IA Model
c. ACEA agreement
d. Inequality

5. In economics, the _________ is used to illustrate the idea that increases in the rate of taxation do not necessarily increase tax revenue. (For instance, whereas a 0% income tax rate will generate no revenue, neither will a 100% rate, as citizens will have no incentive to make money.) Increasing taxes beyond the peak of the curve point will decrease tax revenue.

a. 1921 recession
b. 130-30 fund
c. 100-year flood
d. Laffer curve

6. In economics, the _________ is a graphical representation of the cumulative distribution function of a probability distribution; it is a graph showing the proportion of the distribution assumed by the bottom y% of the values. It is a curve that illustrates income distribution. It is often used to represent income distribution, where it shows for the bottom x% of households, what percentage y% of the total income they have.

a. Phillips curve
b. Kuznets curve
c. Lorenz curve
d. Demand curve

7. A variety of measures of _________ and output are used in economics to estimate total economic activity in a country or region, including gross domestic product (GDP), gross national product (GNP), and net _________

There are three main ways of calculating these numbers; the output approach, the income approach and the expenditure approach. In theory, the three must yield the same, because total expenditures on goods and services must equal the total income paid to the producers (Gnational income), and that must also equal the total value of the output of goods and services (GNP.)

a. Gross world product
b. National income
c. GNI per capita
d. Volume index

8. Total _________ is defined by the United States' Bureau of Economic Analysis as

income received by persons from all sources. It includes income received from participation in production as well as from government and business transfer payments. It is the sum of compensation of employees (received), supplements to wages and salaries, proprietors' income with inventory valuation adjustment (IVA) and capital consumption adjustment (CCAdj), rental income of persons with CCAdj, _________ receipts on assets, and personal current transfer receipts, less contributions for government social insurance.

a. Dividend Discount Model
b. Greater fool theory
c. Personal income
d. Bidding

9. _________ is the shortage of common things such as food, clothing, shelter and safe drinking water, all of which determine the quality of life. It may also include the lack of access to opportunities such as education and employment which aid the escape from _________ and/or allow one to enjoy the respect of fellow citizens. According to Mollie Orshansky who developed the _________ measurements used by the U.S. government, 'to be poor is to be deprived of those goods and services and pleasures which others around us take for granted.' Ongoing debates over causes, effects and best ways to measure _________, directly influence the design and implementation of _________-reduction programs and are therefore relevant to the fields of public administration and international development.

a. Liberal welfare reforms
b. Poverty
c. Poverty map
d. Growth Elasticity of Poverty

10. _________ in political thought refers to economic theories of social organization advocating collective ownership and administration of the means of production and distribution of goods, and a society characterized by equality for all individuals, with an egalitarian method of compensation. Modern _________ originated in the late 19th-century intellectual and working class political movement that criticized the effects of industrialization and private ownership on society. Karl Marx posited that _________ would be achieved via class struggle and a proletarian revolution after a transitional stage from capitalism called the dictatorship of the proletariat.

a. Socialism
b. Adolph Fischer
c. Adam Smith
d. Adolf Hitler

11. There are two main interpretations of the idea of a _________:

- A model in which the state assumes primary responsibility for the welfare of its citizens. This responsibility in theory ought to be comprehensive, because all aspects of welfare are considered and universally applied to citizens as a 'right'. _________ can also mean the creation of a 'social safety net' of minimum standards of varying forms of welfare. Here is found some confusion between a '_________' and a 'welfare society' in common debate about the definition of the term.
- The provision of welfare in society. In many '_________s', especially in continental Europe, welfare is not actually provided by the state, but by a combination of independent, voluntary, mutualist and government services. The functional provider of benefits and services may be a central or state government, a state-sponsored company or agency, a private corporation, a charity or another form of non-profit organization. However, this phenomenon has been more appropriately termed a 'welfare society,' and the term 'welfare system' has been used to describe the range of _________ and welfare society mixes that are found.

The English term '_________' is believed by Asa Briggs to have been coined by Archbishop William Temple during the Second World War, contrasting wartime Britain with the 'warfare state' of Nazi Germany. Friedrich Hayek contends that the term derived from the older German word Wohlfahrtsstaat, which itself was used by nineteenth century historians to describe a variant of the ideal of Polizeistaat . It was fully developed by the German academic Sozialpolitiker--'socialists of the chair'--from 1870 and first implemented through Bismarck's 'state socialism'. Bismarck's policies have also been seen as the creation of a _________.

a. 100-year flood
b. 1921 recession
c. 130-30 fund
d. Welfare state

12. A _________ represents the combinations of goods and services that a consumer can purchase given current prices and his income. Consumer theory uses the concepts of a _________ and a preference map to analyze consumer choices. Both concepts have a ready graphical representation in the two-good case.

a. Joint demand
b. Budget constraint
c. Revealed preference
d. Quality bias

13. The _________ is 'the basic residential unit in which economic production, consumption, inheritance, child rearing, and shelter are organized and carried out'; [the _________] 'may or may not be synonomous with family'.

The _________ is the basic unit of analysis in many social, microeconomic and government models. The term refers to all individuals who live in the same dwelling.

a. 100-year flood
b. Family economics
c. 130-30 fund
d. Household

14. In economics, _________ is how a natione;s total economy is distributed among its population. ._________ has always been a central concern of economic theory and economic policy. Classical economists such as Adam Smith, Thomas Malthus and David Ricardo were mainly concerned with factor _________, that is, the distribution of income between the main factors of production, land, labour and capital.

a. Eco commerce
b. Authorised capital
c. Equipment trust certificate
d. Income distribution

15. In probability theory and statistics, a _________ is described as the number separating the higher half of a sample, a population from the lower half. The _________ of a finite list of numbers can be found by arranging all the observations from lowest value to highest value and picking the middle one. If there is an even number of observations, the _________ is not unique, so one often takes the mean of the two middle values.

a. Median
b. Labour vouchers
c. Fiscal stimulus plans
d. First player wins

16. In business and accounting, _________ are everything of value that is owned by a person or company. It is a claim on the property your income of a borrower. The balance sheet of a firm records the monetary value of the _________ owned by the firm.

a. ACEA agreement
b. Amortization schedule
c. ACCRA Cost of Living Index
d. Assets

17. In economics, the _________ measures the payments that flow between any individual country and all other countries. It is used to summarize all international economic transactions for that country during a specific time period, usually a year. The _________ is determined by the country's exports and imports of goods, services, and financial capital, as well as financial transfers.

a. Gross domestic product per barrel
b. Skyscraper Index
c. Gross world product
d. Balance of payments

18. A _________ is the transfer of wealth from one party (such as a person or company) to another. A _________ is usually made in exchange for the provision of goods, services or both, or to fulfill a legal obligation.

The simplest and oldest form of _________ is barter, the exchange of one good or service for another.

a. Soft count
b. Social gravity
c. Payment
d. Going concern

19. The _________ is a measure of statistical dispersion, commonly used as a measure of inequality of income distribution or inequality of wealth distribution. It is defined as a ratio with values between 0 and 1: A low _________ indicates more equal income or wealth distribution, while a high _________ indicates more unequal distribution. 0 corresponds to perfect equality (everyone having exactly the same income) and 1 corresponds to perfect inequality (where one person has all the income, while everyone else has zero income.)

a. Gini coefficient
b. Suits index
c. Leapfrogging
d. Compensating variation

20. In mathematics, a _________ is a constant multiplicative factor of a certain object. For example, in the expression $9x^2$, the _________ of x^2 is 9.

The object can be such things as a variable, a vector, a function, etc.

a. 130-30 fund
b. 1921 recession
c. 100-year flood
d. Coefficient

21. _________ is a comparison of the wealth of various members or groups in a society. It differs from the distribution of income in a manner analogous to the difference between position and speed.

Wealth is a person's net worth, expressed as:

wealth = assets - liabilities

The word 'wealth' is often confused with 'income'.

a. 130-30 fund
b. Distribution of wealth
c. Wealth condensation
d. 100-year flood

22. In economics, a _________ is the tax on money or property that one living person gives to another. See Gift (law) #Taxation or _________ in the United States.

a. Fiscal drag
b. Succession duty
c. Taxation as slavery
d. Gift tax

23. Inheritance tax, _________ and death duty are the names given to various taxes which arise on the death of an individual. It is a tax on the estate, or total value of the money and property, of a person who has died. In international tax law, there is a distinction between an _________ and an inheritance tax: the former taxes the personal representatives of the deceased, while the latter taxes the beneficiaries of the estate.

a. AD-IA Model
b. ACEA agreement
c. ACCRA Cost of Living Index
d. Estate tax

24. _________, often referred to by his initials _________, was the 32nd President of the United States. He was a central figure of the 20th century during a time of worldwide economic crisis and world war. Elected to four terms in office, he served from 1933 to 1945 and is the only U.S. president to have served more than two terms.

a. Adolf Hitler
b. Franklin Delano Roosevelt
c. Adolph Fischer
d. Adam Smith

25. To _________ is to impose a financial charge or other levy upon a taxpayer by a state or the functional equivalent of a state.

_________es are also imposed by many subnational entities. _________es consist of direct _________ or indirect _________, and may be paid in money or as its labour equivalent (often but not always unpaid.)

a. 1921 recession
b. Tax
c. 100-year flood
d. 130-30 fund

26. To tax is to impose a financial charge or other levy upon a taxpayer by a state or the functional equivalent of a state.

_________ are also imposed by many subnational entities. _________ consist of direct tax or indirect tax, and may be paid in money or as its labour equivalent (often but not always unpaid.)

a. 130-30 fund
b. 100-year flood
c. 1921 recession
d. Taxes

27. _________ is the returns received on factors of production: rent is return on land, wages on labor, interest on capital, and profit on entrepreneurship. It is also known as Net Factor Payments (NFP.)

Part of current account with balance of trade (exports minus imports of goods and services) and net transfer payments (such as foreign aid.)

a. 130-30 fund
b. 100-year flood
c. Redistributive justice
d. Factor income

28. A _________ is a place of residence or refuge and comfort. It is usually a place in which an individual or a family can rest and be able to store personal property. Most modern-day households contain sanitary facilities and a means of preparing food.

a. 100-year flood
b. 130-30 fund
c. 1921 recession
d. Home

29. _________ is the period of time that an individual spends at paid occupational labor. Unpaid labors such as housework are not considered part of the working week. Many countries regulate the work week by law, such as stipulating minimum daily rest periods, annual holidays and a maximum number of working hours per week.

a. 130-30 fund
b. 100-year flood
c. 1921 recession
d. Working time

30. _________ refers to the stock of skills and knowledge embodied in the ability to perform labor so as to produce economic value. It is the skills and knowledge gained by a worker through education and experience.Many early economic theories refer to it simply as labor, one of three factors of production, and consider it to be a fungible resource -- homogeneous and easily interchangeable. Other conceptions of labor dispense with these assumptions.

a. Human capital
b. Price theory
c. General equilibrium
d. Law of increasing costs

31. In economics, the people in the _________ are the suppliers of labor. The _________ is all the nonmilitary people who are employed or unemployed. In 2005, the worldwide _________ was over 3 billion people.

a. Distributed workforce
b. Departmentalization
c. Grenelle agreements
d. Labor force

32. _________ is a term that is used to describe the overall process of invention, innovation and diffusion of technology or processes. The term is redundant with technological development, technological achievement, and technological progress. In essence _________ is the invention of a technology (or a process), the continuous process of improving a technology (in which it often becomes cheaper) and its diffusion throughout industry or society.

a. Technological change
b. 130-30 fund
c. 100-year flood
d. 1921 recession

33. The _________ consists of a number of economic theories which describe the nature of the firm, company including its existence, its behaviour, and its relationship with the market.

In simplified terms, the _________ aims to answer these questions:

1. Existence - why do firms emerge, why are not all transactions in the economy mediated over the market?
2. Boundaries - why the boundary between firms and the market is located exactly there? Which transactions are performed internally and which are negotiated on the market?
3. Organization - why are firms structured in such specific way? What is the interplay of formal and informal relationships?

Despite looking simple, these questions are not answered by the established economic theory, which usually views firms as given, and treats them as black boxes without any internal structure.

The First World War period saw a change of emphasis in economic theory away from industry-level analysis which mainly included analysing markets to analysis at the level of the firm, as it became increasingly clear that perfect competition was no longer an adequate model of how firms behaved. Economic theory till then had focussed on trying to understand markets alone and there had been little study on understanding why firms or organisations exist.

a. Theory of the firm
b. Khazzoom-Brookes postulate
c. Policy Ineffectiveness Proposition
d. Technology gap

34. _________ according to Onuoha (2007) is the practice of starting new organizations or revitalizing mature organizations, particularly new businesses generally in response to identified opportunities. _________ is often a difficult undertaking, as a vast majority of new businesses fail. Entrepreneurial activities are substantially different depending on the type of organization that is being started.

a. ACCRA Cost of Living Index
b. Intrapreneurship
c. ACEA agreement
d. Entrepreneurship

35. In statistics, the _________ problem occurs when one considers a set of statistical inferences simultaneously. Errors in inference, including confidence intervals that fail to include their corresponding population parameters are more likely to occur when one considers the family as a whole. Several statistical techniques have been developed to prevent this from happening, allowing significance levels for single and _________ to be directly compared.

a. Hypotheses suggested by the data
b. False discovery rate
c. Familywise error rate
d. Multiple comparisons

36. _________ is a broad label that refers to any individuals or households that use goods and services generated within the economy. The concept of a _________ is used in different contexts, so that the usage and significance of the term may vary.

Typically when business people and economists talk of _________s they are talking about person as _________, an aggregated commodity item with little individuality other than that expressed in the buy/not-buy decision.

a. 1921 recession
b. Consumer
c. 130-30 fund
d. 100-year flood

37. A _________ is a measure of the average price of consumer goods and services purchased by households. A _________ measures a price change for a constant market basket of goods and services from one period to the next within the same area (city, region, or nation.) It is a price index determined by measuring the price of a standard group of goods meant to represent the typical market basket of a typical urban consumer.

a. Consumer price index
b. CPI
c. Cost-of-living index
d. Lipstick index

38. _________ is a common concept in economics, and gives rise to derived concepts such as consumer debt. Generally _________ is defined by opposition to production. But the precise definition can vary because different schools of economists define production quite differently.

a. Foreclosure data providers
b. Consumption
c. Cash or share options
d. Federal Reserve Bank Notes

39. _________ is the cost of maintaining a certain standard of living. Changes in the _________ over time are often operationalized in a _________ index. _________ calculations are also used to compare the cost of maintaining a certain standard of living in different geographic areas.

a. Decision process tool
b. Restructuring
c. Bear raid
d. Cost of living

40. The _________ is the minimum level of income deemed necessary to achieve an adequate standard of living in a given country. In practice, like the definition of poverty, the official or common understanding of the poverty line is significantly higher in developed countries than in developing countries.

The common international poverty line has been roughly $1 a day, or more precisely $1.08 at 1993 purchasing-power parity (PPP.)

a. Poverty threshold
b. Poverty reduction
c. Poverty map
d. Poverty

41. The _________ is the name for legislation first introduced by United States President Lyndon B. Johnson during his State of the Union address on January 8, 1964. This legislation was proposed by Johnson in response to a national poverty rate of around nineteen percent. The speech led the United States Congress to pass the Economic Opportunity Act, which established the Office of Economic Opportunity (OEO) to administer the local application of federal funds targeted against poverty.

a. 130-30 fund
b. 100-year flood
c. Supplemental Nutrition Assistance Program
d. War on poverty

42. _________ in economics and business is the result of an exchange and from that trade we assign a numerical monetary value to a good, service or asset. If Alice trades Bob 4 apples for an orange, the _________ of an orange is 4 apples. Inversely, the _________ of an apple is 1/4 oranges.

a. Price war
b. Price book
c. Premium pricing
d. Price

43. A _________ is a normalized average (typically a weighted average) of prices for a given class of goods or services in a given region, during a given interval of time. It is a statistic designed to help to compare how these prices, taken as a whole, differ between time periods or geographical locations.

Price indices have several potential uses.

a. Transactional Net Margin Method
b. Product sabotage
c. Two-part tariff
d. Price index

44. _________ is the income of individuals or nations after adjusting for inflation. It is calculated by subtracting inflation from the nominal income. Real variables, such as _________, real GDP, and real interest rate are variables that are measured in physical units, while nominal variables such as nominal income, nominal GDP, and nominal interest rate are measured in monetary units.

a. Real income
b. Windfall gain
c. Family income
d. Net national income

45. A _________ is any worker who has some special skill, knowledge, or (usually acquired) ability in his work. A _________ may have attended a college, university or technical school. Or, a _________ may have learned his skills on the job.

a. Timebar scheduling
b. Global Career Development Facilitator
c. Time and attendance
d. Skilled worker

46. The term '_________' refers to the concept of collecting information and attempting to spot a pattern in the information. In some fields of study, the term '_________' has more formally-defined meanings.

In project management _________ is a mathematical technique that uses historical results to predict future outcome.

a. Probit model
b. Trend analysis
c. Coefficient of determination
d. Quantile regression

47. _________s is the social science that studies the production, distribution, and consumption of goods and services. The term _________s comes from the Ancient Greek οá¼°κονομÎ¯α from οá¼¶κος (oikos, 'house') + νÏŒμος (nomos, 'custom' or 'law'), hence 'rules of the house(hold)'. Current _________ models developed out of the broader field of political economy in the late 19th century, owing to a desire to use an empirical approach more akin to the physical sciences.

a. Energy economics
b. Inflation
c. Economic
d. Opportunity cost

48. _________ to the arrival of new individuals into a habitat or population. It is a biological concept and is important in population ecology, differentiated from emigration and migration.

_________ is a modern phenomenon.

a. ACEA agreement
b. AD-IA Model
c. ACCRA Cost of Living Index
d. Immigration

49. _________ is the increase in the amount of the goods and services produced by an economy over time. It is conventionally measured as the percent rate of increase in real gross domestic product, or real GDP. Growth is usually calculated in real terms, i.e. inflation-adjusted terms, in order to net out the effect of inflation on the price of the goods and services produced.

a. AD-IA Model
b. Economic growth
c. ACCRA Cost of Living Index
d. ACEA agreement

50. _________ is widely regarded as the first modern school of economic thought. It is the idea that free markets can regulate themselves.Its major developers include Adam Smith, David Ricardo, Thomas Malthus and John Stuart Mill. Sometimes the definition of _________ is expanded to include William Petty, Johann Heinrich von Thünen.

a. Tendency of the rate of profit to fall
b. Marginalism
c. Classical economics
d. Schools of economic thought

51. In economics, _________ is the transfer of income, wealth or property from some individuals to others.

One premise of _________ is that money should be distributed to benefit the poorer members of society, and that the rich have an obligation to assist the poor, thus creating a more financially egalitarian society. Another argument is that the rich exploit the poor or otherwise gain unfair benefits.

a. 100-year flood
b. 130-30 fund
c. 1921 recession
d. Redistribution

52. _________ is a term that refers both to:

- a formal discipline used to help appraise, or assess, the case for a project or proposal, which itself is a process known as project appraisal; and
- an informal approach to making decisions of any kind.

Under both definitions the process involves, whether explicitly or implicitly, weighing the total expected costs against the total expected benefits of one or more actions in order to choose the best or most profitable option. The formal process is often referred to as either CBA (_________) or BCost-benefit analysis

A hallmark of CBA is that all benefits and all costs are expressed in money terms, and are adjusted for the time value of money, so that all flows of benefits and flows of project costs over time (which tend to occur at different points in time) are expressed on a common basis in terms of their e;present value.e; Closely related, but slightly different, formal techniques include Cost-effectiveness analysis, Economic impact analysis, Fiscal impact analysis and Social Return on Investment(SROI) analysis. The latter builds upon the logic of _________, but differs in that it is explicitly designed to inform the practical decision-making of enterprise managers and investors focused on optimising their social and environmental impacts.

a. Cost-benefit analysis
b. 130-30 fund
c. Decision theory
d. 100-year flood

53. A _________ is an expression that compares quantities relative to each other. The most common examples involve two quantities, but any number of quantities can be compared. _________s are represented mathematically by separating each quantity with a colon, for example the _________ 2:3, which is read as the _________ 'two to three'.

a. Ratio
b. 100-year flood
c. 130-30 fund
d. Y-intercept

54. _________ or equality of condition is a form of egalitarianism which seeks to reduce or eliminate differences in material condition between individuals or households in a society. This usually means equalizing income and/or total wealth to a certain degree.

In theory, _________ can be distinguished from equal opportunity.

a. ACCRA Cost of Living Index
b. Equality of outcome
c. AD-IA Model
d. ACEA agreement

55.

_________ was a German philosopher, political economist, historian, political theorist, sociologist, communist and revolutionary credited as the founder of communism.

Marx summarized his approach to history and politics in the opening line of the first chapter of The Communist Manifesto : e;The history of all hitherto existing society is the history of class struggles.e; Marx argued that capitalism, like previous socioeconomic systems, will produce internal tensions which will lead to its destruction. Just as capitalism replaced feudalism, socialism will in its turn replace capitalism and lead to a stateless, classless society which will emerge after a transitional period, the 'dictatorship of the proletariat'.

a. Adam Smith
b. Neo-Gramscianism
c. Marxism
d. Karl Heinrich Marx

56. _________ is used to refer to a number of related concepts. It is the using resources in such a way as to maximize the production of goods and services. A system can be called economically efficient if:

- No one can be made better off without making someone else worse off.
- More output cannot be obtained without increasing the amount of inputs.
- Production proceeds at the lowest possible per-unit cost.

These definitions of efficiency are not equivalent, but they are all encompassed by the idea that nothing more can be achieved given the resources available.

An economic system is more efficient if it can provide more goods and services for society without using more resources.

a. Economic efficiency
b. Efficient contract theory
c. ACEA agreement
d. ACCRA Cost of Living Index

57. The _________ is the largest national economy in the world. Its gross domestic product (GDP) was estimated as $14.2 trillion in 2008. The U.S. economy maintains a high level of output per person (GDP per capita, $46,800 in 2008, ranked at around number ten in the world.)

a. Economy of the United States
b. AD-IA Model
c. ACCRA Cost of Living Index
d. ACEA agreement

58. In economics, a _________ is a redistribution of income in the market system. These payments are considered to be nonexhaustive because they do not directly absorb resources or create output. Examples of certain _________s include welfare (financial aid), social security, and government subsidies for certain businesses (firms.)

a. 130-30 fund
b. Transfer payment
c. 100-year flood
d. 1921 recession

59. A _________ is:

- Rewrite _________, in generative grammar and computer science
- Standardization, a formal and widely-accepted statement, fact, definition, or qualification
- Operation, a determinate _________ for performing a mathematical operation and obtaining a certain result (Mathematics, Logic)
    - Unary operation
    - Binary operation
- _________ of inference, a function from sets of formulae to formulae (Mathematics, Logic)
- _________ of thumb, principle with broad application that is not intended to be strictly accurate or reliable for every situation. Also often simply referred to as a _________
- Moral, an atomic element of a moral code for guiding choices in human behavior
- Heuristic, a quantized '_________' which shows a tendency or probability for successful function
- A regulation, as in sports
- A Production _________, as in computer science
- Procedural law, a _________set governing the application of laws to cases
    - A law, which may informally be called a '_________'
    - A court ruling, a decision by a court
- In the U.S. Government, a regulation mandated by Congress, but written or expanded upon by the Executive Branch.
- Norm (sociology), an informal but widely accepted _________, concept, truth, definition, or qualification (social norms, legal norms, coding norms)
- Norm (philosophy), a kind of sentence or a reason to act, feel or believe
- 'Rulership' is the concept of governance by a government:
    - Military _________, governance by a military body
    - Monastic _________, a collection of precepts that guides the life of monks or nuns in a religious order where the superior holds the place of Christ
- Slide _________

- '_________,' a song by Ayumi Hamasaki
- '_________,' a song by rapper Nas
- '_________s,' an album by the band The Whitest Boy Alive
- _________s: Pyaar Ka Superhit Formula, a 2003 Bollywood film
- ruler, an instrument for measuring lengths
- _________, a component of an astrolabe, circumferator or similar instrument
- The _________s, a bestselling self-help book
- _________ Project (Run Up-to-date Linux Everywhere), a project that aims to use up-to-date Linux software on old PCs
- _________ engine, a software system that helps managing business _________s
- Ja _________, a hip hop artist
    - R.U.L.E., a 2005 greatest hits album by rapper Ja _________
- '_________s,' a KMFDM song

a. Procter ' Gamble
b. Technocracy
c. Rule
d. Demand

60. _________ is a voluntary transfer of resources from one country to another, given at least partly with the objective of benefiting the recipient country. It may have other functions as well: it may be given as a signal of diplomatic approval, or to strengthen a military ally, to reward a government for behaviour desired by the donor, to extend the donor's cultural influence, to provide infrastructure needed by the donor for resource extraction from the recipient country, or to gain other kinds of commercial access. Humanitarianism and altruism are, nevertheless, significant motivations for the giving of _________.

a. ACCRA Cost of Living Index
b. AD-IA Model
c. ACEA agreement
d. Aid

61. _________ was a federal assistance program in effect from 1935 to 1997, which was administered by the United States Department of Health and Human Services. This program provided financial assistance to children whose families had low or no income.

The program was created under the name Aid to Dependent Children (ADC) by the Social Security Act of 1935 as part of the New Deal; the words 'families with' were added to the name in 1960, partly due to concern that the program's rules discouraged marriage.

a. AD-IA Model
b. ACCRA Cost of Living Index
c. Aid to Families with Dependent Children
d. ACEA agreement

62. In economics and sociology, an _________ is any factor (financial or non-financial) that enables or motivates a particular course of action, or counts as a reason for preferring one choice to the alternatives. It is an expectation that encourages people to behave in a certain way. Since human beings are purposeful creatures, the study of _________ structures is central to the study of all economic activity (both in terms of individual decision-making and in terms of co-operation and competition within a larger institutional structure.)

a. Incentive
b. Isocost
c. Epstein-Zin preferences
d. Economic reform

63. In the United States, _________ federal benefits is defined as any federal program, project, service, and activity provided by the federal government that directly assists or benefits the American public in the areas of education, health, public safety, public welfare, and public works, among others. The assistance, which can reach to over $400 billion dollars annually, is provided and administered by federal government agencies, such as the U.S. Department of Housing and Urban Development and the U.S. Department of Health and Human Services, through special programs to recipients.

The term assistance is defined by the federal government as:

In order to provide _________ in an organized manner, the federal government provides assistance through federal agencies.

a. State Revolving Fund
b. General Assistance
c. Federal Medical Assistance Percentages
d. Federal assistance

64. A _________ refers to any type debt instrument, such as a loan, bond, mortgage that does not have a fixed rate of interest over the life of the instrument. Such debt typically uses an index or other base rate for establishing the interest rate for each relevant period. One of the most common rates to use as the basis for applying interest rates is the London Inter-bank Offered Rate, or LIBOR

a. Disposal tax effect
b. Money market
c. Floating interest rate
d. Moneylender

65. The term _________ describes two different concepts:

- The first is a recognition of partial payment already made towards taxes due.
- The second is a state benefit paid to workers through the tax system, which has the effect of increasing (rather than reducing) net income.

Within the Australian, Canadian, United Kingdom, and United States tax systems, a _________ is a recognition of partial payment already made towards taxes due. A similar concept exists (fr:Avoir fiscal) in the French tax system. This situation arises, for example, when standard rate tax has been deducted at source , but the tax-payer is subject to further taxation at a higher rate. It also applies in dividend imputation systems.

a. 100-year flood
b. 130-30 fund
c. 1921 recession
d. Tax credit

66. In a federal system of government, a _________ is a large sum of money granted by the national government to a regional government with only general provisions as to the way it is to be spent. This can be contrasted with a categorical grant which has more strict and specific provisions on the way it is to be spent.

An advantage of _________s is that they allow regional governments to experiment with different ways of spending money with the same goal in mind, though it is very difficult to compare the results of such spending and reach a conclusion.

a. Financial Industry Regulatory Authority
b. 100-year flood
c. Block grant
d. Transactions deposit

67. A _________ usually refers to an individual entity seeking a more favorable outcome at the expense of other entities by upsetting an equilibrium to their own favor, only to cause an inevitable retaliation by the other individuals to rebalance the equilibrium, resulting in all participants having an overall less favorable outcome. For example, people may have a tendency to buy increasingly larger, heavier, and often more expensive cars because the additional weight can help make the car safer in a collision with a smaller, lighter car. Thus to keep up with the average vehicle weight for safety's sake, drivers must buy heavier, more expensive, less efficient cars, while safety on the whole does not improve compared to when the average vehicle was lighter.

a. Stylized fact
b. Trailing twelve months
c. Fear factor
d. Race to the bottom

68. _________ is the United States of America's federal assistance program, formerly known as 'welfare'. It began on July 1, 1997, and succeeded the Aid to Families with Dependent Children program, providing cash assistance to indigent American families with dependent children through the United States Department of Health and Human Services. Prior to 1997, the federal government designed the overall program requirements and guidelines, while states administered the program and determined eligibility for benefits.

a. Temporary Assistance for Needy Families
b. 1921 recession
c. 130-30 fund
d. 100-year flood

69. _________ is a company's financial statement that indicates how the revenue is transformed into the net income The purpose of the _________ is to show managers and investors whether the company made or lost money during the period being reported.

The important thing to remember about an _________ is that it represents a period of time.

a. AD-IA Model
b. ACCRA Cost of Living Index
c. Income statement
d. ACEA agreement

70. _________ in economic theory is the use of modern economic tools to study problems that are traditionally in the province of political science.

In particular, it studies the behavior of politicians and government officials as mostly self-interested agents and their interactions in the social system either as such or under alternative constitutional rules. These can be represented a number of ways, including standard constrained utility maximization, game theory, or decision theory.

a. Rational ignorance
b. Paradox of voting
c. Public interest theory
d. Public choice

71. _________ is the branch of economics that incorporates value judgments (that is, normative judgements) about what the economy ought to be like or what particular policy actions ought to be recommended to achieve a desirable goal. _________ looks at the desirability of certain aspects of the economy. It underlies expressions of support for particular economic policies.

a. Nanoeconomics
b. Double bottom line
c. Broad money
d. Normative economics

72. _________ is the branch of economics that concerns the description and explanation of economic phenomena (Wong, 1987, p. 920.) It focuses on facts and cause-and-effect relationships and includes the development and testing of economics theories.

a. Regulatory economics
b. Positive economics
c. 130-30 fund
d. 100-year flood

73. A _________ is the procedure of systematically acquiring and recording information about the members of a given population. It is a regularly occurring and official count of a particular population. The term is used mostly in connection with national 'population and door to door _________es' (to be taken every 10 years according to United Nations recommendations), agriculture, and business _________es.

a. 100-year flood
b. 1921 recession
c. 130-30 fund
d. Census

74. The _________, asbl is a non-profit project which produces a cross-national database of micro-economic income data for social science research. The project started in 1983 and is headquartered in Luxembourg. In 2006 the database included data from 30 countries on four continents, with some countries represented for over 30 years.

a. Leading stock
b. Deutsche Bank
c. Bankruptcy of Lehman Brothers
d. Luxembourg Income Study

1. The _________ was a worldwide economic downturn starting in most places in 1929 and ending at different times in the 1930s or early 1940s for different countries. It was the largest and most important economic depression in the 20th century, and is used in the 21st century as an example of how far the world's economy can fall. The _________ originated in the United States; historians most often use as a starting date the stock market crash on October 29, 1929, known as Black Tuesday.

a. Jarrow March
b. Wall Street Crash of 1929
c. British Empire Economic Conference
d. Great Depression

2. _________, 1st Baron Keynes was a renowned economist from Britain whose many ideas on economic and political theories as well as on many governments' monetary policies influenced America. He advocated a government that played an active role in the lives of people regarding business, economy, etc. In this role, the government would use fiscal measures to reduce the consequences of recessions, economic depressions and booms.

a. Adam Smith
b. Adolf Hitler
c. Adolph Fischer
d. John Maynard Keynes

3. _________ and Keynesian Theory) is a macroeconomic theory based on the ideas of 20th-century British economist John Maynard Keynes. _________ argues that private sector decisions sometimes lead to inefficient macroeconomic outcomes and therefore advocates active policy responses by the public sector, including monetary policy actions by the central bank and fiscal policy actions by the government to stabilize output over the business cycle.

The theories forming the basis of _________ were first presented in The General Theory of Employment, Interest and Money, published in 1936.

a. Deflation
b. Rational choice theory
c. Keynesian economics
d. Market failure

4. _________ is a branch of economics that deals with the performance, structure, and behavior of a national or regional economy as a whole. Along with microeconomics, _________ is one of the two most general fields in economics. It is the study of the behavior and decision-making of entire economies.

a. Macroeconomics
b. New Trade Theory
c. Tobit model
d. Nominal value

5. _________ is a branch of economics that studies how individuals, households and firms and some states make decisions to allocate limited resources, typically in markets where goods or services are being bought and sold. _________ examines how these decisions and behaviours affect the supply and demand for goods and services, which determines prices; and how prices, in turn , determine the supply and demand of goods and services.

Whereas macroeconomics involves the 'sum total of economic activity, dealing with the issues of growth, inflation and unemployment, and with national economic policies relating to these issues' and the effects of government actions on them.

a. Countercyclical
b. New Keynesian economics
c. Recession
d. Microeconomics

6. _________ is an economic situation in which inflation and economic stagnation occur simultaneously and remain unchecked for a period of time. The portmanteau _________ is generally attributed to British politician Iain Macleod, who coined the term in a speech to Parliament in 1965. The concept is notable partly because, in postwar macroeconomic theory, inflation and recession were regarded as mutually exclusive, and also because _________ has generally proven to be difficult and costly to eradicate once it gets started.

a. Chronic inflation
b. Price/wage spiral
c. Real interest rate
d. Stagflation

7. _________ are the inflation-indexed bonds issued by the U.S. Treasury. The principal is adjusted to the Consumer Price Index, the commonly used measure of inflation. The coupon rate is constant, but generates a different amount of interest when multiplied by the inflation-adjusted principal, thus protecting the holder against inflation.

a. 130-30 fund
b. 1921 recession
c. 100-year flood
d. Treasury Inflation-Protected Securities

8. A security is a fungible, negotiable instrument representing financial value. _________ are broadly categorized into debt _________; equity _________, e.g., common stocks; and derivative (finance) contracts such as forwards, futures, options and swaps. The company or other entity issuing the security is called the issuer.

a. Red herring prospectus
b. Pass-Through Certificates
c. Settlement risk
d. Securities

9. _________ refers to discriminatory employment practices such as bias in hiring, promotion, job assignment, termination, and compensation, and various types of harassment.

In many countries, laws prohibit employers from discriminating on the basis of race, color, sex, religion, national origin, physical or mental disability, or age. There is also a growing body of law preventing or occasionally justifying _________ based on sexual orientation or gender identity.

a. Impotent poor
b. Irish competition law
c. Energy Independence and Security Act of 2007
d. Employment discrimination

10. The _________ or gross domestic income (GDI), a basic measure of an economy's economic performance, is the market value of all final goods and services produced within the borders of a nation in a year. _________ can be defined in three ways, all of which are conceptually identical. First, it is equal to the total expenditures for all final goods and services produced within the country in a stipulated period of time (usually a 365-day year.)

a. Market structure
b. Countercyclical
c. Monopolistic competition
d. Gross domestic product

11. _________ in economics and business is the result of an exchange and from that trade we assign a numerical monetary value to a good, service or asset. If Alice trades Bob 4 apples for an orange, the _________ of an orange is 4 apples. Inversely, the _________ of an apple is 1/4 oranges.

a. Price book
b. Price war
c. Premium pricing
d. Price

12. In economics, _________ is a rise in the general level of prices of goods and services in an economy over a period of time. When the general price level rises, each unit of currency buys fewer goods and services; consequently, _________ is also a decline in the real value of money--a loss of purchasing power in the medium of exchange which is also the monetary unit of account in the economy. A chief measure of general price-level _________ is the general _________ rate, which is the percentage change in a general price index (normally the Consumer Price Index) over time.

a. Opportunity cost
b. Energy economics
c. Economic
d. Inflation

13. The _________ is the central banking system of the United States. Created in 1913 by the enactment of the Federal Reserve Act (signed by Woodrow Wilson), it is a quasi-public and quasi-private (government entity with private components) banking system that comprises (1) the presidentially appointed Board of Governors of the _________ in Washington, D.C.; (2) the Federal Open Market Committee; (3) twelve regional Federal Reserve Banks located in major cities throughout the nation acting as fiscal agents for the U.S. Treasury, each with its own nine-member board of directors; (4) numerous other private U.S. member banks, which subscribe to required amounts of non-transferable stock in their regional Federal Reserve Banks; and (5) various advisory councils. Since February 2006, Ben Bernanke has served as the Chairman of the Board of Governors of the _________.

a. Monetary Policy Report to the Congress
b. Federal Reserve System
c. Term auction facility
d. Federal Reserve System Open Market Account

14. The _________ was written by the English economist John Maynard Keynes. The book, generally considered to be his magnum opus, is largely credited with creating the terminology and shape of modern macroeconomics. Published in February 1936 it sought to bring about a revolution, commonly referred to as the 'Keynesian Revolution', in the way economists thought - especially in relation to the proposition that a market economy tends naturally to restore itself to full employment after temporary shocks.

a. The General Theory of Employment, Interest and Money
b. Black Book of Communism
c. General Theory of Employment, Interest and Money
d. Human Action

15. _________ is a fee paid on borrowed assets. It is the price paid for the use of borrowed money , or, money earned by deposited funds . Assets that are sometimes lent with _________ include money, shares, consumer goods through hire purchase, major assets such as aircraft, and even entire factories in finance lease arrangements.

a. Insolvency
b. Asset protection
c. Interest
d. Internal debt

16. A _________ is a situation that involves losing one quality or aspect of something in return for gaining another quality or aspect. It implies a decision to be made with full comprehension of both the upside and downside of a particular choice.

In economics the term is expressed as opportunity cost, referring the most preferred alternative given up.

a. Nonmarket
b. Whitemail
c. Trade-off
d. Friedman-Savage utility function

17. _________s is the social science that studies the production, distribution, and consumption of goods and services. The term _________s comes from the Ancient Greek oá¼°κονομÎ¯α from oá¼¶κος (oikos, 'house') + νÏŒμος (nomos, 'custom' or 'law'), hence 'rules of the house(hold)'. Current _________ models developed out of the broader field of political economy in the late 19th century, owing to a desire to use an empirical approach more akin to the physical sciences.

a. Opportunity cost
b. Economic
c. Energy economics
d. Inflation

18. _________ is the increase in the amount of the goods and services produced by an economy over time. It is conventionally measured as the percent rate of increase in real gross domestic product, or real GDP. Growth is usually calculated in real terms, i.e. inflation-adjusted terms, in order to net out the effect of inflation on the price of the goods and services produced.

a. Economic growth
b. ACCRA Cost of Living Index
c. AD-IA Model
d. ACEA agreement

19. An _________, in economics, is the amount by which the real Gross domestic product exceeds potential GDP. The real GDP is also known as GDP 'adjusted for inflation', 'constant prices' GDP or 'constant dollar' GDP, because it measures the aggregate output in a country's income accounts in a given year, expressed in base-year prices. On the other hand, the potential GDP is the quantity of real GDP when a country's economy is at full-employment.

a. Inflationary gap
b. AD-IA Model
c. ACCRA Cost of Living Index
d. ACEA agreement

20. In economics and finance, _________ is the change in total cost that arises when the quantity produced changes by one unit. It is the cost of producing one more unit of a good. Mathematically, the _________ function is expressed as the first derivative of the total cost (TC) function with respect to quantity (Q.)

a. Variable cost
b. Quality costs
c. Khozraschyot
d. Marginal cost

21. The term _________ refers to economy-wide fluctuations in production or economic activity over several months or years. These fluctuations occur around a long-term growth trend, and typically involve shifts over time between periods of relatively rapid economic growth (expansion or boom), and periods of relative stagnation or decline (contraction or recession.)

These fluctuations are often measured using the growth rate of real gross domestic product.

a. Consumer theory
b. Business cycle
c. Nominal value
d. Tobit model

22. In economics, the people in the _________ are the suppliers of labor. The _________ is all the nonmilitary people who are employed or unemployed. In 2005, the worldwide _________ was over 3 billion people.

a. Departmentalization
b. Distributed workforce
c. Grenelle agreements
d. Labor force

23. _________ is a misspelled phrase from Latin 'pro capite' phrase meaning per head with pro meaning 'per' or 'for each' and capite meaning 'head.' Both words together equate to the phrase 'for each head.'

It is usually used in the field of statistics to indicate the average per person for any given concern, such as income, crime rate, etc.

It is also used in wills to indicate that each of the named beneficiaries should receive, by devise or bequest, equal shares of the estate. This is in contrast to a per stirpes division, in which each branch of the inheriting family inherits an equal share of the estate.

a. False positive rate
b. Sargan test
c. Per capita
d. Population statistics

24. In economics, a _________ is a general slowdown in economic activity over a sustained period of time, or a business cycle contraction. During _________s, many macroeconomic indicators vary in a similar way. Production as measured by Gross Domestic Product (GDP), employment, investment spending, capacity utilization, household incomes and business profits all fall during _________s.

a. Recession
b. Treasury View
c. Monetary economics
d. Leading indicators

25. Unemployment occurs when a person is available to work and seeking work but currently without work. The prevalence of unemployment is usually measured using the _________, which is defined as the percentage of those in the labor force who are unemployed. The _________ is also used in economic studies and economic indexes such as the United States' Conference Board's Index of Leading Indicators as a measure of the state of the macroeconomics.

a. ACCRA Cost of Living Index
b. ACEA agreement
c. Unemployment rate
d. AD-IA Model

26. In economics, the _________ is a measure of inflation, the rate of increase of a price index (for example, a consumer price index.)It is the percentage rate of change in price level over time. The rate of decrease in the purchasing power of money is approximately equal.

It's used to calculate the real interest rate, as well as real increases in wages, and official measurements of this rate act as input variables to COLA adjustments and Inflation derivatives prices.

a. Edgeworth paradox
b. Equity value
c. Interest rate option
d. Inflation rate

27. _________ is a broad label that refers to any individuals or households that use goods and services generated within the economy. The concept of a _________ is used in different contexts, so that the usage and significance of the term may vary.

Typically when business people and economists talk of _________s they are talking about person as _________, an aggregated commodity item with little individuality other than that expressed in the buy/not-buy decision.

a. Consumer
b. 100-year flood
c. 130-30 fund
d. 1921 recession

28. A _________ is a measure of the average price of consumer goods and services purchased by households. A _________ measures a price change for a constant market basket of goods and services from one period to the next within the same area (city, region, or nation.) It is a price index determined by measuring the price of a standard group of goods meant to represent the typical market basket of a typical urban consumer.

a. Lipstick index
b. CPI
c. Cost-of-living index
d. Consumer price index

29. A _________ is a normalized average (typically a weighted average) of prices for a given class of goods or services in a given region, during a given interval of time. It is a statistic designed to help to compare how these prices, taken as a whole, differ between time periods or geographical locations.

Price indices have several potential uses.

a. Two-part tariff
b. Price index
c. Transactional Net Margin Method
d. Product sabotage

30. In economics, the _________ measures the payments that flow between any individual country and all other countries. It is used to summarize all international economic transactions for that country during a specific time period, usually a year. The _________ is determined by the country's exports and imports of goods, services, and financial capital, as well as financial transfers.

a. Gross domestic product per barrel
b. Balance of payments
c. Gross world product
d. Skyscraper Index

31. A _________ is the transfer of wealth from one party (such as a person or company) to another. A _________ is usually made in exchange for the provision of goods, services or both, or to fulfill a legal obligation.

The simplest and oldest form of _________ is barter, the exchange of one good or service for another.

a. Going concern
b. Social gravity
c. Soft count
d. Payment

32. In economics, _________ is a sustained decrease in the general price level of goods and services. _________ occurs when the annual inflation rate falls below zero percent, resulting in an increase in the real value of money -- a negative inflation rate. This should not be confused with disinflation, a slow-down in the inflation rate (i.e. when the inflation decreases, but still remains positive.)

a. Price revolution
b. Literacy rate
c. Tobit model
d. Deflation

33. In economics, _________ is inflation that is very high or 'out of control', a condition in which prices increase rapidly as a currency loses its value. Definitions used by the media vary from a cumulative inflation rate over three years approaching 100% to 'inflation exceeding 50% a month.' In informal usage the term is often applied to much lower rates. As a rule of thumb, normal inflation is reported per year, but _________ is often reported for much shorter intervals, often per month.

a. 100-year flood
b. 130-30 fund
c. Hyperinflation
d. 1921 recession

34. A _________ is an economy based on the division of labor in which the prices of goods and services are determined in a free price system set by supply and demand. This is often contrasted with a planned economy, in which a central government determines the price of goods and services using a fixed price system. Market economies are contrasted with mixed economy where the price system is not entirely free but under some government control that is not extensive enough to constitute a planned economy.

a. Nutritional Economics
b. Commons-based peer production
c. Network Economy
d. Market economy

35. A _________, reserve bank, or monetary authority is the entity responsible for the monetary policy of a country or of a group of member states. It is a bank that can lend money to other banks in times of need. Its primary responsibility is to maintain the stability of the national currency and money supply, but more active duties include controlling subsidized-loan interest rates, and acting as a lender of last resort to the banking sector during times of financial crisis (private banks often being integral to the national financial system.)

a. 1921 recession
b. 130-30 fund
c. 100-year flood
d. Central bank

36. The term _________ refers to government debt, expenditures and revenues, or to finance (particularly financial revenue) in general.

- _________ deficit is the budget deficit of federal or local government
- _________ policy is the discretionary spending of governments. Contrasts with monetary policy.
- _________ year and _________ quarter are reporting periods for firms and other agencies.

.

a. Procter ' Gamble
b. Drawdown
c. Bucket shop
d. Fiscal

37. In economics, _________ is the use of government spending and revenue collection to influence the economy.

_________ can be contrasted with the other main type of economic policy, monetary policy, which attempts to stabilize the economy by controlling interest rates and the supply of money. The two main instruments of _________ are government spending and taxation.

a. 100-year flood
b. Sustainable investment rule
c. Fiscal policy
d. Fiscalism

38. _________ in economic theory is the use of modern economic tools to study problems that are traditionally in the province of political science.

In particular, it studies the behavior of politicians and government officials as mostly self-interested agents and their interactions in the social system either as such or under alternative constitutional rules. These can be represented a number of ways, including standard constrained utility maximization, game theory, or decision theory.

a. Public choice
b. Paradox of voting
c. Rational ignorance
d. Public interest theory

39. In economics, a _________ is a redistribution of income in the market system. These payments are considered to be nonexhaustive because they do not directly absorb resources or create output. Examples of certain _________s include welfare (financial aid), social security, and government subsidies for certain businesses (firms.)

a. 1921 recession
b. 130-30 fund
c. 100-year flood
d. Transfer payment

40. _________ refers to a business or organization attempting to acquire goods or services to accomplish the goals of the enterprise. Though there are several organizations that attempt to set standards in the _________ process, processes can vary greatly between organizations. Typically the word '_________' is not used interchangeably with the word 'procurement', since procurement typically includes Expediting, Supplier Quality, and Traffic and Logistics (T'L) in addition to _________.

a. 100-year flood
b. 130-30 fund
c. Purchasing
d. Free port

41. A _________ is:

- Rewrite _________, in generative grammar and computer science
- Standardization, a formal and widely-accepted statement, fact, definition, or qualification
- Operation, a determinate _________ for performing a mathematical operation and obtaining a certain result (Mathematics, Logic)
  - Unary operation
  - Binary operation
- _________ of inference, a function from sets of formulae to formulae (Mathematics, Logic)
- _________ of thumb, principle with broad application that is not intended to be strictly accurate or reliable for every situation. Also often simply referred to as a _________
- Moral, an atomic element of a moral code for guiding choices in human behavior
- Heuristic, a quantized '_________' which shows a tendency or probability for successful function
- A regulation, as in sports
- A Production _________, as in computer science
- Procedural law, a _________set governing the application of laws to cases
  - A law, which may informally be called a '_________'
  - A court ruling, a decision by a court
- In the U.S. Government, a regulation mandated by Congress, but written or expanded upon by the Executive Branch.
- Norm (sociology), an informal but widely accepted _________, concept, truth, definition, or qualification (social norms, legal norms, coding norms)
- Norm (philosophy), a kind of sentence or a reason to act, feel or believe
- 'Rulership' is the concept of governance by a government:
  - Military _________, governance by a military body
  - Monastic _________, a collection of precepts that guides the life of monks or nuns in a religious order where the superior holds the place of Christ
- Slide _________

- '_________,' a song by Ayumi Hamasaki
- '_________,' a song by rapper Nas
- '_________s,' an album by the band The Whitest Boy Alive
- _________s: Pyaar Ka Superhit Formula, a 2003 Bollywood film
- ruler, an instrument for measuring lengths
- _________, a component of an astrolabe, circumferator or similar instrument
- The _________s, a bestselling self-help book
- _________ Project (Run Up-to-date Linux Everywhere), a project that aims to use up-to-date Linux software on old PCs
- _________ engine, a software system that helps managing business _________s
- Ja _________, a hip hop artist
  - R.U.L.E., a 2005 greatest hits album by rapper Ja _________
- '_________s,' a KMFDM song

a. Procter ' Gamble
b. Rule
c. Demand
d. Technocracy

42. _________ in economics are wage and price controls, most commonly instituted as a response to inflation, and usually below market level.

This type of policy dates to the Old Testament, in which Israelites were instructed not to charge interest to other Israelites. It was tried during the Roman Empire.

a. Employment Cost Index
b. Inflation swap
c. Inflationary Spikes
d. Incomes policies

43. _________ is the process by which the government, central bank (ii) availability of money, and (iii) cost of money or rate of interest, in order to attain a set of objectives oriented towards the growth and stability of the economy. Monetary theory provides insight into how to craft optimal _________.

_________ is referred to as either being an expansionary policy where an expansionary policy increases the total supply of money in the economy, and a contractionary policy decreases the total money supply.

a. Monetary policy
b. 1921 recession
c. 130-30 fund
d. 100-year flood

44. In economics, _________ is the total amount of money available in an economy at a particular point in time. There are several ways to define 'money', but standard measures usually include currency in circulation and demand deposits.

_________ data are recorded and published, usually by the government or the central bank of the country.

a. Veil of money
b. Neutrality of money
c. Velocity of money
d. Money supply

45. A _________ refers to any type debt instrument, such as a loan, bond, mortgage that does not have a fixed rate of interest over the life of the instrument. Such debt typically uses an index or other base rate for establishing the interest rate for each relevant period. One of the most common rates to use as the basis for applying interest rates is the London Inter-bank Offered Rate, or LIBOR

a. Floating interest rate
b. Moneylender
c. Disposal tax effect
d. Money market

46. To _________ is to impose a financial charge or other levy upon a taxpayer by a state or the functional equivalent of a state.

_________es are also imposed by many subnational entities. _________es consist of direct _________ or indirect _________, and may be paid in money or as its labour equivalent (often but not always unpaid.)

a. 100-year flood
b. 130-30 fund
c. 1921 recession
d. Tax

47. The term _________ describes two different concepts:

- The first is a recognition of partial payment already made towards taxes due.
- The second is a state benefit paid to workers through the tax system, which has the effect of increasing (rather than reducing) net income.

Within the Australian, Canadian, United Kingdom, and United States tax systems, a _________ is a recognition of partial payment already made towards taxes due. A similar concept exists (fr:Avoir fiscal) in the French tax system. This situation arises, for example, when standard rate tax has been deducted at source , but the tax-payer is subject to further taxation at a higher rate. It also applies in dividend imputation systems.

a. 1921 recession
b. Tax credit
c. 100-year flood
d. 130-30 fund

48. The _________ is where currency trading takes place. It is where banks and other official institutions facilitate the buying and selling of foreign currencies. FX transactions typically involve one party purchasing a quantity of one currency in exchange for paying a quantity of another.

a. Foreign exchange market
b. Currency swap
c. Covered interest arbitrage
d. Floating currency

49. _________ in its literal sense is the process of transformation of local or regional phenomena into global ones. It can be described as a process by which the people of the world are unified into a single society and function together.

This process is a combination of economic, technological, sociocultural and political forces.

a. Globalization
b. Globally Integrated Enterprise
c. Helsinki Process on Globalisation and Democracy
d. Global Cosmopolitanism

50. The balance of trade (or net exports, sometimes symbolized as NX) is the difference between the monetary value of exports and imports in an economy over a certain period of time. It is the relationship between a nation's imports and exports. A favorable balance of trade is known as a trade surplus and consists of exporting more than is imported; an unfavorable balance of trade is known as a _________ or, informally, a trade gap.

a. Demographics of India
b. Computational economic
c. Trade deficit
d. Complementary asset

51. In economics, _________ refers to the ability of a party to produce a good or service using fewer real resources than another entity producing the same good or service..A party has an _________ when using the same input as another party, it can produce a greater output. Since _________ is determined by a simple comparison of labor productivities, it is possible for a a party to have no _________ in anything. It can be contrasted with the concept of comparative advantage which refers to the ability to produce a particular good at a lower opportunity cost.

a. ACCRA Cost of Living Index
b. International economics
c. Index number
d. Absolute advantage

52. _________ is widely regarded as the first modern school of economic thought. It is the idea that free markets can regulate themselves.Its major developers include Adam Smith, David Ricardo, Thomas Malthus and John Stuart Mill. Sometimes the definition of _________ is expanded to include William Petty, Johann Heinrich von Thünen.

a. Tendency of the rate of profit to fall
b. Classical economics
c. Marginalism
d. Schools of economic thought

53. _________ is that which is owed; usually referencing assets owed, but the term can also cover moral obligations and other interactions not requiring money. In the case of assets, _________ is a means of using future purchasing power in the present before a summation has been earned. Some companies and corporations use _________ as a part of their overall corporate finance strategy.

a. Debt
b. Hard money loan
c. Debenture
d. Collateral Management

54. _________ refers to the actions that governments take in the economic field. It covers the systems for setting interest rates and government deficit as well as the labour market, national ownership, and many other areas of government.

Such policies are often influenced by international institutions like the International Monetary Fund or World Bank as well as political beliefs and the consequent policies of parties.

a. ACEA agreement
b. ACCRA Cost of Living Index
c. Economic policy
d. AD-IA Model

55. In economics, an _________ is any good or commodity, transported from one country to another country in a legitimate fashion, typically for use in trade. _________ goods or services are provided to foreign consumers by domestic producers. _________ is an important part of international trade.

a. ACEA agreement
b. ACCRA Cost of Living Index
c. AD-IA Model
d. Export

56. _________ is that part of the total debt in a country that is owed to creditors outside the country. The debtors can be the government, corporations or private households. The debt includes money owed to private commercial banks, other governments, or international financial institutions such as the IMF and World Bank.

a. Asset protection
b. Internal debt
c. International debt collection
d. External debt

57. In economics, _________ is the total demand for final goods and services in the economy (Y) at a given time and price level. It is the amount of goods and services in the economy that will be purchased at all possible price levels. This is the demand for the gross domestic product of a country when inventory levels are static.

a. Aggregation problem
b. Aggregate supply
c. Aggregate expenditure
d. Aggregate demand

58. In economics, _________ is the total supply of goods and services produced by a national economy during a specific time period. It is the total amount of goods and services in the economy available at all possible price levels.

a. Aggregation problem
b. Aggregate demand
c. Aggregate expenditure
d. Aggregate supply

59. Economics:

- _________,the desire to own something and the ability to pay for it
- _________ curve,a graphic representation of a _________ schedule
- _________ deposit, the money in checking accounts
- _________ pull theory,the theory that inflation occurs when _________ for goods and services exceeds existing supplies
- _________ schedule,a table that lists the quantity of a good a person will buy it each different price
- _________ side economics,the school of economics at believes government spending and tax cuts open economy by raising _________

.

a. McKesson ' Robbins scandal
b. Production
c. Variability
d. Demand

60. In economics, _________ refers to the highest level of real Gross Domestic Product output that can be sustained over the long term. The existence of a limit is due to natural and institutional constraints. If actual GDP rises and stays above _________, then (in the absence of wage and price controls) inflation tends to increase as demand exceeds supply.

a. Fundamental psychological law
b. Potential output
c. Monetary conditions index
d. Monetary policy reaction function

61. A _________ is a hypothetical measure of overall prices for some set of goods and services, in a given region during a given interval, normalized relative to some base set. Typically, a _________ is approximated with a price index.

The classical dichotomy is the assumption that there is a relatively clean distinction between overall increases or decreases in prices and underlying, e;reale; economic variables.

a. Discretionary spending
b. Discouraged worker
c. Price elasticity of supply
d. Price level

62. In economics, the _________ can be defined as the graph depicting the relationship between the price of a certain commodity, and the amount of it that consumers are willing and able to purchase at that given price. It is a graphic representation of a demand schedule. The _________ for all consumers together follows from the _________ of every individual consumer: the individual demands at each price are added together.

a. Demand curve
b. Wage curve
c. Kuznets curve
d. Cost curve

63. In economics, a _________ is a table that lists the quantity of a good a person will buy it each different price See Demand curve.

a. Rational irrationality
b. Free contract
c. Federal Reserve districts
d. Demand schedule

64. _________ theory is a branch of theoretical economics. It seeks to explain the behavior of supply, demand and prices in a whole economy with several or many markets. It is often assumed that agents are price takers and in that setting two common notions of equilibrium exist: Walrasian (or competitive) equilibrium, and its generalization; a price equilibrium with transfers.

a. Rational choice theory
b. Human capital
c. New Keynesian economics
d. General equilibrium

65. In economics, economic equilibrium is simply a state of the world where economic forces are balanced and in the absence of external influences the (equilibrium) values of economic variables will not change. It is the point at which quantity demanded and quantity supplied are equal. _________, for example, refers to a condition where a market price is established through competition such that the amount of goods or services sought by buyers is equal to the amount of goods or services produced by sellers.

a. Product-Market Growth Matrix
b. Market equilibrium
c. Marketization
d. Regulated market

66. _________ is an economic concept with commonplace familiarity. It is the price that a good or service is offered at, or will fetch, in the marketplace. It is of interest mainly in the study of microeconomics.

a. Paper trading
b. Market anomaly
c. Noisy market hypothesis
d. Market price

67. Competition law, known in the United States as _________ law, has three main elements:

- prohibiting agreements or practices that restrict free trading and competition between business entities. This includes in particular the repression of cartels.
- banning abusive behaviour by a firm dominating a market, or anti-competitive practices that tend to lead to such a dominant position. Practices controlled in this way may include predatory pricing, tying, price gouging, refusal to deal, and many others.
- supervising the mergers and acquisitions of large corporations, including some joint ventures. Transactions that are considered to threaten the competitive process can be prohibited altogether, or approved subject to 'remedies' such as an obligation to divest part of the merged business or to offer licences or access to facilities to enable other businesses to continue competing.

The substance and practice of competition law varies from jurisdiction to jurisdiction. Protecting the interests of consumers (consumer welfare) and ensuring that entrepreneurs have an opportunity to compete in the market economy are often treated as important objectives. Competition law is closely connected with law on deregulation of access to markets, state aids and subsidies, the privatisation of state owned assets and the establishment of independent sector regulators. In recent decades, competition law has been viewed as a way to provide better public services.

a. Anti-Inflation Act
b. United Kingdom competition law
c. Intellectual property law
d. Antitrust

68. _________ is an economic model based on price, utility and quantity in a market. It predicts that in a competitive market, price will function to equalize the quantity demanded by consumers, and the quantity supplied by producers, resulting in an economic equilibrium of price and quantity. The model incorporates other factors changing equilibrium as a shift of demand and/or supply.

a. Supply and demand
b. Deferred gratification
c. Rational addiction
d. Joint demand

69. _________ is the a method of technical and economic research of the systems for purpose to optimize a parity between system's consumer functions or properties and expenses to achieve those functions or properties.

This methodology for continuous perfection of production, industrial technologies, organizational structures was developed by Juryj Sobolev in 1948 at the 'Perm telephone factory'

- 1948 Juryj Sobolev - the first success in application of a method analysis at the 'Perm telephone factory' .
- 1949 - the first application for the invention as result of use of the new method.

Today in economically developed countries practically each enterprise or the company use methodology of the kind of functional-cost analysis as a practice of the quality management, most full satisfying to principles of standards of series ISO 9000.

- Interest of consumer not in products itself, but the advantage which it will receive from its usage.
- The consumer aspires to reduce his expenses
- Functions needed by consumer can be executed in the various ways, and, hence, with various efficiency and expenses. Among possible alternatives of realization of functions exist such in which the parity of quality and the price is the optimal for the consumer.

The goal of _________ is achievement of the highest consumer satisfaction of production at simultaneous decrease in all kinds of industrial expenses Classical _________ has three English synonyms - Value Engineering, Value Management, Value Analysis.

a. Staple financing
b. Monopoly wage
c. Willingness to pay
d. Function cost analysis

70. An _________ is the price a borrower pays for the use of money they do not own, for instance a small company might borrow from a bank to kick start their business, and the return a lender receives for deferring the use of funds, by lending it to the borrower. _________s are normally expressed as a percentage rate over the period of one year.

_________s targets are also a vital tool of monetary policy and are used to control variables like investment, inflation, and unemployment.

a. Enterprise value
b. Arrow-Debreu model
c. ACCRA Cost of Living Index
d. Interest rate

71. _________ is a common concept in economics, and gives rise to derived concepts such as consumer debt. Generally _________ is defined by opposition to production. But the precise definition can vary because different schools of economists define production quite differently.

a. Cash or share options
b. Federal Reserve Bank Notes
c. Foreclosure data providers
d. Consumption

72. In microeconomics, _________ is quite simply the conversion of inputs into outputs. It is an economic process that uses resources to create a good or service that is suitable for exchange. This can include manufacturing, storing, shipping, and packaging.

a. Production
b. Solved
c. Red Guards
d. MET

73. A _________ occurs when an entity spends more money than it takes in. The opposite of a _________ is a budget surplus. Debt is essentially an accumulated flow of deficits.

a. Public Financial Management
b. Funding body
c. Budget deficit
d. Lump-sum tax

74. A _________ is a situation in which the government takes in more than it spends.

a. 130-30 fund
b. Budget set
c. Budget surplus
d. 100-year flood

75. _________, or a _________ is the concept of a resulting effect (cf. cause and effect, arising from another action. In general terms, it is used to indicate that all human actions, particularly crime and sin, have profound effects.

a. Rule
b. Variability
c. Solved
d. Consequence

1. The _________ or gross domestic income (GDI), a basic measure of an economy's economic performance, is the market value of all final goods and services produced within the borders of a nation in a year. _________ can be defined in three ways, all of which are conceptually identical. First, it is equal to the total expenditures for all final goods and services produced within the country in a stipulated period of time (usually a 365-day year.)

a. Gross domestic product
b. Market structure
c. Countercyclical
d. Monopolistic competition

2. The _________ was a worldwide economic downturn starting in most places in 1929 and ending at different times in the 1930s or early 1940s for different countries. It was the largest and most important economic depression in the 20th century, and is used in the 21st century as an example of how far the world's economy can fall. The _________ originated in the United States; historians most often use as a starting date the stock market crash on October 29, 1929, known as Black Tuesday.

a. Great Depression
b. British Empire Economic Conference
c. Jarrow March
d. Wall Street Crash of 1929

3. A variety of measures of _________ and output are used in economics to estimate total economic activity in a country or region, including gross domestic product (GDP), gross national product (GNP), and net _________

There are three main ways of calculating these numbers; the output approach, the income approach and the expenditure approach. In theory, the three must yield the same, because total expenditures on goods and services must equal the total income paid to the producers (Gnational income), and that must also equal the total value of the output of goods and services (GNP.)

a. Volume index
b. National income
c. Gross world product
d. GNI per capita

4. _________ use double-entry accounting to report the monetary value and sources of output produced in a country and the distribution of incomes that production generates. Data are available at the national and industry levels.

The NIPA summarizes national income on the left (debit, revenue) side and national product on the right (credit, expense) side of a two-column accounting report.

a. Current account
b. National income and product accounts
c. Gross private domestic investment
d. Net national product

5. _________ is a misspelled phrase from Latin 'pro capite' phrase meaning per head with pro meaning 'per' or 'for each' and capite meaning 'head.' Both words together equate to the phrase 'for each head.'

It is usually used in the field of statistics to indicate the average per person for any given concern, such as income, crime rate, etc.

It is also used in wills to indicate that each of the named beneficiaries should receive, by devise or bequest, equal shares of the estate. This is in contrast to a per stirpes division, in which each branch of the inheriting family inherits an equal share of the estate.

a. False positive rate
b. Population statistics
c. Sargan test
d. Per capita

6. An _________, in economics, is the amount by which the real Gross domestic product exceeds potential GDP. The real GDP is also known as GDP 'adjusted for inflation', 'constant prices' GDP or 'constant dollar' GDP, because it measures the aggregate output in a country's income accounts in a given year, expressed in base-year prices. On the other hand, the potential GDP is the quantity of real GDP when a country's economy is at full-employment.

a. AD-IA Model
b. ACEA agreement
c. ACCRA Cost of Living Index
d. Inflationary gap

7. _________ is a branch of economics that deals with the performance, structure, and behavior of a national or regional economy as a whole. Along with microeconomics, _________ is one of the two most general fields in economics. It is the study of the behavior and decision-making of entire economies.

a. Macroeconomics
b. Nominal value
c. Tobit model
d. New Trade Theory

8. In economics, the term _________ of income or _________ refers to a simple economic model which describes the reciprocal circulation of income between producers and consumers. In the _________ model, the inter-dependent entities of producer and consumer are referred to as 'firms' and 'households' respectively and provide each other with factors in order to facilitate the flow of income. Firms provide consumers with goods and services in exchange for consumer expenditure and 'factors of production' from households.

a. 100-year flood
b. 1921 recession
c. 130-30 fund
d. Circular flow

9. _________ is a specific term used in companies' financial reporting from the company-whole point of view. Because that use excludes the effects of changing ownership interest, an economic measure of _________ is necessary for financial analysis from the shareholders' point of view

_________ is defined by the Financial Accounting Standards Board, or FASB, as e;the change in equity [net assets] of a business enterprise during a period from transactions and other events and circumstances from nonowner sources. It includes all changes in equity during a period except those resulting from investments by owners and distributions to owners.e;

_________ is the sum of net income and other items that must bypass the income statement because they have not been realized, including items like an unrealized holding gain or loss from available for sale securities and foreign currency translation gains or losses.

a. Windfall gain
b. Net national income
c. Real income
d. Comprehensive income

10. A _________ is an object whose consumption increases the utility of the consumer, for which the quantity demanded exceeds the quantity supplied at zero price. _________s are usually modeled as having diminishing marginal utility. The first individual purchase has high utility; the second has less.

a. Composite good
b. Pie method
c. Merit good
d. Good

11. _________ is a common concept in economics, and gives rise to derived concepts such as consumer debt. Generally _________ is defined by opposition to production. But the precise definition can vary because different schools of economists define production quite differently.

a. Consumption
b. Cash or share options
c. Federal Reserve Bank Notes
d. Foreclosure data providers

12. _________ are the prices that the factors of production of a finished item attract.

There has been some economic debate as to what determines these prices. Classical and Marxist economists argued that the _________ decided the value of a product and so value was intrinsic within the product.

a. Factor prices
b. Marginal product of labor
c. Productivity model
d. Marginal product

13. In economics _________s are goods that are ultimately consumed rather than used in the production of another good. For example, a car sold to a consumer is a _________; the components such as tires sold to the car manufacturer are not; they are intermediate goods used to make the _________.

When used in measures of national income and output the term _________s only includes new goods.

a. Substitute good
b. Luxury good
c. Goods and services
d. Final good

14. In economics, economic output is divided into physical goods and intangible services. Consumption of _________ is assumed to produce utility. It is often used when referring to a _________ Tax.

a. Composite good
b. Private good
c. Goods and services
d. Manufactured goods

15. In financial accounting, a _________ or statement of financial position is a summary of a person's or organization's balances. Assets, liabilities and ownership equity are listed as of a specific date, such as the end of its financial year. A _________ is often described as a snapshot of a company's financial condition.

a. 1921 recession
b. 130-30 fund
c. 100-year flood
d. Balance sheet

16. _________ is a theory of aesthetics based on the theories of Karl Marx. It involves a dialectical approach to the application of Marxism to the cultural sphere, specifically areas related to taste such as art, beauty, etc. Marxists believe that economic and social conditions affect every aspect of an individual's life, from religious beliefs to legal systems to cultural frameworks.

a. 130-30 fund
b. Marxist aesthetics
c. 100-year flood
d. 1921 recession

17. _________ in economics and business is the result of an exchange and from that trade we assign a numerical monetary value to a good, service or asset. If Alice trades Bob 4 apples for an orange, the _________ of an orange is 4 apples. Inversely, the _________ of an apple is 1/4 oranges.

a. Premium pricing
b. Price war
c. Price book
d. Price

18. In microeconomics, _________ is quite simply the conversion of inputs into outputs. It is an economic process that uses resources to create a good or service that is suitable for exchange. This can include manufacturing, storing, shipping, and packaging.

a. MET
b. Solved
c. Red Guards
d. Production

19. _________ in economics refers to metrics and measures of output from production processes, per unit of input. Labor _________, for example, is typically measured as a ratio of output per labor-hour, an input. _________ may be conceived of as a metrics of the technical or engineering efficiency of production.

a. Piece work
b. Fordism
c. Production-possibility frontier
d. Productivity

20. _________ is the a method of technical and economic research of the systems for purpose to optimize a parity between system's consumer functions or properties and expenses to achieve those functions or properties.

This methodology for continuous perfection of production, industrial technologies, organizational structures was developed by Juryj Sobolev in 1948 at the 'Perm telephone factory'

- 1948 Juryj Sobolev - the first success in application of a method analysis at the 'Perm telephone factory' .
- 1949 - the first application for the invention as result of use of the new method.

Today in economically developed countries practically each enterprise or the company use methodology of the kind of functional-cost analysis as a practice of the quality management, most full satisfying to principles of standards of series ISO 9000.

- Interest of consumer not in products itself, but the advantage which it will receive from its usage.
- The consumer aspires to reduce his expenses
- Functions needed by consumer can be executed in the various ways, and, hence, with various efficiency and expenses. Among possible alternatives of realization of functions exist such in which the parity of quality and the price is the optimal for the consumer.

The goal of _________ is achievement of the highest consumer satisfaction of production at simultaneous decrease in all kinds of industrial expenses Classical _________ has three English synonyms - Value Engineering, Value Management, Value Analysis.

a. Monopoly wage
b. Staple financing
c. Willingness to pay
d. Function cost analysis

21. _________ or producer goods are goods used as inputs in the production of other goods, such as partly finished goods. They are goods used in production of final goods. A firm may make then use _________, or make then sell, or buy then use them.

a. Economic forecasting
b. Inflation adjustment
c. Intermediate goods
d. Income distribution

22. _________ refers to the additional value of a commodity over the cost of commodities used to produce it from the previous stage of production. An example is the price of gasoline at the pump over the price of the oil in it. In national accounts used in macroeconomics, it refers to the contribution of the factors of production, i.e., land, labor, and capital goods, to raising the value of a product and corresponds to the incomes received by the owners of these factors.

a. Full employment
b. Hodrick-Prescott filter
c. Solow residual
d. Value added

23. A _________ is a normalized average (typically a weighted average) of prices for a given class of goods or services in a given region, during a given interval of time. It is a statistic designed to help to compare how these prices, taken as a whole, differ between time periods or geographical locations.

Price indices have several potential uses.

a. Price index
b. Product sabotage
c. Transactional Net Margin Method
d. Two-part tariff

24. In statistics, a _________ is a value that allows data to be measured over time in terms of some base period ussually through a price index in order to distinguish between changes in the money value of GNP which result from a change in prices and those which result from a change in physical output. It is the measure of the price level for some quantity. A _________ serves as a price index in which the effects of inflation are nulled.

a. Deflator
b. Contingent employment
c. Blanket order
d. Market microstructure

25. _________ is a term used in national accounts statistics and macroeconomics. It basically refers to the net additions to the (physical) capital stock in an accounting period, or, to the value of the increase of the capital stock; though it may occasionally also refer to the (growth of the) total stock of capital formed.

Thus, in UNSNA, _________ equals fixed capital investment, the increase in the value of inventories held, plus (net) lending to foreign countries, during an accounting period.

a. Capital intensity
b. Capital flight
c. Capital formation
d. Consumption of fixed capital

26. _________ is a term used in accounting, economics and finance to spread the cost of an asset over the span of several years.

In simple words we can say that _________ is the reduction in the value of an asset due to usage, passage of time, wear and tear, technological outdating or obsolescence, depletion, inadequacy, rot, rust, decay or other such factors.

In accounting, _________ is a term used to describe any method of attributing the historical or purchase cost of an asset across its useful life, roughly corresponding to normal wear and tear.

a. Net income per employee
b. Historical cost
c. Salvage value
d. Depreciation

27. In economics, _________ refers to an activity of spending which increases the availability of fixed capital goods or means of production. It is the total spending on new fixed investment minus replacement investment, which simply replaces depreciated capital goods.

a. Net investment
b. Greenfield investment
c. Lehman Formula
d. Tangible investments

28. A _________ occurs when an entity spends more money than it takes in. The opposite of a _________ is a budget surplus. Debt is essentially an accumulated flow of deficits.

a. Public Financial Management
b. Lump-sum tax
c. Funding body
d. Budget deficit

29. The term _________ has more than one meaning.

In the colloquial sense, an _________, or goods and services tax (GST)) is a tax collected by an intermediary (such as a retail store) from the person who bears the ultimate economic burden of the tax (such as the customer.) The intermediary later files a tax return and forwards the tax proceeds to government with the return.

a. Olivera-Tanzi effect
b. User charge
c. Indirect tax
d. Optimal tax

30. _________ is a fee paid on borrowed assets. It is the price paid for the use of borrowed money , or, money earned by deposited funds . Assets that are sometimes lent with _________ include money, shares, consumer goods through hire purchase, major assets such as aircraft, and even entire factories in finance lease arrangements.

a. Insolvency
b. Interest
c. Asset protection
d. Internal debt

31. _________ in economic theory is the use of modern economic tools to study problems that are traditionally in the province of political science.

In particular, it studies the behavior of politicians and government officials as mostly self-interested agents and their interactions in the social system either as such or under alternative constitutional rules. These can be represented a number of ways, including standard constrained utility maximization, game theory, or decision theory.

a. Public choice
b. Public interest theory
c. Paradox of voting
d. Rational ignorance

32. A _________ is a consumption tax charged at the point of purchase for certain goods and services. The tax is usually set as a percentage by the government charging the tax. There is usually a list of exemptions.

a. 130-30 fund
b. 100-year flood
c. 1921 recession
d. Sales tax

33. In economics, a _________ is a redistribution of income in the market system. These payments are considered to be nonexhaustive because they do not directly absorb resources or create output. Examples of certain _________s include welfare (financial aid), social security, and government subsidies for certain businesses (firms.)

a. 100-year flood
b. 130-30 fund
c. 1921 recession
d. Transfer payment

34. _________ is that which is owed; usually referencing assets owed, but the term can also cover moral obligations and other interactions not requiring money. In the case of assets, _________ is a means of using future purchasing power in the present before a summation has been earned. Some companies and corporations use _________ as a part of their overall corporate finance strategy.

a. Debt
b. Hard money loan
c. Collateral Management
d. Debenture

35. A _________ is the transfer of wealth from one party (such as a person or company) to another. A _________ is usually made in exchange for the provision of goods, services or both, or to fulfill a legal obligation.

The simplest and oldest form of _________ is barter, the exchange of one good or service for another.

a. Social gravity
b. Soft count
c. Going concern
d. Payment

36. _________ refers to a business or organization attempting to acquire goods or services to accomplish the goals of the enterprise. Though there are several organizations that attempt to set standards in the _________ process, processes can vary greatly between organizations. Typically the word '_________' is not used interchangeably with the word 'procurement', since procurement typically includes Expediting, Supplier Quality, and Traffic and Logistics (T'L) in addition to _________.

a. 100-year flood
b. 130-30 fund
c. Free port
d. Purchasing

37. A _________ is:

- Rewrite _________, in generative grammar and computer science
- Standardization, a formal and widely-accepted statement, fact, definition, or qualification
- Operation, a determinate _________ for performing a mathematical operation and obtaining a certain result (Mathematics, Logic)
    - Unary operation
    - Binary operation
- _________ of inference, a function from sets of formulae to formulae (Mathematics, Logic)
- _________ of thumb, principle with broad application that is not intended to be strictly accurate or reliable for every situation. Also often simply referred to as a _________
- Moral, an atomic element of a moral code for guiding choices in human behavior
- Heuristic, a quantized '_________' which shows a tendency or probability for successful function
- A regulation, as in sports
- A Production _________, as in computer science
- Procedural law, a _________set governing the application of laws to cases
    - A law, which may informally be called a '_________'
    - A court ruling, a decision by a court
- In the U.S. Government, a regulation mandated by Congress, but written or expanded upon by the Executive Branch.
- Norm (sociology), an informal but widely accepted _________, concept, truth, definition, or qualification (social norms, legal norms, coding norms)
- Norm (philosophy), a kind of sentence or a reason to act, feel or believe
- 'Rulership' is the concept of governance by a government:
    - Military _________, governance by a military body
    - Monastic _________, a collection of precepts that guides the life of monks or nuns in a religious order where the superior holds the place of Christ
- Slide _________

- '_________,' a song by Ayumi Hamasaki
- '_________,' a song by rapper Nas
- '_________s,' an album by the band The Whitest Boy Alive
- _________s: Pyaar Ka Superhit Formula, a 2003 Bollywood film
- ruler, an instrument for measuring lengths
- _________, a component of an astrolabe, circumferator or similar instrument
- The _________s, a bestselling self-help book
- _________ Project (Run Up-to-date Linux Everywhere), a project that aims to use up-to-date Linux software on old PCs
- _________ engine, a software system that helps managing business _________s
- Ja _________, a hip hop artist
    - R.U.L.E., a 2005 greatest hits album by rapper Ja _________
- '_________s,' a KMFDM song

a. Technocracy
b. Procter ' Gamble
c. Demand
d. Rule

38. To _________ is to impose a financial charge or other levy upon a taxpayer by a state or the functional equivalent of a state.

_________es are also imposed by many subnational entities. _________es consist of direct _________ or indirect _________, and may be paid in money or as its labour equivalent (often but not always unpaid.)

a. 130-30 fund
b. 100-year flood
c. 1921 recession
d. Tax

39. To tax is to impose a financial charge or other levy upon a taxpayer by a state or the functional equivalent of a state.

_________ are also imposed by many subnational entities. _________ consist of direct tax or indirect tax, and may be paid in money or as its labour equivalent (often but not always unpaid.)

a. 130-30 fund
b. Taxes
c. 1921 recession
d. 100-year flood

40. In economics, an _________ is any good or commodity, transported from one country to another country in a legitimate fashion, typically for use in trade. _________ goods or services are provided to foreign consumers by domestic producers. _________ is an important part of international trade.

a. ACCRA Cost of Living Index
b. ACEA agreement
c. AD-IA Model
d. Export

41. A variety of measures of national income and output are used in economics to estimate total economic activity in a country or region, including gross domestic product (GDP), _________ , and net national income (NNI.)

There are three main ways of calculating these numbers; the output approach, the income approach and the expenditure approach. In theory, the three must yield the same, because total expenditures on goods and services must equal the total income paid to the producers (GNI), and that must also equal the total value of the output of goods and services (_________.)

a. Gross world product
b. Gross national product
c. Household final consumption expenditure
d. Purchasing power parity

42. In economics, an _________ is any good (e.g. a commodity) or service brought into one country from another country in a legitimate fashion, typically for use in trade.It is a good that is brought in from another country for sale. _________ goods or services are provided to domestic consumers by foreign producers. An _________ in the receiving country is an export to the sending country.

a. Economic integration
b. Import
c. Incoterms
d. Import quota

43. The _________ equals the gross domestic product (GDP) minus depreciation on a country's capital goods.

_________ accounts for capital that has been consumed over the year in the form of housing, vehicle, or machinery deterioration. The depreciation accounted for is often referred to as capital consumption allowance and represents the amount needed in order to replace those depreciated assets.

a. Net domestic product
b. Carrying charge
c. Commodity price shocks
d. Cass criterion

44. In economics, _________ refers to the ability of a party to produce a good or service using fewer real resources than another entity producing the same good or service..A party has an _________ when using the same input as another party, it can produce a greater output. Since _________ is determined by a simple comparison of labor productivities, it is possible for a a party to have no _________ in anything. It can be contrasted with the concept of comparative advantage which refers to the ability to produce a particular good at a lower opportunity cost.

a. International economics
b. Index number
c. Absolute advantage
d. ACCRA Cost of Living Index

45. A _________ product is a product designed for cheapness and short-term convenience rather than medium to long-term durability, with most products only intended for single use. The term is also sometimes used for products that may last several months (ex. _________ air filters) to distinguish from similar products that last indefinitely (ex.

a. 130-30 fund
b. 1921 recession
c. 100-year flood
d. Disposable

46. _________ is gross income minus income tax on that income.

Discretionary income is income after subtracting taxes and normal expenses (such as rent or mortgage, utilities, insurance, medical, transportation, property maintenance, child support, inflation, food and sundries, 'c.) to maintain a certain standard of living.

a. Disposable personal income
b. Taxation as theft
c. Stamp Act
d. Disposable income

47. _________ is the measure of investment used to compute GDP. This is an important component of GDP because it provides an indicator of the future productive capacity of the economy. It includes replacement purchases plus net additions to capital assets plus investments in inventories.

a. Gross private domestic investment
b. National Income and Product Accounts
c. Compensation of employees
d. Current account

48. Economic _________ is defined as an excess distribution to any factor in a production process above that which is required to induce the factor into the process or any excess above that which is necessary to keep the factor in its current use..

Classical Factor _________ is primarily concerned with the fee paid for the use of fixed (e.g. natural) resources. The classical definition is expressed as any excess payment above that required to induce or provide for production.

a. 1921 recession
b. Rent
c. 100-year flood
d. 130-30 fund

49. _________ refers to internal and external organizing and correcting factors that provide order to market and other types of societal institutions and organizations - economic, political, social and cultural - so that they may function efficiently and effectively as well as repair their failures.

The expression _________ is increasingly found in the title, abstract and text of articles, chapters and papers in the business, management, organization, strategy, social-issues, political-science and sociology literatures. The ABI/Inform Global source located 1748 such uses of both expressions in October 2008, compared with 31 in 1991 and 247 in 2002.

a. Positive statement
b. Total revenue
c. Private Benefits of Control
d. Nonmarket

50. In finance, _________ is investment originating from other countries.See Foreign direct investment.

a. Horizontal merger
b. Preclusive purchasing
c. Demand side economics
d. Foreign investment

51. In law and economics, the _________, describes the economic efficiency of an economic allocation or outcome in the presence of externalities. The theorem states that when trade in an externality is possible and there are no transaction costs, bargaining will lead to an efficient outcome regardless of the initial allocation of property rights. In practice, obstacles to bargaining or poorly defined property rights can prevent Coasian bargaining.

a. General Mining Act of 1872
b. Means test
c. Coase theorem
d. Prior appropriation water rights

52. In economics, _________ is a rise in the general level of prices of goods and services in an economy over a period of time. When the general price level rises, each unit of currency buys fewer goods and services; consequently, _________ is also a decline in the real value of money--a loss of purchasing power in the medium of exchange which is also the monetary unit of account in the economy. A chief measure of general price-level _________ is the general _________ rate, which is the percentage change in a general price index (normally the Consumer Price Index) over time.

a. Energy economics
b. Economic
c. Opportunity cost
d. Inflation

53. In economics, the _________ is a measure of inflation, the rate of increase of a price index (for example, a consumer price index.)It is the percentage rate of change in price level over time. The rate of decrease in the purchasing power of money is approximately equal.

It's used to calculate the real interest rate, as well as real increases in wages, and official measurements of this rate act as input variables to COLA adjustments and Inflation derivatives prices.

a. Interest rate option
b. Edgeworth paradox
c. Equity value
d. Inflation rate

54. _________s (economically referred to as land or raw materials) occur naturally within environments that exist relatively undisturbed by mankind, in a natural form. A _________'s is often characterized by amounts of biodiversity existent in various ecosystems.

Mining, petroleum extraction, fishing, hunting, and forestry are generally considered natural-resource industries.

a. Natural resource
b. 1921 recession
c. 100-year flood
d. 130-30 fund

55. In economics, the _________ is a historical inverse relation between the rate of unemployment and the rate of inflation in an economy. Stated simply, the lower the unemployment in an economy, the higher the rate of increase in nominal wages in the economy. Rate of Change of Wages against Unemployment, United Kingdom 1913-1948 from Phillips (1958)

William Phillips, a New Zealand born economist, wrote a paper in 1958 titled The Relationship between Unemployment and the Rate of Change of Money Wages in the United Kingdom 1861-1957, which was published in the quarterly journal Economica.

a. Lorenz curve
b. Cost curve
c. Phillips curve
d. Demand curve

56. The _________ or black market is a market where all commerce is conducted without regard to taxation, law or regulations of trade. The term is also often known as the underdog, shadow economy, black economy, parallel economy or phantom trades.

In modern societies the _________ covers a vast array of activities.

a. Underground economy
b. Information markets
c. Information economy
d. Autarky

57. The _________, a unit of the United States Department of Labor, is the principal fact-finding agency for the U.S. government in the broad field of labor economics and statistics. The BLS is an independent national statistical agency that collects, processes, analyzes, and disseminates essential statistical data to the American public, the U.S. Congress, other Federal agencies, State and local governments, business, and labor representatives. The BLS also serves as a statistical resource to the Department of Labor.

a. Gross Regional Product
b. Gross national product
c. Bureau of Labor Statistics
d. Gross world product

58. _________ is a broad label that refers to any individuals or households that use goods and services generated within the economy. The concept of a _________ is used in different contexts, so that the usage and significance of the term may vary.

Typically when business people and economists talk of _________s they are talking about person as _________, an aggregated commodity item with little individuality other than that expressed in the buy/not-buy decision.

a. 1921 recession
b. 100-year flood
c. Consumer
d. 130-30 fund

59. A _________ is a measure of the average price of consumer goods and services purchased by households. A _________ measures a price change for a constant market basket of goods and services from one period to the next within the same area (city, region, or nation.) It is a price index determined by measuring the price of a standard group of goods meant to represent the typical market basket of a typical urban consumer.

a. Lipstick index
b. Consumer price index
c. CPI
d. Cost-of-living index

60. In economics, _________ is a sustained decrease in the general price level of goods and services. _________ occurs when the annual inflation rate falls below zero percent, resulting in an increase in the real value of money -- a negative inflation rate. This should not be confused with disinflation, a slow-down in the inflation rate (i.e. when the inflation decreases, but still remains positive.)

a. Tobit model
b. Deflation
c. Literacy rate
d. Price revolution

61. The term _________ or commodity bundle refers to a fixed list of items used specifically to track the progress of inflation in an economy or specific market.

The most common type of _________ is the basket of consumer goods, used to define the Consumer Price Index (CPI.) Other types of baskets are used to define

- Producer Price Index (PPI), previously known as Wholesale Price Index (WPI)
- various commodity price indices

The term _________ analysis in the retail business refers to research that provides the retailer with information to understand the purchase behaviour of a buyer. This information will enable the retailer to understand the buyer's needs and rewrite the store's layout accordingly, develop cross-promotional programs, or even capture new buyers (much like the cross-selling concept.)

a. Cost-weighted activity index
b. Category Development Index
c. Market basket
d. Robin Hood index

62. A _________ is a hypothetical measure of overall prices for some set of goods and services, in a given region during a given interval, normalized relative to some base set. Typically, a _________ is approximated with a price index.

The classical dichotomy is the assumption that there is a relatively clean distinction between overall increases or decreases in prices and underlying, e;reale; economic variables.

a. Discretionary spending
b. Discouraged worker
c. Price elasticity of supply
d. Price level

63. An _________ is an economic data figure reflecting price or quantity compared with a standard or base value. The base usually equals 100 and the _________ is usually expressed as 100 times the ratio to the base value. For example, if a commodity costs twice as much in 1970 as it did in 1960, its _________ would be 200 relative to 1960.

a. International economics
b. ACCRA Cost of Living Index
c. Economic depreciation
d. Index number

64. A _________ measures average changes in prices received by domestic producers for their output. It is one of several price indices

Its importance is being undermined by the steady decline in manufactured goods as a share of spending.

A number of countries that now report a _________ previously reported a Wholesale Price Index.

a. Hemline index
b. Visible balance
c. Gross national product
d. Producer price index

65. _________ are the divisions at which tax rates change in a progressive tax system (or an explicitly regressive tax system, although this is much rarer.) Essentially, they are the cutoff values for taxable income -- income past a certain point will be taxed at a higher rate.

a. Popiwek
b. Tax farming
c. Tax brackets
d. Disposable income

66. _________s is the social science that studies the production, distribution, and consumption of goods and services. The term _________s comes from the Ancient Greek oá¼°κονομῖα from oá¼¶κος (oikos, 'house') + νϊŒμος (nomos, 'custom' or 'law'), hence 'rules of the house(hold)'. Current _________ models developed out of the broader field of political economy in the late 19th century, owing to a desire to use an empirical approach more akin to the physical sciences.

a. Energy economics
b. Economic
c. Inflation
d. Opportunity cost

1. The term _________ refers to economy-wide fluctuations in production or economic activity over several months or years. These fluctuations occur around a long-term growth trend, and typically involve shifts over time between periods of relatively rapid economic growth (expansion or boom), and periods of relative stagnation or decline (contraction or recession.)

These fluctuations are often measured using the growth rate of real gross domestic product.

a. Tobit model
b. Consumer theory
c. Nominal value
d. Business cycle

2. _________ is a broad label that refers to any individuals or households that use goods and services generated within the economy. The concept of a _________ is used in different contexts, so that the usage and significance of the term may vary.

Typically when business people and economists talk of _________s they are talking about person as _________, an aggregated commodity item with little individuality other than that expressed in the buy/not-buy decision.

a. Consumer
b. 100-year flood
c. 1921 recession
d. 130-30 fund

3. _________ is the degree of optimism that consumers feel about the overall state of the economy and their personal financial situation. How confident people feel about stability of their incomes determines their spending activity and therefore serves as one of the key indicators for the overall shape of the economy. In essence, if _________ is higher, consumers are making more purchases, boosting the economic expansion.

a. Communal marketing
b. Rule Developing Experimentation
c. Consumer behavior
d. Consumer confidence

4. _________ is a common concept in economics, and gives rise to derived concepts such as consumer debt. Generally _________ is defined by opposition to production. But the precise definition can vary because different schools of economists define production quite differently.

a. Cash or share options
b. Federal Reserve Bank Notes
c. Consumption
d. Foreclosure data providers

5. The _________ or gross domestic income (GDI), a basic measure of an economy's economic performance, is the market value of all final goods and services produced within the borders of a nation in a year. _________ can be defined in three ways, all of which are conceptually identical. First, it is equal to the total expenditures for all final goods and services produced within the country in a stipulated period of time (usually a 365-day year.)

a. Market structure
b. Countercyclical
c. Monopolistic competition
d. Gross domestic product

6. _________ is a misspelled phrase from Latin 'pro capite' phrase meaning per head with pro meaning 'per' or 'for each' and capite meaning 'head.' Both words together equate to the phrase 'for each head.'

It is usually used in the field of statistics to indicate the average per person for any given concern, such as income, crime rate, etc.

It is also used in wills to indicate that each of the named beneficiaries should receive, by devise or bequest, equal shares of the estate. This is in contrast to a per stirpes division, in which each branch of the inheriting family inherits an equal share of the estate.

a. Population statistics
b. Sargan test
c. Per capita
d. False positive rate

7. An _________, in economics, is the amount by which the real Gross domestic product exceeds potential GDP. The real GDP is also known as GDP 'adjusted for inflation', 'constant prices' GDP or 'constant dollar' GDP, because it measures the aggregate output in a country's income accounts in a given year, expressed in base-year prices. On the other hand, the potential GDP is the quantity of real GDP when a country's economy is at full-employment.

a. ACEA agreement
b. ACCRA Cost of Living Index
c. AD-IA Model
d. Inflationary gap

8. _________ or consumer demand or consumption is also known as personal consumption expenditure. It is the largest part of aggregate demand or effective demand at the macroeconomic level. There are two variants of consumption in the aggregate demand model, including induced consumption and autonomous consumption.

a. Potential output
b. Complex multiplier
c. Dishoarding
d. Consumer spending

9. _________s is the social science that studies the production, distribution, and consumption of goods and services. The term _________s comes from the Ancient Greek oá¼°κονομÎ¯α from oá¼¶κος (oikos, 'house') + νÏŒμος (nomos, 'custom' or 'law'), hence 'rules of the house(hold)'. Current _________ models developed out of the broader field of political economy in the late 19th century, owing to a desire to use an empirical approach more akin to the physical sciences.

a. Inflation
b. Energy economics
c. Opportunity cost
d. Economic

10. A _________ product is a product designed for cheapness and short-term convenience rather than medium to long-term durability, with most products only intended for single use. The term is also sometimes used for products that may last several months (ex. _________ air filters) to distinguish from similar products that last indefinitely (ex.

a. 100-year flood
b. 130-30 fund
c. 1921 recession
d. Disposable

11. _________ is gross income minus income tax on that income.

Discretionary income is income after subtracting taxes and normal expenses (such as rent or mortgage, utilities, insurance, medical, transportation, property maintenance, child support, inflation, food and sundries, 'c.) to maintain a certain standard of living.

a. Stamp Act
b. Taxation as theft
c. Disposable personal income
d. Disposable income

12. The _________ is 'the basic residential unit in which economic production, consumption, inheritance, child rearing, and shelter are organized and carried out'; [the _________] 'may or may not be synonomous with family'.

The _________ is the basic unit of analysis in many social, microeconomic and government models. The term refers to all individuals who live in the same dwelling.

a. Family economics
b. 100-year flood
c. 130-30 fund
d. Household

13. In business and accounting, _________ are everything of value that is owned by a person or company. It is a claim on the property your income of a borrower. The balance sheet of a firm records the monetary value of the _________ owned by the firm.

a. Amortization schedule
b. Assets
c. ACEA agreement
d. ACCRA Cost of Living Index

14. In economics, the _________ measures the payments that flow between any individual country and all other countries. It is used to summarize all international economic transactions for that country during a specific time period, usually a year. The _________ is determined by the country's exports and imports of goods, services, and financial capital, as well as financial transfers.

a. Skyscraper Index
b. Gross world product
c. Gross domestic product per barrel
d. Balance of payments

15. A _________ is the transfer of wealth from one party (such as a person or company) to another. A _________ is usually made in exchange for the provision of goods, services or both, or to fulfill a legal obligation.

The simplest and oldest form of _________ is barter, the exchange of one good or service for another.

a. Soft count
b. Payment
c. Going concern
d. Social gravity

16. _________ was the American founder of the Ford Motor Company and father of modern assembly lines used in mass production. His introduction of the Model T automobile revolutionized transportation and American industry. He was a prolific inventor and was awarded 161 U.S. patents.

a. Maximilian Carl Emil Weber
b. George Cabot Lodge II
c. Werner Sombart
d. Henry Ford

17. A _________ is an object whose consumption increases the utility of the consumer, for which the quantity demanded exceeds the quantity supplied at zero price. _________s are usually modeled as having diminishing marginal utility. The first individual purchase has high utility; the second has less.

a. Composite good
b. Merit good
c. Pie method
d. Good

18. In economics, economic output is divided into physical goods and intangible services. Consumption of _________ is assumed to produce utility. It is often used when referring to a _________ Tax.

a. Composite good
b. Private good
c. Manufactured goods
d. Goods and services

19. _________ is a term that is used to describe the overall process of invention, innovation and diffusion of technology or processes. The term is redundant with technological development, technological achievement, and technological progress. In essence _________ is the invention of a technology (or a process), the continuous process of improving a technology (in which it often becomes cheaper) and its diffusion throughout industry or society.

a. 1921 recession
b. 100-year flood
c. 130-30 fund
d. Technological change

20. _________ in economics refers to metrics and measures of output from production processes, per unit of input. Labor _________, for example, is typically measured as a ratio of output per labor-hour, an input. _________ may be conceived of as a metrics of the technical or engineering efficiency of production.

a. Fordism
b. Production-possibility frontier
c. Piece work
d. Productivity

21. A variety of measures of _________ and output are used in economics to estimate total economic activity in a country or region, including gross domestic product (GDP), gross national product (GNP), and net _________

There are three main ways of calculating these numbers; the output approach, the income approach and the expenditure approach. In theory, the three must yield the same, because total expenditures on goods and services must equal the total income paid to the producers (Gnational income), and that must also equal the total value of the output of goods and services (GNP.)

a. Gross world product
b. Volume index
c. GNI per capita
d. National income

22. A _________ represents the combinations of goods and services that a consumer can purchase given current prices and his income. Consumer theory uses the concepts of a _________ and a preference map to analyze consumer choices. Both concepts have a ready graphical representation in the two-good case.

a. Quality bias
b. Revealed preference
c. Budget constraint
d. Joint demand

23. In economics and business, specifically cost accounting, the _________ point (BEP) is the point at which cost or expenses and revenue are equal: there is no net loss or gain, and one has 'broken even'. A profit or a loss has not been made, although opportunity costs have been paid, and capital has received the risk-adjusted, expected return.

For example, if the business sells less than 200 tables each month, it will make a loss, if it sells more, it will be a profit.

a. Small numbers game
b. Buffer stock scheme
c. Nonmarket
d. Break-even

24. In economics, the _________ is a single mathematical function used to express consumer spending. It was developed by John Maynard Keynes and detailed most famously in his book The General Theory of Employment, Interest, and Money. The function is used to calculate the amount of total consumption in an economy.

a. Procyclical
b. Consumption function
c. DAD-SAS model
d. Liquidity preference

25. In algebra, a _________ is a function depending on n that associates a scalar, det(A), to an n×n square matrix A. The fundamental geometric meaning of a _________ is a scale factor for measure when A is regarded as a linear transformation. _________s are important both in calculus, where they enter the substitution rule for several variables, and in multilinear algebra.

For a fixed nonnegative integer n, there is a unique _________ function for the n×n matrices over any commutative ring R. In particular, this function exists when R is the field of real or complex numbers.

a. Determinant
b. 100-year flood
c. 1921 recession
d. 130-30 fund

26. _________, 1st Baron Keynes was a renowned economist from Britain whose many ideas on economic and political theories as well as on many governments' monetary policies influenced America. He advocated a government that played an active role in the lives of people regarding business, economy, etc. In this role, the government would use fiscal measures to reduce the consequences of recessions, economic depressions and booms.

a. Adolph Fischer
b. Adam Smith
c. Adolf Hitler
d. John Maynard Keynes

27. In economics, the _________ is an empirical metric that quantifies induced consumption, the concept that the increase in personal consumer spending (consumption) that occurs with an increase in disposable income (income after taxes and transfers.) For example, if a household earns one extra dollar of disposable income, and the _________ is 0.65, then of that dollar, the household will spend 65 cents and save 35 cents.

Mathematically, the _________ (MPC) function is expressed as the derivative of the consumption (C) function with respect to disposable income (Y.)

a. Marginal propensity to import
b. Technology shock
c. Marginal propensity to consume
d. Supply shock

28. The _________ refers to the increase in saving (non-purchase of current goods and services) that results from an increase in income. For example, if a household earns one extra dollar, and the _________ is 0.35, then of that dollar, the household will spend 65 cents and save 35 cents. It can also go the other way, referring to the decrease in saving that results from a decrease in income.

a. Solow residual
b. Robertson lag
c. Real business cycle
d. Marginal propensity to save

29. _________ and Keynesian Theory) is a macroeconomic theory based on the ideas of 20th-century British economist John Maynard Keynes. _________ argues that private sector decisions sometimes lead to inefficient macroeconomic outcomes and therefore advocates active policy responses by the public sector, including monetary policy actions by the central bank and fiscal policy actions by the government to stabilize output over the business cycle.

The theories forming the basis of _________ were first presented in The General Theory of Employment, Interest and Money, published in 1936.

a. Market failure
b. Rational choice theory
c. Deflation
d. Keynesian economics

30. _________ is the point where a person stops employment completely. A person may also semi-retire and keep some sort of _________ job, out of choice rather than necessity. This usually happens upon reaching a determined age, when physical conditions don't allow the person to work any more (by illness or accident), or even for personal choice (usually in the presence of an adequate pension or personal savings.)

a. 100-year flood
b. Termination of employment
c. Layoff
d. Retirement

31. A _________ is a public market for the trading of company stock and derivatives at an agreed price; these are securities listed on a stock exchange as well as those only traded privately.

The size of the world _________ was estimated at about $36.6 trillion US at the beginning of October 2008 . The total world derivatives market has been estimated at about $791 trillion face or nominal value, 11 times the size of the entire world economy.

a. Adolph Fischer
b. Adolf Hitler
c. Stock market
d. Adam Smith

32. A _________ is a sudden dramatic decline of stock prices across a significant cross-section of a stock market. Crashes are driven by panic as much as by underlying economic factors. They often follow speculative stock market bubbles.

a. 100-year flood
b. Stock market crash
c. 1921 recession
d. 130-30 fund

33. The _________ is an economic term, referring to an increase in spending that accompanies an increase or perceived increase in wealth.

The effect would cause changes in the amounts and composition of consumer consumption caused by changes in consumer wealth. People should spend more when one of two things is true: when people actually are richer (by objective measurement, for example, a bonus or a pay raise at work, which would be an income effect), or when people perceive themselves to be 'richer' (for example, the assessed value of their home increases, or a stock they own has gone up in price recently.)

a. 100-year flood
b. Wealth condensation
c. Wealth effect
d. 130-30 fund

34. In economics, a _________ is a mechanism that allows people to easily buy and sell (trade) financial securities (such as stocks and bonds), commodities (such as precious metals or agricultural goods), and other fungible items of value at low transaction costs and at prices that reflect the efficient-market hypothesis.

_________s have evolved significantly over several hundred years and are undergoing constant innovation to improve liquidity.

Both general markets (where many commodities are traded) and specialized markets (where only one commodity is traded) exist.

a. Financial market
b. Noise trader
c. Market anomaly
d. Convertible arbitrage

35. In financial accounting, a _________ or statement of financial position is a summary of a person's or organization's balances. Assets, liabilities and ownership equity are listed as of a specific date, such as the end of its financial year. A _________ is often described as a snapshot of a company's financial condition.

a. 1921 recession
b. 130-30 fund
c. 100-year flood
d. Balance sheet

36. A _________ refers to any type debt instrument, such as a loan, bond, mortgage that does not have a fixed rate of interest over the life of the instrument. Such debt typically uses an index or other base rate for establishing the interest rate for each relevant period. One of the most common rates to use as the basis for applying interest rates is the London Inter-bank Offered Rate, or LIBOR

a. Disposal tax effect
b. Floating interest rate
c. Moneylender
d. Money market

37. _________ is the a method of technical and economic research of the systems for purpose to optimize a parity between system's consumer functions or properties and expenses to achieve those functions or properties.

This methodology for continuous perfection of production, industrial technologies, organizational structures was developed by Juryj Sobolev in 1948 at the 'Perm telephone factory'

- 1948 Juryj Sobolev - the first success in application of a method analysis at the 'Perm telephone factory' .
- 1949 - the first application for the invention as result of use of the new method.

Today in economically developed countries practically each enterprise or the company use methodology of the kind of functional-cost analysis as a practice of the quality management, most full satisfying to principles of standards of series ISO 9000.

- Interest of consumer not in products itself, but the advantage which it will receive from its usage.
- The consumer aspires to reduce his expenses
- Functions needed by consumer can be executed in the various ways, and, hence, with various efficiency and expenses. Among possible alternatives of realization of functions exist such in which the parity of quality and the price is the optimal for the consumer.

The goal of _________ is achievement of the highest consumer satisfaction of production at simultaneous decrease in all kinds of industrial expenses Classical _________ has three English synonyms - Value Engineering, Value Management, Value Analysis.

a. Monopoly wage
b. Willingness to pay
c. Staple financing
d. Function cost analysis

38. _________ is a branch of economics that deals with the performance, structure, and behavior of a national or regional economy as a whole. Along with microeconomics, _________ is one of the two most general fields in economics. It is the study of the behavior and decision-making of entire economies.

a. Nominal value
b. Tobit model
c. New Trade Theory
d. Macroeconomics

39. The _________ is an expected return that the provider of capital plans to earn on their investment.

Capital (money) used for funding a business should earn returns for the capital providers who risk their capital. For an investment to be worthwhile, the expected return on capital must be greater than the _________.

a. Cost of capital
b. Capital expenditure
c. Modigliani-Miller theorem
d. Capital intensive

40. _________ is the measure of investment used to compute GDP. This is an important component of GDP because it provides an indicator of the future productive capacity of the economy. It includes replacement purchases plus net additions to capital assets plus investments in inventories.

a. Gross private domestic investment
b. Compensation of employees
c. National Income and Product Accounts
d. Current account

41. _________ is a fee paid on borrowed assets. It is the price paid for the use of borrowed money , or, money earned by deposited funds . Assets that are sometimes lent with _________ include money, shares, consumer goods through hire purchase, major assets such as aircraft, and even entire factories in finance lease arrangements.

a. Interest
b. Asset protection
c. Insolvency
d. Internal debt

42. An _________ is the price a borrower pays for the use of money they do not own, for instance a small company might borrow from a bank to kick start their business, and the return a lender receives for deferring the use of funds, by lending it to the borrower. _________s are normally expressed as a percentage rate over the period of one year.

_________s targets are also a vital tool of monetary policy and are used to control variables like investment, inflation, and unemployment.

a. ACCRA Cost of Living Index
b. Arrow-Debreu model
c. Enterprise value
d. Interest rate

43. _________ is an assumption used in many contemporary macroeconomic models, and also in other areas of contemporary economics and game theory and in other applications of rational choice theory.

Since most macroeconomic models today study decisions over many periods, the expectations of workers, consumers, and firms about future economic conditions are an essential part of the model. How to model these expectations has long been controversial, and it is well known that the macroeconomic predictions of the model may differ depending on the assumptions made about expectations

a. Potential output
b. Balanced-growth equilibrium
c. Minimum wage
d. Rational expectations

44. An _________ is a tax levied on the financial income of people, corporations, or other legal entities. Various _________ systems exist, with varying degrees of tax incidence. Income taxation can be progressive, proportional, or regressive.

a. Income tax
b. ACEA agreement
c. ACCRA Cost of Living Index
d. AD-IA Model

45. _________ is a concept coined by structuralist inflation theorists. It refers to a situation where all prices in an economy are continuously adjusted with relation to a price index by force of contracts.

Changes in price indices trigger changes in prices of goods.

a. Employment Cost Index
b. Inflationary Spikes
c. Incomes policies
d. Inertial inflation

46. In economics, _________ is a rise in the general level of prices of goods and services in an economy over a period of time. When the general price level rises, each unit of currency buys fewer goods and services; consequently, _________ is also a decline in the real value of money--a loss of purchasing power in the medium of exchange which is also the monetary unit of account in the economy. A chief measure of general price-level _________ is the general _________ rate, which is the percentage change in a general price index (normally the Consumer Price Index) over time.

a. Energy economics
b. Opportunity cost
c. Economic
d. Inflation

47. In economics, _________ is the active redirecting resources from being consumed today so that they may create benefits in the future; the use of assets to earn income or profit._________ is the process of making an investment in order to earn a profit, for example equity investment either through a fund, a 401k plan, or individually. People often invest in order to build up their estate or to accumulate funds for retirement.

To try to predict good stocks to invest in, two main schools of thought exist: technical analysis and fundamentals analysis.

a. AD-IA Model
b. Investing
c. ACCRA Cost of Living Index
d. ACEA agreement

48. To _________ is to impose a financial charge or other levy upon a taxpayer by a state or the functional equivalent of a state.

_________es are also imposed by many subnational entities. _________es consist of direct _________ or indirect _________, and may be paid in money or as its labour equivalent (often but not always unpaid.)

a. 100-year flood
b. 130-30 fund
c. Tax
d. 1921 recession

49. To tax is to impose a financial charge or other levy upon a taxpayer by a state or the functional equivalent of a state.

_________ are also imposed by many subnational entities. _________ consist of direct tax or indirect tax, and may be paid in money or as its labour equivalent (often but not always unpaid.)

a. 1921 recession
b. 130-30 fund
c. 100-year flood
d. Taxes

50. Economics:

- _________,the desire to own something and the ability to pay for it
- _________ curve,a graphic representation of a _________ schedule
- _________ deposit, the money in checking accounts
- _________ pull theory,the theory that inflation occurs when _________ for goods and services exceeds existing supplies
- _________ schedule,a table that lists the quantity of a good a person will buy it each different price
- _________ side economics,the school of economics at believes government spending and tax cuts open economy by raising _________

a. Demand
b. McKesson ' Robbins scandal
c. Production
d. Variability

51. In economics, the _________ can be defined as the graph depicting the relationship between the price of a certain commodity, and the amount of it that consumers are willing and able to purchase at that given price. It is a graphic representation of a demand schedule. The _________ for all consumers together follows from the _________ of every individual consumer: the individual demands at each price are added together.

a. Cost curve
b. Wage curve
c. Kuznets curve
d. Demand curve

52. In economics, _________ is the total demand for final goods and services in the economy (Y) at a given time and price level. It is the amount of goods and services in the economy that will be purchased at all possible price levels. This is the demand for the gross domestic product of a country when inventory levels are static.

a. Aggregate expenditure
b. Aggregate supply
c. Aggregation problem
d. Aggregate demand

53. The _________ was an evolution of developed countries from an industrial/manufacturing-based wealth producing economy into a service sector asset based economy, brought about by globalization and currency manipulation by governments and their central banks. Some analysts claimed that this change in the economic structure of the United States had created a state of permanent steady growth, low unemployment, and immunity to boom and bust macroeconomic cycles. They believed that the change rendered obsolete many business practices.

a. New economy
b. 1921 recession
c. 100-year flood
d. 130-30 fund

54. _________ has several particular meanings:

- in mathematics
  - _________ function
  - Euler _________
  - _________
  - _________ subgroup
  - method of _________s (partial differential equations)
- in physics and engineering
  - any _________ curve that shows the relationship between certain input- and output parameters, e.g.
  - an I-V or current-voltage _________ is the current in a circuit as a function of the applied voltage
  - Receiver-Operator _________
- in fiction
  - in Dungeons ' Dragons, _________ is another name for ability score

.

a. Characteristic
b. Technocracy
c. Russian financial crisis
d. Demand

55. _________ was an American economist, statistician and public intellectual, and a recipient of the Nobel Memorial Prize in Economic Sciences. He is best known among scholars for his theoretical and empirical research, especially consumption analysis, monetary history and theory, and for his demonstration of the complexity of stabilization policy. A global public followed his restatement of a political philosophy that insisted on minimizing the role of government in favor of the private sector.

a. Adam Smith
b. Adolph Fischer
c. Milton Friedman
d. Adolf Hitler

1. In economics, _________ is the total demand for final goods and services in the economy (Y) at a given time and price level. It is the amount of goods and services in the economy that will be purchased at all possible price levels. This is the demand for the gross domestic product of a country when inventory levels are static.

a. Aggregate expenditure
b. Aggregate demand
c. Aggregation problem
d. Aggregate supply

2. The term _________ refers to economy-wide fluctuations in production or economic activity over several months or years. These fluctuations occur around a long-term growth trend, and typically involve shifts over time between periods of relatively rapid economic growth (expansion or boom), and periods of relative stagnation or decline (contraction or recession.)

These fluctuations are often measured using the growth rate of real gross domestic product.

a. Nominal value
b. Consumer theory
c. Tobit model
d. Business cycle

3. _________ is an economic system in which wealth, and the means of producing wealth, are privately owned. Through _________, the land, labor, and capital are owned, operated, and traded for the purpose of generating profits, without force or fraud, by private individuals either singly or jointly, and investments, distribution, income, production, pricing and supply of goods, commodities and services are determined by voluntary private decision in a market economy. A distinguishing feature of _________ is that each person owns his or her own labor and therefore is allowed to sell the use of it to employers.

a. Late capitalism
b. Socialism for the rich and capitalism for the poor
c. Capitalism
d. Creative capitalism

4. The _________ was a worldwide economic downturn starting in most places in 1929 and ending at different times in the 1930s or early 1940s for different countries. It was the largest and most important economic depression in the 20th century, and is used in the 21st century as an example of how far the world's economy can fall. The _________ originated in the United States; historians most often use as a starting date the stock market crash on October 29, 1929, known as Black Tuesday.

a. Wall Street Crash of 1929
b. British Empire Economic Conference
c. Jarrow March
d. Great Depression

5. _________, 1st Baron Keynes was a renowned economist from Britain whose many ideas on economic and political theories as well as on many governments' monetary policies influenced America. He advocated a government that played an active role in the lives of people regarding business, economy, etc. In this role, the government would use fiscal measures to reduce the consequences of recessions, economic depressions and booms.

a. Adam Smith
b. Adolf Hitler
c. Adolph Fischer
d. John Maynard Keynes

6. _________ and Keynesian Theory) is a macroeconomic theory based on the ideas of 20th-century British economist John Maynard Keynes. _________ argues that private sector decisions sometimes lead to inefficient macroeconomic outcomes and therefore advocates active policy responses by the public sector, including monetary policy actions by the central bank and fiscal policy actions by the government to stabilize output over the business cycle.

The theories forming the basis of _________ were first presented in The General Theory of Employment, Interest and Money, published in 1936.

a. Deflation
b. Market failure
c. Keynesian economics
d. Rational choice theory

7. The _________ is the largest national economy in the world. Its gross domestic product (GDP) was estimated as $14.2 trillion in 2008. The U.S. economy maintains a high level of output per person (GDP per capita, $46,800 in 2008, ranked at around number ten in the world.)

a. ACEA agreement
b. ACCRA Cost of Living Index
c. AD-IA Model
d. Economy of the United States

8. In economics, the _________ measures the payments that flow between any individual country and all other countries. It is used to summarize all international economic transactions for that country during a specific time period, usually a year. The _________ is determined by the country's exports and imports of goods, services, and financial capital, as well as financial transfers.

a. Balance of payments
b. Gross domestic product per barrel
c. Gross world product
d. Skyscraper Index

9. Economics:

- _________,the desire to own something and the ability to pay for it
- _________ curve,a graphic representation of a _________ schedule
- _________ deposit, the money in checking accounts
- _________ pull theory,the theory that inflation occurs when _________ for goods and services exceeds existing supplies
- _________ schedule,a table that lists the quantity of a good a person will buy it each different price
- _________ side economics,the school of economics at believes government spending and tax cuts open economy by raising _________

.

a. Demand
b. McKesson ' Robbins scandal
c. Production
d. Variability

10. A _________ is the transfer of wealth from one party (such as a person or company) to another. A _________ is usually made in exchange for the provision of goods, services or both, or to fulfill a legal obligation.

The simplest and oldest form of _________ is barter, the exchange of one good or service for another.

a. Going concern
b. Soft count
c. Social gravity
d. Payment

11. _________s is the social science that studies the production, distribution, and consumption of goods and services. The term _________s comes from the Ancient Greek oá¼°κονομί¯α from oá¼¶κος (oikos, 'house') + νÏŒμος (nomos, 'custom' or 'law'), hence 'rules of the house(hold)'. Current _________ models developed out of the broader field of political economy in the late 19th century, owing to a desire to use an empirical approach more akin to the physical sciences.

a. Energy economics
b. Opportunity cost
c. Inflation
d. Economic

12. The _________ or gross domestic income (GDI), a basic measure of an economy's economic performance, is the market value of all final goods and services produced within the borders of a nation in a year. _________ can be defined in three ways, all of which are conceptually identical. First, it is equal to the total expenditures for all final goods and services produced within the country in a stipulated period of time (usually a 365-day year.)

a. Monopolistic competition
b. Countercyclical
c. Gross domestic product
d. Market structure

13. The _________ is a US private, nonprofit research organization dedicated to studying the science and empirics of economics, especially the American economy. It is 'committed to undertaking and disseminating unbiased economic research among public policymakers, business professionals, and the academic community.' It publishes NBER Working Papers and books. The NBER is located in Cambridge, Massachusetts with branch offices in Palo Alto, California, and New York City.

a. CEFTA
b. Deutsche Bank
c. National Bureau of Economic Research
d. Non-governmental organization

14. An _________, in economics, is the amount by which the real Gross domestic product exceeds potential GDP. The real GDP is also known as GDP 'adjusted for inflation', 'constant prices' GDP or 'constant dollar' GDP, because it measures the aggregate output in a country's income accounts in a given year, expressed in base-year prices. On the other hand, the potential GDP is the quantity of real GDP when a country's economy is at full-employment.

a. ACCRA Cost of Living Index
b. AD-IA Model
c. ACEA agreement
d. Inflationary gap

15. In economics, a _________ is a general slowdown in economic activity over a sustained period of time, or a business cycle contraction. During _________s, many macroeconomic indicators vary in a similar way. Production as measured by Gross Domestic Product (GDP), employment, investment spending, capacity utilization, household incomes and business profits all fall during _________s.

a. Leading indicators
b. Recession
c. Treasury View
d. Monetary economics

16. _________ has several particular meanings:

- in mathematics
  - _________ function
  - Euler _________
  - _________
  - _________ subgroup
  - method of _________s (partial differential equations)
- in physics and engineering
  - any _________ curve that shows the relationship between certain input- and output parameters, e.g.
  - an I-V or current-voltage _________ is the current in a circuit as a function of the applied voltage
  - Receiver-Operator _________
- in fiction
  - in Dungeons ' Dragons, _________ is another name for ability score

a. Demand
b. Technocracy
c. Russian financial crisis
d. Characteristic

17. _________ refers to an action or object coming from outside a system. It is the opposite of endogenous, something generated from within the system.

- In an economic model, an _________ change is one that comes from outside the model and is unexplained by the model. For example, in the simple supply and demand model, a change in consumer tastes or preferences is unexplained by the model and also leads to endogenous changes in demand that lead to changes in the equilibrium price. Put another way, an _________ change involves an alteration of a variable that is autonomous, i.e., unaffected by the workings of the model.

- In linear regression, it means that the variable is independent of all other response values.

- In biology, '_________' refers to an action or object coming from the outside of a system. For example, an _________ contrast agent in medical imaging refers to a liquid injected into the patient intravenously that enhances visibility of a pathology, such as a tumor.

a. Exogenous
b. AD-IA Model
c. ACCRA Cost of Living Index
d. ACEA agreement

18. The _________ was an evolution of developed countries from an industrial/manufacturing-based wealth producing economy into a service sector asset based economy, brought about by globalization and currency manipulation by governments and their central banks. Some analysts claimed that this change in the economic structure of the United States had created a state of permanent steady growth, low unemployment, and immunity to boom and bust macroeconomic cycles. They believed that the change rendered obsolete many business practices.

a. 100-year flood
b. New economy
c. 1921 recession
d. 130-30 fund

19. A _________ is a public market for the trading of company stock and derivatives at an agreed price; these are securities listed on a stock exchange as well as those only traded privately.

The size of the world _________ was estimated at about $36.6 trillion US at the beginning of October 2008 . The total world derivatives market has been estimated at about $791 trillion face or nominal value, 11 times the size of the entire world economy.

a. Adam Smith
b. Adolf Hitler
c. Adolph Fischer
d. Stock market

20. The term _________ refers to a great buildup in the price of a particular commodity or, alternately, the localized rise in an economy, often based upon the value of a single commodity, followed by a downturn as the commodity price falls due to a change in economic circumstances or the collapse of unrealistic expectations.

_________ phenomenon have existed for centuries. During a 'boom' period, buyers find themselves paying increasingly higher prices until the 'bust', at which time the goods and commodities for which they have paid inflated prices may end up as valueless or nearly so.

a. Carrying charge
b. Double bottom line
c. Merchant capitalism
d. Boom and bust

21. _________ in economics and business is the result of an exchange and from that trade we assign a numerical monetary value to a good, service or asset. If Alice trades Bob 4 apples for an orange, the _________ of an orange is 4 apples. Inversely, the _________ of an apple is 1/4 oranges.

a. Price war
b. Price book
c. Premium pricing
d. Price

22. In economics, _________ is the total supply of goods and services produced by a national economy during a specific time period. It is the total amount of goods and services in the economy available at all possible price levels.

a. Aggregate expenditure
b. Aggregate demand
c. Aggregation problem
d. Aggregate supply

23. _________ was an American economist, statistician and public intellectual, and a recipient of the Nobel Memorial Prize in Economic Sciences. He is best known among scholars for his theoretical and empirical research, especially consumption analysis, monetary history and theory, and for his demonstration of the complexity of stabilization policy. A global public followed his restatement of a political philosophy that insisted on minimizing the role of government in favor of the private sector.

a. Adolph Fischer
b. Adolf Hitler
c. Adam Smith
d. Milton Friedman

24. _________ is the view within monetary economics that variation in the money supply has major influences on national output in the short run and the price level over longer periods and that objectives of monetary policy are best met by targeting the growth rate of the money supply.

_________ today is mainly associated with the work of Milton Friedman, who was among the generation of economists to accept Keynesian economics and then criticize it on his own terms. Friedman and Anna Schwartz wrote an influential book, Monetary History of the United States 1867-1960, and argued that 'inflation is always and everywhere a monetary phenomenon.' Friedman advocated a central bank policy aimed at keeping the supply and demand for money at equilibrium, as measured by growth in productivity and demand.

a. Historical school of economics
b. Complexity economics
c. Marginal revenue productivity theory of wages
d. Monetarism

25. _________ is the study of questions about the city, government, politics, liberty, justice, property, rights, law and the enforcement of a legal code by authority: what they are, why (or even if) they are needed, what makes a government legitimate, what rights and freedoms it should protect and why, what form it should take and why, what the law is, and what duties citizens owe to a legitimate government, if any, and when it may be legitimately overthrown--if ever. In a vernacular sense, the term '_________' often refers to a general view, or specific ethic, political belief or attitude, about politics that does not necessarily belong to the technical discipline of philosophy.

_________ can also be understood by analysing it through the perspectives of metaphysics, epistemology and axiology thereby unearthing the ultimate reality side, the knowledge or methodical side and the value aspects of politics.

a. Political philosophy
b. Global justice
c. Deductive logic
d. Materialism

26. A _________ is an event that suddenly changes the price of a commodity or service. It may be caused by a sudden increase or decrease in the supply of a particular good. This sudden change affects the equilibrium price.

a. Friedman rule
b. SIMIC
c. Demand shock
d. Supply shock

27. In economics, the _________ can be defined as the graph depicting the relationship between the price of a certain commodity, and the amount of it that consumers are willing and able to purchase at that given price. It is a graphic representation of a demand schedule. The _________ for all consumers together follows from the _________ of every individual consumer: the individual demands at each price are added together.

a. Wage curve
b. Cost curve
c. Kuznets curve
d. Demand curve

28. _________s is concerned with the tasks of developing and applying quantitative or statistical methods to the study and elucidation of economic principles. _________s combines economic theory with statistics to analyze and test economic relationships. Theoretical _________s considers questions about the statistical properties of estimators and tests, while applied _________s is concerned with the application of _________ methods to assess economic theories.

a. Evolutionary economics
b. Experimental economics
c. Economic
d. Econometric

29. _________s are statistical models used in econometrics. An _________ specifies the statistical relationship that is believed to hold between the various economic quantities pertaining a particular economic phenomena under study. An _________ can be derived from a deterministic economic model by allowing for uncertainty or from an economic model which itself is stochastic.

a. Econometric model
b. Economic statistics
c. ACCRA Cost of Living Index
d. Event study

30. _________ is the process of estimation in unknown situations. Prediction is a similar, but more general term. Both can refer to estimation of time series, cross-sectional or longitudinal data.

a. 130-30 fund
b. 1921 recession
c. 100-year flood
d. Forecasting

31. The _________ is an American economic index intended to estimate future economic activity. It is calculated by The Conference Board, a non-governmental organization, which determines the value of the index from the values of ten key variables. These variables have historically turned downward before a recession and upward before an expansion.

a. Index of dissimilarity
b. Index of diversity
c. Atkinson index
d. Index of leading indicators

32. _________ is a misspelled phrase from Latin 'pro capite' phrase meaning per head with pro meaning 'per' or 'for each' and capite meaning 'head.' Both words together equate to the phrase 'for each head.'

It is usually used in the field of statistics to indicate the average per person for any given concern, such as income, crime rate, etc.

It is also used in wills to indicate that each of the named beneficiaries should receive, by devise or bequest, equal shares of the estate. This is in contrast to a per stirpes division, in which each branch of the inheriting family inherits an equal share of the estate.

a. Sargan test
b. False positive rate
c. Per capita
d. Population statistics

33. In economics, _________ are key economic variables that economists used to predict a new phase of the business cycle. A leading indicator is one that changes before the economy does; a lagging indicator is one that changes after the economy has changed. Examples of _________ include stock prices, which often improve or worsen before a similar change in the economy.

a. Gross domestic product
b. Macroeconomics
c. Medium of exchange
d. Leading indicators

34. _________ is a common concept in economics, and gives rise to derived concepts such as consumer debt. Generally _________ is defined by opposition to production. But the precise definition can vary because different schools of economists define production quite differently.

a. Cash or share options
b. Consumption
c. Foreclosure data providers
d. Federal Reserve Bank Notes

35. The term _________ is an acronym for Non-Accelerating Inflation Rate of Unemployment. It is a concept in economic theory significant in the interplay of macroeconomics and microeconomics. This 'full employment' unemployment rate is sometimes termed the 'inflation-threshold unemployment rate': Actual unemployment cannot fall below the _________, and the inflation rate is likely to rise quickly (accelerate) in times of strong labor demands during periods of growth.

a. Social Credit
b. Coal depletion
c. Cobweb model
d. NAIRU

36. In economics, an _________ is any good or commodity, transported from one country to another country in a legitimate fashion, typically for use in trade. _________ goods or services are provided to foreign consumers by domestic producers. _________ is an important part of international trade.

a. ACCRA Cost of Living Index
b. ACEA agreement
c. Export
d. AD-IA Model

37. _________ refers to a business or organization attempting to acquire goods or services to accomplish the goals of the enterprise. Though there are several organizations that attempt to set standards in the _________ process, processes can vary greatly between organizations. Typically the word '_________' is not used interchangeably with the word 'procurement', since procurement typically includes Expediting, Supplier Quality, and Traffic and Logistics (T'L) in addition to _________.

a. 130-30 fund
b. Free port
c. 100-year flood
d. Purchasing

38. _________ is a fee paid on borrowed assets. It is the price paid for the use of borrowed money , or, money earned by deposited funds . Assets that are sometimes lent with _________ include money, shares, consumer goods through hire purchase, major assets such as aircraft, and even entire factories in finance lease arrangements.

a. Insolvency
b. Internal debt
c. Interest
d. Asset protection

39. An _________ is the price a borrower pays for the use of money they do not own, for instance a small company might borrow from a bank to kick start their business, and the return a lender receives for deferring the use of funds, by lending it to the borrower. _________s are normally expressed as a percentage rate over the period of one year.

_________s targets are also a vital tool of monetary policy and are used to control variables like investment, inflation, and unemployment.

a. Arrow-Debreu model
b. Enterprise value
c. ACCRA Cost of Living Index
d. Interest rate

40. In economics, _________ is the total amount of money available in an economy at a particular point in time. There are several ways to define 'money', but standard measures usually include currency in circulation and demand deposits.

_________ data are recorded and published, usually by the government or the central bank of the country.

a. Veil of money
b. Velocity of money
c. Money supply
d. Neutrality of money

41. A _________ is a hypothetical measure of overall prices for some set of goods and services, in a given region during a given interval, normalized relative to some base set. Typically, a _________ is approximated with a price index.

The classical dichotomy is the assumption that there is a relatively clean distinction between overall increases or decreases in prices and underlying, e;reale; economic variables.

a. Discretionary spending
b. Price level
c. Price elasticity of supply
d. Discouraged worker

42. _________ is the a method of technical and economic research of the systems for purpose to optimize a parity between system's consumer functions or properties and expenses to achieve those functions or properties.

This methodology for continuous perfection of production, industrial technologies, organizational structures was developed by Juryj Sobolev in 1948 at the 'Perm telephone factory'

- 1948 Juryj Sobolev - the first success in application of a method analysis at the 'Perm telephone factory' .
- 1949 - the first application for the invention as result of use of the new method.

Today in economically developed countries practically each enterprise or the company use methodology of the kind of functional-cost analysis as a practice of the quality management, most full satisfying to principles of standards of series ISO 9000.

- Interest of consumer not in products itself, but the advantage which it will receive from its usage.
- The consumer aspires to reduce his expenses
- Functions needed by consumer can be executed in the various ways, and, hence, with various efficiency and expenses. Among possible alternatives of realization of functions exist such in which the parity of quality and the price is the optimal for the consumer.

The goal of _________ is achievement of the highest consumer satisfaction of production at simultaneous decrease in all kinds of industrial expenses Classical _________ has three English synonyms - Value Engineering, Value Management, Value Analysis.

a. Monopoly wage
b. Willingness to pay
c. Function cost analysis
d. Staple financing

43. _________ is defined as the measure of responsiveness in the quantity demanded for a commodity as a result of change in price of the same commodity. It is a measure of how consumers react to a change in price. In other words, it is percentage change in quantity demanded as per the percentage change in price of the same commodity.

a. 130-30 fund
b. 100-year flood
c. 1921 recession
d. Price elasticity of demand

44. _________ is an economic model based on price, utility and quantity in a market. It predicts that in a competitive market, price will function to equalize the quantity demanded by consumers, and the quantity supplied by producers, resulting in an economic equilibrium of price and quantity. The model incorporates other factors changing equilibrium as a shift of demand and/or supply.

a. Rational addiction
b. Joint demand
c. Supply and demand
d. Deferred gratification

45. In economics, _________ is the ratio of the percent change in one variable to the percent change in another variable. It is a tool for measuring the responsiveness of a function to changes in parameters in a relative way. Commonly analyzed are _________ of substitution, price and wealth.

a. ACCRA Cost of Living Index
b. Elasticity of demand
c. ACEA agreement
d. Elasticity

46. Price _________ is defined as the measure of responsiveness in the quantity demanded for a commodity as a result of change in price of the same commodity. It is a measure of how consumers react to a change in price. In other words, it is percentage change in quantity demanded by the percentage change in price of the same commodity.

a. ACEA agreement
b. ACCRA Cost of Living Index
c. Elasticity
d. Elasticity of demand

47. A _________, reserve bank, or monetary authority is the entity responsible for the monetary policy of a country or of a group of member states. It is a bank that can lend money to other banks in times of need. Its primary responsibility is to maintain the stability of the national currency and money supply, but more active duties include controlling subsidized-loan interest rates, and acting as a lender of last resort to the banking sector during times of financial crisis (private banks often being integral to the national financial system.)

a. 1921 recession
b. 100-year flood
c. 130-30 fund
d. Central bank

48. The _________ is the central banking system of the United States. Created in 1913 by the enactment of the Federal Reserve Act (signed by Woodrow Wilson), it is a quasi-public and quasi-private (government entity with private components) banking system that comprises (1) the presidentially appointed Board of Governors of the _________ in Washington, D.C.; (2) the Federal Open Market Committee; (3) twelve regional Federal Reserve Banks located in major cities throughout the nation acting as fiscal agents for the U.S. Treasury, each with its own nine-member board of directors; (4) numerous other private U.S. member banks, which subscribe to required amounts of non-transferable stock in their regional Federal Reserve Banks; and (5) various advisory councils. Since February 2006, Ben Bernanke has served as the Chairman of the Board of Governors of the _________.

a. Term auction facility
b. Federal Reserve System Open Market Account
c. Monetary Policy Report to the Congress
d. Federal Reserve System

49. The term _________ refers to government debt, expenditures and revenues, or to finance (particularly financial revenue) in general.

- _________ deficit is the budget deficit of federal or local government
- _________ policy is the discretionary spending of governments. Contrasts with monetary policy.
- _________ year and _________ quarter are reporting periods for firms and other agencies.

.

a. Fiscal
b. Drawdown
c. Bucket shop
d. Procter ' Gamble

50. In economics, _________ is the use of government spending and revenue collection to influence the economy.

_________ can be contrasted with the other main type of economic policy, monetary policy, which attempts to stabilize the economy by controlling interest rates and the supply of money. The two main instruments of _________ are government spending and taxation.

a. Fiscalism
b. Sustainable investment rule
c. Fiscal policy
d. 100-year flood

51. _________ is widely regarded as the first modern school of economic thought. It is the idea that free markets can regulate themselves.Its major developers include Adam Smith, David Ricardo, Thomas Malthus and John Stuart Mill. Sometimes the definition of _________ is expanded to include William Petty, Johann Heinrich von Thünen.

a. Marginalism
b. Tendency of the rate of profit to fall
c. Schools of economic thought
d. Classical economics

52. In algebra, a _________ is a function depending on n that associates a scalar, det(A), to an n×n square matrix A. The fundamental geometric meaning of a _________ is a scale factor for measure when A is regarded as a linear transformation. _________s are important both in calculus, where they enter the substitution rule for several variables, and in multilinear algebra.

For a fixed nonnegative integer n, there is a unique _________ function for the n×n matrices over any commutative ring R. In particular, this function exists when R is the field of real or complex numbers.

a. 100-year flood
b. 130-30 fund
c. 1921 recession
d. Determinant

53. _________ is a term that is used to describe the overall process of invention, innovation and diffusion of technology or processes. The term is redundant with technological development, technological achievement, and technological progress. In essence _________ is the invention of a technology (or a process), the continuous process of improving a technology (in which it often becomes cheaper) and its diffusion throughout industry or society.

a. 130-30 fund
b. 100-year flood
c. Technological change
d. 1921 recession

54. In economics, a _________ is a sudden event that increases or decreases demand for goods or services temporarily. A positive _________ increases demand and a negative _________ decreases demand. Prices of goods and services are affected in both cases.

a. Lucas-Islands model
b. War economy
c. Robertson lag
d. Demand shock

1. The term _________ refers to economy-wide fluctuations in production or economic activity over several months or years. These fluctuations occur around a long-term growth trend, and typically involve shifts over time between periods of relatively rapid economic growth (expansion or boom), and periods of relative stagnation or decline (contraction or recession.)

These fluctuations are often measured using the growth rate of real gross domestic product.

a. Consumer theory
b. Nominal value
c. Tobit model
d. Business cycle

2. _________, 1st Baron Keynes was a renowned economist from Britain whose many ideas on economic and political theories as well as on many governments' monetary policies influenced America. He advocated a government that played an active role in the lives of people regarding business, economy, etc. In this role, the government would use fiscal measures to reduce the consequences of recessions, economic depressions and booms.

a. Adolph Fischer
b. John Maynard Keynes
c. Adam Smith
d. Adolf Hitler

3. _________ and Keynesian Theory) is a macroeconomic theory based on the ideas of 20th-century British economist John Maynard Keynes. _________ argues that private sector decisions sometimes lead to inefficient macroeconomic outcomes and therefore advocates active policy responses by the public sector, including monetary policy actions by the central bank and fiscal policy actions by the government to stabilize output over the business cycle.

The theories forming the basis of _________ were first presented in The General Theory of Employment, Interest and Money, published in 1936.

a. Deflation
b. Rational choice theory
c. Market failure
d. Keynesian economics

4. _________ is a common concept in economics, and gives rise to derived concepts such as consumer debt. Generally _________ is defined by opposition to production. But the precise definition can vary because different schools of economists define production quite differently.

a. Federal Reserve Bank Notes
b. Foreclosure data providers
c. Cash or share options
d. Consumption

5. In economics, the _________ is a single mathematical function used to express consumer spending. It was developed by John Maynard Keynes and detailed most famously in his book The General Theory of Employment, Interest, and Money. The function is used to calculate the amount of total consumption in an economy.

a. Procyclical
b. Liquidity preference
c. DAD-SAS model
d. Consumption function

6. _________ refers to an action or object coming from outside a system. It is the opposite of endogenous, something generated from within the system.

- In an economic model, an _________ change is one that comes from outside the model and is unexplained by the model. For example, in the simple supply and demand model, a change in consumer tastes or preferences is unexplained by the model and also leads to endogenous changes in demand that lead to changes in the equilibrium price. Put another way, an _________ change involves an alteration of a variable that is autonomous, i.e., unaffected by the workings of the model.

- In linear regression, it means that the variable is independent of all other response values.

- In biology, '_________' refers to an action or object coming from the outside of a system. For example, an _________ contrast agent in medical imaging refers to a liquid injected into the patient intravenously that enhances visibility of a pathology, such as a tumor.

a. AD-IA Model
b. ACEA agreement
c. ACCRA Cost of Living Index
d. Exogenous

7. The _________ or gross domestic income (GDI), a basic measure of an economy's economic performance, is the market value of all final goods and services produced within the borders of a nation in a year. _________ can be defined in three ways, all of which are conceptually identical. First, it is equal to the total expenditures for all final goods and services produced within the country in a stipulated period of time (usually a 365-day year.)

a. Countercyclical
b. Gross domestic product
c. Monopolistic competition
d. Market structure

8. _________ is a misspelled phrase from Latin 'pro capite' phrase meaning per head with pro meaning 'per' or 'for each' and capite meaning 'head.' Both words together equate to the phrase 'for each head.'

It is usually used in the field of statistics to indicate the average per person for any given concern, such as income, crime rate, etc.

It is also used in wills to indicate that each of the named beneficiaries should receive, by devise or bequest, equal shares of the estate. This is in contrast to a per stirpes division, in which each branch of the inheriting family inherits an equal share of the estate.

a. False positive rate
b. Sargan test
c. Population statistics
d. Per capita

9. An _________, in economics, is the amount by which the real Gross domestic product exceeds potential GDP. The real GDP is also known as GDP 'adjusted for inflation', 'constant prices' GDP or 'constant dollar' GDP, because it measures the aggregate output in a country's income accounts in a given year, expressed in base-year prices. On the other hand, the potential GDP is the quantity of real GDP when a country's economy is at full-employment.

a. ACEA agreement
b. ACCRA Cost of Living Index
c. AD-IA Model
d. Inflationary gap

10. In algebra, a _________ is a function depending on n that associates a scalar, det(A), to an n×n square matrix A. The fundamental geometric meaning of a _________ is a scale factor for measure when A is regarded as a linear transformation. _________s are important both in calculus, where they enter the substitution rule for several variables, and in multilinear algebra.

For a fixed nonnegative integer n, there is a unique _________ function for the n×n matrices over any commutative ring R. In particular, this function exists when R is the field of real or complex numbers.

a. 1921 recession
b. Determinant
c. 100-year flood
d. 130-30 fund

11. In economics, the _________ or spending multiplier is the idea that an initial amount of spending (usually by the government) leads to increased consumption spending and so results in an increase in national income greater than the initial amount of spending. In other words, an initial change in aggregate demand causes a change in aggregate output for the economy that is a multiple of the initial change.

The existence of a _________ was initially proposed by Ralph George Hawtrey in 1931.

a. Spending multiplier
b. Keynesian cross
c. Magical triangle
d. Multiplier effect

12. In economics, the multiplier effect or _________ is the idea that an initial amount of spending (usually by the government) leads to increased consumption spending and so results in an increase in national income greater than the initial amount of spending. In other words, an initial change in aggregate demand causes a change in aggregate output for the economy that is a multiple of the initial change.

The existence of a multiplier effect was initially proposed by Ralph George Hawtrey in 1931.

a. Spending Multiplier
b. Neo-Keynesian economics
c. Keynesian formula
d. Multiplier effect

13. _________ is an economic concept with commonplace familiarity. It is the price that a good or service is offered at, or will fetch, in the marketplace. It is of interest mainly in the study of microeconomics.

a. Noisy market hypothesis
b. Market price
c. Market anomaly
d. Paper trading

14. In economics, _________ refers to the highest level of real Gross Domestic Product output that can be sustained over the long term. The existence of a limit is due to natural and institutional constraints. If actual GDP rises and stays above _________, then (in the absence of wage and price controls) inflation tends to increase as demand exceeds supply.

a. Monetary conditions index
b. Fundamental psychological law
c. Monetary policy reaction function
d. Potential output

15. Competition law, known in the United States as _________ law, has three main elements:

- prohibiting agreements or practices that restrict free trading and competition between business entities. This includes in particular the repression of cartels.
- banning abusive behaviour by a firm dominating a market, or anti-competitive practices that tend to lead to such a dominant position. Practices controlled in this way may include predatory pricing, tying, price gouging, refusal to deal, and many others.
- supervising the mergers and acquisitions of large corporations, including some joint ventures. Transactions that are considered to threaten the competitive process can be prohibited altogether, or approved subject to 'remedies' such as an obligation to divest part of the merged business or to offer licences or access to facilities to enable other businesses to continue competing.

The substance and practice of competition law varies from jurisdiction to jurisdiction. Protecting the interests of consumers (consumer welfare) and ensuring that entrepreneurs have an opportunity to compete in the market economy are often treated as important objectives. Competition law is closely connected with law on deregulation of access to markets, state aids and subsidies, the privatisation of state owned assets and the establishment of independent sector regulators. In recent decades, competition law has been viewed as a way to provide better public services.

a. United Kingdom competition law
b. Intellectual property law
c. Anti-Inflation Act
d. Antitrust

16. _________ is widely regarded as the first modern school of economic thought. It is the idea that free markets can regulate themselves.Its major developers include Adam Smith, David Ricardo, Thomas Malthus and John Stuart Mill. Sometimes the definition of _________ is expanded to include William Petty, Johann Heinrich von Thünen.

a. Tendency of the rate of profit to fall
b. Marginalism
c. Schools of economic thought
d. Classical economics

17. _________s is the social science that studies the production, distribution, and consumption of goods and services. The term _________s comes from the Ancient Greek oá¼°κονομÎ¯α from oá¼¶κος (oikos, 'house') + νÏŒμος (nomos, 'custom' or 'law'), hence 'rules of the house(hold)'. Current _________ models developed out of the broader field of political economy in the late 19th century, owing to a desire to use an empirical approach more akin to the physical sciences.

a. Inflation
b. Opportunity cost
c. Energy economics
d. Economic

18. _________ is the increase in the amount of the goods and services produced by an economy over time. It is conventionally measured as the percent rate of increase in real gross domestic product, or real GDP. Growth is usually calculated in real terms, i.e. inflation-adjusted terms, in order to net out the effect of inflation on the price of the goods and services produced.

a. AD-IA Model
b. ACEA agreement
c. ACCRA Cost of Living Index
d. Economic growth

19. In economics and finance, _________ is the change in total cost that arises when the quantity produced changes by one unit. It is the cost of producing one more unit of a good. Mathematically, the _________ function is expressed as the first derivative of the total cost (TC) function with respect to quantity (Q.)

a. Marginal cost
b. Khozraschyot
c. Variable cost
d. Quality costs

20. _________ in economics and business is the result of an exchange and from that trade we assign a numerical monetary value to a good, service or asset. If Alice trades Bob 4 apples for an orange, the _________ of an orange is 4 apples. Inversely, the _________ of an apple is 1/4 oranges.

a. Price book
b. Price war
c. Premium pricing
d. Price

21. The _________ or cash market is a commodities or securities market in which goods are sold for cash and delivered immediately. Contracts bought and sold on these markets are immediately effective. _________s can operate wherever the infrastructure exists to conduct the transaction.

a. Spot market
b. Foreign exchange trading
c. Currency band
d. Triangular arbitrage

22. The term _________ refers to government debt, expenditures and revenues, or to finance (particularly financial revenue) in general.

- _________ deficit is the budget deficit of federal or local government
- _________ policy is the discretionary spending of governments. Contrasts with monetary policy.
- _________ year and _________ quarter are reporting periods for firms and other agencies.

.

a. Fiscal
b. Bucket shop
c. Drawdown
d. Procter ' Gamble

23. In economics, _________ is the use of government spending and revenue collection to influence the economy.

_________ can be contrasted with the other main type of economic policy, monetary policy, which attempts to stabilize the economy by controlling interest rates and the supply of money. The two main instruments of _________ are government spending and taxation.

a. Fiscalism
b. Fiscal policy
c. 100-year flood
d. Sustainable investment rule

24. _________ are the inflation-indexed bonds issued by the U.S. Treasury. The principal is adjusted to the Consumer Price Index, the commonly used measure of inflation. The coupon rate is constant, but generates a different amount of interest when multiplied by the inflation-adjusted principal, thus protecting the holder against inflation.

a. 1921 recession
b. 130-30 fund
c. 100-year flood
d. Treasury Inflation-Protected Securities

25. A _________ is:

- Rewrite _________, in generative grammar and computer science
- Standardization, a formal and widely-accepted statement, fact, definition, or qualification
- Operation, a determinate _________ for performing a mathematical operation and obtaining a certain result (Mathematics, Logic)
    - Unary operation
    - Binary operation
- _________ of inference, a function from sets of formulae to formulae (Mathematics, Logic)
- _________ of thumb, principle with broad application that is not intended to be strictly accurate or reliable for every situation. Also often simply referred to as a _________
- Moral, an atomic element of a moral code for guiding choices in human behavior
- Heuristic, a quantized '_________' which shows a tendency or probability for successful function
- A regulation, as in sports
- A Production _________, as in computer science
- Procedural law, a _________set governing the application of laws to cases
    - A law, which may informally be called a '_________'
    - A court ruling, a decision by a court
- In the U.S. Government, a regulation mandated by Congress, but written or expanded upon by the Executive Branch.
- Norm (sociology), an informal but widely accepted _________, concept, truth, definition, or qualification (social norms, legal norms, coding norms)
- Norm (philosophy), a kind of sentence or a reason to act, feel or believe
- 'Rulership' is the concept of governance by a government:
    - Military _________, governance by a military body
    - Monastic _________, a collection of precepts that guides the life of monks or nuns in a religious order where the superior holds the place of Christ
- Slide _________
- '_________,' a song by Ayumi Hamasaki
- '_________,' a song by rapper Nas
- '_________s,' an album by the band The Whitest Boy Alive
- _________s: Pyaar Ka Superhit Formula, a 2003 Bollywood film
- ruler, an instrument for measuring lengths
- _________, a component of an astrolabe, circumferator or similar instrument
- The _________s, a bestselling self-help book
- _________ Project (Run Up-to-date Linux Everywhere), a project that aims to use up-to-date Linux software on old PCs
- _________ engine, a software system that helps managing business _________s
- Ja _________, a hip hop artist
    - R.U.L.E., a 2005 greatest hits album by rapper Ja _________
- '_________s,' a KMFDM song

a. Demand

b. Procter ' Gamble

c. Technocracy

d. Rule

26. A security is a fungible, negotiable instrument representing financial value. _________ are broadly categorized into debt _________; equity _________, e.g., common stocks; and derivative (finance) contracts such as forwards, futures, options and swaps. The company or other entity issuing the security is called the issuer.

a. Red herring prospectus
b. Settlement risk
c. Pass-Through Certificates
d. Securities

27. A _________ product is a product designed for cheapness and short-term convenience rather than medium to long-term durability, with most products only intended for single use. The term is also sometimes used for products that may last several months (ex. _________ air filters) to distinguish from similar products that last indefinitely (ex.

a. 100-year flood
b. Disposable
c. 1921 recession
d. 130-30 fund

28. _________ is gross income minus income tax on that income.

Discretionary income is income after subtracting taxes and normal expenses (such as rent or mortgage, utilities, insurance, medical, transportation, property maintenance, child support, inflation, food and sundries, 'c.) to maintain a certain standard of living.

a. Stamp Act
b. Disposable personal income
c. Taxation as theft
d. Disposable income

29. In economics, the _________ is used to illustrate the idea that increases in the rate of taxation do not necessarily increase tax revenue. (For instance, whereas a 0% income tax rate will generate no revenue, neither will a 100% rate, as citizens will have no incentive to make money.) Increasing taxes beyond the peak of the curve point will decrease tax revenue.

a. 1921 recession
b. Laffer curve
c. 100-year flood
d. 130-30 fund

30. A _________ is a tax that is a fixed amount no matter what the change in circumstance of the taxed entity. (A lump-sum subsidy or lump-sum redistribution is defined similarly.) It is a regressive tax, such that the lower income is, the higher percentage of income applicable to the tax.

a. Funding body
b. Grant-in-aid
c. Budget deficit
d. Lump-sum tax

31. _________ refers to a business or organization attempting to acquire goods or services to accomplish the goals of the enterprise. Though there are several organizations that attempt to set standards in the _________ process, processes can vary greatly between organizations. Typically the word '_________' is not used interchangeably with the word 'procurement', since procurement typically includes Expediting, Supplier Quality, and Traffic and Logistics (T'L) in addition to _________.

a. 130-30 fund
b. Purchasing
c. Free port
d. 100-year flood

32. Economic _________ is defined as an excess distribution to any factor in a production process above that which is required to induce the factor into the process or any excess above that which is necessary to keep the factor in its current use..

Classical Factor _________ is primarily concerned with the fee paid for the use of fixed (e.g. natural) resources. The classical definition is expressed as any excess payment above that required to induce or provide for production.

a. 1921 recession
b. Rent
c. 100-year flood
d. 130-30 fund

33. To _________ is to impose a financial charge or other levy upon a taxpayer by a state or the functional equivalent of a state.

_________es are also imposed by many subnational entities. _________es consist of direct _________ or indirect _________, and may be paid in money or as its labour equivalent (often but not always unpaid.)

a. 1921 recession
b. 100-year flood
c. Tax
d. 130-30 fund

34. To tax is to impose a financial charge or other levy upon a taxpayer by a state or the functional equivalent of a state.

_________ are also imposed by many subnational entities. _________ consist of direct tax or indirect tax, and may be paid in money or as its labour equivalent (often but not always unpaid.)

a. 100-year flood
b. 130-30 fund
c. 1921 recession
d. Taxes

35. In economics, _________ is the total demand for final goods and services in the economy (Y) at a given time and price level. It is the amount of goods and services in the economy that will be purchased at all possible price levels. This is the demand for the gross domestic product of a country when inventory levels are static.

a. Aggregate demand
b. Aggregation problem
c. Aggregate expenditure
d. Aggregate supply

36. Economics:

- _________,the desire to own something and the ability to pay for it
- _________ curve,a graphic representation of a _________ schedule
- _________ deposit, the money in checking accounts
- _________ pull theory,the theory that inflation occurs when _________ for goods and services exceeds existing supplies
- _________ schedule,a table that lists the quantity of a good a person will buy it each different price
- _________ side economics,the school of economics at believes government spending and tax cuts open economy by raising _________

a. Production
b. Variability
c. Demand
d. McKesson ' Robbins scandal

37. _________ refers to discriminatory employment practices such as bias in hiring, promotion, job assignment, termination, and compensation, and various types of harassment.

In many countries, laws prohibit employers from discriminating on the basis of race, color, sex, religion, national origin, physical or mental disability, or age. There is also a growing body of law preventing or occasionally justifying _________ based on sexual orientation or gender identity.

a. Irish competition law
b. Employment discrimination
c. Energy Independence and Security Act of 2007
d. Impotent poor

38. In macroeconomics, _________ is a condition of the national economy, where all or nearly all persons willing and able to work at the prevailing wages and working conditions are able to do so. It is defined either as 0% unemployment, literally, no unemployment (the rate of unemployment is the fraction of the work force unable to find work), as by James Tobin, or as the level of employment rates when there is no cyclical unemployment. It is defined by the majority of mainstream economists as being an acceptable level of natural unemployment above 0%, the discrepancy from 0% being due to non-cyclical types of unemployment.

a. Harrod-Johnson diagram
b. Demand shock
c. Marginal propensity to consume
d. Full employment

39. The _________ was a worldwide economic downturn starting in most places in 1929 and ending at different times in the 1930s or early 1940s for different countries. It was the largest and most important economic depression in the 20th century, and is used in the 21st century as an example of how far the world's economy can fall. The _________ originated in the United States; historians most often use as a starting date the stock market crash on October 29, 1929, known as Black Tuesday.

a. Great Depression
b. Jarrow March
c. British Empire Economic Conference
d. Wall Street Crash of 1929

40. _________ was a global military conflict which involved a majority of the world's nations, including all of the great powers, organized into two opposing military alliances: the Allies and the Axis. The war involved the mobilization of over 100 million military personnel, making it the most widespread war in history. In a state of 'total war', the major participants placed their entire economic, industrial, and scientific capabilities at the service of the war effort, erasing the distinction between civilian and military resources.

a. 100-year flood
b. 130-30 fund
c. 1921 recession
d. World War II

41. A _________ occurs when an entity spends more money than it takes in. The opposite of a _________ is a budget surplus. Debt is essentially an accumulated flow of deficits.

a. Lump-sum tax
b. Public Financial Management
c. Budget deficit
d. Funding body

42. A _________ is a situation in which the government takes in more than it spends.

a. 130-30 fund
b. 100-year flood
c. Budget set
d. Budget surplus

43. _________ is a school of macroeconomic thought that argues that economic growth can be most effectively created using incentives for people to produce (supply) goods and services, such as adjusting income tax and capital gains tax rates, and by allowing greater flexibility by reducing regulation. Consumers will then benefit from a greater supply of goods and services at lower prices.

The term _________ was coined by journalist Jude Wanniski in 1975, and popularized the ideas of economists Robert Mundell and Arthur Laffer.

a. Supply-side economics
b. Fiscal stimulus plans
c. Clap note
d. Commodity trading advisors

44. A _________ is a reduction in taxes. Economic stimulus via _________s, along with interest rate intervention and deficit spending, are one of the central tenets of Keynesian economics.

The immediate effects of a _________ are, generally, a decrease in the real income of the government and an increase in the real income of those whose tax rate has been lowered.

a. Withholding tax
b. Popiwek
c. Direct taxes
d. Tax cut

45. _________, or a _________ is the concept of a resulting effect (cf. cause and effect, arising from another action. In general terms, it is used to indicate that all human actions, particularly crime and sin, have profound effects.

a. Consequence
b. Solved
c. Rule
d. Variability

46. _________s is concerned with the tasks of developing and applying quantitative or statistical methods to the study and elucidation of economic principles. _________s combines economic theory with statistics to analyze and test economic relationships. Theoretical _________s considers questions about the statistical properties of estimators and tests, while applied _________s is concerned with the application of _________ methods to assess economic theories.

a. Experimental economics
b. Econometric
c. Evolutionary economics
d. Economic

47. _________s are statistical models used in econometrics. An _________ specifies the statistical relationship that is believed to hold between the various economic quantities pertaining a particular economic phenomena under study. An _________ can be derived from a deterministic economic model by allowing for uncertainty or from an economic model which itself is stochastic.

a. ACCRA Cost of Living Index
b. Economic statistics
c. Event study
d. Econometric model

48. An _________ or Å"conomic system is a system that involves the production, distribution and consumption of goods and services between the entities in a particular society. It is the method used by society to produce and distribute goods and services. The _________ is composed of people and institutions, including their relationships to productive resources, such as through the convention of property.

a. Indicative planning
b. Intention economy
c. Information economy
d. Economic system

49. _________ is an economic system in which wealth, and the means of producing wealth, are privately owned. Through _________, the land, labor, and capital are owned, operated, and traded for the purpose of generating profits, without force or fraud, by private individuals either singly or jointly, and investments, distribution, income, production, pricing and supply of goods, commodities and services are determined by voluntary private decision in a market economy. A distinguishing feature of _________ is that each person owns his or her own labor and therefore is allowed to sell the use of it to employers.

a. Late capitalism
b. Creative capitalism
c. Socialism for the rich and capitalism for the poor
d. Capitalism

50. The _________ is a book published by John Maynard Keynes. Keynes attended the Versailles Conference as a delegate of the British Treasury and argued for a much more generous peace. It was a best seller throughout the world and was critical in establishing a general opinion that the Versailles Treaty was a 'Carthaginian peace'.

a. AD-IA Model
b. ACCRA Cost of Living Index
c. ACEA agreement
d. Economic Consequences of the Peace

51. The _________ is the apparent contradiction that although water is on the whole more useful, in terms of survival, than diamonds, diamonds command a higher price in the market. The economist Adam Smith is often considered to be the classic presenter of this paradox. Nicolaus Copernicus, John Locke, John Law and others had previously tried to explain the disparity.

a. Paradox of value
b. 100-year flood
c. St. Petersburg paradox
d. 130-30 fund

52. The _________ is a paradox of economics propounded by John Maynard Keynes. The paradox states that if everyone saves more money during times of recession, then aggregate demand will fall and will in turn lower total savings in the population because of the decrease in consumption and economic growth.

The argument is that, in equilibrium, total income (and thus demand) must equal total output, and that total investment must equal total saving.

a. Keynesian cross
b. Spending multiplier
c. Speculative demand
d. Paradox of thrift

53. A _________ association is a financial institution that specializes in accepting savings deposits and making mortgage and other loans. The S'L or thrift term is mainly used in the United States; similar institutions in the United Kingdom, Ireland and some Commonwealth countries include building societies and trustee savings banks.

They are often mutually held, meaning that the depositors and borrowers are members with voting rights, and have the ability to direct the financial and managerial goals of the organization, similar to the policyholders of a mutual insurance company.

a. Collective investment scheme
b. Fonds commun de placement
c. Participating policy
d. Savings and Loan

1.

A _________ is a type of financial intermediary and a type of bank. Commercial banking is also known as business banking. It is a bank that provides checking accounts, savings accounts, and money market accounts and that accepts time deposits.

a. Bought deal
b. Daylight overdraft
c. Commercial bank
d. Lombard banking

2. In finance, the _________ is the system that allows the transfer of money between savers and borrowers.

Put another way: the _________ is a set of complex and closely interconnected financial institutions, markets, instruments, services, practices, and transactions.

a. Financial system
b. Hedonimetry
c. Lean consumption
d. Foreign investment

3. In business and accounting, _________ are everything of value that is owned by a person or company. It is a claim on the property your income of a borrower. The balance sheet of a firm records the monetary value of the _________ owned by the firm.

a. Assets
b. ACEA agreement
c. Amortization schedule
d. ACCRA Cost of Living Index

4. The _________ consists of a number of economic theories which describe the nature of the firm, company including its existence, its behaviour, and its relationship with the market.

In simplified terms, the _________ aims to answer these questions:

1. Existence - why do firms emerge, why are not all transactions in the economy mediated over the market?
2. Boundaries - why the boundary between firms and the market is located exactly there? Which transactions are performed internally and which are negotiated on the market?
3. Organization - why are firms structured in such specific way? What is the interplay of formal and informal relationships?

Despite looking simple, these questions are not answered by the established economic theory, which usually views firms as given, and treats them as black boxes without any internal structure.

The First World War period saw a change of emphasis in economic theory away from industry-level analysis which mainly included analysing markets to analysis at the level of the firm, as it became increasingly clear that perfect competition was no longer an adequate model of how firms behaved. Economic theory till then had focussed on trying to understand markets alone and there had been little study on understanding why firms or organisations exist.

a. Theory of the firm
b. Policy Ineffectiveness Proposition
c. Technology gap
d. Khazzoom-Brookes postulate

5. The _________ is the central banking system of the United States. Created in 1913 by the enactment of the Federal Reserve Act (signed by Woodrow Wilson), it is a quasi-public and quasi-private (government entity with private components) banking system that comprises (1) the presidentially appointed Board of Governors of the _________ in Washington, D.C.; (2) the Federal Open Market Committee; (3) twelve regional Federal Reserve Banks located in major cities throughout the nation acting as fiscal agents for the U.S. Treasury, each with its own nine-member board of directors; (4) numerous other private U.S. member banks, which subscribe to required amounts of non-transferable stock in their regional Federal Reserve Banks; and (5) various advisory councils. Since February 2006, Ben Bernanke has served as the Chairman of the Board of Governors of the _________.

a. Monetary Policy Report to the Congress
b. Federal Reserve System
c. Term auction facility
d. Federal Reserve System Open Market Account

6. _________s are cash, evidence of an ownership interest in an entity or deliver, cash or another _________.

_________s can be categorized by form depending on whether they are cash instruments or derivative instruments:

- Cash instruments are _________s whose value is determined directly by markets. They can be divided into securities, which are readily transferable, and other cash instruments such as loans and deposits, where both borrower and lender have to agree on a transfer.
- Derivative instruments are _________s which derive their value from the value and characteristics of one or more underlying assets. They can be divided into exchange-traded derivatives and over-the-counter (OTC) derivatives.

Alternatively, _________s can be categorized by 'asset class' depending on whether they are equity based (reflecting ownership of the issuing entity) or debt based (reflecting a loan the investor has made to the issuing entity.) If it is debt, it can be further categorised into short term (less than one year) or long term.

Foreign Exchange instruments and transactions are neither debt nor equity based and belong in their own category.

a. Market liquidity
b. Municipal Bond Arbitrage
c. Fundamentally based indexes
d. Financial instrument

7. _________s are financial contracts whose values are derived from the value of something else (known as the underlying.) The underlying value on which a _________ is based can be an asset (e.g., commodities, equities (stocks), residential mortgages, commercial real estate, loans, bonds), an index (e.g., interest rates, exchange rates, stock market indices, consumer price index (CPI) -- see inflation _________s), weather conditions bonds or other forms of credit.

a. Second derivative
b. 130-30 fund
c. Derivative
d. 100-year flood

8. The cost advantages of using _________ include:

- Reconciling conflicting preferences of lenders and borrowers
- Risk aversion- intermediaries help spread out and decrease the risks
- Economies of scale- using _________ reduces the costs of lending and borrowing
- Economies of scope- intermediaries concentrate on the demands of the lenders and borrowers and are able to enhance their products and services (use same inputs to produce different outputs)

_________ include:

- Banks
- Building societies
- Credit unions
- Financial advisers or brokers
- Insurance companies
- Collective investment schemes
- Pension funds

Financial institutions (intermediaries) perform the vital role of bringing together those economic agents with surplus funds who want to lend, with those with a shortage of funds who want to borrow.

In doing this they offer the major benefits of maturity and risk transformation. It is possible for this to be done by direct contact between the ultimate borrowers, but there are major cost disadvantages of direct finance.

Indeed, one explanation of the existence of specialist _________ is that they have a related (cost) advantage in offering financial services, which not only enables them to make profit, but also raises the overall efficiency of the economy.

a. Collective investment scheme
b. Financial intermediaries
c. SICAV
d. Broker-dealer

9. In economics, a _________ is a mechanism that allows people to easily buy and sell (trade) financial securities (such as stocks and bonds), commodities (such as precious metals or agricultural goods), and other fungible items of value at low transaction costs and at prices that reflect the efficient-market hypothesis.

_________s have evolved significantly over several hundred years and are undergoing constant innovation to improve liquidity.

Both general markets (where many commodities are traded) and specialized markets (where only one commodity is traded) exist.

a. Noise trader
b. Convertible arbitrage
c. Market anomaly
d. Financial market

10. _________, in law and economics, is a form of risk management primarily used to hedge against the risk of a contingent loss. _________ is defined as the equitable transfer of the risk of a loss, from one entity to another, in exchange for a premium, and can be thought of as a guaranteed small loss to prevent a large, possibly devastating loss. An insurer is a company selling the _________; an insured or policyholder is the person or entity buying the _________.

a. ACCRA Cost of Living Index
b. AD-IA Model
c. Insurance
d. ACEA agreement

11. The accounting equation relates assets, _________, and owner's equity:

Assets = _________ + Owner's Equity

The accounting equation is the mathematical structure of the balance sheet.

The Australian Accounting Research Foundation defines _________ as: 'future sacrifice of economic benefits that the entity is presently obliged to make to other entities as a result of past transactions and other past events.'

Probably the most accepted accounting definition of liability is the one used by the International Accounting Standards Board (IASB.) The following is a quotation from IFRS Framework:

A liability is a present obligation of the enterprise arising from past events, the settlement of which is expected to result in an outflow from the enterprise of resources embodying economic benefits

-

Regulations as to the recognition of _________ are different all over the world, but are roughly similar to those of the IASB.

a. Coase theorem
b. Community property
c. Competition law theory
d. Liabilities

12. _________ is the process by which money is produced or issued. There are three different ways to create money:

- manufacturing a new monetary unit, such as paper currency or metal coins (_________)
- loaning out a physical monetary unit multiple times through fractional-reserve lending (credit creation)
- buying of government securities or other financial instruments by central bank through Open market operations (electronic creation)

Coins are produced by manufacturing metal in a factory called a mint.

Banknotes and bank account balances are financial securities issued by a bank.

Similarly, money destruction, i.e., the reverse of _________, can occur in two different ways, depending on how the money was created.

a. Monetary policy of Sweden
b. Money creation
c. Shadow Open Market Committee
d. Second-round effect

13. A _________ is a professionally managed type of collective investment scheme that pools money from many investors and invests it in stocks, bonds, short-term money market instruments, and/or other securities. The _________ will have a fund manager that trades the pooled money on a regular basis. As of early 2008, the worldwide value of all _________s totals more than $26 trillion.

a. Dark pools of liquidity
b. Participating policy
c. Self-invested personal pension
d. Mutual fund

14. _________ is the revenue to a brokerage firm when commissioned securities and insurance salespeople sell a product, whether it is an investment like stocks, bonds or insurance like life insurance or long term care insurance. The commission that the agent receives is usually a percentage of this figure, although some firms like Merrill Lynch use figures called Production Credits, usually smaller than _________, to determine payouts and retain more revenue.

For example, a mutual fund with a 5.75% sales charge is sold to someone who invests $10,000.

a. Number of Shares
b. Monopoly price
c. Discretionary policy
d. Gross Dealer Concession

15. In general, a _________ is an arrangement to provide people with an income when they are no longer earning a regular income from employment.

The terms retirement plan or superannuation refer to a _________ granted upon retirement . Retirement plans may be set up by employers, insurance companies, the government or other institutions such as employer associations or trade unions.

a. Profit-sharing agreement
b. Real wage
c. Superannuation
d. Pension

16. _________ is the identification, assessment, and prioritization of risks followed by coordinated and economical application of resources to minimize, monitor, and control the probability and/or impact of unfortunate events.. Risks can come from uncertainty in financial markets, project failures, legal liabilities, credit risk, accidents, natural causes and disasters as well as deliberate attacks from an adversary. Several _________ standards have been developed including the Project Management Institute, the National Institute of Science ' Technology, actuarial societies, and ISO standards.

a. Regression toward the mean
b. Kanban
c. Penny stock
d. Risk management

17. A security is a fungible, negotiable instrument representing financial value. _________ are broadly categorized into debt _________; equity _________, e.g., common stocks; and derivative (finance) contracts such as forwards, futures, options and swaps. The company or other entity issuing the security is called the issuer.

a. Securities
b. Red herring prospectus
c. Pass-Through Certificates
d. Settlement risk

18. The _________ is 'the basic residential unit in which economic production, consumption, inheritance, child rearing, and shelter are organized and carried out'; [the _________] 'may or may not be synonomous with family'.

The _________ is the basic unit of analysis in many social, microeconomic and government models. The term refers to all individuals who live in the same dwelling.

a. Family economics
b. Household
c. 130-30 fund
d. 100-year flood

19. _________ is a fee paid on borrowed assets. It is the price paid for the use of borrowed money , or, money earned by deposited funds . Assets that are sometimes lent with _________ include money, shares, consumer goods through hire purchase, major assets such as aircraft, and even entire factories in finance lease arrangements.

a. Interest
b. Asset protection
c. Insolvency
d. Internal debt

20. An _________ is the price a borrower pays for the use of money they do not own, for instance a small company might borrow from a bank to kick start their business, and the return a lender receives for deferring the use of funds, by lending it to the borrower. _________s are normally expressed as a percentage rate over the period of one year.

_________s targets are also a vital tool of monetary policy and are used to control variables like investment, inflation, and unemployment.

a. Arrow-Debreu model
b. Enterprise value
c. ACCRA Cost of Living Index
d. Interest rate

21. _________ in economics and business is the result of an exchange and from that trade we assign a numerical monetary value to a good, service or asset. If Alice trades Bob 4 apples for an orange, the _________ of an orange is 4 apples. Inversely, the _________ of an apple is 1/4 oranges.

a. Price book
b. Price war
c. Premium pricing
d. Price

22. _________ is a life of security. It may also refer to the final payment date of a loan or other financial instrument, at which point all remaining interest and principal is due to be paid.

1, 3, 6 months _________ band can be calculated by using 30-day per month periods.

a. Refinancing risk
b. Future-oriented
c. Future value
d. Maturity

23. _________ is the value on a given date of a future payment or series of future payments, discounted to reflect the time value of money and other factors such as investment risk. _________ calculations are widely used in business and economics to provide a means to compare cash flows at different times on a meaningful 'like to like' basis.

Money value fluctuates over time: $100 today are not worth $100 in five years.

a. Future value
b. Present value of costs
c. Tax shield
d. Present value

24. In economics, _________ is a sustained decrease in the general price level of goods and services. _________ occurs when the annual inflation rate falls below zero percent, resulting in an increase in the real value of money -- a negative inflation rate. This should not be confused with disinflation, a slow-down in the inflation rate (i.e. when the inflation decreases, but still remains positive.)

a. Deflation
b. Literacy rate
c. Price revolution
d. Tobit model

25. _________ is the a method of technical and economic research of the systems for purpose to optimize a parity between system's consumer functions or properties and expenses to achieve those functions or properties.

This methodology for continuous perfection of production, industrial technologies, organizational structures was developed by Juryj Sobolev in 1948 at the 'Perm telephone factory'

- 1948 Juryj Sobolev - the first success in application of a method analysis at the 'Perm telephone factory' .
- 1949 - the first application for the invention as result of use of the new method.

Today in economically developed countries practically each enterprise or the company use methodology of the kind of functional-cost analysis as a practice of the quality management, most full satisfying to principles of standards of series ISO 9000.

- Interest of consumer not in products itself, but the advantage which it will receive from its usage.
- The consumer aspires to reduce his expenses
- Functions needed by consumer can be executed in the various ways, and, hence, with various efficiency and expenses. Among possible alternatives of realization of functions exist such in which the parity of quality and the price is the optimal for the consumer.

The goal of _________ is achievement of the highest consumer satisfaction of production at simultaneous decrease in all kinds of industrial expenses Classical _________ has three English synonyms - Value Engineering, Value Management, Value Analysis.

a. Monopoly wage
b. Willingness to pay
c. Staple financing
d. Function cost analysis

26. _________ in economic theory is the use of modern economic tools to study problems that are traditionally in the province of political science.

In particular, it studies the behavior of politicians and government officials as mostly self-interested agents and their interactions in the social system either as such or under alternative constitutional rules. These can be represented a number of ways, including standard constrained utility maximization, game theory, or decision theory.

a. Public interest theory
b. Rational ignorance
c. Paradox of voting
d. Public choice

27. Market _________ is a business, economics or investment term that refers to an asset's ability to be easily converted through an act of buying or selling without causing a significant movement in the price and with minimum loss of value. Money, or cash on hand, is the most liquid asset. An act of exchange of a less liquid asset with a more liquid asset is called liquidation.

a. 130-30 fund
b. 1921 recession
c. 100-year flood
d. Liquidity

28. In finance, a _________ is a debt security, in which the authorized issuer owes the holders a debt and, depending on the terms of the _________, is obliged to pay interest (the coupon) and/or to repay the principal at a later date, termed maturity. A _________ is a formal contract to repay borrowed money with interest at fixed intervals.

Thus a _________ is like a loan: the issuer is the borrower (debtor), the holder is the lender (creditor), and the coupon is the interest.

a. Zero-coupon
b. Callable
c. Prize Bond
d. Bond

29. A _________ is a bond issued by a corporation. It is a bond that a corporation issues to raise money in order to expand its business. The term is usually applied to longer-term debt instruments, generally with a maturity date falling at least a year after their issue date.

a. Bond fund
b. Dirty price
c. Corporate bond
d. Bond valuation

30. In economics, _________ is a rise in the general level of prices of goods and services in an economy over a period of time. When the general price level rises, each unit of currency buys fewer goods and services; consequently, _________ is also a decline in the real value of money--a loss of purchasing power in the medium of exchange which is also the monetary unit of account in the economy. A chief measure of general price-level _________ is the general _________ rate, which is the percentage change in a general price index (normally the Consumer Price Index) over time.

a. Opportunity cost
b. Economic
c. Energy economics
d. Inflation

31. In economics, the _________ is a measure of inflation, the rate of increase of a price index (for example, a consumer price index.)It is the percentage rate of change in price level over time. The rate of decrease in the purchasing power of money is approximately equal.

It's used to calculate the real interest rate, as well as real increases in wages, and official measurements of this rate act as input variables to COLA adjustments and Inflation derivatives prices.

a. Edgeworth paradox
b. Equity value
c. Interest rate option
d. Inflation rate

32. In finance and economics _________ or nominal rate of interest refers to the rate of interest before adjustment for inflation (in contrast with the real interest rate); or, for interest rates 'as stated' without adjustment for the full effect of compounding (also referred to as the nominal annual rate.) An interest rate is called nominal if the frequency of compounding (e.g. a month) is not identical to the basic time unit (normally a year.)

The real interest rate includes compensation for the lender's lost value due to inflation, whereas the _________ excludes inflation.

a. Risk-free interest rate
b. London Interbank Offered Rate
c. Fixed interest
d. Nominal interest rate

33. The '_________' is approximately the nominal interest rate minus the inflation rate Since the inflation rate over the course of a loan is not known initially, volatility in inflation represents a risk to both the lender and the borrower.

In economics and finance, an individual who lends money for repayment at a later point in time expects to be compensated for the time value of money, or not having the use of that money while it is lent.

a. Real interest rate
b. Cost-push inflation
c. Reflation
d. Core inflation

34. _________ is a broad label that refers to any individuals or households that use goods and services generated within the economy. The concept of a _________ is used in different contexts, so that the usage and significance of the term may vary.

Typically when business people and economists talk of _________s they are talking about person as _________, an aggregated commodity item with little individuality other than that expressed in the buy/not-buy decision.

a. 100-year flood
b. Consumer
c. 130-30 fund
d. 1921 recession

35. A _________ is a measure of the average price of consumer goods and services purchased by households. A _________ measures a price change for a constant market basket of goods and services from one period to the next within the same area (city, region, or nation.) It is a price index determined by measuring the price of a standard group of goods meant to represent the typical market basket of a typical urban consumer.

a. Cost-of-living index
b. CPI
c. Lipstick index
d. Consumer price index

36. _________ are the inflation-indexed bonds issued by the U.S. Treasury. The principal is adjusted to the Consumer Price Index, the commonly used measure of inflation. The coupon rate is constant, but generates a different amount of interest when multiplied by the inflation-adjusted principal, thus protecting the holder against inflation.

a. 100-year flood
b. Treasury inflation-protected securities
c. 1921 recession
d. 130-30 fund

37. A _________ is a normalized average (typically a weighted average) of prices for a given class of goods or services in a given region, during a given interval of time. It is a statistic designed to help to compare how these prices, taken as a whole, differ between time periods or geographical locations.

Price indices have several potential uses.

a. Transactional Net Margin Method
b. Two-part tariff
c. Product sabotage
d. Price index

38. A _________, reserve bank, or monetary authority is the entity responsible for the monetary policy of a country or of a group of member states. It is a bank that can lend money to other banks in times of need. Its primary responsibility is to maintain the stability of the national currency and money supply, but more active duties include controlling subsidized-loan interest rates, and acting as a lender of last resort to the banking sector during times of financial crisis (private banks often being integral to the national financial system.)

a. 100-year flood
b. Central bank
c. 1921 recession
d. 130-30 fund

39. _________ is the process by which the government, central bank (ii) availability of money, and (iii) cost of money or rate of interest, in order to attain a set of objectives oriented towards the growth and stability of the economy. Monetary theory provides insight into how to craft optimal _________.

_________ is referred to as either being an expansionary policy where an expansionary policy increases the total supply of money in the economy, and a contractionary policy decreases the total money supply.

a. 130-30 fund
b. 1921 recession
c. 100-year flood
d. Monetary policy

40. Bartering is a medium in which goods or services are directly exchanged for other goods and/or services, without the use of money. It can be bilateral or multilateral, and usually exists parallel to monetary systems in most developed countries, though to a very limited extent. _________ usually replaces money as the method of exchange in times of monetary crisis, when the currency is unstable and devalued by hyperinflation.

a. Barter
b. Community-based economics
c. Meitheal
d. New Economics Foundation

41. A _________ is something for which there is demand, but which is supplied without qualitative differentiation across a market. It is a product that is the same no matter who produces it, such as petroleum, notebook paper, or milk. In other words, copper is copper.

a. 100-year flood
b. Commodity
c. Hard commodity
d. Soft commodity

42. _________ is money whose value comes from a commodity out of which it is made. It is objects that have value in themselves as well as for use as money.

Examples of commodities that have been used as mediums of exchange include gold, silver, copper, salt, peppercorns, large stones, decorated belts, shells, alcohol, cigarettes, cannabis, candy, barley etc.

a. Currency competition
b. Fiat money
c. Reserve currency
d. Commodity money

43. The _________ problem (often 'double _________') is an important category of transaction costs that impose severe limitations on economies lacking money and thus dominated by barter or other in-kind transactions. The problem is caused by the improbability of the wants, needs or events that cause or motivate a transaction occurring at the same time and the same place.

In-kind transactions have several problems, most notably timing constraints.

a. RFM
b. Buy-sell agreement
c. Going concern
d. Coincidence of Wants

44. _________ refers to money or scrip which is exchanged only electronically. Typically, this involves use of computer networks, the internet and digital stored value systems. Electronic Funds Transfer and direct deposit are examples of _________.

a. Electronic money
b. ACCRA Cost of Living Index
c. AD-IA Model
d. ACEA agreement

45. _________ is money declared by a government to be legal tender. The term derives from the Latin fiat, meaning 'let it be done'. _________ achieves value because a government accepts it in payment of taxes and says it can be used within the country as a 'tender' to pay all debts.

a. Currency board
b. Devaluation
c. World currency
d. Fiat money

46. _________ or forced tender is payment that, by law, cannot be refused in settlement of a debt.

_________ is variously defined in different jurisdictions. Formally, it is anything which when offered in payment extinguishes the debt.

a. Landsbanki Freezing Order 2008
b. Legal tender
c. Patent portfolio
d. Leave of absence

47. In economics, _________ is the total amount of money available in an economy at a particular point in time. There are several ways to define 'money', but standard measures usually include currency in circulation and demand deposits.

_________ data are recorded and published, usually by the government or the central bank of the country.

a. Veil of money
b. Neutrality of money
c. Velocity of money
d. Money supply

48. In economics, _________ is the widest measurement of the money supply. It is generally

'One measure of the money supply that includes M1, plus savings and small time deposits, overnight repos at commercial banks, and non-institutional money market accounts. This is a key economic indicator used to forecast inflation, since it is not as narrow as M1 and still relatively easy to track.

a. Buy-side analyst
b. Flight-to-quality
c. Club goods
d. Broad Money

49. _________ is money accepted for exchange of goods in an economy. The prevalence of one money over another arises, usually, when a government designates through decrees that the government shall accept only particular notes and coins in payment for taxes. Typically, money of _________ consists of stamped coins and minted paper bills.

a. Currency
b. Security thread
c. Local currency
d. Totnes pound

50. A _________ is a kind of negotiable instrument, a promissory note made by a bank payable to the bearer on demand, used as money, and in many jurisdictions is legal tender. Along with coins, _________s make up the cash or bearer forms of all modern money. With the exception of non-circulating high-value or precious metal commemorative issues, coins are generally used for lower valued monetary units, while _________s are used for higher values.

a. Local currency
b. Security thread
c. Microprinting
d. Banknote

51. A _________ is an intermediary used in trade to avoid the inconveniences of a pure barter system.

By contrast, as William Stanley Jevons argued, in a barter system there must be a coincidence of wants before two people can trade - one must want exactly what the other has to offer, when and where it is offered, so that the exchange can occur. A _________ permits the value of goods to be assessed and rendered in terms of the intermediary, most often, a form of money widely accepted to buy any other good.

a. Price revolution
b. Consumer theory
c. Medium of exchange
d. Labour economics

52. A _________ is a standard monetary unit of measurement of the market value/cost of goods, services, or assets. It is one of three well-known functions of money. It lends meaning to profits, losses, liability, or assets.

a. ACEA agreement
b. AD-IA Model
c. ACCRA Cost of Living Index
d. Unit of account

53. In economics, _________ is the total demand for final goods and services in the economy (Y) at a given time and price level. It is the amount of goods and services in the economy that will be purchased at all possible price levels. This is the demand for the gross domestic product of a country when inventory levels are static.

a. Aggregate supply
b. Aggregation problem
c. Aggregate expenditure
d. Aggregate demand

54. _________ is the branch of economics concerned with 'the allocation and deployment of economic resources, both spatially and across time, in an uncertain environment' . It is additionally characterised by its 'concentration on monetary activities', in which 'money of one type or another is likely to appear on both sides of a trade' . The questions within _________ are typically framed in terms of 'time, uncertainty, options and information' .

a. Financial economics
b. Price revolution
c. Fixed exchange rate
d. Public economics

55. _________ or economic opportunity loss is the value of the next best alternative foregone as the result of making a decision. _________ analysis is an important part of a company's decision-making processes but is not treated as an actual cost in any financial statement. The next best thing that a person can engage in is referred to as the _________ of doing the best thing and ignoring the next best thing to be done.

a. Economic ideology
b. Economic
c. Industrial organization
d. Opportunity cost

56. _________ is defined as the measure of responsiveness in the quantity demanded for a commodity as a result of change in price of the same commodity. It is a measure of how consumers react to a change in price. In other words, it is percentage change in quantity demanded as per the percentage change in price of the same commodity.

a. 100-year flood
b. 1921 recession
c. Price elasticity of demand
d. 130-30 fund

57. _________ is an economic model based on price, utility and quantity in a market. It predicts that in a competitive market, price will function to equalize the quantity demanded by consumers, and the quantity supplied by producers, resulting in an economic equilibrium of price and quantity. The model incorporates other factors changing equilibrium as a shift of demand and/or supply.

a. Deferred gratification
b. Supply and demand
c. Joint demand
d. Rational addiction

58. _________ is the demand for financial assets, e.g., securities, money or foreign currency. It is used for purposes of business transactions and personal consumption.

The need to accommodate a firm's expected cash transactions.

a. Keynesian cross
b. Multiplier effect
c. Spending multiplier
d. Transactions demand

59. Economics:

- _________,the desire to own something and the ability to pay for it
- _________ curve,a graphic representation of a _________ schedule
- _________ deposit, the money in checking accounts
- _________ pull theory,the theory that inflation occurs when _________ for goods and services exceeds existing supplies
- _________ schedule,a table that lists the quantity of a good a person will buy it each different price
- _________ side economics,the school of economics at believes government spending and tax cuts open economy by raising _________

.

a. Production
b. McKesson ' Robbins scandal
c. Variability
d. Demand

60. The _________ is the desired holding of money balances in the form of cash or bank deposits.

Money is dominated as store of value by interest bearing assets. However, money is necessary to carry out transactions, or in other words, it provides liquidity.

a. Borrowing base
b. Conglomerate merger
c. Market neutral
d. Demand for money

61. _________s is the social science that studies the production, distribution, and consumption of goods and services. The term _________s comes from the Ancient Greek οá¼°κονομÎ¯α from οá¼¶κος (oikos, 'house') + νÏŒμος (nomos, 'custom' or 'law'), hence 'rules of the house(hold)'. Current _________ models developed out of the broader field of political economy in the late 19th century, owing to a desire to use an empirical approach more akin to the physical sciences.

a. Opportunity cost
b. Inflation
c. Energy economics
d. Economic

62. In economics, _________ is the ratio of the percent change in one variable to the percent change in another variable. It is a tool for measuring the responsiveness of a function to changes in parameters in a relative way. Commonly analyzed are _________ of substitution, price and wealth.

a. ACEA agreement
b. Elasticity
c. Elasticity of demand
d. ACCRA Cost of Living Index

63. Price _________ is defined as the measure of responsiveness in the quantity demanded for a commodity as a result of change in price of the same commodity. It is a measure of how consumers react to a change in price. In other words, it is percentage change in quantity demanded by the percentage change in price of the same commodity.

a. ACCRA Cost of Living Index
b. ACEA agreement
c. Elasticity
d. Elasticity of demand

64. In financial accounting, a _________ or statement of financial position is a summary of a person's or organization's balances. Assets, liabilities and ownership equity are listed as of a specific date, such as the end of its financial year. A _________ is often described as a snapshot of a company's financial condition.

a. Balance sheet
b. 100-year flood
c. 1921 recession
d. 130-30 fund

65. In business, _________ is the total liabilitiess minus total outside assets of an individual or a company. For a company, this is called shareholders' prefernce and may be referred to as book value. _________ is stated as at a particular year in time.
a. Net worth
b. Sinking fund
c. Post earnings announcement drift
d. Bond credit rating

66. _________ is the banking practice in which banks keep only a fraction of their deposits in reserve (as cash and other highly liquid assets) and lend out the remainder, while maintaining the simultaneous obligation to redeem all these deposits upon demand. Fractional reserve banking necessarily occurs when banks lend out any fraction of the funds received from demand deposits. This practice is universal in modern banking.
a. Certificate of deposit
b. Bank roll
c. Lender of last resort
d. Fractional-reserve banking

67. _________ theory is a branch of theoretical economics. It seeks to explain the behavior of supply, demand and prices in a whole economy with several or many markets. It is often assumed that agents are price takers and in that setting two common notions of equilibrium exist: Walrasian (or competitive) equilibrium, and its generalization; a price equilibrium with transfers.
a. General equilibrium
b. Rational choice theory
c. New Keynesian economics
d. Human capital

68. In economics, economic equilibrium is simply a state of the world where economic forces are balanced and in the absence of external influences the (equilibrium) values of economic variables will not change. It is the point at which quantity demanded and quantity supplied are equal. _________, for example, refers to a condition where a market price is established through competition such that the amount of goods or services sought by buyers is equal to the amount of goods or services produced by sellers.
a. Marketization
b. Market equilibrium
c. Product-Market Growth Matrix
d. Regulated market

69. In banking, _________ are bank reserves in excess of the reserve requirement set by a central bank (in the United States, the Federal Reserve System, called the Fed; in Canada, the Bank of Canada.) They are reserves of cash more than the required amounts. Holding _________ is generally considered costly and uneconomical as no interest is earned on the excess amount.
a. Excess reserves
b. Annual percentage rate
c. Origination fee
d. Universal bank

70. The _________ was a worldwide economic downturn starting in most places in 1929 and ending at different times in the 1930s or early 1940s for different countries. It was the largest and most important economic depression in the 20th century, and is used in the 21st century as an example of how far the world's economy can fall. The _________ originated in the United States; historians most often use as a starting date the stock market crash on October 29, 1929, known as Black Tuesday.
a. Great Depression
b. Jarrow March
c. British Empire Economic Conference
d. Wall Street Crash of 1929

71. A _________ is an institution willing to extend credit when no one else will.

Originally the term referred to a reserve financial institution that secured other banks or eligible institutions, as a last resort; most often the central bank of a country. The purpose of this loan and lender is to prevent the collapse of institutions that are experiencing financial difficulty, most often near collapse.

a. Transactional account
b. Time deposit
c. Capital requirement
d. Lender of last resort

72. The _________ is an American stock exchange. It is the largest electronic screen-based equity securities trading market in the United States. With approximately 3,800 companies, it has more trading volume per hour than any other stock exchange in the world.

a. NASDAQ
b. 130-30 fund
c. 100-year flood
d. 1921 recession

73. _________ is an equity (stock) exchange located at 11 Wall Street in lower Manhattan, New York, USA. It is the largest stock exchange in the world by dollar value of its listed companies' securities. As of October 2008, the combined capitalization of all domestic _________ listed companies was US$10.1 trillion.

a. New York Stock Exchange
b. 100-year flood
c. 130-30 fund
d. 1921 recession

74. The _________ percentage shows how profitable a company's assets are in generating revenue.

_________ can be computed as:

$$\text{ROA} = \frac{\text{Net Income - Interest Expense - Interest Tax savings}}{\text{Average Total Assets}}$$

This number tells you what the company can do with what it has, i.e. how many dollars of earnings they derive from each dollar of assets they control. Its a useful number for comparing competing companies in the same industry.

a. Capital recovery factor
b. Sustainable growth rate
c. Jaws ratio
d. Return on assets

75. In probability theory and statistics, _________ is a measure of the variability or dispersion of a population, a data set, or a probability distribution. A low _________ indicates that the data points tend to be very close to the same value (the mean), while high _________ indicates that the data are 'spread out' over a large range of values.

For example, the average height for adult men in the United States is about 70 inches, with a _________ of around 3 inches.

a. Standard deviation
b. 130-30 fund
c. 1921 recession
d. 100-year flood

76. A _________ is a corporation or mutual organization which provides trading facilities for stock brokers and traders, to trade stocks and other securities. It may be a physical trading room where the traders gather, or a formalised communications network. Creation of a _________ is a strategy of economic development.

a. Primary shares
b. SEAQ
c. 100-year flood
d. Stock Exchange

77. A _________ is a public market for the trading of company stock and derivatives at an agreed price; these are securities listed on a stock exchange as well as those only traded privately.

The size of the world _________ was estimated at about $36.6 trillion US at the beginning of October 2008 . The total world derivatives market has been estimated at about $791 trillion face or nominal value, 11 times the size of the entire world economy.

a. Stock market
b. Adam Smith
c. Adolph Fischer
d. Adolf Hitler

78. _________, 1st Baron Keynes was a renowned economist from Britain whose many ideas on economic and political theories as well as on many governments' monetary policies influenced America. He advocated a government that played an active role in the lives of people regarding business, economy, etc. In this role, the government would use fiscal measures to reduce the consequences of recessions, economic depressions and booms.

a. Adolf Hitler
b. Adam Smith
c. Adolph Fischer
d. John Maynard Keynes

79. A _________ is a type of economic bubble taking place in stock markets when price of stocks rise and become overvalued by any measure of stock valuation.

The existence of _________s is at odds with the assumptions of efficient market theory which assumes rational investor behaviour. Behavioral finance theory attribute _________s to cognitive biases that lead to groupthink and herd behavior.

a. Scrip issue
b. Growth investing
c. Fill or kill
d. Stock market bubble

80. The _________ is one of several stock market indices, created by nineteenth-century Wall Street Journal editor and Dow Jones ' Company co-founder Charles Dow. It is an index that shows how certain stocks have traded. Dow compiled the index to gauge the performance of the industrial sector of the American stock market.

a. Federal Reserve Bank Notes
b. Commodity fetishism
c. Fama-French three factor model
d. Dow Jones Industrial Average

81. _________ is an American economist and was the Chairman of the Federal Reserve of the United States from 1987 to 2006. He currently works as a private advisor and providing consulting for firms through his company, Greenspan Associates LLC.

First appointed Federal Reserve chairman by President Ronald Reagan in August 1987, he was reappointed at successive four-year intervals until retiring on January 31, 2006 after the second-longest tenure in the position.

a. Alan Greenspan
b. Adolph Fischer
c. Adam Smith
d. Adolf Hitler

82. '_________' is a phrase used by former Federal Reserve Board Chairman Alan Greenspan in a speech given at the American Enterprise Institute during the stock market boom of the 1990s. The phrase was interpreted by financial pundits as a typical extraordinary economy.

Greenspan's comment was made on December 5, 1996 (emphasis added in excerpt):

The presence of the short comment--not repeated by Greenspan since--within a rather dry and complex speech would not normally have been so memorable; however, it was followed by immediate slumps in stock markets worldwide, provoking a strong reaction in financial circles and making its way into colloquial speech.

a. ACEA agreement
b. Irrational exuberance
c. ACCRA Cost of Living Index
d. AD-IA Model

83. The _________ was a British joint stock company that traded in South America during the 18th century. Founded in 1711, the company was granted a monopoly to trade in Spain's South American colonies as part of a treaty during the War of Spanish Succession. In return, the company assumed the national debt England had incurred during the war.

a. Delancey Street Foundation
b. Trade adjustment assistance
c. Financial Crimes Enforcement Network
d. South Sea Company

84. A _________ is a sudden dramatic decline of stock prices across a significant cross-section of a stock market. Crashes are driven by panic as much as by underlying economic factors. They often follow speculative stock market bubbles.

a. Stock market crash
b. 100-year flood
c. 1921 recession
d. 130-30 fund

85. _________ is a concept with somewhat disparate meanings in several fields. It also has a common meaning which has a loose connection with some of those more definite meanings.

Casually, it is typically used to denote a lack of order, or purpose, or cause.

a. Randomness
b. 130-30 fund
c. 100-year flood
d. 1921 recession

86. A _________, sometimes denoted _________, is a mathematical formalization of a trajectory that consists of taking successive random steps. The results of _________ analysis have been applied to computer science, physics, ecology, economics, and a number of other fields as a fundamental model for random processes in time. For example, the path traced by a molecule as it travels in a liquid or a gas, the search path of a foraging animal, the price of a fluctuating stock and the financial status of a gambler can all be modeled as _________s.

a. 1921 recession
b. 130-30 fund
c. 100-year flood
d. Random walk

87. An _________ or index tracker is a collective investment scheme (usually a mutual fund or exchange-traded fund) that aims to replicate the movements of an index of a specific financial market regardless of market conditions.

Tracking can be achieved by trying to hold all of the securities in the index, in the same proportions as the index. Other methods include statistically sampling the market and holding 'representative' securities.

a. Asset management company
b. Unit trust
c. Index fund
d. Investment trust

88. _________ was an American economist, statistician and public intellectual, and a recipient of the Nobel Memorial Prize in Economic Sciences. He is best known among scholars for his theoretical and empirical research, especially consumption analysis, monetary history and theory, and for his demonstration of the complexity of stabilization policy. A global public followed his restatement of a political philosophy that insisted on minimizing the role of government in favor of the private sector.

a. Adolf Hitler
b. Adolph Fischer
c. Adam Smith
d. Milton Friedman

1. The _________ is the central banking system of the United States. Created in 1913 by the enactment of the Federal Reserve Act (signed by Woodrow Wilson), it is a quasi-public and quasi-private (government entity with private components) banking system that comprises (1) the presidentially appointed Board of Governors of the _________ in Washington, D.C.; (2) the Federal Open Market Committee; (3) twelve regional Federal Reserve Banks located in major cities throughout the nation acting as fiscal agents for the U.S. Treasury, each with its own nine-member board of directors; (4) numerous other private U.S. member banks, which subscribe to required amounts of non-transferable stock in their regional Federal Reserve Banks; and (5) various advisory councils. Since February 2006, Ben Bernanke has served as the Chairman of the Board of Governors of the _________.

a. Monetary Policy Report to the Congress
b. Federal Reserve System Open Market Account
c. Federal Reserve System
d. Term auction facility

2. A _________, reserve bank, or monetary authority is the entity responsible for the monetary policy of a country or of a group of member states. It is a bank that can lend money to other banks in times of need. Its primary responsibility is to maintain the stability of the national currency and money supply, but more active duties include controlling subsidized-loan interest rates, and acting as a lender of last resort to the banking sector during times of financial crisis (private banks often being integral to the national financial system.)

a. 130-30 fund
b. 1921 recession
c. 100-year flood
d. Central bank

3. The Federal Reserve System (also the Federal Reserve; informally The Fed) is the central banking system of the United States. Created in 1913 by the enactment of the Federal Reserve Act (signed by Woodrow Wilson), it is a quasi-public and quasi-private (government entity with private components) banking system that comprises (1) the presidentially appointed Board of Governors of the Federal Reserve System in Washington, D.C.; (2) the Federal Open Market Committee; (3) twelve regional _________ located in major cities throughout the nation acting as fiscal agents for the U.S. Treasury, each with its own nine-member board of directors; (4) numerous other private U.S. member banks, which subscribe to required amounts of non-transferable stock in their regional _________; and (5) various advisory councils. Since February 2006, Ben Bernanke has served as the Chairman of the Board of Governors of the Federal Reserve System.

a. Federal funds
b. Federal Open Market Committee
c. Fed Funds Probability
d. Federal Reserve Banks

4. In economics, _________ is the total demand for final goods and services in the economy (Y) at a given time and price level. It is the amount of goods and services in the economy that will be purchased at all possible price levels. This is the demand for the gross domestic product of a country when inventory levels are static.

a. Aggregate supply
b. Aggregate demand
c. Aggregate expenditure
d. Aggregation problem

5. Economics:

- _________,the desire to own something and the ability to pay for it
- _________ curve,a graphic representation of a _________ schedule
- _________ deposit, the money in checking accounts
- _________ pull theory,the theory that inflation occurs when _________ for goods and services exceeds existing supplies
- _________ schedule,a table that lists the quantity of a good a person will buy it each different price
- _________ side economics,the school of economics at believes government spending and tax cuts open economy by raising _________

a. McKesson ' Robbins scandal
b. Production
c. Variability
d. Demand

6. In economics, _________ is a rise in the general level of prices of goods and services in an economy over a period of time. When the general price level rises, each unit of currency buys fewer goods and services; consequently, _________ is also a decline in the real value of money--a loss of purchasing power in the medium of exchange which is also the monetary unit of account in the economy. A chief measure of general price-level _________ is the general _________ rate, which is the percentage change in a general price index (normally the Consumer Price Index) over time.

a. Opportunity cost
b. Economic
c. Inflation
d. Energy economics

7. _________ is the process by which the government, central bank (ii) availability of money, and (iii) cost of money or rate of interest, in order to attain a set of objectives oriented towards the growth and stability of the economy. Monetary theory provides insight into how to craft optimal _________.

_________ is referred to as either being an expansionary policy where an expansionary policy increases the total supply of money in the economy, and a contractionary policy decreases the total money supply.

a. 130-30 fund
b. 1921 recession
c. 100-year flood
d. Monetary policy

8. The _________ , a component of the Federal Reserve System, is charged under United States law with overseeing the nation's open market operations. It is the Federal Reserve Committee that makes key decisions about interest rates and the growth jam of the United States money supply. It is the principal organ of United States national monetary policy.

a. Federal Reserve Transparency Act
b. Fed Funds Probability
c. Primary Dealer Credit Facility
d. Federal Open Market Committee

9. _________ is an American economist and was the Chairman of the Federal Reserve of the United States from 1987 to 2006. He currently works as a private advisor and providing consulting for firms through his company, Greenspan Associates LLC.

First appointed Federal Reserve chairman by President Ronald Reagan in August 1987, he was reappointed at successive four-year intervals until retiring on January 31, 2006 after the second-longest tenure in the position.

a. Alan Greenspan
b. Adolf Hitler
c. Adolph Fischer
d. Adam Smith

10. In economics, the _________ is the term used to refer to the environment in which bonds are bought and sold between a central bank ' its regulated banks. It is not a free market process.

- To intervene in the 'business cycle', a central bank may choose to go into the _________ and buy or sell government bonds, which is known as _________ operations to increase reserves.

a. ACCRA Cost of Living Index
b. Open Market
c. Outside money
d. Inside money

11. In financial accounting, a _________ or statement of financial position is a summary of a person's or organization's balances. Assets, liabilities and ownership equity are listed as of a specific date, such as the end of its financial year. A _________ is often described as a snapshot of a company's financial condition.

a. 100-year flood
b. 130-30 fund
c. 1921 recession
d. Balance sheet

12. _________ are banks' holdings of deposits in accounts with their central bank (for instance the European Central Bank or the Federal Reserve, in the latter case including federal funds), plus currency that is physically held in bank vaults (vault cash.) The central banks of some nations set minimum reserve requirements. Even when no requirements are set, banks commonly wish to hold some reserves, called desired reserves, against unexpected events.

a. Sweep account
b. Bilateral netting
c. Bank reserves
d. Structuring

13. Discounting is a financial mechanism in which a debtor obtains the right to delay payments to a creditor, for a defined period of time, in exchange for a charge or fee. Essentially, the party that owes money in the present purchases the right to delay the payment until some future date. The _________, or charge, is simply the difference between the original amount owed in the present and the amount that has to be paid in the future to settle the debt.

a. Reinsurance
b. Certified Risk Manager
c. Reliability theory
d. Discount

14. The _________ is an interest rate a central bank charges depository institutions that borrow reserves from it.

The term _________ has two meanings:

- the same as interest rate; the term 'discount' does not refer to the meaning of the word, but to the purpose of using the quantity, such as computations of present value, e.g. net present value or discounted cash flow

- the annual effective _________, which is the annual interest divided by the capital including that interest; this rate is lower than the interest rate; it corresponds to using the value after a year as the nominal value, and seeing the initial value as the nominal value minus a discount; it is used for Treasury Bills and similar financial instruments

The annual effective _________ is the annual interest divided by the capital including that interest, which is the interest rate divided by 100% plus the interest rate. It is the annual discount factor to be applied to the future cash flow, to find the discount, subtracted from a future value to find the value one year earlier.

For example, suppose there is a government bond that sells for $95 and pays $100 in a year's time.

a. Perpetuity
b. Johansen test
c. Stochastic volatility
d. Discount rate

15. _________ is a fee paid on borrowed assets. It is the price paid for the use of borrowed money , or, money earned by deposited funds . Assets that are sometimes lent with _________ include money, shares, consumer goods through hire purchase, major assets such as aircraft, and even entire factories in finance lease arrangements.

a. Insolvency
b. Internal debt
c. Interest
d. Asset protection

16. An _________ is the price a borrower pays for the use of money they do not own, for instance a small company might borrow from a bank to kick start their business, and the return a lender receives for deferring the use of funds, by lending it to the borrower. _________s are normally expressed as a percentage rate over the period of one year.

_________s targets are also a vital tool of monetary policy and are used to control variables like investment, inflation, and unemployment.

a. Interest rate
b. Enterprise value
c. ACCRA Cost of Living Index
d. Arrow-Debreu model

17. The accounting equation relates assets, _________, and owner's equity:

Assets = _________ + Owner's Equity

The accounting equation is the mathematical structure of the balance sheet.

The Australian Accounting Research Foundation defines _________ as: 'future sacrifice of economic benefits that the entity is presently obliged to make to other entities as a result of past transactions and other past events.'

Probably the most accepted accounting definition of liability is the one used by the International Accounting Standards Board (IASB.) The following is a quotation from IFRS Framework:

A liability is a present obligation of the enterprise arising from past events, the settlement of which is expected to result in an outflow from the enterprise of resources embodying economic benefits

-

Regulations as to the recognition of _________ are different all over the world, but are roughly similar to those of the IASB.

a. Liabilities
b. Community property
c. Coase theorem
d. Competition law theory

18. _________ are the means of implementing monetary policy by which a central bank controls its national money supply by buying and selling government securities, or other financial instruments. Monetary targets, such as interest rates or exchange rates, are used to guide this implementation.

Since most money is now in the form of electronic records, rather than paper records such as banknotes, _________ are conducted simply by electronically increasing or decreasing ('crediting' or 'debiting') the amount of money that a bank has, e.g., in its reserve account at the central bank, in exchange for a bank selling or buying a financial instrument.

a. ACEA agreement
b. AD-IA Model
c. Open market operations
d. ACCRA Cost of Living Index

19. A _________ is a currency which is held in significant quantities by many governments and institutions as part of their foreign exchange reserves. It also tends to be the international pricing currency for products traded on a global market, such as oil, gold, etc.

This permits the issuing country to purchase the commodities at a marginally cheaper rate than other nations, which must exchange their currency with each purchase and pay a transaction cost.

a. World currency
b. Texas redbacks
c. Currency board
d. Reserve currency

20. _________ is money accepted for exchange of goods in an economy. The prevalence of one money over another arises, usually, when a government designates through decrees that the government shall accept only particular notes and coins in payment for taxes. Typically, money of _________ consists of stamped coins and minted paper bills.

a. Totnes pound
b. Local currency
c. Security thread
d. Currency

21. In economics, _________ is the total amount of money available in an economy at a particular point in time. There are several ways to define 'money', but standard measures usually include currency in circulation and demand deposits.

_________ data are recorded and published, usually by the government or the central bank of the country.

a. Neutrality of money
b. Veil of money
c. Velocity of money
d. Money supply

22. In the United States, _________ are overnight borrowings by banks to maintain their bank reserves at the Federal Reserve. Banks keep reserves at Federal Reserve Banks to meet their reserve requirements and to clear financial transactions. Transactions in the _________ market enable depository institutions with reserve balances in excess of reserve requirements to lend reserves to institutions with reserve deficiencies.

a. Federal Reserve Transparency Act
b. Federal funds rate
c. Term auction facility
d. Federal funds

23. In the United States, the _________ is the interest rate at which private depository institutions (mostly banks) lend balances (federal funds) at the Federal Reserve to other depository institutions, usually overnight. It is the interest rate banks charge each other for loans. Changing the target rate is one way the Chairman of the Federal Reserve can influence the supply of money in the U.S. economy..

a. Federal banking
b. Federal funds rate
c. Monetary Policy Report to the Congress
d. Term auction facility

24. _________ is a financial mechanism in which a debtor obtains the right to delay payments to a creditor, for a defined period of time, in exchange for a charge or fee. Essentially, the party that owes money in the present purchases the right to delay the payment until some future date. The discount, or charge, is simply the difference between the original amount owed in the present and the amount that has to be paid in the future to settle the debt.

a. Maximum life span
b. Generalized linear model
c. Certified Risk Manager
d. Discounting

25. The _________ is a bank regulation that sets the minimum reserves each bank must hold to customer deposits and notes. It would normally be in the form of fiat currency stored in a bank vault (vault cash), or with a central bank.

The reserve ratio is sometimes used as a tool in the monetary policy, influencing the country's economy, borrowing, and interest rates.

a. Fractional-reserve banking
b. Probability of default
c. Private money
d. Reserve requirement

26. The _________ is an instrument of monetary policy (usually controlled by central banks) that allows eligible institutions to borrow money from the central bank, usually on a short-term basis, to meet temporary shortages of liquidity caused by internal or external disruptions. The term originated with the practice of sending a bank representative to a reserve bank teller window when a bank needed to borrow money.

The interest rate charged on such loans by a central bank is called the discount rate, base rate, repo rate, or primary rate.

a. Capital requirement
b. Private money
c. Prime rate
d. Discount window

27. _________ is the banking practice in which banks keep only a fraction of their deposits in reserve (as cash and other highly liquid assets) and lend out the remainder, while maintaining the simultaneous obligation to redeem all these deposits upon demand. Fractional reserve banking necessarily occurs when banks lend out any fraction of the funds received from demand deposits. This practice is universal in modern banking.

a. Bank roll
b. Certificate of deposit
c. Fractional-reserve banking
d. Lender of last resort

28. A _________ is an expression that compares quantities relative to each other. The most common examples involve two quantities, but any number of quantities can be compared. _________s are represented mathematically by separating each quantity with a colon, for example the _________ 2:3, which is read as the _________ 'two to three'.

a. Y-intercept
b. 130-30 fund
c. Ratio
d. 100-year flood

29. The reserve requirement (or required _________) is a bank regulation that sets the minimum reserves each bank must hold to customer deposits and notes. It would normally be in the form of fiat currency stored in a bank vault (vault cash), or with a central bank.

The _________ is sometimes used as a tool in the monetary policy, influencing the country's economy, borrowing, and interest rates.

a. Bank-State-Branch
b. Reserve ratio
c. Dividend unit
d. First player wins

30. The _________ was a worldwide economic downturn starting in most places in 1929 and ending at different times in the 1930s or early 1940s for different countries. It was the largest and most important economic depression in the 20th century, and is used in the 21st century as an example of how far the world's economy can fall. The _________ originated in the United States; historians most often use as a starting date the stock market crash on October 29, 1929, known as Black Tuesday.

a. Wall Street Crash of 1929
b. Great Depression
c. Jarrow March
d. British Empire Economic Conference

31. The term '_________' refers to the concept of collecting information and attempting to spot a pattern in the information. In some fields of study, the term '_________' has more formally-defined meanings.

In project management _________ is a mathematical technique that uses historical results to predict future outcome.

a. Probit model
b. Quantile regression
c. Trend analysis
d. Coefficient of determination

32. Competition law, known in the United States as _________ law, has three main elements:

- prohibiting agreements or practices that restrict free trading and competition between business entities. This includes in particular the repression of cartels.
- banning abusive behaviour by a firm dominating a market, or anti-competitive practices that tend to lead to such a dominant position. Practices controlled in this way may include predatory pricing, tying, price gouging, refusal to deal, and many others.
- supervising the mergers and acquisitions of large corporations, including some joint ventures. Transactions that are considered to threaten the competitive process can be prohibited altogether, or approved subject to 'remedies' such as an obligation to divest part of the merged business or to offer licences or access to facilities to enable other businesses to continue competing.

The substance and practice of competition law varies from jurisdiction to jurisdiction. Protecting the interests of consumers (consumer welfare) and ensuring that entrepreneurs have an opportunity to compete in the market economy are often treated as important objectives. Competition law is closely connected with law on deregulation of access to markets, state aids and subsidies, the privatisation of state owned assets and the establishment of independent sector regulators. In recent decades, competition law has been viewed as a way to provide better public services.

a. Intellectual property law
b. Antitrust
c. Anti-Inflation Act
d. United Kingdom competition law

33. In business and accounting, _________ are everything of value that is owned by a person or company. It is a claim on the property your income of a borrower. The balance sheet of a firm records the monetary value of the _________ owned by the firm.

a. Amortization schedule
b. ACEA agreement
c. ACCRA Cost of Living Index
d. Assets

34. A _________ occurs when a large number of bank customers withdraw their deposits because they believe the bank is insolvent. As a _________ progresses, it generates its own momentum, in a kind of self-fulfilling prophecy: as more people withdraw their deposits, the likelihood of default increases, and this encourages further withdrawals. This can destabilize the bank to the point where it faces bankruptcy.

a. Fractional-reserve banking
b. Tier 1 capital
c. Bank run
d. Funds Transfer Pricing

35. The _________ consists of a number of economic theories which describe the nature of the firm, company including its existence, its behaviour, and its relationship with the market.

In simplified terms, the _________ aims to answer these questions:

1. Existence - why do firms emerge, why are not all transactions in the economy mediated over the market?
2. Boundaries - why the boundary between firms and the market is located exactly there? Which transactions are performed internally and which are negotiated on the market?
3. Organization - why are firms structured in such specific way? What is the interplay of formal and informal relationships?

Despite looking simple, these questions are not answered by the established economic theory, which usually views firms as given, and treats them as black boxes without any internal structure.

The First World War period saw a change of emphasis in economic theory away from industry-level analysis which mainly included analysing markets to analysis at the level of the firm, as it became increasingly clear that perfect competition was no longer an adequate model of how firms behaved. Economic theory till then had focussed on trying to understand markets alone and there had been little study on understanding why firms or organisations exist.

a. Theory of the firm
b. Policy Ineffectiveness Proposition
c. Khazzoom-Brookes postulate
d. Technology gap

36. The _________ is a United States government corporation created by the Glass-Steagall Act of 1933. It provides deposit insurance, which guarantees the safety of deposits in member banks, currently up to $250,000 per depositor per bank. Funds in non-interest bearing transaction accounts are fully insured, with no limit, under the temporary Transaction Account Guarantee Program.

a. Luxembourg Income Study
b. Great Leap Forward
c. Foreign direct investment
d. Federal Deposit Insurance Corporation

37. In economic theory, _________ is the competitive situation in any market where the conditions necessary for perfect competition are not satisfied. It is a market structure that does not meet the conditions of perfect competition.

Forms of _________ include:

- Monopoly, in which there is only one seller of a good.
- Oligopoly, in which there is a small number of sellers.
- Monopolistic competition, in which there are many sellers producing highly differentiated goods.
- Monopsony, in which there is only one buyer of a good.
- Oligopsony, in which there is a small number of buyers.

There may also be _________ in markets due to buyers or sellers lacking information about prices and the goods being traded.

There may also be _________ due to a time lag in a market.

a. Imperfect competition
b. AD-IA Model
c. ACCRA Cost of Living Index
d. ACEA agreement

38. _________, in law and economics, is a form of risk management primarily used to hedge against the risk of a contingent loss. _________ is defined as the equitable transfer of the risk of a loss, from one entity to another, in exchange for a premium, and can be thought of as a guaranteed small loss to prevent a large, possibly devastating loss. An insurer is a company selling the _________; an insured or policyholder is the person or entity buying the _________.

a. AD-IA Model
b. ACEA agreement
c. ACCRA Cost of Living Index
d. Insurance

39. An _________ is an economy in which people, including businesses, can trade in goods and services with other people and businesses in the international community at large. This contrasts with a closed economy in which international trade cannot take place.

The act of selling goods or services to a foreign country is called exporting.

a. Information economy
b. Attention work
c. Indicative planning
d. Open economy

40. In neoclassical economics and microeconomics, _________ describes the perfect being a market in which there are many small firms, all producing homogeneous goods. In the short term, such markets are productively inefficient as output will not occur where mc is equal to ac, but allocatively efficient, as output under _________ will always occur where mc is equal to mr, and therefore where mc equals ar. However, in the long term, such markets are both allocatively and productively efficient.

a. Law of supply
b. Perfect competition
c. Co-operative economics
d. General equilibrium

41. _________ is a common concept in economics, and gives rise to derived concepts such as consumer debt. Generally _________ is defined by opposition to production. But the precise definition can vary because different schools of economists define production quite differently.

a. Consumption
b. Foreclosure data providers
c. Federal Reserve Bank Notes
d. Cash or share options

42. The _________ is an economic and political union of 27 member states, located primarily in Europe. It was established by the Treaty of Maastricht on 1 November 1993, upon the foundations of the pre-existing European Economic Community. With a population of almost 500 million, the _________ generates an estimated 30% share (US$18.4 trillion in 2008) of the nominal gross world product.

a. ACEA agreement
b. European Court of Justice
c. European Union
d. ACCRA Cost of Living Index

43. A _________, sometimes called a pegged exchange rate, is a type of exchange rate regime wherein a currency's value is matched to the value of another single currency or to a basket of other currencies such as gold.

A _________ is usually used to stabilize the value of a currency, vis-a-vis the currency it is pegged to. This facilitates trade and investments between the two countries, and is especially useful for small economies where external trade forms a large part of their GDP.

a. Law of supply
b. Leading indicators
c. Monetary economics
d. Fixed exchange rate

44. In economics, the _________ measures the payments that flow between any individual country and all other countries. It is used to summarize all international economic transactions for that country during a specific time period, usually a year. The _________ is determined by the country's exports and imports of goods, services, and financial capital, as well as financial transfers.

a. Gross world product
b. Gross domestic product per barrel
c. Skyscraper Index
d. Balance of payments

45. _________ is an economic system in which wealth, and the means of producing wealth, are privately owned. Through _________, the land, labor, and capital are owned, operated, and traded for the purpose of generating profits, without force or fraud, by private individuals either singly or jointly, and investments, distribution, income, production, pricing and supply of goods, commodities and services are determined by voluntary private decision in a market economy. A distinguishing feature of _________ is that each person owns his or her own labor and therefore is allowed to sell the use of it to employers.

a. Capitalism
b. Late capitalism
c. Creative capitalism
d. Socialism for the rich and capitalism for the poor

46. _________ is a negative term describing an claimed capitalist economy in which success in business depends on close relationships between businesspeople and government officials. It may be exhibited in the distribution of legal permits, government grants, special tax breaks, and so forth.

_________ is believed to arise when political cronyism spills over into the business world; self-serving friendships and family ties between businessmen and the government influence the economy and society to the extent that it corrupts public-serving economic and political ideals.

a. 100-year flood
b. Good governance
c. 130-30 fund
d. Crony capitalism

47. A _________ is a monetary authority which is required to maintain a fixed exchange rate with a foreign currency. This policy objective requires the conventional objectives of a central bank to be subordinated to the exchange rate target.

The main qualities of an orthodox _________ are:

- A _________'s foreign currency reserves must be sufficient to ensure that all holders of its notes and coins (and all banks creditor of a Reserve Account at the _________) can convert them into the reserve currency (usually 110-115% of the monetary base M0.)
- A _________ maintains absolute, unlimited convertibility between its notes and coins and the currency against which they are pegged (the anchor currency), at a fixed rate of exchange, with no restrictions on current-account or capital-account transactions.
- A _________ only earns profit from interests on foreign reserves (less the expense of note-issuing), and does not engage in forward-exchange transactions. These foreign reserves exist (1) because local notes have been issued in exchange, or (2) because commercial banks must by regulation deposit a minimum reserve at the _________. (1) generates a seignorage revenue. (2) is the revenue on minimum reserves (revenue of investment activities less cost of minimum reserves remuneration)
- A _________ has no discretionary powers to effect monetary policy and does not lend to the government. Governments cannot print money, and can only tax or borrow to meet their spending commitments.
- A _________ does not act as a lender of last resort to commercial banks, and does not regulate reserve requirements.
- A _________ does not attempt to manipulate interest rates by establishing a discount rate like a central bank. The peg with the foreign currency tends to keep interest rates and inflation very closely aligned to those in the country against whose currency the peg is fixed.

The _________ in question will no longer issue fiat money but instead will only issue one unit of local currency for each unit (or decided amount) of foreign currency it has in its vault (often a hard currency such as the U.S. dollar or the euro.) The surplus on the balance of payments of that country is reflected by higher deposits local banks hold at the central bank as well as (initially) higher deposits of the (net) exporting firms at their local banks.

a. Currency board
b. Currency competition
c. Reserve currency
d. Petrodollar

48. A _________, which is also called a balance-of-payments crisis, occurs when the value of a currency changes quickly, undermining its ability to serve as a medium of exchange or a store of value. It is a type of financial crisis and is often associated with a real economic crisis. Currency crises can be especially destructive to small open economies or bigger, but not sufficiently stable ones.

a. Speculative attack
b. Currency crisis
c. 130-30 fund
d. 100-year flood

49. In finance, the _________s between two currencies specifies how much one currency is worth in terms of the other. It is the value of a foreign natione;s currency in terms of the home natione;s currency. For example an _________ of 102 Japanese yen to the United States dollar means that JPY 102 is worth the same as USD 1.

a. ACCRA Cost of Living Index
b. ACEA agreement
c. Interbank market
d. Exchange rate

50. The term _________ is applied broadly to a variety of situations in which some financial institutions or assets suddenly lose a large part of their value. In the 19th and early 20th centuries, many financial crises were associated with banking panics, and many recessions coincided with these panics. Other situations that are often called financial crises include stock market crashes and the bursting of other financial bubbles, currency crises, and sovereign defaults.

a. Co-operative economics
b. Financial crisis
c. Market failure
d. Macroeconomics

51. Market _________ is a business, economics or investment term that refers to an asset's ability to be easily converted through an act of buying or selling without causing a significant movement in the price and with minimum loss of value. Money, or cash on hand, is the most liquid asset. An act of exchange of a less liquid asset with a more liquid asset is called liquidation.

a. 1921 recession
b. Liquidity
c. 100-year flood
d. 130-30 fund

52. A _________ is the transfer of wealth from one party (such as a person or company) to another. A _________ is usually made in exchange for the provision of goods, services or both, or to fulfill a legal obligation.

The simplest and oldest form of _________ is barter, the exchange of one good or service for another.

a. Payment
b. Soft count
c. Going concern
d. Social gravity

53. _________ in economics and business is the result of an exchange and from that trade we assign a numerical monetary value to a good, service or asset. If Alice trades Bob 4 apples for an orange, the _________ of an orange is 4 apples. Inversely, the _________ of an apple is 1/4 oranges.

a. Premium pricing
b. Price
c. Price book
d. Price war

54. In finance, the _________ is the global financial market for short-term borrowing and lending. It provides short-term liquidity funding for the global financial system. The _________ is where short-term obligations such as Treasury bills, commercial paper and bankers' acceptances are bought and sold.

a. Consignment stock
b. T-Model
c. Deferred compensation
d. Money market

55. _________ is defined as the measure of responsiveness in the quantity demanded for a commodity as a result of change in price of the same commodity. It is a measure of how consumers react to a change in price. In other words, it is percentage change in quantity demanded as per the percentage change in price of the same commodity.

a. 1921 recession
b. 100-year flood
c. 130-30 fund
d. Price elasticity of demand

56. _________ is an economic model based on price, utility and quantity in a market. It predicts that in a competitive market, price will function to equalize the quantity demanded by consumers, and the quantity supplied by producers, resulting in an economic equilibrium of price and quantity. The model incorporates other factors changing equilibrium as a shift of demand and/or supply.

a. Supply and demand
b. Deferred gratification
c. Joint demand
d. Rational addiction

57. The _________ is the desired holding of money balances in the form of cash or bank deposits.

Money is dominated as store of value by interest bearing assets. However, money is necessary to carry out transactions, or in other words, it provides liquidity.

a. Borrowing base
b. Demand for Money
c. Market neutral
d. Conglomerate merger

58. In economics, a _________ is a table that lists the quantity of a good a person will buy it each different price See Demand curve.

a. Rational irrationality
b. Federal Reserve districts
c. Free contract
d. Demand schedule

59. In economics, _________ is the ratio of the percent change in one variable to the percent change in another variable. It is a tool for measuring the responsiveness of a function to changes in parameters in a relative way. Commonly analyzed are _________ of substitution, price and wealth.

a. ACEA agreement
b. ACCRA Cost of Living Index
c. Elasticity of demand
d. Elasticity

60. Price _________ is defined as the measure of responsiveness in the quantity demanded for a commodity as a result of change in price of the same commodity. It is a measure of how consumers react to a change in price. In other words, it is percentage change in quantity demanded by the percentage change in price of the same commodity.

a. ACCRA Cost of Living Index
b. Elasticity
c. Elasticity of demand
d. ACEA agreement

61. _________ is the process by which money is produced or issued. There are three different ways to create money:

- manufacturing a new monetary unit, such as paper currency or metal coins (_________)
- loaning out a physical monetary unit multiple times through fractional-reserve lending (credit creation)
- buying of government securities or other financial instruments by central bank through Open market operations (electronic creation)

Coins are produced by manufacturing metal in a factory called a mint.

Banknotes and bank account balances are financial securities issued by a bank.

Similarly, money destruction, i.e., the reverse of _________, can occur in two different ways, depending on how the money was created.

a. Second-round effect
b. Monetary policy of Sweden
c. Money creation
d. Shadow Open Market Committee

62. _________s is the social science that studies the production, distribution, and consumption of goods and services. The term _________s comes from the Ancient Greek οá¼°κονομΐα from οá¼¶κος (oikos, 'house') + νÏŒμος (nomos, 'custom' or 'law'), hence 'rules of the house(hold)'. Current _________ models developed out of the broader field of political economy in the late 19th century, owing to a desire to use an empirical approach more akin to the physical sciences.

a. Opportunity cost
b. Inflation
c. Energy economics
d. Economic

63. The _________ or gross domestic income (GDI), a basic measure of an economy's economic performance, is the market value of all final goods and services produced within the borders of a nation in a year. _________ can be defined in three ways, all of which are conceptually identical. First, it is equal to the total expenditures for all final goods and services produced within the country in a stipulated period of time (usually a 365-day year.)

a. Market structure
b. Monopolistic competition
c. Countercyclical
d. Gross domestic product

64. _________ is a misspelled phrase from Latin 'pro capite' phrase meaning per head with pro meaning 'per' or 'for each' and capite meaning 'head.' Both words together equate to the phrase 'for each head.'

It is usually used in the field of statistics to indicate the average per person for any given concern, such as income, crime rate, etc.

It is also used in wills to indicate that each of the named beneficiaries should receive, by devise or bequest, equal shares of the estate. This is in contrast to a per stirpes division, in which each branch of the inheriting family inherits an equal share of the estate.

a. Per capita
b. Population statistics
c. False positive rate
d. Sargan test

65. An _________, in economics, is the amount by which the real Gross domestic product exceeds potential GDP. The real GDP is also known as GDP 'adjusted for inflation', 'constant prices' GDP or 'constant dollar' GDP, because it measures the aggregate output in a country's income accounts in a given year, expressed in base-year prices. On the other hand, the potential GDP is the quantity of real GDP when a country's economy is at full-employment.

a. AD-IA Model
b. ACEA agreement
c. ACCRA Cost of Living Index
d. Inflationary gap

66. In economics, _________ is a sustained decrease in the general price level of goods and services. _________ occurs when the annual inflation rate falls below zero percent, resulting in an increase in the real value of money -- a negative inflation rate. This should not be confused with disinflation, a slow-down in the inflation rate (i.e. when the inflation decreases, but still remains positive.)

a. Tobit model
b. Literacy rate
c. Price revolution
d. Deflation

67. In economics, a _________ is a sudden event that increases or decreases demand for goods or services temporarily. A positive _________ increases demand and a negative _________ decreases demand. Prices of goods and services are affected in both cases.

a. Lucas-Islands model
b. War economy
c. Robertson lag
d. Demand shock

68. In economics, _________ refers to the ability of a party to produce a good or service using fewer real resources than another entity producing the same good or service..A party has an _________ when using the same input as another party, it can produce a greater output. Since _________ is determined by a simple comparison of labor productivities, it is possible for a a party to have no _________ in anything. It can be contrasted with the concept of comparative advantage which refers to the ability to produce a particular good at a lower opportunity cost.

a. International economics
b. ACCRA Cost of Living Index
c. Index number
d. Absolute advantage

69. _________ is exchange of capital, goods, and services across international borders or territories. In most countries, it represents a significant share of gross domestic product (GDP.) While _________ has been present throughout much of history , its economic, social, and political importance has been on the rise in recent centuries.

a. Import license
b. Intra-industry trade
c. International trade
d. Incoterms

70. In economics, a _________ is a general slowdown in economic activity over a sustained period of time, or a business cycle contraction. During _________s, many macroeconomic indicators vary in a similar way. Production as measured by Gross Domestic Product (GDP), employment, investment spending, capacity utilization, household incomes and business profits all fall during _________s.

a. Leading indicators
b. Monetary economics
c. Treasury View
d. Recession

71. In economics, _________ is the total supply of goods and services produced by a national economy during a specific time period. It is the total amount of goods and services in the economy available at all possible price levels.

a. Aggregate demand
b. Aggregate expenditure
c. Aggregation problem
d. Aggregate supply

72. _________ is monetary policy that seeks to reduce the size of the money supply. They are fiscal policies, like lower spending and higher taxes, that reduce economic growth. In most nations, monetary policy is controlled by either a central bank or a finance ministry.

a. Contractionary monetary policy
b. Shadow Open Market Committee
c. Money creation
d. Monetary policy of Sweden

73. The _________ is one of the world's most important central banks, responsible for monetary policy covering the 16 member States of the Eurozone. It was established by the European Union (EU) in 1998 with its headquarters in Frankfurt, Germany.

The predecessor to the _________ was the European Monetary Institute .

a. ACEA agreement
b. ACCRA Cost of Living Index
c. AD-IA Model
d. European Central Bank

74. _________ is monetary policy that seeks to increase the size of the money supply. In most nations, monetary policy is controlled by either a central bank or a finance ministry

Neoclassical and Keynesian economics significantly differ on the effects and effectiveness of monetary policy on influencing the real economy; there is no clear consensus on how monetary policy affects real economic variables (aggregate output or income, employment.) Both economic schools accept that monetary policy affects monetary variables (price levels, interest rates.)

a. ACCRA Cost of Living Index
b. ACEA agreement
c. AD-IA Model
d. Expansionary monetary policy

75. _________ is widely regarded as the first modern school of economic thought. It is the idea that free markets can regulate themselves.Its major developers include Adam Smith, David Ricardo, Thomas Malthus and John Stuart Mill. Sometimes the definition of _________ is expanded to include William Petty, Johann Heinrich von Thünen.

a. Marginalism
b. Tendency of the rate of profit to fall
c. Schools of economic thought
d. Classical economics

76. _________ refers to an action or object coming from outside a system. It is the opposite of endogenous, something generated from within the system.

- In an economic model, an _________ change is one that comes from outside the model and is unexplained by the model. For example, in the simple supply and demand model, a change in consumer tastes or preferences is unexplained by the model and also leads to endogenous changes in demand that lead to changes in the equilibrium price. Put another way, an _________ change involves an alteration of a variable that is autonomous, i.e., unaffected by the workings of the model.

- In linear regression, it means that the variable is independent of all other response values.

- In biology, '_________' refers to an action or object coming from the outside of a system. For example, an _________ contrast agent in medical imaging refers to a liquid injected into the patient intravenously that enhances visibility of a pathology, such as a tumor.

a. ACEA agreement
b. ACCRA Cost of Living Index
c. AD-IA Model
d. Exogenous

77. In economic models, the _________ time frame assumes no fixed factors of production. Firms can enter or leave the marketplace, and the cost (and availability) of land, labor, raw materials, and capital goods can be assumed to vary. In contrast, in the short-run time frame, certain factors are assumed to be fixed, because there is not sufficient time for them to change.

a. Long-run
b. Productivity world
c. Diseconomies of scale
d. Price/performance ratio

78. _________ is an economic concept with commonplace familiarity. It is the price that a good or service is offered at, or will fetch, in the marketplace. It is of interest mainly in the study of microeconomics.

a. Noisy market hypothesis
b. Paper trading
c. Market price
d. Market anomaly

79. A _________ is a hypothetical measure of overall prices for some set of goods and services, in a given region during a given interval, normalized relative to some base set. Typically, a _________ is approximated with a price index.

The classical dichotomy is the assumption that there is a relatively clean distinction between overall increases or decreases in prices and underlying, e;reale; economic variables.

a. Discretionary spending
b. Discouraged worker
c. Price elasticity of supply
d. Price level

80. The term _________ is used in macroeconomics to refer to a situation where a country's nominal interest rate has been lowered nearly to or equal to zero to avoid a recession, but the liquidity in the market created by these low interest rates does not stimulate the economy to full employment. In this situation, any further increase in the money supply will not stimulate the economy any further. This is because any further injection of liquidity will no longer lower the nominal interest rate, as the nominal interest rate cannot drop below zero.

a. Macroeconomic models
b. Liquidity trap
c. Minimum wage
d. Robertson lag

1. _________s is the social science that studies the production, distribution, and consumption of goods and services. The term _________s comes from the Ancient Greek oá¼°κονομÎ¯α from oá¼¶κος (oikos, 'house') + νÏŒμος (nomos, 'custom' or 'law'), hence 'rules of the house(hold)'. Current _________ models developed out of the broader field of political economy in the late 19th century, owing to a desire to use an empirical approach more akin to the physical sciences.

a. Opportunity cost
b. Energy economics
c. Inflation
d. Economic

2. _________ is the increase in the amount of the goods and services produced by an economy over time. It is conventionally measured as the percent rate of increase in real gross domestic product, or real GDP. Growth is usually calculated in real terms, i.e. inflation-adjusted terms, in order to net out the effect of inflation on the price of the goods and services produced.

a. AD-IA Model
b. ACEA agreement
c. ACCRA Cost of Living Index
d. Economic growth

3. The _________ or gross domestic income (GDI), a basic measure of an economy's economic performance, is the market value of all final goods and services produced within the borders of a nation in a year. _________ can be defined in three ways, all of which are conceptually identical. First, it is equal to the total expenditures for all final goods and services produced within the country in a stipulated period of time (usually a 365-day year.)

a. Gross domestic product
b. Monopolistic competition
c. Market structure
d. Countercyclical

4. In economic models, the _________ time frame assumes no fixed factors of production. Firms can enter or leave the marketplace, and the cost (and availability) of land, labor, raw materials, and capital goods can be assumed to vary. In contrast, in the short-run time frame, certain factors are assumed to be fixed, because there is not sufficient time for them to change.

a. Diseconomies of scale
b. Long-run
c. Price/performance ratio
d. Productivity world

5. _________ is a misspelled phrase from Latin 'pro capite' phrase meaning per head with pro meaning 'per' or 'for each' and capite meaning 'head.' Both words together equate to the phrase 'for each head.'

It is usually used in the field of statistics to indicate the average per person for any given concern, such as income, crime rate, etc.

It is also used in wills to indicate that each of the named beneficiaries should receive, by devise or bequest, equal shares of the estate. This is in contrast to a per stirpes division, in which each branch of the inheriting family inherits an equal share of the estate.

a. Population statistics
b. False positive rate
c. Sargan test
d. Per capita

6. An _________, in economics, is the amount by which the real Gross domestic product exceeds potential GDP. The real GDP is also known as GDP 'adjusted for inflation', 'constant prices' GDP or 'constant dollar' GDP, because it measures the aggregate output in a country's income accounts in a given year, expressed in base-year prices. On the other hand, the potential GDP is the quantity of real GDP when a country's economy is at full-employment.

a. AD-IA Model
b. ACEA agreement
c. ACCRA Cost of Living Index
d. Inflationary gap

7. In economics, the _________ measures the payments that flow between any individual country and all other countries. It is used to summarize all international economic transactions for that country during a specific time period, usually a year. The _________ is determined by the country's exports and imports of goods, services, and financial capital, as well as financial transfers.

a. Skyscraper Index
b. Balance of payments
c. Gross world product
d. Gross domestic product per barrel

8. A _________ is the transfer of wealth from one party (such as a person or company) to another. A _________ is usually made in exchange for the provision of goods, services or both, or to fulfill a legal obligation.

The simplest and oldest form of _________ is barter, the exchange of one good or service for another.

a. Payment
b. Social gravity
c. Soft count
d. Going concern

9. _________ is the period of time that an individual spends at paid occupational labor. Unpaid labors such as housework are not considered part of the working week. Many countries regulate the work week by law, such as stipulating minimum daily rest periods, annual holidays and a maximum number of working hours per week.

a. 100-year flood
b. 1921 recession
c. Working time
d. 130-30 fund

10. In economics, the people in the _________ are the suppliers of labor. The _________ is all the nonmilitary people who are employed or unemployed. In 2005, the worldwide _________ was over 3 billion people.

a. Departmentalization
b. Grenelle agreements
c. Distributed workforce
d. Labor force

11. In financial accounting, the _________ is one of the accounts in shareholders' equity. Sole proprietorships have a single _________ in the owner's equity. Partnerships maintain a _________ for each of the partners.

a. Net national product
b. Current account
c. Compensation of employees
d. Capital account

12. In economics, accounting and Marxian economics, _________ is often equated with investment of profit income, especially in real capital goods. The concentration and centralisation of capital are two of the results of such accumulation

But _________ can refer variously to

- working and consuming less than earned
- relying on the effects of compound interest to increase initial capital
- real investment in tangible means of production.
- financial investment in assets represented on paper.
- investment in non-productive physical assets such as residential real estate that appreciate in value.
- consuming less than produced by productive assets like farm land--saving or accumulating the residual
- 'human _________,' i.e., new education and training increasing the skills of the labour force.

Non-financial and financial _________ is usually needed for economic growth, since additional production usually requires additional funds to enlarge the scale of production. Smarter and more productive organization of production can also increase production without increased capital.

a. Cultural Marxism
b. Productive force
c. Marxian economics
d. Capital accumulation

13. _________ is a term used in national accounts statistics and macroeconomics. It basically refers to the net additions to the (physical) capital stock in an accounting period, or, to the value of the increase of the capital stock; though it may occasionally also refer to the (growth of the) total stock of capital formed.

Thus, in UNSNA, _________ equals fixed capital investment, the increase in the value of inventories held, plus (net) lending to foreign countries, during an accounting period.

a. Capital flight
b. Consumption of fixed capital
c. Capital formation
d. Capital intensity

14. In Marxian economics, _________ originally referred to the means of production. Individuals, organizations and governments use _________ in the production of other goods or commodities. _________ include factories, machinery, tools, equipment, and various buildings which are used to produce other products for consumption.

a. Wealth inequality in the United States
b. Capital deepening
c. Capital goods
d. Capital intensive

15. _________ is the development of economic wealth of countries or regions for the well-being of their inhabitants. It is the process by which a nation improves the economic, political, and social well being of its people. From a policy perspective, _________ can be defined as efforts that seek to improve the economic well-being and quality of life for a community by creating and/or retaining jobs and supporting or growing incomes and the tax base.

a. Economic methodology
b. Experimental economics
c. Economic development
d. Inflation

16. The _________ was a period in the late 18th and early 19th centuries when major changes in agriculture, manufacturing, mining, and transportation had a profound effect on the socioeconomic and cultural conditions in Britain. The changes subsequently spread throughout Europe, North America, and eventually the world. The onset of the _________ marked a major turning point in human society; almost every aspect of daily life was eventually influenced in some way.

a. Adam Smith
b. Industrial Revolution
c. Adolf Hitler
d. Adolph Fischer

17. _________ is the term denoting either an entrance or changes which are inserted into a system and which activate/modify a process. It is an abstract concept, used in the modeling, system(s) design and system(s) exploitation. It is usually connected with other terms, e.g., _________ field, _________ variable, _________ parameter, _________ value, _________ signal, _________ device and _________ file.

a. ACEA agreement
b. ACCRA Cost of Living Index
c. Input
d. AD-IA Model

18. _________s (economically referred to as land or raw materials) occur naturally within environments that exist relatively undisturbed by mankind, in a natural form. A _________'s is often characterized by amounts of biodiversity existent in various ecosystems.

Mining, petroleum extraction, fishing, hunting, and forestry are generally considered natural-resource industries.

a. 1921 recession
b. 130-30 fund
c. Natural resource
d. 100-year flood

19. _________ in economics refers to metrics and measures of output from production processes, per unit of input. Labor _________, for example, is typically measured as a ratio of output per labor-hour, an input. _________ may be conceived of as a metrics of the technical or engineering efficiency of production.

a. Fordism
b. Production-possibility frontier
c. Productivity
d. Piece work

20. In business and accounting, _________ are everything of value that is owned by a person or company. It is a claim on the property your income of a borrower. The balance sheet of a firm records the monetary value of the _________ owned by the firm.

a. ACEA agreement
b. Amortization schedule
c. Assets
d. ACCRA Cost of Living Index

21. _________, in microeconomics, are the cost advantages that a business obtains due to expansion. They are factors that cause a producere;s average cost per unit to fall as scale is increased. _________ is a long run concept and refers to reductions in unit cost as the size of a facility, or scale, increases.

a. Underinvestment employment relationship
b. Isoquant
c. Economies of scale
d. Economic production quantity

22. A _________ is an object whose consumption increases the utility of the consumer, for which the quantity demanded exceeds the quantity supplied at zero price. _________s are usually modeled as having diminishing marginal utility. The first individual purchase has high utility; the second has less.

a. Good
b. Pie method
c. Merit good
d. Composite good

23. _________ is a type of private equity investment, most often a minority investment, in relatively mature companies that are looking for capital to expand or restructure operations, enter new markets or finance a significant acquisition without a change of control of the business.

Companies that seek _________, will often do so in order to finance a transformational event in their lifecycle. These companies are likely to be more mature than venture capital funded companies, able to generate revenue and operating profits but unable to generate sufficient cash to fund major expansions, acquisitions or other investments.

a. Startup company
b. Growth Capital
c. Club deal
d. Seed money

24. In microeconomics, _________ is quite simply the conversion of inputs into outputs. It is an economic process that uses resources to create a good or service that is suitable for exchange. This can include manufacturing, storing, shipping, and packaging.

a. Red Guards
b. MET
c. Solved
d. Production

25. In economics, a _________ is a function that specifies the output of a firm, an industry, or an entire economy for all combinations of inputs. A meta-_________ compares the practice of the existing entities converting inputs X into output y to determine the most efficient practice _________ of the existing entities, whether the most efficient feasible practice production or the most efficient actual practice production. In either case, the maximum output of a technologically-determined production process is a mathematical function of input factors of production.

a. Constant elasticity of substitution
b. Post-Fordism
c. Short-run
d. Production function

26. A _________ is an expression that compares quantities relative to each other. The most common examples involve two quantities, but any number of quantities can be compared. _________s are represented mathematically by separating each quantity with a colon, for example the _________ 2:3, which is read as the _________ 'two to three'.

a. Y-intercept
b. Ratio
c. 130-30 fund
d. 100-year flood

27. _________ is a term that is used to describe the overall process of invention, innovation and diffusion of technology or processes. The term is redundant with technological development, technological achievement, and technological progress. In essence _________ is the invention of a technology (or a process), the continuous process of improving a technology (in which it often becomes cheaper) and its diffusion throughout industry or society.

a. 1921 recession
b. Technological change
c. 100-year flood
d. 130-30 fund

28. _________ , as defined by the _________ Association of America (Information technologyAA), is 'the study, design, development, implementation, support or management of computer-based information systems, particularly software applications and computer hardware.' _________ deals with the use of electronic computers and computer software to convert, store, protect, process, transmit, and securely retrieve information.

Today, the term _________ has ballooned to encompass many aspects of computing and technology, and the term has become very recognizable. The _________ umbrella can be quite large, covering many fields.

a. ACCRA Cost of Living Index
b. ACEA agreement
c. AD-IA Model
d. Information technology

29. In economics and sociology, an _________ is any factor (financial or non-financial) that enables or motivates a particular course of action, or counts as a reason for preferring one choice to the alternatives. It is an expectation that encourages people to behave in a certain way. Since human beings are purposeful creatures, the study of _________ structures is central to the study of all economic activity (both in terms of individual decision-making and in terms of co-operation and competition within a larger institutional structure.)

a. Epstein-Zin preferences
b. Isocost
c. Economic reform
d. Incentive

30. _________ was a survey conducted by the U.S. Department of Justice to gauge the prevalence of alcohol and illegal drug use among prior arrestees. It was a reformulation of the prior Drug Use Forecasting (DUF) program, focused on five drugs in particular: cocaine, marijuana, methamphetamine, opiates, and PCP.

Participants were randomly selected from arrest records in major metropolitan areas; because no personally identifying information is taken from each record chosen, the resulting data can be correlated to arrest rates, but not to the total population of persons charged.

a. AD-IA Model
b. Arrestee Drug Abuse Monitoring
c. ACCRA Cost of Living Index
d. ACEA agreement

31. The _________ is a heterodox school of economics that emphasizes the spontaneous organizing power of the price mechanism. It holds that the complexity of subjective human choices makes mathematical modelling of the evolving market extremely difficult and advocates a laissez faire approach to the economy. _________ economists advocate the enforcement of voluntary contractual agreements between economic agents, but otherwise the smallest imposition of coercive force on commercial transactions.

a. ACEA agreement
b. Austrian School
c. Economic calculation problem
d. ACCRA Cost of Living Index

32. _________ is widely regarded as the first modern school of economic thought. It is the idea that free markets can regulate themselves.Its major developers include Adam Smith, David Ricardo, Thomas Malthus and John Stuart Mill. Sometimes the definition of _________ is expanded to include William Petty, Johann Heinrich von Thünen.

a. Tendency of the rate of profit to fall
b. Classical economics
c. Schools of economic thought
d. Marginalism

33. The _________ is a derogatory alternative name for economics devised by the Victorian historian Thomas Carlyle in the 19th century. The term is an inversion of the phrase 'gay science,' meaning 'life-enhancing knowledge.' This was a familiar expression at the time, and was later adopted as the title of a book by Nietzsche

It is often stated that Carlyle gave economics the nickname '_________' as a response to the late 18th century writings of The Reverend Thomas Robert Malthus, who grimly predicted that starvation would result as projected population growth exceeded the rate of increase in the food supply.

a. 1921 recession
b. 130-30 fund
c. 100-year flood
d. Dismal science

34. _________ was a Scottish moral philosopher and a pioneer of political economy. One of the key figures of the Scottish Enlightenment, Smith is the author of The Theory of Moral Sentiments and An Inquiry into the Nature and Causes of the Wealth of Nations. The latter, usually abbreviated as The Wealth of Nations, is considered his magnum opus and the first modern work of economics.

a. Adolf Hitler
b. Alan Greenspan
c. Adolph Fischer
d. Adam Smith

35. An Inquiry into the Nature and Causes of the _________ is the magnum opus of the Scottish economist Adam Smith. It is a clearly written account of economics at the dawn of the Industrial Revolution, as well as a rhetorical piece written for the generally educated individual of the 18th century - advocating a free market economy as more productive and more beneficial to society.

The work is credited as a watershed in history and economics due to its comprehensive, largely accurate characterization of economic mechanisms that survive in modern economics; and also for its effective use of rhetorical technique, including structuring the work to contrast real world examples of free and fettered markets.

a. Wealth of Nations
b. Black Book of Communism
c. The Rise and Fall of the Great Powers
d. The Bell Curve

36. _________ is any long-term change in the patterns of average weather of a specific region or the Earth as a whole. _________ reflects abnormal variations to the Earth's climate and subsequent effects on other parts of the Earth, such as in the ice caps over durations ranging from decades to millions of years.

In recent usage, especially in the context of environmental policy, _________ usually refers to changes in modern climate

a. 130-30 fund
b. 1921 recession
c. 100-year flood
d. Climate change

37. The _________ is a 1972 book modeling the consequences of a rapidly growing world population and finite resource supplies, commissioned by the Club of Rome. Its authors were Donella H. Meadows, Dennis L. Meadows, Jørgen Randers, and William W. Behrens III. The book used the World3 model to simulate the consequence of interactions between the Earth's and human systems.

a. Principles of Political Economy and Taxation
b. The Wealth of Nations
c. Fail-Safe Investing
d. Limits to growth

38. The _________ was a phase of the Industrial Revolution; sometimes labeled as the separate Technical Revolution. From a technological and a social point of view there is no clean break between the two.

Major innovations during the period occurred in the chemical, electrical, petroleum, and steel industries.

a. 1921 recession
b. 130-30 fund
c. Second Industrial Revolution
d. 100-year flood

39. _________ is a term used in economics to describe an economy where capital per worker is increasing. A process of increasing the amount of capital per worker. It is an increase in the capital intensity.

a. Capital formation
b. Capital expenditure
c. Capital deepening
d. Firm-specific infrastructure

40. _________ are the prices that the factors of production of a finished item attract.

There has been some economic debate as to what determines these prices. Classical and Marxist economists argued that the _________ decided the value of a product and so value was intrinsic within the product.

a. Marginal product of labor
b. Factor prices
c. Marginal product
d. Productivity model

41. In economics, the _________ or marginal physical product is the extra output produced by one more unit of an input (for instance, the difference in output when a firm's labour is increased from five to six units.) Assuming that no other inputs to production change, the _________ of a given input (X) can be expressed as:

_________ = ΔY/ΔX = (the change of Y)/(the change of X.)

-
  -
    - Pending approval by Thomas Sowell***

In neoclassical economics, this is the mathematical derivative of the production function.... Note that the 'product' (Y) is typically defined ignoring external costs and benefits.

a. Labor problem
b. Productive capacity
c. Marginal product
d. Factor prices

42. _________ is the additional output resulting from the use of an additional unit of capital (ceteris paribus assuming all other factors are fixed.) It equals to 1 divided by the Incremental Capital-Output Ratio.

a. CAN SLIM
b. Buy-write
c. Loan officer
d. Marginal product of capital

43. _________ in economics and business is the result of an exchange and from that trade we assign a numerical monetary value to a good, service or asset. If Alice trades Bob 4 apples for an orange, the _________ of an orange is 4 apples. Inversely, the _________ of an apple is 1/4 oranges.

a. Price war
b. Premium pricing
c. Price book
d. Price

44. In economics, endogenous growth theory or _________ was developed in the 1980s as a response to criticism of the neo-classical growth model.

In neo-classical growth models, the long-run rate of growth is exogenously determined by either assuming a savings rate (the Harrod-Domar model) or a rate of technical progress (Solow model.) However, the savings rate and rate of technological progress remain unexplained.

a. Cobweb model
b. Real prices and ideal prices
c. Kondratiev waves
d. New growth theory

45. In economics, a _________ is a good that is non-rivaled and non-excludable. This means, respectively, that consumption of the good by one individual does not reduce availability of the good for consumption by others; and that no one can be effectively excluded from using the good. In the real world, there may be no such thing as an absolutely non-rivaled and non-excludable good; but economists think that some goods approximate the concept closely enough for the analysis to be economically useful.

a. Public good
b. Neoclassical synthesis
c. Happiness economics
d. Demand-pull theory

46. _________ is that which is owed; usually referencing assets owed, but the term can also cover moral obligations and other interactions not requiring money. In the case of assets, _________ is a means of using future purchasing power in the present before a summation has been earned. Some companies and corporations use _________ as a part of their overall corporate finance strategy.

a. Debenture
b. Hard money loan
c. Debt
d. Collateral Management

47. _________ are legal property rights over creations of the mind, both artistic and commercial, and the corresponding fields of law. Under _________ law, owners are granted certain exclusive rights to a variety of intangible assets, such as musical, literary, and artistic works; ideas, discoveries and inventions; and words, phrases, symbols, and designs. Common types of _________ include copyrights, trademarks, patents, industrial design rights and trade secrets.

a. Intellectual property
b. Expedited Funds Availability Act
c. Independent contractor
d. Ease of Doing Business Index

48. In economics, a _________ exists when the production or use of goods and services by the market is not efficient. That is, there exists another outcome where all involved can be made better off. _________s can be viewed as scenarios where individuals' pursuit of pure self-interest leads to results that are not efficient - that can be improved upon from the societal point-of-view.

a. Financial economics
b. Fixed exchange rate
c. Market failure
d. General equilibrium

49. _________ data refers to selected population characteristics as used in government, marketing or opinion research, or the _________ profiles used in such research. Note the distinction from the term 'demography' Commonly-used _________s include race, age, income, disabilities, mobility (in terms of travel time to work or number of vehicles available), educational attainment, home ownership, employment status, and even location.

a. NEET
b. Demographic warfare
c. Generation Z
d. Demographic

50. The _________ model (Demographic transitionM) is a model used to represent the process of explaining the transformation of countries from high birth rates and high death rates to low birth rates and low death rates as part of the economic development of a country from a pre-industrial to an industrialized economy. It is based on an interpretation begun in 1929 by the American demographer Warren Thompson of prior observed changes, or transitions, in birth and death rates in industrialized societies over the past two hundred years.

Most developed countries are beyond stage three of the model; the majority of developing countries are in stage 2 or stage 3.

a. Demographic economics
b. Population mobility
c. Demographic transition
d. Healthy Life Years

51. _________ is the change in population over time, and can be quantified as the change in the number of individuals in a population using 'per unit time' for measurement. The term _________ can technically refer to any species, but almost always refers to humans, and it is often used informally for the more specific demographic term _________ rate , and is often used to refer specifically to the growth of the population of the world.

Simple models of _________ include the Malthusian Growth Model and the logistic model.

a. 100-year flood
b. Population growth
c. Population dynamics
d. 130-30 fund

52. A _________ is the exclusive authority to determine how a resource is used, whether that resource is owned by government or by individuals. All economic goods have a _________s attribute. This attribute has three broad components

1. The right to use the good
2. The right to earn income from the good
3. The right to transfer the good to others

The concept of _________s as used by economists and legal scholars are related but distinct. The distinction is largely seen in the economists' focus on the ability of an individual or collective to control the use of the good.

a. Property right
b. Holder in due course
c. High-reeve
d. Post-sale restraint

53. The '_________' is approximately the nominal interest rate minus the inflation rate Since the inflation rate over the course of a loan is not known initially, volatility in inflation represents a risk to both the lender and the borrower.

In economics and finance, an individual who lends money for repayment at a later point in time expects to be compensated for the time value of money, or not having the use of that money while it is lent.

a. Reflation
b. Cost-push inflation
c. Core inflation
d. Real interest rate

54. _________ is a fee paid on borrowed assets. It is the price paid for the use of borrowed money , or, money earned by deposited funds . Assets that are sometimes lent with _________ include money, shares, consumer goods through hire purchase, major assets such as aircraft, and even entire factories in finance lease arrangements.

a. Interest
b. Insolvency
c. Asset protection
d. Internal debt

55. An _________ is the price a borrower pays for the use of money they do not own, for instance a small company might borrow from a bank to kick start their business, and the return a lender receives for deferring the use of funds, by lending it to the borrower. _________s are normally expressed as a percentage rate over the period of one year.

_________s targets are also a vital tool of monetary policy and are used to control variables like investment, inflation, and unemployment.

a. ACCRA Cost of Living Index
b. Arrow-Debreu model
c. Enterprise value
d. Interest rate

56. In business, _________, Overhead cost or _________ expense refers to an ongoing expense of operating a business. The term _________ is usually used to group expenses that are necessary to the continued functioning of the business, but do not directly generate profits.

_________ expenses are all costs on the income statement except for direct labor and direct materials.

a. Overhead
b. ACEA agreement
c. AD-IA Model
d. ACCRA Cost of Living Index

57. The term '_________' refers to the concept of collecting information and attempting to spot a pattern in the information. In some fields of study, the term '_________' has more formally-defined meanings.

In project management _________ is a mathematical technique that uses historical results to predict future outcome.

a. Quantile regression
b. Trend analysis
c. Coefficient of determination
d. Probit model

58. _________ is a procedure used in economics to measure the contribution of different factors to economic growth and to indirectly compute the rate of technological progress, measured as a residual, in an economy.

_________ decomposes the growth rate of economy's total output into that which is due to increases in the amount of factors used - usually the increase in the amount of capital and labor - and that which cannot be accounted for by observable changes in factor utilization. The unexplained part of growth in GDP is then taken to represent increases in productivity (getting more output with the same amounts of inputs) or a measure of broadly defined technological progress.

a. Reaganomics
b. Spillover effect
c. Growth accounting
d. Cobb-Douglas

59. In economics, _________ are the resources employed to produce goods and services. They facilitate production but do not become part of the product (as with raw materials) or significantly transformed by the production process (as with fuel used to power machinery.) To 19th century economists, the _________ were land (natural resources, gifts from nature), labor (the ability to work), and capital goods (human-made tools and equipment.)

a. Product Pipeline
b. Factors of production
c. Long-run
d. Hicks-neutral technical change

60. In economics, _________ (TFP) is a variable which accounts for effects in total output not caused by inputs. For example, a year with unusually good weather will tend to have higher output, because bad weather hinders agricultural output. A variable like weather does not directly relate to unit inputs, so weather is considered a _________ variable.

a. Human rights
b. Flow to Equity-Approach
c. 35-hour working week
d. Total-factor productivity

61. _________ or amortisation is the process of increasing an amount over a period of time. The word comes from Middle English amortisen to kill, alienate in mortmain, from Anglo-French amorteser, alteration of amortir, from Vulgar Latin admortire to kill, from Latin ad- + mort-, mors death. Particular instances of the term include:

- _________, the allocation of a lump sum amount to different time periods, particularly for loans and other forms of finance, including related interest or other finance charges.
  - _________ schedule, a table detailing each periodic payment on a loan (typically a mortgage), as generated by an _________ calculator.
  - Negative _________, an _________ schedule where the loan amount actually increases through not paying the full interest
- Amortized analysis, analyzing the execution cost of algorithms over a sequence of operations.
- _________ of capital expenditures of certain assets under accounting rules, particularly intangible assets, in a manner analogous to depreciation.
- _________ (tax law)

_________ is also used in the context of zoning regulations and describes the time in which a property owner has to relocate when the property's use constitutes a preexisting nonconforming use under zoning regulations.

a. Economic miracle
b. Amortization
c. Augmentation
d. Oslo Agreements

62. In economics and finance, _________ is the change in total cost that arises when the quantity produced changes by one unit. It is the cost of producing one more unit of a good. Mathematically, the _________ function is expressed as the first derivative of the total cost (TC) function with respect to quantity (Q.)

a. Marginal cost
b. Khozraschyot
c. Variable cost
d. Quality costs

63. The term _________s refers to wages that have been adjusted for inflation. This term is used in contrast to nominal wages or unadjusted wages.

The use of adjusted figures is in undertaking some form of economic analysis.

a. Living wage
b. Real wage
c. Profit sharing
d. Federal Wage System

64. _________ is an American economist and was the Chairman of the Federal Reserve of the United States from 1987 to 2006. He currently works as a private advisor and providing consulting for firms through his company, Greenspan Associates LLC.

First appointed Federal Reserve chairman by President Ronald Reagan in August 1987, he was reappointed at successive four-year intervals until retiring on January 31, 2006 after the second-longest tenure in the position.

a. Alan Greenspan
b. Adam Smith
c. Adolf Hitler
d. Adolph Fischer

65. The _________ was an evolution of developed countries from an industrial/manufacturing-based wealth producing economy into a service sector asset based economy, brought about by globalization and currency manipulation by governments and their central banks. Some analysts claimed that this change in the economic structure of the United States had created a state of permanent steady growth, low unemployment, and immunity to boom and bust macroeconomic cycles. They believed that the change rendered obsolete many business practices.

a. 130-30 fund
b. 100-year flood
c. 1921 recession
d. New economy

1. _________s is the social science that studies the production, distribution, and consumption of goods and services. The term _________s comes from the Ancient Greek oá¼°κονομΐα from oá¼¶κος (oikos, 'house') + νΪŒμος (nomos, 'custom' or 'law'), hence 'rules of the house(hold)'. Current _________ models developed out of the broader field of political economy in the late 19th century, owing to a desire to use an empirical approach more akin to the physical sciences.

a. Inflation
b. Energy economics
c. Opportunity cost
d. Economic

2. _________ is the development of economic wealth of countries or regions for the well-being of their inhabitants. It is the process by which a nation improves the economic, political, and social well being of its people. From a policy perspective, _________ can be defined as efforts that seek to improve the economic well-being and quality of life for a community by creating and/or retaining jobs and supporting or growing incomes and the tax base.

a. Economic development
b. Experimental economics
c. Economic methodology
d. Inflation

3. _________ is the increase in the amount of the goods and services produced by an economy over time. It is conventionally measured as the percent rate of increase in real gross domestic product, or real GDP. Growth is usually calculated in real terms, i.e. inflation-adjusted terms, in order to net out the effect of inflation on the price of the goods and services produced.

a. ACCRA Cost of Living Index
b. Economic growth
c. AD-IA Model
d. ACEA agreement

4. The _________ or gross domestic income (GDI), a basic measure of an economy's economic performance, is the market value of all final goods and services produced within the borders of a nation in a year. _________ can be defined in three ways, all of which are conceptually identical. First, it is equal to the total expenditures for all final goods and services produced within the country in a stipulated period of time (usually a 365-day year.)

a. Monopolistic competition
b. Countercyclical
c. Market structure
d. Gross domestic product

5. _________ is a misspelled phrase from Latin 'pro capite' phrase meaning per head with pro meaning 'per' or 'for each' and capite meaning 'head.' Both words together equate to the phrase 'for each head.'

It is usually used in the field of statistics to indicate the average per person for any given concern, such as income, crime rate, etc.

It is also used in wills to indicate that each of the named beneficiaries should receive, by devise or bequest, equal shares of the estate. This is in contrast to a per stirpes division, in which each branch of the inheriting family inherits an equal share of the estate.

a. Population statistics
b. Per capita
c. Sargan test
d. False positive rate

6. _________ refers to a business or organization attempting to acquire goods or services to accomplish the goals of the enterprise. Though there are several organizations that attempt to set standards in the _________ process, processes can vary greatly between organizations. Typically the word '_________' is not used interchangeably with the word 'procurement', since procurement typically includes Expediting, Supplier Quality, and Traffic and Logistics (T'L) in addition to _________.

a. Free port
b. 100-year flood
c. 130-30 fund
d. Purchasing

7. _________ is the number of goods/services that can be purchased with a unit of currency. For example, if you had taken one dollar to a store in the 1950s, you would have been able to buy a greater number of items than you would today, indicating that you would have had a greater _________ in the 1950s. Currency can be either a commodity money, like gold or silver, or fiat currency like US dollars.

a. Compliance cost
b. Genuine progress indicator
c. Human Poverty Index
d. Purchasing power

8. The _________ theory uses the long-term equilibrium exchange rate of two currencies to equalize their purchasing power. Developed by Gustav Cassel in 1920, it is based on the law of one price: the theory states that, in ideally efficient markets, identical goods should have only one price.

This purchasing power SEM rate equalizes the purchasing power of different currencies in their home countries for a given basket of goods.

a. Purchasing power parity
b. Bureau of Labor Statistics
c. Measures of national income and output
d. Gross national product

9. _________ data refers to selected population characteristics as used in government, marketing or opinion research, or the _________ profiles used in such research. Note the distinction from the term 'demography' Commonly-used _________s include race, age, income, disabilities, mobility (in terms of travel time to work or number of vehicles available), educational attainment, home ownership, employment status, and even location.

a. NEET
b. Demographic warfare
c. Generation Z
d. Demographic

10. The _________ model (Demographic transitionM) is a model used to represent the process of explaining the transformation of countries from high birth rates and high death rates to low birth rates and low death rates as part of the economic development of a country from a pre-industrial to an industrialized economy. It is based on an interpretation begun in 1929 by the American demographer Warren Thompson of prior observed changes, or transitions, in birth and death rates in industrialized societies over the past two hundred years.

Most developed countries are beyond stage three of the model; the majority of developing countries are in stage 2 or stage 3.

a. Demographic economics
b. Population mobility
c. Healthy Life Years
d. Demographic transition

11. _________ is the use of statistics to analyze characteristics or changes to a population. It is related to social demography and demography.

_________ can analyze anything from global demographic changes to local small scale changes.

a. Markov logic network
b. Nonparametric regression
c. Dynamic Bayesian network
d. Population statistics

12. In microeconomics, _________ is quite simply the conversion of inputs into outputs. It is an economic process that uses resources to create a good or service that is suitable for exchange. This can include manufacturing, storing, shipping, and packaging.

a. Solved
b. MET
c. Red Guards
d. Production

13. In economics, a _________ is a function that specifies the output of a firm, an industry, or an entire economy for all combinations of inputs. A meta-_________ compares the practice of the existing entities converting inputs X into output y to determine the most efficient practice _________ of the existing entities, whether the most efficient feasible practice production or the most efficient actual practice production. In either case, the maximum output of a technologically-determined production process is a mathematical function of input factors of production.

a. Post-Fordism
b. Production function
c. Short-run
d. Constant elasticity of substitution

14. _________ is a voluntary transfer of resources from one country to another, given at least partly with the objective of benefiting the recipient country. It may have other functions as well: it may be given as a signal of diplomatic approval, or to strengthen a military ally, to reward a government for behaviour desired by the donor, to extend the donor's cultural influence, to provide infrastructure needed by the donor for resource extraction from the recipient country, or to gain other kinds of commercial access. Humanitarianism and altruism are, nevertheless, significant motivations for the giving of _________.

a. AD-IA Model
b. ACEA agreement
c. AID
d. ACCRA Cost of Living Index

15. A _________ product is a product designed for cheapness and short-term convenience rather than medium to long-term durability, with most products only intended for single use. The term is also sometimes used for products that may last several months (ex. _________ air filters) to distinguish from similar products that last indefinitely (ex.

a. 1921 recession
b. 100-year flood
c. Disposable
d. 130-30 fund

16. _________ is gross income minus income tax on that income.

Discretionary income is income after subtracting taxes and normal expenses (such as rent or mortgage, utilities, insurance, medical, transportation, property maintenance, child support, inflation, food and sundries, 'c.) to maintain a certain standard of living.

a. Taxation as theft
b. Stamp Act
c. Disposable personal income
d. Disposable income

17. A variety of measures of _________ and output are used in economics to estimate total economic activity in a country or region, including gross domestic product (GDP), gross national product (GNP), and net _________

There are three main ways of calculating these numbers; the output approach, the income approach and the expenditure approach. In theory, the three must yield the same, because total expenditures on goods and services must equal the total income paid to the producers (Gnational income), and that must also equal the total value of the output of goods and services (GNP.)

a. Gross world product
b. Volume index
c. GNI per capita
d. National income

18. A _________ represents the combinations of goods and services that a consumer can purchase given current prices and his income. Consumer theory uses the concepts of a _________ and a preference map to analyze consumer choices. Both concepts have a ready graphical representation in the two-good case.

a. Quality bias
b. Joint demand
c. Budget constraint
d. Revealed preference

19. _________ is a socioeconomic structure and political ideology that promotes the establishment of an egalitarian, classless, stateless society based on common ownership and control of the means of production and property in general. In political science, the term '_________' is sometimes used to refer to communist states, a form of government in which the state operates under a one-party system and declares allegiance to Marxism-Leninism or a derivative thereof, even if the party does not actually claim that it has already reached _________.

Forerunners of communist ideas existed in antiquity and particularly in the 18th and early 19th century France, with thinkers such as Jean-Jacques Rousseau and the more radical Gracchus Babeuf.

a. Democratic centralism
b. Social fascism
c. New Communist Movement
d. Communism

20. Crude _________ is the nativity or childbirths per 1,000 people per year.

It can be represented by number of childbirths in that year, and p is the current population. This figure is combined with the crude death rate to produce the rate of natural population growth (natural in that it does not take into account net migration.)

a. Neo-Malthusianism
b. Birth rate
c. Depensation
d. Malthusian equilibrium

21. _________ refers to the stock of skills and knowledge embodied in the ability to perform labor so as to produce economic value. It is the skills and knowledge gained by a worker through education and experience.Many early economic theories refer to it simply as labor, one of three factors of production, and consider it to be a fungible resource -- homogeneous and easily interchangeable. Other conceptions of labor dispense with these assumptions.

a. Law of increasing costs
b. General equilibrium
c. Price theory
d. Human capital

22. The traditional definition of _________ is considered to be the ability to use language to read, write, listen, and speak. In modern contexts, the word refers to reading and writing at a level adequate for communication, or at a level that lets one understand and communicate ideas in a literate society, so as to take part in that society. The United Nations Educational, Scientific and Cultural Organization (UNESCO) has drafted the following definition: "_________' is the ability to identify, understand, interpret, create, communicate, compute and use printed and written materials associated with varying contexts.

a. Literacy
b. 130-30 fund
c. 100-year flood
d. 1921 recession

23. _________ is a term used in national accounts statistics and macroeconomics. It basically refers to the net additions to the (physical) capital stock in an accounting period, or, to the value of the increase of the capital stock; though it may occasionally also refer to the (growth of the) total stock of capital formed.

Thus, in UNSNA, _________ equals fixed capital investment, the increase in the value of inventories held, plus (net) lending to foreign countries, during an accounting period.

a. Capital intensity
b. Capital flight
c. Consumption of fixed capital
d. Capital formation

24. _________s (economically referred to as land or raw materials) occur naturally within environments that exist relatively undisturbed by mankind, in a natural form. A _________'s is often characterized by amounts of biodiversity existent in various ecosystems.

Mining, petroleum extraction, fishing, hunting, and forestry are generally considered natural-resource industries.

a. 1921 recession
b. 130-30 fund
c. Natural resource
d. 100-year flood

25. The term _________ is used to describe a nation's social or business activity in the process of rapid growth and industrialization. Currently, there are approximately 28 _________ in the world, with the economies of China and India considered to be two of the largest. According to The Economist many people find the term dated, but a new term has yet to gain much traction.

a. Emerging markets
b. Asymmetric price transmission
c. Occupational welfare
d. Affinity diagram

26. The _________ is an international organization that oversees the global financial system by following the macroeconomic policies of its member countries, in particular those with an impact on exchange rates and the balance of payments. It is an organization formed to stabilize international exchange rates and facilitate development. It also offers financial and technical assistance to its members, making it an international lender of last resort.

a. Office of Thrift Supervision
b. International Monetary Fund
c. ACCRA Cost of Living Index
d. ACEA agreement

27. _________ is a term that is used to describe the overall process of invention, innovation and diffusion of technology or processes. The term is redundant with technological development, technological achievement, and technological progress. In essence _________ is the invention of a technology (or a process), the continuous process of improving a technology (in which it often becomes cheaper) and its diffusion throughout industry or society.

a. 1921 recession
b. 100-year flood
c. 130-30 fund
d. Technological change

28. In business and accounting, _________ are everything of value that is owned by a person or company. It is a claim on the property your income of a borrower. The balance sheet of a firm records the monetary value of the _________ owned by the firm.

a. ACCRA Cost of Living Index
b. ACEA agreement
c. Amortization schedule
d. Assets

29. _________ is an economic system in which wealth, and the means of producing wealth, are privately owned. Through _________, the land, labor, and capital are owned, operated, and traded for the purpose of generating profits, without force or fraud, by private individuals either singly or jointly, and investments, distribution, income, production, pricing and supply of goods, commodities and services are determined by voluntary private decision in a market economy. A distinguishing feature of _________ is that each person owns his or her own labor and therefore is allowed to sell the use of it to employers.

a. Creative capitalism
b. Late capitalism
c. Socialism for the rich and capitalism for the poor
d. Capitalism

30. _________ is a negative term describing an claimed capitalist economy in which success in business depends on close relationships between businesspeople and government officials. It may be exhibited in the distribution of legal permits, government grants, special tax breaks, and so forth.

_________ is believed to arise when political cronyism spills over into the business world; self-serving friendships and family ties between businessmen and the government influence the economy and society to the extent that it corrupts public-serving economic and political ideals.

a. 100-year flood
b. 130-30 fund
c. Good governance
d. Crony capitalism

31. The term financial crisis is applied broadly to a variety of situations in which some financial institutions or assets suddenly lose a large part of their value. In the 19th and early 20th centuries, many _________ were associated with banking panics, and many recessions coincided with these panics. Other situations that are often called _________ include stock market crashes and the bursting of other financial bubbles, currency crises, and sovereign defaults.

a. General equilibrium
b. Financial crises
c. Microeconomics
d. Georgism

32. The term _________ is applied broadly to a variety of situations in which some financial institutions or assets suddenly lose a large part of their value. In the 19th and early 20th centuries, many financial crises were associated with banking panics, and many recessions coincided with these panics. Other situations that are often called financial crises include stock market crashes and the bursting of other financial bubbles, currency crises, and sovereign defaults.

a. Financial crisis
b. Co-operative economics
c. Macroeconomics
d. Market failure

33. The _________ percentage shows how profitable a company's assets are in generating revenue.

_________ can be computed as:

$$\text{ROA} = \frac{\text{Net Income - Interest Expense - Interest Tax savings}}{\text{Average Total Assets}}$$

This number tells you what the company can do with what it has, i.e. how many dollars of earnings they derive from each dollar of assets they control. Its a useful number for comparing competing companies in the same industry.

a. Capital recovery factor
b. Jaws ratio
c. Return on assets
d. Sustainable growth rate

34. _________ according to Onuoha (2007) is the practice of starting new organizations or revitalizing mature organizations, particularly new businesses generally in response to identified opportunities. _________ is often a difficult undertaking, as a vast majority of new businesses fail. Entrepreneurial activities are substantially different depending on the type of organization that is being started.

a. ACEA agreement
b. ACCRA Cost of Living Index
c. Intrapreneurship
d. Entrepreneurship

35. _________ ndustrialization in North America, is the process of social and economic change whereby a human group is transformed from a pre-industrial society into an industrial one. _________ t is a part of a wider modernisation process, where social change and economic development are closely related with technological innovation, particularly with the development of large-scale energy and metallurgy production. _________ t is the extensive organisation of an economy for the purpose of manufacturing.

a. AD-IA Model
b. ACCRA Cost of Living Index
c. Industrialization
d. ACEA agreement

36. In economics, the _________ measures the payments that flow between any individual country and all other countries. It is used to summarize all international economic transactions for that country during a specific time period, usually a year. The _________ is determined by the country's exports and imports of goods, services, and financial capital, as well as financial transfers.

a. Skyscraper Index
b. Gross domestic product per barrel
c. Gross world product
d. Balance of payments

37. A _________ is the transfer of wealth from one party (such as a person or company) to another. A _________ is usually made in exchange for the provision of goods, services or both, or to fulfill a legal obligation.

The simplest and oldest form of _________ is barter, the exchange of one good or service for another.

a. Social gravity
b. Going concern
c. Soft count
d. Payment

38. _________ is the shortage of common things such as food, clothing, shelter and safe drinking water, all of which determine the quality of life. It may also include the lack of access to opportunities such as education and employment which aid the escape from _________ and/or allow one to enjoy the respect of fellow citizens. According to Mollie Orshansky who developed the _________ measurements used by the U.S. government, 'to be poor is to be deprived of those goods and services and pleasures which others around us take for granted.' Ongoing debates over causes, effects and best ways to measure _________, directly influence the design and implementation of _________-reduction programs and are therefore relevant to the fields of public administration and international development.

a. Poverty
b. Liberal welfare reforms
c. Poverty map
d. Growth Elasticity of Poverty

39. A economically backward economy is defined as one which makes less progress than normal. USSR leader Gorbachev once said e;If you done;t move forward, sooner or later you begin to move backward.e; The _________ model is a theory of economic growth created by Alexander Gerschenkron. The model postulates that the more backward an economy is at the outset of economic development, the more likely certain conditions are to occur.

a. Triangle model
b. LoopCo
c. Backwardness
d. Baker Cube

40. _________ was a German lawyer, politician, scholar, political economist and sociologist, who profoundly influenced sociological theory.

Weber's major works deal with rationalization in sociology of religion, government, organizational theory, and behavior. His most famous work is his essay The Protestant Ethic and the Spirit of Capitalism, which began his work in the sociology of religion.

a. Martin Luther
b. Maximilian Carl Emil Weber
c. George Cabot Lodge II
d. Peter Ferdinand Drucker

41. In economics, an _________ is any good (e.g. a commodity) or service brought into one country from another country in a legitimate fashion, typically for use in trade.It is a good that is brought in from another country for sale. _________ goods or services are provided to domestic consumers by foreign producers. An _________ in the receiving country is an export to the sending country.

a. Economic integration
b. Import
c. Incoterms
d. Import quota

42. _________ industrialization is a trade and economic policy based on the premise that a country should attempt to reduce its foreign dependency through the local production of industrialized products. Adopted in many Latin American countries from the 1930s until the late 1980s, and in some Asian and African countries from the 1950s on, Import substitutionI was theoretically organized in the works of Raúl Prebisch, Hans Singer, Celso Furtado and other structural economic thinkers, and gained prominence with the creation of the United Nations Economic Commission for Latin America and the Caribbean . Insofar as its suggestion of state-induced industrialization through governmental spending, it is largely influenced by Keynesian thinking, as well as the infant industry arguments adopted by some highly industrialized countries, such as the United States, until the 1940s.

a. ACCRA Cost of Living Index
b. ACEA agreement
c. AD-IA Model
d. Import substitution

43. An _________ is an economy in which people, including businesses, can trade in goods and services with other people and businesses in the international community at large. This contrasts with a closed economy in which international trade cannot take place.

The act of selling goods or services to a foreign country is called exporting.

a. Indicative planning
b. Information economy
c. Open economy
d. Attention work

44. _________ in economic theory is the use of modern economic tools to study problems that are traditionally in the province of political science.

In particular, it studies the behavior of politicians and government officials as mostly self-interested agents and their interactions in the social system either as such or under alternative constitutional rules. These can be represented a number of ways, including standard constrained utility maximization, game theory, or decision theory.

a. Public interest theory
b. Public choice
c. Paradox of voting
d. Rational ignorance

45. A _________ is a general term that describes any government policy or regulation that restricts international trade. The barriers can take many forms, including the following terms that include many restrictions in international trade within multiple countries that import and export any items of trade.

- Import duty
- Import licenses
- Export licenses
- Import quotas
- Tariffs
- Subsidies
- Non-tariff barriers to trade
- Voluntary Export Restraints
- Local Content Requirements
- Embargo

Most _________s work on the same principle: the imposition of some sort of cost on trade that raises the price of the traded products. If two or more nations repeatedly use _________s against each other, then a trade war results.

a. Trade barrier
b. Global financial system
c. Certificate of origin
d. National Foreign Trade Council

46. In economics, _________ refers to the ability of a party to produce a good or service using fewer real resources than another entity producing the same good or service..A party has an _________ when using the same input as another party, it can produce a greater output. Since _________ is determined by a simple comparison of labor productivities, it is possible for a a party to have no _________ in anything. It can be contrasted with the concept of comparative advantage which refers to the ability to produce a particular good at a lower opportunity cost.

a. International economics
b. Index number
c. ACCRA Cost of Living Index
d. Absolute advantage

47. An autarky is an economy that is self-sufficient and does not take part in international trade, or severely limits trade with the outside world. Likewise the term refers to an ecosystem not affected by influences from the outside, which relies entirely on its own resources. In the economic meaning, it is also referred to as a _________.

a. Digital economy
b. Transition economy
c. Network Economy
d. Closed economy

48. A _________ or directed economy is an economic system in which the government or workers' councils manages the economy. It is an economic system in which the central government makes all decisions on the production and consumption of goods and services. Its most extensive form is referred to as a _________, centrally planned economy, or command and control economy.

a. Subsistence economy
b. Command economy
c. Transition economy
d. Nutritional Economics

49. An _________ or Å"conomic system is a system that involves the production, distribution and consumption of goods and services between the entities in a particular society. It is the method used by society to produce and distribute goods and services. The _________ is composed of people and institutions, including their relationships to productive resources, such as through the convention of property.

a. Intention economy
b. Economic system
c. Information economy
d. Indicative planning

50. A _________ is an economy based on the division of labor in which the prices of goods and services are determined in a free price system set by supply and demand. This is often contrasted with a planned economy, in which a central government determines the price of goods and services using a fixed price system. Market economies are contrasted with mixed economy where the price system is not entirely free but under some government control that is not extensive enough to constitute a planned economy.

a. Commons-based peer production
b. Nutritional Economics
c. Network Economy
d. Market economy

51. _________ in political thought refers to economic theories of social organization advocating collective ownership and administration of the means of production and distribution of goods, and a society characterized by equality for all individuals, with an egalitarian method of compensation. Modern _________ originated in the late 19th-century intellectual and working class political movement that criticized the effects of industrialization and private ownership on society. Karl Marx posited that _________ would be achieved via class struggle and a proletarian revolution after a transitional stage from capitalism called the dictatorship of the proletariat.

a. Adolph Fischer
b. Adam Smith
c. Socialism
d. Adolf Hitler

52. The _________ is an international financial institution that provides financial and technical assistance to developing countries for development programs (e.g. bridges, roads, schools, etc.) with the stated goal of reducing poverty.

The _________ differs from the _________ Group, in that the _________ comprises only two institutions:

- International Bank for Reconstruction and Development (IBRD)
- International Development Association (IDA)

Whereas the latter incorporates these two in addition to three more:

- International Finance Corporation (IFC)
- Multilateral Investment Guarantee Agency (MIGA)
- International Centre for Settlement of Investment Disputes (ICSID)

John Maynard Keynes (right) represented the UK at the conference, and Harry Dexter White represented the US.

The _________ is one of two major financial institutions created as a result of the Bretton Woods Conference in 1944. The International Monetary Fund, a related but separate institution, is the second.

a. Bank-State-Branch
b. Financial costs of the 2003 Iraq War
c. Flow to Equity-Approach
d. World Bank

53. The Great Proletarian _________ in the People's Republic of China was a period of widespread social and political upheaval; the nation-wide chaos and economic disarray engulfed much of Chinese society between 1966 and 1976.

It was launched by Mao Zedong, the chairman of the Communist Party of China, on May 16, 1966, who alleged that liberal bourgeoisie elements were dominating the party and insisted that they needed to be removed through post-revolutionary class struggle by mobilizing the thoughts and actions of China's youth, who formed Red Guards groups around the country. Although Mao himself officially declared the _________ to have ended in 1969, today it is widely believed that the power struggles and political instability between 1969 and the arrest of the Gang of Four as well as the death of Mao in 1976 were also part of the Revolution.

a. 130-30 fund
b. 1921 recession
c. 100-year flood
d. Cultural Revolution

54. An _________, in economics, is the amount by which the real Gross domestic product exceeds potential GDP. The real GDP is also known as GDP 'adjusted for inflation', 'constant prices' GDP or 'constant dollar' GDP, because it measures the aggregate output in a country's income accounts in a given year, expressed in base-year prices. On the other hand, the potential GDP is the quantity of real GDP when a country's economy is at full-employment.

a. ACCRA Cost of Living Index
b. Inflationary gap
c. ACEA agreement
d. AD-IA Model

55. _________ has several particular meanings:

- in mathematics
  - _________ function
  - Euler _________
  - _________
  - _________ subgroup
  - method of _________s (partial differential equations)
- in physics and engineering
  - any _________ curve that shows the relationship between certain input- and output parameters, e.g.
  - an I-V or current-voltage _________ is the current in a circuit as a function of the applied voltage
  - Receiver-Operator _________
- in fiction
  - in Dungeons ' Dragons, _________ is another name for ability score

.

a. Russian financial crisis
b. Demand
c. Technocracy
d. Characteristic

56. In economics, an _________ is any good or commodity, transported from one country to another country in a legitimate fashion, typically for use in trade. _________ goods or services are provided to foreign consumers by domestic producers. _________ is an important part of international trade.

a. AD-IA Model
b. Export
c. ACCRA Cost of Living Index
d. ACEA agreement

57. The _________ is the market for securities, where companies and governments can raise longterm funds. It is a market in which money is lent for periods longer than a year. The _________ includes the stock market and the bond market.

a. Performance attribution
b. Financial instrument
c. Capital market
d. Multi-family office

58. Manifesto of the Communist Party , often referred to as The _________, was first published on February 21, 1848, and is one of the world's most influential political manuscripts. Commissioned by the Communist League and written by communist theorists Karl Marx and Friedrich Engels, it laid out the League's purposes and program. It presents an analytical approach to the class struggle and the problems of capitalism, rather than a prediction of communism's potential future forms.

a. Differential and Absolute Ground Rent
b. Communist Manifesto
c. Labour power
d. Dialectical materialism

59.

_________ was a German philosopher, political economist, historian, political theorist, sociologist, communist and revolutionary credited as the founder of communism.

Marx summarized his approach to history and politics in the opening line of the first chapter of The Communist Manifesto : e;The history of all hitherto existing society is the history of class struggles.e; Marx argued that capitalism, like previous socioeconomic systems, will produce internal tensions which will lead to its destruction. Just as capitalism replaced feudalism, socialism will in its turn replace capitalism and lead to a stateless, classless society which will emerge after a transitional period, the 'dictatorship of the proletariat'.

a. Marxism
b. Neo-Gramscianism
c. Adam Smith
d. Karl Heinrich Marx

60. There are two main interpretations of the idea of a _________:

- A model in which the state assumes primary responsibility for the welfare of its citizens. This responsibility in theory ought to be comprehensive, because all aspects of welfare are considered and universally applied to citizens as a 'right'. _________ can also mean the creation of a 'social safety net' of minimum standards of varying forms of welfare. Here is found some confusion between a '_________' and a 'welfare society' in common debate about the definition of the term.
- The provision of welfare in society. In many '_________s', especially in continental Europe, welfare is not actually provided by the state, but by a combination of independent, voluntary, mutualist and government services. The functional provider of benefits and services may be a central or state government, a state-sponsored company or agency, a private corporation, a charity or another form of non-profit organization. However, this phenomenon has been more appropriately termed a 'welfare society,' and the term 'welfare system' has been used to describe the range of _________ and welfare society mixes that are found.

The English term '_________' is believed by Asa Briggs to have been coined by Archbishop William Temple during the Second World War, contrasting wartime Britain with the 'warfare state' of Nazi Germany. Friedrich Hayek contends that the term derived from the older German word Wohlfahrtsstaat, which itself was used by nineteenth century historians to describe a variant of the ideal of Polizeistaat . It was fully developed by the German academic Sozialpolitiker--'socialists of the chair'--from 1870 and first implemented through Bismarck's 'state socialism'. Bismarck's policies have also been seen as the creation of a _________.

a. 130-30 fund
b. 100-year flood
c. Welfare state
d. 1921 recession

61. In financial accounting, a _________ or statement of financial position is a summary of a person's or organization's balances. Assets, liabilities and ownership equity are listed as of a specific date, such as the end of its financial year. A _________ is often described as a snapshot of a company's financial condition.

a. 100-year flood
b. 130-30 fund
c. 1921 recession
d. Balance sheet

62. In finance, the _________ of a financial asset measures the sensitivity of the asset's price to interest rate movements. There are various definitions of _________ and derived quantities, discussed below. If not otherwise specified, '_________' generally means the Macaulay _________, as defined below.

a. 100-year flood
b. Time value of money
c. Newtonian time
d. Duration

63. To _________ is to impose a financial charge or other levy upon a taxpayer by a state or the functional equivalent of a state.

_________es are also imposed by many subnational entities. _________es consist of direct _________ or indirect _________, and may be paid in money or as its labour equivalent (often but not always unpaid.)

a. 100-year flood
b. 1921 recession
c. 130-30 fund
d. Tax

64. _________ is the a method of technical and economic research of the systems for purpose to optimize a parity between system's consumer functions or properties and expenses to achieve those functions or properties.

This methodology for continuous perfection of production, industrial technologies, organizational structures was developed by Juryj Sobolev in 1948 at the 'Perm telephone factory'

- 1948 Juryj Sobolev - the first success in application of a method analysis at the 'Perm telephone factory' .
- 1949 - the first application for the invention as result of use of the new method.

Today in economically developed countries practically each enterprise or the company use methodology of the kind of functional-cost analysis as a practice of the quality management, most full satisfying to principles of standards of series ISO 9000.

- Interest of consumer not in products itself, but the advantage which it will receive from its usage.
- The consumer aspires to reduce his expenses
- Functions needed by consumer can be executed in the various ways, and, hence, with various efficiency and expenses. Among possible alternatives of realization of functions exist such in which the parity of quality and the price is the optimal for the consumer.

The goal of _________ is achievement of the highest consumer satisfaction of production at simultaneous decrease in all kinds of industrial expenses Classical _________ has three English synonyms - Value Engineering, Value Management, Value Analysis.

a. Function cost analysis
b. Monopoly wage
c. Staple financing
d. Willingness to pay

65. _________ in the Soviet Union was a policy pursued under Stalin, between 1928 and 1940, to consolidate individual land and labour into collective farms . The Soviet leadership was confident that the replacement of individual peasant farms by kolkhozy would immediately increase food supplies for the urban population, the supply of raw materials for processing industry, and agricultural exports generally. _________ was thus regarded as the solution to the crisis in agricultural distribution that had developed since 1927 and was becoming more acute as the Soviet Union pressed ahead with its ambitious industrialization program.

a. 100-year flood
b. Collectivization
c. 1921 recession
d. 130-30 fund

66. _________ was the General Secretary of the Communist Party of the Soviet Union's Central Committee from 1922 until his death in 1953. In the years following Lenin's death in 1924, he rose to become the leader of the Soviet Union.

Stalin launched a command economy, replacing the New Economic Policy of the 1920s with Five-Year Plans and launching a period of rapid industrialization and economic collectivization.

a. Adolph Fischer
b. Josef Stalin
c. Adam Smith
d. Adolf Hitler

67. In economics, the _________ is a historical inverse relation between the rate of unemployment and the rate of inflation in an economy. Stated simply, the lower the unemployment in an economy, the higher the rate of increase in nominal wages in the economy. Rate of Change of Wages against Unemployment, United Kingdom 1913-1948 from Phillips (1958)

William Phillips, a New Zealand born economist, wrote a paper in 1958 titled The Relationship between Unemployment and the Rate of Change of Money Wages in the United Kingdom 1861-1957, which was published in the quarterly journal Economica.

a. Lorenz curve
b. Cost curve
c. Phillips curve
d. Demand curve

68. In political science and economics, the _________ or agency dilemma treats the difficulties that arise under conditions of incomplete and asymmetric information when a principal hires an agent, such as the problem that the two may not have the same interests, while the principal is, presumably, hiring the agent to pursue the interests of the former.

Various mechanisms may be used to try to align the interests of the agent with those of the principal, such as piece rates/commissions, profit sharing, efficiency wages, performance measurement (including financial statements), the agent posting a bond, or fear of firing. The _________ is found in most employer/employee relationships, for example, when stockholders hire top executives of corporations.

a. 1921 recession
b. 100-year flood
c. 130-30 fund
d. Principal-agent problem

69. In economics, _________ is a rise in the general level of prices of goods and services in an economy over a period of time. When the general price level rises, each unit of currency buys fewer goods and services; consequently, _________ is also a decline in the real value of money--a loss of purchasing power in the medium of exchange which is also the monetary unit of account in the economy. A chief measure of general price-level _________ is the general _________ rate, which is the percentage change in a general price index (normally the Consumer Price Index) over time.

a. Opportunity cost
b. Energy economics
c. Economic
d. Inflation

70. _________ in economics and business is the result of an exchange and from that trade we assign a numerical monetary value to a good, service or asset. If Alice trades Bob 4 apples for an orange, the _________ of an orange is 4 apples. Inversely, the _________ of an apple is 1/4 oranges.

a. Price book
b. Premium pricing
c. Price war
d. Price

71. _________ is one of the four Ps of the marketing mix. The other three aspects are product, promotion, and place. It is also a key variable in microeconomic price allocation theory.

a. Guaranteed Maximum Price
b. Pricing
c. Point of total assumption
d. Premium pricing

72. _________ is the incidence or process of transferring ownership of a business, enterprise, agency or public service from the public sector (government) to the private sector (business.) In a broader sense, _________ refers to transfer of any government function to the private sector including governmental functions like revenue collection and law enforcement.

The term '_________' also has been used to describe two unrelated transactions.

a. Privatization
b. Ricardian equivalence
c. Compound empowerment
d. Performance reports

73. In economics, _________ is equal to total cost divided by the number of goods produced (the output quantity, Q.) It is also equal to the sum of average variable costs (total variable costs divided by Q) plus average fixed costs (total fixed costs divided by Q.) _________s may be dependent on the time period considered (increasing production may be expensive or impossible in the short term, for example.)

a. Explicit cost
b. Average fixed cost
c. Average variable cost
d. Average cost

74. _________ is a social science concept used in business, economics, organizational behaviour, political science, public health and sociology that refers to connections within and between social networks. Though there are a variety of related definitions, which have been described as 'something of a cure-all' for the problems of modern society, they tend to share the core idea 'that social networks have value. Just as a screwdriver (physical capital) or a college education (human capital) can increase productivity (both individual and collective), so do social contacts affect the productivity of individuals and groups'.

a. Pre-industrial society
b. Social capital
c. Social inequality
d. Diversity training

1. _________s is the social science that studies the production, distribution, and consumption of goods and services. The term _________s comes from the Ancient Greek oá¼°κονομÎ¯α from oá¼¶κος (oikos, 'house') + νÏŒμος (nomos, 'custom' or 'law'), hence 'rules of the house(hold)'. Current _________ models developed out of the broader field of political economy in the late 19th century, owing to a desire to use an empirical approach more akin to the physical sciences.

a. Opportunity cost
b. Energy economics
c. Inflation
d. Economic

2. _________ is a term used to describe how different aspects between economies are integrated. The basics of this theory were written by the Hungarian Economist Béla Balassa in the 1960s. As _________ increases, the barriers of trade between markets diminishes.

a. Inward investment
b. Economic integration
c. Import license
d. Import

3. _________ was an arrangement established in 1979 under the Jenkins European Commission where most nations of the European Economic Community (EEC) linked their currencies to prevent large fluctuations relative to one another.

After the collapse of the Bretton Woods system in 1971, most of the EEC countries agreed in 1972 to maintain stable exchange rates by preventing exchange fluctuations of more than 2.25% (the European 'currency snake'.) In March 1979, this system was replaced by the _________, and the European Currency Unit (ECU) was defined.

a. European Monetary System
b. European Monetary Union
c. Euro Interbank Offered Rate
d. Exchange rate mechanism

4. The _________ is an economic and political union of 27 member states, located primarily in Europe. It was established by the Treaty of Maastricht on 1 November 1993, upon the foundations of the pre-existing European Economic Community. With a population of almost 500 million, the _________ generates an estimated 30% share (US$18.4 trillion in 2008) of the nominal gross world product.

a. ACEA agreement
b. ACCRA Cost of Living Index
c. European Union
d. European Court of Justice

5. The term financial crisis is applied broadly to a variety of situations in which some financial institutions or assets suddenly lose a large part of their value. In the 19th and early 20th centuries, many _________ were associated with banking panics, and many recessions coincided with these panics. Other situations that are often called _________ include stock market crashes and the bursting of other financial bubbles, currency crises, and sovereign defaults.

a. Financial crises
b. Microeconomics
c. General equilibrium
d. Georgism

6. The _________ or gross domestic income (GDI), a basic measure of an economy's economic performance, is the market value of all final goods and services produced within the borders of a nation in a year. _________ can be defined in three ways, all of which are conceptually identical. First, it is equal to the total expenditures for all final goods and services produced within the country in a stipulated period of time (usually a 365-day year.)

a. Monopolistic competition
b. Market structure
c. Countercyclical
d. Gross domestic product

7. A _________ secures the proper functioning of money by regulating economic agents, transaction types, and money supply.

_________s are traditionally formed by the policy decisions of individual governments and administrated as a domestic economic issue.

The current trend, however, is to use international trade and investment to alter the policy and legislation of individual governments.

a. Financial rand
b. Netting
c. Consumer basket
d. Monetary System

8. In economics, _________ refers to the ability of a party to produce a good or service using fewer real resources than another entity producing the same good or service..A party has an _________ when using the same input as another party, it can produce a greater output. Since _________ is determined by a simple comparison of labor productivities, it is possible for a a party to have no _________ in anything. It can be contrasted with the concept of comparative advantage which refers to the ability to produce a particular good at a lower opportunity cost.

a. ACCRA Cost of Living Index
b. Index number
c. International economics
d. Absolute advantage

9. _________ is an economic system in which wealth, and the means of producing wealth, are privately owned. Through _________, the land, labor, and capital are owned, operated, and traded for the purpose of generating profits, without force or fraud, by private individuals either singly or jointly, and investments, distribution, income, production, pricing and supply of goods, commodities and services are determined by voluntary private decision in a market economy. A distinguishing feature of _________ is that each person owns his or her own labor and therefore is allowed to sell the use of it to employers.

a. Capitalism
b. Late capitalism
c. Socialism for the rich and capitalism for the poor
d. Creative capitalism

10. _________ is a negative term describing an claimed capitalist economy in which success in business depends on close relationships between businesspeople and government officials. It may be exhibited in the distribution of legal permits, government grants, special tax breaks, and so forth.

_________ is believed to arise when political cronyism spills over into the business world; self-serving friendships and family ties between businessmen and the government influence the economy and society to the extent that it corrupts public-serving economic and political ideals.

a. Good governance
b. 130-30 fund
c. 100-year flood
d. Crony capitalism

11. _________ is money accepted for exchange of goods in an economy. The prevalence of one money over another arises, usually, when a government designates through decrees that the government shall accept only particular notes and coins in payment for taxes. Typically, money of _________ consists of stamped coins and minted paper bills.

a. Totnes pound
b. Security thread
c. Local currency
d. Currency

12. A _________ is a monetary authority which is required to maintain a fixed exchange rate with a foreign currency. This policy objective requires the conventional objectives of a central bank to be subordinated to the exchange rate target.

The main qualities of an orthodox _________ are:

- A _________'s foreign currency reserves must be sufficient to ensure that all holders of its notes and coins (and all banks creditor of a Reserve Account at the _________) can convert them into the reserve currency (usually 110-115% of the monetary base M0.)
- A _________ maintains absolute, unlimited convertibility between its notes and coins and the currency against which they are pegged (the anchor currency), at a fixed rate of exchange, with no restrictions on current-account or capital-account transactions.
- A _________ only earns profit from interests on foreign reserves (less the expense of note-issuing), and does not engage in forward-exchange transactions. These foreign reserves exist (1) because local notes have been issued in exchange, or (2) because commercial banks must by regulation deposit a minimum reserve at the _________. (1) generates a seignorage revenue. (2) is the revenue on minimum reserves (revenue of investment activities less cost of minimum reserves remuneration)
- A _________ has no discretionary powers to effect monetary policy and does not lend to the government. Governments cannot print money, and can only tax or borrow to meet their spending commitments.
- A _________ does not act as a lender of last resort to commercial banks, and does not regulate reserve requirements.
- A _________ does not attempt to manipulate interest rates by establishing a discount rate like a central bank. The peg with the foreign currency tends to keep interest rates and inflation very closely aligned to those in the country against whose currency the peg is fixed.

The _________ in question will no longer issue fiat money but instead will only issue one unit of local currency for each unit (or decided amount) of foreign currency it has in its vault (often a hard currency such as the U.S. dollar or the euro.) The surplus on the balance of payments of that country is reflected by higher deposits local banks hold at the central bank as well as (initially) higher deposits of the (net) exporting firms at their local banks.

a. Currency board
b. Reserve currency
c. Currency competition
d. Petrodollar

13. A currency crisis, which is also called a balance-of-payments crisis, occurs when the value of a currency changes quickly, undermining its ability to serve as a medium of exchange or a store of value. It is a type of financial crisis and is often associated with a real economic crisis. _________ can be especially destructive to small open economies or bigger, but not sufficiently stable ones.

a. 100-year flood
b. 130-30 fund
c. 1921 recession
d. Currency crises

14. A _________, which is also called a balance-of-payments crisis, occurs when the value of a currency changes quickly, undermining its ability to serve as a medium of exchange or a store of value. It is a type of financial crisis and is often associated with a real economic crisis. Currency crises can be especially destructive to small open economies or bigger, but not sufficiently stable ones.

a. 130-30 fund
b. Currency crisis
c. Speculative attack
d. 100-year flood

15. _________ is that which is owed; usually referencing assets owed, but the term can also cover moral obligations and other interactions not requiring money. In the case of assets, _________ is a means of using future purchasing power in the present before a summation has been earned. Some companies and corporations use _________ as a part of their overall corporate finance strategy.

a. Debenture
b. Hard money loan
c. Collateral Management
d. Debt

16. _________ is the increase in the amount of the goods and services produced by an economy over time. It is conventionally measured as the percent rate of increase in real gross domestic product, or real GDP. Growth is usually calculated in real terms, i.e. inflation-adjusted terms, in order to net out the effect of inflation on the price of the goods and services produced.

a. Economic growth
b. ACEA agreement
c. AD-IA Model
d. ACCRA Cost of Living Index

17. The term _________ is applied broadly to a variety of situations in which some financial institutions or assets suddenly lose a large part of their value. In the 19th and early 20th centuries, many financial crises were associated with banking panics, and many recessions coincided with these panics. Other situations that are often called financial crises include stock market crashes and the bursting of other financial bubbles, currency crises, and sovereign defaults.

a. Macroeconomics
b. Financial crisis
c. Market failure
d. Co-operative economics

18. In finance, the _________ is the system that allows the transfer of money between savers and borrowers.

Put another way: the _________ is a set of complex and closely interconnected financial institutions, markets, instruments, services, practices, and transactions.

a. Hedonimetry
b. Foreign investment
c. Lean consumption
d. Financial system

19. A _________ is the transfer of wealth from one party (such as a person or company) to another. A _________ is usually made in exchange for the provision of goods, services or both, or to fulfill a legal obligation.

The simplest and oldest form of _________ is barter, the exchange of one good or service for another.

a. Soft count
b. Going concern
c. Payment
d. Social gravity

20. An _________ is an economy in which people, including businesses, can trade in goods and services with other people and businesses in the international community at large. This contrasts with a closed economy in which international trade cannot take place.

The act of selling goods or services to a foreign country is called exporting.

a. Attention work
b. Information economy
c. Indicative planning
d. Open economy

21. _________ is a misspelled phrase from Latin 'pro capite' phrase meaning per head with pro meaning 'per' or 'for each' and capite meaning 'head.' Both words together equate to the phrase 'for each head.'

It is usually used in the field of statistics to indicate the average per person for any given concern, such as income, crime rate, etc.

It is also used in wills to indicate that each of the named beneficiaries should receive, by devise or bequest, equal shares of the estate. This is in contrast to a per stirpes division, in which each branch of the inheriting family inherits an equal share of the estate.

a. Per capita
b. Population statistics
c. False positive rate
d. Sargan test

22. An _________, in economics, is the amount by which the real Gross domestic product exceeds potential GDP. The real GDP is also known as GDP 'adjusted for inflation', 'constant prices' GDP or 'constant dollar' GDP, because it measures the aggregate output in a country's income accounts in a given year, expressed in base-year prices. On the other hand, the potential GDP is the quantity of real GDP when a country's economy is at full-employment.

a. AD-IA Model
b. ACCRA Cost of Living Index
c. Inflationary gap
d. ACEA agreement

23. In economics, the _________ measures the payments that flow between any individual country and all other countries. It is used to summarize all international economic transactions for that country during a specific time period, usually a year. The _________ is determined by the country's exports and imports of goods, services, and financial capital, as well as financial transfers.

a. Gross domestic product per barrel
b. Gross world product
c. Skyscraper Index
d. Balance of payments

24. _________ is the development of economic wealth of countries or regions for the well-being of their inhabitants. It is the process by which a nation improves the economic, political, and social well being of its people. From a policy perspective, _________ can be defined as efforts that seek to improve the economic well-being and quality of life for a community by creating and/or retaining jobs and supporting or growing incomes and the tax base.

a. Experimental economics
b. Economic methodology
c. Inflation
d. Economic development

25. The term '_________' refers to the concept of collecting information and attempting to spot a pattern in the information. In some fields of study, the term '_________' has more formally-defined meanings.

In project management _________ is a mathematical technique that uses historical results to predict future outcome.

a. Quantile regression
b. Probit model
c. Coefficient of determination
d. Trend analysis

26. A _________ refers to any type debt instrument, such as a loan, bond, mortgage that does not have a fixed rate of interest over the life of the instrument. Such debt typically uses an index or other base rate for establishing the interest rate for each relevant period. One of the most common rates to use as the basis for applying interest rates is the London Inter-bank Offered Rate, or LIBOR

a. Money market
b. Floating interest rate
c. Disposal tax effect
d. Moneylender

27. In economics, the _________ is one of the two primary components of the balance of payments, the other being the capital account. It is the sum of the balance of trade (exports minus imports of goods and services), net factor income (such as interest and dividends) and net transfer payments (such as foreign aid.)

$$\begin{aligned}\text{Current account} = {} & \text{Balance of trade} \\ & + \text{Net factor income from abroad} \\ & + \text{Net unilateral transfers from abroad}\end{aligned}$$

The _________ balance is one of two major metrics of the nature of a country's foreign trade (the other being the net capital outflow.)

a. National Income and Product Accounts
b. Gross private domestic investment
c. Compensation of employees
d. Current account

28. In economics, an _________ is any good (e.g. a commodity) or service brought into one country from another country in a legitimate fashion, typically for use in trade.It is a good that is brought in from another country for sale. _________ goods or services are provided to domestic consumers by foreign producers. An _________ in the receiving country is an export to the sending country.

a. Import quota
b. Incoterms
c. Economic integration
d. Import

29. _________ and Keynesian Theory) is a macroeconomic theory based on the ideas of 20th-century British economist John Maynard Keynes. _________ argues that private sector decisions sometimes lead to inefficient macroeconomic outcomes and therefore advocates active policy responses by the public sector, including monetary policy actions by the central bank and fiscal policy actions by the government to stabilize output over the business cycle.

The theories forming the basis of _________ were first presented in The General Theory of Employment, Interest and Money, published in 1936.

a. Market failure
b. Deflation
c. Rational choice theory
d. Keynesian economics

30. _________ is an economic theory that holds that the prosperity of a nation is dependent upon its supply of capital, and that the global volume of international trade is 'unchangeable.' Economic assets or capital, are represented by bullion (gold, silver, and trade value) held by the state, which is best increased through a positive balance of trade with other nations (exports minus imports.) _________ suggests that the ruling government should advance these goals by playing a protectionist role in the economy; by encouraging exports and discouraging imports, notably through the use of tariffs and subsidies.

_________ was the dominant school of thought throughout the early modern period (from the 16th to the 18th century.)

a. Consumer theory
b. Nominal value
c. General equilibrium theory
d. Mercantilism

31. The balance of trade (or net exports, sometimes symbolized as NX) is the difference between the monetary value of exports and imports in an economy over a certain period of time. It is the relationship between a nation's imports and exports. A favorable balance of trade is known as a trade surplus and consists of exporting more than is imported; an unfavorable balance of trade is known as a _________ or, informally, a trade gap.

a. Complementary asset
b. Demographics of India
c. Trade deficit
d. Computational economic

32. In economics, an _________ is any good or commodity, transported from one country to another country in a legitimate fashion, typically for use in trade. _________ goods or services are provided to foreign consumers by domestic producers. _________ is an important part of international trade.

a. AD-IA Model
b. ACEA agreement
c. Export
d. ACCRA Cost of Living Index

33. _________ is exchange of capital, goods, and services across international borders or territories. In most countries, it represents a significant share of gross domestic product (GDP.) While _________ has been present throughout much of history , its economic, social, and political importance has been on the rise in recent centuries.

a. Import license
b. Incoterms
c. Intra-industry trade
d. International trade

34. In economics a _________ is an entity that owes a debt to someone else. The entity may be an individual, a firm, a government, a company or other legal person. The counterparty is called a creditor.

a. Duration gap
b. Decision process tool
c. Senior stretch loan
d. Debtor

35. A _________, sometimes called a pegged exchange rate, is a type of exchange rate regime wherein a currency's value is matched to the value of another single currency or to a basket of other currencies such as gold.

A _________ is usually used to stabilize the value of a currency, vis-a-vis the currency it is pegged to. This facilitates trade and investments between the two countries, and is especially useful for small economies where external trade forms a large part of their GDP.

a. Leading indicators
b. Law of supply
c. Monetary economics
d. Fixed exchange rate

36. In financial accounting, the _________ is one of the accounts in shareholders' equity. Sole proprietorships have a single _________ in the owner's equity. Partnerships maintain a _________ for each of the partners.

a. Current account
b. Net national product
c. Compensation of employees
d. Capital account

37. In finance, the _________s between two currencies specifies how much one currency is worth in terms of the other. It is the value of a foreign natione;s currency in terms of the home natione;s currency. For example an _________ of 102 Japanese yen to the United States dollar means that JPY 102 is worth the same as USD 1.

a. ACCRA Cost of Living Index
b. ACEA agreement
c. Interbank market
d. Exchange rate

38. In economics, _________ is the total demand for final goods and services in the economy (Y) at a given time and price level. It is the amount of goods and services in the economy that will be purchased at all possible price levels. This is the demand for the gross domestic product of a country when inventory levels are static.

a. Aggregate expenditure
b. Aggregate supply
c. Aggregate demand
d. Aggregation problem

39. In economics, _________ is the total supply of goods and services produced by a national economy during a specific time period. It is the total amount of goods and services in the economy available at all possible price levels.

a. Aggregate expenditure
b. Aggregate demand
c. Aggregation problem
d. Aggregate supply

40. The _________ is the official currency of 16 of the 27 member states of the European Union (EU.) The states, known collectively as the Eurozone, are Austria, Belgium, Cyprus, Finland, France, Germany, Greece, Ireland, Italy, Luxembourg, Malta, the Netherlands, Portugal, Slovakia, Slovenia, and Spain. The currency is also used in a further five European countries, with and without formal agreements and is consequently used daily by some 327 million Europeans.

a. Euro
b. IRS Code 3401
c. Import and Export Price Indices
d. Equity capital market

41. The _________ is where currency trading takes place. It is where banks and other official institutions facilitate the buying and selling of foreign currencies. FX transactions typically involve one party purchasing a quantity of one currency in exchange for paying a quantity of another.

a. Floating currency
b. Currency swap
c. Foreign exchange market
d. Covered interest arbitrage

42. _________ in economics and business is the result of an exchange and from that trade we assign a numerical monetary value to a good, service or asset. If Alice trades Bob 4 apples for an orange, the _________ of an orange is 4 apples. Inversely, the _________ of an apple is 1/4 oranges.

a. Price war
b. Price
c. Price book
d. Premium pricing

43. _________ is defined as the measure of responsiveness in the quantity demanded for a commodity as a result of change in price of the same commodity. It is a measure of how consumers react to a change in price. In other words, it is percentage change in quantity demanded as per the percentage change in price of the same commodity.

a. Price elasticity of demand
b. 100-year flood
c. 1921 recession
d. 130-30 fund

44. In economics, the _________ is defined as a numerical measure of the responsiveness of the quantity supplied of product (A) to a change in price of product (A) alone. It is the measure of the way quantity supplied reacts to a change in price.

>

For example, if, in response to a 10% rise in the price of a good, the quantity supplied increases by 20%, the _________ would be 20%/10% = 2.

a. Price elasticity of supply
b. Passive income
c. Hedonimetry
d. Demand shaping

45. _________ is an economic model based on price, utility and quantity in a market. It predicts that in a competitive market, price will function to equalize the quantity demanded by consumers, and the quantity supplied by producers, resulting in an economic equilibrium of price and quantity. The model incorporates other factors changing equilibrium as a shift of demand and/or supply.

a. Deferred gratification
b. Rational addiction
c. Joint demand
d. Supply and demand

46. Economics:

- _________,the desire to own something and the ability to pay for it
- _________ curve,a graphic representation of a _________ schedule
- _________ deposit, the money in checking accounts
- _________ pull theory,the theory that inflation occurs when _________ for goods and services exceeds existing supplies
- _________ schedule,a table that lists the quantity of a good a person will buy it each different price
- _________ side economics,the school of economics at believes government spending and tax cuts open economy by raising _________

a. Variability
b. Production
c. McKesson ' Robbins scandal
d. Demand

47. In economics, _________ is the ratio of the percent change in one variable to the percent change in another variable. It is a tool for measuring the responsiveness of a function to changes in parameters in a relative way. Commonly analyzed are _________ of substitution, price and wealth.

a. ACEA agreement
b. ACCRA Cost of Living Index
c. Elasticity of demand
d. Elasticity

48. Price _________ is defined as the measure of responsiveness in the quantity demanded for a commodity as a result of change in price of the same commodity. It is a measure of how consumers react to a change in price. In other words, it is percentage change in quantity demanded by the percentage change in price of the same commodity.

a. Elasticity of demand
b. ACCRA Cost of Living Index
c. Elasticity
d. ACEA agreement

49. _________ is a term used in accounting relating to the increase in value of an asset. In this sense it is the reverse of depreciation, which measures the fall in value of assets over their normal life-time.

_________ is a rise of a currency in a floating exchange rate.

a. ACEA agreement
b. AD-IA Model
c. ACCRA Cost of Living Index
d. Appreciation

50. _________ is a term used in accounting, economics and finance to spread the cost of an asset over the span of several years.

In simple words we can say that _________ is the reduction in the value of an asset due to usage, passage of time, wear and tear, technological outdating or obsolescence, depletion, inadequacy, rot, rust, decay or other such factors.

In accounting, _________ is a term used to describe any method of attributing the historical or purchase cost of an asset across its useful life, roughly corresponding to normal wear and tear.

a. Historical cost
b. Depreciation
c. Net income per employee
d. Salvage value

51. _________ is a reduction in the value of a currency with respect to other monetary units. In common modern usage, it specifically implies an official lowering of the value of a country's currency within a fixed exchange rate system, by which the monetary authority formally sets a new fixed rate with respect to a foreign reference currency. In contrast, (currency) depreciation is used for the unofficial decrease in the exchange rate in a floating exchange rate system.

a. Petrodollar recycling
b. Devaluation
c. Reserve currency
d. Texas redbacks

52. _________ means a rise of a price of goods or products. This term is specially used as _________ of a currency, where it means a rise of currency to the relation with a foreign currency in a fixed exchange rate. In floating exchange rate correct term would be appreciation.

a. Legal monopoly
b. Revaluation
c. Deglobalization
d. Death spiral financing

53. A _________, reserve bank, or monetary authority is the entity responsible for the monetary policy of a country or of a group of member states. It is a bank that can lend money to other banks in times of need. Its primary responsibility is to maintain the stability of the national currency and money supply, but more active duties include controlling subsidized-loan interest rates, and acting as a lender of last resort to the banking sector during times of financial crisis (private banks often being integral to the national financial system.)

a. 1921 recession
b. 130-30 fund
c. 100-year flood
d. Central bank

54. The _________ is the central banking system of the United States. Created in 1913 by the enactment of the Federal Reserve Act (signed by Woodrow Wilson), it is a quasi-public and quasi-private (government entity with private components) banking system that comprises (1) the presidentially appointed Board of Governors of the _________ in Washington, D.C.; (2) the Federal Open Market Committee; (3) twelve regional Federal Reserve Banks located in major cities throughout the nation acting as fiscal agents for the U.S. Treasury, each with its own nine-member board of directors; (4) numerous other private U.S. member banks, which subscribe to required amounts of non-transferable stock in their regional Federal Reserve Banks; and (5) various advisory councils. Since February 2006, Ben Bernanke has served as the Chairman of the Board of Governors of the _________.

a. Federal Reserve System
b. Monetary Policy Report to the Congress
c. Term auction facility
d. Federal Reserve System Open Market Account

55. The term _________ or commodity bundle refers to a fixed list of items used specifically to track the progress of inflation in an economy or specific market.

The most common type of _________ is the basket of consumer goods, used to define the Consumer Price Index (CPI.) Other types of baskets are used to define

- Producer Price Index (PPI), previously known as Wholesale Price Index (WPI)
- various commodity price indices

The term _________ analysis in the retail business refers to research that provides the retailer with information to understand the purchase behaviour of a buyer. This information will enable the retailer to understand the buyer's needs and rewrite the store's layout accordingly, develop cross-promotional programs, or even capture new buyers (much like the cross-selling concept.)

a. Category Development Index
b. Robin Hood index
c. Market basket
d. Cost-weighted activity index

56. _________ is an economic concept with commonplace familiarity. It is the price that a good or service is offered at, or will fetch, in the marketplace. It is of interest mainly in the study of microeconomics.

a. Market anomaly
b. Paper trading
c. Noisy market hypothesis
d. Market price

57. _________ refers to a business or organization attempting to acquire goods or services to accomplish the goals of the enterprise. Though there are several organizations that attempt to set standards in the _________ process, processes can vary greatly between organizations. Typically the word '_________' is not used interchangeably with the word 'procurement', since procurement typically includes Expediting, Supplier Quality, and Traffic and Logistics (T'L) in addition to _________.

a. Free port
b. 100-year flood
c. 130-30 fund
d. Purchasing

58. _________ is the number of goods/services that can be purchased with a unit of currency. For example, if you had taken one dollar to a store in the 1950s, you would have been able to buy a greater number of items than you would today, indicating that you would have had a greater _________ in the 1950s. Currency can be either a commodity money, like gold or silver, or fiat currency like US dollars.

a. Human Poverty Index
b. Genuine progress indicator
c. Purchasing power
d. Compliance cost

59. The _________ theory uses the long-term equilibrium exchange rate of two currencies to equalize their purchasing power. Developed by Gustav Cassel in 1920, it is based on the law of one price: the theory states that, in ideally efficient markets, identical goods should have only one price.

This purchasing power SEM rate equalizes the purchasing power of different currencies in their home countries for a given basket of goods.

a. Gross national product
b. Bureau of Labor Statistics
c. Measures of national income and output
d. Purchasing power parity

60. Competition law, known in the United States as _________ law, has three main elements:

- prohibiting agreements or practices that restrict free trading and competition between business entities. This includes in particular the repression of cartels.
- banning abusive behaviour by a firm dominating a market, or anti-competitive practices that tend to lead to such a dominant position. Practices controlled in this way may include predatory pricing, tying, price gouging, refusal to deal, and many others.
- supervising the mergers and acquisitions of large corporations, including some joint ventures. Transactions that are considered to threaten the competitive process can be prohibited altogether, or approved subject to 'remedies' such as an obligation to divest part of the merged business or to offer licences or access to facilities to enable other businesses to continue competing.

The substance and practice of competition law varies from jurisdiction to jurisdiction. Protecting the interests of consumers (consumer welfare) and ensuring that entrepreneurs have an opportunity to compete in the market economy are often treated as important objectives. Competition law is closely connected with law on deregulation of access to markets, state aids and subsidies, the privatisation of state owned assets and the establishment of independent sector regulators. In recent decades, competition law has been viewed as a way to provide better public services.

a. Intellectual property law
b. United Kingdom competition law
c. Anti-Inflation Act
d. Antitrust

61. A _________ is an object whose consumption increases the utility of the consumer, for which the quantity demanded exceeds the quantity supplied at zero price. _________s are usually modeled as having diminishing marginal utility. The first individual purchase has high utility; the second has less.

a. Composite good
b. Pie method
c. Merit good
d. Good

62. _________ is the process by which the government, central bank (ii) availability of money, and (iii) cost of money or rate of interest, in order to attain a set of objectives oriented towards the growth and stability of the economy. Monetary theory provides insight into how to craft optimal _________.

_________ is referred to as either being an expansionary policy where an expansionary policy increases the total supply of money in the economy, and a contractionary policy decreases the total money supply.

a. 100-year flood
b. 130-30 fund
c. 1921 recession
d. Monetary policy

63. In economics, _________ is a rise in the general level of prices of goods and services in an economy over a period of time. When the general price level rises, each unit of currency buys fewer goods and services; consequently, _________ is also a decline in the real value of money--a loss of purchasing power in the medium of exchange which is also the monetary unit of account in the economy. A chief measure of general price-level _________ is the general _________ rate, which is the percentage change in a general price index (normally the Consumer Price Index) over time.

a. Energy economics
b. Opportunity cost
c. Economic
d. Inflation

64. In economics, the _________ is a measure of inflation, the rate of increase of a price index (for example, a consumer price index.)It is the percentage rate of change in price level over time. The rate of decrease in the purchasing power of money is approximately equal.

It's used to calculate the real interest rate, as well as real increases in wages, and official measurements of this rate act as input variables to COLA adjustments and Inflation derivatives prices.

a. Interest rate option
b. Edgeworth paradox
c. Equity value
d. Inflation rate

65. The _________ is a monetary system in which a region's common medium of exchange are paper notes that are normally freely convertible into pre-set, fixed quantities of gold. The _________ is not currently used by any government, having been replaced completely by fiat currency. Gold certificates were used as paper currency in the United States from 1882 to 1933, these certificates were freely convertable into gold coins.

In the 1790s Britain suffered a massive shortage of silver coinage and ceased to mint larger silver coins.

a. 100-year flood
b. 1921 recession
c. 130-30 fund
d. Gold standard

66. _________, Jr. (January 29, 1843 - September 14, 1901) was the 25th President of the United States, and the last veteran of the American Civil War to be elected.

By the 1880s, McKinley was a national Republican leader; his signature issue was high tariffs on imports as a formula for prosperity, as typified by his McKinley Tariff of 1890.

a. Adolf Hitler
b. Adolph Fischer
c. Adam Smith
d. William McKinley

67. In economics, the _________ of money is a theory emphasizing the positive relationship of overall prices or the nominal value of expenditures to the quantity of money.

It is the mainstream economic theory of the price level. Alternative theories include the real bills doctrine and the more recent fiscal theory of the price level.

a. Quantity theory
b. Romer Model
c. Real business cycle
d. Dishoarding

68. _________ is the a method of technical and economic research of the systems for purpose to optimize a parity between system's consumer functions or properties and expenses to achieve those functions or properties.

This methodology for continuous perfection of production, industrial technologies, organizational structures was developed by Juryj Sobolev in 1948 at the 'Perm telephone factory'

- 1948 Juryj Sobolev - the first success in application of a method analysis at the 'Perm telephone factory' .
- 1949 - the first application for the invention as result of use of the new method.

Today in economically developed countries practically each enterprise or the company use methodology of the kind of functional-cost analysis as a practice of the quality management, most full satisfying to principles of standards of series ISO 9000.

- Interest of consumer not in products itself, but the advantage which it will receive from its usage.
- The consumer aspires to reduce his expenses
- Functions needed by consumer can be executed in the various ways, and, hence, with various efficiency and expenses. Among possible alternatives of realization of functions exist such in which the parity of quality and the price is the optimal for the consumer.

The goal of _________ is achievement of the highest consumer satisfaction of production at simultaneous decrease in all kinds of industrial expenses Classical _________ has three English synonyms - Value Engineering, Value Management, Value Analysis.

a. Function cost analysis
b. Staple financing
c. Monopoly wage
d. Willingness to pay

69. In economics, _________ is the total amount of money available in an economy at a particular point in time. There are several ways to define 'money', but standard measures usually include currency in circulation and demand deposits.

_________ data are recorded and published, usually by the government or the central bank of the country.

a. Veil of money
b. Neutrality of money
c. Velocity of money
d. Money supply

70. _________ refers to discriminatory employment practices such as bias in hiring, promotion, job assignment, termination, and compensation, and various types of harassment.

In many countries, laws prohibit employers from discriminating on the basis of race, color, sex, religion, national origin, physical or mental disability, or age. There is also a growing body of law preventing or occasionally justifying _________ based on sexual orientation or gender identity.

a. Irish competition law
b. Energy Independence and Security Act of 2007
c. Impotent poor
d. Employment discrimination

71. The _________ was the outcome of the failure of negotiating governments to create the International Trade Organization (ITO.) GATT was formed in 1947 and lasted until 1994, when it was replaced by the World Trade Organization. The Bretton Woods Conference had introduced the idea for an organization to regulate trade as part of a larger plan for economic recovery after World War II.

a. GATT
b. Dutch-Scandinavian Economic Pact
c. General Agreement on Trade in Services
d. General Agreement on Tariffs and Trade

72. The _________ is an international organization that oversees the global financial system by following the macroeconomic policies of its member countries, in particular those with an impact on exchange rates and the balance of payments. It is an organization formed to stabilize international exchange rates and facilitate development. It also offers financial and technical assistance to its members, making it an international lender of last resort.

a. ACEA agreement
b. Office of Thrift Supervision
c. ACCRA Cost of Living Index
d. International Monetary Fund

73. A _________ is a duty imposed on goods when they are moved across a political boundary. They are usually associated with protectionism, the economic policy of restraining trade between nations. For political reasons, _________s are usually imposed on imported goods, although they may also be imposed on exported goods.

a. Tariff
b. 130-30 fund
c. 1921 recession
d. 100-year flood

74. The _________ is an international financial institution that provides financial and technical assistance to developing countries for development programs (e.g. bridges, roads, schools, etc.) with the stated goal of reducing poverty.

The _________ differs from the _________ Group, in that the _________ comprises only two institutions:

- International Bank for Reconstruction and Development (IBRD)
- International Development Association (IDA)

Whereas the latter incorporates these two in addition to three more:

- International Finance Corporation (IFC)
- Multilateral Investment Guarantee Agency (MIGA)
- International Centre for Settlement of Investment Disputes (ICSID)

John Maynard Keynes (right) represented the UK at the conference, and Harry Dexter White represented the US.

The _________ is one of two major financial institutions created as a result of the Bretton Woods Conference in 1944. The International Monetary Fund, a related but separate institution, is the second.

a. World Bank
b. Bank-State-Branch
c. Flow to Equity-Approach
d. Financial costs of the 2003 Iraq War

75. The _________ is an important selective, mainly private, international organization designed by its founders to supervise and liberalize international trade. The organization officially commenced on 1 January 1995, under the Marrakesh Agreement, succeeding the 1947 General Agreement on Tariffs and Trade (GATT.)

The _________ deals with regulation of trade between participating countries; it provides a framework for negotiating and formalising trade agreements, and a dispute resolution process aimed at enforcing participants' adherence to _________ agreements which are signed by representatives of member governments and ratified by their parliaments.

a. World Trade Organization
b. Bio-energy village
c. 2009 G-20 London summit protests
d. Backus-Kehoe-Kydland consumption correlation puzzle

76. In economics, the concept of the _________ refers to the decision-making time frame of a firm in which at least one factor of production is fixed. Costs which are fixed in the _________ have no impact on a firms decisions. For example a firm can raise output by increasing the amount of labour through overtime.

a. Product Pipeline
b. Hicks-neutral technical change
c. Short-run
d. Productivity model

77. The _________ of monetary management established the rules for commercial and financial relations among the world's major industrial states in the mid 20th Century. The _________ was the first example of a fully negotiated monetary order intended to govern monetary relations among independent nation-states.

Preparing to rebuild the international economic system as World War II was still raging, 730 delegates from all 44 Allied nations gathered at the Mount Washington Hotel in Bretton Woods, New Hampshire, United States, for the United Nations Monetary and Financial Conference.

a. Bretton Woods system
b. 1921 recession
c. 100-year flood
d. 130-30 fund

78. _________ is sometimes referred to as _________, actually it means Economic Monetary Union.

First ideas of an economic and monetary union in Europe were raised well before establishing the European Communities. For example, already in the League of Nations, Gustav Stresemann asked in 1929 for a European currency (Link) against the background of an increased economic division due to a number of new nation states in Europe after WWI.

a. Euro Interbank Offered Rate
b. European Monetary System
c. Exchange rate mechanism
d. European Monetary Union

79. _________, 1st Baron Keynes was a renowned economist from Britain whose many ideas on economic and political theories as well as on many governments' monetary policies influenced America. He advocated a government that played an active role in the lives of people regarding business, economy, etc. In this role, the government would use fiscal measures to reduce the consequences of recessions, economic depressions and booms.

a. Adolph Fischer
b. Adam Smith
c. John Maynard Keynes
d. Adolf Hitler

80. An economic and _________ is a single market with a common currency. It is to be distinguished from a mere currency union , which does not involve a single market. This is the fifth stage of economic integration.

a. Customs union
b. Free trade zone
c. Commercial invoice
d. Monetary Union

81. A _________ is the massive selling of a country's currency assets by both domestic and foreign investors. Countries that utilize a fixed exchange rate are more susceptible to a _________ than countries utilizing a floating exchange rate. This is because of the large amount of reserves necessary to hold the fixed exchange rate in place at that fixed level.

a. 100-year flood
b. 130-30 fund
c. Currency crisis
d. Speculative attack

82. _________ theory is a branch of theoretical economics. It seeks to explain the behavior of supply, demand and prices in a whole economy with several or many markets. It is often assumed that agents are price takers and in that setting two common notions of equilibrium exist: Walrasian (or competitive) equilibrium, and its generalization; a price equilibrium with transfers.

a. Human capital
b. New Keynesian economics
c. Rational choice theory
d. General equilibrium

83. In economics, economic equilibrium is simply a state of the world where economic forces are balanced and in the absence of external influences the (equilibrium) values of economic variables will not change. It is the point at which quantity demanded and quantity supplied are equal. _________, for example, refers to a condition where a market price is established through competition such that the amount of goods or services sought by buyers is equal to the amount of goods or services produced by sellers.

a. Marketization
b. Regulated market
c. Product-Market Growth Matrix
d. Market equilibrium

84. _________ in economic theory is the use of modern economic tools to study problems that are traditionally in the province of political science.

In particular, it studies the behavior of politicians and government officials as mostly self-interested agents and their interactions in the social system either as such or under alternative constitutional rules. These can be represented a number of ways, including standard constrained utility maximization, game theory, or decision theory.

a. Paradox of voting
b. Public interest theory
c. Rational ignorance
d. Public choice

85. In economics, the term _________ of income or _________ refers to a simple economic model which describes the reciprocal circulation of income between producers and consumers. In the _________ model, the inter-dependent entities of producer and consumer are referred to as 'firms' and 'households' respectively and provide each other with factors in order to facilitate the flow of income. Firms provide consumers with goods and services in exchange for consumer expenditure and 'factors of production' from households.

a. 1921 recession
b. 100-year flood
c. 130-30 fund
d. Circular flow

1. The term _________ refers to economy-wide fluctuations in production or economic activity over several months or years. These fluctuations occur around a long-term growth trend, and typically involve shifts over time between periods of relatively rapid economic growth (expansion or boom), and periods of relative stagnation or decline (contraction or recession.)

These fluctuations are often measured using the growth rate of real gross domestic product.

a. Consumer theory
b. Tobit model
c. Business cycle
d. Nominal value

2. In economics, an _________ is any good or commodity, transported from one country to another country in a legitimate fashion, typically for use in trade. _________ goods or services are provided to foreign consumers by domestic producers. _________ is an important part of international trade.

a. ACEA agreement
b. ACCRA Cost of Living Index
c. AD-IA Model
d. Export

3. In macroeconomics, _________ is a condition of the national economy, where all or nearly all persons willing and able to work at the prevailing wages and working conditions are able to do so. It is defined either as 0% unemployment, literally, no unemployment (the rate of unemployment is the fraction of the work force unable to find work), as by James Tobin, or as the level of employment rates when there is no cyclical unemployment. It is defined by the majority of mainstream economists as being an acceptable level of natural unemployment above 0%, the discrepancy from 0% being due to non-cyclical types of unemployment.

a. Marginal propensity to consume
b. Full employment
c. Demand shock
d. Harrod-Johnson diagram

4. In economics, an _________ is any good (e.g. a commodity) or service brought into one country from another country in a legitimate fashion, typically for use in trade.It is a good that is brought in from another country for sale. _________ goods or services are provided to domestic consumers by foreign producers. An _________ in the receiving country is an export to the sending country.

a. Incoterms
b. Import quota
c. Economic integration
d. Import

5. _________ is a term used to collectively describe topics relating to the operations of firms with interests in multiple countries. Such firms are sometimes called multinational corporations . Well known MNCs include fast food companies McDonald's and Yum Brands, vehicle manufacturers such as General Motors and Toyota, consumer electronics companies like Samsung, LG and Sony, and energy companies such as ExxonMobil and BP.

a. ACCRA Cost of Living Index
b. International business
c. AD-IA Model
d. ACEA agreement

6. An _________ is an economy in which people, including businesses, can trade in goods and services with other people and businesses in the international community at large. This contrasts with a closed economy in which international trade cannot take place.

The act of selling goods or services to a foreign country is called exporting.

a. Attention work
b. Indicative planning
c. Information economy
d. Open economy

7. In economics, _________ refers to the ability of a party to produce a good or service using fewer real resources than another entity producing the same good or service..A party has an _________ when using the same input as another party, it can produce a greater output. Since _________ is determined by a simple comparison of labor productivities, it is possible for a a party to have no _________ in anything. It can be contrasted with the concept of comparative advantage which refers to the ability to produce a particular good at a lower opportunity cost.

a. Absolute advantage
b. ACCRA Cost of Living Index
c. Index number
d. International economics

8. In finance, _________ is investment originating from other countries.See Foreign direct investment.

a. Foreign investment
b. Demand side economics
c. Preclusive purchasing
d. Horizontal merger

9. _________ is a branch of economics that deals with the performance, structure, and behavior of a national or regional economy as a whole. Along with microeconomics, _________ is one of the two most general fields in economics. It is the study of the behavior and decision-making of entire economies.

a. Tobit model
b. Nominal value
c. New Trade Theory
d. Macroeconomics

10. In economics and finance, _________ is the change in total cost that arises when the quantity produced changes by one unit. It is the cost of producing one more unit of a good. Mathematically, the _________ function is expressed as the first derivative of the total cost (TC) function with respect to quantity (Q.)

a. Marginal cost
b. Variable cost
c. Khozraschyot
d. Quality costs

11. A _________ is the transfer of wealth from one party (such as a person or company) to another. A _________ is usually made in exchange for the provision of goods, services or both, or to fulfill a legal obligation.

The simplest and oldest form of _________ is barter, the exchange of one good or service for another.

a. Payment
b. Soft count
c. Social gravity
d. Going concern

12. In law and economics, the _________, describes the economic efficiency of an economic allocation or outcome in the presence of externalities. The theorem states that when trade in an externality is possible and there are no transaction costs, bargaining will lead to an efficient outcome regardless of the initial allocation of property rights. In practice, obstacles to bargaining or poorly defined property rights can prevent Coasian bargaining.

a. Means test
b. Prior appropriation water rights
c. General Mining Act of 1872
d. Coase theorem

13. _________ is a common concept in economics, and gives rise to derived concepts such as consumer debt. Generally _________ is defined by opposition to production. But the precise definition can vary because different schools of economists define production quite differently.

a. Cash or share options
b. Federal Reserve Bank Notes
c. Foreclosure data providers
d. Consumption

14. The _________ is a group of three respected economists who advise the President of the United States on economic policy. It is a part of the Executive Office of the President of the United States, and provides much of the economic policy of the White House. The council prepares the annual Economic Report of the President.

a. Council of Economic Advisers
b. Constrained Pareto optimality
c. Hybrid renewable energy systems
d. Federal Reserve Bank Notes

15. _________s is the social science that studies the production, distribution, and consumption of goods and services. The term _________s comes from the Ancient Greek οá¼°κονομΐα from οá¼¶κος (oikos, 'house') + νÏŒμος (nomos, 'custom' or 'law'), hence 'rules of the house(hold)'. Current _________ models developed out of the broader field of political economy in the late 19th century, owing to a desire to use an empirical approach more akin to the physical sciences.

a. Inflation
b. Economic
c. Energy economics
d. Opportunity cost

16. A _________ is an object whose consumption increases the utility of the consumer, for which the quantity demanded exceeds the quantity supplied at zero price. _________s are usually modeled as having diminishing marginal utility. The first individual purchase has high utility; the second has less.

a. Composite good
b. Pie method
c. Good
d. Merit good

17. In economics, economic output is divided into physical goods and intangible services. Consumption of _________ is assumed to produce utility. It is often used when referring to a _________ Tax.

a. Private good
b. Manufactured goods
c. Composite good
d. Goods and services

18. The balance of trade (or net exports, sometimes symbolized as NX) is the difference between the monetary value of exports and imports in an economy over a certain period of time. It is the relationship between a nation's imports and exports. A favorable balance of trade is known as a trade surplus and consists of exporting more than is imported; an unfavorable balance of trade is known as a _________ or, informally, a trade gap.

a. Demographics of India
b. Computational economic
c. Trade deficit
d. Complementary asset

19. In economics, the _________ measures the payments that flow between any individual country and all other countries. It is used to summarize all international economic transactions for that country during a specific time period, usually a year. The _________ is determined by the country's exports and imports of goods, services, and financial capital, as well as financial transfers.

a. Gross domestic product per barrel
b. Gross world product
c. Skyscraper Index
d. Balance of payments

20. Economics:

- _________,the desire to own something and the ability to pay for it
- _________ curve,a graphic representation of a _________ schedule
- _________ deposit, the money in checking accounts
- _________ pull theory,the theory that inflation occurs when _________ for goods and services exceeds existing supplies
- _________ schedule,a table that lists the quantity of a good a person will buy it each different price
- _________ side economics,the school of economics at believes government spending and tax cuts open economy by raising _________

.

a. Demand
b. Variability
c. McKesson ' Robbins scandal
d. Production

21. In algebra, a _________ is a function depending on n that associates a scalar, det(A), to an n×n square matrix A. The fundamental geometric meaning of a _________ is a scale factor for measure when A is regarded as a linear transformation. _________s are important both in calculus, where they enter the substitution rule for several variables, and in multilinear algebra.

For a fixed nonnegative integer n, there is a unique _________ function for the n×n matrices over any commutative ring R. In particular, this function exists when R is the field of real or complex numbers.

a. 1921 recession
b. 100-year flood
c. Determinant
d. 130-30 fund

22. _________ in economics refers to metrics and measures of output from production processes, per unit of input. Labor _________, for example, is typically measured as a ratio of output per labor-hour, an input. _________ may be conceived of as a metrics of the technical or engineering efficiency of production.

a. Piece work
b. Production-possibility frontier
c. Fordism
d. Productivity

23. The _________ or gross domestic income (GDI), a basic measure of an economy's economic performance, is the market value of all final goods and services produced within the borders of a nation in a year. _________ can be defined in three ways, all of which are conceptually identical. First, it is equal to the total expenditures for all final goods and services produced within the country in a stipulated period of time (usually a 365-day year.)

a. Gross domestic product
b. Market structure
c. Countercyclical
d. Monopolistic competition

24. In economics, the concept of the _________ refers to the decision-making time frame of a firm in which at least one factor of production is fixed. Costs which are fixed in the _________ have no impact on a firms decisions. For example a firm can raise output by increasing the amount of labour through overtime.

a. Productivity model
b. Hicks-neutral technical change
c. Product Pipeline
d. Short-run

25. In economics, _________ is the total demand for final goods and services in the economy (Y) at a given time and price level. It is the amount of goods and services in the economy that will be purchased at all possible price levels. This is the demand for the gross domestic product of a country when inventory levels are static.

a. Aggregate supply
b. Aggregate demand
c. Aggregation problem
d. Aggregate expenditure

26. The _________ refers to the change in import expenditure that occurs with a change in disposable income (income after taxes and transfers.) For example, if a household earns one extra dollar of disposable income, and the _________ is 0.2, then of that dollar, the household will spend 20 cents of that dollar on imported goods and services.

Mathematically, the _________ (MPI) function is expressed as the derivative of the import (I) function with respect to disposable income (Y.)

a. Hodrick-Prescott filter
b. Complex multiplier
c. Minimum wage
d. Marginal propensity to import

27. The _________ refers to the increase in saving (non-purchase of current goods and services) that results from an increase in income. For example, if a household earns one extra dollar, and the _________ is 0.35, then of that dollar, the household will spend 65 cents and save 35 cents. It can also go the other way, referring to the decrease in saving that results from a decrease in income.

a. Solow residual
b. Robertson lag
c. Marginal propensity to save
d. Real business cycle

28. In economics, the _________ is an empirical metric that quantifies induced consumption, the concept that the increase in personal consumer spending (consumption) that occurs with an increase in disposable income (income after taxes and transfers.) For example, if a household earns one extra dollar of disposable income, and the _________ is 0.65, then of that dollar, the household will spend 65 cents and save 35 cents.

Mathematically, the _________ (MPC) function is expressed as the derivative of the consumption (C) function with respect to disposable income (Y.)

a. Marginal propensity to import
b. Supply shock
c. Technology shock
d. Marginal propensity to consume

29. _________ is a misspelled phrase from Latin 'pro capite' phrase meaning per head with pro meaning 'per' or 'for each' and capite meaning 'head.' Both words together equate to the phrase 'for each head.'

It is usually used in the field of statistics to indicate the average per person for any given concern, such as income, crime rate, etc.

It is also used in wills to indicate that each of the named beneficiaries should receive, by devise or bequest, equal shares of the estate. This is in contrast to a per stirpes division, in which each branch of the inheriting family inherits an equal share of the estate.

a. Population statistics
b. False positive rate
c. Sargan test
d. Per capita

30. An _________, in economics, is the amount by which the real Gross domestic product exceeds potential GDP. The real GDP is also known as GDP 'adjusted for inflation', 'constant prices' GDP or 'constant dollar' GDP, because it measures the aggregate output in a country's income accounts in a given year, expressed in base-year prices. On the other hand, the potential GDP is the quantity of real GDP when a country's economy is at full-employment.

a. AD-IA Model
b. ACCRA Cost of Living Index
c. ACEA agreement
d. Inflationary gap

31. _________ is sometimes referred to as _________, actually it means Economic Monetary Union.

First ideas of an economic and monetary union in Europe were raised well before establishing the European Communities. For example, already in the League of Nations, Gustav Stresemann asked in 1929 for a European currency (Link) against the background of an increased economic division due to a number of new nation states in Europe after WWI.

a. Exchange rate mechanism
b. Euro Interbank Offered Rate
c. European Monetary Union
d. European Monetary System

32. A _________, sometimes called a pegged exchange rate, is a type of exchange rate regime wherein a currency's value is matched to the value of another single currency or to a basket of other currencies such as gold.

A _________ is usually used to stabilize the value of a currency, vis-a-vis the currency it is pegged to. This facilitates trade and investments between the two countries, and is especially useful for small economies where external trade forms a large part of their GDP.

a. Fixed exchange rate
b. Monetary economics
c. Leading indicators
d. Law of supply

33. _________ is a fee paid on borrowed assets. It is the price paid for the use of borrowed money , or, money earned by deposited funds . Assets that are sometimes lent with _________ include money, shares, consumer goods through hire purchase, major assets such as aircraft, and even entire factories in finance lease arrangements.

a. Interest
b. Insolvency
c. Asset protection
d. Internal debt

34. An _________ is the price a borrower pays for the use of money they do not own, for instance a small company might borrow from a bank to kick start their business, and the return a lender receives for deferring the use of funds, by lending it to the borrower. _________s are normally expressed as a percentage rate over the period of one year.

_________s targets are also a vital tool of monetary policy and are used to control variables like investment, inflation, and unemployment.

a. Arrow-Debreu model
b. ACCRA Cost of Living Index
c. Enterprise value
d. Interest rate

35. An economic and _________ is a single market with a common currency. It is to be distinguished from a mere currency union , which does not involve a single market. This is the fifth stage of economic integration.

a. Customs union
b. Free trade zone
c. Commercial invoice
d. Monetary Union

36. In finance, the _________s between two currencies specifies how much one currency is worth in terms of the other. It is the value of a foreign natione;s currency in terms of the home natione;s currency. For example an _________ of 102 Japanese yen to the United States dollar means that JPY 102 is worth the same as USD 1.

a. ACCRA Cost of Living Index
b. ACEA agreement
c. Interbank market
d. Exchange rate

37. _________ is exchange of capital, goods, and services across international borders or territories. In most countries, it represents a significant share of gross domestic product (GDP.) While _________ has been present throughout much of history , its economic, social, and political importance has been on the rise in recent centuries.

a. Incoterms
b. Intra-industry trade
c. Import license
d. International trade

38. The _________ of monetary management established the rules for commercial and financial relations among the world's major industrial states in the mid 20th Century. The _________ was the first example of a fully negotiated monetary order intended to govern monetary relations among independent nation-states.

Preparing to rebuild the international economic system as World War II was still raging, 730 delegates from all 44 Allied nations gathered at the Mount Washington Hotel in Bretton Woods, New Hampshire, United States, for the United Nations Monetary and Financial Conference.

a. 100-year flood
b. 130-30 fund
c. 1921 recession
d. Bretton Woods system

39. _________ is money accepted for exchange of goods in an economy. The prevalence of one money over another arises, usually, when a government designates through decrees that the government shall accept only particular notes and coins in payment for taxes. Typically, money of _________ consists of stamped coins and minted paper bills.

a. Local currency
b. Security thread
c. Totnes pound
d. Currency

40. _________ is the a method of technical and economic research of the systems for purpose to optimize a parity between system's consumer functions or properties and expenses to achieve those functions or properties.

This methodology for continuous perfection of production, industrial technologies, organizational structures was developed by Juryj Sobolev in 1948 at the 'Perm telephone factory'

- 1948 Juryj Sobolev - the first success in application of a method analysis at the 'Perm telephone factory' .
- 1949 - the first application for the invention as result of use of the new method.

Today in economically developed countries practically each enterprise or the company use methodology of the kind of functional-cost analysis as a practice of the quality management, most full satisfying to principles of standards of series ISO 9000.

- Interest of consumer not in products itself, but the advantage which it will receive from its usage.
- The consumer aspires to reduce his expenses
- Functions needed by consumer can be executed in the various ways, and, hence, with various efficiency and expenses. Among possible alternatives of realization of functions exist such in which the parity of quality and the price is the optimal for the consumer.

The goal of _________ is achievement of the highest consumer satisfaction of production at simultaneous decrease in all kinds of industrial expenses Classical _________ has three English synonyms - Value Engineering, Value Management, Value Analysis.

a. Staple financing
b. Function cost analysis
c. Monopoly wage
d. Willingness to pay

41. _________ is a term used in economics to describe how an economic quantity is related to economic fluctuations. It is the opposite of procyclical. However, it has more than one meaning.

a. Mathematical economics
b. Countercyclical
c. Law of comparative advantage
d. Price revolution

42. _________ is the increase in the amount of the goods and services produced by an economy over time. It is conventionally measured as the percent rate of increase in real gross domestic product, or real GDP. Growth is usually calculated in real terms, i.e. inflation-adjusted terms, in order to net out the effect of inflation on the price of the goods and services produced.

a. ACCRA Cost of Living Index
b. ACEA agreement
c. AD-IA Model
d. Economic growth

43. An autarky is an economy that is self-sufficient and does not take part in international trade, or severely limits trade with the outside world. Likewise the term refers to an ecosystem not affected by influences from the outside, which relies entirely on its own resources. In the economic meaning, it is also referred to as a _________.

a. Network Economy
b. Digital economy
c. Closed economy
d. Transition economy

44. A _________ occurs when an entity spends more money than it takes in. The opposite of a _________ is a budget surplus. Debt is essentially an accumulated flow of deficits.

a. Budget deficit
b. Lump-sum tax
c. Public Financial Management
d. Funding body

45. _________, or a _________ is the concept of a resulting effect (cf. cause and effect, arising from another action. In general terms, it is used to indicate that all human actions, particularly crime and sin, have profound effects.

a. Variability
b. Solved
c. Consequence
d. Rule

46. In finance, the _________ is the system that allows the transfer of money between savers and borrowers.

Put another way: the _________ is a set of complex and closely interconnected financial institutions, markets, instruments, services, practices, and transactions.

a. Lean consumption
b. Hedonimetry
c. Foreign investment
d. Financial system

47. _________, in economics, occurs when assets and/or money rapidly flow out of a country, due to an economic event that disturbs investors and causes them to lower their valuation of the assets in that country, or otherwise to lose confidence in its economic strength. This leads to a disappearance of wealth and is usually accompanied by a sharp drop in the exchange rate of the affected country (depreciation in a variable exchange rate regime, or a forced devaluation in a fixed exchange rate regime.)

This fall is particularly damaging when the capital belongs to the people of the affected country, because not only are the citizens now burdened by the loss of faith in the economy and devaluation of their currency, but probably also their assets have lost much of their nominal value.

a. Liquid capital
b. Capital formation
c. Capital flight
d. Firm-specific infrastructure

48. _________ is the act of leaving one's native country or region to settle in another. It is the same as immigration but from the perspective of the country of origin. Human movement before the establishment of political boundaries or within one state, is termed migration.

a. ACCRA Cost of Living Index
b. AD-IA Model
c. ACEA agreement
d. Emigration

49. _________ according to Onuoha (2007) is the practice of starting new organizations or revitalizing mature organizations, particularly new businesses generally in response to identified opportunities. _________ is often a difficult undertaking, as a vast majority of new businesses fail. Entrepreneurial activities are substantially different depending on the type of organization that is being started.

a. ACEA agreement
b. ACCRA Cost of Living Index
c. Entrepreneurship
d. Intrapreneurship

50. _________ to the arrival of new individuals into a habitat or population. It is a biological concept and is important in population ecology, differentiated from emigration and migration.

_________ is a modern phenomenon.

a. AD-IA Model
b. Immigration
c. ACCRA Cost of Living Index
d. ACEA agreement

51. _________ are legal property rights over creations of the mind, both artistic and commercial, and the corresponding fields of law. Under _________ law, owners are granted certain exclusive rights to a variety of intangible assets, such as musical, literary, and artistic works; ideas, discoveries and inventions; and words, phrases, symbols, and designs. Common types of _________ include copyrights, trademarks, patents, industrial design rights and trade secrets.

a. Expedited Funds Availability Act
b. Ease of Doing Business Index
c. Independent contractor
d. Intellectual property

52. In economics, the people in the _________ are the suppliers of labor. The _________ is all the nonmilitary people who are employed or unemployed. In 2005, the worldwide _________ was over 3 billion people.

a. Distributed workforce
b. Labor force
c. Grenelle agreements
d. Departmentalization

53. A _________ is the exclusive authority to determine how a resource is used, whether that resource is owned by government or by individuals. All economic goods have a _________s attribute. This attribute has three broad components

1. The right to use the good
2. The right to earn income from the good
3. The right to transfer the good to others

The concept of _________s as used by economists and legal scholars are related but distinct. The distinction is largely seen in the economists' focus on the ability of an individual or collective to control the use of the good.

a. Holder in due course
b. Post-sale restraint
c. Property right
d. High-reeve

54. In microeconomics, _________ is quite simply the conversion of inputs into outputs. It is an economic process that uses resources to create a good or service that is suitable for exchange. This can include manufacturing, storing, shipping, and packaging.

a. Production
b. Solved
c. MET
d. Red Guards

55. In economics, a _________ is a function that specifies the output of a firm, an industry, or an entire economy for all combinations of inputs. A meta-_________ compares the practice of the existing entities converting inputs X into output y to determine the most efficient practice _________ of the existing entities, whether the most efficient feasible practice production or the most efficient actual practice production. In either case, the maximum output of a technologically-determined production process is a mathematical function of input factors of production.

a. Short-run
b. Constant elasticity of substitution
c. Post-Fordism
d. Production function

56. A _________ is the minimum difference a person requires to be willing to take an uncertain bet, between the expected value of the bet and the certain value that he is indifferent to.

The certainty equivalent is the guaranteed payoff at which a person is 'indifferent' between accepting the guaranteed payoff and a higher but uncertain payoff. (It is the amount of the higher payout minus the _________.)

a. Workers compensation
b. Linear model
c. Ruin theory
d. Risk premium

57. _________ is a comparative concept of the ability and performance of a firm, sub-sector or country to sell and supply goods and/or services in a given market. Although widely used in economics and business management, the usefulness of the concept, particularly in the context of national _________, is vigorously disputed by economists, such as Paul Krugman .

The term may also be applied to markets, where it is used to refer to the extent to which the market structure may be regarded as perfectly competitive.

a. Countervailing duties
b. Competitiveness
c. Quota share
d. Debt moratorium

58. _________ is an economic concept with commonplace familiarity. It is the price that a good or service is offered at, or will fetch, in the marketplace. It is of interest mainly in the study of microeconomics.

a. Market price
b. Market anomaly
c. Paper trading
d. Noisy market hypothesis

59. _________ is the income of individuals or nations after adjusting for inflation. It is calculated by subtracting inflation from the nominal income. Real variables, such as _________, real GDP, and real interest rate are variables that are measured in physical units, while nominal variables such as nominal income, nominal GDP, and nominal interest rate are measured in monetary units.

a. Windfall gain
b. Family income
c. Net national income
d. Real income

60. The balance of trade (or net exports, sometimes symbolized as NX) is the difference between the monetary value of exports and imports in an economy over a certain period of time. It is the relationship between a nation's imports and exports. A favorable balance of trade is known as a _________ and consists of exporting more than is imported; an unfavorable balance of trade is known as a trade deficit or, informally, a trade gap.

a. Dividend unit
b. Business valuation standards
c. Trade surplus
d. Black-Scholes

61. Competition law, known in the United States as _________ law, has three main elements:

- prohibiting agreements or practices that restrict free trading and competition between business entities. This includes in particular the repression of cartels.
- banning abusive behaviour by a firm dominating a market, or anti-competitive practices that tend to lead to such a dominant position. Practices controlled in this way may include predatory pricing, tying, price gouging, refusal to deal, and many others.
- supervising the mergers and acquisitions of large corporations, including some joint ventures. Transactions that are considered to threaten the competitive process can be prohibited altogether, or approved subject to 'remedies' such as an obligation to divest part of the merged business or to offer licences or access to facilities to enable other businesses to continue competing.

The substance and practice of competition law varies from jurisdiction to jurisdiction. Protecting the interests of consumers (consumer welfare) and ensuring that entrepreneurs have an opportunity to compete in the market economy are often treated as important objectives. Competition law is closely connected with law on deregulation of access to markets, state aids and subsidies, the privatisation of state owned assets and the establishment of independent sector regulators. In recent decades, competition law has been viewed as a way to provide better public services.

a. Anti-Inflation Act
b. Antitrust
c. Intellectual property law
d. United Kingdom competition law

62. _________ in economics and business is the result of an exchange and from that trade we assign a numerical monetary value to a good, service or asset. If Alice trades Bob 4 apples for an orange, the _________ of an orange is 4 apples. Inversely, the _________ of an apple is 1/4 oranges.

a. Price book
b. Price
c. Premium pricing
d. Price war

63. The term '_________' refers to the concept of collecting information and attempting to spot a pattern in the information. In some fields of study, the term '_________' has more formally-defined meanings.

In project management _________ is a mathematical technique that uses historical results to predict future outcome.

a. Probit model
b. Coefficient of determination
c. Quantile regression
d. Trend analysis

64. _________ was an arrangement established in 1979 under the Jenkins European Commission where most nations of the European Economic Community (EEC) linked their currencies to prevent large fluctuations relative to one another.

After the collapse of the Bretton Woods system in 1971, most of the EEC countries agreed in 1972 to maintain stable exchange rates by preventing exchange fluctuations of more than 2.25% (the European 'currency snake'.) In March 1979, this system was replaced by the _________, and the European Currency Unit (ECU) was defined.

a. Euro Interbank Offered Rate
b. European Monetary Union
c. Exchange rate mechanism
d. European Monetary System

65. _________ in its classic form is defined as a company from one country making a physical investment into building a factory in another country. It is the establishment of an enterprise by a foreigner. Its definition can be extended to include investments made to acquire lasting interest in enterprises operating outside of the economy of the investor.

a. Financial Stability Forum
b. Federal Deposit Insurance Corporation
c. Non-governmental organization
d. Foreign direct investment

66. In economic theory, _________ is the competitive situation in any market where the conditions necessary for perfect competition are not satisfied. It is a market structure that does not meet the conditions of perfect competition.

Forms of _________ include:

- Monopoly, in which there is only one seller of a good.
- Oligopoly, in which there is a small number of sellers.
- Monopolistic competition, in which there are many sellers producing highly differentiated goods.
- Monopsony, in which there is only one buyer of a good.
- Oligopsony, in which there is a small number of buyers.

There may also be _________ in markets due to buyers or sellers lacking information about prices and the goods being traded.

There may also be _________ due to a time lag in a market.

a. ACEA agreement
b. AD-IA Model
c. ACCRA Cost of Living Index
d. Imperfect competition

67. A _________ secures the proper functioning of money by regulating economic agents, transaction types, and money supply.

_________s are traditionally formed by the policy decisions of individual governments and administrated as a domestic economic issue.

The current trend, however, is to use international trade and investment to alter the policy and legislation of individual governments.

a. Netting
b. Financial rand
c. Consumer basket
d. Monetary System

68. In neoclassical economics and microeconomics, _________ describes the perfect being a market in which there are many small firms, all producing homogeneous goods. In the short term, such markets are productively inefficient as output will not occur where mc is equal to ac, but allocatively efficient, as output under _________ will always occur where mc is equal to mr, and therefore where mc equals ar. However, in the long term, such markets are both allocatively and productively efficient.

a. General equilibrium
b. Co-operative economics
c. Perfect competition
d. Law of supply

69. A _________ is the massive selling of a country's currency assets by both domestic and foreign investors. Countries that utilize a fixed exchange rate are more susceptible to a _________ than countries utilizing a floating exchange rate. This is because of the large amount of reserves necessary to hold the fixed exchange rate in place at that fixed level.

a. Currency crisis
b. Speculative attack
c. 130-30 fund
d. 100-year flood

70. A _________, reserve bank, or monetary authority is the entity responsible for the monetary policy of a country or of a group of member states. It is a bank that can lend money to other banks in times of need. Its primary responsibility is to maintain the stability of the national currency and money supply, but more active duties include controlling subsidized-loan interest rates, and acting as a lender of last resort to the banking sector during times of financial crisis (private banks often being integral to the national financial system.)

a. 100-year flood
b. Central bank
c. 130-30 fund
d. 1921 recession

71. _________ has several particular meanings:

- in mathematics
  - _________ function
  - Euler _________
  - _________
  - _________ subgroup
  - method of _________s (partial differential equations)
- in physics and engineering
  - any _________ curve that shows the relationship between certain input- and output parameters, e.g.
  - an I-V or current-voltage _________ is the current in a circuit as a function of the applied voltage
  - Receiver-Operator _________
- in fiction
  - in Dungeons ' Dragons, _________ is another name for ability score

.

a. Technocracy
b. Russian financial crisis
c. Demand
d. Characteristic

72. _________ is a term used to describe how different aspects between economies are integrated. The basics of this theory were written by the Hungarian Economist Béla Balassa in the 1960s. As _________ increases, the barriers of trade between markets diminishes.

a. Import
b. Import license
c. Inward investment
d. Economic integration

73. The _________ is the official currency of 16 of the 27 member states of the European Union (EU.) The states, known collectively as the Eurozone, are Austria, Belgium, Cyprus, Finland, France, Germany, Greece, Ireland, Italy, Luxembourg, Malta, the Netherlands, Portugal, Slovakia, Slovenia, and Spain. The currency is also used in a further five European countries, with and without formal agreements and is consequently used daily by some 327 million Europeans.

a. Equity capital market
b. Import and Export Price Indices
c. Euro
d. IRS Code 3401

74. The _________ is an economic and political union of 27 member states, located primarily in Europe. It was established by the Treaty of Maastricht on 1 November 1993, upon the foundations of the pre-existing European Economic Community. With a population of almost 500 million, the _________ generates an estimated 30% share (US$18.4 trillion in 2008) of the nominal gross world product.

a. ACCRA Cost of Living Index
b. ACEA agreement
c. European Union
d. European Court of Justice

75. _________ is a term that refers both to:

- a formal discipline used to help appraise, or assess, the case for a project or proposal, which itself is a process known as project appraisal; and
- an informal approach to making decisions of any kind.

Under both definitions the process involves, whether explicitly or implicitly, weighing the total expected costs against the total expected benefits of one or more actions in order to choose the best or most profitable option. The formal process is often referred to as either CBA (_________) or BCost-benefit analysis

A hallmark of CBA is that all benefits and all costs are expressed in money terms, and are adjusted for the time value of money, so that all flows of benefits and flows of project costs over time (which tend to occur at different points in time) are expressed on a common basis in terms of their e;present value.e; Closely related, but slightly different, formal techniques include Cost-effectiveness analysis, Economic impact analysis, Fiscal impact analysis and Social Return on Investment(SROI) analysis. The latter builds upon the logic of _________, but differs in that it is explicitly designed to inform the practical decision-making of enterprise managers and investors focused on optimising their social and environmental impacts.

a. 100-year flood
b. Decision theory
c. 130-30 fund
d. Cost-benefit analysis

76. The _________ is one of the world's most important central banks, responsible for monetary policy covering the 16 member States of the Eurozone. It was established by the European Union (EU) in 1998 with its headquarters in Frankfurt, Germany.

The predecessor to the _________ was the European Monetary Institute .

a. ACEA agreement
b. ACCRA Cost of Living Index
c. AD-IA Model
d. European Central Bank

77. _________ is a broad label that refers to any individuals or households that use goods and services generated within the economy. The concept of a _________ is used in different contexts, so that the usage and significance of the term may vary.

Typically when business people and economists talk of _________s they are talking about person as _________, an aggregated commodity item with little individuality other than that expressed in the buy/not-buy decision.

a. 100-year flood
b. 1921 recession
c. 130-30 fund
d. Consumer

78. The term surplus is used in economics for several related quantities. The _________ is the amount that consumers benefit by being able to purchase a product for a price that is less than they would be willing to pay. The producer surplus is the amount that producers benefit by selling at a market price mechanism that is higher than they would be willing to sell for.

a. Microeconomic reform
b. Necessity good
c. Consumer surplus
d. Marginal rate of technical substitution

79. A _________ is a theoretical term that economists use to describe a market which is free from government intervention (i.e. no regulation, no subsidization, no single monetary system and no governmental monopolies.) In a _________, property rights are voluntarily exchanged at a price arranged solely by the mutual consent of sellers and buyers. By definition, buyers and sellers do not coerce each other, in the sense that they obtain each other's property without the use of physical force, threat of physical force, or fraud, nor is the coerced by a third party (such as by government via transfer payments) and they engage in trade simply because they both consent and believe that it is a good enough choice.

a. Third camp
b. Free market
c. Leninism
d. Delegation

1. In economics, _________ is the total supply of goods and services produced by a national economy during a specific time period. It is the total amount of goods and services in the economy available at all possible price levels.

a. Aggregate demand
b. Aggregation problem
c. Aggregate expenditure
d. Aggregate supply

2. In economic models, the _________ time frame assumes no fixed factors of production. Firms can enter or leave the marketplace, and the cost (and availability) of land, labor, raw materials, and capital goods can be assumed to vary. In contrast, in the short-run time frame, certain factors are assumed to be fixed, because there is not sufficient time for them to change.

a. Diseconomies of scale
b. Productivity world
c. Price/performance ratio
d. Long-run

3. In economics, a _________ is a general slowdown in economic activity over a sustained period of time, or a business cycle contraction. During _________s, many macroeconomic indicators vary in a similar way. Production as measured by Gross Domestic Product (GDP), employment, investment spending, capacity utilization, household incomes and business profits all fall during _________s.

a. Leading indicators
b. Recession
c. Treasury View
d. Monetary economics

4. In economics, the concept of the _________ refers to the decision-making time frame of a firm in which at least one factor of production is fixed. Costs which are fixed in the _________ have no impact on a firms decisions. For example a firm can raise output by increasing the amount of labour through overtime.

a. Productivity model
b. Hicks-neutral technical change
c. Short-run
d. Product Pipeline

5. In economics, the _________ measures the payments that flow between any individual country and all other countries. It is used to summarize all international economic transactions for that country during a specific time period, usually a year. The _________ is determined by the country's exports and imports of goods, services, and financial capital, as well as financial transfers.

a. Gross world product
b. Balance of payments
c. Gross domestic product per barrel
d. Skyscraper Index

6. A _________ is the transfer of wealth from one party (such as a person or company) to another. A _________ is usually made in exchange for the provision of goods, services or both, or to fulfill a legal obligation.

The simplest and oldest form of _________ is barter, the exchange of one good or service for another.

a. Payment
b. Soft count
c. Going concern
d. Social gravity

7. The _________ or gross domestic income (GDI), a basic measure of an economy's economic performance, is the market value of all final goods and services produced within the borders of a nation in a year. _________ can be defined in three ways, all of which are conceptually identical. First, it is equal to the total expenditures for all final goods and services produced within the country in a stipulated period of time (usually a 365-day year.)

a. Market structure
b. Gross domestic product
c. Monopolistic competition
d. Countercyclical

8. In economics, _________ refers to the highest level of real Gross Domestic Product output that can be sustained over the long term. The existence of a limit is due to natural and institutional constraints. If actual GDP rises and stays above _________, then (in the absence of wage and price controls) inflation tends to increase as demand exceeds supply.

a. Potential output
b. Monetary conditions index
c. Monetary policy reaction function
d. Fundamental psychological law

9. In algebra, a _________ is a function depending on n that associates a scalar, det(A), to an n×n square matrix A. The fundamental geometric meaning of a _________ is a scale factor for measure when A is regarded as a linear transformation. _________s are important both in calculus, where they enter the substitution rule for several variables, and in multilinear algebra.

For a fixed nonnegative integer n, there is a unique _________ function for the n×n matrices over any commutative ring R. In particular, this function exists when R is the field of real or complex numbers.

a. Determinant
b. 130-30 fund
c. 100-year flood
d. 1921 recession

10. In economics, _________ is a rise in the general level of prices of goods and services in an economy over a period of time. When the general price level rises, each unit of currency buys fewer goods and services; consequently, _________ is also a decline in the real value of money--a loss of purchasing power in the medium of exchange which is also the monetary unit of account in the economy. A chief measure of general price-level _________ is the general _________ rate, which is the percentage change in a general price index (normally the Consumer Price Index) over time.

a. Economic
b. Opportunity cost
c. Energy economics
d. Inflation

11. In economics, the _________ is a measure of inflation, the rate of increase of a price index (for example, a consumer price index.)It is the percentage rate of change in price level over time. The rate of decrease in the purchasing power of money is approximately equal.

It's used to calculate the real interest rate, as well as real increases in wages, and official measurements of this rate act as input variables to COLA adjustments and Inflation derivatives prices.

a. Equity value
b. Interest rate option
c. Edgeworth paradox
d. Inflation rate

12. In economics and finance, _________ is the change in total cost that arises when the quantity produced changes by one unit. It is the cost of producing one more unit of a good. Mathematically, the _________ function is expressed as the first derivative of the total cost (TC) function with respect to quantity (Q.)

a. Variable cost
b. Khozraschyot
c. Quality costs
d. Marginal cost

13. _________ is the term denoting either an entrance or changes which are inserted into a system and which activate/modify a process. It is an abstract concept, used in the modeling, system(s) design and system(s) exploitation. It is usually connected with other terms, e.g., _________ field, _________ variable, _________ parameter, _________ value, _________ signal, _________ device and _________ file.

a. Input
b. AD-IA Model
c. ACCRA Cost of Living Index
d. ACEA agreement

14. In microeconomics, _________ is quite simply the conversion of inputs into outputs. It is an economic process that uses resources to create a good or service that is suitable for exchange. This can include manufacturing, storing, shipping, and packaging.

a. Red Guards
b. MET
c. Production
d. Solved

15. In economics, _________ is the total demand for final goods and services in the economy (Y) at a given time and price level. It is the amount of goods and services in the economy that will be purchased at all possible price levels. This is the demand for the gross domestic product of a country when inventory levels are static.

a. Aggregate expenditure
b. Aggregation problem
c. Aggregate demand
d. Aggregate supply

16. _________ is widely regarded as the first modern school of economic thought. It is the idea that free markets can regulate themselves.Its major developers include Adam Smith, David Ricardo, Thomas Malthus and John Stuart Mill. Sometimes the definition of _________ is expanded to include William Petty, Johann Heinrich von Thünen.

a. Tendency of the rate of profit to fall
b. Schools of economic thought
c. Marginalism
d. Classical economics

17. _________ and Keynesian Theory) is a macroeconomic theory based on the ideas of 20th-century British economist John Maynard Keynes. _________ argues that private sector decisions sometimes lead to inefficient macroeconomic outcomes and therefore advocates active policy responses by the public sector, including monetary policy actions by the central bank and fiscal policy actions by the government to stabilize output over the business cycle.

The theories forming the basis of _________ were first presented in The General Theory of Employment, Interest and Money, published in 1936.

a. Deflation
b. Keynesian economics
c. Rational choice theory
d. Market failure

18. Economics:

- _________,the desire to own something and the ability to pay for it
- _________ curve,a graphic representation of a _________ schedule
- _________ deposit, the money in checking accounts
- _________ pull theory,the theory that inflation occurs when _________ for goods and services exceeds existing supplies
- _________ schedule,a table that lists the quantity of a good a person will buy it each different price
- _________ side economics,the school of economics at believes government spending and tax cuts open economy by raising _________

a. Demand
b. McKesson ' Robbins scandal
c. Production
d. Variability

19. _________s is the social science that studies the production, distribution, and consumption of goods and services. The term _________s comes from the Ancient Greek oá¼°κονομÎ¯α from oá¼¶κος (oikos, 'house') + vÏŒμος (nomos, 'custom' or 'law'), hence 'rules of the house(hold)'. Current _________ models developed out of the broader field of political economy in the late 19th century, owing to a desire to use an empirical approach more akin to the physical sciences.

a. Energy economics
b. Economic
c. Inflation
d. Opportunity cost

20. The _________ was a worldwide economic downturn starting in most places in 1929 and ending at different times in the 1930s or early 1940s for different countries. It was the largest and most important economic depression in the 20th century, and is used in the 21st century as an example of how far the world's economy can fall. The _________ originated in the United States; historians most often use as a starting date the stock market crash on October 29, 1929, known as Black Tuesday.

a. Jarrow March
b. British Empire Economic Conference
c. Wall Street Crash of 1929
d. Great Depression

21. Though there have been several definitions of voluntary and _________ in the economics literature, a simple distinction is often applied. Voluntary unemployment is attributed to the individual's decisions, whereas _________ exists because of the socio-economic environment (including the market structure, government intervention, and the level of aggregate demand) in which individuals operate. In these terms, much or most of frictional unemployment is voluntary, since it reflects individual search behavior.

a. AD-IA Model
b. ACCRA Cost of Living Index
c. Involuntary unemployment
d. ACEA agreement

22. In economics, the _________ is a historical inverse relation between the rate of unemployment and the rate of inflation in an economy. Stated simply, the lower the unemployment in an economy, the higher the rate of increase in nominal wages in the economy. Rate of Change of Wages against Unemployment, United Kingdom 1913-1948 from Phillips (1958)

William Phillips, a New Zealand born economist, wrote a paper in 1958 titled The Relationship between Unemployment and the Rate of Change of Money Wages in the United Kingdom 1861-1957, which was published in the quarterly journal Economica.

a. Lorenz curve
b. Demand curve
c. Phillips curve
d. Cost curve

23. _________ in economics and business is the result of an exchange and from that trade we assign a numerical monetary value to a good, service or asset. If Alice trades Bob 4 apples for an orange, the _________ of an orange is 4 apples. Inversely, the _________ of an apple is 1/4 oranges.

a. Premium pricing
b. Price war
c. Price book
d. Price

24. In economics, the people in the _________ are the suppliers of labor. The _________ is all the nonmilitary people who are employed or unemployed. In 2005, the worldwide _________ was over 3 billion people.

a. Departmentalization
b. Distributed workforce
c. Labor force
d. Grenelle agreements

25. A _________ is an economy based on the division of labor in which the prices of goods and services are determined in a free price system set by supply and demand. This is often contrasted with a planned economy, in which a central government determines the price of goods and services using a fixed price system. Market economies are contrasted with mixed economy where the price system is not entirely free but under some government control that is not extensive enough to constitute a planned economy.

a. Market economy
b. Nutritional Economics
c. Commons-based peer production
d. Network Economy

26. _________ is a concept with somewhat disparate meanings in several fields. It also has a common meaning which has a loose connection with some of those more definite meanings.

Casually, it is typically used to denote a lack of order, or purpose, or cause.

a. 100-year flood
b. Randomness
c. 1921 recession
d. 130-30 fund

27. Unemployment occurs when a person is available to work and seeking work but currently without work. The prevalence of unemployment is usually measured using the _________, which is defined as the percentage of those in the labor force who are unemployed. The _________ is also used in economic studies and economic indexes such as the United States' Conference Board's Index of Leading Indicators as a measure of the state of the macroeconomics.

a. ACEA agreement
b. ACCRA Cost of Living Index
c. AD-IA Model
d. Unemployment rate

28. Economists distinguish between various types of unemployment, including cyclical unemployment, _________, structural unemployment and classical unemployment. Some additional types of unemployment that are occasionally mentioned are seasonal unemployment, hardcore unemployment, and hidden unemployment. Real-world unemployment may combine different types.

a. Seasonal unemployment
b. Types of unemployment
c. Structural unemployment
d. Frictional unemployment

29. _________ was an American economist, statistician and public intellectual, and a recipient of the Nobel Memorial Prize in Economic Sciences. He is best known among scholars for his theoretical and empirical research, especially consumption analysis, monetary history and theory, and for his demonstration of the complexity of stabilization policy. A global public followed his restatement of a political philosophy that insisted on minimizing the role of government in favor of the private sector.

a. Milton Friedman
b. Adolph Fischer
c. Adolf Hitler
d. Adam Smith

30. _________ is the view within monetary economics that variation in the money supply has major influences on national output in the short run and the price level over longer periods and that objectives of monetary policy are best met by targeting the growth rate of the money supply.

_________ today is mainly associated with the work of Milton Friedman, who was among the generation of economists to accept Keynesian economics and then criticize it on his own terms. Friedman and Anna Schwartz wrote an influential book, Monetary History of the United States 1867-1960, and argued that 'inflation is always and everywhere a monetary phenomenon.' Friedman advocated a central bank policy aimed at keeping the supply and demand for money at equilibrium, as measured by growth in productivity and demand.

a. Historical school of economics
b. Complexity economics
c. Marginal revenue productivity theory of wages
d. Monetarism

31. Economists distinguish between various types of unemployment, including _________, frictional unemployment, structural unemployment and classical unemployment. Some additional types of unemployment that are occasionally mentioned are seasonal unemployment, hardcore unemployment, and hidden unemployment. Real-world unemployment may combine different types.

a. Types of unemployment
b. Structural unemployment
c. Seasonal unemployment
d. Cyclical unemployment

32. _________ is long-term and chronic unemployment arising from imbalances between the skills and other characteristics of workers in the market and the needs of employers. It involves a mismatch between workers looking for jobs and the vacancies available often despite the number of vacancies being similar to the number of unemployed people. In this case, the unemployed workers lack the specific skills required for the jobs, or are located in a different geographical region to the vacant jobs.

a. Seasonal unemployment
b. Types of unemployment
c. Frictional unemployment
d. Structural unemployment

33. _________ is a branch of economics that deals with the performance, structure, and behavior of a national or regional economy as a whole. Along with microeconomics, _________ is one of the two most general fields in economics. It is the study of the behavior and decision-making of entire economies.

a. Nominal value
b. Tobit model
c. New Trade Theory
d. Macroeconomics

34. _________, 1st Baron Keynes was a renowned economist from Britain whose many ideas on economic and political theories as well as on many governments' monetary policies influenced America. He advocated a government that played an active role in the lives of people regarding business, economy, etc. In this role, the government would use fiscal measures to reduce the consequences of recessions, economic depressions and booms.

a. Adam Smith
b. John Maynard Keynes
c. Adolph Fischer
d. Adolf Hitler

35. The _________, established in 1848, is the world's oldest futures and options exchange. More than 50 different options and futures contracts are traded by over 3,600 _________ members through open outcry and eTrading. Volumes at the exchange in 2003 were a record breaking 454 million contracts.

a. Chicago Board of Trade
b. 100-year flood
c. 130-30 fund
d. New York Mercantile Exchange

36. The _________ consists of a number of economic theories which describe the nature of the firm, company including its existence, its behaviour, and its relationship with the market

In simplified terms, the _________ aims to answer these questions:

1. Existence - why do firms emerge, why are not all transactions in the economy mediated over the market?
2. Boundaries - why the boundary between firms and the market is located exactly there? Which transactions are performed internally and which are negotiated on the market?
3. Organization - why are firms structured in such specific way? What is the interplay of formal and informal relationships?

Despite looking simple, these questions are not answered by the established economic theory, which usually views firms as given, and treats them as black boxes without any internal structure.

The First World War period saw a change of emphasis in economic theory away from industry-level analysis which mainly included analysing markets to analysis at the level of the firm, as it became increasingly clear that perfect competition was no longer an adequate model of how firms behaved. Economic theory till then had focussed on trying to understand markets alone and there had been little study on understanding why firms or organisations exist.

a. Theory of the firm
b. Technology gap
c. Policy Ineffectiveness Proposition
d. Khazzoom-Brookes postulate

37. A _________ is a group of people who share or are motivated by at least one common issue or interest, or work together on a specific project(s) to achieve a common objective. _________s are also characterised by attempts to share and exercise political and social power and to make decisions on a consensus-driven and egalitarian basis. _________s differ from cooperatives in that they are not necessarily focused upon an economic benefit or saving (but can be that as well.)

a. 1921 recession
b. 100-year flood
c. 130-30 fund
d. Collective

38. In organized labor, _________ is the method whereby workers organize together (usually in unions) to meet, converse, and negotiate upon the work conditions with their employers normally resulting in a written contract setting forth the wages, hours, and other conditions to be observed for a stipulated period.It is the practice in which union and company representatives meet to negotiate a new labor contract. In various national labor and employment law contexts, _________ takes on a more specific legal meaning and so, in a broad sense, however, it is the coming together of workers to negotiate their employment.

A collective agreement is a labor contract between an employer and one or more unions.

a. Designated Suppliers Program
b. Strikebreaker
c. Collective bargaining
d. Demarcation dispute

39. _________ data refers to selected population characteristics as used in government, marketing or opinion research, or the _________ profiles used in such research. Note the distinction from the term 'demography' Commonly-used _________s include race, age, income, disabilities, mobility (in terms of travel time to work or number of vehicles available), educational attainment, home ownership, employment status, and even location.

a. Demographic warfare
b. Generation Z
c. NEET
d. Demographic

40. In finance, the _________ of a financial asset measures the sensitivity of the asset's price to interest rate movements. There are various definitions of _________ and derived quantities, discussed below. If not otherwise specified, '_________' generally means the Macaulay _________, as defined below.

a. Time value of money
b. 100-year flood
c. Newtonian time
d. Duration

41. The term _________ refers to economy-wide fluctuations in production or economic activity over several months or years. These fluctuations occur around a long-term growth trend, and typically involve shifts over time between periods of relatively rapid economic growth (expansion or boom), and periods of relative stagnation or decline (contraction or recession.)

These fluctuations are often measured using the growth rate of real gross domestic product.

a. Consumer theory
b. Nominal value
c. Tobit model
d. Business cycle

42. _________ is the shortage of common things such as food, clothing, shelter and safe drinking water, all of which determine the quality of life. It may also include the lack of access to opportunities such as education and employment which aid the escape from _________ and/or allow one to enjoy the respect of fellow citizens. According to Mollie Orshansky who developed the _________ measurements used by the U.S. government, 'to be poor is to be deprived of those goods and services and pleasures which others around us take for granted.' Ongoing debates over causes, effects and best ways to measure _________, directly influence the design and implementation of _________-reduction programs and are therefore relevant to the fields of public administration and international development.

a. Liberal welfare reforms
b. Growth Elasticity of Poverty
c. Poverty map
d. Poverty

43. The _________ is the central banking system of the United States. Created in 1913 by the enactment of the Federal Reserve Act (signed by Woodrow Wilson), it is a quasi-public and quasi-private (government entity with private components) banking system that comprises (1) the presidentially appointed Board of Governors of the _________ in Washington, D.C.; (2) the Federal Open Market Committee; (3) twelve regional Federal Reserve Banks located in major cities throughout the nation acting as fiscal agents for the U.S. Treasury, each with its own nine-member board of directors; (4) numerous other private U.S. member banks, which subscribe to required amounts of non-transferable stock in their regional Federal Reserve Banks; and (5) various advisory councils. Since February 2006, Ben Bernanke has served as the Chairman of the Board of Governors of the _________.

a. Federal Reserve System Open Market Account
b. Federal Reserve System
c. Term auction facility
d. Monetary Policy Report to the Congress

44. A _________ is the lowest hourly, daily or monthly wage that employers may legally pay to employees or workers. Equivalently, it is the lowest wage at which workers may sell their labor. Although _________ laws are in effect in a great many jurisdictions, there are differences of opinion about the benefits and drawbacks of a _________.

a. Marginal propensity to consume
b. Minimum wage
c. Permanent war economy
d. Microfoundations

45. A _________, reserve bank, or monetary authority is the entity responsible for the monetary policy of a country or of a group of member states. It is a bank that can lend money to other banks in times of need. Its primary responsibility is to maintain the stability of the national currency and money supply, but more active duties include controlling subsidized-loan interest rates, and acting as a lender of last resort to the banking sector during times of financial crisis (private banks often being integral to the national financial system.)

a. 1921 recession
b. 100-year flood
c. 130-30 fund
d. Central Bank

46. In economics, _________ is the art or science of controlling economic demand to avoid a recession. In natural resources management and environmental policy more generally, it refers to policies to control consumer demand for environmentally sensitive or harmful goods such as water and energy. Within manufacturing firms the term is used to describe the activities of demand forecasting, planning and order fulfillment.

a. Cobra effect
b. Demand management
c. Fiscal imbalance
d. Peak-load pricing

47. The _________ is one of the world's most important central banks, responsible for monetary policy covering the 16 member States of the Eurozone. It was established by the European Union (EU) in 1998 with its headquarters in Frankfurt, Germany.

The predecessor to the _________ was the European Monetary Institute .

a. ACCRA Cost of Living Index
b. AD-IA Model
c. European Central Bank
d. ACEA agreement

48. _________ was an arrangement established in 1979 under the Jenkins European Commission where most nations of the European Economic Community (EEC) linked their currencies to prevent large fluctuations relative to one another.

After the collapse of the Bretton Woods system in 1971, most of the EEC countries agreed in 1972 to maintain stable exchange rates by preventing exchange fluctuations of more than 2.25% (the European 'currency snake'.) In March 1979, this system was replaced by the _________, and the European Currency Unit (ECU) was defined.

a. Euro Interbank Offered Rate
b. Exchange rate mechanism
c. European Monetary Union
d. European Monetary System

49. A _________ secures the proper functioning of money by regulating economic agents, transaction types, and money supply.

_________s are traditionally formed by the policy decisions of individual governments and administrated as a domestic economic issue.

The current trend, however, is to use international trade and investment to alter the policy and legislation of individual governments.

a. Netting
b. Consumer basket
c. Financial rand
d. Monetary System

50. The term _________s refers to wages that have been adjusted for inflation. This term is used in contrast to nominal wages or unadjusted wages.

The use of adjusted figures is in undertaking some form of economic analysis.

a. Real wage
b. Living wage
c. Profit sharing
d. Federal Wage System

51. There are two main interpretations of the idea of a _________:

- A model in which the state assumes primary responsibility for the welfare of its citizens. This responsibility in theory ought to be comprehensive, because all aspects of welfare are considered and universally applied to citizens as a 'right'. _________ can also mean the creation of a 'social safety net' of minimum standards of varying forms of welfare. Here is found some confusion between a '_________' and a 'welfare society' in common debate about the definition of the term.
- The provision of welfare in society. In many '_________s', especially in continental Europe, welfare is not actually provided by the state, but by a combination of independent, voluntary, mutualist and government services. The functional provider of benefits and services may be a central or state government, a state-sponsored company or agency, a private corporation, a charity or another form of non-profit organization. However, this phenomenon has been more appropriately termed a 'welfare society,' and the term 'welfare system' has been used to describe the range of _________ and welfare society mixes that are found.

The English term '_________' is believed by Asa Briggs to have been coined by Archbishop William Temple during the Second World War, contrasting wartime Britain with the 'warfare state' of Nazi Germany. Friedrich Hayek contends that the term derived from the older German word Wohlfahrtsstaat, which itself was used by nineteenth century historians to describe a variant of the ideal of Polizeistaat . It was fully developed by the German academic Sozialpolitiker--'socialists of the chair'--from 1870 and first implemented through Bismarck's 'state socialism'. Bismarck's policies have also been seen as the creation of a _________.

a. 1921 recession
b. 100-year flood
c. 130-30 fund
d. Welfare state

1. In law and economics, the _________, describes the economic efficiency of an economic allocation or outcome in the presence of externalities. The theorem states that when trade in an externality is possible and there are no transaction costs, bargaining will lead to an efficient outcome regardless of the initial allocation of property rights. In practice, obstacles to bargaining or poorly defined property rights can prevent Coasian bargaining.

a. Prior appropriation water rights
b. Means test
c. General Mining Act of 1872
d. Coase theorem

2. _________ is a broad label that refers to any individuals or households that use goods and services generated within the economy. The concept of a _________ is used in different contexts, so that the usage and significance of the term may vary.

Typically when business people and economists talk of _________s they are talking about person as _________, an aggregated commodity item with little individuality other than that expressed in the buy/not-buy decision.

a. 100-year flood
b. Consumer
c. 1921 recession
d. 130-30 fund

3. A _________ is a measure of the average price of consumer goods and services purchased by households. A _________ measures a price change for a constant market basket of goods and services from one period to the next within the same area (city, region, or nation.) It is a price index determined by measuring the price of a standard group of goods meant to represent the typical market basket of a typical urban consumer.

a. CPI
b. Consumer price index
c. Cost-of-living index
d. Lipstick index

4. The _________ or gross domestic income (GDI), a basic measure of an economy's economic performance, is the market value of all final goods and services produced within the borders of a nation in a year. _________ can be defined in three ways, all of which are conceptually identical. First, it is equal to the total expenditures for all final goods and services produced within the country in a stipulated period of time (usually a 365-day year.)

a. Monopolistic competition
b. Market structure
c. Countercyclical
d. Gross domestic product

5. _________ in its literal sense is the process of transformation of local or regional phenomena into global ones. It can be described as a process by which the people of the world are unified into a single society and function together.

This process is a combination of economic, technological, sociocultural and political forces.

a. Globally Integrated Enterprise
b. Global Cosmopolitanism
c. Helsinki Process on Globalisation and Democracy
d. Globalization

6. In economics, the _________ is a historical inverse relation between the rate of unemployment and the rate of inflation in an economy. Stated simply, the lower the unemployment in an economy, the higher the rate of increase in nominal wages in the economy. Rate of Change of Wages against Unemployment, United Kingdom 1913-1948 from Phillips (1958)

William Phillips, a New Zealand born economist, wrote a paper in 1958 titled The Relationship between Unemployment and the Rate of Change of Money Wages in the United Kingdom 1861-1957, which was published in the quarterly journal Economica.

a. Cost curve
b. Lorenz curve
c. Demand curve
d. Phillips curve

7. In statistics, a _________ is a value that allows data to be measured over time in terms of some base period ussually through a price index in order to distinguish between changes in the money value of GNP which result from a change in prices and those which result from a change in physical output. It is the measure of the price level for some quantity. A _________ serves as a price index in which the effects of inflation are nulled.

a. Market microstructure
b. Contingent employment
c. Blanket order
d. Deflator

8. In economics, _________ is a rise in the general level of prices of goods and services in an economy over a period of time. When the general price level rises, each unit of currency buys fewer goods and services; consequently, _________ is also a decline in the real value of money--a loss of purchasing power in the medium of exchange which is also the monetary unit of account in the economy. A chief measure of general price-level _________ is the general _________ rate, which is the percentage change in a general price index (normally the Consumer Price Index) over time.

a. Inflation
b. Energy economics
c. Economic
d. Opportunity cost

9. _________ in economics and business is the result of an exchange and from that trade we assign a numerical monetary value to a good, service or asset. If Alice trades Bob 4 apples for an orange, the _________ of an orange is 4 apples. Inversely, the _________ of an apple is 1/4 oranges.

a. Premium pricing
b. Price
c. Price book
d. Price war

10. A _________ is a normalized average (typically a weighted average) of prices for a given class of goods or services in a given region, during a given interval of time. It is a statistic designed to help to compare how these prices, taken as a whole, differ between time periods or geographical locations.

Price indices have several potential uses.

a. Product sabotage
b. Transactional Net Margin Method
c. Price index
d. Two-part tariff

11. In microeconomics, _________ is quite simply the conversion of inputs into outputs. It is an economic process that uses resources to create a good or service that is suitable for exchange. This can include manufacturing, storing, shipping, and packaging.

a. Production
b. Red Guards
c. MET
d. Solved

12. In economics, the _________ is a measure of inflation, the rate of increase of a price index (for example, a consumer price index.)It is the percentage rate of change in price level over time. The rate of decrease in the purchasing power of money is approximately equal.

It's used to calculate the real interest rate, as well as real increases in wages, and official measurements of this rate act as input variables to COLA adjustments and Inflation derivatives prices.

a. Interest rate option
b. Edgeworth paradox
c. Inflation rate
d. Equity value

13. _________, 1st Baron Keynes was a renowned economist from Britain whose many ideas on economic and political theories as well as on many governments' monetary policies influenced America. He advocated a government that played an active role in the lives of people regarding business, economy, etc. In this role, the government would use fiscal measures to reduce the consequences of recessions, economic depressions and booms.

a. Adolph Fischer
b. Adam Smith
c. Adolf Hitler
d. John Maynard Keynes

14. _________s is the social science that studies the production, distribution, and consumption of goods and services. The term _________s comes from the Ancient Greek οἀ¼°κονομΐα from οἀ¼¶κος (oikos, 'house') + νΪŒμος (nomos, 'custom' or 'law'), hence 'rules of the house(hold)'. Current _________ models developed out of the broader field of political economy in the late 19th century, owing to a desire to use an empirical approach more akin to the physical sciences.

a. Energy economics
b. Opportunity cost
c. Inflation
d. Economic

15. _________ refers to the actions that governments take in the economic field. It covers the systems for setting interest rates and government deficit as well as the labour market, national ownership, and many other areas of government.

Such policies are often influenced by international institutions like the International Monetary Fund or World Bank as well as political beliefs and the consequent policies of parties.

a. Economic policy
b. ACCRA Cost of Living Index
c. AD-IA Model
d. ACEA agreement

16. A _________ is a hypothetical measure of overall prices for some set of goods and services, in a given region during a given interval, normalized relative to some base set. Typically, a _________ is approximated with a price index.

The classical dichotomy is the assumption that there is a relatively clean distinction between overall increases or decreases in prices and underlying, e;reale; economic variables.

a. Discretionary spending
b. Discouraged worker
c. Price elasticity of supply
d. Price level

17. The term _________s refers to wages that have been adjusted for inflation. This term is used in contrast to nominal wages or unadjusted wages.

The use of adjusted figures is in undertaking some form of economic analysis.

a. Federal Wage System
b. Living wage
c. Real wage
d. Profit sharing

18. _________ is an economic concept with commonplace familiarity. It is the price that a good or service is offered at, or will fetch, in the marketplace. It is of interest mainly in the study of microeconomics.

a. Market anomaly
b. Market price
c. Noisy market hypothesis
d. Paper trading

19. Competition law, known in the United States as _________ law, has three main elements:

- prohibiting agreements or practices that restrict free trading and competition between business entities. This includes in particular the repression of cartels.
- banning abusive behaviour by a firm dominating a market, or anti-competitive practices that tend to lead to such a dominant position. Practices controlled in this way may include predatory pricing, tying, price gouging, refusal to deal, and many others.
- supervising the mergers and acquisitions of large corporations, including some joint ventures. Transactions that are considered to threaten the competitive process can be prohibited altogether, or approved subject to 'remedies' such as an obligation to divest part of the merged business or to offer licences or access to facilities to enable other businesses to continue competing.

The substance and practice of competition law varies from jurisdiction to jurisdiction. Protecting the interests of consumers (consumer welfare) and ensuring that entrepreneurs have an opportunity to compete in the market economy are often treated as important objectives. Competition law is closely connected with law on deregulation of access to markets, state aids and subsidies, the privatisation of state owned assets and the establishment of independent sector regulators. In recent decades, competition law has been viewed as a way to provide better public services.

a. United Kingdom competition law
b. Intellectual property law
c. Anti-Inflation Act
d. Antitrust

20. In economics, the _________ measures the payments that flow between any individual country and all other countries. It is used to summarize all international economic transactions for that country during a specific time period, usually a year. The _________ is determined by the country's exports and imports of goods, services, and financial capital, as well as financial transfers.

a. Skyscraper Index
b. Gross domestic product per barrel
c. Gross world product
d. Balance of payments

21. A _________, reserve bank, or monetary authority is the entity responsible for the monetary policy of a country or of a group of member states. It is a bank that can lend money to other banks in times of need. Its primary responsibility is to maintain the stability of the national currency and money supply, but more active duties include controlling subsidized-loan interest rates, and acting as a lender of last resort to the banking sector during times of financial crisis (private banks often being integral to the national financial system.)

a. 130-30 fund
b. 100-year flood
c. 1921 recession
d. Central bank

22. In economics, _________ is inflation that is very high or 'out of control', a condition in which prices increase rapidly as a currency loses its value. Definitions used by the media vary from a cumulative inflation rate over three years approaching 100% to 'inflation exceeding 50% a month.' In informal usage the term is often applied to much lower rates. As a rule of thumb, normal inflation is reported per year, but _________ is often reported for much shorter intervals, often per month.

a. 130-30 fund
b. 100-year flood
c. 1921 recession
d. Hyperinflation

23. A _________ is the transfer of wealth from one party (such as a person or company) to another. A _________ is usually made in exchange for the provision of goods, services or both, or to fulfill a legal obligation.

The simplest and oldest form of _________ is barter, the exchange of one good or service for another.

a. Social gravity
b. Soft count
c. Going concern
d. Payment

24. In business and accounting, _________ are everything of value that is owned by a person or company. It is a claim on the property your income of a borrower. The balance sheet of a firm records the monetary value of the _________ owned by the firm.

a. ACEA agreement
b. Assets
c. Amortization schedule
d. ACCRA Cost of Living Index

25. In economics, _________ is a sustained decrease in the general price level of goods and services. _________ occurs when the annual inflation rate falls below zero percent, resulting in an increase in the real value of money -- a negative inflation rate. This should not be confused with disinflation, a slow-down in the inflation rate (i.e. when the inflation decreases, but still remains positive.)

a. Tobit model
b. Price revolution
c. Deflation
d. Literacy rate

26. _________ is a fee paid on borrowed assets. It is the price paid for the use of borrowed money , or, money earned by deposited funds . Assets that are sometimes lent with _________ include money, shares, consumer goods through hire purchase, major assets such as aircraft, and even entire factories in finance lease arrangements.

a. Internal debt
b. Asset protection
c. Interest
d. Insolvency

27. An _________ is the price a borrower pays for the use of money they do not own, for instance a small company might borrow from a bank to kick start their business, and the return a lender receives for deferring the use of funds, by lending it to the borrower. _________s are normally expressed as a percentage rate over the period of one year.

_________s targets are also a vital tool of monetary policy and are used to control variables like investment, inflation, and unemployment.

a. Enterprise value
b. Arrow-Debreu model
c. Interest rate
d. ACCRA Cost of Living Index

28. Market _________ is a business, economics or investment term that refers to an asset's ability to be easily converted through an act of buying or selling without causing a significant movement in the price and with minimum loss of value. Money, or cash on hand, is the most liquid asset. An act of exchange of a less liquid asset with a more liquid asset is called liquidation.

a. 100-year flood
b. 1921 recession
c. 130-30 fund
d. Liquidity

29. The term _________ is used in macroeconomics to refer to a situation where a country's nominal interest rate has been lowered nearly to or equal to zero to avoid a recession, but the liquidity in the market created by these low interest rates does not stimulate the economy to full employment. In this situation, any further increase in the money supply will not stimulate the economy any further. This is because any further injection of liquidity will no longer lower the nominal interest rate, as the nominal interest rate cannot drop below zero.

a. Minimum wage
b. Liquidity trap
c. Macroeconomic models
d. Robertson lag

30. In finance and economics _________ or nominal rate of interest refers to the rate of interest before adjustment for inflation (in contrast with the real interest rate); or, for interest rates 'as stated' without adjustment for the full effect of compounding (also referred to as the nominal annual rate.) An interest rate is called nominal if the frequency of compounding (e.g. a month) is not identical to the basic time unit (normally a year.)

The real interest rate includes compensation for the lender's lost value due to inflation, whereas the _________ excludes inflation.

a. Nominal interest rate
b. Risk-free interest rate
c. London Interbank Offered Rate
d. Fixed interest

31. The '_________' is approximately the nominal interest rate minus the inflation rate Since the inflation rate over the course of a loan is not known initially, volatility in inflation represents a risk to both the lender and the borrower.

In economics and finance, an individual who lends money for repayment at a later point in time expects to be compensated for the time value of money, or not having the use of that money while it is lent.

a. Reflation
b. Core inflation
c. Cost-push inflation
d. Real interest rate

32. The term _________ refers to government debt, expenditures and revenues, or to finance (particularly financial revenue) in general.

- _________ deficit is the budget deficit of federal or local government
- _________ policy is the discretionary spending of governments. Contrasts with monetary policy.
- _________ year and _________ quarter are reporting periods for firms and other agencies.

.

a. Bucket shop
b. Drawdown
c. Procter ' Gamble
d. Fiscal

33. In economics, _________ is the use of government spending and revenue collection to influence the economy.

_________ can be contrasted with the other main type of economic policy, monetary policy, which attempts to stabilize the economy by controlling interest rates and the supply of money. The two main instruments of _________ are government spending and taxation.

a. Fiscalism
b. Sustainable investment rule
c. 100-year flood
d. Fiscal policy

34. In economics, _________ is how a natione;s total economy is distributed among its population. ._________ has always been a central concern of economic theory and economic policy. Classical economists such as Adam Smith, Thomas Malthus and David Ricardo were mainly concerned with factor _________, that is, the distribution of income between the main factors of production, land, labour and capital.

a. Equipment trust certificate
b. Eco commerce
c. Authorised capital
d. Income distribution

35. In economics, _________ is the transfer of income, wealth or property from some individuals to others.

One premise of _________ is that money should be distributed to benefit the poorer members of society, and that the rich have an obligation to assist the poor, thus creating a more financially egalitarian society. Another argument is that the rich exploit the poor or otherwise gain unfair benefits.

a. Redistribution
b. 100-year flood
c. 1921 recession
d. 130-30 fund

36. The _________ is an economic term, referring to an increase in spending that accompanies an increase or perceived increase in wealth.

The effect would cause changes in the amounts and composition of consumer consumption caused by changes in consumer wealth. People should spend more when one of two things is true: when people actually are richer (by objective measurement, for example, a bonus or a pay raise at work, which would be an income effect), or when people perceive themselves to be 'richer' (for example, the assessed value of their home increases, or a stock they own has gone up in price recently.)

a. 100-year flood
b. Wealth effect
c. 130-30 fund
d. Wealth condensation

37. _________ is a term that refers both to:

- a formal discipline used to help appraise, or assess, the case for a project or proposal, which itself is a process known as project appraisal; and
- an informal approach to making decisions of any kind.

Under both definitions the process involves, whether explicitly or implicitly, weighing the total expected costs against the total expected benefits of one or more actions in order to choose the best or most profitable option. The formal process is often referred to as either CBA (_________) or BCost-benefit analysis

A hallmark of CBA is that all benefits and all costs are expressed in money terms, and are adjusted for the time value of money, so that all flows of benefits and flows of project costs over time (which tend to occur at different points in time) are expressed on a common basis in terms of their e;present value.e; Closely related, but slightly different, formal techniques include Cost-effectiveness analysis, Economic impact analysis, Fiscal impact analysis and Social Return on Investment(SROI) analysis. The latter builds upon the logic of _________, but differs in that it is explicitly designed to inform the practical decision-making of enterprise managers and investors focused on optimising their social and environmental impacts.

a. 130-30 fund
b. 100-year flood
c. Decision theory
d. Cost-benefit analysis

38. _________ is a situation in which the limited resources of a firm are allocated in accordance with the wishes of consumers. An allocatively efficient economy produces an 'optimal mix' of commodities. A firm is allocatively efficient when its price is equal to its marginal costs (that is, P = MC) in a perfect market.

a. Economic efficiency
b. ACCRA Cost of Living Index
c. ACEA agreement
d. Allocative efficiency

39. A _________ is message sent to consumers and producers in the form of a price charged for a commodity; this is seen as indicating a signal for producers to increase supplies and/or consumers to reduce demand.

For example, in a free price system, rising prices may indicate a shortage of supply, increase in demand, or a rise in input costs. Regardless of the underlying reason--and without the consumer needing to know the cause--the price increase communicates the notion that consumer demand (at this new, higher price) should recede or that supplies should increase.

a. Market demand schedule
b. Threshold population
c. Mohring effect
d. Price signal

40. To _________ is to impose a financial charge or other levy upon a taxpayer by a state or the functional equivalent of a state.

_________es are also imposed by many subnational entities. _________es consist of direct _________ or indirect _________, and may be paid in money or as its labour equivalent (often but not always unpaid.)

a. 100-year flood
b. Tax
c. 130-30 fund
d. 1921 recession

41. _________ are the divisions at which tax rates change in a progressive tax system (or an explicitly regressive tax system, although this is much rarer.) Essentially, they are the cutoff values for taxable income -- income past a certain point will be taxed at a higher rate.

a. Disposable income
b. Tax farming
c. Popiwek
d. Tax brackets

42. In economics, _________ is the total demand for final goods and services in the economy (Y) at a given time and price level. It is the amount of goods and services in the economy that will be purchased at all possible price levels. This is the demand for the gross domestic product of a country when inventory levels are static.

a. Aggregate supply
b. Aggregation problem
c. Aggregate expenditure
d. Aggregate demand

43. _________ arises when aggregate demand in an economy outpaces aggregate supply. It involves inflation rising as real gross domestic product rises and unemployment falls, as the economy moves along the Phillips curve. This is commonly described as 'too much money chasing too few goods'.

a. Kinked demand
b. Kinked demand curve
c. Marshallian demand function
d. Demand-pull inflation

44. _________ is widely regarded as the first modern school of economic thought. It is the idea that free markets can regulate themselves.Its major developers include Adam Smith, David Ricardo, Thomas Malthus and John Stuart Mill. Sometimes the definition of _________ is expanded to include William Petty, Johann Heinrich von Thünen.

a. Tendency of the rate of profit to fall
b. Schools of economic thought
c. Marginalism
d. Classical economics

45. Economics:

- _________,the desire to own something and the ability to pay for it
- _________ curve,a graphic representation of a _________ schedule
- _________ deposit, the money in checking accounts
- _________ pull theory,the theory that inflation occurs when _________ for goods and services exceeds existing supplies
- _________ schedule,a table that lists the quantity of a good a person will buy it each different price
- _________ side economics,the school of economics at believes government spending and tax cuts open economy by raising _________

.

a. Production
b. Variability
c. McKesson ' Robbins scandal
d. Demand

46. _________ is a concept coined by structuralist inflation theorists. It refers to a situation where all prices in an economy are continuously adjusted with relation to a price index by force of contracts.

Changes in price indices trigger changes in prices of goods.

a. Incomes policies
b. Inflationary Spikes
c. Inertial Inflation
d. Employment Cost Index

47. _________ is a type of inflation caused by substantial increases in the cost of important goods or services where no suitable alternative is available. A situation that has been often cited of this was the oil crisis of the 1970s, which some economists see as a major cause of the inflation experienced in the Western world in that decade. It is argued that this inflation resulted from increases in the cost of petroleum imposed by the member states of OPEC.

a. Cost-push inflation
b. Headline inflation
c. Chronic inflation
d. Mundell-Tobin effect

48. _________ is an assumption used in many contemporary macroeconomic models, and also in other areas of contemporary economics and game theory and in other applications of rational choice theory.

Since most macroeconomic models today study decisions over many periods, the expectations of workers, consumers, and firms about future economic conditions are an essential part of the model. How to model these expectations has long been controversial, and it is well known that the macroeconomic predictions of the model may differ depending on the assumptions made about expectations

a. Rational expectations
b. Potential output
c. Balanced-growth equilibrium
d. Minimum wage

49. In economics, _________ is the total supply of goods and services produced by a national economy during a specific time period. It is the total amount of goods and services in the economy available at all possible price levels.

a. Aggregation problem
b. Aggregate expenditure
c. Aggregate demand
d. Aggregate supply

50. In economics, a _________ is a sudden event that increases or decreases demand for goods or services temporarily. A positive _________ increases demand and a negative _________ decreases demand. Prices of goods and services are affected in both cases.

a. Lucas-Islands model
b. War economy
c. Robertson lag
d. Demand shock

51. A _________ is an event that suddenly changes the price of a commodity or service. It may be caused by a sudden increase or decrease in the supply of a particular good. This sudden change affects the equilibrium price.

a. SIMIC
b. Supply shock
c. Demand shock
d. Friedman rule

52. _________ in economics refers to metrics and measures of output from production processes, per unit of input. Labor _________, for example, is typically measured as a ratio of output per labor-hour, an input. _________ may be conceived of as a metrics of the technical or engineering efficiency of production.

a. Fordism
b. Productivity
c. Piece work
d. Production-possibility frontier

53. In economics, the concept of the _________ refers to the decision-making time frame of a firm in which at least one factor of production is fixed. Costs which are fixed in the _________ have no impact on a firms decisions. For example a firm can raise output by increasing the amount of labour through overtime.

a. Productivity model
b. Hicks-neutral technical change
c. Product Pipeline
d. Short-run

54. In economics, _________ is when quantity demanded is more than quantity supplied.See Economic shortage.

a. Excess demand
b. AD-IA Model
c. ACCRA Cost of Living Index
d. ACEA agreement

55. _________ was an American economist, statistician and public intellectual, and a recipient of the Nobel Memorial Prize in Economic Sciences. He is best known among scholars for his theoretical and empirical research, especially consumption analysis, monetary history and theory, and for his demonstration of the complexity of stabilization policy. A global public followed his restatement of a political philosophy that insisted on minimizing the role of government in favor of the private sector.

a. Adam Smith
b. Adolph Fischer
c. Milton Friedman
d. Adolf Hitler

56. _________ and Keynesian Theory) is a macroeconomic theory based on the ideas of 20th-century British economist John Maynard Keynes. _________ argues that private sector decisions sometimes lead to inefficient macroeconomic outcomes and therefore advocates active policy responses by the public sector, including monetary policy actions by the central bank and fiscal policy actions by the government to stabilize output over the business cycle.

The theories forming the basis of _________ were first presented in The General Theory of Employment, Interest and Money, published in 1936.

a. Deflation
b. Keynesian economics
c. Rational choice theory
d. Market failure

57. In economic models, the _________ time frame assumes no fixed factors of production. Firms can enter or leave the marketplace, and the cost (and availability) of land, labor, raw materials, and capital goods can be assumed to vary. In contrast, in the short-run time frame, certain factors are assumed to be fixed, because there is not sufficient time for them to change.

a. Price/performance ratio
b. Diseconomies of scale
c. Long-run
d. Productivity world

58. The term _________ is an acronym for Non-Accelerating Inflation Rate of Unemployment. It is a concept in economic theory significant in the interplay of macroeconomics and microeconomics. This 'full employment' unemployment rate is sometimes termed the 'inflation-threshold unemployment rate': Actual unemployment cannot fall below the _________, and the inflation rate is likely to rise quickly (accelerate) in times of strong labor demands during periods of growth.

a. Coal depletion
b. Social Credit
c. NAIRU
d. Cobweb model

59. In economics, a _________ is a general slowdown in economic activity over a sustained period of time, or a business cycle contraction. During _________s, many macroeconomic indicators vary in a similar way. Production as measured by Gross Domestic Product (GDP), employment, investment spending, capacity utilization, household incomes and business profits all fall during _________s.

a. Monetary economics
b. Leading indicators
c. Treasury View
d. Recession

60. _________ is an American economist and was the Chairman of the Federal Reserve of the United States from 1987 to 2006. He currently works as a private advisor and providing consulting for firms through his company, Greenspan Associates LLC.

First appointed Federal Reserve chairman by President Ronald Reagan in August 1987, he was reappointed at successive four-year intervals until retiring on January 31, 2006 after the second-longest tenure in the position.

a. Alan Greenspan
b. Adolf Hitler
c. Adam Smith
d. Adolph Fischer

61. _________ is a school of macroeconomic thought that argues that economic growth can be most effectively created using incentives for people to produce (supply) goods and services, such as adjusting income tax and capital gains tax rates, and by allowing greater flexibility by reducing regulation. Consumers will then benefit from a greater supply of goods and services at lower prices.

The term _________ was coined by journalist Jude Wanniski in 1975, and popularized the ideas of economists Robert Mundell and Arthur Laffer.

a. Clap note
b. Fiscal stimulus plans
c. Commodity trading advisors
d. Supply-side economics

62. _________ is a decrease in the rate of inflation. This phase of the business cycle, in which retailers can no longer pass on higher prices to their customers, often occurs during a recession. In contrast, deflation occurs when prices are actually dropping.

a. Mundell-Tobin effect
b. Stealth inflation
c. Reflation
d. Disinflation

63. In finance, the _________ of a financial asset measures the sensitivity of the asset's price to interest rate movements. There are various definitions of _________ and derived quantities, discussed below. If not otherwise specified, '_________' generally means the Macaulay _________, as defined below.

a. Duration
b. 100-year flood
c. Newtonian time
d. Time value of money

64. _________ refers to the objective and subjective components of the believability of a source or message.

Traditionally, _________ has two key components: trustworthiness and expertise, which both have objective and subjective components. Trustworthiness is a based more on subjective factors, but can include objective measurements such as established reliability.

a. 1921 recession
b. 100-year flood
c. 130-30 fund
d. Credibility

65. The _________ is the central banking system of the United States. Created in 1913 by the enactment of the Federal Reserve Act (signed by Woodrow Wilson), it is a quasi-public and quasi-private (government entity with private components) banking system that comprises (1) the presidentially appointed Board of Governors of the _________ in Washington, D.C.; (2) the Federal Open Market Committee; (3) twelve regional Federal Reserve Banks located in major cities throughout the nation acting as fiscal agents for the U.S. Treasury, each with its own nine-member board of directors; (4) numerous other private U.S. member banks, which subscribe to required amounts of non-transferable stock in their regional Federal Reserve Banks; and (5) various advisory councils. Since February 2006, Ben Bernanke has served as the Chairman of the Board of Governors of the _________.

a. Term auction facility
b. Monetary Policy Report to the Congress
c. Federal Reserve System Open Market Account
d. Federal Reserve System

66. _________ in economic theory is the use of modern economic tools to study problems that are traditionally in the province of political science.

In particular, it studies the behavior of politicians and government officials as mostly self-interested agents and their interactions in the social system either as such or under alternative constitutional rules. These can be represented a number of ways, including standard constrained utility maximization, game theory, or decision theory.

a. Rational ignorance
b. Public interest theory
c. Paradox of voting
d. Public choice

1. _________ originally was the term for studying production, buying and selling, and their relations with law, custom, and government. _________ originated in moral philosophy. It developed in the 18th century as the study of the economies of states -- polities, hence _________.

a. Geoeconomics
b. Productive and unproductive labour
c. Dirigisme
d. Political Economy

2. _________ by John Stuart Mill was the most important economics or political economy textbook of the mid nineteenth century. It was revised until its seventh edition in 1871, shortly before Mill's death in 1873, and republished in numerous other editions.

Mill's Principles were written in a style of prose far flung from the introductory texts of today.

a. Limits to Growth
b. Principles of Political Economy
c. Principles of Political Economy and Taxation
d. The Rise and Fall of the Great Powers

3. _________ is widely regarded as the first modern school of economic thought. It is the idea that free markets can regulate themselves.Its major developers include Adam Smith, David Ricardo, Thomas Malthus and John Stuart Mill. Sometimes the definition of _________ is expanded to include William Petty, Johann Heinrich von Thünen.

a. Marginalism
b. Tendency of the rate of profit to fall
c. Schools of economic thought
d. Classical economics

4. In macroeconomics, _________ is a condition of the national economy, where all or nearly all persons willing and able to work at the prevailing wages and working conditions are able to do so. It is defined either as 0% unemployment, literally, no unemployment (the rate of unemployment is the fraction of the work force unable to find work), as by James Tobin, or as the level of employment rates when there is no cyclical unemployment. It is defined by the majority of mainstream economists as being an acceptable level of natural unemployment above 0%, the discrepancy from 0% being due to non-cyclical types of unemployment.

a. Harrod-Johnson diagram
b. Marginal propensity to consume
c. Demand shock
d. Full employment

5. _________, 1st Baron Keynes was a renowned economist from Britain whose many ideas on economic and political theories as well as on many governments' monetary policies influenced America. He advocated a government that played an active role in the lives of people regarding business, economy, etc. In this role, the government would use fiscal measures to reduce the consequences of recessions, economic depressions and booms.

a. Adolph Fischer
b. Adam Smith
c. John Maynard Keynes
d. Adolf Hitler

6. A _________ is an economy based on the division of labor in which the prices of goods and services are determined in a free price system set by supply and demand. This is often contrasted with a planned economy, in which a central government determines the price of goods and services using a fixed price system. Market economies are contrasted with mixed economy where the price system is not entirely free but under some government control that is not extensive enough to constitute a planned economy.

a. Commons-based peer production
b. Nutritional Economics
c. Network Economy
d. Market economy

7. _________ is an economic concept with commonplace familiarity. It is the price that a good or service is offered at, or will fetch, in the marketplace. It is of interest mainly in the study of microeconomics.

a. Paper trading
b. Noisy market hypothesis
c. Market anomaly
d. Market price

8. The term _________s refers to wages that have been adjusted for inflation. This term is used in contrast to nominal wages or unadjusted wages.

The use of adjusted figures is in undertaking some form of economic analysis.

a. Living wage
b. Federal Wage System
c. Profit sharing
d. Real wage

9. Competition law, known in the United States as _________ law, has three main elements:

- prohibiting agreements or practices that restrict free trading and competition between business entities. This includes in particular the repression of cartels.
- banning abusive behaviour by a firm dominating a market, or anti-competitive practices that tend to lead to such a dominant position. Practices controlled in this way may include predatory pricing, tying, price gouging, refusal to deal, and many others.
- supervising the mergers and acquisitions of large corporations, including some joint ventures. Transactions that are considered to threaten the competitive process can be prohibited altogether, or approved subject to 'remedies' such as an obligation to divest part of the merged business or to offer licences or access to facilities to enable other businesses to continue competing.

The substance and practice of competition law varies from jurisdiction to jurisdiction. Protecting the interests of consumers (consumer welfare) and ensuring that entrepreneurs have an opportunity to compete in the market economy are often treated as important objectives. Competition law is closely connected with law on deregulation of access to markets, state aids and subsidies, the privatisation of state owned assets and the establishment of independent sector regulators. In recent decades, competition law has been viewed as a way to provide better public services.

a. United Kingdom competition law
b. Antitrust
c. Intellectual property law
d. Anti-Inflation Act

10. _________s is the social science that studies the production, distribution, and consumption of goods and services. The term _________s comes from the Ancient Greek οá¼°κονομῖα from οá¼¶κος (oikos, 'house') + νÏŒμος (nomos, 'custom' or 'law'), hence 'rules of the house(hold)'. Current _________ models developed out of the broader field of political economy in the late 19th century, owing to a desire to use an empirical approach more akin to the physical sciences.

a. Inflation
b. Opportunity cost
c. Energy economics
d. Economic

11. _________ in economics and business is the result of an exchange and from that trade we assign a numerical monetary value to a good, service or asset. If Alice trades Bob 4 apples for an orange, the _________ of an orange is 4 apples. Inversely, the _________ of an apple is 1/4 oranges.

a. Price book
b. Price
c. Premium pricing
d. Price war

12. A _________, reserve bank, or monetary authority is the entity responsible for the monetary policy of a country or of a group of member states. It is a bank that can lend money to other banks in times of need. Its primary responsibility is to maintain the stability of the national currency and money supply, but more active duties include controlling subsidized-loan interest rates, and acting as a lender of last resort to the banking sector during times of financial crisis (private banks often being integral to the national financial system.)

a. 100-year flood
b. 130-30 fund
c. 1921 recession
d. Central bank

13. The _________ is the central banking system of the United States. Created in 1913 by the enactment of the Federal Reserve Act (signed by Woodrow Wilson), it is a quasi-public and quasi-private (government entity with private components) banking system that comprises (1) the presidentially appointed Board of Governors of the _________ in Washington, D.C.; (2) the Federal Open Market Committee; (3) twelve regional Federal Reserve Banks located in major cities throughout the nation acting as fiscal agents for the U.S. Treasury, each with its own nine-member board of directors; (4) numerous other private U.S. member banks, which subscribe to required amounts of non-transferable stock in their regional Federal Reserve Banks; and (5) various advisory councils. Since February 2006, Ben Bernanke has served as the Chairman of the Board of Governors of the _________.

a. Federal Reserve System
b. Monetary Policy Report to the Congress
c. Term auction facility
d. Federal Reserve System Open Market Account

14. The term _________ refers to government debt, expenditures and revenues, or to finance (particularly financial revenue) in general.

- _________ deficit is the budget deficit of federal or local government
- _________ policy is the discretionary spending of governments. Contrasts with monetary policy.
- _________ year and _________ quarter are reporting periods for firms and other agencies.

.

a. Fiscal
b. Bucket shop
c. Procter ' Gamble
d. Drawdown

15. In economics, _________ is the use of government spending and revenue collection to influence the economy.

_________ can be contrasted with the other main type of economic policy, monetary policy, which attempts to stabilize the economy by controlling interest rates and the supply of money. The two main instruments of _________ are government spending and taxation.

a. Sustainable investment rule
b. Fiscalism
c. 100-year flood
d. Fiscal policy

16. The _________ was written by the English economist John Maynard Keynes. The book, generally considered to be his magnum opus, is largely credited with creating the terminology and shape of modern macroeconomics. Published in February 1936 it sought to bring about a revolution, commonly referred to as the 'Keynesian Revolution', in the way economists thought - especially in relation to the proposition that a market economy tends naturally to restore itself to full employment after temporary shocks.

a. Black Book of Communism
b. Human Action
c. General Theory of Employment, Interest and Money
d. The General Theory of Employment, Interest and Money

17. _________ is a fee paid on borrowed assets. It is the price paid for the use of borrowed money , or, money earned by deposited funds . Assets that are sometimes lent with _________ include money, shares, consumer goods through hire purchase, major assets such as aircraft, and even entire factories in finance lease arrangements.

a. Interest
b. Asset protection
c. Insolvency
d. Internal debt

18. _________ and Keynesian Theory) is a macroeconomic theory based on the ideas of 20th-century British economist John Maynard Keynes. _________ argues that private sector decisions sometimes lead to inefficient macroeconomic outcomes and therefore advocates active policy responses by the public sector, including monetary policy actions by the central bank and fiscal policy actions by the government to stabilize output over the business cycle.

The theories forming the basis of _________ were first presented in The General Theory of Employment, Interest and Money, published in 1936.

a. Rational choice theory
b. Deflation
c. Market failure
d. Keynesian economics

19. The _________ was a fundamental reworking of economic theory concerning the factors determining employment levels in the overall economy. The revolution was set against the orthodox classical economic framework, which based on Say's Law argued that unless special conditions prevailed the free market would naturally establish full employment equilibrium with no need for government intervention. Employers will be able to make a profit by employing all available workers as long as workers drop their wages below the value of the total output they are able to produce - and classical economics assumed that in a free market workers would be willing to lower their wage demands accordingly , because they are rational agents who would rather work for less than face unemployment.

a. Military Keynesianism
b. Keynesian revolution
c. Neo-Keynesian economics
d. Speculative demand

20. _________ emerged as a school in macroeconomics during the 1970s. As opposed to Keynesian macroeconomics, it builds its analysis on an entirely neoclassical framework. Specifically, _________ emphasises the importance of rigorous foundations, in which the macroeconomic model is built in analogy to the actions of individual agents, whose behaviour is modelled by microeconomics.

a. Developmentalism
b. New classical macroeconomics
c. Henry George Theorem
d. Dominant Design

21. In economics, _________ is the total demand for final goods and services in the economy (Y) at a given time and price level. It is the amount of goods and services in the economy that will be purchased at all possible price levels. This is the demand for the gross domestic product of a country when inventory levels are static.

a. Aggregate demand
b. Aggregation problem
c. Aggregate supply
d. Aggregate expenditure

22. _________, or a _________ is the concept of a resulting effect (cf. cause and effect, arising from another action. In general terms, it is used to indicate that all human actions, particularly crime and sin, have profound effects.

a. Solved
b. Variability
c. Consequence
d. Rule

23. Economics:

- _________,the desire to own something and the ability to pay for it
- _________ curve,a graphic representation of a _________ schedule
- _________ deposit, the money in checking accounts
- _________ pull theory,the theory that inflation occurs when _________ for goods and services exceeds existing supplies
- _________ schedule,a table that lists the quantity of a good a person will buy it each different price
- _________ side economics,the school of economics at believes government spending and tax cuts open economy by raising _________

.

a. Production
b. Variability
c. Demand
d. McKesson ' Robbins scandal

24. _________ is a branch of economics that deals with the performance, structure, and behavior of a national or regional economy as a whole. Along with microeconomics, _________ is one of the two most general fields in economics. It is the study of the behavior and decision-making of entire economies.

a. Macroeconomics
b. New Trade Theory
c. Tobit model
d. Nominal value

25. The _________ was a worldwide economic downturn starting in most places in 1929 and ending at different times in the 1930s or early 1940s for different countries. It was the largest and most important economic depression in the 20th century, and is used in the 21st century as an example of how far the world's economy can fall. The _________ originated in the United States; historians most often use as a starting date the stock market crash on October 29, 1929, known as Black Tuesday.

a. British Empire Economic Conference
b. Wall Street Crash of 1929
c. Jarrow March
d. Great Depression

26. In economics, the term _________ has three different distinct meanings and applications. While it is related to unemployment, a situation in which a person who is searching for work cannot find a job, in the case of _________, a person is working. All three of the definitions of '_________' involve underutilization of labor that critics say is missed by most official (governmental agency) definitions and measurements of unemployment.

a. Employability
b. Underemployment
c. Informational interview
d. Encore career

27. In Keynesian economics, _________ refers to a situation with a persistent shortfall relative to full employment and potential output so that unemployment is higher than at the NAIRU or the 'natural' rate of unemployment. This situation is not seen as solvable via laissez-faire polices of 'letting nature take its course' (price adjustment.) Instead, fiscal policy (i.e., deficit spending) or monetary policy is needed to 'prime the pump' or 'jump-start the economy' to abolish cyclical unemployment and the 'GDP gap.' .

a. ACEA agreement
b. ACCRA Cost of Living Index
c. Underemployment equilibrium
d. AD-IA Model

28. The _________ says that it is naïve to try to predict the effects of a change in economic policy entirely on the basis of relationships observed in historical data, especially highly aggregated historical data.

The basic idea pre-dates Lucas's contribution, but in a 1976 paper he drove home the point that this simple notion invalidated policy advice based on conclusions drawn from estimated system of equation models. Because the parameters of those models were not structural - that is, not policy-invariant - they would necessarily change whenever policy - the rules of the game - was changed.

a. Peak-load pricing
b. Dahrendorf hypothesis
c. Demand management
d. Lucas critique

29. _________ is the view within monetary economics that variation in the money supply has major influences on national output in the short run and the price level over longer periods and that objectives of monetary policy are best met by targeting the growth rate of the money supply.

_________ today is mainly associated with the work of Milton Friedman, who was among the generation of economists to accept Keynesian economics and then criticize it on his own terms. Friedman and Anna Schwartz wrote an influential book, Monetary History of the United States 1867-1960, and argued that 'inflation is always and everywhere a monetary phenomenon.' Friedman advocated a central bank policy aimed at keeping the supply and demand for money at equilibrium, as measured by growth in productivity and demand.

a. Marginal revenue productivity theory of wages
b. Complexity economics
c. Historical school of economics
d. Monetarism

30. In economics, _________ is the total amount of money available in an economy at a particular point in time. There are several ways to define 'money', but standard measures usually include currency in circulation and demand deposits.

_________ data are recorded and published, usually by the government or the central bank of the country.

a. Veil of money
b. Money supply
c. Velocity of money
d. Neutrality of money

31. In economics, the _________ is the relation:

$$M \cdot V = P \cdot Q$$

where, for a given period,

M is the total amount of money in circulation on average in an economy.
V is the velocity of money, that is the average frequency with which a unit of money is spent.
P is the price level.

a. ACCRA Cost of Living Index
b. Outside money
c. Open market
d. Equation of exchange

32. The _________ is the average frequency with which a unit of money is spent in a specific period of time. Velocity associates the amount of economic activity associated with a given money supply. When the period is understood, the velocity may be present as a pure number; otherwise it should be given as a pure number over time.

a. Money supply
b. Neutrality of money
c. Velocity of Money
d. Chartalism

33. In economics, the _________ of money is a theory emphasizing the positive relationship of overall prices or the nominal value of expenditures to the quantity of money.

It is the mainstream economic theory of the price level. Alternative theories include the real bills doctrine and the more recent fiscal theory of the price level.

a. Dishoarding
b. Romer Model
c. Real business cycle
d. Quantity theory

34. In economics, the _________ is a theory emphasizing the positive relationship of overall prices or the nominal value of expenditures to the quantity of money.

It is the mainstream economic theory of the price level. Alternative theories include the real bills doctrine and the more recent fiscal theory of the price level.

a. Fundamental psychological law
b. Quantity theory of money
c. Consumer spending
d. Microsimulation

35. _________ is an economic system in which wealth, and the means of producing wealth, are privately owned. Through _________, the land, labor, and capital are owned, operated, and traded for the purpose of generating profits, without force or fraud, by private individuals either singly or jointly, and investments, distribution, income, production, pricing and supply of goods, commodities and services are determined by voluntary private decision in a market economy. A distinguishing feature of _________ is that each person owns his or her own labor and therefore is allowed to sell the use of it to employers.

a. Capitalism
b. Late capitalism
c. Socialism for the rich and capitalism for the poor
d. Creative capitalism

36. _________ was an American economist, statistician and public intellectual, and a recipient of the Nobel Memorial Prize in Economic Sciences. He is best known among scholars for his theoretical and empirical research, especially consumption analysis, monetary history and theory, and for his demonstration of the complexity of stabilization policy. A global public followed his restatement of a political philosophy that insisted on minimizing the role of government in favor of the private sector.

a. Adam Smith
b. Adolph Fischer
c. Adolf Hitler
d. Milton Friedman

37. A _________ is an object whose consumption increases the utility of the consumer, for which the quantity demanded exceeds the quantity supplied at zero price. _________s are usually modeled as having diminishing marginal utility. The first individual purchase has high utility; the second has less.

a. Pie method
b. Good
c. Composite good
d. Merit good

38. In economics, economic output is divided into physical goods and intangible services. Consumption of _________ is assumed to produce utility. It is often used when referring to a _________ Tax.

a. Composite good
b. Private good
c. Manufactured goods
d. Goods and services

39. In economics, _________ is inflation that is very high or 'out of control', a condition in which prices increase rapidly as a currency loses its value. Definitions used by the media vary from a cumulative inflation rate over three years approaching 100% to 'inflation exceeding 50% a month.' In informal usage the term is often applied to much lower rates. As a rule of thumb, normal inflation is reported per year, but _________ is often reported for much shorter intervals, often per month.

a. 130-30 fund
b. 100-year flood
c. Hyperinflation
d. 1921 recession

40. _________ in economics refers to metrics and measures of output from production processes, per unit of input. Labor _________, for example, is typically measured as a ratio of output per labor-hour, an input. _________ may be conceived of as a metrics of the technical or engineering efficiency of production.

a. Production-possibility frontier
b. Fordism
c. Piece work
d. Productivity

41. In economics, the _________ is a historical inverse relation between the rate of unemployment and the rate of inflation in an economy. Stated simply, the lower the unemployment in an economy, the higher the rate of increase in nominal wages in the economy. Rate of Change of Wages against Unemployment, United Kingdom 1913-1948 from Phillips (1958)

William Phillips, a New Zealand born economist, wrote a paper in 1958 titled The Relationship between Unemployment and the Rate of Change of Money Wages in the United Kingdom 1861-1957, which was published in the quarterly journal Economica.

a. Demand curve
b. Phillips curve
c. Lorenz curve
d. Cost curve

42. In economics, _________ is the total supply of goods and services produced by a national economy during a specific time period. It is the total amount of goods and services in the economy available at all possible price levels.

a. Aggregate expenditure
b. Aggregate supply
c. Aggregate demand
d. Aggregation problem

43. The _________ or gross domestic income (GDI), a basic measure of an economy's economic performance, is the market value of all final goods and services produced within the borders of a nation in a year. _________ can be defined in three ways, all of which are conceptually identical. First, it is equal to the total expenditures for all final goods and services produced within the country in a stipulated period of time (usually a 365-day year.)

a. Countercyclical
b. Gross domestic product
c. Market structure
d. Monopolistic competition

44. _________ is a misspelled phrase from Latin 'pro capite' phrase meaning per head with pro meaning 'per' or 'for each' and capite meaning 'head.' Both words together equate to the phrase 'for each head.'

It is usually used in the field of statistics to indicate the average per person for any given concern, such as income, crime rate, etc.

It is also used in wills to indicate that each of the named beneficiaries should receive, by devise or bequest, equal shares of the estate. This is in contrast to a per stirpes division, in which each branch of the inheriting family inherits an equal share of the estate.

a. Per capita
b. False positive rate
c. Population statistics
d. Sargan test

45. An _________, in economics, is the amount by which the real Gross domestic product exceeds potential GDP. The real GDP is also known as GDP 'adjusted for inflation', 'constant prices' GDP or 'constant dollar' GDP, because it measures the aggregate output in a country's income accounts in a given year, expressed in base-year prices. On the other hand, the potential GDP is the quantity of real GDP when a country's economy is at full-employment.

a. AD-IA Model
b. ACEA agreement
c. ACCRA Cost of Living Index
d. Inflationary gap

46. A _________ is:

- Rewrite _________, in generative grammar and computer science
- Standardization, a formal and widely-accepted statement, fact, definition, or qualification
- Operation, a determinate _________ for performing a mathematical operation and obtaining a certain result (Mathematics, Logic)
    - Unary operation
    - Binary operation
- _________ of inference, a function from sets of formulae to formulae (Mathematics, Logic)
- _________ of thumb, principle with broad application that is not intended to be strictly accurate or reliable for every situation. Also often simply referred to as a _________
- Moral, an atomic element of a moral code for guiding choices in human behavior
- Heuristic, a quantized '_________' which shows a tendency or probability for successful function
- A regulation, as in sports
- A Production _________, as in computer science
- Procedural law, a _________set governing the application of laws to cases
    - A law, which may informally be called a '_________'
    - A court ruling, a decision by a court
- In the U.S. Government, a regulation mandated by Congress, but written or expanded upon by the Executive Branch.
- Norm (sociology), an informal but widely accepted _________, concept, truth, definition, or qualification (social norms, legal norms, coding norms)
- Norm (philosophy), a kind of sentence or a reason to act, feel or believe
- 'Rulership' is the concept of governance by a government:
    - Military _________, governance by a military body
    - Monastic _________, a collection of precepts that guides the life of monks or nuns in a religious order where the superior holds the place of Christ
- Slide _________

- '_________,' a song by Ayumi Hamasaki
- '_________,' a song by rapper Nas
- '_________s,' an album by the band The Whitest Boy Alive
- _________s: Pyaar Ka Superhit Formula, a 2003 Bollywood film
- ruler, an instrument for measuring lengths
- _________, a component of an astrolabe, circumferator or similar instrument
- The _________s, a bestselling self-help book
- _________ Project (Run Up-to-date Linux Everywhere), a project that aims to use up-to-date Linux software on old PCs
- _________ engine, a software system that helps managing business _________s
- Ja _________, a hip hop artist
    - R.U.L.E., a 2005 greatest hits album by rapper Ja _________
- '_________s,' a KMFDM song

a. Procter ' Gamble
b. Technocracy
c. Demand
d. Rule

47. The _________ , a component of the Federal Reserve System, is charged under United States law with overseeing the nation's open market operations. It is the Federal Reserve Committee that makes key decisions about interest rates and the growth jam of the United States money supply. It is the principal organ of United States national monetary policy.

a. Fed Funds Probability
b. Federal Reserve Transparency Act
c. Primary Dealer Credit Facility
d. Federal Open Market Committee

48. In economics, the _________ is the term used to refer to the environment in which bonds are bought and sold between a central bank ' its regulated banks. It is not a free market process.

- To intervene in the 'business cycle', a central bank may choose to go into the _________ and buy or sell government bonds, which is known as _________ operations to increase reserves.

a. ACCRA Cost of Living Index
b. Open Market
c. Inside money
d. Outside money

49. _________ is the process of estimation in unknown situations. Prediction is a similar, but more general term. Both can refer to estimation of time series, cross-sectional or longitudinal data.

a. 1921 recession
b. 100-year flood
c. 130-30 fund
d. Forecasting

50. _________ is an assumption used in many contemporary macroeconomic models, and also in other areas of contemporary economics and game theory and in other applications of rational choice theory.

Since most macroeconomic models today study decisions over many periods, the expectations of workers, consumers, and firms about future economic conditions are an essential part of the model. How to model these expectations has long been controversial, and it is well known that the macroeconomic predictions of the model may differ depending on the assumptions made about expectations

a. Rational expectations
b. Balanced-growth equilibrium
c. Potential output
d. Minimum wage

51. _________ is a term used to described a tendency or preference towards a particular perspective, ideology or result, especially when the tendency interferes with the ability to be impartial, unprejudiced, or objective. The term _________ed is used to describe an action, judgment, or other outcome influenced by a prejudged perspective. It is also used to refer to a person or body of people whose actions or judgments exhibit _________.

a. 1921 recession
b. 130-30 fund
c. 100-year flood
d. Bias

52. The term _________ refers to economy-wide fluctuations in production or economic activity over several months or years. These fluctuations occur around a long-term growth trend, and typically involve shifts over time between periods of relatively rapid economic growth (expansion or boom), and periods of relative stagnation or decline (contraction or recession.)

These fluctuations are often measured using the growth rate of real gross domestic product.

a. Consumer theory
b. Tobit model
c. Nominal value
d. Business cycle

53. _________s is concerned with the tasks of developing and applying quantitative or statistical methods to the study and elucidation of economic principles. _________s combines economic theory with statistics to analyze and test economic relationships. Theoretical _________s considers questions about the statistical properties of estimators and tests, while applied _________s is concerned with the application of _________ methods to assess economic theories.

a. Experimental economics
b. Economic
c. Econometric
d. Evolutionary economics

54. _________s are statistical models used in econometrics. An _________ specifies the statistical relationship that is believed to hold between the various economic quantities pertaining a particular economic phenomena under study. An _________ can be derived from a deterministic economic model by allowing for uncertainty or from an economic model which itself is stochastic.

a. Event study
b. Economic statistics
c. ACCRA Cost of Living Index
d. Econometric model

55. A _________ is an event that suddenly changes the price of a commodity or service. It may be caused by a sudden increase or decrease in the supply of a particular good. This sudden change affects the equilibrium price.

a. Friedman rule
b. Demand shock
c. SIMIC
d. Supply shock

56. In labor economics, the _________ hypothesis argues that wages, at least in some markets, are determined by more than simply supply and demand. Specifically, it points to the incentive for managers to pay their employees more than the market-clearing wage in order to increase their productivity or efficiency. This increased labor productivity pays for the relatively higher wages.

a. Inflatable rats
b. Efficiency wage
c. Earnings calls
d. Exogenous growth model

57. In economics, _________ is a rise in the general level of prices of goods and services in an economy over a period of time. When the general price level rises, each unit of currency buys fewer goods and services; consequently, _________ is also a decline in the real value of money--a loss of purchasing power in the medium of exchange which is also the monetary unit of account in the economy. A chief measure of general price-level _________ is the general _________ rate, which is the percentage change in a general price index (normally the Consumer Price Index) over time.

a. Opportunity cost
b. Energy economics
c. Economic
d. Inflation

58. In economics, the _________ is a measure of inflation, the rate of increase of a price index (for example, a consumer price index.)It is the percentage rate of change in price level over time. The rate of decrease in the purchasing power of money is approximately equal.

It's used to calculate the real interest rate, as well as real increases in wages, and official measurements of this rate act as input variables to COLA adjustments and Inflation derivatives prices.

a. Edgeworth paradox
b. Interest rate option
c. Equity value
d. Inflation rate

59. In microeconomics, _________ is quite simply the conversion of inputs into outputs. It is an economic process that uses resources to create a good or service that is suitable for exchange. This can include manufacturing, storing, shipping, and packaging.

a. Red Guards
b. MET
c. Solved
d. Production

60. In economics, a _________ is a function that specifies the output of a firm, an industry, or an entire economy for all combinations of inputs. A meta-_________ compares the practice of the existing entities converting inputs X into output y to determine the most efficient practice _________ of the existing entities, whether the most efficient feasible practice production or the most efficient actual practice production. In either case, the maximum output of a technologically-determined production process is a mathematical function of input factors of production.

a. Post-Fordism
b. Production function
c. Short-run
d. Constant elasticity of substitution

61. Though there have been several definitions of voluntary and _________ in the economics literature, a simple distinction is often applied. Voluntary unemployment is attributed to the individual's decisions, whereas _________ exists because of the socio-economic environment (including the market structure, government intervention, and the level of aggregate demand) in which individuals operate. In these terms, much or most of frictional unemployment is voluntary, since it reflects individual search behavior.

a. AD-IA Model
b. Involuntary unemployment
c. ACCRA Cost of Living Index
d. ACEA agreement

62. In economics, the _________ is used to illustrate the idea that increases in the rate of taxation do not necessarily increase tax revenue. (For instance, whereas a 0% income tax rate will generate no revenue, neither will a 100% rate, as citizens will have no incentive to make money.) Increasing taxes beyond the peak of the curve point will decrease tax revenue.

a. Laffer curve
b. 1921 recession
c. 100-year flood
d. 130-30 fund

63. _________ is a school of macroeconomic thought that argues that economic growth can be most effectively created using incentives for people to produce (supply) goods and services, such as adjusting income tax and capital gains tax rates, and by allowing greater flexibility by reducing regulation. Consumers will then benefit from a greater supply of goods and services at lower prices.

The term _________ was coined by journalist Jude Wanniski in 1975, and popularized the ideas of economists Robert Mundell and Arthur Laffer.

a. Fiscal stimulus plans
b. Commodity trading advisors
c. Supply-side economics
d. Clap note

64. In economics, _________ is a measure of the relative satisfaction from consumption of various goods and services. Given this measure, one may speak meaningfully of increasing or decreasing _________, and thereby explain economic behavior in terms of attempts to increase one's _________. For illustrative purposes, changes in _________ are sometimes expressed in units called utils

a. Utility function
b. Expected utility hypothesis
c. Ordinal utility
d. Utility

65. In economics, _________ means that people form their expectations about what will happen in the future based on what has happened in the past. For example, if inflation has been higher than expected in the past, people would revise expectations for the future.

One simple version of _________ is stated in the following equation, where p^e is the next year's rate of inflation that is currently expected; p^e_{-1} is this year's rate of inflation that was expected last year; and p is this year's actual rate of inflation:

$$p^e = p^e_{-1} + \lambda(p_{-1} - p^e_{-1})$$

With λ is between 0 and 1, this says that current expectations of future inflation reflect past expectations and an 'error-adjustment' term, in which current expectations are raised (or lowered) according to the gap between actual inflation and previous expectations.

a. Investment-specific technological progress
b. AD-IA Model
c. Economic interdependence
d. Adaptive expectations

66. A model in macroeconomics is a logical, mathematical, and/or computational framework designed to describe the operation of a national or regional economy, and especially the dynamics of aggregate quantities such as the total amount of goods and services produced, total income earned, the level of employment of productive resources, and the level of prices.

There are different types of _________ that serve different purposes and have different advantages and disadvantages. Models are used to clarify and illustrate basic theoretical principles in macroeconomics; they are used to test, compare, and quantify different theories of the macroeconomy; they are used to produce 'what if' scenarios, and especially to evaluate the possible effects of changes in monetary, fiscal, or other macroeconomic policies; and they are used for generating economic forecasts.

a. Macroeconomic models
b. Factor shares
c. Natural rate of unemployment
d. High-powered money

67. _________ refers to discriminatory employment practices such as bias in hiring, promotion, job assignment, termination, and compensation, and various types of harassment.

In many countries, laws prohibit employers from discriminating on the basis of race, color, sex, religion, national origin, physical or mental disability, or age. There is also a growing body of law preventing or occasionally justifying _________ based on sexual orientation or gender identity.

a. Energy Independence and Security Act of 2007
b. Impotent poor
c. Irish competition law
d. Employment discrimination

68. In economic models, the _________ time frame assumes no fixed factors of production. Firms can enter or leave the marketplace, and the cost (and availability) of land, labor, raw materials, and capital goods can be assumed to vary. In contrast, in the short-run time frame, certain factors are assumed to be fixed, because there is not sufficient time for them to change.

a. Productivity world
b. Diseconomies of scale
c. Price/performance ratio
d. Long-run

69. _________ is the increase in the amount of the goods and services produced by an economy over time. It is conventionally measured as the percent rate of increase in real gross domestic product, or real GDP. Growth is usually calculated in real terms, i.e. inflation-adjusted terms, in order to net out the effect of inflation on the price of the goods and services produced.

a. AD-IA Model
b. Economic growth
c. ACCRA Cost of Living Index
d. ACEA agreement

70. In economics and finance, _________ is the change in total cost that arises when the quantity produced changes by one unit. It is the cost of producing one more unit of a good. Mathematically, the _________ function is expressed as the first derivative of the total cost (TC) function with respect to quantity (Q.)

a. Khozraschyot
b. Marginal cost
c. Quality costs
d. Variable cost

71. In economics, the concept of the _________ refers to the decision-making time frame of a firm in which at least one factor of production is fixed. Costs which are fixed in the _________ have no impact on a firms decisions. For example a firm can raise output by increasing the amount of labour through overtime.

a. Hicks-neutral technical change
b. Productivity model
c. Product Pipeline
d. Short-run

72. A _________ is a situation that involves losing one quality or aspect of something in return for gaining another quality or aspect. It implies a decision to be made with full comprehension of both the upside and downside of a particular choice.

In economics the term is expressed as opportunity cost, referring the most preferred alternative given up.

a. Nonmarket
b. Friedman-Savage utility function
c. Trade-off
d. Whitemail

1. A _________ occurs when an entity spends more money than it takes in. The opposite of a _________ is a budget surplus. Debt is essentially an accumulated flow of deficits.

a. Public Financial Management
b. Funding body
c. Lump-sum tax
d. Budget deficit

2. _________ and Keynesian Theory) is a macroeconomic theory based on the ideas of 20th-century British economist John Maynard Keynes. _________ argues that private sector decisions sometimes lead to inefficient macroeconomic outcomes and therefore advocates active policy responses by the public sector, including monetary policy actions by the central bank and fiscal policy actions by the government to stabilize output over the business cycle.

The theories forming the basis of _________ were first presented in The General Theory of Employment, Interest and Money, published in 1936.

a. Market failure
b. Deflation
c. Rational choice theory
d. Keynesian economics

3. In economics, the _________ measures the payments that flow between any individual country and all other countries. It is used to summarize all international economic transactions for that country during a specific time period, usually a year. The _________ is determined by the country's exports and imports of goods, services, and financial capital, as well as financial transfers.

a. Gross domestic product per barrel
b. Balance of payments
c. Gross world product
d. Skyscraper Index

4. _________, or a _________ is the concept of a resulting effect (cf. cause and effect, arising from another action. In general terms, it is used to indicate that all human actions, particularly crime and sin, have profound effects.

a. Solved
b. Rule
c. Variability
d. Consequence

5. _________s is the social science that studies the production, distribution, and consumption of goods and services. The term _________s comes from the Ancient Greek οá¼°κονομÎ¯α from οá¼¶κος (oikos, 'house') + νÏŒμος (nomos, 'custom' or 'law'), hence 'rules of the house(hold)'. Current _________ models developed out of the broader field of political economy in the late 19th century, owing to a desire to use an empirical approach more akin to the physical sciences.

a. Energy economics
b. Economic
c. Inflation
d. Opportunity cost

6. A _________ is the transfer of wealth from one party (such as a person or company) to another. A _________ is usually made in exchange for the provision of goods, services or both, or to fulfill a legal obligation.

The simplest and oldest form of _________ is barter, the exchange of one good or service for another.

a. Social gravity
b. Going concern
c. Payment
d. Soft count

7. From a Keynesian point of view, a _________ in the public sector is achieved when the government equates the revenues with expenditure over the business cycles. In other words, a government's budget is balanced if its income is equal to its expenditure. It is a budget in which revenues are equal to spending.

a. Budget theory
b. Budget support
c. Budget crisis
d. Balanced budget

8. A _________ is a situation in which the government takes in more than it spends.

a. Budget set
b. 100-year flood
c. 130-30 fund
d. Budget surplus

9. _________ is a school of macroeconomic thought that argues that economic growth can be most effectively created using incentives for people to produce (supply) goods and services, such as adjusting income tax and capital gains tax rates, and by allowing greater flexibility by reducing regulation. Consumers will then benefit from a greater supply of goods and services at lower prices.

The term _________ was coined by journalist Jude Wanniski in 1975, and popularized the ideas of economists Robert Mundell and Arthur Laffer.

a. Supply-side economics
b. Clap note
c. Fiscal stimulus plans
d. Commodity trading advisors

10. _________ is that which is owed; usually referencing assets owed, but the term can also cover moral obligations and other interactions not requiring money. In the case of assets, _________ is a means of using future purchasing power in the present before a summation has been earned. Some companies and corporations use _________ as a part of their overall corporate finance strategy.

a. Debt
b. Hard money loan
c. Debenture
d. Collateral Management

11. The term _________ refers to government debt, expenditures and revenues, or to finance (particularly financial revenue) in general.

- _________ deficit is the budget deficit of federal or local government
- _________ policy is the discretionary spending of governments. Contrasts with monetary policy.
- _________ year and _________ quarter are reporting periods for firms and other agencies.

.

a. Fiscal
b. Drawdown
c. Procter ' Gamble
d. Bucket shop

12. To _________ is to impose a financial charge or other levy upon a taxpayer by a state or the functional equivalent of a state.

_________es are also imposed by many subnational entities. _________es consist of direct _________ or indirect _________, and may be paid in money or as its labour equivalent (often but not always unpaid.)

a. 130-30 fund
b. 1921 recession
c. 100-year flood
d. Tax

13. A _________ is a reduction in taxes. Economic stimulus via _________s, along with interest rate intervention and deficit spending, are one of the central tenets of Keynesian economics.

The immediate effects of a _________ are, generally, a decrease in the real income of the government and an increase in the real income of those whose tax rate has been lowered.

a. Withholding tax
b. Direct taxes
c. Popiwek
d. Tax cut

14. In economics, _________ is the total demand for final goods and services in the economy (Y) at a given time and price level. It is the amount of goods and services in the economy that will be purchased at all possible price levels. This is the demand for the gross domestic product of a country when inventory levels are static.

a. Aggregate supply
b. Aggregate demand
c. Aggregation problem
d. Aggregate expenditure

15. In economics, _________ is the use of government spending and revenue collection to influence the economy.

_________ can be contrasted with the other main type of economic policy, monetary policy, which attempts to stabilize the economy by controlling interest rates and the supply of money. The two main instruments of _________ are government spending and taxation.

a. Fiscal policy
b. Sustainable investment rule
c. 100-year flood
d. Fiscalism

16. The _________ or gross domestic income (GDI), a basic measure of an economy's economic performance, is the market value of all final goods and services produced within the borders of a nation in a year. _________ can be defined in three ways, all of which are conceptually identical. First, it is equal to the total expenditures for all final goods and services produced within the country in a stipulated period of time (usually a 365-day year.)

a. Countercyclical
b. Monopolistic competition
c. Gross domestic product
d. Market structure

17. _________, 1st Baron Keynes was a renowned economist from Britain whose many ideas on economic and political theories as well as on many governments' monetary policies influenced America. He advocated a government that played an active role in the lives of people regarding business, economy, etc. In this role, the government would use fiscal measures to reduce the consequences of recessions, economic depressions and booms.

a. John Maynard Keynes
b. Adam Smith
c. Adolph Fischer
d. Adolf Hitler

18. _________ is a misspelled phrase from Latin 'pro capite' phrase meaning per head with pro meaning 'per' or 'for each' and capite meaning 'head.' Both words together equate to the phrase 'for each head.'

It is usually used in the field of statistics to indicate the average per person for any given concern, such as income, crime rate, etc.

It is also used in wills to indicate that each of the named beneficiaries should receive, by devise or bequest, equal shares of the estate. This is in contrast to a per stirpes division, in which each branch of the inheriting family inherits an equal share of the estate.

a. Per capita
b. Sargan test
c. False positive rate
d. Population statistics

19. An _________, in economics, is the amount by which the real Gross domestic product exceeds potential GDP. The real GDP is also known as GDP 'adjusted for inflation', 'constant prices' GDP or 'constant dollar' GDP, because it measures the aggregate output in a country's income accounts in a given year, expressed in base-year prices. On the other hand, the potential GDP is the quantity of real GDP when a country's economy is at full-employment.

a. ACCRA Cost of Living Index
b. AD-IA Model
c. ACEA agreement
d. Inflationary gap

20. The term _________ refers to economy-wide fluctuations in production or economic activity over several months or years. These fluctuations occur around a long-term growth trend, and typically involve shifts over time between periods of relatively rapid economic growth (expansion or boom), and periods of relative stagnation or decline (contraction or recession.)

These fluctuations are often measured using the growth rate of real gross domestic product.

a. Nominal value
b. Tobit model
c. Business cycle
d. Consumer theory

21. Economics:

- _________,the desire to own something and the ability to pay for it
- _________ curve,a graphic representation of a _________ schedule
- _________ deposit, the money in checking accounts
- _________ pull theory,the theory that inflation occurs when _________ for goods and services exceeds existing supplies
- _________ schedule,a table that lists the quantity of a good a person will buy it each different price
- _________ side economics,the school of economics at believes government spending and tax cuts open economy by raising _________

.

a. Variability
b. McKesson ' Robbins scandal
c. Production
d. Demand

22. The term '_________' refers to the concept of collecting information and attempting to spot a pattern in the information. In some fields of study, the term '_________' has more formally-defined meanings.

In project management _________ is a mathematical technique that uses historical results to predict future outcome.

a. Quantile regression
b. Coefficient of determination
c. Probit model
d. Trend analysis

23. In economic models, the _________ time frame assumes no fixed factors of production. Firms can enter or leave the marketplace, and the cost (and availability) of land, labor, raw materials, and capital goods can be assumed to vary. In contrast, in the short-run time frame, certain factors are assumed to be fixed, because there is not sufficient time for them to change.

a. Long-run
b. Diseconomies of scale
c. Price/performance ratio
d. Productivity world

24. In economics, the concept of the _________ refers to the decision-making time frame of a firm in which at least one factor of production is fixed. Costs which are fixed in the _________ have no impact on a firms decisions. For example a firm can raise output by increasing the amount of labour through overtime.

a. Productivity model
b. Hicks-neutral technical change
c. Product Pipeline
d. Short-run

25. In economics and sociology, an _________ is any factor (financial or non-financial) that enables or motivates a particular course of action, or counts as a reason for preferring one choice to the alternatives. It is an expectation that encourages people to behave in a certain way. Since human beings are purposeful creatures, the study of _________ structures is central to the study of all economic activity (both in terms of individual decision-making and in terms of co-operation and competition within a larger institutional structure.)

a. Economic reform
b. Epstein-Zin preferences
c. Incentive
d. Isocost

26. _________ is the part of a country's debts that is owed to creditors who are citizens of that country.

It is a form of fiat creation of money, in which the government obtains cash not by printing it, but by borrowing it. The money created is in the form of treasury securities or securities borrowed from the central bank.

a. External debt
b. International debt collection
c. Interest
d. Internal debt

27. A _________ is an expression that compares quantities relative to each other. The most common examples involve two quantities, but any number of quantities can be compared. _________s are represented mathematically by separating each quantity with a colon, for example the _________ 2:3, which is read as the _________ 'two to three'.

a. 100-year flood
b. 130-30 fund
c. Y-intercept
d. Ratio

28. To tax is to impose a financial charge or other levy upon a taxpayer by a state or the functional equivalent of a state.

_________ are also imposed by many subnational entities. _________ consist of direct tax or indirect tax, and may be paid in money or as its labour equivalent (often but not always unpaid.)

a. 100-year flood
b. 1921 recession
c. 130-30 fund
d. Taxes

29. In business and accounting, _________ are everything of value that is owned by a person or company. It is a claim on the property your income of a borrower. The balance sheet of a firm records the monetary value of the _________ owned by the firm.

a. Assets
b. Amortization schedule
c. ACCRA Cost of Living Index
d. ACEA agreement

30. _________ is an economic model based on price, utility and quantity in a market. It predicts that in a competitive market, price will function to equalize the quantity demanded by consumers, and the quantity supplied by producers, resulting in an economic equilibrium of price and quantity. The model incorporates other factors changing equilibrium as a shift of demand and/or supply.

a. Deferred gratification
b. Joint demand
c. Rational addiction
d. Supply and demand

31. _________ is the capital that a business raises by taking out a loan. It is a loan made to a company that is normally repaid at some future date. _________ differs from equity or share capital because subscribers to _________ do not become part owners of the business, but are merely creditors, and the suppliers of _________ usually receive a contractually fixed annual percentage return on their loan, and this is known as the coupon rate.

a. Blank endorsement
b. Financial rand
c. Debt cash flow
d. Debt Capital

32. _________ is the increase in the amount of the goods and services produced by an economy over time. It is conventionally measured as the percent rate of increase in real gross domestic product, or real GDP. Growth is usually calculated in real terms, i.e. inflation-adjusted terms, in order to net out the effect of inflation on the price of the goods and services produced.

a. ACEA agreement
b. ACCRA Cost of Living Index
c. AD-IA Model
d. Economic growth

33. _________ is a type of private equity investment, most often a minority investment, in relatively mature companies that are looking for capital to expand or restructure operations, enter new markets or finance a significant acquisition without a change of control of the business.

Companies that seek _________, will often do so in order to finance a transformational event in their lifecycle. These companies are likely to be more mature than venture capital funded companies, able to generate revenue and operating profits but unable to generate sufficient cash to fund major expansions, acquisitions or other investments.

a. Seed money
b. Club deal
c. Growth capital
d. Startup company

34. In economics, _________ is a rise in the general level of prices of goods and services in an economy over a period of time. When the general price level rises, each unit of currency buys fewer goods and services; consequently, _________ is also a decline in the real value of money--a loss of purchasing power in the medium of exchange which is also the monetary unit of account in the economy. A chief measure of general price-level _________ is the general _________ rate, which is the percentage change in a general price index (normally the Consumer Price Index) over time.

a. Economic
b. Inflation
c. Energy economics
d. Opportunity cost

35. In economics, the _________ is a measure of inflation, the rate of increase of a price index (for example, a consumer price index.)It is the percentage rate of change in price level over time. The rate of decrease in the purchasing power of money is approximately equal.

It's used to calculate the real interest rate, as well as real increases in wages, and official measurements of this rate act as input variables to COLA adjustments and Inflation derivatives prices.

a. Edgeworth paradox
b. Equity value
c. Interest rate option
d. Inflation rate

36. In economics, _________ is the art or science of controlling economic demand to avoid a recession. In natural resources management and environmental policy more generally, it refers to policies to control consumer demand for environmentally sensitive or harmful goods such as water and energy. Within manufacturing firms the term is used to describe the activities of demand forecasting, planning and order fulfillment.

a. Cobra effect
b. Fiscal imbalance
c. Peak-load pricing
d. Demand management

37. The _________ was a fundamental reworking of economic theory concerning the factors determining employment levels in the overall economy. The revolution was set against the orthodox classical economic framework, which based on Say's Law argued that unless special conditions prevailed the free market would naturally establish full employment equilibrium with no need for government intervention. Employers will be able to make a profit by employing all available workers as long as workers drop their wages below the value of the total output they are able to produce - and classical economics assumed that in a free market workers would be willing to lower their wage demands accordingly , because they are rational agents who would rather work for less than face unemployment.

a. Speculative demand
b. Keynesian revolution
c. Neo-Keynesian economics
d. Military Keynesianism

38. _________ is an economic system in which wealth, and the means of producing wealth, are privately owned. Through _________, the land, labor, and capital are owned, operated, and traded for the purpose of generating profits, without force or fraud, by private individuals either singly or jointly, and investments, distribution, income, production, pricing and supply of goods, commodities and services are determined by voluntary private decision in a market economy. A distinguishing feature of _________ is that each person owns his or her own labor and therefore is allowed to sell the use of it to employers.

a. Capitalism
b. Socialism for the rich and capitalism for the poor
c. Creative capitalism
d. Late capitalism

39. _________ is a negative term describing an claimed capitalist economy in which success in business depends on close relationships between businesspeople and government officials. It may be exhibited in the distribution of legal permits, government grants, special tax breaks, and so forth.

_________ is believed to arise when political cronyism spills over into the business world; self-serving friendships and family ties between businessmen and the government influence the economy and society to the extent that it corrupts public-serving economic and political ideals.

a. Crony capitalism
b. 100-year flood
c. 130-30 fund
d. Good governance

40. In finance, the _________ of a financial asset measures the sensitivity of the asset's price to interest rate movements. There are various definitions of _________ and derived quantities, discussed below. If not otherwise specified, '_________' generally means the Macaulay _________, as defined below.

a. 100-year flood
b. Newtonian time
c. Time value of money
d. Duration

41. The term _________ is applied broadly to a variety of situations in which some financial institutions or assets suddenly lose a large part of their value. In the 19th and early 20th centuries, many financial crises were associated with banking panics, and many recessions coincided with these panics. Other situations that are often called financial crises include stock market crashes and the bursting of other financial bubbles, currency crises, and sovereign defaults.

a. Market failure
b. Macroeconomics
c. Co-operative economics
d. Financial crisis

42. _________ refers to the state of not requiring any outside aid, support for survival; it is therefore a type of personal or collective autonomy. On a large scale, a totally self-sufficient economy that does not trade with the outside world is called an autarky.

The term _________ is usually applied to varieties of sustainable living in which nothing is consumed outside of what is produced by the self-sufficient individuals.

a. Sustainable forest management
b. Global Reporting Initiative
c. Sustainability science
d. Self-sufficiency

43. _________ is the process by which the government, central bank (ii) availability of money, and (iii) cost of money or rate of interest, in order to attain a set of objectives oriented towards the growth and stability of the economy. Monetary theory provides insight into how to craft optimal _________.

_________ is referred to as either being an expansionary policy where an expansionary policy increases the total supply of money in the economy, and a contractionary policy decreases the total money supply.

a. Monetary policy
b. 1921 recession
c. 100-year flood
d. 130-30 fund

44. A _________, reserve bank, or monetary authority is the entity responsible for the monetary policy of a country or of a group of member states. It is a bank that can lend money to other banks in times of need. Its primary responsibility is to maintain the stability of the national currency and money supply, but more active duties include controlling subsidized-loan interest rates, and acting as a lender of last resort to the banking sector during times of financial crisis (private banks often being integral to the national financial system.)

a. 1921 recession
b. 100-year flood
c. Central bank
d. 130-30 fund

45. The _________ is the central banking system of the United States. Created in 1913 by the enactment of the Federal Reserve Act (signed by Woodrow Wilson), it is a quasi-public and quasi-private (government entity with private components) banking system that comprises (1) the presidentially appointed Board of Governors of the _________ in Washington, D.C.; (2) the Federal Open Market Committee; (3) twelve regional Federal Reserve Banks located in major cities throughout the nation acting as fiscal agents for the U.S. Treasury, each with its own nine-member board of directors; (4) numerous other private U.S. member banks, which subscribe to required amounts of non-transferable stock in their regional Federal Reserve Banks; and (5) various advisory councils. Since February 2006, Ben Bernanke has served as the Chairman of the Board of Governors of the _________.

a. Term auction facility
b. Federal Reserve System Open Market Account
c. Monetary Policy Report to the Congress
d. Federal Reserve System

46. _________ is an economic concept with commonplace familiarity. It is the price that a good or service is offered at, or will fetch, in the marketplace. It is of interest mainly in the study of microeconomics.

a. Paper trading
b. Noisy market hypothesis
c. Market anomaly
d. Market price

47. In economics, _________ is the total amount of money available in an economy at a particular point in time. There are several ways to define 'money', but standard measures usually include currency in circulation and demand deposits.

_________ data are recorded and published, usually by the government or the central bank of the country.

a. Money supply
b. Veil of money
c. Velocity of money
d. Neutrality of money

48. Competition law, known in the United States as _________ law, has three main elements:

- prohibiting agreements or practices that restrict free trading and competition between business entities. This includes in particular the repression of cartels.
- banning abusive behaviour by a firm dominating a market, or anti-competitive practices that tend to lead to such a dominant position. Practices controlled in this way may include predatory pricing, tying, price gouging, refusal to deal, and many others.
- supervising the mergers and acquisitions of large corporations, including some joint ventures. Transactions that are considered to threaten the competitive process can be prohibited altogether, or approved subject to 'remedies' such as an obligation to divest part of the merged business or to offer licences or access to facilities to enable other businesses to continue competing.

The substance and practice of competition law varies from jurisdiction to jurisdiction. Protecting the interests of consumers (consumer welfare) and ensuring that entrepreneurs have an opportunity to compete in the market economy are often treated as important objectives. Competition law is closely connected with law on deregulation of access to markets, state aids and subsidies, the privatisation of state owned assets and the establishment of independent sector regulators. In recent decades, competition law has been viewed as a way to provide better public services.

a. Intellectual property law
b. United Kingdom competition law
c. Anti-Inflation Act
d. Antitrust

49. _________ in economics and business is the result of an exchange and from that trade we assign a numerical monetary value to a good, service or asset. If Alice trades Bob 4 apples for an orange, the _________ of an orange is 4 apples. Inversely, the _________ of an apple is 1/4 oranges.

a. Premium pricing
b. Price war
c. Price book
d. Price

50. _________s is concerned with the tasks of developing and applying quantitative or statistical methods to the study and elucidation of economic principles. _________s combines economic theory with statistics to analyze and test economic relationships. Theoretical _________s considers questions about the statistical properties of estimators and tests, while applied _________s is concerned with the application of _________ methods to assess economic theories.

a. Evolutionary economics
b. Experimental economics
c. Economic
d. Econometric

51. _________s are statistical models used in econometrics. An _________ specifies the statistical relationship that is believed to hold between the various economic quantities pertaining a particular economic phenomena under study. An _________ can be derived from a deterministic economic model by allowing for uncertainty or from an economic model which itself is stochastic.

a. Event study
b. ACCRA Cost of Living Index
c. Economic statistics
d. Econometric model

52. In economics, an _________ is any good or commodity, transported from one country to another country in a legitimate fashion, typically for use in trade. _________ goods or services are provided to foreign consumers by domestic producers. _________ is an important part of international trade.

a. ACCRA Cost of Living Index
b. ACEA agreement
c. AD-IA Model
d. Export

53. A _________ represents the combinations of goods and services that a consumer can purchase given current prices and his income. Consumer theory uses the concepts of a _________ and a preference map to analyze consumer choices. Both concepts have a ready graphical representation in the two-good case.

a. Joint demand
b. Revealed preference
c. Budget constraint
d. Quality bias

54. A _________ is:

- Rewrite _________, in generative grammar and computer science
- Standardization, a formal and widely-accepted statement, fact, definition, or qualification
- Operation, a determinate _________ for performing a mathematical operation and obtaining a certain result (Mathematics, Logic)
  - Unary operation
  - Binary operation
- _________ of inference, a function from sets of formulae to formulae (Mathematics, Logic)
- _________ of thumb, principle with broad application that is not intended to be strictly accurate or reliable for every situation. Also often simply referred to as a _________
- Moral, an atomic element of a moral code for guiding choices in human behavior
- Heuristic, a quantized '_________' which shows a tendency or probability for successful function
- A regulation, as in sports
- A Production _________, as in computer science
- Procedural law, a _________set governing the application of laws to cases
  - A law, which may informally be called a '_________'
  - A court ruling, a decision by a court
- In the U.S. Government, a regulation mandated by Congress, but written or expanded upon by the Executive Branch.
- Norm (sociology), an informal but widely accepted _________, concept, truth, definition, or qualification (social norms, legal norms, coding norms)
- Norm (philosophy), a kind of sentence or a reason to act, feel or believe
- 'Rulership' is the concept of governance by a government:
  - Military _________, governance by a military body
  - Monastic _________, a collection of precepts that guides the life of monks or nuns in a religious order where the superior holds the place of Christ
- Slide _________

- '_________,' a song by Ayumi Hamasaki
- '_________,' a song by rapper Nas
- '_________s,' an album by the band The Whitest Boy Alive
- _________s: Pyaar Ka Superhit Formula, a 2003 Bollywood film
- ruler, an instrument for measuring lengths
- _________, a component of an astrolabe, circumferator or similar instrument
- The _________s, a bestselling self-help book
- _________ Project (Run Up-to-date Linux Everywhere), a project that aims to use up-to-date Linux software on old PCs
- _________ engine, a software system that helps managing business _________s
- Ja _________, a hip hop artist
  - R.U.L.E., a 2005 greatest hits album by rapper Ja _________
- '_________s,' a KMFDM song

a. Technocracy
b. Demand
c. Rule
d. Procter ' Gamble

55. _________ is a common concept in economics, and gives rise to derived concepts such as consumer debt. Generally _________ is defined by opposition to production. But the precise definition can vary because different schools of economists define production quite differently.

a. Cash or share options
b. Federal Reserve Bank Notes
c. Foreclosure data providers
d. Consumption

56. The _________ is one of the world's most important central banks, responsible for monetary policy covering the 16 member States of the Eurozone. It was established by the European Union (EU) in 1998 with its headquarters in Frankfurt, Germany.

The predecessor to the _________ was the European Monetary Institute .

a. ACEA agreement
b. European Central Bank
c. AD-IA Model
d. ACCRA Cost of Living Index

57. _________ is an economic policy in which a central bank estimates and makes public a projected, or 'target,' inflation rate and then attempts to steer actual inflation towards the target through the use of interest rate changes and other monetary tools.

Because interest rates and the inflation rate tend to be inversely related, the likely moves of the central bank to raise or lower interest rates become more transparent under the policy of _________. Examples:

- if inflation appears to be above the target, the bank is likely to raise interest rates. This usually (but not always) has the effect over time of cooling the economy and bringing down inflation.

- if inflation appears to be below the target, the bank is likely to lower interest rates. This usually (again, not always) has the effect over time of accelerating the economy and raising inflation.

a. Employment Cost Index
b. Inflation swap
c. Inflation targeting
d. Incomes policies

58. A _________ product is a product designed for cheapness and short-term convenience rather than medium to long-term durability, with most products only intended for single use. The term is also sometimes used for products that may last several months (ex. _________ air filters) to distinguish from similar products that last indefinitely (ex.

a. 1921 recession
b. 130-30 fund
c. Disposable
d. 100-year flood

59. _________ is gross income minus income tax on that income.

Discretionary income is income after subtracting taxes and normal expenses (such as rent or mortgage, utilities, insurance, medical, transportation, property maintenance, child support, inflation, food and sundries, 'c.) to maintain a certain standard of living.

a. Stamp Act
b. Taxation as theft
c. Disposable personal income
d. Disposable income

60. _________ is an American economist and was the Chairman of the Federal Reserve of the United States from 1987 to 2006. He currently works as a private advisor and providing consulting for firms through his company, Greenspan Associates LLC.

First appointed Federal Reserve chairman by President Ronald Reagan in August 1987, he was reappointed at successive four-year intervals until retiring on January 31, 2006 after the second-longest tenure in the position.

a. Adolf Hitler
b. Adam Smith
c. Alan Greenspan
d. Adolph Fischer

61. A variety of measures of _________ and output are used in economics to estimate total economic activity in a country or region, including gross domestic product (GDP), gross national product (GNP), and net _________

There are three main ways of calculating these numbers; the output approach, the income approach and the expenditure approach. In theory, the three must yield the same, because total expenditures on goods and services must equal the total income paid to the producers (Gnational income), and that must also equal the total value of the output of goods and services (GNP.)

a. Volume index
b. GNI per capita
c. Gross world product
d. National income

62. _________ refers to a business or organization attempting to acquire goods or services to accomplish the goals of the enterprise. Though there are several organizations that attempt to set standards in the _________ process, processes can vary greatly between organizations. Typically the word '_________' is not used interchangeably with the word 'procurement', since procurement typically includes Expediting, Supplier Quality, and Traffic and Logistics (T'L) in addition to _________.

a. Free port
b. Purchasing
c. 100-year flood
d. 130-30 fund

63. _________ is the number of goods/services that can be purchased with a unit of currency. For example, if you had taken one dollar to a store in the 1950s, you would have been able to buy a greater number of items than you would today, indicating that you would have had a greater _________ in the 1950s. Currency can be either a commodity money, like gold or silver, or fiat currency like US dollars.

a. Compliance cost
b. Purchasing power
c. Genuine progress indicator
d. Human Poverty Index

64. The _________ theory uses the long-term equilibrium exchange rate of two currencies to equalize their purchasing power. Developed by Gustav Cassel in 1920, it is based on the law of one price: the theory states that, in ideally efficient markets, identical goods should have only one price.

This purchasing power SEM rate equalizes the purchasing power of different currencies in their home countries for a given basket of goods.

a. Gross national product
b. Bureau of Labor Statistics
c. Purchasing power parity
d. Measures of national income and output

65. A _________ or directed economy is an economic system in which the government or workers' councils manages the economy. It is an economic system in which the central government makes all decisions on the production and consumption of goods and services. Its most extensive form is referred to as a _________, centrally planned economy, or command and control economy.

a. Command economy
b. Subsistence economy
c. Transition economy
d. Nutritional Economics

66. A _________ is a theoretical term that economists use to describe a market which is free from government intervention (i.e. no regulation, no subsidization, no single monetary system and no governmental monopolies.) In a _________, property rights are voluntarily exchanged at a price arranged solely by the mutual consent of sellers and buyers. By definition, buyers and sellers do not coerce each other, in the sense that they obtain each other's property without the use of physical force, threat of physical force, or fraud, nor is the coerced by a third party (such as by government via transfer payments) and they engage in trade simply because they both consent and believe that it is a good enough choice.

a. Third camp
b. Leninism
c. Free market
d. Delegation

67. In economic theory, _________ is the competitive situation in any market where the conditions necessary for perfect competition are not satisfied. It is a market structure that does not meet the conditions of perfect competition.

Forms of _________ include:

- Monopoly, in which there is only one seller of a good.
- Oligopoly, in which there is a small number of sellers.
- Monopolistic competition, in which there are many sellers producing highly differentiated goods.
- Monopsony, in which there is only one buyer of a good.
- Oligopsony, in which there is a small number of buyers.

There may also be _________ in markets due to buyers or sellers lacking information about prices and the goods being traded.

There may also be _________ due to a time lag in a market.

a. ACEA agreement
b. AD-IA Model
c. Imperfect competition
d. ACCRA Cost of Living Index

68. _________ means how much each individual receives, in monetary terms, of the yearly income generated in the country. This is what each citizen is to receive if the yearly national income is divided equally among everyone. _________ is usually reported in units of currency per year.

a. Real income
b. Lerman ratio
c. Family income
d. Per capita income

69. In neoclassical economics and microeconomics, _________ describes the perfect being a market in which there are many small firms, all producing homogeneous goods. In the short term, such markets are productively inefficient as output will not occur where mc is equal to ac, but allocatively efficient, as output under _________ will always occur where mc is equal to mr, and therefore where mc equals ar. However, in the long term, such markets are both allocatively and productively efficient.

a. Co-operative economics
b. Perfect competition
c. General equilibrium
d. Law of supply

70. _________ is defined as the measure of responsiveness in the quantity demanded for a commodity as a result of change in price of the same commodity. It is a measure of how consumers react to a change in price. In other words, it is percentage change in quantity demanded as per the percentage change in price of the same commodity.

a. 1921 recession
b. 130-30 fund
c. 100-year flood
d. Price elasticity of demand

71. _________ in political thought refers to economic theories of social organization advocating collective ownership and administration of the means of production and distribution of goods, and a society characterized by equality for all individuals, with an egalitarian method of compensation. Modern _________ originated in the late 19th-century intellectual and working class political movement that criticized the effects of industrialization and private ownership on society. Karl Marx posited that _________ would be achieved via class struggle and a proletarian revolution after a transitional stage from capitalism called the dictatorship of the proletariat.

a. Adolf Hitler
b. Adolph Fischer
c. Socialism
d. Adam Smith

72. _________ is a term that is used to describe the overall process of invention, innovation and diffusion of technology or processes. The term is redundant with technological development, technological achievement, and technological progress. In essence _________ is the invention of a technology (or a process), the continuous process of improving a technology (in which it often becomes cheaper) and its diffusion throughout industry or society.

a. 130-30 fund
b. 1921 recession
c. Technological change
d. 100-year flood

73. _________ is the development of economic wealth of countries or regions for the well-being of their inhabitants. It is the process by which a nation improves the economic, political, and social well being of its people. From a policy perspective, _________ can be defined as efforts that seek to improve the economic well-being and quality of life for a community by creating and/or retaining jobs and supporting or growing incomes and the tax base.

a. Economic methodology
b. Experimental economics
c. Economic development
d. Inflation

74. In economics, _________ is the ratio of the percent change in one variable to the percent change in another variable. It is a tool for measuring the responsiveness of a function to changes in parameters in a relative way. Commonly analyzed are _________ of substitution, price and wealth.

a. ACCRA Cost of Living Index
b. ACEA agreement
c. Elasticity of demand
d. Elasticity

75. Price _________ is defined as the measure of responsiveness in the quantity demanded for a commodity as a result of change in price of the same commodity. It is a measure of how consumers react to a change in price. In other words, it is percentage change in quantity demanded by the percentage change in price of the same commodity.

a. ACEA agreement
b. Elasticity of demand
c. Elasticity
d. ACCRA Cost of Living Index

76. In economics, _________ is the total supply of goods and services produced by a national economy during a specific time period. It is the total amount of goods and services in the economy available at all possible price levels.

a. Aggregation problem
b. Aggregate demand
c. Aggregate supply
d. Aggregate expenditure

77. The _________ consists of a number of economic theories which describe the nature of the firm, company including its existence, its behaviour, and its relationship with the market.

In simplified terms, the _________ aims to answer these questions:

1. Existence - why do firms emerge, why are not all transactions in the economy mediated over the market?
2. Boundaries - why the boundary between firms and the market is located exactly there? Which transactions are performed internally and which are negotiated on the market?
3. Organization - why are firms structured in such specific way? What is the interplay of formal and informal relationships?

Despite looking simple, these questions are not answered by the established economic theory, which usually views firms as given, and treats them as black boxes without any internal structure.

The First World War period saw a change of emphasis in economic theory away from industry-level analysis which mainly included analysing markets to analysis at the level of the firm, as it became increasingly clear that perfect competition was no longer an adequate model of how firms behaved. Economic theory till then had focussed on trying to understand markets alone and there had been little study on understanding why firms or organisations exist.

a. Policy Ineffectiveness Proposition
b. Technology gap
c. Khazzoom-Brookes postulate
d. Theory of the firm

78. In finance, _________ is investment originating from other countries.See Foreign direct investment.

a. Horizontal merger
b. Preclusive purchasing
c. Demand side economics
d. Foreign investment

79. A _________ is an economy based on the division of labor in which the prices of goods and services are determined in a free price system set by supply and demand. This is often contrasted with a planned economy, in which a central government determines the price of goods and services using a fixed price system. Market economies are contrasted with mixed economy where the price system is not entirely free but under some government control that is not extensive enough to constitute a planned economy.

a. Network Economy
b. Market economy
c. Nutritional Economics
d. Commons-based peer production

80. In economics, the _________ is defined as a numerical measure of the responsiveness of the quantity supplied of product (A) to a change in price of product (A) alone. It is the measure of the way quantity supplied reacts to a change in price.

For example, if, in response to a 10% rise in the price of a good, the quantity supplied increases by 20%, the _________ would be 20%/10% = 2.

a. Passive income
b. Hedonimetry
c. Demand shaping
d. Price elasticity of supply

81. In economics, _________ is the active redirecting resources from being consumed today so that they may create benefits in the future; the use of assets to earn income or profit._________ is the process of making an investment in order to earn a profit, for example equity investment either through a fund, a 401k plan, or individually. People often invest in order to build up their estate or to accumulate funds for retirement.

To try to predict good stocks to invest in, two main schools of thought exist: technical analysis and fundamentals analysis.

a. AD-IA Model
b. Investing
c. ACCRA Cost of Living Index
d. ACEA agreement

Chapter 1

1. d	2. d	3. a	4. d	5. c	6. b	7. d	8. c	9. d	10. c
11. a	12. a	13. b	14. c	15. d	16. a	17. d	18. d	19. b	20. d
21. d	22. d	23. b	24. c	25. b	26. c	27. c	28. d	29. d	30. a
31. c	32. a	33. a	34. a	35. d	36. b	37. d	38. d	39. d	40. d
41. d	42. d	43. b	44. d	45. c	46. d	47. d	48. d	49. d	50. a
51. d	52. c	53. d	54. d	55. b	56. d	57. d	58. b	59. d	60. d
61. c	62. c								

Chapter 2

1. d	2. d	3. d	4. d	5. a	6. a	7. d	8. d	9. c	10. c
11. a	12. d	13. b	14. d	15. d	16. c	17. d	18. d	19. c	20. d
21. a	22. b	23. b	24. d	25. d	26. d	27. c	28. d	29. a	30. d
31. a	32. d	33. d	34. d	35. d	36. d	37. b	38. b	39. b	40. d
41. c	42. d	43. d	44. c	45. c	46. d	47. c	48. d	49. b	50. d
51. d	52. d	53. c	54. d	55. d	56. d	57. a	58. d	59. d	60. d
61. d	62. d	63. d	64. d	65. d	66. c	67. b	68. d	69. d	70. d
71. c	72. b	73. d	74. b	75. b	76. b	77. d	78. a	79. a	80. a
81. b	82. c	83. a	84. d	85. a	86. c	87. c	88. d	89. a	90. b
91. c	92. c	93. a	94. a	95. c	96. a	97. b	98. d	99. d	100. b
101. b	102. a	103. c	104. a	105. d	106. a	107. d	108. d	109. c	110. a
111. a	112. d	113. d	114. d	115. d	116. c	117. d	118. d	119. b	

Chapter 3

1. a	2. d	3. b	4. d	5. c	6. c	7. a	8. c	9. a	10. d
11. a	12. b	13. b	14. a	15. d	16. d	17. d	18. b	19. b	20. b
21. d	22. d	23. a	24. d	25. d	26. c	27. d	28. d	29. b	30. c
31. a	32. a	33. d	34. a	35. c	36. d	37. d	38. c	39. b	40. d
41. c	42. d								

Chapter 4

1. d	2. d	3. d	4. a	5. b	6. b	7. d	8. c	9. d	10. c
11. a	12. d	13. d	14. d	15. a	16. d	17. c	18. d	19. d	20. d
21. b	22. c	23. a	24. d	25. a	26. d	27. c	28. c	29. a	30. b
31. d	32. c	33. b	34. d	35. b	36. b	37. d	38. d	39. d	40. c
41. b	42. c	43. c	44. d	45. a	46. b	47. b	48. c	49. d	50. c
51. a	52. c	53. a	54. d	55. d	56. d				

Chapter 5

1. a	2. b	3. a	4. c	5. d	6. d	7. b	8. b	9. d	10. d
11. b	12. d	13. d	14. d	15. b	16. d	17. d	18. a	19. d	20. b
21. a	22. b	23. a	24. c	25. a	26. b	27. a	28. a	29. d	30. d
31. d	32. d	33. d	34. c	35. d	36. b	37. d	38. a	39. a	40. b
41. c	42. d	43. b	44. b	45. d	46. a	47. c	48. d	49. d	50. d
51. d	52. d	53. c	54. d	55. a	56. c				

Chapter 6

1. b	2. a	3. d	4. c	5. c	6. a	7. c	8. d	9. d	10. c
11. b	12. b	13. a	14. a	15. c	16. a	17. b	18. d	19. b	20. c
21. d	22. d	23. d	24. d	25. c	26. d	27. d	28. d	29. d	30. d
31. d	32. d	33. d	34. b	35. c	36. b	37. d	38. d	39. a	40. c
41. d	42. d	43. b	44. d	45. b	46. d	47. d	48. d	49. d	50. b
51. a	52. c	53. a	54. d	55. c	56. d	57. a	58. b	59. d	60. c

Chapter 7

1. d	2. c	3. c	4. a	5. d	6. d	7. d	8. d	9. d	10. a
11. c	12. b	13. d	14. d	15. d	16. d	17. c	18. b	19. d	20. b
21. d	22. b	23. c	24. c	25. b	26. b	27. c	28. b	29. d	30. d
31. d	32. a	33. d	34. c	35. a	36. b	37. d	38. d	39. a	40. b
41. a	42. a	43. b	44. b	45. d	46. a	47. d	48. b	49. d	50. c

Chapter 8

1. c	2. d	3. a	4. c	5. a	6. c	7. d	8. d	9. d	10. b
11. c	12. d	13. d	14. b	15. d	16. a	17. a	18. d	19. d	20. c
21. b	22. b	23. d	24. d	25. d	26. d	27. d	28. a	29. d	30. d
31. d	32. a	33. d	34. d	35. d	36. b	37. d	38. b	39. b	40. d
41. d	42. d	43. c	44. d	45. d	46. d	47. d	48. c	49. b	50. d
51. c	52. d	53. d	54. d	55. b	56. b	57. d	58. d	59. d	

Chapter 9

1. b	2. c	3. a	4. a	5. d	6. b	7. a	8. b	9. d	10. d
11. d	12. c	13. a	14. d	15. d	16. d	17. d	18. d	19. b	20. d
21. d	22. d	23. a	24. a	25. c	26. d	27. d	28. c	29. b	30. d
31. a	32. a	33. c	34. d	35. c	36. d	37. b	38. c	39. d	40. c
41. c	42. d	43. d	44. a	45. d	46. d	47. d	48. a	49. b	50. d
51. d	52. d	53. b	54. b	55. c	56. d	57. d	58. a	59. d	60. b
61. d	62. d	63. b							

Chapter 10

1. d	2. d	3. d	4. d	5. d	6. b	7. b	8. b	9. d	10. d
11. c	12. b	13. c	14. d	15. d	16. c	17. d	18. a	19. d	20. d
21. a	22. b	23. b	24. d	25. d	26. a	27. a	28. b	29. b	30. d
31. d	32. d	33. b	34. c	35. b	36. a	37. d	38. b	39. b	40. d
41. d	42. d	43. d	44. b	45. a	46. d	47. d	48. d	49. d	50. d
51. d	52. d	53. d	54. a	55. d	56. b	57. c	58. c	59. d	60. d
61. b	62. a	63. c	64. d	65. d	66. d	67. d	68. a	69. b	70. d
71. d	72. d	73. d	74. d	75. d					

Chapter 11

1. d	2. b	3. b	4. d	5. a	6. d	7. c	8. a	9. d	10. a
11. a	12. c	13. d	14. a	15. b	16. b	17. b	18. a	19. d	20. a
21. d	22. d	23. c	24. a	25. d	26. d	27. d	28. a	29. d	30. d
31. d	32. c	33. c	34. c	35. b	36. a	37. d	38. d	39. d	40. c
41. d	42. d	43. b	44. a	45. d	46. d	47. d	48. c	49. b	50. d
51. d	52. d	53. d	54. d	55. a	56. a				

Chapter 12

1. c	2. a	3. d	4. d	5. d	6. b	7. d	8. d	9. a	10. d
11. d	12. a	13. a	14. d	15. a	16. d	17. b	18. a	19. a	20. b
21. d	22. c	23. d	24. d	25. c	26. a	27. d	28. d	29. d	30. d
31. a	32. d	33. d	34. b	35. b	36. b	37. d	38. a	39. c	40. d
41. d	42. d	43. c	44. c	45. d	46. d	47. c	48. d	49. d	50. a
51. d	52. a	53. d	54. d	55. d	56. d	57. d	58. a	59. d	60. a
61. d	62. b	63. d							

Chapter 13

1. d	2. a	3. d	4. b	5. d	6. c	7. c	8. b	9. c	10. d
11. d	12. d	13. b	14. d	15. d	16. d	17. b	18. b	19. a	20. a
21. d	22. b	23. d	24. b	25. d	26. d	27. d	28. b	29. a	30. a
31. d	32. d	33. d	34. d	35. a	36. d	37. b	38. d	39. c	40. a
41. b	42. d	43. c	44. d	45. c	46. b	47. d	48. d	49. d	50. a
51. d	52. b	53. a	54. b	55. d	56. c	57. a	58. c	59. d	

Chapter 14

1. d	2. d	3. d	4. b	5. b	6. c	7. b	8. c	9. b	10. c
11. b	12. c	13. d	14. a	15. d	16. d	17. d	18. b	19. a	20. c
21. d	22. b	23. b	24. d	25. a	26. d	27. c	28. b	29. b	30. b
31. d	32. c	33. d	34. b	35. d	36. d	37. d	38. a	39. d	40. a
41. c	42. d	43. b	44. d	45. a	46. a	47. b	48. b	49. c	50. c
51. d	52. d	53. d	54. c	55. a	56. c	57. d	58. c	59. d	60. b
61. d	62. a	63. d	64. a	65. d	66. d	67. a	68. d	69. d	70. a
71. a	72. d	73. d	74. b	75. d	76. d	77. d	78. d	79. d	80. d
81. b	82. d	83. b	84. c	85. a	86. b	87. b	88. c	89. d	90. d
91. d	92. d	93. d	94. d	95. c					

Chapter 15

1. a	2. c	3. c	4. d	5. d	6. d	7. d	8. d	9. a	10. d
11. a	12. b	13. a	14. a	15. d	16. c	17. d	18. c	19. b	20. d
21. c	22. a	23. d	24. c	25. d	26. a	27. d	28. c	29. d	30. a
31. b	32. d	33. c	34. d	35. d	36. d	37. d	38. a	39. b	40. d
41. d	42. c	43. b	44. d	45. b	46. d	47. a	48. d	49. c	50. a
51. a	52. d	53. d	54. d	55. b	56. d	57. a	58. d	59. d	60. d
61. d	62. b	63. d	64. c	65. d	66. b	67. a	68. d	69. d	70. d
71. d	72. d	73. c	74. d	75. d	76. d				

Chapter 16

1. d	2. d	3. d	4. b	5. b	6. a	7. d	8. d	9. a	10. d
11. d	12. c	13. d	14. a	15. d	16. c	17. a	18. b	19. a	20. a
21. b	22. c	23. d	24. a	25. b	26. d	27. d	28. b	29. b	30. d
31. d	32. d	33. d	34. d	35. d	36. a	37. a	38. d	39. b	40. d
41. d	42. d	43. d	44. d	45. d	46. c	47. c	48. d	49. a	50. d
51. b	52. d	53. c	54. c	55. d	56. d	57. c	58. c	59. c	60. b
61. a	62. c	63. d	64. d	65. d	66. c	67. d	68. d	69. b	70. d
71. d	72. d	73. b	74. c	75. a	76. d	77. b	78. d	79. c	80. a
81. c	82. b	83. d	84. c	85. c	86. a	87. a	88. d	89. d	90. b
91. b	92. b	93. d	94. d	95. a	96. d	97. a	98. b	99. a	

Chapter 17

1. d	2. d	3. b	4. d	5. d	6. d	7. a	8. b	9. d	10. b
11. d	12. d	13. d	14. d	15. d	16. b	17. d	18. a	19. c	20. d
21. a	22. d	23. d	24. d	25. c	26. a	27. b	28. d	29. d	30. c
31. d	32. c	33. d	34. b	35. b	36. d	37. d	38. a	39. a	40. c
41. c	42. d	43. d	44. d	45. a	46. a	47. a	48. c	49. a	50. d
51. d	52. d	53. a	54. d	55. a	56. c	57. d	58. d	59. c	60. d
61. c	62. d	63. b	64. d	65. c	66. c	67. b	68. a		

Chapter 18

1. a	2. d	3. d	4. d	5. d	6. a	7. c	8. b	9. c	10. d
11. a	12. d	13. d	14. d	15. b	16. c	17. d	18. b	19. c	20. c
21. d	22. b	23. c	24. a	25. d	26. d	27. c	28. a	29. d	30. a
31. b	32. d	33. c	34. b	35. d	36. d	37. b	38. c	39. c	40. d
41. d	42. d	43. d	44. d	45. a	46. b	47. d	48. d	49. c	50. d
51. d	52. d	53. c							

Chapter 19

1. d	2. c	3. c	4. d	5. d	6. c	7. b	8. c	9. b	10. a
11. d	12. b	13. d	14. d	15. a	16. d	17. d	18. c	19. a	20. d
21. b	22. d	23. d	24. b	25. b	26. d	27. d	28. d	29. d	30. a
31. d	32. a	33. a	34. d	35. d	36. b	37. a	38. b	39. d	40. a
41. d	42. d	43. d	44. a	45. d	46. b	47. c	48. d	49. b	50. c
51. d	52. a	53. a	54. b	55. d	56. a	57. a	58. b	59. c	60. d
61. c	62. a	63. d	64. c	65. d	66. c	67. d	68. a	69. c	70. d
71. d	72. b	73. d	74. d						

Chapter 20

1. d	2. d	3. c	4. a	5. d	6. d	7. d	8. d	9. d	10. d
11. d	12. d	13. b	14. c	15. c	16. c	17. b	18. a	19. a	20. d
21. b	22. d	23. c	24. a	25. c	26. d	27. a	28. d	29. b	30. b
31. d	32. d	33. c	34. d	35. d	36. d	37. c	38. a	39. d	40. c
41. b	42. d	43. a	44. d	45. a	46. d	47. b	48. a	49. a	50. c
51. d	52. b	53. a	54. c	55. d	56. d	57. d	58. d	59. d	60. b
61. d	62. a	63. d	64. d	65. b	66. d	67. d	68. a	69. d	70. d
71. d	72. a	73. c	74. c	75. d					

Chapter 21

1. a	2. a	3. b	4. b	5. d	6. d	7. a	8. d	9. d	10. d
11. a	12. a	13. d	14. c	15. d	16. b	17. d	18. d	19. d	20. d
21. c	22. d	23. a	24. a	25. c	26. d	27. a	28. d	29. c	30. b
31. a	32. d	33. d	34. a	35. d	36. d	37. d	38. d	39. b	40. d
41. b	42. b	43. a	44. c	45. d	46. d	47. a	48. b	49. d	50. d
51. c	52. d	53. d	54. a	55. c	56. a	57. c	58. c	59. b	60. b
61. c	62. d	63. d	64. d	65. c	66. b				

Chapter 22

1. d	2. a	3. d	4. c	5. d	6. c	7. d	8. d	9. d	10. d
11. d	12. d	13. b	14. d	15. b	16. d	17. d	18. d	19. d	20. d
21. d	22. c	23. d	24. b	25. a	26. d	27. c	28. d	29. d	30. d
31. c	32. b	33. c	34. a	35. d	36. b	37. d	38. d	39. a	40. a
41. a	42. d	43. d	44. a	45. d	46. d	47. b	48. c	49. d	50. a
51. d	52. d	53. a	54. a	55. c					

Chapter 23

1. b	2. d	3. c	4. d	5. d	6. c	7. d	8. a	9. a	10. d
11. d	12. c	13. c	14. d	15. b	16. d	17. a	18. b	19. d	20. d
21. d	22. d	23. d	24. d	25. a	26. d	27. d	28. d	29. a	30. d
31. d	32. c	33. d	34. b	35. d	36. c	37. d	38. c	39. d	40. c
41. b	42. c	43. d	44. c	45. d	46. d	47. d	48. d	49. a	50. c
51. d	52. d	53. c	54. d						

Chapter 24

1. d	2. b	3. d	4. d	5. d	6. d	7. b	8. d	9. d	10. b
11. d	12. a	13. b	14. d	15. d	16. d	17. d	18. d	19. a	20. d
21. a	22. a	23. b	24. d	25. d	26. d	27. b	28. d	29. b	30. d
31. b	32. b	33. c	34. d	35. a	36. c	37. b	38. d	39. a	40. d
41. c	42. d	43. a	44. d	45. a	46. b	47. d	48. d	49. d	50. d
51. a	52. d	53. d							

Chapter 25

1. c	2. a	3. a	4. a	5. b	6. d	7. c	8. b	9. d	10. c
11. d	12. b	13. d	14. d	15. d	16. d	17. a	18. b	19. a	20. d
21. d	22. d	23. d	24. a	25. d	26. d	27. d	28. d	29. c	30. d
31. d	32. d	33. a	34. b	35. d	36. b	37. d	38. b	39. d	40. a
41. b	42. d	43. d	44. a	45. d	46. b	47. d	48. d	49. a	50. d
51. c	52. d	53. d	54. a	55. d	56. c	57. b	58. d	59. d	60. d
61. d	62. b	63. d	64. a	65. a	66. d	67. a	68. b	69. a	70. a
71. d	72. a	73. a	74. d	75. a	76. d	77. a	78. d	79. d	80. d
81. a	82. b	83. d	84. a	85. a	86. d	87. c	88. d		

Chapter 26

1. c	2. d	3. d	4. b	5. d	6. c	7. d	8. d	9. a	10. b
11. d	12. c	13. d	14. d	15. c	16. a	17. a	18. c	19. d	20. d
21. d	22. d	23. b	24. d	25. d	26. d	27. c	28. c	29. b	30. b
31. c	32. b	33. d	34. c	35. a	36. d	37. a	38. d	39. d	40. b
41. a	42. c	43. d	44. d	45. a	46. d	47. a	48. b	49. d	50. b
51. b	52. a	53. b	54. d	55. d	56. a	57. b	58. d	59. d	60. c
61. c	62. d	63. d	64. a	65. d	66. d	67. d	68. d	69. c	70. d
71. d	72. a	73. d	74. d	75. d	76. d	77. a	78. c	79. d	80. b

Chapter 27

1. d	2. d	3. a	4. b	5. d	6. d	7. b	8. a	9. c	10. d
11. d	12. d	13. c	14. c	15. c	16. b	17. c	18. c	19. c	20. c
21. c	22. a	23. b	24. d	25. d	26. b	27. b	28. d	29. d	30. b
31. b	32. b	33. d	34. d	35. a	36. d	37. d	38. c	39. c	40. b
41. c	42. d	43. d	44. d	45. a	46. c	47. a	48. c	49. d	50. c
51. b	52. a	53. d	54. a	55. d	56. a	57. b	58. c	59. b	60. d
61. b	62. a	63. b	64. a	65. d					

Chapter 28

1. d	2. a	3. b	4. d	5. b	6. d	7. d	8. a	9. d	10. d
11. d	12. d	13. b	14. c	15. c	16. d	17. d	18. c	19. d	20. b
21. d	22. a	23. d	24. c	25. a	26. b	27. d	28. d	29. d	30. d
31. b	32. a	33. c	34. d	35. c	36. d	37. d	38. a	39. c	40. b
41. b	42. d	43. c	44. b	45. a	46. d	47. d	48. b	49. b	50. d
51. c	52. d	53. d	54. b	55. d	56. b	57. c	58. b	59. d	60. c
61. d	62. d	63. d	64. a	65. b	66. b	67. c	68. d	69. d	70. d
71. b	72. a	73. d	74. b						

Chapter 29

1. d	2. b	3. a	4. c	5. a	6. d	7. d	8. d	9. a	10. d
11. d	12. a	13. d	14. b	15. d	16. a	17. b	18. d	19. c	20. d
21. a	22. c	23. d	24. d	25. d	26. b	27. d	28. d	29. d	30. d
31. c	32. c	33. d	34. d	35. d	36. d	37. d	38. c	39. d	40. a
41. c	42. b	43. a	44. a	45. d	46. d	47. d	48. a	49. d	50. b
51. b	52. b	53. d	54. a	55. c	56. d	57. d	58. c	59. d	60. d
61. d	62. d	63. d	64. d	65. d	66. d	67. a	68. a	69. d	70. d
71. d	72. d	73. a	74. a	75. a	76. c	77. a	78. d	79. c	80. d
81. d	82. d	83. d	84. d	85. d					

Chapter 30

1. c	2. d	3. b	4. d	5. b	6. d	7. a	8. a	9. d	10. a
11. a	12. d	13. d	14. a	15. b	16. c	17. d	18. c	19. d	20. a
21. c	22. d	23. a	24. d	25. b	26. d	27. c	28. d	29. d	30. d
31. c	32. a	33. a	34. d	35. d	36. d	37. d	38. d	39. d	40. b
41. b	42. d	43. c	44. a	45. c	46. d	47. c	48. d	49. c	50. b
51. d	52. b	53. c	54. a	55. d	56. d	57. b	58. a	59. d	60. c
61. b	62. b	63. d	64. d	65. d	66. d	67. d	68. c	69. b	70. b
71. d	72. d	73. c	74. c	75. d	76. d	77. d	78. c	79. b	

Chapter 31

1. d	2. d	3. b	4. c	5. b	6. a	7. b	8. a	9. a	10. d
11. d	12. d	13. a	14. c	15. c	16. d	17. b	18. a	19. b	20. d
21. c	22. c	23. d	24. c	25. a	26. b	27. d	28. d	29. a	30. d
31. d	32. d	33. d	34. b	35. a	36. a	37. d	38. c	39. d	40. d
41. d	42. d	43. b	44. b	45. d	46. b	47. c	48. d	49. d	50. a
51. d									

Chapter 32

1. d	2. b	3. b	4. d	5. d	6. d	7. d	8. a	9. b	10. c
11. a	12. c	13. d	14. d	15. a	16. d	17. c	18. b	19. d	20. d
21. d	22. d	23. d	24. b	25. c	26. c	27. c	28. d	29. b	30. a
31. d	32. d	33. d	34. d	35. a	36. b	37. d	38. d	39. d	40. b
41. d	42. d	43. d	44. d	45. d	46. c	47. a	48. a	49. d	50. d
51. b	52. b	53. d	54. a	55. c	56. b	57. c	58. c	59. d	60. a
61. d	62. d	63. a	64. d	65. d	66. d				

Chapter 33

1. d	2. b	3. d	4. d	5. c	6. d	7. d	8. d	9. b	10. d
11. b	12. d	13. a	14. a	15. d	16. c	17. a	18. d	19. b	20. b
21. a	22. c	23. c	24. a	25. d	26. b	27. c	28. d	29. d	30. b
31. d	32. c	33. d	34. b	35. a	36. d	37. b	38. d	39. c	40. d
41. b	42. b	43. b	44. a	45. d	46. d	47. d	48. b	49. d	50. a
51. d	52. d	53. c	54. d	55. d	56. b	57. d	58. d	59. d	60. b
61. b	62. a	63. c	64. d	65. d	66. a	67. d	68. d	69. b	70. b
71. d	72. c								

Chapter 34

1. d	2. d	3. b	4. d	5. b	6. c	7. d	8. d	9. a	10. a
11. a	12. d	13. d	14. b	15. a	16. c	17. a	18. a	19. d	20. c
21. d	22. d	23. a	24. d	25. c	26. d	27. d	28. d	29. a	30. d
31. d	32. d	33. c	34. b	35. d	36. d	37. b	38. a	39. a	40. d
41. d	42. d	43. a	44. c	45. d	46. d	47. a	48. d	49. d	50. d
51. d	52. d	53. c	54. c	55. d	56. b	57. c	58. c	59. d	60. c
61. d	62. b	63. b	64. c	65. a	66. c	67. c	68. d	69. b	70. d
71. c	72. c	73. c	74. d	75. b	76. c	77. d	78. d	79. b	80. d
81. b									

www.ingramcontent.com/pod-product-compliance
Lightning Source LLC
Chambersburg PA
CBHW080933300426
44115CB00017B/2797